Active Math

Strands 1–5

Michael Keating, Derek Mulvany and James O'Loughlin

Special Advisors:
Oliver Murphy, Colin Townsend and Jim McElroy

FOLENS

Contents

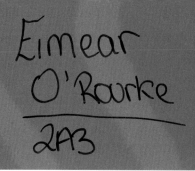

Eimear
O'Rourke
2A3

Introduction

Active Maths 2 is the second part of a two-book series covering the **complete Junior Certificate course at Higher Level**. On completing *Active Maths 1*, Higher Level students continue the Junior Certificate Higher Level course with *Active Maths 2*.

Active Maths 2 covers all five strands of the new Project Maths syllabus.

Active Maths 2 reflects the much greater emphasis in the new syllabus on:

- understanding mathematical concepts;
- relating mathematics to everyday experience;
- developing problem-solving skills.

Teachers and students will find that they have the new syllabus fully covered.

- A separate **free Activity Book** provides a wealth of activities designed to develop students' understanding of each topic in a hands-on way. The textbooks are linked throughout with the Activity Book to introduce topics and emphasise key Learning Outcomes.

Active Maths 2 is packed with student-friendly features:

- Prepares students for the new style of exam question with comprehensive **graded exercises** on each topic and **end-of-chapter revision exercises** include Project Maths-type exam questions based on all material that has been released by the NCCA and SEC.

- **Learning Outcomes** from the new syllabus are stated at the beginning of each chapter.

- Each chapter includes a **You Should Remember** section so that students can check they are fully prepared before starting the chapter.

- A list of **Key Words** at the start of each chapter helps students to consolidate learning. On first occurrence in each chapter, key words are set apart in **Definition boxes** to reinforce the importance of understanding their meaning.

- Clear and concise **Worked Examples** show students how to set out their answers, including step-by-step instructions with excellent diagrams to explain constructions.

- Essential formulae are set apart in **Formula boxes**.

- **Answers** to exercises are given at the end of each book.

   Additional **teacher resources, including digital activities** and **fully worked-out solutions** for the textbooks, will be available online at www.folensonline.ie.

Active Maths 2 allows teachers to meet the challenge of the new syllabus for Junior Certificate, and encourages students to discover for themselves that mathematics can be enjoyable and relevant to everyday life.

NB: Constructions in this book are numbered according to the NCCA syllabus for Project Maths at Junior Certificate Higher Level.

chapter 1

Sets

Learning Outcomes

In this chapter, you will:

- ➲ Learn about union, intersection, set difference and complement for three sets
- ➲ Solve problems involving/using three sets
- ➲ Investigate the associative property for intersection, union and set difference
- ➲ Investigate the distributive property of union over intersection and intersection over union

A **set** is a collection of well-defined objects. The objects in the set are called **elements**.

The symbol ∈ is used to denote **is an element of.**

The symbol ∉ is used to denote **is not an element of.**

For example, $1 \in \{1, 3, 5, 7\}$ and $2 \notin \{1, 3, 5, 7\}$.

Worked Example 1.1

Which of the following sets are well defined?

(i)   The set of all counties in Connacht

(ii) The set of all great Munster rugby teams

(iii) The set of all whole numbers greater than 4 and less than or equal to 10

Solution

(i)   This set is well defined.

It is the set {Galway, Leitrim, Mayo, Roscommon, Sligo}.

(ii) This set is not well defined. The set of great Munster rugby teams is a matter of opinion. Some people might say that the present Munster rugby team belongs to the set, while others may disagree. We cannot properly define what is meant by a 'great Munster rugby team'.

(iii) This set is well defined. It is the set {5, 6, 7, 8, 9, 10}.

The **cardinal number** of a set A is the number of elements in the set A and is denoted by #A or |A|.

If a set has no elements, then it is called the **null set** or the **empty set**.

It is denoted by the symbol ∅ or { }.

The cardinal number of the null set is 0.

YOU SHOULD REMEMBER...

- The definition of a set
- The cardinal number of a set
- How to describe a set using the Rule Method
- Subsets
- The universal set
- How to represent sets on a Venn diagram
- The union of two sets
- The intersection of two sets
- The commutative property of union and intersection
- Set difference
- The complement of a set
- How to solve problems using two sets

KEY WORDS

- **Element**
- **Cardinal number**
- **Null set**
- **Venn diagram**
- **Union**
- **Intersection**
- **Universal set**
- **Set difference**
- **Complement**
- **Commutative property**
- **Associative property**
- **Distributive property**

Two sets are equal if they each have the same elements.

For example, the sets A = {1, 2, 3, 4} and B = {4, 3, 2, 1} are equal. We can write A = B.

If all the elements of a set A are also in a set B, then we say that A is a **subset** of B. The symbol for subset is ⊂.

A = {2, 3, 4}

B = {1, 2, 3, 4, 5}

∴ A ⊂ B

If A is a subset of B and A contains all the elements of B, then A is an **improper subset** of B.
If A is a subset of B but A does not contain all the elements of B, then A is a **proper subset** of B.

The null set and the set A itself are both subsets of A.

If #A = n, then A has 2^n subsets.

ACTIVITY 1.1

Worked Example 1.2

A = {x | 0 < x < 10, x ∈ N, x is even}

(i) List the elements of A.

(ii) What is #A?

(iii) Write down all the subsets of A containing two elements.

(iv) How many subsets does A have?

(v) How many of these are proper subsets of A?

Solution

(i) A = {2, 4, 6, 8}

(ii) #A = 4

(iii) {2, 4}, {2, 6}, {2, 8}, {4, 6}, {4, 8}, {6, 8}

(iv) 2^4 = 16

(v) A has one improper subset – itself.

∴ Number of proper subsets = 16 – 1

= 15

Venn Diagrams, Union and Intersection

Sets can also be represented using Venn diagrams.
The Venn diagram shown represents the set A = {2, 3, 5, 7}.

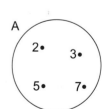

In a Venn diagram, the **universal set** can be represented by a rectangle. The letter U is used to denote the universal set.

The **universal set** is the set that contains all elements.
Every set is a subset of the universal set.

...o sets A and B have elements in common, then the sets A and B are represented by overlapping circles.

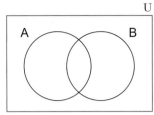

If two sets A and B have no elements in common, they are usually represented by non-overlapping circles. If two sets have no elements in common, then they are called **mutually exclusive sets** or **disjoint sets**.

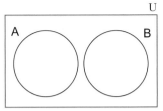

The **union** of two sets is the set of elements contained in either set. The union of the two sets A and B is written as A ∪ B.

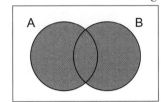

So, A ∪ B is the set of elements in A **or** in B **or** in both.

The **intersection** of two sets is the set of elements that are common to both sets. The intersection of the two sets A and B is written as A ∩ B.

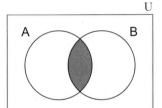

So, A ∩ B is the set of elements that are in both A **and** B.

Worked Example 1.3

U = {1, 2, 3, 4, 5, 6, 7, 8, 9, 10, 11, 12}

A = {1, 3, 5, 7, 9}

B = {2, 3, 5, 7, 11}

  (i) Represent the sets on a Venn diagram.

  (ii) List the elements of A ∪ B.

  (iii) List the elements of A ∩ B.

  (iv) Which of the following statements is false?

    (a) 3 ∈ A ∩ B

    (b) {2, 9} ⊂ A ∪ B

    (c) 2 ∉ B

Solution

(i)

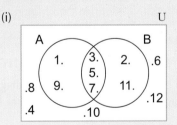

(ii) A ∪ B = {1, 2, 3, 5, 7, 9, 11}

(iii) A ∩ B = {3, 5, 7}

(iv) Only (c) is false, as 2 ∈ B.

Complement of a Set

> The **complement** of a set A is the set of all elements outside set A.

The complement of a set A is denoted by A' or A^C.

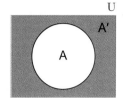

Set Difference

> **A \ B** is the set of elements that are in A but not in B.

A \ B can be pronounced 'A less B'.

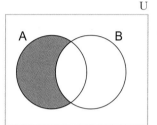

Worked Example 1.4

U = {a, b, c, d, e, f, g}, A = {a, b, c, d} and B = {c, d, e, f}.

   (i)   Represent the sets on a Venn diagram.

   (ii) Show that set difference is not commutative for the given sets A and B.

   (iii) List the elements of (A ∪ B)'.

   (iv) Give one other name for (A ∪ B)'.

Solution

(i)

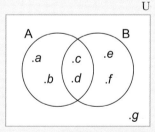

(ii) If set difference is commutative, then A \ B = B \ A.

$$A \setminus B = \{a, b\}$$

$$B \setminus A = \{e, f\}$$

$$\therefore A \setminus B \neq B \setminus A$$

⇒ Set difference is not commutative.

(iii) (A ∪ B)' = {g}

(iv) (A ∪ B)' = U \ (A ∪ B)

We can use sets to answer practical problems.

When doing so, we usually place the cardinal number of each set within a Venn diagram.

We do **not** place a dot beside the cardinal number when doing this, although we do use dots when listing elements within a Venn diagram.

Worked Example 1.5

Thirty students in Transition Year in Cantor Community College were asked if they watched *The Voice of Ireland* or *The X Factor*. Fifteen students said they watched *The Voice of Ireland*. Thirteen students said they watched *The X Factor*.

Twice as many students watched neither programme as watched both programmes. How many students watched neither programme?

Solution

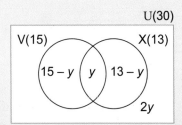

U(30)
V(15)   X(13)
15 − y   y   13 − y
2y

$\# V = 15$

$\# X = 13$

Let $\# (V \cap X) = y$

$\therefore \# (V \cup X)' = 2y$

$\# U = 30$

$(15 - y) + y + (13 - y) + 2y = 30$

$$28 + y = 30$$

$$y = 2$$

$\therefore$ Answer $= 2y$

$= 2(2)$

$= 4$ students watched neither programme.

Exercise 1.1

1. State whether the following sets are well defined or not:

   (i) The set of all inexpensive phones

   (ii) The set of all prime numbers

   (iii) The set of all large numbers

   (iv) The set of all integers

2. $U = \{0, 1, 2, 3, 4, 5, 6, 7, 8\}$, $A = \{2, 3, 5, 7\}$ and $B = \{0, 2, 4, 6, 8\}$.

   List the elements of:

   (i) $A \cup B$ (v) $A \setminus B$

   (ii) $A \cap B$ (vi) $B \setminus A$

   (iii) A' (vii) $(A \cup B)'$

   (iv) B' (viii) $A' \cup B$

3. $U = \{20, 21, 22, 23, 24, 25\}$, $A = \{21, 23, 25\}$ and $B = \{23\}$.

   (a) Represent the sets using a Venn diagram.

   (b) List the elements of:

   (i) $A \cup B$ (v) $(A \cap B)'$

   (ii) $A \cap B$ (vi) $A' \cup B'$

   (iii) A' (vii) $B \setminus A$

   (iv) B' (viii) $(A \setminus B) \cup (B \setminus A)$

   (c) Is $A \setminus B' = B \setminus A'$?

   (d) As $B = A \cap B$, what is the relationship between sets A and B?

   (e) Explain why, for any two sets A and B, $\# (A \cup B) \geqslant \# (A \cap B)$.

4. $A = \{x, y, z\}$

   (i) How many subsets does A have?

   (ii) Write out all the subsets of A.

   (iii) Which of the subsets listed in part (ii) is the only improper subset of A?

5. Name the shaded region in each of the following diagrams:

   (i)
   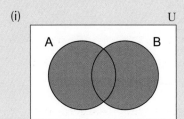

   (ii)
   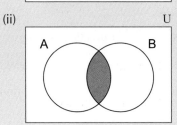

(iii)

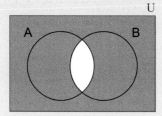

(iv)

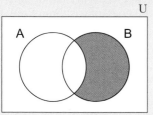

6. Copy the following Venn diagram four times and shade the following sets:

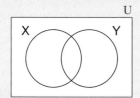

(i) X

(ii) X′

(iii) X \ Y

(iv) (X ∪ Y) \ (X ∩ Y)

7. U = {x | x ≤ 8, x ∈ N},
O = {x | x ≤ 8, x ∈ N, x is odd}, and
P = {x | 2 ≤ x ≤ 8, x ∈ N, x is odd}.

(a) List the elements of sets U, O and P.

(b) Represent the sets U, O and P using a Venn diagram.

(c) Find:

(i) #O

(ii) #P

(iii) #(O ∩ P)

(iv) #(O \ P)

(v) #(O ∪ P)

(vi) #(O ∪ P)′

(d) Complete the following statement:

If A ⊂ B, then #A _____ #(A ∩ B) and #B _____ #(A ∪ B).

8. In a recent survey, 500 teenagers were asked to tick the appropriate box or boxes in the following questionnaire:

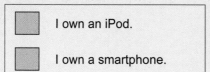

| | I own an iPod. |
| | I own a smartphone. |

The results were as follows: 103 teenagers ticked the iPod box, 146 ticked the smartphone box, and 20 ticked both boxes.

(i) Draw a Venn diagram illustrating the results of the survey.

(ii) What percentage of these teenagers owned a smartphone or an iPod but not both?

9. In a recent health survey, 400 men in their forties were asked to tick the appropriate box or boxes in the following questionnaire:

| | I go to the gym at least twice a week. |
| | I am a vegetarian. |

The results were as follows: 150 ticked the gym box, 100 ticked the vegetarian box and 170 ticked neither box.

(i) Draw a Venn diagram illustrating the results of the survey.

(ii) How many men ticked both boxes?

(iii) What percentage of those surveyed are vegetarians but do not visit the gym at least twice a week?

(iv) Assuming that the sample of 400 is representative of the whole population, i.e. all males in their forties who live in Ireland, what is the probability that a randomly selected male from this population visits the gym at least twice a week or is a vegetarian?

10. Answer the following questions using complete sentences / statements.

(i) What is the difference between {0} and ∅?

(ii) What is the difference between 0 and {0}?

(iii) If X ∩ Y = ∅, what is the relationship between the sets X and Y?

(iv) If X ∪ Y = ∅, what can you say about sets X and Y?

(v) If X ⊂ Y, then what is X ∩ Y?

(vi) If X ⊂ Y, then what is X ∪ Y?

(vii) If X ⊂ Y and Y ⊂ X, then what is the relationship between the sets X and Y?

11. Draw diagrams to simplify and identify the following sets:

   (i) $A \setminus (B \setminus A)$ (iii) $A \cup (B \setminus A)$

   (ii) $A \setminus (A \setminus B)$ (iv) $A \cap (B \setminus A)$

12. The symmetric difference of two sets A and B is the set D of all elements that belong to either A or B but not both.

   (i) Using a Venn diagram, represent the set $(A \setminus B) \cup (B \setminus A)$.

   (ii) Using a Venn diagram, represent the set $(A \cup B) \setminus (A \cap B)$.

   (iii) Hence, what conclusion can you reach about the sets D, $(A \setminus B) \cup (B \setminus A)$ and $(A \cup B) \setminus (A \cap B)$?

13. For each $n \in N$, let $A_n = \{(n + 1)k : k \in N\}$.

   (i) List the first five elements of A_3.

   (ii) $A_1 \cap A_2 = A_p$, where p is some natural number. Find the value of p.

14. In a school of 430 students, 250 students study History and 240 students study Geography.

Let x represent the number of students who study neither History nor Geography.

The number of students who study both History and Geography is three times the number who study neither of these subjects.

   (i) Represent this information on a Venn diagram.

   (ii) Write down and simplify an expression in x for the total number of students in the school.

   (iii) Use this expression to find the number of students who study neither History nor Geography.

1.2 WORKING WITH THREE SETS

We are now going to explore the operations of union, intersection, set difference and complement for three sets. The Venn diagram representation for three sets is shown.

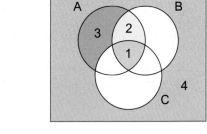

- Region 1, the centre of the Venn diagram, contains the elements common to all three sets: $A \cap B \cap C$.

- Region 2 contains the elements common to A and B only: $(A \cap B) \setminus C$.

- Region 3 contains the elements of A that are not elements of B or C: $A \setminus (B \cup C)$.

- Region 4 contains the elements that do not belong to A, B or C: $(A \cup B \cup C)'$.

ACTIVITY 1.2

Worked Example 1.6

$U = \{x \mid x < 11, x \in N, \}$, A = {the first five natural numbers}, B = {2, 4, 5, 6, 8} and C = {3, 5, 7, 8}.

Represent the above sets using a Venn diagram.

Solution

Step 1   U = {1, 2, 3, 4, 5, 6, 7, 8, 9, 10}
            A = {1, 2, 3, 4, 5}
            B = {2, 4, 5, 6, 8}
            C = {3, 5, 7, 8}

Step 2   Fill in the elements that are common to all three sets; i.e. A ∩ B ∩ C.

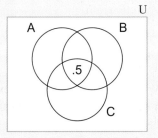

Step 3   Fill in the elements that are common to two sets only; i.e. (A ∩ B) \ C, (A ∩ C) \ B and (B ∩ C) \ A.

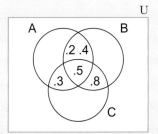

Step 4   Fill in the elements of the sets: A \ (B ∪ C), B \ (A ∪ C) and C \ (A ∪ B).

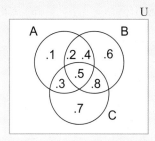

Step 5   Fill in the elements of (A ∪ B ∪ C)′.

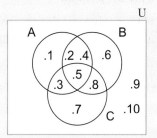

 Exercise 1.2

1. Copy the Venn diagram shown and shade in the following areas: (Use a separate diagram for each part.)

   (i)   A ∩ B ∩ C
   (ii)   A \ (B ∩ C)
   (iii)   (A ∪ B) \ C
   (iv)   (B ∪ C) \ A
   (v)   A ∪ B ∪ C
   (vi)   (A ∪ B ∪ C)′

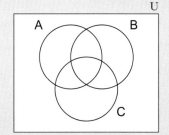

2. Use set notation to name each coloured region in the diagram.

   (i)   Red
   (ii)   Blue
   (iii)   Yellow
   (iv)   Green

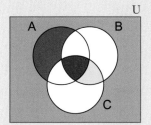

3. Using the Venn diagram shown, list the elements of each of the following sets:

   (i)   A \ B
   (ii)   A ∩ B
   (iii)   (A ∩ B) \ C
   (iv)   A ∩ B ∩ C
   (v)   A ∪ B ∪ C
   (vi)   (A ∪ B ∪ C)′

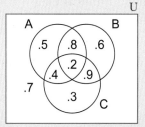

4. Using the Venn diagram shown, list the elements of each of the following sets:

   (i)   P ∪ Q ∪ R
   (ii)   P ∩ Q ∩ R
   (iii)   (R ∩ Q) \ P
   (iv)   (R ∩ P) \ Q
   (v)   (P ∪ Q) ∩ R
   (vi)   U \ (P ∪ Q ∪ R)

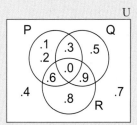

5. Use set notation to name each coloured region in the diagram.

   (i) Red   (iii) Yellow

   (ii) Blue   (iv) Grey

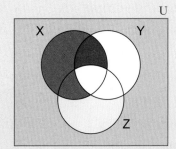

6. Represent the following sets using a Venn diagram:

$U = \{0, 1, 2, 3, 4, 5, 6, 7\}$, $X = \{1, 2, 3, 4\}$, $Y = \{0, 3, 4, 5\}$, $Z = \{1, 3, 5, 6\}$

7. $U = \{1, 2, 3, 4, 5, 6, 7, 8\}$, $P = \{1, 2, 6\}$, $Q = \{2, 3, 4, 5, 6\}$ and $R = \{5, 6, 7\}$.

  (a) Represent the above sets using a Venn diagram.

  (b) List the elements of each of the following sets:

     (i) $P \setminus Q$ (vii) $P \setminus (Q \cup R)$

     (ii) $Q \cap R$ (viii) $(P \cap R) \setminus Q$

     (iii) $P \cup Q \cup R$ (ix) Q^c

     (iv) $P \cap Q \cap R$ (x) $(P \setminus Q) \cup R$

     (v) P' (xi) $P \setminus (Q \setminus R)$

     (vi) $(P \cup Q \cup R)'$ (xii) $(P \setminus Q) \setminus R$

8. $X = \{a, b, c, d\}$, $Y = \{b, c, e\}$ and $Z = \{c, d, f\}$

  (i) Represent the sets X, Y and Z on a Venn diagram.

  (ii) List the elements of $X \cap Y$.

  (iii) List the elements of $(X \cap Z) \setminus Y$.

  (iv) What is $\#(X \cup Y \cup Z)$?

  (v) Identify, using set notation, the set that is empty.

9. $U = \{x \mid 0 < x < 10, x \in N\}$

$A = \{x \mid x \text{ is a prime number less than } 10\}$

$B = \{x \mid x \text{ is an even natural number less than } 10\}$

$C = \{x \mid x \text{ is an odd natural number less than } 10\}$

  (i) Represent the sets U, A, B and C on a Venn diagram.

  (ii) List the elements of $A \cap C$.

  (iii) List the elements of $A \cap B$.

  (iv) Show that $\#(A \cup B \cup C) = \#U$.

  (v) Identify, using set notation, four different sets that are empty.

10. $U = \{x \mid 1 \leqslant x \leqslant 12, x \in N\}$

$A = \{x \mid x \text{ is a prime factor of } 12\}$

$B = \{x \mid x \text{ is a divisor of } 12\}$

$C = \{x \mid x = 2^m, 0 \leqslant m \leqslant 3, m \in Z\}$

  (i) List the elements of sets A, B and C.

  (ii) Represent the sets U, A, B and C on a Venn diagram.

  (iii) List the elements of $B \cap C$.

  (iv) List the elements of $A \cap B \cap C$.

  (v) Find $\#(A \cup B \cup C)$.

  (vi) Identify, using set notation, two different sets that are empty.

11. Consider the Venn diagram below:

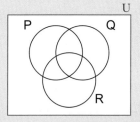

Name the smallest set that each of the following elements are in:

  (i) An element common to P, Q and R

  (ii) An element in P, Q or R

  (iii) An element in Q

  (iv) An element in Q only

  (v) An element in P and R

  (vi) An element in P and Q but not in R

  (vii) An element not in R

  (viii) An element in none of P, Q or R

12. In the Venn diagram below:

$P = \{x \mid x \text{ is a prime number}\}$
$N = \{x \mid x \text{ is a natural number}\}$
$Z = \{x \mid x \text{ is an integer}\}$
$U = \{x \mid x \text{ is any number}\}$

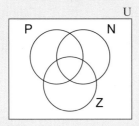

(i) Copy the Venn diagram and insert the following elements:

(a) 0   (e) 4   (i) $\frac{1}{2}$

(b) 1   (f) 5   (j) $\sqrt{3}$

(c) 2   (g) –2   (k) 9.0321

(d) 3   (h) –10   (l) 2^3

(ii) Hence, or otherwise, write down the names of all of the empty sets from the Venn diagram.

(iii) Hence, what conclusions can you make about the relationship between each of the following sets:

(a) P and N

(b) N and Z

13. Let $A = \{k : k \in N, k \leqslant 20\}$,
$B = \{3k - 1 : k \in N\}$ and
$C = \{2k + 1 : k \in N\}$.

Determine the sets:

(a) $A \cap B \cap C$

(b) $(A \cap B) \setminus C$

(c) $(A \cap C) \setminus B$

1.3 PROBLEM-SOLVING WITH THREE SETS

In *Active Maths 1*, we solved problems with two sets. We will now investigate problems that require working with three sets.

Worked Example 1.7

One hundred people took part in a survey. Here is one of the questions posed in the survey:

> Do you listen to:
>
> ☐   Radio 555
>
> ☐   Radio Citytalk
>
> ☐   Radio Riverside

The results of the survey were as follows:

- Four people listen to all three stations.
- Seven people listen to Radio 555 and Radio Citytalk.
- Nine people listen to Radio 555 and Radio Riverside.
- Fourteen people listen to Radio Riverside and Radio Citytalk.
- Thirty-seven people listen to Radio 555, 49 listen to Radio Riverside and 34 listen to Radio Citytalk.

(i) Represent this information on a Venn diagram.

(ii) How many people listen to none of these radio stations?

Solution

Step 1 Let A = {people who listen to Radio 555}.

Let B = {people who listen to Radio Citytalk}.

Let C = {people who listen to Radio Riverside}.

$\#(A \cap B \cap C) = 4$

$\#(A \cap B) = 7$; therefore,
$\#(A \cap B) \setminus C = 7 - 4 = 3$

$\#(A \cap C) = 9$; therefore,
$\#(A \cap C) \setminus B = 9 - 4 = 5$

$\#(C \cap B) = 14$; therefore,
$\#(C \cap B) \setminus A = 14 - 4 = 10$

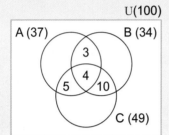

Step 2 $\#(A \setminus (B \cup C)) = 37 - (3 + 4 + 5) = 25$

$\#(B \setminus (A \cup C)) = 34 - (3 + 4 + 10) = 17$

$\#(C \setminus (A \cup B)) = 49 - (10 + 4 + 5) = 30$

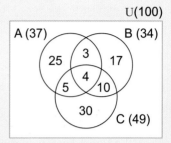

Step 3 $\#(A \cup B \cup C)'$
$= 100 - (37 + 30 + 10 + 17)$
$= 6$

(i)

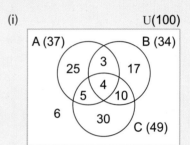

(ii) Six people listen to none of these radio stations.

Worked Example 1.8

A survey was conducted to examine patterns in ownership of iMacs, iPads and iPhones.

The following data was obtained:

- 213 people had an iMac, 295 had an iPad and 337 had an iPhone.

- 109 had all three and 64 had none.

- 198 had an iPhone and an iPad, 382 had an iMac or an iPad, and 61 had an iMac and an iPhone but not an iPad.

(i) Represent this information on a suitable Venn diagram.

(ii) How many people in total were surveyed?

(iii) What percentage of those surveyed own exactly two of the three devices? Answer correct to two decimal places.

Solution

(i) **Step 1** A Venn diagram with three sets consists of eight different regions. In the diagram below, each region has been given a unique colour.

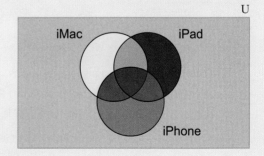

To begin, we examine the cardinal numbers given in the problem, and any numbers that are associated with any one of the eight regions are filled in on the diagram. In this problem, 109 belongs to the red region, 64 to the grey region and 61 to the purple region.

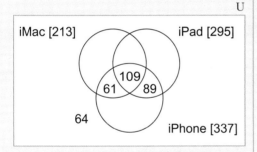

Step 2 Look for numbers that cover two regions. We know that 198 people had an iPhone and an iPad, but 109 people had all three.
Therefore, 198 – 109 = 89 people had an iPhone and an iPad, but not an iMac.

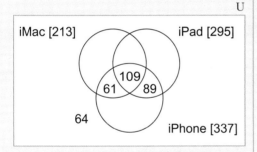

Step 3 We know that 337 had an iPhone. Therefore, 337 – (61 + 109 + 89) = 78 people had an iPhone but not an iMac or an iPod.

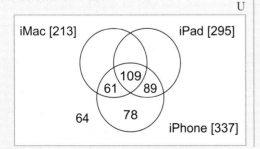

Step 4 The figure of 382 covers six different regions, i.e. every region except the orange region and the grey region. We already have values for three of these six regions. If we let the number in the green region be x, then:

Yellow = $213 – (61 + 109 + x) = 43 – x$

Brown = $295 – (109 + 89 + x) = 97 – x$

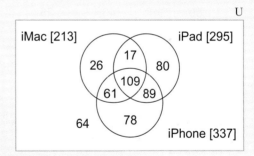

Step 5 Solve for x:

$$213 + 89 + 97 – x = 382$$
$$399 – x = 382$$
$$-x = -17$$
$$x = 17$$

Step 6 Complete the Venn diagram.

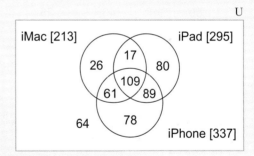

(ii) Total number surveyed:
$$213 + 80 + 89 + 78 + 64$$
$$= 524 \text{ people}$$

(iii) $17 + 61 + 89 = 167$
$$\frac{167}{524} \times \frac{100}{1} \% \approx 31.87\%$$

Exercise 1.3

1. The Venn diagram shows the instruments played by 47 students at a music academy.

   How many students at this academy:

   (i)   Play all three instruments

   (ii) Play piano but not guitar or violin

   (iii) Play violin

   (iv) Play violin only

   (v)   Play piano and one other instrument

   (vi) Play just one instrument

   (vii) Play two or more instruments

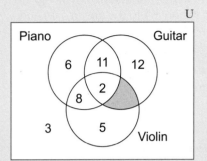

2. A shopkeeper had 70 customers on a particular day. He kept a record of those who bought milk, bread or sugar on that day.

Milk	Bread	Sugar	Sugar & milk	Bread & milk	Bread & sugar	All three items
35	30	37	15	13	12	5

   (i) Represent the results of the survey on a Venn diagram.

   (ii) How many customers bought none of these items?

3. In a survey, 100 people were asked which car colour they liked: red, silver or blue. The results of the survey are given in the table below:

Red	Silver	Blue	Red & silver	Red & blue	Blue & silver	All three colours
55	48	43	25	18	19	10

   (i) Display the results of the survey on a Venn diagram.

   (ii) Use the diagram to find the number of people who liked none of these colours.

4. In a class of 30 pupils, 15 study French, 19 study Irish and 12 study German. Seven pupils study French and Irish, eight pupils study French and German, and seven pupils study Irish and German. Five pupils study all three languages.

   (i)   Represent the information on a Venn diagram.

   (ii) How many pupils study French only?

   (iii) How many pupils study German only?

   (iv) A pupil is chosen at random. What is the probability that the chosen pupil does not study any of these subjects?

5. A shop sells three types of lottery tickets: Lotto, Lotto Plus 1 and Lotto Plus 2. On a particular day:

   ■ Twenty-three people bought a Lotto Plus 1 ticket, 21 people bought a Lotto Plus 2 ticket, and 31 people bought a Lotto ticket.

   ■ Ten people bought a Lotto and a Lotto Plus 2 ticket.

   ■ Nine people bought a Lotto Plus 1 and a Lotto Plus 2 ticket.

   ■ Eleven people bought a Lotto Plus 1 and a Lotto ticket.

   ■ Five people bought a Lotto, a Lotto Plus 1 and a Lotto Plus 2 ticket.

   (i) Represent the information on a Venn diagram.

   (ii) How many people bought a Lotto ticket only?

6. In the Venn diagram below, #U = 50 and the cardinal number of each of the other regions is given.

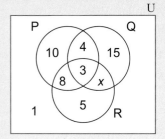

(i) Find the value of *x*.

(ii) Write down #(Q ∩ R).

7. In the Venn diagram below, #U = 45 and the cardinal number of each of the other regions is given.

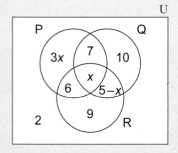

(i) Find the value of *x*.

(ii) Write down #R.

8. Forty members of a youth club are asked if they like to play pool, table tennis or chess.

■ Two members like all three games.

■ Eight like pool and chess.

■ Four like table tennis and chess.

■ Nineteen like pool.

■ Sixteen like table tennis.

■ Eighteen like chess.

■ Six like none of these games.

Let *x* represent the number who like pool and table tennis but not chess.

(i)   Represent the information on a Venn diagram.

(ii) Find the value of *x*.

(iii) How many liked pool but not table tennis or chess?

(iv) One of the members is chosen at random. What is the probability that this member likes all three games?

(v)   What is the probability that a randomly selected member likes pool or table tennis?

(vi) What is the probability that a randomly selected member likes pool or table tennis but not both?

9. One hundred people are asked if they like adventure, science fiction or comedy films.

■ Twenty like adventure and science fiction.

■ Nine like science fiction and comedy.

■ Sixteen like adventure and comedy but not science fiction.

■ Forty-one like adventure.

■ Fifty like comedy.

■ Twenty-five like science fiction but not adventure or comedy.

■ Two do not like any of these kinds of films.

Let *x* represent the number of people who like all three types.

(i)   Represent the information on a Venn diagram.

(ii) Find the value of *x*.

(iii) How many like adventure and science fiction but not comedy?

(iv) How many like science fiction?

(v)   How many like two or more of these types of film?

(vi) What is the probability that a randomly selected person from the group likes science fiction or comedy?

(vii) What is the probability that a randomly selected person likes science fiction or comedy but not adventure?

10. Thirty-nine students were asked if they liked peas, Brussels sprouts or cauliflower.

- Twenty-three liked peas.
- Eighteen liked Brussels sprouts.
- Three liked cauliflower only.
- Nine liked peas and Brussels sprouts.
- Seven liked Brussels sprouts and cauliflower but not peas.
- Eleven liked peas and cauliflower.
- Four did not like any of the vegetables.
- Six liked peas only.

Let x represent the number who liked all three types.

(i) Represent the information on a Venn diagram.

(ii) Find the value of x.

(iii) How many liked Brussels sprouts only?

(iv) How many liked Brussels sprouts and peas but not cauliflower?

11. Forty people were asked whether they grew roses, tulips or daffodils in their garden.

- Five people did not grow any of these flowers.
- Six grew roses or daffodils but not tulips.
- Twenty-eight grew roses.
- Thirty grew at least two of the three flowers.
- Twenty grew roses and tulips but not daffodils.
- Seven grew tulips and daffodils.
- Four grew all three.

(i) Represent the information on a Venn diagram.

(ii) Find the probability that a person chosen at random from the group grew roses or daffodils.

(iii) Find the probability that a person chosen at random from the group grew roses and daffodils but not tulips.

12. Thirty-five people coming back from the USA were asked if they had visited New York, Boston or San Francisco. The results were as follows:

- Twenty had visited New York.
- Thirteen had visited Boston.
- Sixteen had visited San Francisco.
- Seven had been to all three cities.
- Three had been to both New York and San Francisco, but not Boston.
- One had been to both New York and Boston, but not San Francisco.
- Eight had been to Boston and San Francisco.

(i) Display this information in a Venn diagram.

(ii) If one person is chosen at random from the group, what is the probability that the person had not visited any of the three cities?

(iii) If one person is chosen at random, what is the probability that the person had visited New York only?

(iv) If one person is chosen at random, what is the probability that the person had visited Boston or New York?

SEC Sample Paper, JCHL

1.4 THE ASSOCIATIVE AND DISTRIBUTIVE PROPERTIES

Two basic properties of the rational numbers are the associative property and the distributive property.

$(a + b) + c = a + (b + c)$ (Associative property of addition)

$(a \times b) \times c = a \times (b \times c)$ (Associative property of multiplication)

$a \times (b + c) = a \times b + a \times c$ (Distributive property of multiplication over addition)

There are similar properties for union and intersection of sets, which you can investigate in the next activities.

 **ACTIVITIES 1.3, 1.4, 1.5**

Associative properties

> (i) $(A \cup B) \cup C = A \cup (B \cup C)$ (ii) $(A \cap B) \cap C = A \cap (B \cap C)$

Distributive properties

> (i) $A \cup (B \cap C) = (A \cup B) \cap (A \cup C)$ (Union distributes over intersection)
>
> (ii) $A \cap (B \cup C) = (A \cap B) \cup (A \cap C)$ (Intersection distributes over union)

In *Active Maths 1*, we dealt with the commutative properties.

Commutative properties

> (i) $A \cup B = B \cup A$ (ii) $A \cap B = B \cap A$

Worked Example 1.9

$U = \{1, 2, 3, 4, 5, 6, 7, 8\}$, $A = \{1, 2, 3, 4\}$,

$B = \{3, 4, 5, 8\}$ and $C = \{1, 3, 5, 7\}$.

  (i) Represent these sets on a Venn diagram.

 (ii) Show that $(A \cup B) \cup C = A \cup (B \cup C)$.

(iii) Show that $(A \cap B) \cap C = A \cap (B \cap C)$.

(iv) Show that $(A \setminus B) \setminus C \neq A \setminus (B \setminus C)$.

Solution

(i)

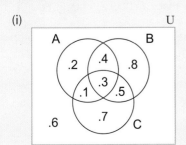

(ii) $(A \cup B) \cup C$

$= \{1, 2, 3, 4, 5, 8\} \cup \{1, 3, 5, 7\}$

$= \{1, 2, 3, 4, 5, 7, 8\}$

$A \cup (B \cup C)$

$= \{1, 2, 3, 4\} \cup \{1, 3, 4, 5, 7, 8\}$

$= \{1, 2, 3, 4, 5, 7, 8\}$

$\therefore (A \cup B) \cup C = A \cup (B \cup C)$

(iii) $(A \cap B) \cap C = \{3, 4\} \cap \{1, 3, 5, 7\} = \{3\}$

$A \cap (B \cap C) = \{1, 2, 3, 4\} \cap \{3, 5\} = \{3\}$

$\therefore (A \cap B) \cap C = A \cap (B \cap C)$

(iv) $(A \setminus B) \setminus C = \{1, 2\} \setminus \{1, 3, 5, 7\} = \{2\}$

$A \setminus (B \setminus C) = \{1, 2, 3, 4\} \setminus \{4, 8\} = \{1, 2, 3\}$

$\therefore (A \setminus B) \setminus C \neq A \setminus (B \setminus C)$

Worked Example 1.10

U = {a, b, c, d, e, f, g, h}, A = {a, b, c, d},

B = {c, d, e, h} and C = {a, c, e, g}.

(i) Represent these sets on a Venn diagram.

(ii) Show that A ∪ (B ∩ C) = (A ∪ B) ∩ (A ∪ C).

(iii) Show that A ∩ (B ∪ C) = (A ∩ B) ∪ (A ∩ C).

Solution

(i)

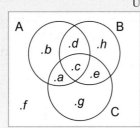

(ii) A ∪ (B ∩ C) = {a, b, c, d} ∪ {c, e}
     = {a, b, c, d, e}

(A ∪ B) ∩ (A ∪ C)

= {a, b, c, d, e, h} ∩ {a, b, c, d, e, g}

= {a, b, c, d, e}

∴ A ∪ (B ∩ C) = (A ∪ B) ∩ (A ∪ C)

(iii) A ∩ (B ∪ C)

= {a, b, c, d} ∩ {a, c, d, e, g, h}

= {a, c, d}

(A ∩ B) ∪ (A ∩ C)

= {c, d} ∪ {a, c}

= {a, c, d}

∴ A ∩ (B ∪ C) = (A ∩ B) ∪ (A ∩ C)

Worked Example 1.11

Use the associative and commutative properties to show that (A ∪ C) ∪ B = (A ∪ B) ∪ C.

Solution

(A ∪ C) ∪ B = A ∪ (C ∪ B)   (Associative property)

= A ∪ (B ∪ C)   (Commutative property)

= (A ∪ B) ∪ C   (Associative property)

Exercise 1.4

1. U = {0, 1, 2, 3, 4, 5, 6, 7, 8, 9},
   A = {2, 3, 7, 8}, B = {0, 4, 5, 7, 8, 9} and
   C = {1, 2, 6, 7, 8, 9}.

   (i) Represent the above sets on a Venn diagram.

   (ii) Show that (A ∪ B) ∪ C = A ∪ (B ∪ C).

   (iii) Show that (A ∩ B) ∩ C = A ∩ (B ∩ C).

   (iv) Show that (A \ B) \ C ≠ A \ (B \ C).

2. U = {0, 1, 2, 3, 4, 5, 6, 7, 8, 9, 10},
   A = {0, 2, 4, 5, 9}, B = {1, 2, 7, 8, 9}
   and C = {2, 4, 8, 10}.

   (i) Represent the above sets on a Venn diagram.

   (ii) Show that A ∪ (B ∩ C) = (A ∪ B) ∩ (A ∪ C).

   (iii) Show that A ∩ (B ∪ C) = (A ∩ B) ∪ (A ∩ C).

3. U = {a, b, c, d, e, f, g, h}, P = {b, c, d, e, f},
   Q = {e, f, g, h} and R = {a, b, c, h}.

   (i) Show that (P ∪ Q) ∪ R = P ∪ (Q ∪ R).

   (ii) Show that (P ∩ Q) ∩ R = P ∩ (Q ∩ R).

4. U = {s, t, u, v, w, x, y, z}, X = {s, t, v, w},
   Y = {u, w, y, z} and Z = {s, u, x, z}

   (i) Show that X ∪ (Y ∩ Z) = (X ∪ Y) ∩ (X ∪ Z).

   (ii) Show that X ∩ (Y ∪ Z) = (X ∩ Y) ∪ (X ∩ Z).

5. Use the associative and commutative properties to show that (X ∪ Z) ∪ Y = (X ∪ Y) ∪ Z.

6. Name a set that you would use along with (M ∪ N) ∩ (M ∪ O) to show that union distributes over intersection.

7. Name a set that you would use along with $T \cap (R \cup S)$ to show that intersection distributes over union.

8. A and B are two sets and U is the universal set.

(i) Name the set shaded yellow.

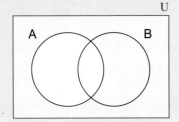

(ii) Name the set shaded green.

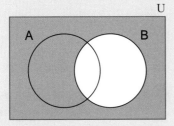

(iii) If the diagram from part (i) is superimposed on the diagram from part (ii), which region(s) (numbered 1–4 below) would contain yellow shading and green shading, i.e. find the intersection of (i) and (ii).

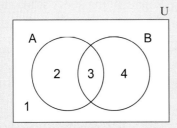

(iv) Using your results from parts (i)–(iii), explain what relationship exists between $(A \cup B)'$ and $A' \cap B'$.

(v) Name the set shaded grey.

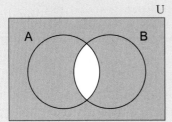

(vi) Using the results from parts (i), (ii) and (v), explain what relationship exists between $(A \cap B)'$ and $A' \cup B'$.

$U \setminus (A \cup B) = (U \setminus A) \cap (U \setminus B)$ and $U \setminus (A \cap B) = (U \setminus A) \cup (U \setminus B)$ are known as de Morgan's Laws. Augustus de Morgan (1806–1871) was born in Madras, India, and educated at Cambridge.
At the age of 22, he became the first professor of mathematics at the newly opened University of London. He contributed to many different areas of mathematics, including set theory, algebra, calculus and probability.

9. $U = \{1, 2, 3, 4, 5, 6, 7, 8, 9, 10\}$, $A = \{2, 3, 5, 7\}$, $B = \{4, 5, 7, 8, 9, 10\}$ and $C = \{2, 4, 6, 8, 10\}$. Show that:

(i) $(A \cup B)' = A' \cap B'$

(ii) $(A \cap C)' = A' \cup C'$

(iii) $(A')' = A$

(iv) $A \cup (B \cap C) = (A \cup B) \cap (A \cup C)$

(v) $A \cap (B \cup C) = (A \cap B) \cup (A \cap C)$

10. $U = \{1, 2, 3, 4, 5, 6, 7, 8, 9, 10\}$, $A = \{2, 3, 7, 8\}$ and $B = \{4, 5, 7, 8, 9, 10\}$.

Use de Morgan's Laws to find:

(i) $(A' \cup B)'$

(ii) $(A \cap B')'$

Use a Venn diagram to verify your answers to parts (i) and (ii).

1. $U = \{x \mid 1 \leqslant x < 21, x \in N\}$,

$A = \{x \mid x \text{ is a factor of } 20\}$ and

$B = \{x \mid x < 21 \text{ and } x \text{ is a multiple of } 2\}$.

  (a) Represent the above sets using a Venn diagram.

  (b) List the elements of:

    (i) $A \cup B$ (v) $(A \cap B)'$

    (ii) $A \cap B$ (vi) $A' \cup B'$

    (iii) A' (vii) $(A \setminus B) \cup (B \setminus A)$

    (iv) B' (viii) $(A \setminus B) \cap (B \setminus A)$

2. $U = \{1, 2, 3, 4, 5, 6, 7, 8\}$, $P = \{1, 3, 5, 7\}$ and $Q = \{2, 3, 4, 5\}$. Find:

  (i) $\#P$ (iv) $\#(P \setminus Q)$

  (ii) $\#Q$ (v) $\#(P \cup Q)$

  (iii) $\#(P \cap Q)$ (vi) $\#(P \cup Q)'$

3. $X = \{s, t, u, w, x, y, z\}$, $Y = \{w, y, z\}$ and $Z = \{v, w, y, z\}$.

  (i) Represent the sets X, Y and Z on a Venn diagram.

  (ii) List the elements of $X \cap Y$.

  (iii) List the elements of $(X \cap Z) \setminus Y$.

  (iv) What is $\#(X \cup Y \cup Z)$?

  (v) Identify, using set notation, the set containing four elements.

  (vi) Name four distinct empty regions.

4. Recently, *Black Eyed Peas*, *Take That* and *JLS* had concert tours. A large group of teenagers was surveyed and the following information was obtained:

- 762 teenagers saw *Black Eyed Peas*.
- 1,248 saw *Take That*.
- 1,424 saw *JLS*.
- 222 saw all three.
- 1,026 saw none.
- 480 saw only *JLS*.
- 754 saw *JLS* and *Take That*.
- 234 saw *Take That* and *Black Eyed Peas* but not *JLS*.

  (i) Represent the information on a Venn diagram.

  (ii) How many teenagers were surveyed?

  (iii) What percentage of the group saw at least one of the bands? Answer correct to two places of decimals.

  (iv) What percentage of the group saw exactly one of the bands? Answer correct to two places of decimals.

  (v) What percentage of the group saw *Take That* or *JLS*? Answer correct to the nearest whole number.

5. $U = \{2, 3, 4, 5, ..., 30\}$,
$A = \{x \mid x \text{ is a multiple of } 2, x \leqslant 30\}$,
$B = \{x \mid x \text{ is a multiple of } 3, x \leqslant 30\}$ and
$C = \{x \mid x \text{ is a multiple of } 5, x \leqslant 30\}$.

  (i) Represent the above sets on a Venn diagram.

  (ii) Show that $(A \cup B) \cup C = A \cup (B \cup C)$.

  (iii) Show that $(A \cap B) \cap C = A \cap (B \cap C)$.

  (iv) Show that $(A \setminus B) \setminus C \neq A \setminus (B \setminus C)$.

  (v) Show that $A \cup (B \cap C) = (A \cup B) \cap (A \cup C)$.

  (vi) Show that $A \cap (B \cup C) = (A \cap B) \cup (A \cap C)$.

6. A group of 49 students was asked which fruit each liked.

- Twenty-eight said they liked apples, 25 said they liked pears while 26 said they liked oranges.
- Eight said they liked all three types of fruit.
- Seventeen said they liked pears and oranges; 11 said they liked apples and oranges.
- Five said they did not like any of the three types of fruit.

Let x represent those students who liked apples and pears but not oranges.

(i) Represent the above information on a Venn diagram.

(ii) Calculate the value of x.

(iii) Calculate the percentage of students who liked one type of fruit only.

Give your answer correct to the nearest whole number.

7. U is the universal set and P and Q are two subsets of U.

$\#U = 30$, $\#P = 16$ and $\#Q = 6$.

(i) Find with the aid of a Venn diagram the minimum value of $\#(P \cup Q)'$.

(ii) Find with the aid of a Venn diagram the maximum value of $\#(P \cup Q)'$.

$\#U = u$, $\#P = p$, $\#Q = q$ and $\#(P \cup Q)' = x$.

(iii) Show, with the aid of a Venn diagram, that if $p > q$ and x is a maximum, then $u = p + x$.

SEC 2011, JCHL

8. The following information was obtained from a group of pet owners:

■ Twenty-three own a fish.

■ Twenty-five own a bird.

■ Thirty-one own a cat.

■ Forty-three own a bird or a cat.

■ Thirty-eight own a bird or a fish.

■ Eight own a fish, a bird and a cat.

■ Seven own a cat only.

(i) Represent this information on a Venn diagram.

(ii) How many pet owners were surveyed?

(iii) What percentage of the group own at least two pets? (Answer to the nearest whole number.)

(iv) What percentage of the group own one pet only? (Answer to the nearest whole number.)

9.

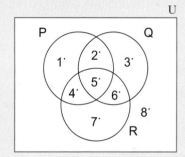

(a) From the Venn diagram above, list the elements of:

(i) $P \cup Q$ (ii) $Q \cap R$ (iii) $P \cup (Q \cap R)$

(b) Miriam says, 'For all sets, union is distributive over intersection.' Name a set that you would use along with $P \cup (Q \cap R)$ to show that Miriam's claim is true for the sets P, Q and R in the Venn diagram above.

SEC Sample Paper, JCHL

10. $U = \{2, 3, 4, 5, ..., 30\}$, $A = \{$multiples of 2$\}$, $B = \{$multiples of 3$\}$, $C = \{$multiples of 5$\}$

(a) Find $\#[(A \cup B \cup C)']$, the number of elements in the complement of the set $A \cup B \cup C$.

(b) How many divisors does each of the numbers in $(A \cup B \cup C)'$ have?

(c) What name is given to numbers that have this many divisors?

SEC Sample Paper, JCHL

11. A group of 100 students were surveyed to find whether they drank tea (T), coffee (C) or a soft drink (D) at any time in the previous week.

- Twenty-four had not drunk any of the three.
- Fifty-one drank tea or coffee but not a soft drink.
- Forty-one drank tea.
- Twenty drank at least two of the three.
- Eight drank tea and a soft drink but not coffee.
- Nine drank a soft drink and coffee.
- Four drank all three.

(a) Represent the above information on the Venn diagram shown below.

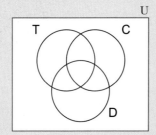

(b) Find the probability that a student chosen at random from the group had drunk tea or coffee.

(c) Find the probability that a student chosen at random from the group had drunk tea and coffee but not a soft drink.

SEC Sample Paper, JCHL

12. (i) A = {1, 2, 3, 4}, B = {2, 3, 5} and C = {1, 3, 4, 5, 6}.

List the elements of (A \ B) ∪ (C ∩ B) and the elements of (A ∪ B) ∩ (C \ B).

(ii) U is the universal set, and P and Q are two subsets of U.

$\#U = 20$ $\#((P \cup Q)') = 4$

$\#(P \cap Q) = x$ $\#Q = 2(\#P)$

$\#(P \setminus Q) = 2x$

Represent the above information on a Venn diagram and hence find #Q.

13. (a) A leisure centre has 110 members. The weights room (W) is used by 82 members and the swimming pool (S) is used by 57 members; 15 members do not use either facility.

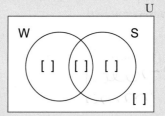

Copy the above Venn diagram and complete it to show the number of members in each part of each set.

(b) U is the universal set, and A and B are two subsets of U.

$\#U = u$ $\#(A \cap B) = x$

$\#A = a$ $\#((A \cup B)') = y$

$\#B = b$

(i) Represent this information on a Venn diagram and hence express u in terms of a, b, x and y.

(ii) Show that if $a > b$, then the minimum possible value of u is $y + a$.

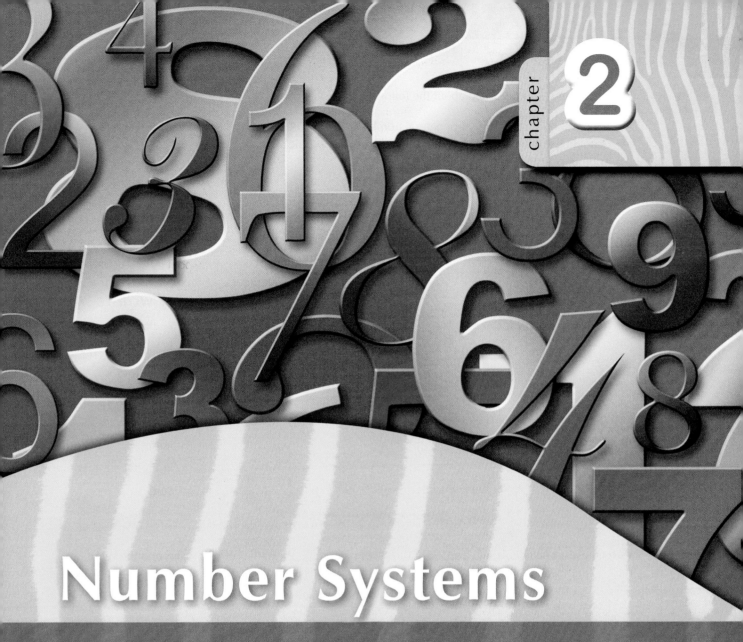

chapter 2

Number Systems

Learning Outcomes

In this chapter you will learn:

- ➲ About irrational numbers
- ➲ About the real number system
- ➲ The meaning of the term surd
- ➲ How to operate on the set of irrational numbers $R \setminus Q$

2.1 REVIEW

In *Active Maths* 1, you learned about the following number systems:

1. **Natural numbers:** The set of natural numbers is the set of counting numbers. They are also called the positive whole numbers.

$$N = \{1, 2, 3, 4, \ldots\}$$

2. **Integers:** The set of integers is the set of all whole numbers (positive, negative and zero).

$$Z = \{\ldots, -3, -2, -1, 0, 1, 2, 3, \ldots\}$$
$$\text{OR}$$
$$Z = \{0, 1, -1, 2, -2, 3, -3, \ldots\}$$

3. **Rational numbers:** The rational numbers are numbers that can be written in the form $\frac{a}{b}$, where $a, b \in Z$ and $b \neq 0$.

$$Q = \{\text{Any number of the form } \frac{a}{b}, \text{ where } a, b \in Z, b \neq 0\}$$

YOU SHOULD REMEMBER...

- Prime numbers
- Natural numbers, integers and rational numbers
- LCM and HCF
- Commutative, associative and distributive properties

KEY WORDS

- **Factor**
- **Multiple**
- **Prime factor**
- **Product of prime factors**
- **HCF**
- **LCM**
- **Irrational number**
- **Surd**

We can use a Venn diagram to represent the set of natural numbers, the set of integers and the set of rational numbers.

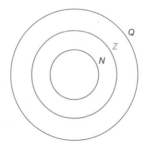

Every natural number is an integer. So $N \subset Z$. Every integer is a rational number. So $Z \subset Q$. Therefore:

$$N \subset Z \subset Q$$

An important subset of the natural numbers is the set of **prime numbers**.

A **prime number** is a natural number greater than 1 whose only positive factors are 1 and itself.

Every natural number greater than 1 is either a prime number or can be written uniquely as a product of prime numbers.

Worked Example 2.1

Write 525 as a product of prime numbers.

Solution

3	525
5	175
5	35
7	7
	1

$525 = 3 \times 5^2 \times 7$

 Worked Example 2.2

Find the highest common factor (HCF) of 102 and 170.

Solution

Write each of 102 and 170 as a product of primes.

2	102
3	51
17	17
	1

2	170
5	85
17	17
	1

$102 = ②\times 3 \times ⑰$ $170 = ②\times 5 \times ⑰$

The common factors are 2 and 17.

Therefore, HCF(102,170) = 2 × 17 = 34.

 Worked Example 2.3

Find the lowest common multiple (LCM) of 60 and 42.

Solution

Write each number as a product of prime factors.

2	60
2	30
3	15
5	5
	1

2	42
3	21
7	7
	1

- 2^2 is the bigger of the factors 2 and 2^2.
- 3 is a common factor of both 60 and 42.
- 5 and 7 are the non-common factors.

∴ LCM = $2^2 \times 3 \times 5 \times 7$

∴ LCM = 420

$60 = 2^2 \times 3 \times 5$

$42 = 2 \times 3 \times 7$

The Commutative, Associative and Distributive Properties

If $a, b, c \in N$, then:

(i) $a + b = b + a$ (Addition is commutative)

(ii) $a \times b = b \times a$ (Multiplication is commutative)

(iii) $(a + b) + c = a + (b + c)$ (Addition is associative)

(iv) $(a \times b) \times c = a \times (b \times c)$ (Multiplication is associative)

(v) $a \times (b + c) = a \times b + a \times c$ (Multiplication distributes over addition)

These properties also apply to Z, the set of integers, and to Q, the set of rational numbers.

BIMDAS

In maths, the order of operations is the order in which things are done. It is important to have order, otherwise answers will differ.

We can use the guide shown to help us remember the order in which operations are carried out.

These letters stand for **B**rackets, **I**ndex, **M**ultiplication, **D**ivision, **A**ddition and **S**ubtraction. We start at the top of the triangle and work down. Therefore, Brackets come first, then Indices (powers and roots), Multiplication/Division and finally Addition/Subtraction.

$$\boxed{B} \to \boxed{I} \to \boxed{MD} \to \boxed{AS}$$

For $\boxed{MD}$ and $\boxed{AS}$ read left to right.

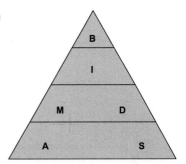

Worked Example 2.4

Evaluate $4\left(\dfrac{5}{2} - 3\right)^2 - 6\left(\dfrac{1}{4} \div 2\right)^3 + 6(-2)^4$.

Solution

$$4\left(\frac{5}{2} - 3\right)^2 - 6\left(\frac{1}{4} \div 2\right)^3 + 6(-2)^4 = 4\left(-\frac{1}{2}\right)^2 - 6\left(\frac{1}{8}\right)^3 + 6(-2)^4 \qquad \text{(Brackets)}$$

$$= 4\left(\frac{1}{4}\right) - 6\left(\frac{1}{512}\right) + 6(16) \qquad \text{(Indices)}$$

$$= 1 - \frac{3}{256} + 96 \qquad \text{(Multiplication)}$$

$$= 96\frac{253}{256} \qquad \text{(Addition and subtraction)}$$

Exercise 2.1

1. (a) Define each of the following sets as a single set, where N is the set of natural numbers, Z the set of integers and Q the set of rational numbers:

   (i) $N \cup Z$ (iv) $Q \cap Z$

   (ii) $N \cap Z$ (v) $Q \cap Z \cap N$

   (iii) $Q \cup Z$ (vi) $(N \cap Z) \cap (Z \cap Q)$

   (b) Represent each answer above on a suitable Venn diagram.

2. (a) List, in order, the first 15 prime numbers.

   (b) Write each of the following numbers as a product of prime numbers:

   (i) 1,320   (iv) 2,310

   (ii) 5,200   (v) 7,776

   (iii) 1,452   (vi) 2,666

3. (a) Using a number line, evaluate each of the following products by skip counting:

   (i) 4×3 (iii) 8×3

   (ii) 3×5 (iv) 2×6

   (b) Use area models to evaluate each of the following products:

   (i) 24×42 (iv) 15×124

   (ii) 38×62 (v) 122×451

   (iii) 42×71 (vi) 215×512

4. Use a number line to evaluate each of the following:

   (i) $-3 + 5$ (iv) $-7 + 3$

   (ii) $5 - 7$ (v) $-8 - 3$

   (iii) $-3 - 5$ (vi) $2 - 5$

5. (a) Use fraction strips to evaluate each of the following:

  (i) $\frac{1}{2} + \frac{2}{5}$ (ii) $\frac{3}{4} + \frac{3}{16}$ (iii) $\frac{2}{3} + \frac{1}{2}$ (iv) $\frac{5}{8} + \frac{3}{4}$

  (b)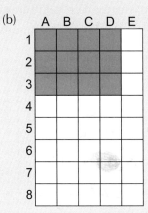

  Study the diagram, and answer the following questions:

  (i) What fraction of row 1 is shaded?

  (ii) What fraction of column A is shaded?

  (iii) Use the diagram to calculate the result when the fractions in parts (i) and (ii) above are multiplied together.

6. (a) The diagram below shows three-fifths of a rectangle. Complete the rectangle on the grid.

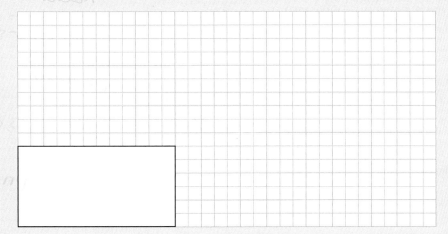

  (b) By shading appropriate sections of the strips below, show that $\frac{1}{3} + \frac{2}{6} \neq \frac{3}{9}$

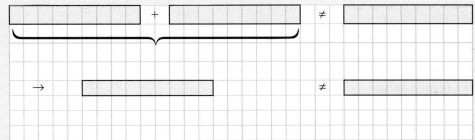

SEC 2012, JCHL

7. Find the HCF and LCM of each of the following by first writing each number as a product of primes:

  (i) 69 and 123   (iii) 1,144 and 680   (v) 1,056 and 2,208

  (ii) 368 and 621   (iv) 4,185 and 4,437   (vi) 789 and 1,635

8. Which properties of the rational numbers are being illustrated in the following:

  (i) $\frac{1}{2} + 3 = 3 + \frac{1}{2}$ (iv) $(3.4 \times 2.8) \times 3.6 = 3.4 \times (2.8 \times 3.6)$

  (ii) $5 \times 4 = 4 \times 5$ (v) $5 \times (2 + 8) = 5 \times 2 + 5 \times 8$

  (iii) $\left(\frac{1}{2} + \frac{1}{4}\right) + \frac{1}{3} = \frac{1}{2} + \left(\frac{1}{4} + \frac{1}{3}\right)$

9. Evaluate each of the following:

(i) $2(5 - 3)^3 - 4(6 \div 3)^2 + 5(4)^3$

(ii) $\dfrac{2^3 \times 3 - 50}{(3 \div 2)^3 - 5}$

(iii) $6\sqrt{\dfrac{1}{4}} - 5\left(\dfrac{1}{2} - \dfrac{3}{8}\right)^2 + 16 \times \sqrt{\dfrac{1}{64}}$

(iv) $5\sqrt{\dfrac{9}{25}} + 7\left(\dfrac{3}{28} - \dfrac{1}{14}\right) + \dfrac{5}{\sqrt{\dfrac{16}{625}}}$

10. The values of w, x, y and z are 6, 7, 8 and 9, but not necessarily in that order. Determine the largest possible value of $w(x)^2 + zw + y^3w$.

11. The three-digit number 5M4 is divisible by 4, and the three-digit number 37N is divisible by 3. What is the largest possible difference between 5M4 and 37N?

12. In the expression $\dfrac{p}{q} + \dfrac{r}{s} + \dfrac{t}{u}$, each letter is replaced with a different digit from the set $\{1, 2, 3, 4, 5, 6, 7, 8, 9\}$.

(a) What is the largest possible value of the expression?

(b) What is the smallest possible value?

13. A container contains 45 litres of wine. Nine litres of wine are removed from the container and replaced with 9 litres of water. Nine litres of the mixture are then removed and replaced with 9 litres of water.

What is the ratio of wine to water in the new mixture?

14. A piece of wire 80 cm in length is to be cut into two parts in the ratio 5 : 11. Each part is bent to form a square. Determine the ratio of the area of the larger square to the area of the smaller square.

15. Consider the Venn diagram below:

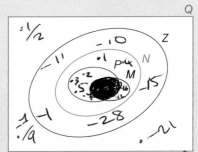

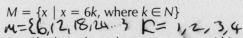

$Q = \{x \mid x = \dfrac{a}{b}, \text{ where } a, b \in Z, b \neq 0\}$ *rational*

$Z = \{0, 1, -1, 2, -2, ...\}$ *integers*

$N = \{1, 2, 3, 4, ...\}$ *Natural*

$P = \{x \mid x \text{ is prime}\}$ *prime*

$M = \{x \mid x = 6k, \text{ where } k \in N\}$
$M = \{6, 12, 18, 24...\}$ $k = 1, 2, 3, 4$

(a) Shade in the only empty region within the Venn diagram above.

(b) What is the name of this region? $P \cap M$

(c) Explain why this region is empty.

(d) Draw the Venn diagram above in your copy book and insert the following numbers into the diagram:

2	4	6	0
-5	$\sqrt{9}$	$\dfrac{1}{2}$	$(-2)^3$
-2^2	$\dfrac{10}{2}$	97	$((-1)^2)^3$

2.2 IRRATIONAL NUMBERS

The length x of the diagonal of the unit square can be found using the theorem of Pythagoras.

$x^2 = 1^2 + 1^2$

$x^2 = 1 + 1$

$x^2 = 2$

$x = \sqrt{2}$ (as $x > 0$)

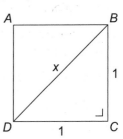

Can $\sqrt{2}$ be written as a fraction? In other words, do there exist integers a and b such that $\sqrt{2} = \dfrac{a}{b}$?

This problem preoccupied ancient Greek mathematicians for many years, among them the famous philosopher and mathematician Pythagoras, who lived in the sixth century BC. Around 500 BC, Hippasus, a follower of Pythagoras, is said to have proved that $\sqrt{2}$ could not be written as a fraction. Pythagoras, who did not believe in the existence of irrational numbers, was apparently so enraged by this proof that he had Hippasus thrown overboard from a ship, causing him to drown. $\sqrt{2}$ became the first known irrational number.

Pythagoras

π, the ratio of the circumference of a circle to its diameter, is also an irrational number. It was not until the 18th century that Johann Heinrich Lambert, a Swiss mathematician, proved that π is irrational.

Johann Heinrich Lambert (1728–1777)

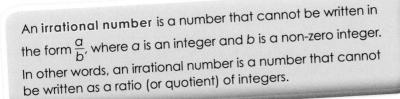

An irrational number is a number that cannot be written in the form $\frac{a}{b}$, where a is an integer and b is a non-zero integer. In other words, an irrational number is a number that cannot be written as a ratio (or quotient) of integers.

While $\sqrt{2}$ cannot be written as a rational number, it is possible to find an approximation for $\sqrt{2}$. A calculator gives the approximation $\sqrt{2} = 1.414213562$, but this decimal goes on forever with no pattern or repetition.

Real Numbers

The rational and irrational numbers together make up the real number system.

A number is real if its square is non-negative.

$$R = \{x \mid x^2 \geqslant 0\}$$

The commutative, associative and distributive properties of the rational numbers also apply to the real number system.

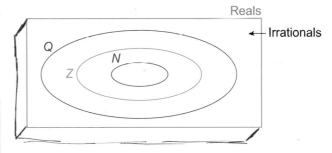

Surds

Some irrational numbers can be written as the root of a rational number. These numbers are called **surds**.

$\sqrt{2}$ and $\sqrt{3}$ are examples of surds. They are both irrational and can both be written as the root of a rational number.

Consider the following numbers:

$\sqrt{9}$ π $\sqrt[3]{8}$ $\sqrt{5}$

Which of these numbers is a surd?

$\sqrt{9}$ is not a surd as $\sqrt{9} = 3$, which is rational.

π is not a surd as π cannot be written as the root of a rational number. (π is, of course, irrational.)

$\sqrt[3]{8}$ is not a surd. Although $\sqrt[3]{8}$ is the cube root of a rational number, $\sqrt[3]{8} = 2$, which is rational.

$\sqrt{5}$ is a surd as it is both irrational and can be written as the root of a rational number.

> **A surd** is an irrational number that can be written as the root of a rational number.

In Activities 2.1 and 2.2, you will derive two Laws of Surds.

 **ACTIVITIES** 2.1, 2.2

FORMULA

Law 1 $\sqrt{a}\sqrt{b} = \sqrt{ab}$

Law 2 $\dfrac{\sqrt{a}}{\sqrt{b}} = \sqrt{\dfrac{a}{b}}$

Law 3 $(a^p)^q = a^{pq}$

The word 'surd' comes from the Latin word *surdus* (meaning 'deaf' or 'mute'). The Latin term was itself a translation from Arabic, as Arab mathematicians liked to think of rational numbers as being 'audible' and irrational numbers as being 'inaudible'.

Worked Example 2.5

What is $\sqrt{a^2}$, $a \geqslant 0$, $a \in R$?

Solution

$\sqrt{a^2} = (a^2)^{\frac{1}{2}}$

$\quad = a^1$ (Law 3 of Indices)

$\quad = a$

Worked Example 2.6

What is $\sqrt{a}\sqrt{a}$, $a \geqslant 0$, $a \in R$?

Solution

$\sqrt{a}\sqrt{a} = \sqrt{(a)(a)}$ (Law 1 of Surds)

$\quad = \sqrt{a^2}$

$\quad = a$

Reducing Surds

Square roots can be reduced or simplified if the number under the radical sign (square root sign) has a perfect square number greater than 1 as a factor. The perfect squares greater than 1 are 4, 9, 16, 25, 36, ... etc.

Example: $\sqrt{128} = \sqrt{64 \times 2} = \sqrt{64}\sqrt{2} = 8\sqrt{2}$.

Worked Example 2.7

Reduce $\sqrt{45}$ to its simplest surd form.

Solution

Step 1

Find the largest square number that is a factor of 45.

9 is the largest square factor of 45.

Step 2

$\sqrt{45} = \sqrt{9 \times 5}$

$\quad = \sqrt{9}\sqrt{5}$

$\quad = 3\sqrt{5}$

Worked Example 2.8

Simplify $\sqrt{50} + \sqrt{8} - \sqrt{32}$.

Solution

$$\sqrt{50} + \sqrt{8} - \sqrt{32} = \sqrt{25}\sqrt{2} + \sqrt{4}\sqrt{2} - \sqrt{16}\sqrt{2}$$
$$= 5\sqrt{2} + 2\sqrt{2} - 4\sqrt{2}$$
$$= 3\sqrt{2}$$

- 25 is the largest square factor of 50
- 4 is the largest square factor of 8
- 16 is the largest square factor of 32

Worked Example 2.9

Show that $(a\sqrt{b})^2 = a^2b$ where $a \in Q$ and $b \in Q^+$.
Hence, evaluate $(3\sqrt{5})^2$.

Note: Q^+ is the set of positive rational numbers.

Solution

$$(a\sqrt{b})^2 = (a\sqrt{b})(a\sqrt{b})$$
$$= (a)(a)(\sqrt{b})(\sqrt{b})$$
$$= a^2b$$

$$(3\sqrt{5})^2 = 3^2(5)$$
$$= 9(5)$$
$$= 45$$

Exercise 2.2

1. Which of the following numbers are irrational:

   $\sqrt{7}, \quad \sqrt{4}, \quad 101, \quad \dfrac{3}{5}, \quad 3 - \sqrt{9}$

2. For each of the following numbers, say whether it is or is not a surd and explain your reasoning.

   (i) $\sqrt{5}$ (iv) π (vii) $\sqrt{324}$

   (ii) $\sqrt{64}$ (v) $\sqrt{\pi^2}$ (viii) $\sqrt{648}$

   (iii) $\sqrt{19}$ (vi) $\sqrt{2500}$ (ix) $\sqrt[3]{\pi^3}$

3. Evaluate each of the following without using a calculator:

   (i) $(\sqrt{5})^2$ (vi) $(3\sqrt{3})^2$

   (ii) $(\sqrt{11})^2$ (vii) $(5\sqrt{10})^2$

   (iii) $(\sqrt{17})^2$ (viii) $\left(\dfrac{1}{3}\sqrt{29}\right)^2$

   (iv) $(\sqrt{27})^2$ (ix) $\left(\dfrac{1}{4}\sqrt{65}\right)^2$

   (v) $(\sqrt{34})^2$ (x) $\left(\dfrac{3}{8}\sqrt{19}\right)^2$

4. Say if each of the following is true or false:

   (i) $\sqrt{2} + \sqrt{7} = \sqrt{9}$ (iii) $\sqrt{7}\sqrt{2} = \sqrt{14}$

   (ii) $\sqrt{7} - \sqrt{2} = \sqrt{5}$ (iv) $\dfrac{\sqrt{35}}{\sqrt{7}} = \sqrt{5}$

5. Explain why each of the following is true:

   (i) $\sqrt{2} + \sqrt{3} = \sqrt{3} + \sqrt{2}$

   (ii) $(\sqrt{3} \times \sqrt{5}) \times \sqrt{6} = \sqrt{3} \times (\sqrt{5} \times \sqrt{6})$

   (iii) $\sqrt{11}(\sqrt{2} + \sqrt{5}) = \sqrt{22} + \sqrt{55}$

6. Give one example to illustrate each of the following properties:

   (i) The commutative property of multiplication

   (ii) The associative property of addition

   (iii) The distributive property of multiplication over addition

7. Evaluate each of the following without the use of a calculator:

   (i) $\sqrt{12}\sqrt{3}$ (iii) $\sqrt{2}\sqrt{8}$ (v) $\sqrt{50}\sqrt{2}$

   (ii) $\sqrt{20}\sqrt{5}$ (iv) $\sqrt{2}\sqrt{32}$ (vi) $\sqrt{24}\sqrt{6}$

8. Evaluate each of the following without the use of a calculator:

   (i) $\dfrac{\sqrt{27}}{\sqrt{3}}$ (iii) $\dfrac{\sqrt{28}}{\sqrt{7}}$ (v) $\dfrac{\sqrt{200}}{\sqrt{8}}$

   (ii) $\dfrac{\sqrt{50}}{\sqrt{2}}$ (iv) $\dfrac{\sqrt{72}}{\sqrt{8}}$ (vi) $\dfrac{\sqrt{1,000}}{\sqrt{10}}$

9. Simplify these surds:

   (i) $\sqrt{8}$ (v) $\sqrt{32}$ (ix) $\sqrt{75}$

   (ii) $\sqrt{45}$ (vi) $\sqrt{500}$ (x) $\sqrt{98}$

   (iii) $\sqrt{300}$ (vii) $\sqrt{27}$

   (iv) $\sqrt{12}$ (viii) $\sqrt{54}$

10. Write $\sqrt{50} + \sqrt{8}$ in the form $k\sqrt{2}, k \in Q$.

11. Write $\sqrt{27} + \sqrt{12}$ in the form $k\sqrt{3}, k \in Q$.

12. Write $\sqrt{125} + \sqrt{20}$ in the form $k\sqrt{5}, k \in Q$.

13. If $\sqrt{99} - \sqrt{44} = n\sqrt{11}$, find n, where $n \in N$.

14. Write $\sqrt{288} - \sqrt{8}$ in the form $k\sqrt{2}$, where $k \in N$.

15. Write $\sqrt{243} - \sqrt{27}$ in the form $k\sqrt{3}$, where $k \in N$.

16. (i) Write down two different surds which, when added, give a surd.

    (ii) Write down two surds which, when added, do not give a surd.

17. (i) Write down a rational number between 5 and 6 and not including 5 or 6.

    (ii) Write down an irrational number between 5 and 6 and not including 5 or 6.

    (iii) Write down a rational number that has a rational square root.

    (iv) Write down a rational number that has an irrational square root.

18. Write down three irrational numbers between 1 and 2 and not including 1 or 2.

19. The rectangle shown has sides of length $\sqrt{5}$ and $\sqrt{2}$.

    (i) Find the area of the rectangle in the form $\sqrt{k}, k \in N$.

    (ii) If the perimeter of the rectangle is $a(\sqrt{5} + \sqrt{2})$, find the value of a.

20. Show that the area of the triangle below is rational.

    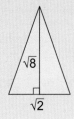

21. Find the area of the parallelogram shown in the form $k\sqrt{2}, k \in N$.

    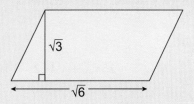

22. Two squares are shown. The area of the smaller square is 7 square metres, and the area of the larger square is 28 square metres. Show that the side length of the larger square is twice the side length of the smaller square.

    7

    28

23. Joe is working out the height (in metres) of a blind for a window. His calculator displays the answer $2 + \sqrt{3}$.

    Without using a calculator, explain why the height of the blind is between 3 m and 4 m.

24. An engineer uses a formula to calculate the number of metres of cable he needs to complete a job. His calculator displays the answer as $10\sqrt{70}$. He is unable to use his calculator to convert this to a decimal.

    He has 80 m of cable. Without using a calculator, decide whether he has enough cable. Show clearly how you decide.

25. Copy the Venn diagram shown and insert each of the following numbers in its correct region on the diagram.

    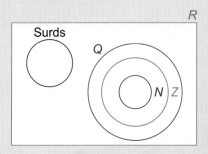

    (i) $\frac{3}{4}$ (vi) -8

    (ii) $\sqrt{3}$ (vii) $\frac{14}{2}$

    (iii) $\frac{5}{2}$ (viii) π

    (iv) $\sqrt{5}$ (ix) 5π

    (v) $\sqrt{144}$ (x) $(\sqrt{3})^2$

26. Let $a = \sqrt{3}$. Copy the table shown below.

Number	Rational	Irrational
a		
a^2		
$a^2 - 1$		
$2a$		

(a) For each of the numbers in the table, tick the correct box to say whether it is rational or irrational.

(b) Verify that $a = \sqrt{3}$ is a solution to the equation $a^2 + (2 - \sqrt{3})a - 2\sqrt{3} = 0$

27. Show that $\sqrt{2}$ is a solution of the equation $x^3 - 2x = 0$, $x \in R$.

2.3 MULTIPLYING AND DIVIDING NUMBERS OF THE FORM $a \pm b\sqrt{c}$, $a, b \in Q$, $c \in Q^+$

Worked Example 2.10

Use an area model to simplify the following:

(i) $\sqrt{3}(\sqrt{7} + 1)$ (ii) $(2 + \sqrt{3})(\sqrt{2} + 3)$ (iii) $(1 + \sqrt{5})^2$

Solution

(i) We can obtain the solution by finding the area of a rectangle of width $\sqrt{3}$ and length $\sqrt{7} + 1$. The rectangle can be subdivided into two smaller rectangles, as shown in the diagram.

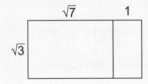

Summing the area of the two smaller rectangles gives the solution.

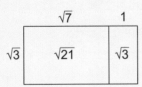

$$\sqrt{3}(\sqrt{7} + 1) = \sqrt{21} + \sqrt{3}$$

(ii) We can obtain the solution by finding the area of a rectangle of length $2 + \sqrt{3}$ and width $\sqrt{2} + 3$. The rectangle can be subdivided into four smaller rectangles, as shown in the diagram.

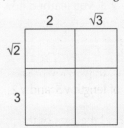

Summing the area of the four smaller rectangles gives the solution.

	2	$\sqrt{3}$
$\sqrt{2}$	$2\sqrt{2}$	$\sqrt{6}$
3	6	$3\sqrt{3}$

$$(2 + \sqrt{3})(\sqrt{2} + 3) = 2\sqrt{2} + \sqrt{6} + 3\sqrt{3} + 6$$

(iii) We can obtain the solution by finding the area of a square of length $1 + \sqrt{5}$. The square can be subdivided into four rectangles as shown in the diagram.

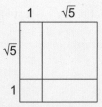

Summing the area of the four rectangles gives the solution.

$$(1 + \sqrt{5})^2 = 1 + \sqrt{5} + \sqrt{5} + 5$$
$$= 6 + 2\sqrt{5}$$

Worked Example 2.11

Use the distributive property of the real numbers to simplify each of the following:

(i) $\sqrt{2}(3 + 4\sqrt{2})$

(ii) $(1 + \sqrt{3})(1 - \sqrt{3})$

Solution

(i) $\sqrt{2}(3 + 4\sqrt{2}) = 3\sqrt{2} + 4\sqrt{2}\sqrt{2}$
$= 3\sqrt{2} + 4(2)$
$= 8 + 3\sqrt{2}$

(ii) $(1 + \sqrt{3})(1 - \sqrt{3}) = 1(1 - \sqrt{3}) + \sqrt{3}(1 - \sqrt{3})$
$= 1 - \sqrt{3} + \sqrt{3} - 3$
$= -2$

Rationalising the Denominator

When dividing a real number by an irrational number, we may be required to rationalise the denominator.

In Activity 2.3, you learned how to rationalise numbers of the type $a \pm b\sqrt{c}$.

$$(a + b\sqrt{c})(a - b\sqrt{c}) = a^2 - b^2c$$

The method of eliminating a surd from the denominator in order to simplify an expression is known as **rationalising the denominator**.

 ACTIVITY 2.3

Worked Example 2.12

Simplify $\dfrac{1}{\sqrt{2}}$.

Solution

Rationalise the denominator by multiplying both the numerator and denominator by $\sqrt{2}$.

$$\frac{1}{\sqrt{2}} = \frac{1(\sqrt{2})}{\sqrt{2}(\sqrt{2})}$$
$$= \frac{\sqrt{2}}{2}$$

Worked Example 2.13

Simplify $\dfrac{3}{1 + \sqrt{3}}$.

Solution

$$\frac{3}{1 + \sqrt{3}} = \frac{3(1 - \sqrt{3})}{(1 + \sqrt{3})(1 - \sqrt{3})}$$

$(1 + \sqrt{3})(1 - \sqrt{3}) = 1^2 - (\sqrt{3})^2 = 1 - 3 = -2$

Therefore, $\dfrac{3}{1 + \sqrt{3}} = \dfrac{3 - 3\sqrt{3}}{-2}$
$$= -\frac{3}{2} + \frac{3}{2}\sqrt{3}$$

Exercise 2.3

1. Use an area model to simplify each of the following:

   (i) $\sqrt{2}(1 + \sqrt{5})$

   (ii) $(2 + \sqrt{5})(3 + \sqrt{5})$

   (iii) $(3 + \sqrt{6})^2$

   (iv) $2(1 + \sqrt{2})^2$

2. Use the distributive property of the real numbers to simplify the following:

   (i) $\sqrt{13}(\sqrt{2} + 1)$

   (ii) $\sqrt{5}(1 - \sqrt{5})$

   (iii) $(\sqrt{2} - 1)\sqrt{2}$

   (iv) $(1 + \sqrt{7})^2$

3. Use the distributive property of the real numbers to simplify the following:

   (i) $(1 + \sqrt{3})(2 - \sqrt{3})$

   (ii) $(3 - \sqrt{7})(5 + 2\sqrt{7})$

   (iii) $(5 + \sqrt{2})^2$

   (iv) $(a + b)^2$ where $a, b \in R$

4. Simplify:

   (i) $3(1 + \sqrt{2}) - (3 + \sqrt{2})(1 - 3\sqrt{2})$

   (ii) $(1 + \sqrt{5})^2 + (3 - \sqrt{5})(3 + \sqrt{5})$

5. Simplify each of the following by rationalising the denominator:

   (i) $\dfrac{1}{\sqrt{3}}$

   (ii) $\dfrac{2}{\sqrt{5}}$

   (iii) $\dfrac{2}{\sqrt{2}}$

   (iv) $\dfrac{7}{\sqrt{7}}$

   (v) $\dfrac{3\sqrt{3}}{\sqrt{7}}$

   (vi) $\dfrac{4}{3\sqrt{6}}$

   (vii) $\dfrac{\sqrt{5}}{\sqrt{75}}$

   (viii) $\dfrac{\sqrt{32}}{\sqrt{256}}$

6. Simplify each of the following by rationalising the denominator:

   (i) $\dfrac{2}{1 + \sqrt{5}}$

   (ii) $\dfrac{5}{1 - \sqrt{3}}$

   (iii) $\dfrac{12}{5 - \sqrt{2}}$

   (iv) $\dfrac{\sqrt{3}}{1 - \sqrt{3}}$

   (v) $\dfrac{1 + \sqrt{5}}{1 - \sqrt{5}}$

   (vi) $\dfrac{3 - \sqrt{3}}{3 + \sqrt{3}}$

7. Express $\dfrac{2\sqrt{2}}{\sqrt{3} - 1} - \dfrac{2\sqrt{3}}{\sqrt{2} + 1}$ in the form $x\sqrt{6} + y\sqrt{3} + z\sqrt{2}$, where x, y and $z \in Z$.

8. Solve the following equations, giving your answers in the form $a + b\sqrt{c}$, where $a, b, c \in Q$:

   (i) $\sqrt{5}x = 6$

   (ii) $(1 - \sqrt{3})x = 2$

   (iii) $(2 + \sqrt{3}) + (1 + 3\sqrt{3})x = 5$

9. Find the area of the rectangle below in the form $a + b\sqrt{2}$, where $a, b \in N$.

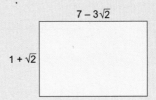

$7 - 3\sqrt{2}$

$1 + \sqrt{2}$

10. A triangle has a base length (in metres) as given. The area of the triangle is 12 m². Find the perpendicular height of the triangle in the form $a + b\sqrt{5}$, where $a, b \in Z$.

   $1 + \sqrt{5}$

11. Calculate the area of these rectangles, simplifying your answers where possible:

   (a) $1 + \sqrt{2}$ cm

   $2 - \sqrt{2}$ cm

   (b) $\sqrt{3}$ cm

   $2 + \sqrt{7}$ cm

12. A rectangle has sides of length $5 + \sqrt{3}$ and $5 - \sqrt{3}$ units.

   Calculate, in their most simplified form:

   (i) The perimeter of the rectangle

   (ii) The area of the rectangle

   (iii) The length of a diagonal of the rectangle

13. The diagram below represents a right-angled triangle ABC.

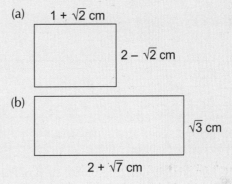

$\sqrt{7} - 2$

C

L

A

$\sqrt{7} + 2$

B

$|AB| = \sqrt{7} + 2$ units and $|AC| = \sqrt{7} - 2$ units.

Work out, leaving any appropriate answers in surd form:

   (a) The area of triangle ABC

   (b) The length of BC

NUMBER SYSTEMS

1. Copy the Venn diagram shown and insert each of the following numbers in its correct region on the diagram.

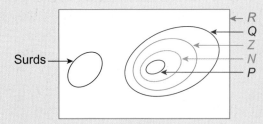

Note: R = reals, Q = rationals, Z = integers, N = naturals, P = primes

(i) −4

(ii) 5

(iii) 9

(iv) $\sqrt{11}$

(v) $\dfrac{1}{4}$

(vi) π

(vii) $-\sqrt{196}$

(viii) $\sqrt{18}$

2. (a) Use fraction strips to evaluate each of the following:

(i) $\dfrac{1}{3} + \dfrac{1}{6}$

(ii) $\dfrac{3}{4} - \dfrac{1}{2}$

(iii) $\dfrac{7}{8} - \dfrac{3}{4}$

(iv) $\dfrac{2}{5} + \dfrac{3}{10}$

(b) Use area models to evaluate each of the following products:

(i) 24×25

(ii) 32×41

(iii) 22×124

(iv) 128×215

3. Find the HCF and LCM of each of the following by first writing each number as a product of primes:

(i) 69 and 234

(ii) 408 and 1,105

(iii) 594 and 418

(iv) 680 and 1,196

4. Evaluate each of the following, without the use of a calculator:

(i) $\sqrt{48}\sqrt{3}$

(ii) $\sqrt{50}\sqrt{5}$

(iii) $\sqrt{2}\sqrt{8}$

(iv) $\sqrt{12}\sqrt{108}$

(v) $\sqrt{150}\sqrt{6}$

(vi) $\sqrt{14}\sqrt{8}$

5. Simplify $\sqrt{ab}\sqrt{ab^2}$, where $a, b \in R^+$.

6. Evaluate each of the following without the use of a calculator:

(i) $\dfrac{\sqrt{147}}{\sqrt{3}}$

(ii) $\dfrac{\sqrt{162}}{\sqrt{2}}$

(iii) $\dfrac{\sqrt{448}}{\sqrt{7}}$

(iv) $\dfrac{\sqrt{288}}{\sqrt{72}}$

7. Simplify these surds:

(i) $\sqrt{90}$

(ii) $\sqrt{45}$

(iii) $\sqrt{800}$

(iv) $\sqrt{192}$

(v) $\sqrt{160}$

(vi) $\sqrt{2,250}$

8. Which properties of the rational numbers are being illustrated in the following:

(i) $\dfrac{3}{2} \times 5 = 5 \times \dfrac{3}{2}$

(ii) $\left(\dfrac{1}{2} + 2\right) + \dfrac{5}{8} = \dfrac{1}{2} + \left(2 + \dfrac{5}{8}\right)$

(iii) $2 \times (3 + 4) = 2 \times 3 + 2 \times 4$

(iv) $\dfrac{1}{5} + \dfrac{1}{4} = \dfrac{1}{4} + \dfrac{1}{5}$

(v) $\dfrac{1}{2} \times \left(\dfrac{1}{3} \times \dfrac{1}{4}\right) = \left(\dfrac{1}{2} \times \dfrac{1}{3}\right) \times \dfrac{1}{4}$

9. Evaluate each of the following:

(i) $5(6 - 4)^4 - 3(6 \div 2)^2 + 8 \times 5$

(ii) $\dfrac{5^2 \times 2 - 20}{3 + 4 \times 2 - 12 \div 2}$

(iii) $3 \times \sqrt{\dfrac{36}{25}} + 4\left(\dfrac{11}{56} - \dfrac{3}{28}\right) + 3 \times 2^2$

(iv) $\dfrac{5 - 3 \times 7 + \sqrt{144}}{(11 - 9)^2}$

10. The first four square numbers greater than 1 are 4, 9, 16 and 25.

(i) Write each of the numbers 4, 9, 16 and 25 as a product of primes.

(ii) The number 5,929 is a square number. Find its prime factorisation.

(iii) If x is a square number and its prime factorisation is $a^p b^q c^r$, what sort of numbers are p, q and r?

(iv) Determine the smallest square number that has four prime numbers in its prime factorisation.

11. Use the distributive property of the real numbers to simplify the following:

   (i) $(1 + \sqrt{6})(2 - \sqrt{6})$

   (ii) $(2 - \sqrt{15})(5 + 2\sqrt{45})$

   (iii) $(6 + \sqrt{2})^2$

12. Simplify each of the following by rationalising the denominator:

   (i) $\dfrac{2}{3 + \sqrt{7}}$ (iv) $\dfrac{\sqrt{3}}{3 - \sqrt{3}}$

   (ii) $\dfrac{3}{4 - \sqrt{3}}$ (v) $\dfrac{1 + \sqrt{13}}{1 - \sqrt{13}}$

   (iii) $\dfrac{11}{11 - \sqrt{11}}$ (vi) $\dfrac{5}{\sqrt{2} + \sqrt{3}}$

13. (a) Using $(a + b)^2 = a^2 + 2ab + b^2$, or otherwise, show that $(\sqrt{2} + \sqrt{8})^2 = 18$.

   (b) Tracey says,

     '$(\sqrt{2} + \sqrt{8})$ is an irrational number.

     $(\sqrt{2} + \sqrt{8})^2 = 18$.

     I think that if you square an irrational number, you will always get a rational number.'

     Use an example to show that Tracey is wrong.

14. Sort the following into four pairs of equal value:

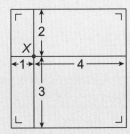

$\dfrac{1}{\sqrt{2}}$ 6 $\sqrt{8} \times \sqrt{5}$ $3\sqrt{4}$ $\dfrac{\sqrt{40}}{\sqrt{10}}$ 2 $\dfrac{\sqrt{8}}{4}$ $\sqrt{40}$

15. A square has side length 5. X is a point inside the square such that the distances from X to the four sides of the square are 1, 2, 3 and 4.

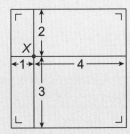

   (i) Show that three of the distances from X to the vertices of the square are irrational and that the fourth distance is of integer length.

   (ii) If the product of the four distances is written in the form $ab^2\sqrt{10}$, where a and b are prime, find the value of a and the value of b.

16. Three cans of juice fill two-thirds of a one-litre jug. How many cans of juice are needed to fill eight one-litre jugs?

17. There are two girls and six boys playing a game. How many additional girls must join the game so that $\frac{5}{8}$ of the players will be girls?

18. The rectangle and square below have the same area. The dimensions of both are in centimetres. The diagrams are not drawn to scale.

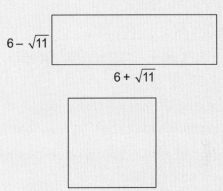

   (a) Find the area of the rectangle.

   (b) Find the length of one side of the square.

              SEC Sample Paper, JCHL

19. (a) Find the value of $16^{\frac{1}{2}}$.

   (b) Given that $40 = k\sqrt{10}$, find the value of k.

   (c) A large rectangular piece of card is $(\sqrt{5} + \sqrt{20})$ cm long and $\sqrt{8}$ cm wide.

     A small rectangle $\sqrt{2}$ cm long and $\sqrt{5}$ cm wide is cut out of the piece of card.

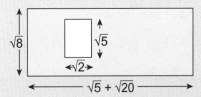

     Express the area of the card that is left as a percentage of the area of the large rectangle.

20. Given any two positive integers m and n ($n > m$), it is possible to form three numbers a, b and c where:

$$a = n^2 - m^2 \quad b = 2nm \quad c = n^2 + m^2$$

These three numbers a, b and c are then known as a 'Pythagorean triple'.

(a) For $m = 3$ and $n = 5$, calculate a, b and c.

(b) If the values of a, b and c from part (a) are the lengths of the sides of a triangle, show that the triangle is right-angled.

(c) If $n^2 - m^2$, $2nm$ and $n^2 + m^2$ are the lengths of the sides of a triangle, show that the triangle is right-angled.

SEC Sample Paper, JCHL

21. The Euclidean Algorithm uses repeated division to find the highest common factor (HCF) of two natural numbers.

Example: Find HCF (1050, 330).

$$1050 \div 330 = 3 \ \ R \ \ 60 \quad \leftarrow \quad \text{('3 remainder 60')}$$
$$330 \div 60 = 5 \ \ R \ \ \boxed{30} \quad \leftarrow \quad \text{HCF is the last non-zero remainder.}$$
$$60 \div \boxed{30} = 2 \ \ R \ \ 0$$

$\therefore$ HCF (1050, 330) = 30.

(i) Use the Euclidean Algorithm to find HCF (2520, 154).

(ii) By first writing each of 2520 and 154 as a product of primes, verify your answer to part (i).

(iii) Use the Euclidean Algorithm to show that 143 and 210 are relatively prime.

> Note: Relative prime natural numbers have a HCF of 1.
> They share no common prime factors.

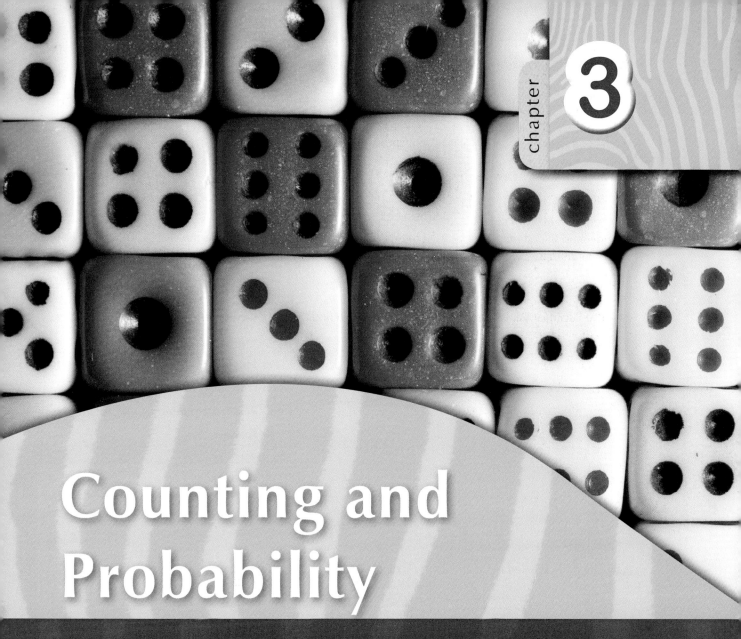

Counting and Probability

Learning Outcomes

In this chapter, you will:

- ➲ Revise counting and probability from the Ordinary Level course
- ➲ Use binary/counting methods to solve problems involving successive random events where only two possible outcomes apply to each event
- ➲ Use set theory to discuss experiments, outcomes and sample spaces

3.1 REVISION OF COUNTING AND PROBABILITY

Probability deals with the likelihood or chance that an event might occur. We may describe the probability of a certain event using words or, much more commonly, using numbers.

Fundamental Principle of Counting

The **Fundamental Principle of Counting** is a quick and easy method to determine the number of outcomes from two or more trials.

FORMULA

If one trial has m possible outcomes and a second trial has n possible outcomes, then the total number of possible outcomes from the first trial followed by the second trial is $m \times n$.

It is important to remember it is the **number of outcomes** that we multiply each time.

KEY WORDS

- Fundamental Principle of Counting
- Trial
- Outcome
- Event
- Sample space
- Probability scale
- Relative frequency
- Fairness
- Equally likely
- Theoretical probability
- Expected frequency
- Systematic listing
- Two-way table
- Tree diagram
- Set theory

Worked Example 3.1

A six-sided die is rolled twice and a coin is flipped twice. How many outcomes are possible?

Solution

Die has six possible outcomes.

Coin has two possible outcomes.

Trial	1st Roll		2nd Roll		1st Flip		2nd Flip		
No. of outcomes	6	×	6	×	2	×	2	=	144 possible outcomes

PROBABILITY

Terms That You Need to Know

A **trial** is the act of doing an experiment in probability.

The rolling of a die is an example of a **trial**.

An **outcome** is one of the possible results of a trial.

An **event** is the occurrence of one or more specific outcomes.

On a six-sided die the possible outcomes are 1, 2, 3, 4, 5 or 6.

Rolling a prime number on a die would be an example of an event.

Likelihood Scale

We use the **likelihood scale** when we use words to describe the probability of an event. We use words such as:

| Impossible | Unlikely | Evens | Likely | Certain |

Using words to describe the probability of an event can be problematic. Saying an event is 'likely' is open to many different interpretations.

Probability Scale

Using numbers to describe the probability of an event is a much better approach.

Probability is the numerical measure of the chance of an event happening.

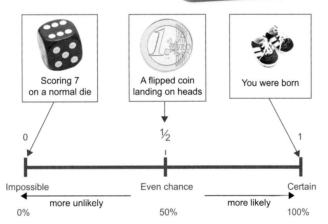

A probability scale using percentages ranges from 0% (impossible) to 100% (certain).
A probability scale using decimals ranges from 0 (impossible) to 1 (certain).

It is also important to remember that the probabilities of all outcomes of a particular experiment will add up to 1. Example: Dublin vs Tyrone in the All-Ireland football final.

Outcomes	Dublin win	Tyrone win	Draw	Total
Probabilities	0.45	0.5	0.05	1

Relative Frequency (Experimental Probability)

We may determine the probability of an event occurring using **statistical data** derived from experiments or observation.

Relative frequency is an estimate of the probability an event.

$$\text{Relative frequency} = \frac{\text{Frequency or number of times the event happens in trials}}{\text{Total number of trials}}$$

Worked Example 3.2

In a survey of 1,000 households, it was found that 650 households had a pet. If a household is selected at random, find the relative frequency that the household does have a pet.

Solution

Relative frequency = $\dfrac{\text{Number of households that have a pet}}{\text{Number of households surveyed}} = \dfrac{650}{1,000} = \dfrac{13}{20}$ or 0.65 or 65%

Fairness and Expected Frequency

If all outcomes are equally likely to occur then the trial or experiment is considered to be **fair or unbiased.**

A fair coin, as there are only two outcomes, should land on tails around 50% of the time and on heads around 50% of the time. Likewise, an unbiased six-sided die would be expected to land on 1 around $16\frac{2}{3}$% of the time, on 2 around $16\frac{2}{3}$% of the time, etc.

To determine if a trial or experiment is fair, it must be repeated a sufficiently large number of times. It is important to note that as the number of trials carried out increases, the closer the relative frequency will be to the actual probability of an event.

Expected Frequency

If the relative frequency or probability of an event is known, we can estimate how many times that event would happen over a certain number of trials. This is called the **expected frequency**.

Expected frequency = (number of trials) × (relative frequency or probability)

Worked Example 3.3

A six-sided die is rolled 600 times. The number 1 is shown 150 times.

  (i) Do you think the die is fair? Explain.

  (ii) If the die is rolled another 200 times, how many times in total would you expect it to show a one?

Solution

  (i) Relative frequency of die showing a one = $\dfrac{150}{600} = \dfrac{1}{4}$ or 0.25

   We would expect a die to land on a one around $\dfrac{1}{6}$ of the time, if the die were fair.

   ∴ The die does not appear to be fair.

   Also, the number of trials is sufficiently large to justify this conclusion.

(ii) Total number of rolls = 600 + 200

$$= 800 \text{ rolls}$$

Expected frequency = $800 \times \frac{1}{4} = 200$ times

Theoretical Probability

If all outcomes are equally likely to occur, then we can calculate the probability of an event happening. This type of probability is sometimes referred to as **theoretical probability**.

Theoretical probability is the ratio of the number of desirable outcomes to the total number of all possible outcomes.

$$\text{Probability} = \frac{\text{Number of desirable outcomes}}{\text{Total number of all possible outcomes}}$$

 Worked Example 3.4

A bag contains 4 white marbles, 6 red marbles, 4 green and 2 blue marbles. A marble is taken from the bag at random. Calculate the probability that this marble will be:

   (i)   White   (iii) Not blue

  (ii)   Blue   (iv) Red or blue

Solution

(i) P(white) = $\dfrac{\text{Number of white marbles}}{\text{Total number of marbles}} = \dfrac{4}{16} = \dfrac{1}{4}$ or 0.25 or 25%

(ii) P(blue) = $\dfrac{\text{Number of blue marbles}}{\text{Total number of marbles}} = \dfrac{2}{16} = \dfrac{1}{8}$ or 0.125 or 12.5%

(iii) There are 14 marbles in the bag that are not blue

P(not blue) = $\dfrac{\text{Number of marbles not blue}}{\text{Total number of marbles}} = \dfrac{14}{16} = \dfrac{7}{8}$ or 0.875 or 87.5%

Alternatively, if P(blue) = $\dfrac{1}{8}$, then P(not blue) = 1 − P(blue)

$$= 1 - \frac{1}{8}$$

$$= \frac{7}{8} \text{ or } 0.875 \text{ or } 87.5\%$$

The probability of an event **not** happening = 1 − the probability that the event **will** happen.

(iv) We count the number of marbles that are red or blue, which is 8 in total.

P(red or blue) = $\dfrac{\text{Number of red or blue marbles}}{\text{Total number of marbles}} = \dfrac{8}{16} = \dfrac{1}{2}$ or 0.5 or 50%

COUNTING OUTCOMES

Sample Spaces

The list of all possible outcomes is referred to as the **sample space**.

When listing all the outcomes (the sample space), three main methods can be used:

■ **Systematic listing**

Systematic listing involves writing down all the possible outcomes.

■ **Two-way tables**

Two-way tables are used to write down all the possible outcomes when one trial is followed by a second trial.

■ **Tree diagrams**

Tree diagrams are used to write down all the possible outcomes when two or more trials are involved.

Worked Example 3.5

A coin is flipped twice. Show all the possible outcomes using:

(i) Systematic listing   (ii) A two-way table   (iii) A tree diagram

Solution

(i) Systematic listing

Head is written as H, and tail is written as T.

The possible outcomes are: {HH, HT, TH, TT}.

(ii) Two-way table

		Second flip	
		Head	Tail
First flip	Head	HH	HT
	Tail	TH	TT

The list of outcomes is {HH, HT, TH, TT}.

(iii) Tree diagram

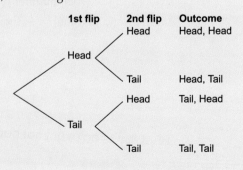

1st flip	2nd flip	Outcome

The list of outcomes is {HH, HT, TH, TT}.

Combined Events

A **combined event** is where two or more trials occur and their outcomes are combined together.

It is advisable to use a two-way table or tree diagram when dealing with the probability of combined events with equally likely outcomes.

 Worked Example 3.6

A four-sided die and a six-sided die are rolled. Both dice are fair. The outcomes for the first die are 1, 2, 3 or 4. The outcomes for the second die are 1, 2, 3, 4, 5 or 6. The score from the first die is added to the score from the second die. Use a two-way table to show all the possible outcomes.

What is the probability that the score from the two dice will be:

(i) An odd number

(ii) A prime number

(iii) A composite number

(iv) Divisible by both 2 and 3

(v) Divisible by 2 or 3

(vi) Not divisible by 2 or 3

Solution

We must first draw a two-way table to show all the outcomes.

First die		Second die					
		1	2	3	4	5	6
	1	2	3	4	5	6	7
	2	3	4	5	6	7	8
	3	4	5	6	7	8	9
	4	5	6	7	8	9	10

We then count the total number of possible outcomes, which in this case is 24. Of course, we can use the fundamental principle of counting here: $4 \times 6 = 24$

(i) A total of 12 outcomes give an odd number (coloured green).

First die		Second die					
		1	2	3	4	5	6
	1	2	3	4	5	6	7
	2	3	4	5	6	7	8
	3	4	5	6	7	8	9
	4	5	6	7	8	9	10

$$P(\text{odd}) = \frac{\text{Number of outcomes that are odd numbers}}{\text{Total number of possible outcomes}} = \frac{12}{24} = \frac{1}{2}$$

COUNTING AND PROBABILITY

(ii) A total of 11 outcomes give a prime number (coloured red).

		Second die					
		1	2	3	4	5	6
First die	1	2	3	4	5	6	7
	2	3	4	5	6	7	8
	3	4	5	6	7	8	9
	4	5	6	7	8	9	10

$$P(\text{prime}) = \frac{\text{Number of outcomes that are prime numbers}}{\text{Total number of possible outcomes}} = \frac{11}{24}$$

(iii) If 11 outcomes are prime numbers then 24 − 11 = 13 are composite numbers.

$$P(\text{composite}) = \frac{13}{24}$$

Alternatively we could count them in a two-way table as we did in parts (i) and (ii) or we could use the rule P(not event) = 1 − P(event).

$$\text{So, } P(\text{composite}) = P(\text{not prime})$$
$$= 1 - P(\text{prime})$$
$$= 1 - \frac{11}{24}$$
$$= \frac{13}{24}$$

(iv) A total of four outcomes are numbers that are divisible by both 2 **AND** 3 (coloured blue).

		Second die					
		1	2	3	4	5	6
First die	1	2	3	4	5	6	7
	2	3	4	5	6	7	8
	3	4	5	6	7	8	9
	4	5	6	7	8	9	10

$$P(\div \text{ by 2 and 3}) = \frac{4}{24} = \frac{1}{6}$$

(v) A total of 16 outcomes are numbers that are divisible by 2 **OR** 3 (coloured brown).

		Second die					
		1	2	3	4	5	6
First die	1	2	3	4	5	6	7
	2	3	4	5	6	7	8
	3	4	5	6	7	8	9
	4	5	6	7	8	9	10

$$P(\div \text{ by 2 or 3}) = \frac{16}{24} = \frac{2}{3}$$

(vi) P(not ÷ by 2 or 3) = 1 − P(÷ by 2 or 3)
$$= 1 - \frac{2}{3}$$
$$= \frac{1}{3}$$

COUNTING AND PROBABILITY

Worked Example 3.7

An unbiased coin is flipped three times.
Use a tree diagram to list all the possible outcomes.
Find the probability that:

    (i)   The coin will land on heads three times.   (iii) The coin will land on tails at least twice.

    (ii) The coin will land on heads exactly twice.   (iv) The coin will land on heads once and tails twice.

Solution

We must first draw a tree diagram to show all the outcomes.
We then count the total number of possible outcomes, which in this case is 8.

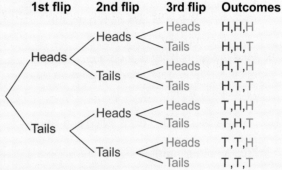

    (i)   One outcome has three heads: HHH

$$\therefore P(\text{three heads}) = \frac{1}{8}$$

    (ii) Count the number of outcomes that have exactly two heads: HHT, HTH, THH

$$\therefore P(\text{exactly two heads}) = \frac{3}{8}$$

    (iii) We count the number of outcomes that have at least two (two or more) tails:
HTT, THT, TTH, TTT

$$\therefore P(\text{at least two tails}) = \frac{4}{8} = \frac{1}{2}$$

    (iv) In this question, the order is not specified.

          Three outcomes have one head and two tails: HTT, THT, TTH

$$\therefore P(\text{one head and two tails}) = \frac{3}{8}$$

Exercise 3.1

1. In a restaurant, there are five choices of starter, eight choices of main course and four choices of dessert. How many different three course meals could be eaten at this restaurant?

2. Give an example of an event that has the following likelihood:

    (i)   Impossible   (iv) Unlikely

    (ii) Certain   (v)   Evens

    (iii) Likely

3. How many ways are there of arranging all the letters of the words shown below?

    (i)   To   (iii) From

    (ii) Any   (iv) Rugby

4. How many ways are there of arranging the letters of WORKED if the letters are taken:

    (i)   Three at a time   (iii) Six at a time

    (ii) Four at a time   (iv) Two at a time

5. A lock has a four-digit code, 1078 for example. How many different codes are possible:

    (i)   If a digit can be used only once

    (ii) If a digit can be used more than once

    (iii) If a digit can be used only once and the code has to end with a prime digit

6. A coin is flipped six times. How many outcomes are possible?

7. Tickets in a raffle have a code printed on them. The code is a capital letter, followed by a digit, followed by a capital letter. (For example: A2C, F7F, etc)

   How many different codes are possible?

8. A spinner numbered 1, 3, 5, 7 and 9 is spun three times, and a coin is flipped twice. How many different outcomes are possible? Give an example of one such outcome.

9. Find the probability of the stated event in each part below and mark its position on a probability scale.

   A single fair six-sided die is rolled and lands on:

   (i) A natural number

   (ii) The number 1

   (iii) An even number

   (iv) A number greater than 5

10. A die is rolled 100 times. The number 4 occurs 35 times. What is the relative frequency of:

    (i) Rolling a 4

    (ii) Not rolling a 4

11. 55,000 students sit an exam. 15,000 of these students get a C grade.

    What is the relative frequency of a student getting a C grade?

12. A six-sided die is rolled 50 times and lands on a 5 six times. In your opinion, is the die fair?

    Give a reason for your answer.

13. A coin is flipped 1,000 times. It lands on heads 430 times. What is the relative frequency of the coin landing on:

    (i) Heads

    (ii) Tails

    Do you think that the coin is unbiased? Explain your answer.

14. Last season, Jonas scored 12 penalties out of 18.

    (i) What was the relative frequency of Jonas scoring a penalty (give your answer as a percentage)?

    (ii) If Jonas takes 24 penalties next season, how many would you expect him to score, if the relative frequency remains the same?

15. Last year there were 167 school days and Myles was late for school 26 times.

    (i) Calculate the relative frequency of 'late days' for Myles for the school year, as a percentage (to the nearest per cent).

    (ii) The following year, Myles is late three times in 24 school days. Has Myles's punctuality improved? Give a reason for your answer.

16. A six-sided die was rolled and the number of times it landed on the number one was recorded at regular intervals.

    (i) Copy and complete the following table:

Number of rolls	20	40	60	80	100
Number of ones	1	5	14	15	24
Relative frequency of one	$\frac{1}{20}$ or 5%				

    (ii) Explain which result gives the best estimate for the probability of rolling a one on this die.

    (iii) Is this die biased? Explain your answer.

17. A manufacturing company determines that the probability of a machine part being produced with a fault is 0.02%. If the manufacturer produces 25,000 parts, how many would you expect to have a fault?

18. In a maths class there are twelve boys and eleven girls. A student is chosen at random. What is the probability that this student will be:

(i) A boy   (ii) A girl

19. A bag contains five red marbles, four blue marbles and nine white marbles. A marble is taken from the bag at random. What is the probability that this marble will be:

(i) White   (iv) Not red

(ii) Blue   (v) Red or white

(iii) White or blue

20. A fair six-sided die is rolled once. Find the probability that you roll:

(i) The number 2

(ii) The number 7

(iii) An odd number

(iv) A prime number

(v) A number less than 4

(vi) A number that is even and prime

21. A letter is chosen at random from the word PERPENDICULAR. Find the probability that the letter chosen will be:

(i) A vowel   (iii) P

(ii) E   (iv) Not P

22. A single card is selected at random from a normal pack of playing cards. What is the probability that the card selected is:

(i) Red

(ii) Black

(iii) Red or Black

(iv) A Queen and Black

(v) A Queen or Black

(vi) A picture card

23. A fair six-sided die is rolled.

(i) What is the probability of getting a number greater than 3?

(ii) If this die is rolled 60 times, how many times would you expect to get a number greater than 4?

24. A five-sided spinner labelled with sectors P, Q, R, S and T is spun 400 times.

Some of the relative frequencies of the spinner landing on certain lettered sectors are shown. Landing on sector P has the same relative frequency as landing on sector Q. The probability that the spinner lands on sector R is one and half times that of landing on sector P.

(i) Copy and complete the following table:

Sector	Relative frequency
P	
Q	
R	
S	.20
T	.17

(ii) Is the spinner fair? Give a reason for your answer.

(iii) If the spinner is spun 1,000 times, how often would you expect it to land on sector Q?

25. A card is drawn from a standard pack of cards and replaced. This is done 520 times. How many times would you expect to get:

(i) A red card   (iii) A King

(ii) A picture card   (iv) A black Jack

26. The probability of Zahra not attending her school council meeting is 0.06 and the probability of her arriving on time is $\frac{6}{7}$. What is the probability, as a percentage to the nearest whole number, that she will be late for the school council meeting?

27. In a class there are 10 boys and 20 girls. Four of the boys and five of the girls are from town A and the rest are from town B.

(a) A student is chosen at random from this class.

Find the probability that this student will be:

(i) A girl

(ii) A boy

(iii) A student from town B

(iv) A girl from town A

(b) A boy is picked at random from the class. What is the probability that he will be from town A?

(c) If a person is chosen at random from this same class every day for 180 days, on how many days would you expect this person to be a girl who is from town B?

28. A spinner with 20 equal sectors numbered 1–20 is spun once.

Find the probability that it lands on:

(i) 6

(ii) An odd number

(iii) A single-digit number

(iv) A single-digit even number

(v) A prime number greater than 16

(vi) A prime number or a number greater than 16

(vii) A number that is even and divisible by 6

29. A fair six-sided die is rolled twice. Copy and complete the following two-way table:

			Second roll			
		1	2	3	4	5	6
First roll	1						
	2						
	3		(3, 2)				
	4						
	5						
	6						

What is the probability that:

(i) An odd number is obtained on both rolls of the die.

(ii) The same number is obtained on both rolls of the die.

(iii) A different number is obtained on both rolls of the die.

(iv) The product of the numbers obtained from each roll is odd.

Explain why the answers to parts (i) and (iv) had to be the same.

30. A spinner, as shown, is spun three times. The spinner consists of four equally-sized sectors.

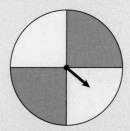

Using a tree diagram, determine the probability of the spinner landing on:

(i) A blue sector each time

(ii) A blue sector followed by two yellow sectors

(iii) A blue and two yellow sectors in any order

(iv) At least two blue sectors

31. Two fair six-sided dice, one coloured red and the other black, are rolled. The score from the red die is added to the score from the black die. Use a two-way table to show all the possible outcomes.

Find the probability that the score on the two dice will add up to:

(i) 6

(ii) An even number

(iii) A prime number

(iv) A number divisible by 2 or 5

(v) A number divisible by both 2 and 5

(vi) A factor of 6

32. The table below shows information about 100 cars advertised for sale in a local paper:

	Ford	Honda	Nissan	Volvo	Total
Petrol	11	7		13	
Diesel			12	9	58
Total		27	23		

(i) Copy and complete the table.

A car is chosen at random.

(ii) What fuel is this car most likely to use?
(iii) Find the probability that is a Honda.
(iv) Find the probability that is a Volvo.
(v) Find the probability that is a diesel car.
(vi) Find the probability that it is a Nissan petrol car.

A diesel car is chosen at random. What is the probability that it is:

(vii) A Ford car
(viii) Not a Nissan

33. Two fair six-sided dice are thrown and the scores are multiplied together. Draw a two-way table to show all possible outcomes.

Find the probability that the product of the scores on the two dice is:

(i) 15
(ii) Less than 9
(iii) A prime number
(iv) Even or divisible by 3
(v) Even and divisible by 3
(vi) A factor of 28

34. A spinner, as shown, is spun twice. All sectors are of equal size. Draw a tree diagram to show all possible outcomes.

What is the probability that after both spins the spinner has landed on:

(i) The green sector both times
(ii) The green sector only once
(iii) The red sector at least once
(iv) The same colour sector each time
(v) A different colour sector each time

35. In a group of 125 students, each student names the country they most want to visit.

Complete the following two-way table:

	Spain	France	Italy	UK	USA	Total
Boy	16	8		14		60
Girl	12		10		15	
Total		26		24	32	125

A student is selected at random. What is the probability that the student:

(i) Is a boy
(ii) Wants to visit France
(iii) Is a girl who wants to visit the UK
(iv) Did not give Italy as the country they most wanted to visit

A boy is selected at random. What is the probability that he:

(v) Wants to visit Italy
(vi) Did not give France as the country he most wanted to visit

A girl is selected at random. What is the probability that she:

(vii) Gave a European country as the country she most wanted to visit

36. Apples are to be shipped to a wholesaler. Each box contains 30 apples and the wholesaler requires 100 boxes. A sample box of 30 apples was examined. The weight (to the nearest gram) of each apple is shown.

105	96	101	102	111	92	106	95	101	88
101	82	118	109	105	83	84	114	109	103
118	115	80	93	103	99	95	100	90	87

(a) Draw a stem-and-leaf diagram to show the weights of the apples.

(b) An apple is picked at random. What is the experimental probability that it weighs:

    (i)   Over 90 grams

    (ii)   Under 100 grams

    (iii)   Over 85 grams but less than 105 grams

(c) Estimate the number of apples per 100 boxes that you would expect to weigh more than 110 grams.

37. Karen and Jason roll two fair six-sided dice and add the scores. They do this 36 times altogether and record their results in the accompanying table.

11	10	4	2	2	9	12	10	9
4	3	6	7	6	3	6	8	3
8	4	7	7	4	6	10	5	8
2	8	3	2	12	12	3	3	6

    (i)   Copy and complete the following frequency table:

Combined score	2	3	4	5	6	7	8	9	10	11	12
Frequency											

    (ii)   What is the experimental probability of a combined score of 6?

    (iii)   Use the frequency table above to draw a bar chart displaying the frequency of each combined score.

    (iv)   Draw a two-way table to show all the possible outcomes from rolling the two dice and then adding their scores.

    (v)   What is the theoretical probability of a combined score of 6?

    (vi)   Use the two-way table to draw a bar chart showing the frequencies based on the theoretical probability.

    (vii)   Explain the difference between experimental and theoretical probability.

    (viii)   What would Karen and Jason have to do so that the bar chart obtained in part (iii) would more closely resemble the bar chart from part (vi)?

    (ix)   A game consists of rolling two fair six-sided dice and then adding their scores.

       ■ Player A wins if the combined score is 2, 3, 4, 10, 11 or 12.

       ■ Player B wins if the combined score is 5, 6, 7, 8 or 9.

       Are the rules of this game fair? Explain your answer clearly.

38. Records for a local library show for each book whether it is in the fiction, non-fiction or classics category and whether it is a hardback or softback version.

When the library closed on Wednesday last week, 2,700 books were out on loan.

Of the books on loan, 72% were in the fiction category.

Of the 620 hardback books on loan, 55% were in the non-fiction category and 25% were in the classics category.

In total, 176 classics books were on loan.

(a) Complete the table, entering the number of books on loan in each case.

Category	Version		Totals
	Hardback	Softback	
Fiction			
Non-fiction			
Classics			176
Totals	620		2,700

(b) A library record for a book on loan is chosen at random. Use the table to calculate the probability that the book is:

   (i)   Non-fiction and a softback version

   (ii) Non-fiction or a hardback version

   (iii) Fiction, given that it is a softback version

(c) How many of the first 200 books taken out on loan on the following day would you expect to be hardback classics?

39. A bag contains 20 marbles: three blue, eight yellow and the remainder green. If one marble is drawn at random from the bag, what is the probability that it is:

   (i)   Green   (ii) Not green

A number of yellow marbles are added, so that the probability of getting a yellow marble is increased by 50%.

   (iii) How many yellow marbles were added?

40. A cat is about to have a litter of kittens. The chance of a male or female kitten is **equally likely**.

   (i)   Explain what the term 'equally likely' means.

   (ii)   Draw a tree diagram to show the possible outcomes for the first kitten.

   (iii) What is the probability that the first kitten will be female?

   (iv)   Using the same tree diagram, show the possible outcomes for the second kitten.

   (v)   What is the probability that the second kitten will be male?

   (vi)   Again using the same tree diagram, show the possible outcomes for the third kitten.

   (vii) What is the probability that the third kitten will be female?

   (viii) What is the probability that all three kittens will be female?

   (ix)   What is the probability that the first two kittens will be female and the last kitten will be male?

   (x)   What is the probability that there will be two female kittens and one male kitten?

3.2 COMBINED EVENTS WITH UNEQUALLY LIKELY OUTCOMES

 Worked Example 3.8

In a game, a fair six-sided die is rolled. To win, a player must score a 3. What is the probability that the player wins on the second roll?

Solution

In this case, the player must fail to get a 3 on the first roll of the die and then get a 3 on the second roll.

We first draw our tree diagram as normal, noting that there are two possible outcomes which we are interested in – rolling a 3 or not rolling a 3.

Note: F stands for Failed (to roll a 3)

1st Roll	2nd Roll	Outcome
3	3	3, 3
	F	3, F
F	3	F, 3
	F	F, F

We next fill in the probability of the two events on the tree diagram at every branch where these events occur.

Rolling a 3 $\rightarrow \dfrac{1}{6}$

Failing to roll a 3 $\rightarrow \dfrac{5}{6}$

1st Roll	2nd Roll	Outcome
$\frac{1}{6}$ → 3	$\frac{1}{6}$ → 3	3, 3
	$\frac{5}{6}$ → F	3, F
$\frac{5}{6}$ → F	$\frac{1}{6}$ → 3	F, 3
	$\frac{5}{6}$ → F	F, F

The outcome we are looking for is F, 3.

We follow the branches of the tree diagram, noting the probabilities from the desired outcome to the start. The probability of getting a 3 after first getting an F is $\dfrac{5}{6}$ of $\dfrac{1}{6}$.

$\therefore$ P(player wins on second roll) $= \dfrac{5}{6} \times \dfrac{1}{6}$

$= \dfrac{5}{36}$

(Remember that in maths 'of' means 'to multiply'.)

Worked Example 3.9

A game is played with 10 marbles in a bag: seven blue and three yellow. A player picks a marble at random out of the bag. If a yellow marble is picked, the player wins the game. If a blue marble is picked, it is returned to the bag (replaced), and the player gets another attempt at picking a yellow marble and winning the game.

(i) What is the probability that the player wins the game on the second go?

(ii) What is the probability that the player does not win the game?

Solution

(i) It is important to note that after each trial the marble is returned to the bag (replaced). This means that the outcome of the first trial does not affect the outcome of the second trial. Such events are referred to as **independent events**.

Therefore, the probability of picking say, a blue marble is the same for the first pick and for the second pick.

We draw our tree diagram noting that there are two possible outcomes that we are interested in – picking a blue marble or picking a yellow marble:

1st Pick	2nd Pick	Outcome
B	B	B, B
	Y	B, Y
Y	B	Y, B
	Y	Y, Y

We next fill in the probability of the two events on the tree diagram at every branch where these events occur:

A blue marble → $\frac{7}{10}$ or 0.7

A yellow marble → $\frac{3}{10}$ or 0.3

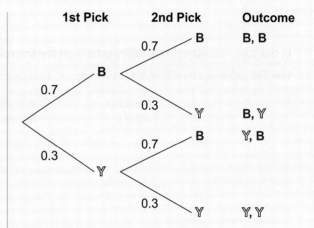

For the player to win on the second attempt, they must have picked a blue marble on the first go. The outcome we are looking for is blue, yellow (B, Y).

$P(B, Y) = 0.7 \times 0.3$

$\qquad = 0.21$ (or 21%)

(ii) The player does not win if they pick a blue marble on both goes.

$P(B, B) = 0.7 \times 0.7$

$\qquad = 0.49$ (or 49%)

Alternatively, the player wins if they pick a yellow on the first go **or** a blue on the first go and a yellow on the second go.

$P(\text{wins}) = P(Y) + P(B, Y)$

$\qquad = 0.3 + 0.21$

$\qquad = 0.51$

$\therefore P(\text{loses}) = 1 - P(\text{wins})$

$\qquad = 1 - 0.51$

$\qquad = 0.49$ (or 49%)

Worked Example 3.10

John walks past two sets of traffic lights on his way to work. The probability of the traffic lights showing a red light is $\frac{3}{4}$ and of showing a green light is $\frac{1}{4}$. What is the probability that when John passes by both sets of lights:

(i) They both show a red light.

(ii) A red light shows at the first set of traffic lights and a green light shows at the second set.

(iii) One shows a red light and the other shows a green light.

(iv) They both show the same colour.

Solution

We draw our tree diagram with green and red as our two outcomes and the probability for each outcome clearly shown on each branch.

1st Traffic lights	2nd Traffic lights	Outcome	Probability
	G	G, G	$\frac{1}{4} \times \frac{1}{4} = \frac{1}{16}$
	R	G, R	$\frac{1}{4} \times \frac{3}{4} = \frac{3}{16}$
	G	R, G	$\frac{3}{4} \times \frac{1}{4} = \frac{3}{16}$
	R	R, R	$\frac{3}{4} \times \frac{3}{4} = \frac{9}{16}$

(i) $P(R, R) = \frac{3}{4} \times \frac{3}{4} = \frac{9}{16}$

(ii) $P(R, G) = \frac{3}{4} \times \frac{1}{4} = \frac{3}{16}$

Notice that $\frac{1}{16} + \frac{3}{16} + \frac{3}{16} + \frac{9}{16} = \frac{16}{16} = 1$.

(iii) Note that the order of the lights is not specified.

This means we could have Red, Green OR Green, Red as our outcomes.

$P(R, G \text{ or } G, R) = \left(\frac{3}{4} \times \frac{1}{4}\right) + \left(\frac{1}{4} \times \frac{3}{4}\right)$

$= \frac{3}{16} + \frac{3}{16}$

$= \frac{6}{16}$

$= \frac{3}{8}$

(iv) The lights could be Red, Red OR Green, Green.

$P(RR \text{ or } GG) = P(R, R) + P(G, G)$

$= \left(\frac{3}{4} \times \frac{3}{4}\right) + \left(\frac{1}{4} \times \frac{1}{4}\right)$

$= \frac{9}{16} + \frac{1}{16}$

$= \frac{10}{16}$

$= \frac{5}{8}$

Remember 'OR' means 'to add'.

COUNTING AND PROBABILITY

1. A spinner with four equal sectors is spun twice. The spinner has three sectors coloured blue and one sector coloured white.

   What is the probability that the spinner first lands on a blue sector and then lands on a white sector?

2. The probability that Josh will be on time for school on any given day is 0.7.

   (i) What is the probability that he will be late for school?

   (ii) What is the probability that Josh will be late on two consecutive school days?

3. A bag contains five 50c coins and three 20c coins. A coin is taken at random from the bag and then put back. A second coin is then taken out.

   What is the probability that two 20c coins are taken out of the bag?

4. A box contains four red dice and three black dice. A die is picked at random from the box and then returned. A second die is then picked at random.

   What is the probability that a black die and then a red die are picked?

5. A game is played with an unfair coin. The coin is biased so that the probability of getting a head is 0.8 and the probability of getting a tail is 0.2.

   The coin is flipped twice. The game is won if the player gets two tails. What is the probability of winning the game?

6. Hat A contains five marbles, of which one is red and four are white. Hat B contains 10 marbles of which eight are red and two are black. A marble is drawn at random from Hat A and then from Hat B.

What is the probability that a red marble from Hat A and a black marble from Hat B are drawn?

7. A student plays two tennis matches. The probability that she wins the first match is 0.6, and the probability of winning the second match is 0.4.

   What is the probability that she loses the first match but wins the second?

8. A spinner with equal sectors numbered 1 to 9 is spun twice.

   What is the probability that the number it lands on will be divisible by three on both spins?

9. There are three girls and seven boys in a class. A student's name is picked at random from a hat to answer a question. The name is then returned to the hat and another name is then picked out of the hat.

Copy and complete the following probability tree diagram.

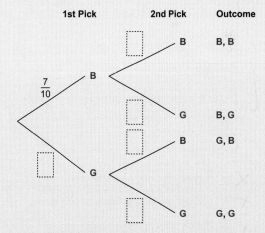

Find the probability that:

   (i) A boy is picked on both occasions.

   (ii) A girl and then a boy are picked.

   (iii) A girl and a boy are picked.

10. A bag contains 10 blue tokens and 15 green tokens. A token is picked at random from the bag and then returned. A second token is then picked at random.

    What is the probability of picking:

    (i) A green token followed by a blue token

    (ii) A blue token followed by a green token

    (iii) Two blue tokens

    (iv) Two tokens of the same colour

    (v) Two tokens of different colour

11. A bag contains fourteen 50c coins and eight 10c coins. A coin is taken at random from the bag and then put back. A second coin is then taken out. What is the probability of selecting:

    (i) Two 10c coins

    (ii) Two 50c coins

    (iii) Two coins of the same value

    (iv) Two coins of different value

    (v) Two coins worth 60c or more in total

12. Met Éireann calculate the probability that it will rain over the next two days:

    Monday – 40%

    Tuesday – 60%

    Draw a tree diagram to show all possible outcomes and probabilities.

    Calculate the probability that:

    (i) It doesn't rain on either day.

    (ii) It rains on at least one of the days.

    (iii) It only rains on one day.

13. A fair coin is flipped three times. A player wins if the coin lands on a head. What is the probability that the player wins for the first time on the:

    (i) First flip

    (ii) Second flip

    (iii) Third flip

    What is the probability that the player doesn't win?

14. A manufacturing company determines that the probability of a machine part being produced with a fault is 0.05. Two parts are picked at random. Draw a tree diagram to show all possible outcomes.

    Calculate the probability that

    (i) Both parts are faulty.

    (ii) Neither part is faulty.

    (iii) At least one part is faulty.

15. A fair six-sided die is rolled up to three times.

    A player wins if a roll of 4 is scored. What is the probability that the player wins on the:

    (i) First turn

    (ii) Second turn

    (iii) Third turn

    What is the probability that the player doesn't win?

16. A token is chosen at random from a box which contains five red tokens and two blue tokens. A second token is chosen at random from a box containing one red token and two green tokens.

    Draw a tree diagram to show all the possible outcomes and probabilities.

    What is the probability of selecting:

    (i) Two tokens of the same colour

    (ii) Two tokens of different colour

    A game is played in which two players compete.

    ■ Player A wins if they pick the same colour token from each box.

    ■ Player B wins if they pick different coloured tokens from each box.

    Is this a fair game? Explain your answer clearly.

17. A company manufactures watches using parts from two different companies. Watch R Us supplies 70% of the parts used and Best Watches supplies the rest. Both companies test their parts for faults. Watch R Us knows that 2% of all its parts supplied are faulty, while 5% of the parts supplied by Best Watches are faulty.

(i) Represent this information on a tree diagram.

A watch is selected at random.

(ii) Find the probability that it is not faulty.

18. On a school day chosen at random, the probability that Jim will travel to school by car is 15%. If Jim does not travel to school by car, he walks. The probability of Jim being late when using the car is 30% and when walking is 11%.

(i) Draw a tree diagram to represent this information.

Find the probability that on a randomly chosen school day:

(ii) Jim travels by car and is late.

(iii) Jim is not late.

If Jim is on time:

(iv) Find the probability that he did not travel by car.

19. The probability that a climber reaches the top of a mountain on a dry day is $\frac{3}{4}$. The probability that he reaches the top on a wet day is $\frac{1}{5}$. Records from the mountain top show that the probability that it rains on any particular day is $\frac{2}{3}$.

(i) Draw a tree diagram to show all outcomes.

(ii) Find the probability that on a day chosen at random, the climber reaches the top of the mountain.

(iii) If the climber reached the top of the mountain, find the probability that it was a dry day.

20. Dylan is trying to knock down a coconut at a coconut shy at a funfair.

The probability that he knocks down a coconut on his first throw is $\frac{1}{3}$.

If he misses on the first throw the probability that he knocks down a coconut on his second throw is $\frac{1}{5}$.

If he knocks down a coconut on his first throw, the probability that he knocks down a coconut on his second throw is $\frac{1}{2}$.

Draw a tree diagram to show all possible outcomes.

Find the probability that Dylan knocks down:

(i) One coconut

(ii) Both coconuts

(iii) At least one coconut

(iv) No coconuts

3.3 SET THEORY AND PROBABILITY

Set theory is very useful when trying to solve questions on probability.
A Venn diagram can be used to represent the sample space, and individual probabilities can then be easily read from the diagram.

Consider two **mutually exclusive** events, A and B. When two sets (A and B) have no elements in common, we say that A and B are mutually exclusive events. They can be represented by two non-overlapping circles. Such non-overlapping sets are called **disjoint sets**. For two disjoint sets A and B, A ∩ B = ∅.

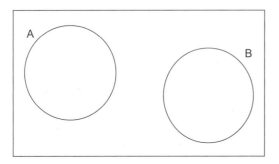

Disjoint sets are sets that have no elements in common.

If the sets do have elements in common, these elements are represented by the areas where the circles overlap:

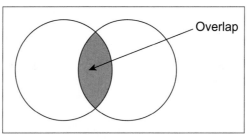

The following Venn diagrams have two sets, A and B.

In the diagram below, the shaded area indicates elements that are in Set A:

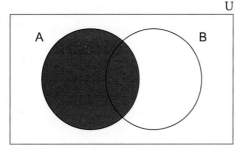

In the diagram below, the shaded area indicates elements that are in Set B:

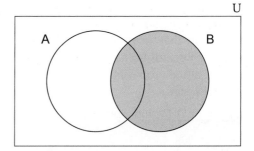

The elements that are shared by Set A **AND** Set B can be shown as follows:

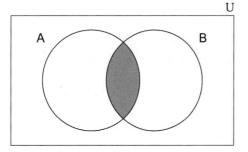

This is written as A ∩ B.

The elements that are in Set A **OR** Set B can be shown as follows:

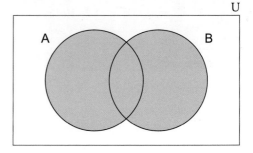

This is written as A ∪ B.

The elements that are neither in Set A nor Set B can be shown as follows:

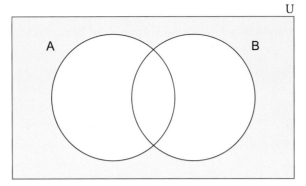

This is written as (A ∪ B)′ or as U \ (A ∪ B).

Elements that are in Set A but not in Set B can be shown as follows:

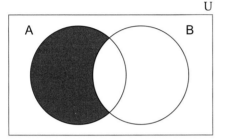

This is written as A\B.

Elements that are in Set B but not in Set A can be shown as follows:

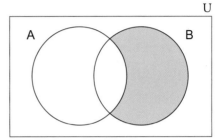

This is written as B\A.

Worked Example 3.11

A survey is conducted to find out how many households have an LCD TV or a plasma TV. The Venn diagram shows the results. Set A contains those households that have an LCD TV, and Set B contains those households that have a plasma TV.

Find the probability that a household chosen at random has:

(i) A TV

(ii) An LCD TV and a plasma TV

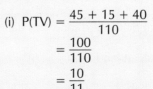

Solution

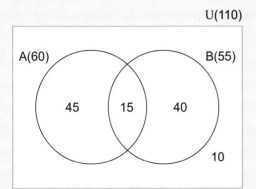

(i) $P(TV) = \dfrac{45 + 15 + 40}{110}$

$= \dfrac{100}{110}$

$= \dfrac{10}{11}$

(ii) In set notation we are looking for $\dfrac{\#(A \cap B)}{\#U}$

$P(\text{LCD TV and Plasma TV}) = \dfrac{15}{110}$

$= \dfrac{3}{22}$

Worked Example 3.12

In a class of 22 students, 15 study French, eight study Spanish and four study neither of these subjects.

(a) Show this information on a Venn diagram.

(b) What is the probability that a student chosen at random:

   (i) Studies French only

   (ii) Studies Spanish only

   (iii) Does not study French

Solution

(a) $15 + 8 + 4 = 27$ students

   But there are only 22 students in the class.

   $\therefore$ Five people have been counted twice.

   So, $\#(F \cap S) = 5$

   $\therefore \#(F \setminus S) = 15 - 5 = 10$

   and $\#(S \setminus F) = 8 - 5 = 3$

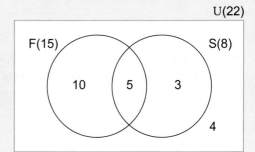

(b) (i) The probability that a student chosen at random studies French only $= \dfrac{10}{22} = \dfrac{5}{11}$.

   (ii) The probability that a student chosen at random studies Spanish only $= \dfrac{3}{22}$.

   (iii) The probability that a student chosen at random does not study French $= \dfrac{7}{22}$.

    There is another way to calculate this probability. Can you think of it?

ACTIVITIES 3.3, 3.4

Worked Example 3.13

In a survey, students were asked what brand of energy drink they liked. The probability that a student liked Brand C was 0.6, and the probability that a student liked Brand P was 0.5. The probability that they liked neither drink was 0.1.

   (i) Draw a Venn diagram to show this data.

  A student is picked at random.

   (ii) Find the probability that the student liked Brand C and Brand P.

   (iii) Find the probability that the student liked Brand P only.

Solution

(i) We know that all the probabilities should add up to 1.

$0.6 + 0.5 + 0.1 = 1.2$

$1.2 - 1 = 0.2$

So the probability that a student liked both Brand C and Brand P is 0.2.

Liked Brand C only $= 0.6 - 0.2$

$= 0.4$

Liked Brand P only $= 0.5 - 0.2$

$= 0.3$

COUNTING AND PROBABILITY

We can now draw the Venn diagram.

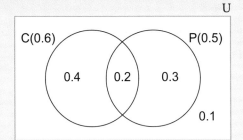

(ii) Probability that the student liked Brand C and Brand P = 0.2.

(iii) Probability that the student liked Brand P only = 0.3.

Worked Example 3.14

Forty-five customers of a computer gaming store were asked which of the following gaming consoles they own: Xbox 360, Nintendo Wii or Sony PS3.

Twenty-one owned an Xbox 360, 19 owned a Nintendo Wii and 16 people owned a Sony PS3.

Seven owned an Xbox 360 and a Sony PS3, six owned an Xbox 360 and a Nintendo Wii and three owned a Nintendo Wii and a Sony PS3 but not an Xbox 360. Five did not own any of the three gaming consoles listed and four owned all three.

(i) Represent this information on a Venn diagram.

A customer is picked at random. Find the probability that this customer owns:

(ii) A Sony PS3 but not an Xbox 360 or a Nintendo Wii

(iii) At least two types of console

Solution

(i)

6 Xbox 360 and Nintendo Wii – 4 who own all 3

21 – 3 – 4 – 2 = 12

Own all 3

U (45)

X (21)   N (19)

12   2   10   ⟶ 19 – 2 – 4 – 3 = 10

4

3   3   ⟶ Own Nintendo Wii and Sony PS3 but not Xbox 360

7 Xbox 360 and Sony PS3 – 4 who own all 3

6

5 ⟶ do not own any

S (16)

16 – 3 – 4 – 3 = 6

Our completed Venn diagram is now ready to be used to help answer the other parts of the question.

(ii) Six people own a Sony PS3 only

Probability (own Sony PS3 only) $= \dfrac{6}{45} = \dfrac{2}{15}$

(iii) We are looking for the number of customers who own two or more consoles.

$3 + 4 + 2 + 3 = 12$

Probability (own at least two types) $= \dfrac{12}{45} = \dfrac{4}{15}$

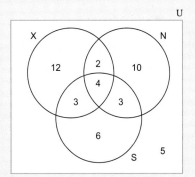

Exercise 3.3

1. This Venn diagram shows the number of teenagers in a group who like tea or coffee.

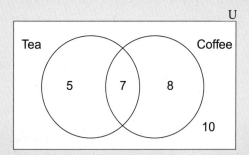

Find the probability that a teenager chosen at random:

(i) Likes tea

(ii) Likes coffee

(iii) Likes tea and coffee

(iv) Likes neither tea nor coffee

2. The Venn diagram below represents the number of students in a college who study zoology or botany.

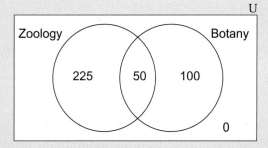

Calculate the probability that a student chosen at random:

(i) Studies zoology

(ii) Studies botany

(iii) Studies zoology and botany

3. For each of the Venn diagrams shown, find the probability of selecting at random an element from:

(i) $R \cup Q$ (ii) $R \cap Q$ (iii) $R \setminus Q$ (iv) $(R \cup Q)'$

(a)
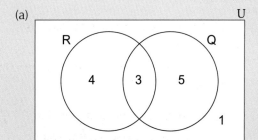

(b)
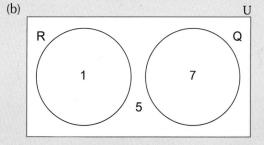

4. The Venn diagram below shows the response to a survey carried out in a supermarket. Forty-five customers were asked what brand of washing powder they purchased.

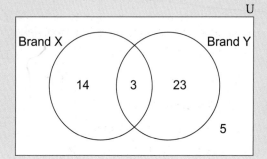

A customer is selected at random. What is the probability that he or she:

(i) Bought Brand X

(ii) Did not buy Brand X

(iii) Bought neither brand

5. Students are asked which of two strands of the new maths syllabus they prefer. The Venn diagram below shows the results:

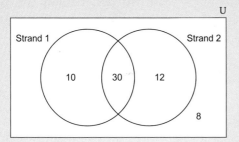

What is the probability that a student selected at random prefers:

(i) Strand 1

(ii) Strand 1 and Strand 2

(iii) Strand 1 or Strand 2

(iv) Neither of the two strands

6. In a survey of 12 people, six people liked Brand A and five people liked Brand B. Five people liked neither brand.

(a) Copy and complete the Venn diagram below.

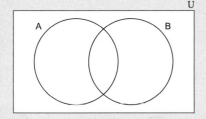

(b) Use the Venn diagram to find the following:

(i) The number of people who liked Brand A or Brand B

(ii) The number of people who liked Brand A only

(iii) The number of people who liked one brand only

A person is picked at random from the group. What is the probability that it is a person who likes:

(iv) Brand A or Brand B

(v) Brand A only

(vi) One brand only

7. In a litter of puppies, all the pups are born with spots on their coats. The spots are coloured black or white. The probability that a pup will have black spots is 0.4. The probability that the pup will have black and white spots is 0.1.

(i) Show this data on a Venn diagram.

(ii) Find the probability that a pup will have white spots only.

8. Michael plays both soccer (S) and rugby (R). The probability that he will get picked for the soccer team is 0.4 and the probability that he will get picked for the rugby team is 0.5. The probability that he will get picked for both teams is 0.1.

(i) Draw a Venn diagram to show these probabilities.

(ii) Find the probability that he will not get picked for either team.

9. Ryan attempts two maths questions. The probability that Ryan gets the first question correct is 0.5. The probability that Ryan gets the second question correct is 0.6. The probability of him getting both questions wrong is 0.2.

(i) Draw a Venn diagram to show these probabilities.

Using the Venn diagram, find the probability that he:

(ii) Correctly answers both questions

(iii) Correctly answers the first question only

10. A survey of 100 people is carried out and shows that 35 listen to classical music, 50 listen to rock music and 20 listen to neither. A person from the survey is selected at random. What is the probability that this person listens to:

(i) Rock music

(ii) Classical music only

(iii) Rock and classical music

(iv) Rock or classical music

11. There are 50 students in a club: 27 play hurling, 34 play football and three play neither of these sports. Fill out a Venn diagram to illustrate this data.

Find the probability that a student selected at random from the club will play:

(i) Hurling

(ii) Football

(iii) Both football and hurling

(iv) Hurling only

> In the following questions, each Venn diagram has three main sets. Try to complete Activities 3.5 and 3.6 before attempting these questions.

 **ACTIVITIES 3.5, 3.6**

12. Thirty people were asked what type of film they like: comedy (C), drama (D) or horror (H). The Venn diagram below shows the results:

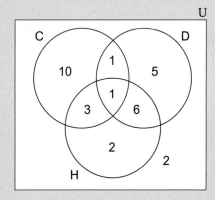

A person is selected at random.
Find the probability that this person likes:

(i) Comedy

(ii) Drama only

(iii) All three film types

(iv) Comedy and horror

(v) Comedy and horror only

(vi) None of these types of films

13. The Venn diagram below shows the number of people who read newspapers P, Q or R.

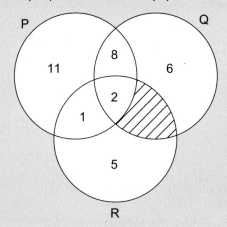

What is the probability that a person selected at random reads:

(i) Paper P

(ii) Paper Q only

(iii) Paper Q and Paper R

(iv) Paper Q or Paper R

14. A total of 85 shoppers were surveyed at a shopping centre. The survey found that 72 people shopped at Amazing Value, 22 shopped at Best Bargains and 19 shopped at Crazy Value. Seventeen people shopped at Amazing Value and Best Bargains, 10 shopped at Best Bargains and Crazy Value, and 12 shopped at Amazing Value and Crazy Value. Seven shopped at all three stores.

(i) Represent this information on a Venn diagram.

A shopper is picked at random. Find the probability that he or she shopped at:

(ii) Amazing Value only

(iii) Amazing Value and Best Bargains only

(iv) Any of these stores

(v) None of these stores

15. In a survey, 45 university students were asked what country they had visited during their summer holidays – England, France or Germany. No one had been to all three countries, but 13 had been to England, 19 to France and 13 to Germany; 13 had visited none of these countries, one had been to England and Germany only, and four had been to England and France only.

  (i) Represent this on a Venn diagram.

A student is selected at random. What is the probability that this student visited:

  (ii) At least one country

  (iii) One country only

  (iv) Two countries

16. A music school has 100 students. Fifty students play the cello, 20 play the trumpet, 60 play the violin, 10 play all three instruments, 15 play both the cello and the violin but not the trumpet, five play both the cello and the trumpet but not the violin, and two play both the trumpet and the violin but not the cello.

  (a) Draw a Venn diagram to represent this information.

  (b) What is the probability that a student chosen at random does not play any of the three instruments mentioned.

  (c) Calculate the probability that a randomly chosen student plays only one instrument.

17. A, B and C are three sets.

$$\#(A \cup B \cup C) = 28$$

$$\#(A) = 10 \quad \#(B) = 18 \quad \#(C) = 18$$

$$\#(A \cap C) = 5 \quad \#(B \cap C) = 9 \quad \#(A \cap B \cap C) = 2$$

Show this information on a Venn diagram and find the following probabilities:

  (i) $P[(A \cap B) \backslash C]$

  (ii) $P[(A \cup B) \backslash C]$

  (iii) $P(B')$

Revision Exercises

1. (a) A fair six-sided white die and a fair six-sided black die are thrown.

  (i) Use a two-way table to show all the possible outcomes.

  (ii) How many outcomes are possible?

Find the probability of getting:

  (iii) A 2 on the white die and a 4 on the black die

  (iv) A 6 on the white die and a 6 on the black die

  (v) A 1 on the white die and an odd number on the black die

  (vi) An even number on the white die and an odd number on the black die

  (vii) A 4 or greater on the white die and a 3 or less on the black die

(b) Urn A contains three yellow and four blue tokens. Urn B contains five yellow and two blue tokens.

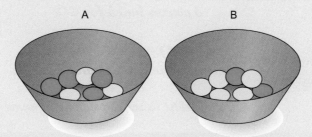

A   B

(i) A token is taken first from Urn A and then from Urn B. Copy and complete the tree diagram to show all the possible outcomes.

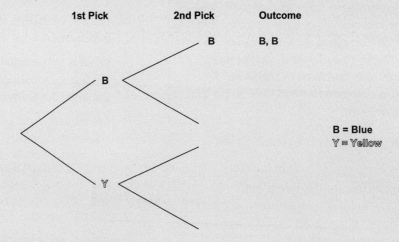

1st Pick   **2nd Pick**   **Outcome**

B   B, B

B

Y

B = Blue
Y = Yellow

(ii) Find the probability of getting:

- Two blue tokens
- Two yellow tokens
- A blue token followed by a yellow token
- Two tokens of the same colour

(c) A bag contains three yellow balls, two blue balls and one orange ball. A ball is taken from the bag at random. The ball is then put back. This is repeated a further two times until three balls have been taken from the bag. What is the probability that the order of the balls picked is yellow, blue and orange?

2. A, B, C, D and E represent the probabilities of certain events occuring.

(a) Write the probability of each of the events listed into the table below.

Event		Probability
A club is selected in a random draw from a pack of playing cards	A	
A tossed fair coin shows a tail on landing	B	
The sun will rise in the east tomorrow	C	
May will follow directly after June	D	
A randomly selected person was born on a Thursday	E	

(b) Place each of the letters A, B, C, D and E at its correct position on the probability scale below.

```
├─────────────────────────────────────────┤
0                                          1
```

SEC 2012, JCHL

3. (a) A restaurant advertises its lunch menu using the sign below.

3 course lunch for €15

Choose from our range of starters, main courses and desserts

180 different lunches to choose from!

(i) The menu has a choice of five starters and nine main courses. How many items must appear on the dessert menu to justify the above claim of 180 different lunches?

(ii) On a particular day one of the starters and one of the main courses is not available. How many different three-course lunches is it possible to have on that day?

SEC 2011, JCHL

(b) The percentage distribution of blood groups in the Irish population is given in the table below. The table also gives information about which types of blood can be safely used when people need to be given blood during an operation.

Blood Group	Percentage in Irish population	Blood groups to which transfusions can be safely given	Blood groups from which transfusions can be safely received
O–	8	All	O–
O+	47	O+, AB+, A+, B+	O+ and O–
A–	5	A–, A+, AB+, AB–	A– and O–
A+	26	A+ and AB+	A+, O–, O+, A–
B–	2	B–, B+, AB–, AB+	B– and O–
B+	9	B+ and AB+	B+, B–, O–, O+
AB–	1	AB– and AB+	AB–, O–, A–, B–
AB+	2	AB+	all

Source: Irish Blood Transfusion Service

(i) If an Irish person is chosen at random, what is the probability that that person will have blood group AB–?

(ii) Mary has blood group B–. If a person is chosen at random from the population, what is the probability that Mary could safely receive blood from that person?

(iii) Aaron has blood group O+ and donates blood. What is the probability that his blood can be given to a person randomly chosen from the population?

(iv) The *Irish Blood Transfusion Service* recently asked that people with blood group O– should give blood as regularly as possible. Give a reason why this might be the case.

SEC 2011, JCHL

4. (a) The colour of 500 cars that pass a particular set of traffic lights during a two-hour period is recorded by a group of students.

Colour	Frequency	Relative frequency	Daily frequency (Part (v) below)
Red	70		
Blue	100		
Yellow	45		
White	55		
Black			
Silver	140		
Total	500		

(i)   Calculate the number of black cars and write it into the table.

(ii)   Calculate the relative frequency of each colour and write these into the table.

(iii) Suggest a method to check that your relative frequency calculations are correct. Perform this check.

(iv)   What is the probability that the next car to pass the lights is red?

(v)   Use the information to estimate the frequency of each colour if 2,400 cars pass the lights in a full day. Write this information into the table.

(vi)   The data collected by the students is not a random sample of the cars passing throughout the day. Do you think that this makes your estimates in part (v) above unreliable? Give a reason for your answer.

SEC 2011, JCHL

(b) In an experiment, Anne tossed a die 600 times. The results are partially recorded in the table below.

Number on die	1	2	3	4	5	6
Frequency	92	101	115	98		105

(i)   Calculate the number of times that a 5 appeared. Write your answer in the table above.

(ii)   After looking at the results, Anne claims that the die is unbiased (fair). Do you agree with her? Give a reason for your answer.

(iii) If this die is tossed 300 times, how many times would you expect to get an even number as a result? Give a reason for your answer.

SEC Sample Paper, JCHL

5. (a) Of the people attending a concert, one is chosen at random to win a prize.

The probability that the chosen person is male is 0.515.

The probability that the chosen person is married is 0.048.

The probability that the chosen person is a married male is 0.029.

What is the probability that the chosen person is an unmarried female?

(b) Harry rolls a six-sided die and keeps a record of the number of 4s after every 10 throws.

Number of Throws	10	20	30	40	50	60	70	80	90	100	110	120
Number of 4s	1	5	8	10	10	12	13	13	15	15	16	18

(i)   Find the relative frequency after every 10 throws.

(ii)   Plot a graph of the relative frequencies against the number of throws taken.

(iii) What does the graph show about the relative frequency values?

6. (a) A bag contains one red and one white ball. A second bag contains one green and one red ball. A third bag contains one red and one white ball.

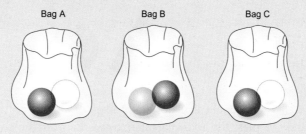

Bag A   Bag B   Bag C

A ball is chosen at random from each bag in turn. Use a tree diagram to list all possible outcomes. Find the probability:

(i)   That the three balls selected will be of the same colour

(ii) That the three balls selected will be of a different colour

(iii) That the first two balls will be of the same colour

(iv) That at least one red ball will be chosen

(b) The probability of Kieran passing his driver theory test is 0.4 at each attempt. He is only allowed two attempts per day.

(i) Copy and complete the following tree diagram. [*Note:* P = Pass, F = Fail]

1st Test   **2nd Test**   **Outcome**

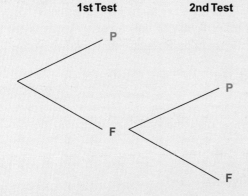

(ii) Calculate the probability that Kieran, on a given day:

- Passes his test on the first attempt
- Fails his test on both attempts
- Passes his test on the second attempt

(c) Shane places two red marbles and three blue marbles into a bag. He picks a marble at random from the bag.

(i) Find the probability that he picks a red marble.

Shane returns his marble to the bag and Nicola adds five blue marbles to the bag. She picks a marble at random from the bag.

(ii) Find the probability that she picks a red marble.

Nicola returns her marble to the bag and Shane adds five more marbles to the bag. The probability that he now picks a red marble is $\frac{1}{3}$.

(iii) How many red marbles did he add to the bag?

7. (a) A fair four-sided die and a fair six-sided die are rolled. The outcome for the first die can be 1, 2, 3 or 4. The outcome for the second die can be 1, 2, 3, 4, 5 or 6.

After rolling the dice, a student calculates the product of the two outcomes by multiplying their scores. Copy and complete the following table, by working out the products each time:

		Second die					
		1	2	3	4	5	6
First die	1	1					
	2		4				
	3						
	4						

What is the probability that the product of the outcomes will be:

(i) Even   (iii) A prime number   (v) A perfect square

(ii) Odd   (iv) Less than 12   (vi) A perfect cube

(b) A driver has to pass through three sets of traffic lights on her way to work. The probability that the first set of traffic lights is green is 0.7; that the second set of traffic lights is green is 0.5; and that the third set of traffic lights is green is 0.3. If traffic lights can only be either green or red calculate the probability that the driver goes through the set of traffic lights in the following order:

(i) Green, green, green   (ii) Red, red, red   (iii) Green, red, green

(c) In a class of 25 students, 20 students own a dog and seven own a cat. Three students own a dog and a cat. Show this information on a Venn diagram, and use the Venn diagram to find the following:

(i) The number of students who own a cat only

(ii) The number of students who own neither type of pet

A student is picked at random from the class. Find the probability that this student owns:

(iii) A cat only

(iv) Neither type of pet

8. (a) A calculator is set up to show the numbers 1 and 7 at random. A number is shown every time the EXE key is pressed.

The EXE key is pressed three times.

What is the probability that:

(i) The number 1 is shown each time

(ii) The same number is shown each time

NCCA 2011, Pre-JCHL

(b) At a press conference at the 2012 Eurovision song contest in Baku, Azerbaijan, journalists were allowed to interview participants from three different countries.

The countries were assigned to three groups (A, B and C) and each journalist was allowed to interview one country from each group.

SONG CONTEST
BAKU 2012

The groups were:

Group A	Group B	Group C
Azerbaijan	Iceland	Serbia
France	Greece	Ukraine
Germany	Albania	Sweden
Italy	Romania	Turkey
Spain	Cyprus	Norway
UK	Denmark	
	Russia	
	Hungary	
	Moldova	
	Ireland	

(i) List two possible sets of countries that a journalist could have chosen to interview.

(ii) How many different sets of countries could be chosen?

(iii) If instead of being allowed to choose a set of countries themselves, a computer was used to randomly select a set of countries, then which country would you expect to be chosen more often, Russia or Turkey? Explain your answer.

(c) Loaded dice are dice that are unfair. They are more likely to land on some sides than on others.

John and Sandeep are two students. Their maths teacher gives them a die and asks them to describe a way in which they could investigate if the die is loaded or not.

(i) Describe, in detail, how the two students could investigate if the die is loaded or not. In your answer you must refer to the total **number of trials** and to **relative frequencies**.

(ii) John and Sandeep roll the die 500 times and record the results in the table below:

Outcome	1	2	3	4	5	6
Frequency	83	85	80	71		81

Complete the table by filling in the missing frequency.

(iii) Do you think that the die John and Sandeep were given is fair? Clearly explain your answer.

9. (a) A man records the colour of different sets of traffic lights he has to pass every morning on his way to work.

Colour	Number
Red	75
Amber	24
Green	32

(i) Calculate the relative frequency to three significant figures of each colour.

(ii) Hence estimate how many more red lights than green lights he would expect in 250 journeys to work.

(b) When Samantha walked into her local shopping centre, she saw a competition taking place. Samantha decided to take part. A poster for the competition read:

> Roll two dice, get a total of 11 and win €10!
> Only €1 to enter.

(i) Draw the sample space diagram for this event. Each die is fair and six-sided.

(ii) What is the probability of winning €10?

(iii) How many goes should she have in order to expect to win at least once?

(iv) If she had 40 goes, how many times could she expect to have won?

(v) If she plays the game three times, what is the chance that she wins every time?

(vi) If she plays the game three times, what is the chance that she wins at least once?

(vii) What is the chance that she wins at least twice?

10. (a) A group of 150 students were asked which daily newspaper(s) they read.

The results are shown in the diagram.

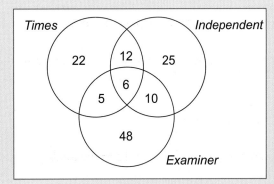

(i) Find the probability that a student chosen at random reads:

(1) The *Times*

(2) Only one of the papers

(3) None of the three papers

(4) The *Independent* or the *Times* or both but not the *Examiner*

(ii) One of the students, Gemma, reads the *Examiner*.

Find the probability that she also reads the *Times*.

(iii) State whether each of the following variables is qualitative, discrete or continuous:

(1) The number of pages in each newspaper

(2) The length of time spent reading each newspaper

(b) The Venn diagram below shows the probability of events A, B and C happening.

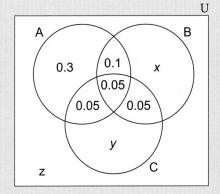

P(B) = 0.4 and P(C) = 0.35

Calculate *x*, *y*, and *z*.

11. (a) Six women and three men go for an interview for two job vacancies. A man and then a woman were chosen for the job. Each man is equally likely to be chosen and each woman is equally likely to be chosen. Use the sample space diagram below to show all the possible outcomes:

	Dee (D)	Elie (E)	Fiona (F)	Gemma (G)	Holly (H)	Isabel (I)
Andy (A)				AG		
Bob (B)			BF			
Charles (C)						

Find the probability that:

(i) Bob and Gemma are chosen for the job.

(ii) Andy gets the job.

(iii) Charles does not get the job.

(b) A consultancy firm surveyed 200 people to determine how they learned about a new product. 150 people learned about the product through word of mouth, 125 from the television, 70 from the Internet, 80 from word of mouth and television, 55 from word of mouth and the Internet, 20 from television and the Internet, and 10 from all three.

A person is selected at random. Calculate the probability that this person learned about the product from:

   (i) The Internet only

   (ii) Any source but the Internet

   (iii) The television and word of mouth

   (iv) Word of mouth and the Internet but not the television

(c) The probability of Alex winning a prize in a game is 0.4. The probability of Beth winning a prize is 0.3. The probability of them both winning a prize is 0.1.

   (i) Use a Venn diagram to determine the probability that neither wins a prize.

In a new game only one of them can win a prize.

   (ii) Use a new Venn diagram to determine the probability that neither wins a prize.

12. Sophie and Amy were designing a game of chance to raise money for charity in their school. They agreed on the following

■ They would call the game *Spin and Win.*

■ They would charge 50c to play.

■ The rule would be: Roll a fair six-sided die and spin the spinner shown and add the totals.

 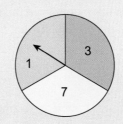

They could not, however, agree on the outcomes that would result in a win, loss or money back.

Sophie's Idea	**Amy's Idea**
Money back: Get total of 13	**Money back:** Even number total
Win €1: Even number total	**Win €1:** Odd total, but not prime
Lose: Anything else	**Lose:** Anything else

(i) Given that there are 180 students in the school and that every student will play the game at least once, create a sample space showing all the possible outcomes of the game and make an argument to support either Sophie or Amy's idea.

(ii) Without changing the rule, make your own set of criteria for **win**, **lose** or **money back** that may generate more money for the chosen charity. Justify your ideas.

NCCA 2011, Pre-JCHL

13. (a) An unbiased coin is flipped four times. List the sample space.
Hence, or otherwise, find the probability that:

    (i) The result will be HHHH.

    (ii) There will be exactly three heads.

    (iii) There will be two or more heads.

    (iv) There will be less than two heads.

    (v) There will be no heads.

(b) A competition is organised to raise money for a charity. To win a prize in the competition, you must pick the number 3 token from each box.

- Box A contains 10 tokens numbered 1 to 10.
- Box B contains five tokens numbered 1 to 5.

    (i) Draw a tree diagram to show all the possible outcomes.
       (*Note:* Treat the outcomes as '3', 'Not a 3'.)

    (ii) Using the tree diagram, calculate the probability of winning a prize.

    (iii) Do you think that people will want to buy a ticket for this raffle? Explain your answer.

Due to poor sales of tickets for the competition, it is decided to change the ways of winning a prize. To win a prize, you now have to pick an even-numbered token from Box A and the number 3 token from Box B.

    (iv) Calculate the probability of now winning a prize.

(c) A bag contains four chocolate and five strawberry cakes.

Two cakes are taken at random from the bag one at a time. Using a tree diagram, find the probability that the two cakes chosen are:

    (i) Both chocolate

    (ii) Both strawberry

    (iii) Chocolate first and strawberry second

    (iv) Chocolate and strawberry

14. A fair circular spinner consists of three equal sectors. Two are coloured blue and one is coloured red.

The spinner is spun and a fair coin is tossed.

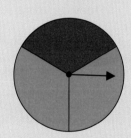

(a) What is the probability of the spinner landing on a blue sector?

(b) Find the probability of getting a head and a red.

(c) Find the probability of getting a tail and a blue.

SEC 2012, JCHL

15. (a) What is the probability of getting a 1 when a fair six-sided die is tossed?

A fair six-sided die is tossed 500 times.

The results are partially recorded in the table below.

Number on die	1	2	3	4	5	6
Frequency	70	82		90	91	81
Relative frequency						

(b) Calculate the number of times a 3 appeared. Write your answer in the table above.

(c) Calculate the relative frequency of each outcome and write it into the table above.
Give your answers correct to two decimal places.

(d) Give a possible reason for the difference in value between the relative frequency for 1 in the table and your answer to part (a)

SEC 2012, JCHL

Number Patterns

Learning Outcomes

In this chapter you will learn how to:

- Use tables to represent a repeating pattern situation

- Generalise and explain patterns and relationships in words and numbers

- Write arithmetic expressions for particular terms in a sequence

- Find the underlying formula algebraically from which the data is derived (linear and quadratic relations)

- Recognise distinguishing features of linear, quadratic and exponential patterns

- Use graphs, tables and diagrams as tools for representing and analysing linear, quadratic and exponential patterns and relations

- Understand rate of change and the y-intercept, with regard to linear graphs

- Recognise proportional relationships

4.1 LINEAR PATTERNS

Mathematics has been referred to as the 'science of patterns'. Mathematicians seek out patterns to help understand the world around us.

A pattern, from the French word *patron*, is a set of numbers, objects or diagrams that repeat in a predictable manner.

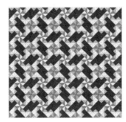

YOU SHOULD REMEMBER...

■ Number patterns from *Active Maths 1*

■ How to graph number patterns from *Active Maths 1*

■ The co-ordinate geometry of the line from *Active Maths 1*

A pattern that is given as an ordered list is called a **sequence**.

A pattern of numbers is called a **number sequence**.

KEY WORDS

■ **Pattern**
■ **Sequence**
■ **Linear**
■ **Quadratic**
■ **Exponential**
■ **Starting value**
■ **Term**
■ **General term**
■ **First difference, first change, common difference**
■ **Second difference**

Worked Example 4.1

A five-marble repeating pattern, made up of coloured marbles, is shown.

  (i)   What colour is the 89th marble?

 (ii)   What colour is the 100th marble?

(iii)   How many times does a blue marble appear in the first 32 marbles of this pattern?

Solution

We can draw a table to help us.

Marble	Colour
1	Blue
2	Blue
3	Red
4	Green
5	Red

The pattern repeats every five marbles.

(i) The 89th marble
$89 \div 5 = 17$, with a remainder of 4.

(17 repeating blocks of five marbles and four extra marbles)

The fourth marble is green.
∴ The 89th marble is green.

(ii) The 100th marble
$100 \div 5 = 20$ R0.   (R0 = Remainder of 0)

(20 repeating blocks of five marbles)

∴ 100 is a multiple of 5.

Every multiple of 5 is red.
∴ The 100th marble is red.

(iii) $32 \div 5 = 6$ R2.

Six complete patterns = $6 \times 2 = 12$ blue marbles.

The remainder of 2 represents the next two marbles, both of which are blue.

∴ A blue marble appears $12 + 2 = 14$ times.

Linear Sequences

In any linear pattern or sequence, the difference or change between one term and the next is always the same number. This means that change in a linear sequence is **constant** (has the same value).

20, 25, 30, 35 ... is an example of a linear sequence.

1st Term	2nd Term	3rd Term	4th Term
T_1	T_2	T_3	T_4
20	25	30	35

+5   +5   +5

This difference between each term can be referred to as the **common difference**, **first difference** or **first change**.

Worked Example 4.2

(i) 4, 7, 10, 13...

(ii) 7, 2, –3, –8...

For each of the above linear sequences:

(a) Write down the start term (T_1).

(b) Find the first difference.

(c) Write down the next three terms.

(d) Describe the sequence in your own words.

Solution

(i) 4, 7, 10, 13...

(a) $T_1 = 4$

(b) 4   7   10   13

+3   +3   +3

The first difference is +3.

(c)

T_4	13
T_5	13 + 3 = 16
T_6	16 + 3 = 19
T_7	19 + 3 = 22

∴ Answer = 16, 19, 22

(d) Start with 4 and then add 3 every term.

(ii) 7, 2, –3, –8...

(a) $T_1 = 7$

(b) 7   2   –3   –8

–5   –5   –5

The first difference is –5.

(c)

T_4	–8
T_5	–8 – 5 = –13
T_6	–13 – 5 = –18
T_7	–18 – 5 = –23

∴ Answer = –13, –18, –23

(d) Start with 7 and then subtract 5 every term.

General Term of a Linear Sequence

It can be more useful to know a rule that would allow us to find the value of any term of a sequence.

This is referred to as finding the general term, or T_n (pronounced nth term), of a sequence.

The **general term of a sequence** (T_n), is a formula that can be used to find the value of any term of the sequence.

NUMBER PATTERNS

Worked Example 4.3

Find the general term of each of the following linear sequences and, hence, find the 25th term of each.

(i) 8, 19, 30, 41...   (ii) 15, 11, 7, 3...

Solution

(i) 8, 19, 30, 41...

The common difference is +11.

Term number			Term value
T_1	11 × 1 = 11	11 − 3 = 8	8
T_2	11 × 2 = 22	22 − 3 = 19	19
T_n	11 × n = 11n	11n − 3	11n − 3

$\therefore T_n = 11n - 3$

$\therefore T_{25} = 11(25) - 3$

$\qquad = 275 - 3$

$\qquad = 272$

(ii) 15, 11, 7, 3...

The common difference is −4.

Term number			Term value
T_1	−4 × 1 = −4	−4 + 19 = 15	15
T_2	−4 × 2 = −8	−8 + 19 = 11	11
T_n	−4 × n = −4n	−4n + 19	19 − 4n

$\therefore T_n = 19 - 4n$

$\therefore T_{25} = 19 - 4(25)$

$\qquad = 19 - 100$

$\qquad = -81$

Worked Example 4.4

A pattern of triangles is built up from matchsticks as follows:

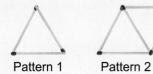 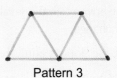

Pattern 1   Pattern 2   Pattern 3

(i) Write down a formula that represents the number of matchsticks for each pattern. Clearly explain all the letters used in your formula.

(ii) How many matchsticks will Pattern 200 need?

(iii) What number pattern will require 147 matchsticks?

Solution

(i) Count the number of matchsticks in each pattern.

Pattern	Number of matchsticks	First Difference
1	3	
2	5	2
3	7	2

As the first difference is constant (= 2), the pattern is linear.

We now find the general term.

Pattern number			Matchsticks required
T_1	$2 \times 1 = 2$	$2 + 1 = 3$	3
T_2	$2 \times 2 = 4$	$4 + 1 = 5$	5
T_n	$2 \times n = 2n$	$2n + 1$	$2n + 1$

$\therefore T_n = 2n + 1$

We must explain what letters we will use for our formula.

Let m = number of matchsticks needed and let n = pattern number.

$\therefore m = 2n + 1$

(ii) Let $n = 200$

As $m = 2n + 1$,

$\therefore m = 2(200) + 1$

$m = 400 + 1$

$m = 401$

$\therefore$ 401 matchsticks are required for Pattern 200.

(iii) Let $m = 147$

As $m = 2n + 1$,

$\therefore 147 = 2n + 1$

$146 = 2n$

$73 = n$

$\therefore$ The 73rd pattern requires 147 matchsticks.

Graphs of Linear Patterns

When graphing linear patterns we must be able to:

- Recognise what the value of the slope of the line represents.

  Remember, the slope of a line equals the rise over the run:

  $\text{Slope} = \dfrac{\text{Rise}}{\text{Run}}$

  The slope tells us by how much the y-value changes when the x-value increases by one unit. It is equal to the rate of change.

  For a linear pattern, the slope is equivalent to the first difference.

- Find the equation of a line.

  The equation of a line can be used to write a formula that represents the linear pattern.

- Identify directly proportional graphs.

  Directly proportional quantities can be represented as a line through the origin (0,0). Such lines are of the form $y = mx$, where m is the slope of the line. In the case of directly proportional graphs, m = the constant of proportionality.

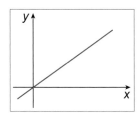

Direct proportion graphs always pass through the point (0,0).

Two quantities are directly proportional if, as one increases, the other increases by the same factor or percentage.

For example, we are told that the price of item A is directly proportional to the price of item B. If the price of item A doubles, then the price of item B will also double.

■ Tell what the point of intersection represents for the particular graph.

Worked Example 4.5

A table representing how two plants grew over a seven-day period is shown.
Plant A grew at a rate of 1.4 cm per day. Plant B grew at a rate of 2 cm per day.

	Plant A	Plant B
Start Height (cm)	3	0
Day 1	4.4	
Day 2	5.8	
Day 3		
Day 4		
Day 5		
Day 6		
Day 7		

(a) Complete the table and graph the height of each plant over the seven-day period on a single diagram. Let the x-axis represent the time in days and the y-axis represent the height of each plant.

(b) Use your graphs to identify:

  (i) Which plant grows at a directly proportional rate

  (ii) The day at which the two plants are at the same height

(c) Write down a formula to represent the height of each plant. State the meaning of any letters used in your formulae.

(d) Write down a formula to represent the difference between the two plant heights for any given day.
Hence, or otherwise, find the difference in height between the two plants on Day 18.
You may assume that the plants keep growing at the same rate.

Solution

(a)

	Plant A	Plant B
Start height	3	0
Day 1	4.4	2
Day 2	5.8	4
Day 3	7.2	6
Day 4	8.6	8
Day 5	10	10
Day 6	11.4	12
Day 7	12.8	14

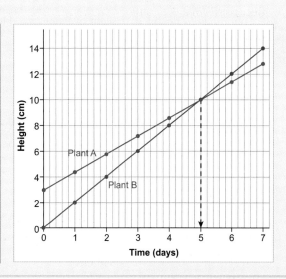

(b) (i) Plant B: As the line for this plant's growth goes through the origin.

(ii) At Day 5, both plants are at the same height.

(c) There are two methods that we can use to determine the formulae.

Method 1

Equation of a line: $y = mx + c$

where m = slope and c = y-intercept

Plant A	Plant B
We must explain what each letter in our formula represents: y = height of the plant x = day number	
Slope (m) = 1.4 (plant grows 1.4 cm per day) y-intercept (c) = 3 (at Day 0) Equation of a line: $y = 1.4x + 3$	Slope (m) = 2 (plant grows 2 cm per day) y-intercept (c) = 0 (at Day 0) Equation of a line: $y = 2x$

Method 2
General term

Plant A	Plant B
We must explain what each letter of our formula represents: h = height of the plant d = day number	
First difference = 1.4 (plant grows 1.4 cm per day) $h_0 = 1.4\,(0) + 3 = 3$ $h_1 = 1.4\,(1) + 3 = 4.4$ $\therefore h = 1.4d + 3$	First difference = 2 (plant grows 2 cm per day) $h_0 = 2(0) + 0 = 0$ $h_1 = 2(1) + 0 = 2$ $\therefore h = 2d$

(d) Difference in height = (Height of Plant A) – (Height of Plant B)

OR

(Height of Plant B) – (Height of Plant A)

From part (a), we can tell that Plant B is taller than Plant A on Day 18. So we will use:

Difference in height = (Height of Plant B) – (Height of Plant A)

$$= 2d - (1.4d + 3)$$

$$= 2d - 1.4d - 3$$

$$= 0.6d - 3$$

On Day 18, difference = $0.6(18) - 3$

$$= 10.8 - 3$$

$$= 7.8 \text{ cm}$$

ACTIVITY 4.1

NUMBER PATTERNS

4

1. A five-tile repeating pattern, made up of shaped tiles, is shown.

   (i) What shape is the 12th tile?

   (ii) What shape is the 35th tile?

   (iii) What shape is the 105th tile?

   (iv) What shape is the 206th tile?

2. A six-marble repeating pattern made up of coloured marbles is shown.

   (i) What colour is the 22nd marble?

   (ii) What colour is the 61st marble?

   (iii) How many times does a red marble appear in the first 27 marbles of this pattern?

3. A repeating pattern is made up of matchsticks.

   (i) How many matchsticks will Pattern 4 need?

   (ii) How many matchsticks will Pattern 5 need?

   (iii) Draw Patterns 4 and 5.

   (iv) How many matchsticks are needed to make the first seven patterns?

4. For each of the linear sequences shown below:

  (a) Write down the start term.

  (b) Find the common difference.

  (c) Write down the next three terms.

  (d) Describe each sequence in your own words.

    (i) 2, 6, 10, 14...

    (ii) 7, 19, 31, 43...

    (iii) 9, 24, 39, 54...

    (iv) 3, −5, −13, −21...

    (v) 1, −10, −21, −32...

5. For each of the following linear sequences, find:

  (a) The start term

  (b) The first difference

  (c) The nth term (general term)

  (d) The value of the stated term

    (i) 6, 9, 12, 15...   Find 9th term.

    (ii) 9, 14, 19, 24...   Find 13th term.

    (iii) 0, −3, −6, −9...   Find 19th term.

    (iv) −10, −7, −4, −1... Find 52nd term.

    (v) 1000, 748, 496, 244... Find 100th term.

6. For each of the following linear sequences, find:

  (a) T_1 (b) T_3 (c) T_{45}

    (i) $T_n = 3n$ (iv) $T_n = 4 - n$

    (ii) $T_n = 2n + 5$ (v) $T_n = 9n - 1$

    (iii) $T_n = n - 3$ (vi) $T_n = 3 - 2n$

7. The graphs of three patterns are shown. Each graph represents the amount of money saved by a student and put into their savings account over a six-week period.

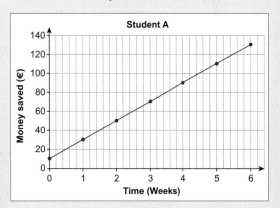

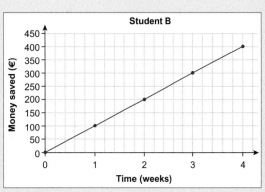

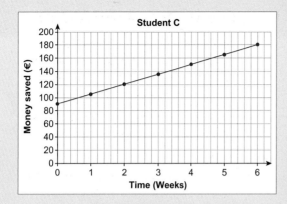

Student C

For each graph:

(i) Estimate how much each student had in their savings account at the start and end of the six weeks.

(ii) Write down a formula that represents the amount of money saved at any given time. State the meaning of all letters used in your formula.

(iii) Assuming that each student continued saving as before, calculate the total amount of money in their savings account after 12 weeks.

(iv) Identify the directly proportional graph. Give a reason for your answer.

(v) Calculate the constant of proportionality. Explain in the context of the question what the constant of proportionality represents.

8. A repeating pattern is made up of matchsticks.

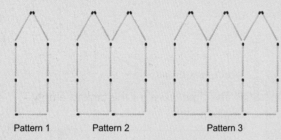

Pattern 1   Pattern 2   Pattern 3

(i) How many matchsticks will Pattern 6 need?

(ii) Write down a formula which shows the number of matchsticks for any pattern. Clearly explain all letters used in your formula.

(iii) Describe the formula you have derived using your own words.

(iv) How many matchsticks will Pattern 25 need?

(v) Which pattern will require 182 matchsticks?

9. A repeating pattern made up of marbles is shown.

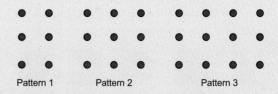

Pattern 1   Pattern 2   Pattern 3

(i) How many marbles will the fifth pattern need?

(ii) How many marbles will the nth pattern need?

(iii) Describe in words the number of marbles needed for any pattern in the sequence.

(iv) What pattern number will require 93 marbles?

10. The first three patterns of a linear sequence is shown. An art student is decorating a mural using coins laid in the same pattern.

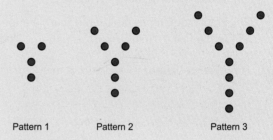

Pattern 1   Pattern 2   Pattern 3

(i) How many coins will the seventh pattern need?

(ii) How many coins will the nth pattern need?

(iii) The student will stop once the pattern requires more than 50 coins. How many complete patterns will she have made by then?

11. Jenny has the option of two phone companies from which to buy a phone. The graphs below show the call costs for each company.

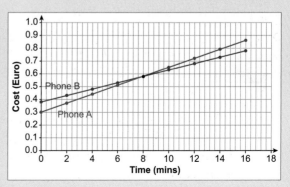

NUMBER PATTERNS

(i) Copy and complete the following table.

Time (mins)	Cost (€) Company A	Cost (€) Company B
0	0.3	0.38
2	0.37	0.43
4	0.44	0.48
6		
8		
10		
12		
14		
16		

(ii) How much does Company A charge per minute?

(iii) How much does Company B charge per minute?

(iv) Each company charges a connection fee per call. Which company has the higher connection fee, and by how much?

(v) Describe in words the cost of making a call for each company.

(vi) Write a formula for the cost of a call per minute for each company. Let c = cost (Euro) and m = number of minutes in your formula.

(vii) How long is a call for which both companies charge the same price?

(viii) Check your answer to (vii) above using algebra.

(ix) How much would each company charge for a 23-minute call?

12. A teacher is organising a coach tour for his students. He gets quotes from two tour companies for a coach. The graphs show the cost of a trip for each company.

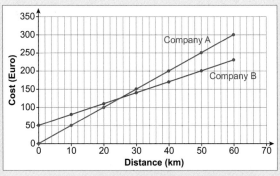

(i) Calculate the charge per kilometre for each company.

(ii) Which company has a standing charge?

(iii) Explain in words the cost of each trip.

(iv) Write a formula for the cost of the journey per kilometre for each company. In your formula let c = cost (euro) and d = kilometres travelled.

(v) Estimate from the graphs the distance at which both companies charge the same price.

(vi) Check your answer to part (v) by using your formulae from part (iv).

(vii) The teacher has budgeted €500 for the tour. Which company will he use if he wishes to travel the farthest? Estimate the total distance covered on such a tour.

(viii) Which coach company has a pricing policy that is proportional in relation to distance travelled?

13. A water storage tank, full to a capacity of 50 litres, starts to leak at a rate of 2.5 litres per hour.

(i) Use a table to show how much the tank leaks over a period of eight hours.

(ii) Draw a graph that illustrates this information.

(iii) Write a formula for the volume of water left in the tank (V) after t hours.

(iv) Explain in your own words the formula you have written.

Use your formula to find:

(v) The volume of water left in the tank after six hours

(vi) The time taken for the tank to empty completely

14. A car manufacturer's factory builds 20 cars for every 8 tonnes of metal used. The relationship between the production of cars and the amount of metal used is directly proportional.

(i) Draw a graph that represents the number of cars built for up to 8 tonnes of metal. Let the x-axis represent the weight of metal in tonnes and let the y-axis represent the number of cars built.

(ii) Calculate the constant of proportionality.

(iii) Explain what the constant of proportionality means in this context.

(iv) Write a formula for the number of cars (c) produced per tonne of metal (m) used.

(v) Write a formula for weight of metal (m) needed per car built.

(vi) Find the number of cars that can be built for 525 tonnes of metal.

(vii) Find the weight of metal needed to build 125 cars.

15. Andreas wishes to hire an electrician to fix an electrical fault in his apartment. He has the choice of two electricians.

Electrician A: call-out charge of €50 plus an hourly rate of €40

Electrician B: hourly rate of €60 with no call-out charge

(i) Draw a graph to show how much each electrician charges for working up to five hours.

(ii) Which graph represents a directly proportional relationship between the two values? Explain your answer.

(iii) Write a formula for the cost of hiring each electrician. Let c = cost (euro) and t = time (in hours) worked.

16. Both Carla and Alvaro are saving for a holiday. Carla saves €25 per week and already has €150 in her account. Alvaro saves €40 per week, on top of the €60 that was originally in his account.

(i) Show how much each will have saved in four weeks, using a table and two graphs. Let the x-axis represent time in weeks and let the y-axis represent euros saved.

(ii) Write a formula for the amount saved by each person. State the meaning of all the letters used.

(iii) After how many weeks will they both have the same amount in their accounts?

(iv) After 11 weeks Alvaro stopped saving. Counting from the time he stopped saving, how long will it take Carla to have the same amount as Alvaro in her account?

(v) If Alvaro had continued saving, they would have combined their two amounts to pay for their holiday. Write a formula to show how much they would have saved together.

17. Two students, Siobhán and Máire, travel from their homes to their school. The table of their travelling times and distances to the school is shown below.

Time (minutes)	Máire Distance to school (m)	Siobhán Distance to school (m)
0	300	500
1	250	400
2	200	300
3		
4		
5		
6		

(i) Copy and complete the above table. Assume that the speed of each student does not change during their journey.

(ii) Using the same axes and scales, draw two graphs to represent the information shown in the table. Let the x-axis represent time and let the y-axis represent distance from the school.

(iii) Who arrives at the school first?

(iv) Calculate the speed of each student.

(v) Who lives the farthest from the school? Give a reason for your answer.

(vi) At what time are the students the same distance from the school?

(vii) Write a formula for each student's distance from the school at any given time. State the meaning of all the letters used in your formula.

(viii) At what two times were the students 25 m apart?

18. The letters of the alphabet are written as the pattern: A BB CCC DDDD EEEEE... so that the number of times each letter is written matches its place in the alphabet. When the pattern gets to the 26th Z, it repeats. What will be the 1,000th letter in the pattern?

19. Two sequences are: 79, 74, 69, 64, 59... and 7, 11, 15, 19, 23.... The mth term of both sequences is the same number.

(a) Find, algebraically, which term this is.

(b) What is the value of this mth term?

20. The cost (C) of building a certain type of shed is directly proportional to the area it covers (A). For every 1 m² increase in area, the cost of the shed increases by €75.

(i) Copy and complete the following table:

Area (m²)	Cost (€)
1	
2	
3	
4	
5	
6	
7	

(ii) Draw a graph that represents the cost of building a shed up to an area of 7 m².

(iii) Calculate the constant of proportionality.

(iv) Write a formula that relates the cost (C) of building a shed to the area (A) that it covers.

(v) Find the cost of building a shed that covers an area of 12 m².

(vi) Find the area covered by a shed that costs €4,500.

Another company builds the same type of shed. The cost of building the shed is still directly proportional to its area, but this company charges €1,170 for a shed with an area of 18 m².

(vii) Find the relationship between the area of the shed and its cost for this company.

(viii) Which company charges less to build a shed of 30 m², and by how much?

21. A repeating pattern, made from blue and red counters, is shown.

Pattern 1   Pattern 2   Pattern 3

(i) How many blue counters will be in Pattern 6?

(ii) How many red counters will be in Pattern 7?

(iii) How many counters in total will Pattern 9 need?

(iv) How many counters are there in T_n, the nth pattern?

(v) How many red counters are there in T_n, the nth pattern?

(vi) How many blue counters are there in T_n, the nth pattern?

(vii) Describe in your own words the formula you have derived for the number of:

(a) Red counters in the pattern

(b) Blue counters in the pattern

22. A pattern made from floor tiles is shown.

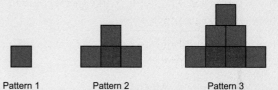

Pattern 1   Pattern 2   Pattern 3

(i) How many blue tiles will be in Pattern 11?

(ii) How many tiles will be in Pattern 20?

(iii) Write down a formula for each of the following. Explain all the letters used in your formulae.

(a) Number of red tiles for any pattern

(b) Number of blue tiles for any pattern

(c) Number of tiles for any pattern

(iv) A decorator has only 30 blue tiles and 15 red tiles. How many complete patterns will she be able to make?

23. Henry buys $2,000 for €1,600. The next week he receives €640 for $800. Assuming that the exchange rate has not changed and that no charges were incurred:

(i) Draw a graph to represent the above information. Let the x-axis represent euros and let the y-axis represent dollars.

(ii) Explain with the aid of your graph why the relationship between dollars and euro is directly proportional.

(iii) Write a formula to exchange euros into dollars. State the meaning of all the letters used in your formula.

(iv) From your formula, find the constant of proportionality.

(v) In this context, explain what the constant of proportionality signifies.

(vi) Use your graph to find out how many dollars Henry will receive in exchange for €800.

(vii) Verify your answer to part (vi) using your formula.

24. Isabelle needs to get her car fixed. She has the choice of two mechanics. Mechanic A charges a call-out fee plus an hourly rate.

Mechanic A

€150 for 3 hours' work

€200 for 5 hours' work

Mechanic B

€100 for 2 hours' work

€200 for 4 hours' work

(i) Using the same axes and scales, draw two graphs to represent the above information. Let the x-axis represent time, and let the y-axis represent cost.

(ii) Calculate the call-out fee for Mechanic A.

(iii) Write a formula for the cost of hiring each mechanic. Clearly explain the meaning of all letters used in your formulae.

(iv) Who is the cheapest mechanic to hire if it takes six hours to fix the car?

25. A 10-year building programme for new council houses began in 1991 and finished in 2000. The number of houses built each year followed a linear sequence.

If 500 houses were built in 1995 and 150 houses were built in 2000, calculate:

(i) The increase or decrease in the number of houses built per year

(ii) The number of houses built in 1991

(iii) The number of houses built over the 10-year period

26. Bill and Jenny are two athletes running in the same direction at steady speeds on a race-track. Tina is standing beside the track. At a particular time, Bill has gone 7 m beyond Tina and his speed is 2 m/s. At the same instant Jenny has gone 2 m beyond Tina and her speed is 3 m/s.

(a) Complete the table below to show the distance between the two runners and Tina over the next 10 seconds.

Time	Bill's distance (m)	Jenny's distance (m)
0	7	2
1	9	
2		
3		
4		
5		
6		
7		
8		
9		
10		

(b) On the grid below, draw graphs for the distance between Bill and Tina and the distance between Jenny and Tina over the 10 seconds.

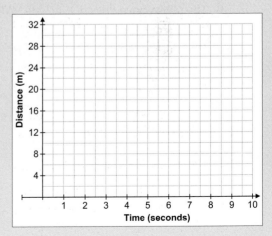

(c) After how many seconds will both runners be the same distance from Tina?

(d) After 9 seconds, which runner is furthest from Tina and what is the distance between the runners?

(e) Write down a formula to represent the distance between Bill and Tina for any given time. State clearly the meaning of any letters used in your formula.

(f) Write down a formula to represent the distance between Jenny and Tina for any given time.

(g) Use your formulas from (e) and (f) to verify the answer that you gave to part (c) above.

(h) After 1 minute, Jenny stops suddenly. From the time she stops, how long will it be until Bill is again level with her?

(i) If Jenny had not stopped, how long in total would it be until the runners are 100 m apart?

SEC Sample Paper, JCHL

27. Lisa is on a particular payment plan called 'Plan A' for her electricity. She pays a standing charge each month even if no electricity is used. She also pays a rate per unit used. The table shows the cost, including the standing charge, of using different amounts of units, in a month.

Units used	Plan A cost in euro
100	38
200	56
300	74
400	92
500	110
600	128
700	146
800	164

(a) Use the data in the table to show that the relationship between the number of units used and the cost is linear.

(b) Draw a graph to show the relationship between the number of units used and the cost of electricity. Let the x-axis represent units used and the y-axis represent cost in euro.

(c) Use your graph to estimate the standing charge.

(d) Write down a different method of finding the standing charge. Find the standing charge using your method.

(e) Write down a formula to represent the relationship between the number of units used and the cost for any given number of units.

(f) The table above does not include VAT. One month Lisa used 650 units. Her total bill for that month, including VAT, was €155.50. Find the VAT rate on electricity, correct to one decimal place.

(g) Lisa is offered a new plan, 'Plan B', where the standing charge is €36 and the rate per unit used is 15.5 cent. Complete the following table for Plan B.

Units Used	100	200	300	400	500	600	700	800
Plan B Cost in euro								

(h) Which plan do you think Lisa should choose? Give a reason for your answer.

(i) On your diagram for part (b), draw a graph to show the relationship between the number of units used and the cost of electricity for Plan B. Label this graph 'Plan B'.

(j) Use your diagram to find the number of units for which both plans have the same cost.

SEC 2012, JCHL

4.2 NON-LINEAR PATTERNS

In a linear sequence or pattern, the first difference between consecutive terms is always constant.

In a non-linear sequence or pattern, the first difference between consecutive terms is not constant.

Quadratic Patterns

If we consider the number sequence: 7, 8, 12, 19, ...
we notice that the second difference is the same value each time.
In this case, the pattern is referred to as a quadratic pattern.

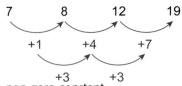

In a quadratic sequence or pattern, the second difference or change is a non-zero constant.

The graph of a quadratic pattern will be a ∪-shaped or ∩-shaped curve called a parabola.

> Every quadratic pattern **eventually** increases or decreases to a certain maximum or minimum value before its starts to decrease or increase again.

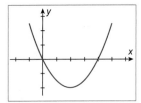
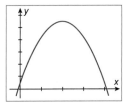

Worked Example 4.6

For each quadratic sequence given below, find:

(a) The start term   (b) The second difference   (c) The next three terms

(i) 2, 5, 12, 23...

(ii) −1, 2, 0, −7...

Solution

(i) 2, 5, 12, 23...

(a) The start term is 2.

(b)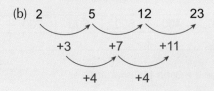

Second difference = +4

(c)

T_1	2
T_2	2 + 3 = 5
T_3	5 + 7 = 12
T_4	12 + 11 = 23
T_5	23 + 15 = 38
T_6	38 + 19 = 57
T_7	57 + 23 = 80

∴ The next three terms are: 38, 57, 80

(ii) −1, 2, 0, −7...

(a) The start term is −1.

(b)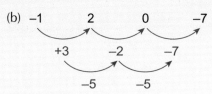

Second difference = −5

(c)

T_1	−1
T_2	−1 + 3 = 2
T_3	2 − 2 = 0
T_4	0 − 7 = −7
T_5	−7 − 12 = −19
T_6	−19 − 17 = −36
T_7	−36 − 22 = −58

∴ The next three terms are: −19, −36, −58

General Term of a Quadratic Sequence

The general term of any quadratic sequence will be of the form $T_n = an^2 + bn + c$, where $a, b, c \in R$, $a \neq 0$.

The quadratic sequence 4, 13, 28, 49 can be generated using the general term $T_n = 3n^2 + 1$.

Term	$T_n = 3n^2 + 1$	Value	First difference	Second difference
1	$3(1)^2 + 1$	4		
2	$3(2)^2 + 1$	13	9	
3	$3(3)^2 + 1$	28	15	6
4	$3(4)^2 + 1$	49	21	6

The second difference is 6.

$T_n = 3n^2 + 1$ for this sequence which, when compared with $T_n = an^2 + bn + c$, tells us that $a = 3$ and $6 = 2(3)$ or second difference = 2 (coefficient of n^2 term).

Now do Activity 4.2 to investigate if this is always true.

It has been shown from our activity that for any quadratic sequence $T_n = an^2 + bn + c$, where $a, b, c \in R$, $a \neq 0$, the second difference is twice the value of a.

So, if the second difference is 10, then for the general term, $T_n = an^2 + bn + c$, $a = 5$.

If the second difference is 15, then $a = 7.5$.

We can use this fact to help us find the nth term of a quadratic sequence.

 **ACTIVITY 4.2**

> For quadratic patterns:
>
> $T_n = an^2 + bn + c$ where $a, b, c \in R$, $a \neq 0$ and the second difference = $2a$.

 Worked Example 4.7

Find T_n, the nth term, for the following quadratic sequence: 13, 17, 29, 49...

Solution

Step 1 Find the second difference.

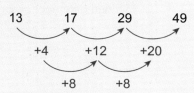

Second difference = +8

Step 2 Find the value of a.

Second difference = 2a

8 = 2a

∴ 4 = a

Step 3   Use $T_n = an^2 + bn + c$ to form two equations, remembering that n = term number and that $a = 4$.

$T_1 = 13$

$T_1 \Rightarrow 4(1)^2 + b(1) + c = 13$

$\qquad 4 + b + c = 13$

$\qquad \therefore b + c = 9$

$T_2 = 17$

$T_2 \Rightarrow 4(2)^2 + b(2) + c = 17$

$\qquad 16 + 2b + c = 17$

$\qquad \therefore 2b + c = 1$

Step 4   Solve the simultaneous equations:

$$b + c = 9$$
$$\underline{-(2b + c = 1)}$$
$$-b = 8$$
$$\Rightarrow b = -8$$

$$b + c = 9$$
$$\Rightarrow -8 + c = 9$$
$$\Rightarrow c = 17$$
$$\therefore T_n = 4n^2 - 8n + 17$$

Worked Example 4.8

The number of computers sold per day for a major retailer over a five-day period is recorded in the table below. Day 1 is Monday, Day 2 is Tuesday, etc.

Time	Numbers sold per day
Day 1	10
Day 2	16
Day 3	18
Day 4	16
Day 5	10

(i)   Draw a graph to illustrate the information in this table.

Let the x-axis represent days and let the y-axis represent the number of computers sold.

(ii)   Verify that the pattern is quadratic and find a formula that describes the number of computers sold (s) for any given day (d).

(iii)   From your graph what is the busiest day for computer sales?

(iv)   The manager expects the sales of computers to continue to follow the same pattern over the weekend. Use your graph to explain if she should consider opening the store on a Saturday.

(v)   Check your answer to part (iv) using the formula derived in part (ii).

Solution

(i)   The pattern appears to be quadratic.

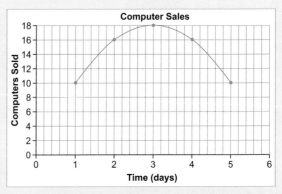

(ii)   **Step 1**   Find the second difference.

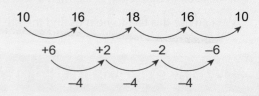

Second difference = -4

$\therefore$ Pattern is quadratic.

Step 2   Find the value of a.

$$\text{Second difference} = 2a$$
$$-4 = 2a$$
$$\therefore -2 = a$$

Step 3 Use $T_n = an^2 + bn + c$ to form equations, remembering that n = term number and that $a = -2$.

$T_1 = 10$

$T_1 \Rightarrow -2(1)^2 + b(1) + c = 10$

$\qquad -2 + b + c = 10$

$\qquad \therefore b + c = 12$

$T_2 = 16$

$T_2 \Rightarrow -2(2)^2 + b(2) + c = 16$

$\qquad -8 + 2b + c = 16$

$\qquad \therefore 2b + c = 24$

Step 4 Solve the simultaneous equations:

$\qquad b + c = 12$

$\qquad \underline{-(2b + c = 24)}$

$\qquad\qquad -b = -12$

$\qquad\qquad \Rightarrow b = 12$

$\qquad b + c = 12$

$\qquad \Rightarrow 12 + c = 12$

$\Rightarrow c = 0$

$\therefore T_n = -2n^2 + 12n$

We now use the letters that the question specified.

$\qquad \therefore s = -2d^2 + 12d$

(iii) Wednesday, as this has the highest point on the graph.

(iv) As this is a negative quadratic graph that has reached it highest point (maximum), the sales of computers will continue to decrease.

We can conclude that it may not be worth her while opening on Saturday.

(v) Check: Saturday $\Rightarrow d = 6$

$\qquad \therefore s = -2(6)^2 + 12(6)$

$\qquad\qquad = -72 + 72$

$\qquad\qquad = 0$

This confirms that the manager should not open on Saturday. If she opened the shop on Saturday, she would sell no computers.

Exponential Patterns

Consider the number sequence: 10, 20, 40, 80...

We notice that the first and second differences are not constant.

However, each term is double the previous term.

This type of pattern is called an exponential pattern.

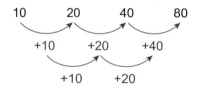

> Patterns that involve doubling, tripling, etc. are referred to as **exponential patterns**.

> Note: **Exponential patterns** on our course are limited to patterns which involve doubling or tripling.

Worked Example 4.9

Show that the sequence 7, 21, 63, 189... is exponential and find the next three terms.

Solution

$7 \times 3 = 21$, $21 \times 3 = 63$, $63 \times 3 = 189$

This sequence is exponential, as terms are tripled each time.

T_1	7
T_2	$7 \times 3 = 21$
T_3	$21 \times 3 = 63$
T_4	$63 \times 3 = 189$
T_5	$189 \times 3 = 567$
T_6	$567 \times 3 = 1701$
T_7	$1701 \times 3 = 5103$

$\therefore$ The next three terms are: 567, 1701, 5103

Exercise 4.2

1. For each quadratic sequence, find:

   (a) The start term

   (b) The first and second differences

   (c) The next three terms

       (i) 14, 15, 21, 32...

       (ii) 16, 26, 42, 64...

       (iii) 0, 4, 11, 21...

       (iv) 5, 7, 6, 2...

       (v) −8, −12, −10, −2...

2. For each exponential sequence:

   (a) Determine whether it doubles or triples.

   (b) Find the next three terms.

       (i) 3, 6, 12, 24...

       (ii) 13, 39, 117, 351...

       (iii) $\frac{1}{8}, \frac{1}{4}, \frac{1}{2}, 1...$

       (iv) $\frac{1}{81}, \frac{1}{27}, \frac{1}{9}, \frac{1}{3}...$

       (v) −2.5, −7.5, −22.5, −67.5...

3. Determine whether the following sequences are linear, quadratic or exponential. In each case, give a reason for your answer.

       (i) 4, 11, 22, 37...   (iv) 2, 4, 8, 16...

       (ii) 23, 26, 29, 32...   (v) −11, −8, −5, −2...

       (iii) 1, 3, 8, 16...

4. An exponential pattern made of blocks is shown.

   Diagram 1   Diagram 2   Diagram 3

       (i) How many blocks will be needed for Diagram 4?

       (ii) How many blocks will be needed for Diagram 5?

       (iii) How many blocks will be needed for Diagram 10?

   If the pattern was quadratic instead of exponential:

       (iv) How many blocks would be needed for Diagram 4?

       (v) How many blocks would be needed for Diagram 5?

5. The nth term (general term) of some sequences are given below. In each case, find:
   (a) T_1, (b) T_2 and (c) T_3

       (i) $T_n = n^2 + 1$

       (ii) $T_n = 2n^2 + n - 2$

       (iii) $T_n = -n^2 - 3n$

       (iv) $T_n = -n^2 - 4n + 1$

       (v) $T_n = 3^n$

   Now describe the general term of each sequence using words.

6. Find T_n, the nth term for each of the following quadratic sequences:

       (i) 18, 21, 28, 39...

       (ii) 2, 7, 17, 32...

       (iii) 0, 2, 11, 27...

       (iv) 1, −3, −4, −2...

       (v) −10, −9, −14, −25...

7. The first three terms of a quadratic pattern of building blocks are shown.

   Pattern 1   Pattern 2   Pattern 3

       (i) Copy and complete the following table:

Pattern	Number of blocks
1	
2	
3	

       (ii) Draw the next pattern of the sequence.

       (iii) How many blocks are there in T_n, the nth term?

       (iv) How many blocks are there in T_{10}, the tenth term?

       (v) Explain in words the number of blocks needed for the nth pattern.

8. The first three patterns of a quadratic sequence are shown below and the sequence continues in the same way.

  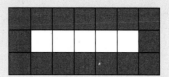

Pattern 1   Pattern 2   Pattern 3

(i) Copy and complete the table below, showing the number of tiles needed for each of the first five patterns.

Pattern	1	2	3	4	5
Number of tiles	9	12			

(ii) Find, in terms of n, a formula that gives the number of tiles needed to make the nth pattern.

(iii) How many tiles are in the 12th pattern?

(iv) If there are 201 tiles, what is the biggest pattern in the sequence that can be made?

9. The first three patterns of a sequence are shown.

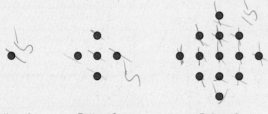

Pattern 1   Pattern 2   Pattern 3

(i) Draw the next pattern in the sequence.

(ii) Describe the sequence of numbers generated by the pattern.

(iii) How many red discs are there in T_7, the seventh pattern?

(iv) Find the formula for T_n, the nth pattern.

(v) Using your formula, or otherwise, find the number of discs in the 20th pattern.

10. A toy rocket is fired into the air. The height (h) of the rocket (in metres) is recorded for a period of 4 seconds. A table is produced to show these heights.

Seconds (t)	Height (h)
1	20
2	30
3	30
4	20

(i) Find, in terms of t, a formula that gives the height of the rocket at any time.

Let height = h and let time = t.

(ii) Draw a graph to represent the information contained in this table.

(iii) Find, using both your graph and the general term, the height of the rocket after 3.5 seconds.

(iv) Find the two times at which the rocket was at ground level.

11. A pipe bursts and starts to flood an area of ground. The area covered by the flood is shown in the table below.

Days	Area covered (m²)
1	1.5
2	4.5
3	13.5
4	40.5

(i) Draw a graph to represent the information contained in this table.

(ii) What type of pattern does the data in the table follow? Explain your answer.

(iii) If the water from the pipe continues to cover the area in the same pattern, how much area will be covered in 11 days?

12. The table below shows the number of seagulls in a colony over a period of four weeks.

Time	Number (thousands)
Week 1	6
Week 2	10
Week 3	12
Week 4	12

(i) What type of pattern do you see in the above table?

(ii) Draw a graph to represent the data. Let the x-axis represent time and let the y-axis represent the number of seagulls.

(iii) From your graph, estimate the maximum number of seagulls in the colony.

(iv) Find the general term of this sequence.

(v) Assuming that the seagull numbers continue to follow the same pattern as before, at what times will there be no seagulls left in the colony?

13. The speed of a car is recorded over a 4-second period. The resulting data is displayed below.

Time (seconds)	Speed (m/s)
1	11
2	17
3	19
4	17

(i) Draw a graph that displays this data.

Let the x-axis represent time and let the y-axis represent speed.

(ii) What type of pattern does the speed of the car follow? Explain your answer with reference to the graph and/or the table.

(iii) Find a formula that describes the speed of the car (v) for any given time (t).

(iv) From your graph, estimate the speed of the car at 2.5 seconds. Verify your answer using your formula.

(v) Using your formula, calculate the times when the speed of the car is 1 m/s.

14. The total number of a particular amoeba (N) over a period of hours (t) can be modelled by the formula, $N = 2^t$.

(i) Copy and complete the table below to show the number of amoebas over a period of 6 hours.

Time	Number
Hour 0	
Hour 1	
Hour 2	
Hour 3	
Hour 4	
Hour 5	
Hour 6	

(ii) Draw a graph to represent the data contained in this table.

(iii) From your graph, estimate how many amoebas will be present after 4.5 hours.

(iv) Verify your answer to part (iii) using your formula .

(v) After how many hours will the there be a total of 65,536 amoebas?

15. An artist is designing a mosaic for a new building. He places a red tile in the shape of a square and surrounds this tile with similar green square tiles. The first three patterns are shown.

Pattern 1

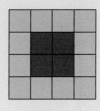
Pattern 2

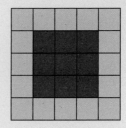
Pattern 3

(i) Copy and complete the following table:

Pattern	Number of green tiles	Number of red tiles	Total number of tiles
1			
2			
3			

(ii) How many green tiles will Pattern 6 need?

(iii) How many red tiles will Pattern 7 need?

(iv) How many tiles in total will Pattern 8 need?

(v) How many green tiles are there in T_n, the nth pattern?

(vi) How many red tiles are there in T_n, the nth pattern?

(vii) How many tiles are there in T_n, the nth pattern?

16. A repeating pattern made from blue and red counters is shown.

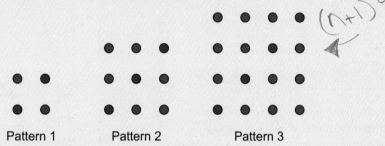

$(n+1)^2$

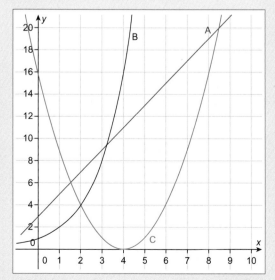

Pattern 1   Pattern 2   Pattern 3

(i) How many blue tiles are there in T_n, the nth pattern?

(ii) How many blue tiles are needed for the 10th pattern?

(iii) How many red tiles are there in T_n, the nth pattern?

(iv) How many red tiles are needed for the 17th pattern?

(v) Write an expression for the total number of tiles for each pattern.

(vi) If there are 650 tiles in total, how many complete patterns could be made?

17. Identify which graph represents a linear, exponential and quadratic pattern. For each, explain how you got your answer.

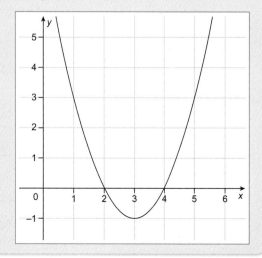

18. Barry releases a paper aeroplane from a nearby building. The graph below shows part of the flight of the paper aeroplane. The x-axis represents the flight time (in seconds) and the y-axis represents the height above sea level (in metres).

(i) Does this graph represent a quadratic pattern? Give a reason for your answer.

(ii) The paper aeroplane flies into a valley and then out again. Locate at what time this happens on the graph.

(iii) Find a formula that describes the height of the paper aeroplane (*h*) for any given time (*t*).

(iv) Using your formula, calculate the height of the paper aeroplane at the moment it was released.

Barry uses this formula to calculate the height of the paper aeroplane after 20 seconds.

(v) What height does Barry calculate the aeroplane will reach after 20 seconds?

(vi) What assumption has Barry made?

(vii) Is Barry correct in making this assumption? Give your opinion.

19. (a) Which of the following graphs represent a quadratic pattern? In each case, give a reason for your answer. Ensure you check that the whole of the graph represents a quadratic pattern.

(i)

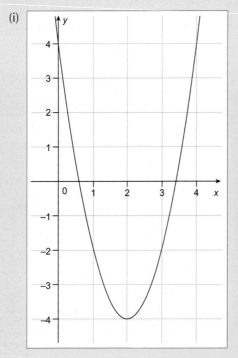

(ii)

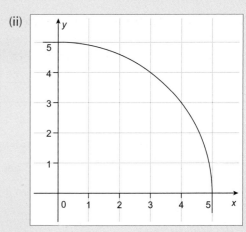

(iii)

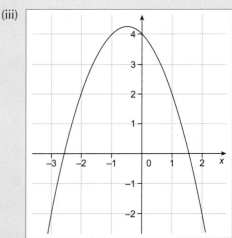

(b) If the graph shown below is quadratic, find T_n, the *n*th term of the quadratic sequence. Assume that T_1 is at $x = 1$, T_2 is at $x = 2$ and so on.

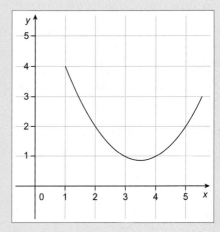

20. The picture below shows the top section of the Spanish Arch in Galway city. George wants to see if the arch can be described by a function. He puts a co-ordinate grid over the arch as shown.

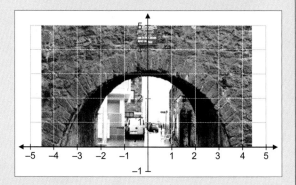

(a) Complete the table below to show the value of y for each of the given values of x.

x	y
−3	
−2	
−1	
0	
1	
2	
3	

(b) Is it possible to represent this section of the Spanish Arch by a quadratic function? Give a reason for your answer.

SEC Sample Paper, JCHL

21. A broker invests a sum of money into share options. The total value of the shares for the first three months is shown.

Month	Total amount (€)
1	800
2	860
3	912
4	956

Assume that the total value of the shares continues in the same pattern.

(i) How much will the shares be worth after five months?

(ii) Find a formula that describes the value of the shares (v) for any given month (m).

(iii) How much was originally invested?

(iv) After how many months will the shares be worth €1,056?

(v) The broker advises that the shares be sold after the ninth month. Give one reason why this recommendation was made.

22. A student drops a coin from the observation deck of a skyscraper. The distance the coin falls is shown in the table below.

Time (s)	Distance fallen (m)
1	5
2	20
3	45

Assume that the data continues in the same pattern.

(i) Does this table represent a quadratic pattern? Give a reason for your answer.

(ii) How far has the coin fallen after 4 seconds?

(iii) Derive a formula that describes how far the coin falls (f) for any given time (t).

(iv) If the observation deck on the skyscraper is 200 metres above ground, how long did it take the coin to hit the ground?

Another student produces a table that shows the height of the coin above the ground.

(v) Copy and complete the following table:

Time (s)	Height above ground (m)
0	200
0.5	
1	
1.5	

(vi) Derive a formula that describes the height of the coin (h) above the ground for any given time (t).

(vii) At what time is the coin 50 metres above the ground?

(viii) From what height (to the nearest metre) would the coin have been dropped if it hit the ground after 20 seconds?

(ix) If the coin fell at the same rate from a height of 10 km, how long (to the nearest second) would it take to hit the ground?

Algebra I: Expressions

Learning Outcomes

In this chapter you will learn to:

- Evaluate algebraic expressions; in particular, those of the form:
  - $ax^2 + bx + c$
  - $x^3 + bx^2 + cx + d$
    where $a, b, c, d, x \in Q$

- Add and subtract simple algebraic expressions; in particular, those of the form:
  - $(ax + by + c) \pm \ldots \pm (dx + ey + f)$
  - $(ax^2 + bx + c) \pm \ldots \pm (dx^2 + ex + f)$
    where $a, b, c, d, e, f \in Z$

- Use the associative, distributive and commutative properties to simplify expressions; in particular, those of the form:
  - $(x + y)(x + y)$
  - $(x - y)(x - y)$
  - $a(bx + cy + d) + \ldots + e(fx + gy + h)$
    where $a, b, c, d, e, f, g, h \in Z$

- Multiply expressions; in particular, those of the form:
  - $(ax + b)(cx^2 + dx + e)$
    where $a, b, c, d, e \in Z$

5.1 EVALUATING ALGEBRAIC EXPRESSIONS

$3x^2 + 5x - 6$ is an example of an algebraic expression.

■ x is a **variable**. This means that x can take on different values.

■ 6 is a **constant**. This means that it always has the same value.

The expression $3x^2 + 5x - 6$ has three **terms**:

1st term	2nd term	3rd term
$3x^2$	$5x$	6

The first term, $3x^2$, is added to the second term, $5x$, and then the third term, 6, is subtracted from their sum.

What value does the expression have if $x = 0$?

Answer: $3(0)^2 + 5(0) - 6$

$\quad = 3(0) + 5(0) - 6$

$\quad = 0 + 0 - 6$

$\quad = -6$

What value does the expression have if $x = -3$?

Answer: $3(-3)^2 + 5(-3) - 6$

$\quad = 3(9) + 5(-3) - 6$

$\quad = 27 - 15 - 6$

$\quad = 12 - 6$

$\quad = 6$

Remember BIMDAS:

Brackets

Index

Multiplication/**D**ivision

Addition/**S**ubtraction

To **evaluate** an expression means to find the value of the expression given specific values for any variable(s).

x^2 Worked Example 5.1

If $x = 4$, $y = -3$ and $z = 2$, find the value of the following expressions:

(i) $2x + 3y$

(ii) $4(x + y)$

(iii) $x^2 + zx - 2$

(iv) $\dfrac{x + 2y}{3x - zy}$

(v) xyz

Solution

(i) $2x + 3y$

$\quad = 2(4) + 3(-3)$

$\quad = 8 - 9$

$\quad = -1$

(ii) $4(x + y)$

$\quad = 4(4 - 3)$

$\quad = 4(1)$

$\quad = 4$

We rewrite the expression, replacing the variables with their specified values.

(iii) $x^2 + zx - 2$

$\quad = (4)^2 + (2)(4) - 2$

$\quad = 16 + (2)(4) - 2$

$\quad = 16 + 8 - 2$

$\quad = 24 - 2$

$\quad = 22$

(iv) $\dfrac{x + 2y}{3x - zy}$

Top: $4 + 2(-3)$

$= 4 - 6$

$= -2$

Bottom: $3(4) - (2)(-3)$

$= 12 + 6$

$= 18$

$\therefore \dfrac{\text{Top}}{\text{Bottom}} = \dfrac{-2}{18}$

$= -\dfrac{1}{9}$

(v) xyz

$= (4)(-3)(2)$

$= -24$

x^2 Worked Example 5.2

If $a = -1$, $b = \dfrac{1}{3}$, $c = -7$, $d = 2$ and $x = -\dfrac{1}{2}$, evaluate:

(i) $ax^2 + bx + c$

(ii) $x^3 + bx^2 + cx + d$

Solution

(i) $ax^2 + bx + c$

$= (-1)\left(-\dfrac{1}{2}\right)^2 + \left(\dfrac{1}{3}\right)\left(-\dfrac{1}{2}\right) + (-7)$ (Replace variables with specified values)

$= (-1)\left(\dfrac{1}{4}\right) + \left(\dfrac{1}{3}\right)\left(-\dfrac{1}{2}\right) + (-7)$ (Index)

$= -\dfrac{1}{4} - \dfrac{1}{6} - 7$ (Multiplication)

$= -\dfrac{6}{24} - \dfrac{4}{24} - \dfrac{168}{24}$ (Common denominator for subtraction of fractions)

$= -\dfrac{178}{24}$ (Single fraction)

$= -7\dfrac{5}{12}$

(ii) $x^3 + bx^2 + cx + d$

$= \left(-\dfrac{1}{2}\right)^3 + \left(\dfrac{1}{3}\right)\left(-\dfrac{1}{2}\right)^2 + (-7)\left(-\dfrac{1}{2}\right) + (2)$ (Replace variables with specified values)

$= -\dfrac{1}{8} + \left(\dfrac{1}{3}\right)\left(\dfrac{1}{4}\right) + (-7)\left(-\dfrac{1}{2}\right) + (2)$ (Index)

$= -\dfrac{1}{8} + \dfrac{1}{12} + \dfrac{7}{2} + 2$ (Multiplication)

$= -\dfrac{3}{24} + \dfrac{2}{24} + \dfrac{84}{24} + \dfrac{48}{24}$ (Common denominator for addition/subtraction of fractions)

$= \dfrac{131}{24}$ (Single fraction)

$= 5\dfrac{11}{24}$

Exercise 5.1

1. If $a = 1$ and $b = 2$, find the value of:

   (i) a^3 (iv) $4ab$

   (ii) $2b^2$ (v) a^2b

   (iii) $-6a^2$ (vi) $(ab)^2$

2. If $a = 3$, $b = -1$ and $c = 4$, evaluate:

   (i) $ab + bc$ (iv) $\dfrac{a + b}{b - c}$

   (ii) $b(a - c)$ (v) abc

   (iii) $a^2 + ba + c$ (vi) $\dfrac{ac - b}{ac + bc}$

3. If $a = 1$, $b = 4$, $c = -5$ and $x = 2$, find the value of:

   (i) $ax^2 - b$ (iv) $x^3 - bx^2 + cx + a$

   (ii) $ax^2 + bx + c$ (v) $x^3 + ax^2 + bx - c$

   (iii) $bx^2 + ax - c$ (vi) $x^3 - cx^2 + cx - b$

4. Insert $=$ or $>$ or $<$ between each of these pairs of expressions, where $x = 3$:

   (i) $x + x \ldots 2x$

   (ii) $2x^2 \ldots (2x)^2$

   (iii) $(x + 1)^2 \ldots x^2 + 1$

   (iv) $13x - 3x \ldots 10x$

   (v) $x \ldots x^3 - x^2$

   (vi) $(x + 2)^2 \ldots x^2 + 4x + 4$

5. If $x = 1$, $y = 3$ and $z = -4$, find the value of:

   (i) $\dfrac{1}{x} + \dfrac{1}{y}$ (iii) $\dfrac{x + y}{z - x}$

   (ii) $\dfrac{1}{x} - \dfrac{3}{y} + \dfrac{2}{z}$ (iv) $\dfrac{2x - 3z}{y^2}$

6. If $x = 2$, $p = 4$, $q = -3$ and $r = -2$, evaluate:

   (i) $x^2 + px + q$

   (ii) $x^3 + 2qx^2 + 4px - 2r$

   (iii) $(2x + p)(rq - p)$

   (iv) $3\sqrt{x(4x^2 - 3r^2)}$

7. If $y = 3$, $a = \dfrac{1}{2}$, $b = \dfrac{1}{5}$ and $c = -\dfrac{4}{3}$, evaluate:

   (i) $y^2 - 3ay - 4b$ (iii) $by^3 + cy^2 + ay + b$

   (ii) $y^3 + aby$ (iv) $ay^2 - cy + b$

8. A cone, as shown, has three dimensions, which can be used to find its curved surface area.

$r = $ radius, $h = $ perpendicular height and $l = $ slant height.

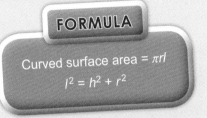

FORMULA

Curved surface area $= \pi r l$

$l^2 = h^2 + r^2$

Using the formulae given above, calculate the curved surface area of each cone described in the following table:

Cone	π	r	h
1	3.14	14 cm	48 cm
2	$\dfrac{22}{7}$	24 m	70 m
3	3.14	63 cm	16 cm
4	$\dfrac{22}{7}$	25 mm	60 mm

9. Heron's formula is used to calculate the area of a triangle with sides a, b and c. To use this formula one must first calculate the semi-perimeter, s.

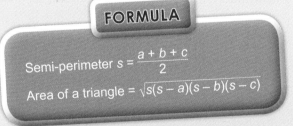

FORMULA

Semi-perimeter $s = \dfrac{a + b + c}{2}$

Area of a triangle $= \sqrt{s(s - a)(s - b)(s - c)}$

Find the area of each of the following triangles, to two decimal places:

Triangle	a	b	c
1	4	3	2
2	10	11.5	10.3
3	$\dfrac{1}{2}$	$\dfrac{1}{3}$	$\dfrac{2}{3}$

All side lengths are in centimetres.

5.2 SIMPLIFYING ALGEBRAIC EXPRESSIONS: ADDING, SUBTRACTING AND MULTIPLYING

In this section we will focus on simplification of expressions involving addition, subtraction or multiplication only. We will examine division in a later chapter.

Addition and Subtraction

When adding or subtracting simple algebraic expressions, remember that we can only add or subtract like terms.

x^2 Worked Example 5.3

Simplify: (i) $(2x + 3y - 7) - (x - 5y - 6)$

(ii) $(x + y + 1) + (3x - 7y + 2) - (-x + 3y - 5)$

(iii) $(3x^2 + 2x + 1) - (x^2 - x - 1)$

(iv) $(x^2 + 6) - (x^2 - x) + (2x^2 + x - 11)$

Solution

(i) $(2x + 3y - 7) - (x - 5y - 6)$
$= 2x + 3y - 7 - x + 5y + 6$
$= 2x - x + 3y + 5y - 7 + 6$
$= x + 8y - 1$

(ii) $(x + y + 1) + (3x - 7y + 2) - (-x + 3y - 5)$
$= x + y + 1 + 3x - 7y + 2 + x - 3y + 5$
$= x + 3x + x + y - 7y - 3y + 1 + 2 + 5$
$= 5x - 9y + 8$

(iii) $(3x^2 + 2x + 1) - (x^2 - x - 1)$
$= 3x^2 + 2x + 1 - x^2 + x + 1$
$= 3x^2 - x^2 + 2x + x + 1 + 1$
$= 2x^2 + 3x + 2$

(iv) $(x^2 + 6) - (x^2 - x) + (2x^2 + x - 11)$
$= x^2 + 6 - x^2 + x + 2x^2 + x - 11$
$= x^2 - x^2 + 2x^2 + x + x + 6 - 11$
$= 2x^2 + 2x - 5$

The Associative, Distributive and Commutative Properties

Remember the associative, distributive and commutative properties of the real number system:

$(a + b) + c = a + (b + c)$ **Associative property of addition**

$(ab)c = a(bc)$ **Associative property of multiplication**

$a(b + c) = ab + ac$ **Distributive property of multiplication over addition**

$a + b = b + a$ **Commutative property of addition**

$ab = ba$ **Commutative property of multiplication**

All of these properties can be used when simplifying algebraic expressions.

x^2 Worked Example 5.4

Simplify: (i) $2(3x - 2y - 4) + 3(7x + 5y - 11)$ (ii) $5(2x^2 - 3x - 6)$ (iii) $3x(4x^2 - 1)$

Solution

(i) $2(3x - 2y - 4) + 3(7x + 5y - 11)$

$= 2(3x) + 2(-2y) + 2(-4) + 3(7x) + 3(5y) + 3(-11)$ (Distributive property)

$= 6x - 4y - 8 + 21x + 15y - 33$ (Associative property of multiplication)

$= 27x + 11y - 41$ (Add/subtract like terms)

(ii) $5(2x^2 - 3x - 6)$

$= 5(2x^2) + 5(-3x) + 5(-6)$

$= 10x^2 - 15x - 30$

(iii) $3x(4x^2 - 1)$

$= 3x(4x^2) + 3x(-1)$

$= 12x^3 - 3x$

Multiplication

x^2 Worked Example 5.5

Simplify: (i) $(x + y)^2$ (ii) $(x - y)^2$

Solution

(i) $(x + y)^2$

$= (x + y)(x + y)$ (By definition)

$= (x + y)(x) + (x + y)(y)$ (Distributive property)

$= x(x + y) + y(x + y)$ (Commutative property of multiplication)

$= x^2 + xy + yx + y^2$ (Distributive property)

$= x^2 + xy + xy + y^2$ (Commutative property of multiplication)

$= x^2 + 2xy + y^2$ (Add like terms)

(ii) $(x - y)^2$

$= (x - y)(x - y)$

$= x(x - y) - y(x - y)$

$= x^2 - xy - xy + y^2$

$= x^2 - 2xy + y^2$

> Remember: $(x + y)^2 = x^2 + 2xy + y^2$
>
> $(x - y)^2 = x^2 - 2xy + y^2$

Having seen the use of applying the associative, distributive and commutative properties in the multiplication of algebraic expressions, we now consider further examples and methods.

ACTIVITY 5.1

x^2 **Worked Example 5.6**

   (i) Simplify $(2x - 3y)(5x - 2y)$.

   (ii) Simplify $(2x - 3y)(5x - 2y)$ using an area model where $2x - 3y$ and $5x - 2y$ are the dimensions of a rectangle and $x > 0$, $y < 0$.

   (iii) Simplify $(2x - 3y)(5x - 2y)$ using an area model where $2x - 3y$ and $5x - 2y$ are the dimensions of a rectangle and $y > 0$.

Solution

   (i) $(2x - 3y)(5x - 2y)$

      $= 2x(5x - 2y) - 3y(5x - 2y)$

      $= 10x^2 - 4xy - 15xy + 6y^2$

      $= 10x^2 - 19xy + 6y^2$

   (ii)

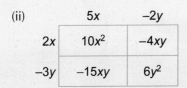

	$5x$	$-2y$
$2x$	$10x^2$	$-4xy$
$-3y$	$-15xy$	$6y^2$

Area of whole rectangle
$= (2x - 3y)(5x - 2y)$

Area of four smaller rectangles
$= 10x^2 - 19xy + 6y^2$

$\therefore (2x - 3y)(5x - 2y) = 10x^2 - 19xy + 6y^2$

   (iii)

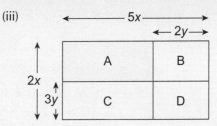

Area of whole rectangle $= (2x)(5x)$

$= 10x^2$

Area $(B + D) = (2x)(2y)$

$= 4xy$

Area $(C + D) = (5x)(3y)$

$= 15xy$

Area $D = (3y)(2y)$

$= 6y^2$

$\therefore$ Area $(B + C + D) = 4xy + 15xy - 6y^2$

$= 19xy - 6y^2$

$\therefore$ Area $A = (2x - 3y)(5x - 2y)$

$= 10x^2 - (19xy - 6y^2)$

$= 10x^2 - 19xy + 6y^2$

---

x^2 **Worked Example 5.7**

Simplify $(3p - 2)(2p^2 + 4p - 1)$.

Solution

Method 1

Use an approach similar to/based on the area model.

	$2p^2$	$4p$	-1
$3p$	$6p^3$	$12p^2$	$-3p$
-2	$-4p^2$	$-8p$	2

$\therefore (3p - 2)(2p^2 + 4p - 1)$

$= 6p^3 + 12p^2 - 4p^2 - 3p - 8p + 2$

$= 6p^3 + 8p^2 - 11p + 2$

Method 2

Use your knowledge of properties.

$(3p - 2)(2p^2 + 4p - 1)$

$= 3p(2p^2 + 4p - 1) - 2(2p^2 + 4p - 1)$

$= 6p^3 + 12p^2 - 3p - 4p^2 - 8p + 2$

$= 6p^3 + 8p^2 - 11p + 2$

Exercise 5.2

Expand and simplify the expressions in Questions 1–7.

1. (i) $(2x + 4y) + 2(x - 2y)$

   (ii) $(3a - b + c) - (2b + c)$

   (iii) $(4x^2 - 2x + 1) - (3x^2 - 4x + 2)$

   (iv) $(b^2 + 2c + 4) - (b^2 - 3c + 5)$

   (v) $(x^2 + x) - (2x^2 + 3x) + (x + 3x^2)$

2. (i) $3(2a + b + 4) + 2(3a - 2b + 5)$

   (ii) $12(p + q - 5) - 8(p - 2q + 1)$

   (iii) $-3(2x + y + 2) - (5x - 3y - 1)$

   (iv) $4(8x^2 - 3x + 2)$

   (v) $5x(2x^2 - 4)$

   (vi) $-11a(5a^2 + 1)$

3. (i) $2(a + b + 3) - 2(5a - 3b + 2)$
     $- (3a + 5b - 3)$

   (ii) $3x(2x + 2) + 2x(x + 3)$

   (iii) $p(1 - 2p) + 2p(p - 1)$

   (iv) $-5(x + 4y - 8) + 3(x + y + 1)$
      $- 2(4 - y - 2x)$

4. (i) $(x + 2)(x + 1)$

   (ii) $(2x - 1)(x + 3)$

   (iii) $(3x - 2)(2x - 1)$

   (iv) $(2a - 5)(a + 2)$

   (v) $(2a - 2)(3a - 2)$

   (vi) $(x - y)(x + y)$

   (vii) $(m - n)(m - n)$

   (viii) $(2a - 3)(5a - 4)$

   (ix) $(1 - 2a)(1 + 2a)$

   (x) $(7 + 3a)(3a - 2)$

5. (i) $(x - 3)^2$

   (ii) $(5x + 1)^2$

   (iii) $(3y - 2)^2$

   (iv) $(4y + 5)^2$

   (v) $[2(2x - 3)]^2$

6. (i) $(x + 1)(x^2 + 2x + 3)$

   (ii) $(x + 2)(2x^2 + 3x - 1)$

   (iii) $(2x + 2)(3x^2 + 2x - 3)$

   (iv) $(a^2 + 2a - 2)(2a - 3)$

   (v) $(3a^2 - 4a - 1)(3a - 1)$

   (vi) $(1 - a)(4 - 3a - a^2)$

7. (i) *1st* $x(x + 1)(x + 3)$

   (ii) $-2a(a + 1)(2a - 3)$

   (iii) $-p(p - 1)(p + 1)$

8. Copy and complete the following algebraic pyramid. The missing values are found by adding the values from the two blocks below.

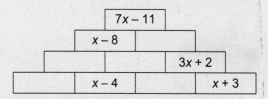

9. A garden has a small rectangular lawn surrounded by a flower-bed of equal width. The lawn measures 5 metres by 12 metres and the flower-bed has a width of x metres. Write an expression for the area of the:

   (i) Garden   (ii) Flower-bed

10. A rectangular playing field has a length of $2x$ metres and width of $(x - 5)$ metres. Write down an expression in x for:

   (i) The area of the field

   (ii) The perimeter of the field

Half of the field is to be used for training.

   (iii) Write an expression in x to show how much of the field is used.

11. A rectangle is $(x + 7)$ cm long by $(x - 1)$ cm wide. A square of side length 4 cm is cut from each corner of the rectangle as shown. The sides are then folded along the dotted line to make an open-topped box.

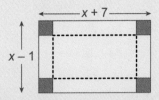

(i) Write an expression in x for the surface area of this box.

(ii) Write an expression in x for the volume of this box.

12. Write an expression in terms of x for the area and perimeter of each of the shapes below.

(i)

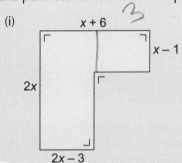

(ii)

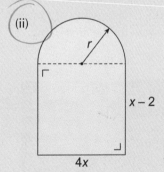

(iii)

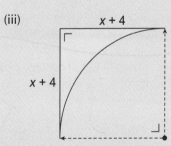

Note: Area of a circle $= \pi r^2$
Circumference of a circle $= 2\pi r$
Take π to be 3.14.

13. (a) A square has a side length of $2x$ units. What is the area of the square?

(b) A rectangle (A), 3 units wide, is cut from the square and placed at the side of the remaining rectangle (B).

A square (C) is then cut from the bottom of rectangle A to leave a final rectangle (D), as shown in the diagram.

(i) What is the area of rectangle B?

(ii) What is the area of square C?

(c) By calculating the area of rectangle D, explain why $(2x + 3)(2x - 3) = 4x^2 - 9$.

14. Each of the four cards A, B, C and D has an algebraic expression on it.

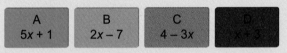

(a) Expand and simplify:

(i) B + 2C

(ii) AC + BD

(iii) ABC

(b) Show that B + C + D = 0.

(c) What combination of three of these cards gives an answer of 12?

15. The area of a rectangle is $12x^2 + 16x$.

One possible expression in x for the product of the length and the width of the rectangle is $x(12x + 16)$.

Write down two more possible expressions for this product.

Revision Exercises

1. (a) If $a = 6$, $b = 4$ and $c = 1$, evaluate:

    (i) ab

    (ii) $ab + c$

    (iii) $b^2 + ab + c$

    (iv) $c^2 + bc + a$

    (v) $\dfrac{ab}{bc + ab}$

(b) Simplify the following:

    (i) $3(2a + 5b)$

    (ii) $4(6b - c)$

    (iii) $7(3x - 2y)$

    (iv) $-2(2x + 7y)$

    (v) $-3(x - y)$

(c) Simplify the following:

    (i) $(5x^2 - 2x) + (2x^2 - 3x) + (4x - 2)$

    (ii) $(8x^2 + 2x + 3) - (6x^2 + 4x - 1)$

    (iii) $(6a^2 + 3a - 2) + (7a^2 - 2a + 4)$
        $- (3a^2 + 4a - 1)$

    (iv) $(11b^2 - 2b + 7) - (8b - 3)$
        $- (4 - 3b + 8b^2) - 3b$

(d) Multiply out the following and simplify:

    (i) $(x + 3)(x + 4)$

    (ii) $(x + 2)(x + 5)$

    (iii) $(x + 10)(x + 3)$

    (iv) $(y + 2)(y + 7)$

    (v) $(2y + 1)(y + 3)$

2. (a) If $x = -1$, $a = 3$, $b = 2$, $c = -4$ and $d = \dfrac{1}{2}$, evaluate:

    (i) $ax + bx + c$

    (ii) $ax^2 + cx - d$

    (iii) $x^3 - bx^2 + cx + a$

    (iv) $x^3 - ax^2 - dx + d$

    (v) $xd^3 + ad^2 - cd + c$

(b) Simplify the following:

    (i) $-10(2x - 5y)$ (iv) $a(12a - 4)$

    (ii) $-(x - y + z)$ (v) $3a(7a - 2b)$

    (iii) $x(2x + 5)$ (vi) $-2x(3 - x)$

(c) Expand and simplify:

    (i) $(3x - 7)(2x + 1)$

    (ii) $(2a - 4)(3a - 5)$

    (iii) $(3y + 2)^2$

    (iv) $(8x - 1)^2$

    (v) $(x - 10)^2$

3. Expand and simplify:

    (i) $x(x + 4)(x + 5)$

    (ii) $x(x - 3)(x + 8)$

    (iii) $(x - 1)(x + 1)(x + 5)$

    (iv) $(x + 1)^2$

    (v) $(x + 1)^3$

    (vi) $(2x - 1)^2$

    (vii) $(2x - 1)^3$

4. (a) Simplify the following:

    (i) $3(a + b) + 2(3a - 4b)$

    (ii) $3(x + 4y + 1) - (x + y - 11)$

    (iii) $-5x(2x^2 - 4)$

    (iv) $\dfrac{1}{3}(9x - 3y + 2) + 2(x + 2y - 1)$

    (v) $\dfrac{1}{2}(10x - 8y + 6) - (5x - 4y + 3)$

(b) Multiply out the following and simplify:

    (i) $(x - 2)(x^2 + x + 5)$

    (ii) $(x + 3)(2x^2 - x - 1)$

    (iii) $(x - 2)(x^2 + 2x + 4)$

    (iv) $(2x + 3)(4x^2 - 6x + 9)$

    (v) $(x + y)^4$

5. (a) If $x = -1$ and $y = -2$, find the value of

    (i) $x + y$ (iii) $5xy$

    (ii) $2x - y$ (iv) $3x + 4y$

(b) Expand and simplify:

    (i) $(4a + 2)(4a^2 - 2a - 7)$

    (ii) $(6y - 1)(2y^2 - 3y - 5)$

    (iii) $(y - 3)(-2y^2 - 4y - 2)$

    (iv) $(1 + 2x)(x^2 + x - 3)$

ALGEBRA I: EXPRESSIONS

6. (a) If $a = 6$, insert $<$, $>$ or $=$ between each pair of expressions:

  (i) $5a \ldots 6a - a$

  (ii) $(a + 2)^2 \ldots a^2 + 4$

  (iii) $\frac{1}{2}a \ldots \frac{a}{2}$

  (iv) $(a + 1)^2 \ldots a^2 + 2a + 1$

  (v) $\left(\frac{1}{2}a\right)^2 \ldots \frac{1}{2}a^2$

(b) If $p = x^2 - x + 2$ and $q = x^2 + 3x - 3$, write the following in terms of x:

  (i) $p + q$ (iii) $3p + q$

  (ii) $p - q$ (iv) $3p - 2q$

(c) If $p = x^2 + 5$ and $q = 2x - 1$, write the following in terms of x:

  (i) $p + q$ (ii) pq (iii) pq^2

7. This rectangle is made up of four parts with areas of x^2, $4x$, $3x$ and 12 square units.

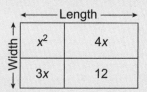

Write down an expression in x for:

  (i) The length of the rectangle

  (ii) The width of the rectangle

  (iii) The perimeter of the rectangle

  (iv) The area of a rectangle that has a perimeter double the perimeter of the rectangle above

8. This square has an area of x^2 square units.

It is split into four rectangles.

(a) Fill in the table below to show the dimensions and area of each rectangle.

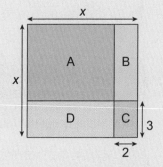

Rectangle	Length	Width	Area
A	$x - 2$	$x - 3$	$(x - 2)(x - 3)$
B			
C			
D			

(b) Add together the areas of rectangles B, C and D. Expand any brackets and simplify.

(c) Use the results from parts (a) and (b) to explain why $(x - 2)(x - 3) = x^2 - 5x + 6$.

9. A two-carriage train has f first-class seats and $2s$ standard-class seats.

A three-carriage train has $2f$ first-class seats and $3s$ standard-class seats.

On a weekday, six two-carriage trains and four three-carriage trains travel from Cork to Limerick.

(a) Write down an expression for the total number of first-class and standard-class seats available during the day.

(b) On average in any day, half of the first-class seats are used at a cost of €60 per seat.
On average in any day, three-quarters of the standard-class seats are used at a cost of €40 per seat.
How much money does the rail company earn in an average day on this route? Give your answer in terms of f and s.

(c) $f = 16$ and $s = 90$. It costs the rail company €25,000 per day to operate this route.
How much profit does the company make on an average day?

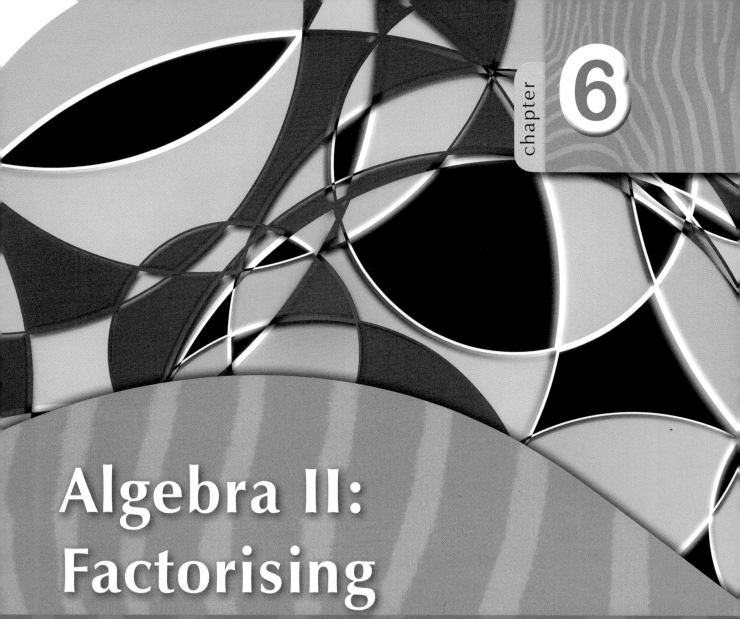

chapter 6

Algebra II: Factorising

Learning Outcomes

In this chapter you will learn to:

- Factorise an expression by:
  - Highest common factor
  - Grouping
  - Difference of two squares
- Factorise a quadratic trinomial where the coefficient of x^2 is a natural number

6.1 HIGHEST COMMON FACTOR

YOU SHOULD REMEMBER...

■ How to factorise expressions from *Active Maths 1*

Factorising is the reverse of expanding. We turn the given expression into a **product**.

$x(x - 3) = x^2 - 3x$ Expanding

$x^2 - 3x = x(x - 3)$ Factorising

One method of factorising that we can sometimes use is the method of taking the highest common factor (HCF) from an algebraic expression.

KEY WORDS

■ **Factors**

■ **Highest Common Factor**

■ **Grouping**

■ **Quadratic trinomials**

■ **Difference of two squares**

x^2 Worked Example 6.1

Factorise fully the following expressions:

(i) $x^2 + 2x^3$ (ii) $3a^2b - 6ba$ (iii) $4xy - 8y^2 + 16yz$

Solution

(i) $x^2 + 2x^3$

     $= x^2(1 + 2x)$ (as x^2 is the HCF)

(ii) $3a^2b - 6ba$

     $= 3ab(a - 2)$ (as $3ab$ is the HCF)

(iii) $4xy - 8y^2 + 16yz$

     $= 4y(x - 2y + 4z)$ (as $4y$ is the HCF)

Exercise 6.1

Factorise fully the expressions in Questions 1–16.

1. $5a + 10$

2. $x^2 + 4x$

3. $y^2 - 7y$

4. $xy - 5y$

5. $x^2 - 3x$

6. $-2pq + 4p$

7. $4xy - 2y$

8. $3ab - 12bd$

9. $x - 4x^2$

10. $21ab^2 + 14ab$

11. $-9xy^2 - xy$

12. $6p - 12p^2q$

13. $-8ab + 10b^2a$

14. $2x^3 + 6x^2 - 2x$

15. $a^2b + ab^2 - 3bc$

16. $-20x^2y^2z + 5x^3y + 10x^2y^2$

17. Simplify and factorise fully
   $(x + 1)(y - 5) + (2x - 1)(y + 1)$.

6.2 GROUPING FACTORS

Consider the product $(x + y)(a - b)$, where a, b, x, y are variable.

If we expand this, we get:

$$x(a - b) + y(a - b)$$
$$= ax - bx + ay - by$$

This expanded expression has four terms.

Sometimes we will encounter algebraic expressions with four terms, and a method of factorising such expressions is by grouping.

x^2 Worked Example 6.2

Factorise fully:

    (i) $3ab - 6by + ax - 2xy$ (ii) $xy - y - 4x + 4$

Solution

    (i) $3ab - 6by + ax - 2xy$

        $= 3b(a - 2y) + x(a - 2y)$ ($3b$ is the HCF of the first pair of terms; x is the HCF of the second pair)

        $= (a - 2y)(3b + x)$ ($(a - 2y)$ is the HCF)

    (ii) $xy - y - 4x + 4$

        $= y(x - 1) - 4(x - 1)$ (y is the HCF of the first pair and -4 is a HCF of the second pair)

> We must be careful with the signs: $-4(x - 1) = -4x + 4$

        $= (x - 1)(y - 4)$ ($(x - 1)$ is the HCF)

x^2 Worked Example 6.3

Factorise $12pr + 2st - 3pt - 8rs$

Solution

Sometimes, we may have to rearrange the terms first so as to be able to factorise the expression.

Method 1	**Method 2**
$12pr + 2st - 3pt - 8rs$	$12pr + 2st - 3pt - 8rs$
$= 12pr - 3pt - 8rs + 2st$ (Rearranging the terms)	$= 12pr - 8rs - 3pt + 2st$ (Rearranging the terms)
$= 3p(4r - t) - 2s(4r - t)$ ($3p$ and $-2s$ are HCFs)	$= 4r(3p - 2s) - t(3p - 2s)$ ($4r$ and $-t$ are HCFs)
$= (4r - t)(3p - 2s)$ ($(4r - t)$ is the HCF)	$= (3p - 2s)(4r - t)$ ($(3p - 2s)$ is the HCF)

Exercise 6.2

| Factorise fully the expressions in Questions 1–10. | Rearrange the following expressions, when necessary, and factorise. |

1. $ad + ac + bd + bc$

2. $ap + aq + bp + bq$

3. $xy - 4x + 3y - 12$

4. $ab + 4a - 2b - 8$

5. $rw + 2w - 3r - 6$

6. $ax + 2bx + ay + 2by$

7. $2qr - rs - 10pq + 5ps$

8. $6ad - 3ae + 2bd - be$

9. $6x^2 - 2xz - 3xy + yz$

10. $40ac - 12a^2 - 70bc + 21ab$

11. $pm + nq + np + mq$

12. $3a + xb + 3b + xa$

13. $ac - bd - ad + bc$

14. $mx + 24by - 2my - 12bx$

15. $2x^2 - 10ay - 5xy + 4ax$

16. $x^2 - 2y - 2x + xy$

17. $3a^2 - 3bc - ab + 9ac$

18. $10xy + z + 2yz + 5x$

19. $3p^2 + 2q - 6pq - p$

20. $ab + b - 1 - a$

21. $x - y + 2y(y - x)$

22. $p(q - r) + r - q$

6.3 QUADRATIC TRINOMIALS I

When we multiply the two expressions $(x - 2)$ and $(x + 3)$ together, we end up with a type of expression called a **quadratic trinomial**.

$(x - 2)(x + 3)$

$= x(x + 3) - 2(x + 3)$

$= x^2 + 3x - 2x - 6$

$= x^2 + x - 6$

> A quadratic trinomial in x has an x^2 term, an x term and a constant.

x^2 Worked Example 6.4

Factorise:

    (i) $x^2 + 11x + 24$

    (ii) $x^2 + 6x - 16$

    (iii) $x^2 - 7x + 12$

Solution

    (i) $x^2 + 11x + 24$

      Method 1

      We need to find the factors of $+24$ that add to up $+11$.

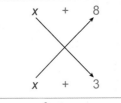

$x \times x = x^2$ ✓

$8 \times 3 = 24$ ✓

We now use the arrows:

$x \times 3 = 3x$

$x \times 8 = \underline{8x}$

        $11x$ ✓

$\therefore x^2 + 11x + 24 = (x + 8)(x + 3)$

Note: It is good practice to check your work by expanding your answer in rough work.

There are several different ways of factorising a quadratic trinomial. Here, we will demonstrate two more methods:

- The Guide Number Method
- A method based on area models

Method 2 (Guide Number Method)

$x^2 + 11x + 24$

The coefficient of x^2 is 1.

The constant term is 24.

$(1)(24) = 24$

The factors of 24, in pairs, are:

1, 24

2, 12

③, ⑧ ← Use this third factor pair.

4, 6

$11x$ can be written as $3x + 8x$.

So, $x^2 + 11x + 24$

$= x^2 + 3x + 8x + 24$

$= x(x + 3) + 8(x + 3)$ (We factorise by grouping)

$= (x + 3)(x + 8)$

$\therefore x^2 + 11x + 24 = (x + 3)(x + 8)$

Method 3 (Based on area models)

Consider a larger rectangle (not to scale) divided into four smaller rectangles. (We ignore the fact that area can never be negative.)

Let $x^2 + 11x + 24 =$ the area of the larger rectangle.

A	B
C	D

Call Area A = x^2.

Call Area D = 24.

x^2	B
C	24

The remaining two areas (of B and C) need to add up to $11x$.

Consider the factor pairs of 24:

1, 24

2, 12

③, ⑧ ← Use this third factor pair.

4, 6

$11x = 3x + 8x$

So, we have:

x^2	$3x$
$8x$	24

The HCF of the first row is x.

The HCF of the second row is 8.

The HCF of the first column is x.

The HCF of the second column is 3.

This gives us:

	x	3
x	x^2	$3x$
8	$8x$	24

The dimensions of the larger rectangle are $(x + 3)$ and $(x + 8)$.

So, area $= x^2 + 11x + 24$

$= (x + 3)(x + 8)$

$\therefore x^2 + 11x + 24 = (x + 3)(x + 8)$

(ii) $x^2 + 6x - 16$

Method 1

Find factors of −16 that add up to 6.

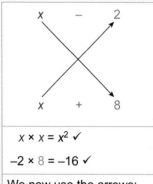

$x \times x = x^2$ ✓

$-2 \times 8 = -16$ ✓

We now use the arrows:

$x \times 8 = 8x$

$x \times -2 = \underline{-2x}$

$\qquad\quad 6x$ ✓

$\therefore x^2 + 6x - 16 = (x - 2)(x + 8)$

Method 2 (Guide Number Method)

Step 1 Multiply the coefficient of x^2 by the constant.

$$x^2 + 6x - 16$$

$$(1)(-16) = -16$$

Step 2 Find two factors of -16 that add to give the coefficient of the middle term, $6x$:

$$+8 \quad \text{and} \quad -2$$

Step 3 Use the answers from Step 2 to rewrite $x^2 + 6x - 16$:

$$x^2 + 8x - 2x - 16$$

$$= x(x + 8) - 2(x + 8)$$
$$\text{(Factorise by grouping)}$$

$$= (x + 8)(x - 2)$$

$$\therefore x^2 + 6x - 16 = (x + 8)(x - 2)$$

Method 3 (Based on area models)

Step 1 Let $x^2 + 6x - 16 = $ Area of the larger rectangle.

x^2	B
C	-16

Step 2 Area of B + Area of C = $6x$

Find the factors of -16 that add up to 6:

$$8 \quad \text{and} \quad -2$$

$$6x = 8x - 2x$$

x^2	$-2x$
$8x$	-16

Step 3 We now find the HCF of each column and row.

	x	-2
x	x^2	$-2x$
8	$8x$	-16

The dimensions of the larger rectangle are $(x + 8)$ and $(x - 2)$.

So, area $= x^2 + 6x - 16$

$$= (x + 8)(x - 2)$$

$$\therefore x^2 + 6x - 16 = (x + 8)(x - 2)$$

 **ACTIVITY 6.1**

(iii) $x^2 - 7x + 12$

Method 1

We are looking for factors of 12 that add up to -7.

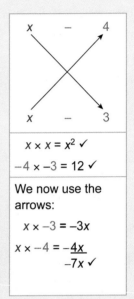

$x \times x = x^2$ ✓

$-4 \times -3 = 12$ ✓

We now use the arrows:

$x \times -3 = -3x$

$x \times -4 = \underline{-4x}$

$\qquad\qquad -7x$ ✓

$$\therefore x^2 - 7x + 12 = (x - 4)(x - 3)$$

Method 2 (Guide Number Method)

Step 1 Multiply the coefficient of x^2 by the constant.

$$x^2 - 7x + 12$$

$$(1)(12) = 12$$

Step 2 Find two factors of 12 that add to give the coefficient of the middle term, $-7x$:

$$-4 \quad \text{and} \quad -3$$

Step 3 Use the answers from Step 2 to rewrite $x^2 - 7x + 12$:

$x^2 - 4x - 3x + 12$

$= x(x - 4) - 3(x - 4)$ (Factorise by grouping)

$= (x - 4)(x - 3)$

$\therefore x^2 - 7x + 12 = (x - 4)(x - 3)$

Method 3 (Based on area models)

Step 1 Let $x^2 - 7x + 12 = $ Area of the larger rectangle.

x^2	B
C	12

Step 2 Area of B + Area of C $= -7x$

Find the factors of 12 that add up to -7:

-4 and -3

$-7x = -4x - 3x$

x^2	$-4x$
$-3x$	12

Step 3 We now find the HCF of each column and row.

	x	-4
x	x^2	$-4x$
-3	$-3x$	12

The dimensions of the larger rectangle are $(x - 4)$ and $(x - 3)$.

So, the area of the larger rectangle
$= x^2 - 7x + 12$

$= (x - 4)(x - 3)$

$\therefore x^2 - 7x + 12 = (x - 4)(x - 3)$

Exercise 6.3

In Questions 1–9, factorise using the method based on area models.	In Questions 10–18, factorise using the Guide Number Method.	In Questions 19–27, factorise using a method of your choice.
1. $x^2 + 4x + 3$	**10.** $x^2 - 2x - 35$	**19.** $x^2 - 13x + 42$
2. $x^2 - 4x - 12$	**11.** $x^2 + 5x - 14$	**20.** $x^2 - 8x + 7$
3. $x^2 + 5x + 4$	**12.** $x^2 + 7x + 6$	**21.** $x^2 - 4x - 21$
4. $x^2 + 5x + 6$	**13.** $x^2 - 7x - 18$	**22.** $x^2 + 12x + 27$
5. $x^2 - 3x + 2$	**14.** $x^2 - 11x + 28$	**23.** $x^2 - 11x + 18$
6. $x^2 - 5x + 4$	**15.** $x^2 + 4x - 21$	**24.** $x^2 + 4x - 12$
7. $x^2 - 6x + 8$	**16.** $x^2 - 8x + 15$	**25.** $x^2 + x - 56$
8. $x^2 + 8x + 16$	**17.** $x^2 + 2x - 35$	**26.** $x^2 + 24x + 108$
9. $x^2 + x - 12$	**18.** $x^2 + 8x + 7$	**27.** $x^2 - x - 132$

6.4 QUADRATIC TRINOMIALS II

In the previous section we factorised quadratic trinomials that had an x^2 coefficient of 1. We now extend our knowledge to consider quadratic trinomials where the x^2 coefficient can be any natural number.

x^2 Worked Example 6.5

Factorise fully the following expressions:

(i) $2x^2 + 5x + 3$

(ii) $7x^2 + 13x - 2$

(iii) $5x^2 - 8x - 4$

Solution

(i) $2x^2 + 5x + 3$

Guide Number Method

The coefficient of x^2 is 2.

The constant term is 3.

$(2)(3) = 6$

The factors of 6, in pairs, are:

1, 6

②,③ → Use this second factor pair.

$5x$ can be written as $2x + 3x$.

So, $2x^2 + 5x + 3$

$= 2x^2 + 2x + 3x + 3$

$= 2x(x + 1) + 3(x + 1)$ (We factorise by grouping)

$= (x + 1)(2x + 3)$

∴ $2x^2 + 5x + 3 = (x + 1)(2x + 3)$

> Note: Check your work in rough work by expanding your answer.

(ii) $7x^2 + 13x - 2$

Step 1   Multiply the coefficient of x^2 by the constant.

$$7x^2 + 13x - 2$$

7 by $-2 = -14$

Step 2   Find two factors of -14 that add to give the coefficient of the middle term, i.e. 13.

$+14$ and -1

Step 3 Use the answers from Step 2 to rewrite $7x^2 + 13x - 2$ as follows:

$7x^2 + 14x - x - 2$

$7x(x + 2) -1(x + 2)$ (Factorise by grouping)

$(x + 2)(7x - 1)$

$\therefore 7x^2 + 13x - 2 = (x + 2)(7x - 1)$.

(iii) This time, we will not use the Guide Number Method, as students need to be familiar with a variety of methods.

$5x^2 - 8x - 4$

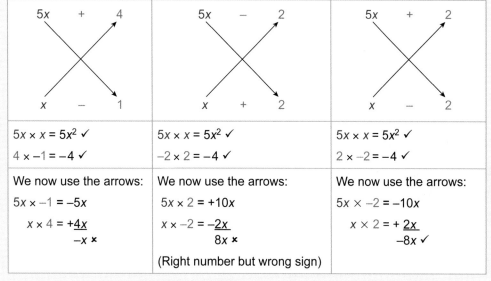

$5x \times x = 5x^2$ ✓	$5x \times x = 5x^2$ ✓	$5x \times x = 5x^2$ ✓
$4 \times -1 = -4$ ✓	$-2 \times 2 = -4$ ✓	$2 \times -2 = -4$ ✓
We now use the arrows:	We now use the arrows:	We now use the arrows:
$5x \times -1 = -5x$	$5x \times 2 = +10x$	$5x \times -2 = -10x$
$x \times 4 = +\underline{4x}$	$x \times -2 = -\underline{2x}$	$x \times 2 = +\underline{2x}$
$-x$ ✗	$8x$ ✗	$-8x$ ✓
	(Right number but wrong sign)	

$\therefore 5x^2 - 8x - 4 = (5x + 2)(x - 2)$

When solving a quadratic trinomial where the coefficient of x^2 is a composite (non-prime) number, it may be easiest to use the Guide Number Method.

 ACTIVITIES 6.2, 6.3

 Worked Example 6.6

Factorise $4x^2 - 5x - 6$.

Solution

Step 1 Multiply the coefficient of x^2 by the constant.

$4x^2 - 5x - 6$

$(4)(-6) = -24$

Step 2 Find two factors of -24 that add to give the coefficient of the middle term, i.e. -5.

-8 and $+3$

Step 3 Use the answers from Step 2 to rewrite $4x^2 - 5x - 6$ as follows:

$4x^2 - 8x + 3x - 6$

$4x(x - 2) + 3(x - 2)$ (Factorise by grouping)

$(4x + 3)(x - 2)$

$\therefore 4x^2 - 5x - 6 = (4x + 3)(x - 2)$

Exercise 6.4

Factorise the expressions in Questions 1–32.

1. $2x^2 + 7x + 3$
2. $3x^2 + 8x - 3$
3. $11x^2 - 12x + 1$
4. $2x^2 + x - 3$
5. $2x^2 - 7x + 5$
6. $3x^2 + x - 2$
7. $2x^2 - 5x + 3$
8. $5x^2 + 7x + 2$
9. $2x^2 - 9x + 4$
10. $5x^2 - 4x - 1$
11. $5x^2 + 13x - 6$
12. $7x^2 - 18x - 9$

13. $5x^2 - 7x + 2$
14. $3x^2 + x - 4$
15. $2x^2 + 11x + 12$
16. $2x^2 + 9x + 9$
17. $5x^2 - 7x - 6$
18. $3x^2 + 14x + 8$
19. $3x^2 - 8x - 16$
20. $5x^2 - 13x - 6$
21. $3x^2 - 2x - 1$
22. $13x^2 - 35x - 12$
23. $2x^2 - 3x - 20$
24. $4x^2 + 3x - 1$

25. $8x^2 + 57x + 7$
26. $4x^2 - 12x + 5$
27. $8x^2 - 5x - 3$
28. $18x^2 - 27x + 4$
29. $4x^2 - 9x - 9$
30. $4x^2 + 19x + 12$
31. $4x^2 - 63x - 16$
32. $12x^2 - 61x + 70$

33. Simplify
$(2x + 1)^2 + (x - 1)^2 - 2(7x - 1)$
and factorise the simplified expression.

6.5 THE DIFFERENCE OF TWO SQUARES

Consider the expression $x^2 - 25$. This can be written as a difference of two squares:

$x^2 - 25 = (x)^2 - (5)^2$

What is the significance of this?

Consider the product $(x + y)(x - y)$. When we expand this, we get:

$$(x + y)(x - y) = x(x - y) + y(x - y)$$
$$= x^2 - xy + xy - y^2$$
$$= x^2 - y^2$$

Therefore, $x^2 - y^2 = (x + y)(x - y)$.

On our course three conditions must be met if the difference of two squares method of factorisation is to work:

(1) There must be two terms.

(2) Each term must be a perfect square.

(3) There must be a minus sign between the two terms.

If these three conditions are met, the factorisation is:

FORMULA

$x^2 - y^2 = (x + y)(x - y)$

OR

$a^2x^2 - b^2y^2 = (ax + by)(ax - by)$

So, $x^2 - 25$

$= (x)^2 - (5)^2$

$= (x + 5)(x - 5)$

x^2 Worked Example 6.7

Factorise fully:

    (i) $x^2 - 36$ (iii) $121a^2 - 49y^2$

    (ii) $16x^2 - 81$ (iv) $x^4 - y^4$

Solution

    (i) $x^2 - 36$

        $= (x)^2 - (6)^2$

        $= (x + 6)(x - 6)$

    (ii) $16x^2 - 81$

        $= (4x)^2 - (9)^2$

        $= (4x + 9)(4x - 9)$

    (iii) $121a^2 - 49y^2$

        $= (11a)^2 - (7y)^2$

        $= (11a + 7y)(11a - 7y)$

    (iv) $x^4 - y^4$

        $= (x^2)^2 - (y^2)^2$ (Since $(x^2)^2 = x^4$, etc.)

        $= (x^2 + y^2)(x^2 - y^2)$

        $= (x^2 + y^2)(x + y)(x - y)$ (Since $x^2 - y^2 = (x + y)(x - y)$)

Exercise 6.5

> Factorise fully the expressions in Questions 1–27.

1. $x^2 - 169$	**10.** $36x^2 - 25$	**19.** $16x^2 - 9y^2$
2. $x^2 - 100$	**11.** $81y^2 - 64$	**20.** $49x^2 - 4y^2$
3. $x^2 - 144$	**12.** $144x^2 - 49$	**21.** $256x^2 - 625y^2$
4. $36 - x^2$	**13.** $81 - 4x^2$	**22.** $9q^2 - 25p^2$
5. $x^2 - 81$	**14.** $196q^2 - 1$	**23.** $900x^2 - 196y^2$
6. $p^2 - 121$	**15.** $121x^2 - 25y^2$	**24.** $16b^2 - a^2$
7. $196 - a^2$	**16.** $169a^2 - 81b^2$	**25.** $x^2 - 441y^2$
8. $9x^2 - 289$	**17.** $100x^2 - 49y^2$	**26.** $361x^2 - 289y^2$
9. $16x^2 - 81$	**18.** $121a^2 - 25b^2$	**27.** $16a^4 - b^4$

28. (i) Factorise and hence evaluate $501^2 - 499^2$.

    (ii) Verify your answer using a calculator.

29. (i) Factorise and evaluate $40.6^2 - 39.4^2$.

    (ii) Verify your answer using a calculator.

30. Simplify $(a - 4b)(a + b) + 3ab$ and factorise the simplified expression.

6.6 FURTHER FACTORISATION

Sometimes, to factorise an expression fully, we may first have to find the highest common factor (HCF) and then factorise again using a different method.

x^2 Worked Example 6.8

Factorise fully the following expressions:

   (i) $12x^2 + 2x - 2$

   (ii) $20ap + 30aq - 12bp - 18bq$

   (iii) $8p^3 - 32p$

Solution

   (i) $12x^2 + 2x - 2$

    Step 1 Take out the HCF:

      $2(6x^2 + x - 1)$

    Step 2 Factorise $6x^2 + x - 1$:

      $6x^2 + x - 1 = (3x - 1)(2x + 1)$

    Step 3 Write out the fully factorised expression:

      $12x^2 + 2x - 2 = 2(3x - 1)(2x + 1)$

   (ii) $20ap + 30aq - 12bp - 18bq$

    Step 1 Take out the HCF:

      $2(10ap + 15aq - 6bp - 9bq)$

    Step 2 Factorise $10ap + 15aq - 6bp - 9bq$:

      $= 5a(2p + 3q) - 3b(2p + 3q)$

      $= (2p + 3q)(5a - 3b)$

    Step 3 Write out the fully factorised expression:

      $20ap + 30aq - 12bp - 18bq$
      $= 2(2p + 3q)(5a - 3b)$

   (iii) $8p^3 - 32p$

    Step 1 Take out the HCF:

      $8p(p^2 - 4)$

    Step 2 Factorise $p^2 - 4$:

      $= (p)^2 - (2)^2$

      $= (p + 2)(p - 2)$

    Step 3 Write out the fully factorised expression:

      $8p^3 - 32p = 8p(p + 2)(p - 2)$

Exercise 6.6

> In Questions 1–20, factorise the expressions fully.

1. $2x^2 - 8$

2. $3y^2 - 300$

3. $2ac - 2ad + 2bc - 2bd$

4. $20x^2 + 20x + 5$

5. $4x^2 - 8x - 12$

6. $y^3 - 25y$

7. $3ax^2 + 6ax - 24a$

8. $5x^3 - 80x$

9. $5x^2 - 10qx + 10px - 20pq$

10. $5a^4 - 45a^2$

11. $2x^3 + x^2 - 15x$

12. $3a^3 - 9a^2c - 6a^2b + 18abc$

13. $3p^2 - 3p - 18$

14. $36x^2 + 68x - 8$

15. $18x^2 - 8$

16. $8q^2 - 44q + 20$

17. $a^4 - 25a^2b^2$

18. $60y^3 - 70y^2 - 30y$

19. $40p^2r - 30p^2s + 20pqr - 15pqs$

20. $40y^2 - 14y - 6$

21. Simplify $(2x + a)(4x - 2a) - (3y + a)(6y - 2a)$ and fully factorise the simplified expression.

22. Simplify $(x - 3)(x^2 + 4) + 3(x - 2)^2 - 17x$ and factorise fully the simplified expression.

23. Simplify $(2a - b)(6a + 3b) - (3c - 3b)(c + b)$ and factorise fully the simplified expression.

24. Simplify $(x^2 - 20)(x^2 - 5) - 4x^2$ and factorise fully the simplified expression.

In Questions 1–39, factorise the expressions fully.

1. $xy + 2x$

2. $3x + 3$

3. $10x^2 + 2x$

4. $5a^2 - a$

5. $ad + ae + cd + ce$

6. $y^2 - 49$

7. $x^2 + 8x + 7$

8. $x^2 + 13x + 30$

9. $mp - mq + np - nq$

10. $g^2 + 4g - 12$

11. $p^2 - 16$

12. $k^2 - 21k - 100$

13. $mx - 2my - 12bx + 24by$

14. $x^2 - x - 20$

15. $c^2 - 25$

16. $14x^2y - 21xy^2$

17. $a^2 + 2a - 8$

18. $m^2 - 5m + 6$

19. $7x^2 + 9x + 2$

20. $ax + 2ay - 5bx - 10by$

21. $2x^2 - 3x + 1$

22. $3x^2 + 14x - 5$

23. $144r^2 - 121s^2$

24. $7x^2 + 26x - 45$

25. $5x^2 + 13x - 6$

26. $36y^2 - z^2$

27. $15km - 6kn - 5m + 2n$

28. $3x^2 + x - 10$

29. $pr + sq - qr - ps$

30. $a^2b^2 - 4x^2y^2$

31. $5x^2 - x - 4$

32. $ac - ad - bc + bd$

33. $6x^2 + 15ab - 10bx - 9ax$

34. $4x^2 + 8x + 3$

35. $10x^2 + 51x + 5$

36. $ax + cy - ay - cx$

37. $8x^2 - 26x - 15$

38. $100y^2 - 81x^2$

39. $6x^2 + 26x - 20$

In Questions 40–47, find the three factors for each expression.

40. $x^3 - 2x^2 - 3x$

41. $2a^2 - 18b^2$

42. $2x^2 + 10x - 28$

43. $x^3 + x^2 - 56x$

44. $pqs - pqt + prs - prt$

45. $30x^2 - 46x + 8$

46. $3x - ax + 3x^2 - ax^2$

47. $x^4 - 16$

48. This rectangle is made up of four parts. Two of the parts have areas of x^2 and 12 square units.

x^2	
	12

The sides of the rectangle are of the form $x + a$ and $x + b$, where $a, b \in Z$.

Find two sets of solutions for a and b. For each set of solutions copy and complete the areas in the other parts of the rectangle.

49. (i) Expand $(x + a)(x + b)$.

(ii) If $x^2 + 8x + 15 = (x + r)(x + t)$, use your answer to part (i) to write down the values of:
   (a) $r + t$
   (b) rt

50. (i) Expand and simplify $(x + 3)^2 - (x + 2)^2$.

(ii) Factorise $a^2 - b^2$.

(iii) In your answer for part (ii), replace a with $(x + 3)$ and b with $(x + 2)$.

(iv) What do you notice about the answer to parts (i) and (iii)?

(v) Simplify $(x + 4)^2 - (x + 1)^2$.

51. Three students are asked to factorise the expression $6x^2 + 36x + 30$.

Sophie	Tara	Viggo
$(6x + 6)(x + 5)$	$(2x + 2)(3x + 15)$	$(3x + 3)(2x + 10)$

(i) Are all the answers correctly factorised? Explain.

(ii) Explain why one quadratic expression may have more than one correct factorisation.

(iii) Factorise fully $6x^2 + 36x + 30$.

52. The factors of $x^2 + kx + 8$ are $(x + a)(x + b)$, where a and b are positive integers. Show that there are two possible values of k.

53. The factors of $x^2 + kx - 8$ are $(x + a)(x + b)$, where a and b are integers. Show that there are four possible values of k.

54. One of the factors of $3x^2 + kx - 15$ is $(x - 5)$. Find the value of k.

55. One of the factors of $5x^2 - x - k$ is $(5x + 1)$. Find the value of k.

chapter 7

Constructions

Learning Outcomes

In this chapter, you will do the following:

⊃ Construct a line perpendicular to a given line *l*, passing through a given point not on *l*

⊃ Divide a line segment into any number of equal segments, without measuring it

⊃ Revise all Junior Certificate Ordinary Level constructions

7.1 CONSTRUCTIONS: REVISION

KEY WORDS

■ **Perpendicular**

■ **Parallel**

■ **Bisect**

■ **Perpendicular bisector**

■ **Segments**

In *Active Maths 1*, the following constructions were studied:

■ Construction 1: The bisector of any given angle, using only a compass and a straight edge

■ Construction 2: The perpendicular bisector of a line segment, using only a compass and a straight edge

■ Construction 4: A line perpendicular to a given line *l*, passing through a given point on *l*

■ Construction 5: A line parallel to a given line, passing through a given point

■ Construction 6: Division of a line segment into two or three equal segments without measuring it

■ Construction 8: A line segment of a given length on a given ray

■ Construction 9: An angle of a given number of degrees with a given ray as one arm

■ Construction 10: A triangle, given the lengths of three sides (SSS)

■ Construction 11: A triangle, given two sides and the angle between these two sides (SAS)

■ Construction 12: A triangle, given two angles and the side between these two angles (ASA)

■ Construction 13: A right-angled triangle, given the length of the hypotenuse and one other side (RHS)

■ Construction 14: A right-angled triangle, given one side and one of the acute angles

■ Construction 15: A rectangle, given side lengths

Students at Higher Level must also be able to complete:

■ Construction 3: A line perpendicular to a given line *l*, passing through a given point not on *l*

■ Construction 7: Division of a line segment into any number of equal segments without measuring it

Students at Higher Level must know all 15 constructions.

7.2 CONSTRUCTION 3

A Line Perpendicular to a Given Line *l*, Passing Through a Given Point Not on *l*

Two methods are shown, both of which should be known.

Worked Example 7.1

Construct a line perpendicular to the line *l*, passing through the point *A* not on the line *l*.

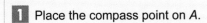

A •

_____

l

Solution Using a Compass and Straight Edge

1 Place the compass point on *A*.

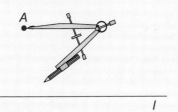

2 Draw an arc that intersects the line *l* at two points. Label them *P*, *Q*.

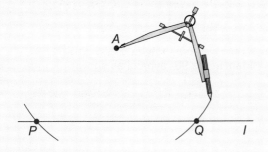

3 Place the compass point on *P* and draw an arc below the line.

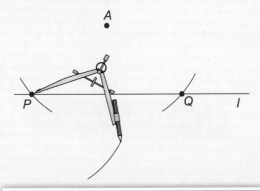

Note: The compass width must be more than half the distance from *P* to *Q*.

4 Without changing the compass width, place the compass point on *Q* and draw an overlapping arc.

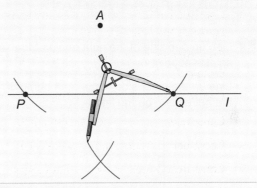

5 Mark the point where the arcs intersect.

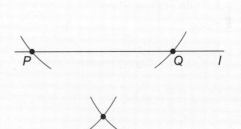

6 Using a straight edge, draw a line through this point and the point *A*.

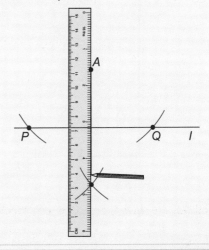

7 This line is perpendicular to the line *l* and passes through the point *A*.

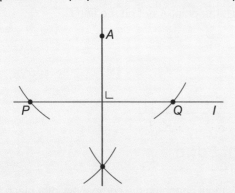

Mark in the 90° symbol as shown.

Check your work:

- Verify, with your protractor, the 90° angle.
- Verify, with your ruler or compass, that [*PQ*] is bisected.

Solution Using a Set Square

1 Line up one side of the right angle of the set square at point *A*.

Line up the other side of the right angle of the set square on the line *l*.

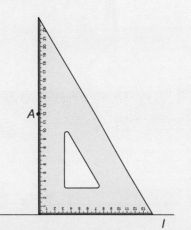

2 Draw a line from the line *l* through the point *A*.

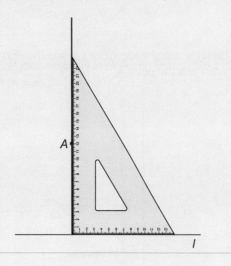

3 This line is perpendicular to the line *l* and passes through the point *A*.

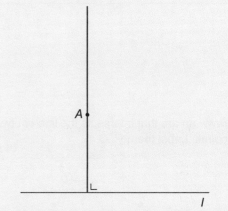

Mark in the 90° symbol as shown.

ACTIVITIES 7.1, 7.2

7.3 CONSTRUCTION 7

Division of a Line Segment into Any Number of Equal Segments, Without Measuring It

Worked Example 7.2

Divide the line segment [AB] into **five** equal segments, without measuring it.

Solution

1 From point A, draw a ray at an acute angle to the given line segment. (Note: The larger the number of equal segments, the less acute the angle.)

2 Place the compass point on A.

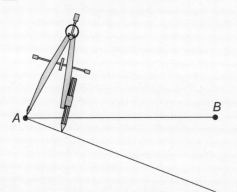

3 Using the same compass width, mark off **five** equal arcs along the ray. (Use a suitable compass width.)

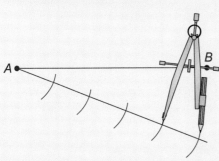

4 Label the points of intersection R, S, T, U and V.

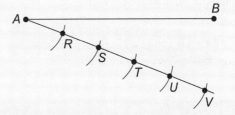

5 Join the last point V to the point B on the line segment, using a straight edge.

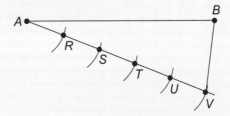

6 Line the set square up with the line segment [VB], and line the straight edge up with the set square as shown.

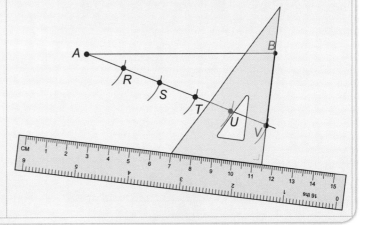

CONSTRUCTIONS

7

7 Slide the set square along using the straight edge as a base. Draw a line segment from *U, T, S* and *R* to the line segment [*AB*] using the set square.
(Keep the straight edge fixed while doing this.)

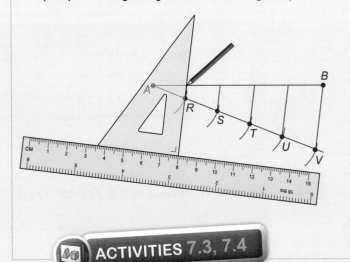

ACTIVITIES 7.3, 7.4

8 Label the points of intersection with the line segment [*AB*] as points *C, D, E* and *F*.

The line segment [*AB*] is now divided into five equal segments.

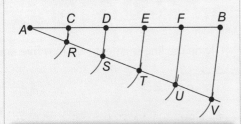

Note: Make sure to mark in the required points of intersection on the given line segment [*AB*]. Check your work using a ruler or compass.

Exercise 7.1

1. Copy the following figures into your copybook. Construct a line perpendicular to the given line passing through the given point (that is not on the line), **using only a compass and a straight edge**.

(i)

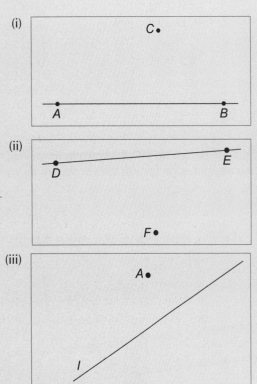

(ii)

(iii)

(iv)

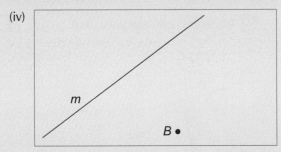

(v)

(vi)

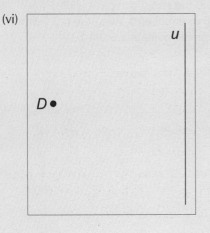

2. Copy the following figures into your copybook. In each case construct lines perpendicular to the given line passing through each of the given points **using a set square**.

(i)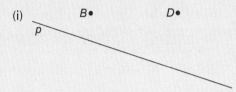

(ii)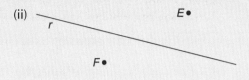

3. Draw a line segment [GH] of length 7.5 cm. Divide this line segment into four equal parts without measuring it.

4. Draw a line segment [AB] of length 11 cm. Divide this line segment into three equal parts without measuring it.

5. Draw a line segment [CD] of length 6 cm. Divide this line segment into four equal segments using only a compass, a straight edge and a set square.

6. Draw a line *l*, and then mark a point A that is 5 cm above this line and mark a point B that is 5 cm below the line. Construct a line through A that is perpendicular to *l*, and also construct a line through B that is perpendicular to *l*.

7. Draw a line segment [EF] of length 13 cm. Divide this line segment into five equal segments without measuring it.

---

8. (i) Draw a line segment [CD] where |CD| = 10 cm.

(ii) Mark a point X that is 5 cm above [CD] as shown.

X

C ———————————————— D

(iii) Using only a compass and straight edge, construct a line perpendicular to CD through the point X.

(iv) Construct a line that is parallel to CD through the point X.

(v) Mark a point Y on this line to the right of the point X, so that |XY| = 10 cm.

(vi) Draw the line segment [DY].

(vii) What type of quadrilateral is the shape CXYD?

9. Draw a line segment [XY] of length 9 cm. Divide this line segment into six equal parts without measuring it.

10. Two new roads are to be built, linking two towns to a motorway as shown. The roads must connect to the motorway using the shortest distance possible.

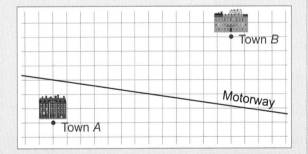

(i) Using only a compass and a straight edge, show the possible locations of the two roads.

(ii) A new road is to run through town A, parallel to the motorway. Show on your construction the location of this new road.

11. (a) (i) Construct the line segment [AB] where |AB| = 8 cm.

   (ii) Without measuring, divide this line segment into four equal parts.

   (iii) Check your construction using a ruler.

(b) Lauren tells her friend Mia that she uses a different method to divide a line segment into four equal parts. She explains that she uses the method for the perpendicular bisector of a line segment.

   (i) Attempt to divide a line segment of 8 cm into four equal parts using this method.

   (ii) Lauren claims that she can divide any line segment into *n* equal parts using the above method. Mia objects, saying that this method will only work for certain values of *n*. Who is correct? In your answer, explain what you think Mia's objection is.

12. A map/plan showing the beginning of Runway 5 at Mombasa Airport, Kenya, is shown below.

To make a safe landing, an aeroplane must travel in a straight line that is perpendicular to the front edge of the runway and that passes over the approach beacon.

Using only a compass and a straight edge, construct the flight path for a safe final approach.

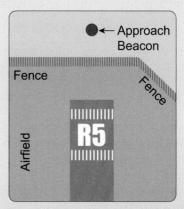

Revision Exercises

1. Construct the following angles using a protractor and a straight edge:

   (i) 45°   (ii) 105°   (iii) 290°

   Bisect each of the constructed angles using only a compass and a straight edge.

2. Draw the following line segments and construct the perpendicular bisector of each line segment:

   (i) [AB], where |AB| = 6 cm

   (ii) [CD], where |CD| = 105 mm

3. Draw a line XY and the points P and Q as shown.

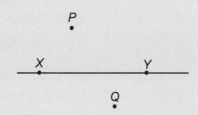

   (i) Construct a line perpendicular to XY through the point P, using only a compass and a straight edge.

   (ii) Construct a line perpendicular to XY through the point Q, using a set square.

4. Copy the figure below into your copybook.

A   C   B   D

   (i) Construct a line perpendicular to AB through the point C, using only a compass and a straight edge.

   (ii) Construct a line perpendicular to AB through the point D, using a set square.

5. Copy the following figure into your copybook.

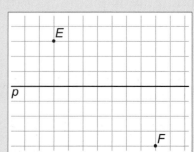

Construct a line through E, parallel to the given line, using only a compass and a straight edge. Do the same for point F.

6. Draw a line *s*, and then mark a point *T*, 4 cm above this line, and a point *U*, 5 cm below this line. Using only a compass and a straight edge:

   (i) Construct a line parallel to the line *s* passing through the point *T*.

   (ii) Construct a line parallel to the line *s* passing through the point *U*.

7. Draw a line segment [*PQ*] of length 11 cm. Divide this line segment into five equal segments without measuring it.

8. Draw a line segment [*AB*] of length 10 cm. Divide this line segment into four equal segments without measuring it.

   Explain an alternative method to divide a line segment into four equal segments without measuring it.

9. Copy the following figures into your copybook. In each case, construct the given line segment on the given ray.

   (i)

   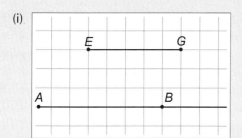

   (ii)

   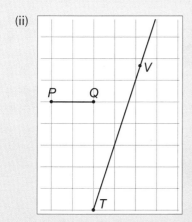

10. Construct the following angles using a protractor:

    (i) |∠*ABC*| = 80° on the ray [*AB*.

    (ii) |∠*DEF*| = 145° on the ray *EF*].

    (iii) |∠*PQR*| = 260° on the ray *PQ*].

    (iv) |∠*XYZ*| = 310° on the ray *XY*].

Construct the following triangles in Questions 11–23. Don't forget to check that your constructions have the correct dimensions. Diagrams are not to scale.

11. Triangle *DEF* where |*DE*| = 6 cm, |*EF*| = 10 cm and |*DF*| = 9 cm.

    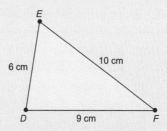

12. Triangle *DEF*, using the measurements shown in the diagram.

    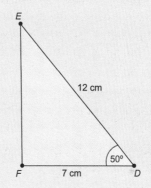

13. Triangle *DEF* where |∠*EDF*| = 40°, |∠*DFE*| = 50° and |*DF*| = 11 cm.

    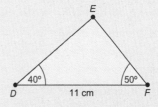

14. Triangle *DEF*, using the measurements shown in the diagram.

    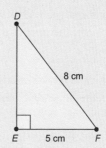

15. Triangle *DEF* where |∠*DEF*| = 55°,
|∠*EFD*| = 90° and |*EF*| = 6 cm.

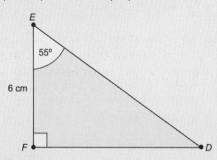

16. Triangle *GHI*, using the measurements shown in the diagram.

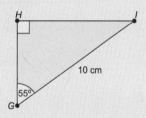

17. Triangle *GHI* where |*GI*| = 12.5 cm,
|*GH*| = 6 cm and |*HI*| = 8 cm.

18. Triangle *ABC* where |*AB*| = 8 cm,
|*BC*| = $\frac{5}{4}$|*AB*| and |*AC*| = $\frac{3}{4}$|*AB*|.

19. Triangle *TUV* where |*TV*| = 3.5 cm,
|*UV*| = 2.5 cm and |∠*TVU*| = 80°.

20. Triangle *JKL* where |∠*KJL*| = 75°,
|∠*JLK*| = 35° and |*JL*| = 6 cm.

21. Triangle *PQR* where |∠*PQR*| = 90°,
|*PQ*| = 9.5 cm and |*PR*| = 10 cm.

22. Triangle *STU* where |*ST*| = 45 mm,
|∠*STU*| = 90° and |∠*SUT*| = 45°.

23. Triangle *ABC* where |∠*ACB*| = 45°,
|*CA*| = 6 cm and |∠*CBA*| = 90°.

24. Construct the square *IJKL* where |*IJ*| = 5 cm.

25. Construct the rectangle *UVWX* where
|*UV*| = 5 cm and the area of the rectangle
UVWX is 30 cm².

26. (i) Using a protractor and straight edge,
construct the angle *ABC* such that
|∠*ABC*| = 75°.

(ii) Show, using only a compass and a straight
edge, how to construct the angle *DEF*
where |∠*DEF*| = |∠*ABC*|.

27. (i) Construct a circle of diameter 12 cm
with centre *O*.

(ii) Draw a chord [*AB*] of the circle as
shown in the diagram below.

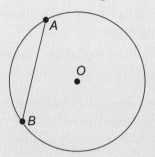

(iii) Construct a line perpendicular to [*AB*]
through the point *O*.

(iv) Label as *X* the point where this
perpendicular line intersects the line
segment [*AB*].

(v) Find |*AX*| and |*XB*|.
What do your measurements tell you
about these line segments?

(vi) Draw another chord [*BC*].

(vii) Construct the perpendicular bisector
of [*BC*].

(viii) Does this line pass through the point *O*?

28. A town planner wishes to build a shopping
centre that is the same distance from three
towns.

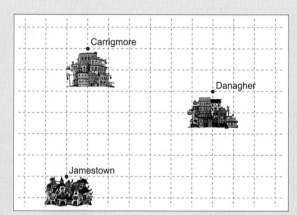

(i) Show by construction, and using an
appropriate scale, how this could be
achieved.

(*Note:* You can set your own figures for
the distance between the towns.)

(ii) Using your construction, find the
distance between the shopping centre
and any one of these towns.

29. A cable anchor 8 m long connects to the top of a vertical flagpole as shown on the diagram.

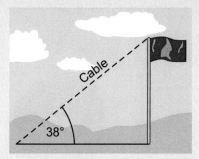

- (i) Construct the triangle shown in the diagram, using an appropriate scale.
- (ii) Find the perpendicular height of the flagpole, using a ruler.
- (iii) Use trigonometry to check your answer.

30. A diagram (not to scale) with dimensions for a piece of a metal for a machine is shown. Construct a scaled drawing of the metal piece.

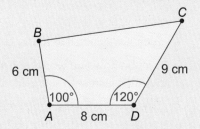

A machinist must drill two holes into this piece.

The first hole must be drilled midway between the points A and C.

The second hole must be drilled 3 cm away from B and at an equal distance from the sides $[AB]$ and $[BC]$.

Mark the position for both drill holes, using only a straight edge and a compass.

31. A ship is at a point C, 35 km from a harbour at A and 60 km from a harbour at B. The angle between the ship and the two harbours is 130°.

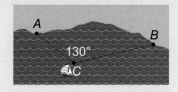

- (i) Construct this diagram, using an appropriate scale.
- (ii) Using measurements taken from your construction, find the shortest distance between the two harbours. (Give your answer to the nearest kilometre.)

- (iii) Show the path a ship would have to travel along if it was, at all times, to keep an equal distance from each harbour.

32. Lucy is to cut semicircular sheets of metal of radius 7 cm into four equal sectors. Using only a compass and a straight edge, divide the semicircle into four equal sectors.

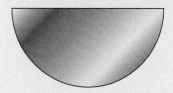

33. A field is in the shape of a rhombus. The sides of this field each measure 45 m.

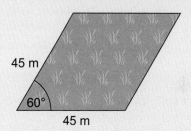

- (i) Construct an appropriately scaled diagram of this field. Explain each step of your construction.
- (ii) Using measurements taken from your construction, find the shortest distance between two parallel sides of the field.

34. The position of three railway stations on a circular model railway track is shown on a Cartesian plane.

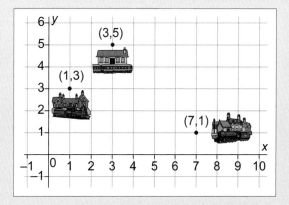

Find, using only a straight edge and a compass, the centre of the circular railway track and hence, construct the railway track.

(*Note:* Ensure that the scale for the *x*-axis and *y*-axis is in the ratio 1 : 1.)

35. A design for a new storage container is shown. Construct this diagram, using an appropriate scale.

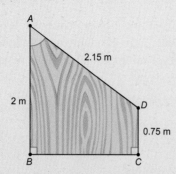

Use your construction to find the length [BC].

36. (i) Construct the following diagram of a square lawn inscribed in a circular garden of radius 8 m, using an appropriate scale. O is the centre of the garden.

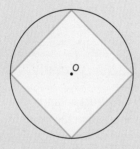

(ii) Using measurements from your construction, find the dimensions of the lawn to one decimal place.

(iii) Check your answer using algebra.

(iv) What percentage of the garden is not lawn? Answer correct to the nearest whole number.

37. By constructing a right-angled triangle, find $\sqrt{52}$ to one decimal place. Explain all steps of your construction.

38. (i) Construct a line parallel to the given line through the given point, in the diagram below. You may only use a straight edge and compass.

• Y

l

(ii) In your copybook, draw an acute angle and bisect it. You may only use a straight edge and compass.

(iii) In 1832, the French mathematician Évariste Galois proved that it is impossible to trisect an angle (divide an angle into three equal parts) using only a compass and straight edge.

His proof was ground-breaking, as the Greek mathematician Archimedes had claimed that trisection in this way was possible.

Now, imagine we lived in a world in which it **was** possible to trisect an angle.

Describe how you would construct an angle 20 degrees in size using only a compass and straight edge.

39. Ronan O'Gara is preparing to take a kick at goal as represented in the diagram below. Construct the ray that would represent the flight path of the ball if his kick was perfectly straight and passed midway between the posts.

Ball

Post   Post

40.

In 2008, Beijing hosted the Olympic Summer Games. The iconic Bird's Nest stadium (above) played host to the track and field events.

A standard Olympic athletics track is approximately composed of two 87-metre straights connected by two semicircular bends each of radius length 36 metres.

(i) Using a scale of 1 cm = 6 m, construct a diagram of a standard Olympic athletics track.

(ii) Hence, calculate, to the nearest metre, the straight-line distance between the start line (at the end of the home straight) and the half-way point on the track (at the end of the back straight).

8 chapter

Statistics

Learning Outcomes

In this chapter you will learn:

- ➲ How to evaluate the reliability of data and data sources

- ➲ How to select a sample from a population (simple random sample)

- ➲ How sampling variability influences the use of sample information to make statements about the population

- ➲ How to recognise the importance of representativeness so as to avoid biased samples

- ➲ How to use back-to-back stem-and-leaf plots

- ➲ How to recognise the existence of outliers

- ➲ How to find the mean of a grouped frequency distribution

- ➲ How to calculate quartiles and the interquartile range and use these to describe data

- ➲ How to draw conclusions from graphical and numerical summaries of data, recognising assumptions and limitations

8.1 COLLECTING DATA

The subject of **statistics** is largely about using sample data to make generalisations about the whole population.

> The **population** is the entire group that is being studied.

> A **sample** is a group that is selected from the population.

Types of Data

All data collected is either categorical or numerical. Questions that cannot be answered with numbers provide **categorical data**. For example, 'What is your favourite band?' Questions that can be answered with numbers provide **numerical data**. For example, 'How many houses were built in Ireland in 2011?' All categorical data is either **nominal** or **ordered**. All numerical data is either **discrete** or **continuous**.

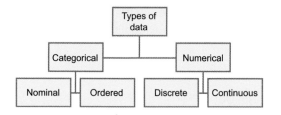

> Numerical data that consists of values that move in steps within a specified range is called **discrete numerical data**. For example, values that move in units. The question 'How many books are in your school bag?' generates discrete numerical data. Or, say, values that move in halves. The question 'What is your shoe size?' generates discrete numerical data, since answers would be of the form ... 6, $6\frac{1}{2}$, 7, $7\frac{1}{2}$, ...

> Numerical data that can take on any value within a specified range is called **continuous numerical data**. For example, 'What height are you?' or 'How long does it take you to travel to school in the morning?' are questions that generate continuous numerical data.

> Categorical data that can be ordered is called **ordered categorical data**. For example, 'What grade did you get in your last maths exam?' generates ordered categorical data.

> Categorical data that cannot be ordered is called **nominal categorical data**. For example, 'What is your favourite colour?' generates nominal categorical data.

Worked Example 8.1

A machine fills packets with salt. The label on each packet says that the contents weigh 1,500 g.
Here is a list of words:

> continuous   ordered   discrete   nominal   numerical   categorical

Use words from the list to complete the following sentences:

   (i)   The weights of the packets of salt are _____ and _____ data.

   (ii) The number of packets of salt filled by the machine is _____ and _____ data.

   (iii) The names of the countries in which the salt could be manufactured are _____ and
         _____ data.

Solution

   (i)   The weights of the packets of salt are numerical and continuous data.

   (ii) The number of packets of salt filled by the machine is numerical and discrete data.

   (iii) The names of the countries in which the salt could be manufactured are categorical and
         nominal data.

Sampling

Obtaining information from part of a population is called **sampling**. Collecting data from every member of a population is not always practical as it might require too much time and effort, or may not even be possible. So sampling is necessary. For example, a company producing batteries for TV remote controls wants to find out the average lifetime of its batteries. If it tested the entire population, there would be no batteries left to sell! So it needs to test a sample.

> A **census** is a survey of the whole population.

Biased Samples

Biased samples are samples that do not represent the population from which they are taken. A sample that is not representative of the population is of no use. Such a sample should never be used in any statistical investigation.

Surveys conducted through the Internet, telephone call-in surveys to radio stations and television programmes, or mail-in surveys generate biased samples. This is because they produce 'self-selected' samples – people take part in the surveys on their own initiative rather than being selected by a researcher. Generally speaking, people with strong opinions are more likely to take part in such surveys. People who do not have strong opinions are less likely to respond, hence the sample is biased.

How can we eliminate bias? Bias can be eliminated by taking a **random sample**. Every member of the population has an equal chance of being included in a random sample.

> A **sampling frame** is a list of all those within a population who can be sampled.

A random sample of size *n* is a **simple random sample** if every possible sample of size *n* within the population has an equal chance of being selected. In a simple random sample, every member of the population has an equal chance of being selected.

Consider a classroom with 60 students arranged in six rows of 10 students each. A teacher selects a sample of 10 students by rolling a die and selecting the row corresponding to the outcome. Every student has an equal chance of being in the sample, but not every possible group of 10 has a chance of being in the sample. For example, a student from Row 1 and a student from Row 6 can never be together in a sample. Therefore, this is not a simple random sample.

Worked Example 8.2

Here is a random number table:

51	19	53	84	38
63	9	93	11	54
31	93	90	66	65
56	92	15	46	93
92	11	27	6	9

John wants to take a random sample of five people from a list of 50 people. He starts from the top left of the table and works across the table row by row.

(i) Write down the set of numbers John could use.

(ii) Explain how John could use these numbers to get his sample.

Solution

(i) As the population size is 50, John will accept only numbers between 1 and 50. The first number, 51, has to be discarded, as it is greater than 50. So the first number John could use is 19. The next two numbers, 53 and 84, have to be discarded, as they are greater than 50, so the second number of use is 38. Continuing in this fashion, we obtain the following list of numbers: 19, 38, 9, 11, 31.

(ii) John could sort the list of 50 names in alphabetical order and designate the first person on the list as number 1, the second person as number 2, and so on. The people assigned the numbers 19, 38, 9, 11 and 31 will make up the sample.

Sampling Variability

Suppose the mean height of all 16-year-old males in the country is 176 cm. (In a real problem, of course, you would never know exactly this value.) Then, suppose you take a random sample from this population and compute the mean height of the sample. Will it be exactly 176 cm? Probably not. Most likely it will be close to 176 cm, especially if the sample size is large. If another sample is taken, will the mean height of the new sample be exactly the same as the mean of the original sample? Again, probably not. The difference between the mean height of a sample and the mean of the population is known as the **sampling error**. In practice we never know the sampling error, as we never know the mean of the population. (After all, we are looking for an estimate of the mean of the population.)

Sampling variability refers to the difference between sample statistics from different samples (e.g. the difference between one sample mean and another sample mean).

STATISTICS

Sampling error refers to the difference between a sample statistic and a true population parameter (e.g. the difference between a sample mean and the true population mean).

Reducing the amount of sampling error helps us make more accurate generalisations about the whole population when using sample data. One way in which this can often be done is by increasing the sample size.

 ACTIVITY 8.1

Worked Example 8.3

A group of five boys measured each other's heights in centimetres. The results are: 168, 175, 178, 182, 190.

The boys are investigating the concept of sampling variability. They decide to select all possible samples of size 3 from the five measurements. Their results are shown in the table below:

Sample 1	168	175	178
Sample 2	168	175	182
Sample 3	168	175	190
Sample 4	168	178	182
Sample 5	168	178	190
Sample 6	168	182	190
Sample 7	175	178	182
Sample 8	175	178	190
Sample 9	175	182	190
Sample 10	178	182	190

(i) Calculate the mean height of the five boys.

(ii) Calculate each sample mean height (correct to two decimal places).

(iii) Calculate the mean value of the means. What do you notice?

(iv) What is the probability of selecting a random sample of size 3 whose mean is within 1 cm of the true mean?

(v) What is the probability of selecting a random sample of size 3 whose mean is greater than 1 cm but less than 2 cm from the true mean?

Solution

(i) Mean $= \dfrac{168 + 175 + 178 + 182 + 190}{5} = 178.6$ cm

(ii)

				Mean (cm)
Sample 1	168	175	178	173.67
Sample 2	168	175	182	175
Sample 3	168	175	190	177.67
Sample 4	168	178	182	176
Sample 5	168	178	190	178.67
Sample 6	168	182	190	180
Sample 7	175	178	182	178.33
Sample 8	175	178	190	181
Sample 9	175	182	190	182.33
Sample 10	178	182	190	183.33

(iii) Mean $= \dfrac{173.67 + 175 + 177.67 + 176 + 178.67 + 180 + 178.33 + 181 + 182.33 + 183.33}{10}$

$= 178.6$ cm

Therefore, the mean of the means is equal to the mean of the population.

(iv) There are three samples whose mean is within 1 cm of the true mean (Samples 3, 5 and 7). Therefore, the probability of selecting a sample within 1 cm of the true mean is $\frac{3}{10} = 0.3$.

(v) There is just one sample (Sample 6) whose mean is greater than 1 cm but less than 2 cm from the true mean. Therefore, the probability of selecting a sample whose mean is greater than 1 cm but less than 2 cm from the true mean is $\frac{1}{10} = 0.1$.

 Exercise 8.1

1. A shop sells shoes. Use the most appropriate words from the list below to complete the sentences.

   sample   ordered   discrete   numerical   continuous   categorical   nominal

   (i) The number of pairs of shoes sold by the shop is ~~Discrete~~ *numerical* data. *categorical*

   (ii) The colour of the shoes is ~~nominal~~ data.

   (iii) The weight of the shoes is ~~continuous~~ *numerical*

   (iv) A selection of shoes chosen from the back of the shop is called a ____ *sample*

2. The manager of a factory wants to carry out a survey to find out the workers' views on the sale of overalls at the factory. There are 1,800 workers in the factory.

   (i) Give two reasons why the manager would take a sample rather than a census to find out the workers' views.

   (ii) The manager has decided to use a questionnaire to find out the workers' views on the sale of overalls at the factory. One of the questions on the questionnaire is shown below:

   > Give one reason why you support the idea of having overalls sold at the factory.

   Write down one criticism of this question.

   (iii) The manager's assistant distributes the questionnaire to the first 30 workers to arrive at the factory on a particular morning. Will the assistant's sample be representative of all workers, or will it be biased? Explain your answer in detail.

3. Dublin Bus wishes to obtain opinions on the quality of its service.

   (i) Explain why a sample of its customers should be taken, rather than a census.

   (ii) The general manager of Dublin Bus suggests that everyone on the 46A bus on Monday morning should be surveyed. Give two possible sources of bias in this sample.

   (iii) An afternoon radio programme asks listeners to call in with their views on the quality of the Dublin Bus company's services. Why might the views of those calling into the programme not be representative of all Dublin Bus customers? Give two possible reasons.

   (iv) Describe a suitable way in which Dublin Bus might select a representative sample of its customers.

4. Eoin wants to choose a sample of size 8 from his class. He writes down all the students' names on pieces of paper, puts all the boys' names in one bag and all the girls' names in another bag. He then chooses, without looking, four pieces of paper from each bag.

   (i) Explain why Eoin's sample is random.

   (ii) Explain why Eoin's sample is not a simple random sample.

   (iii) Explain how Eoin could obtain a simple random sample of eight students from his class.

5. Here is an extract from a table of random numbers.

86	13	84	10	7	30	39	5	97	96	88	7	37	26	4	89	13	48	19	20
60	78	48	12	99	47	9	46	91	33	17	21	3	94	79	0	8	50	40	16
78	48	6	37	82	26	1	6	64	65	94	41	17	26	74	66	61	93	14	97

   (i) Starting from the first line and the fifth column with the number 7, and reading across the table, from left to right, write down ten random numbers betweeen 0 and 69.

   (ii) Explain how you could use the above table of random numbers to select a sample of 12 students from 80 students.

6. Thomas is investigating if distance from a polling station affects whether people usually vote in his town. He decides to select a simple random sample of 50 people from the register of electors, use the telephone directory to find the telephone numbers of the people in the sample and then carry out a telephone survey.

   (i) Define the population for this survey.

   (ii) What obstacles could Thomas encounter in carrying out this survey?

   (iii) One question he uses is, 'What is the distance from your house to the polling station?' Give one criticism of this question.

7. Bob wants to find out what is the most popular PlayStation game in his school. He randomly selects a group of First Year boys and asks them to name their favourite PlayStation game. Using his results, he concludes that *Call of Duty* is the most popular game in the school.

   (i) Define the population for this survey.
   (ii) Why is the sample that Bob uses non-representative of the school population?
   (iii) Describe an improved way in which Bob could select a suitable sample for his study.

8. A researcher determines that she needs results from at least 400 subjects to conduct a study. To compensate for low return rates, she mails the survey to 5,000 subjects. She receives 750 responses. Is the sample of 750 responses a good sample for her to use? Explain.

9. Give one example of each of the following:

   (i) A non-random sample
   (ii) A simple random sample
   (iii) A random sample that is not a simple random sample

10. Using stopwatches, a group of five girls asked each other to estimate 80 seconds. The results (in seconds) are: 68, 75, 78, 82, 87.

   The girls are investigating the concept of sampling variability. They decide to select all possible samples of size 3 from the five estimates. Their results are shown in the table below:

Sample 1	68	75	78
Sample 2	68	75	82
Sample 3	68	75	87
Sample 4	68	78	82
Sample 5	68	78	87
Sample 6	68	82	87
Sample 7	75	78	82
Sample 8	75	78	87
Sample 9	75	82	87
Sample 10	78	82	87

(i) Calculate the mean estimated time for the five girls.

(ii) Calculate the mean estimated time of each sample.

(iii) Calculate the mean value of the means. What do you notice?

(iv) What is the probability of selecting a random sample of size 3 whose mean is within 1 second of the true mean?

(v) What is the probability of selecting a random sample of size 3 whose mean is greater than 1 second but less than 2 seconds from the true mean?

11. A company making light bulbs advertises that less than 1% of its bulbs have defects. To guarantee this claim the company tests a percentage of bulbs produced every day.

There are three different testing methods currently in use to check daily production:

Method 1: Test every 400th bulb produced.

Method 2: Test 200 randomly selected bulbs at the end of the day. A computer program selects the bulbs at random by batch number. Each bulb has a unique batch number.

Method 3: Test every bulb produced between 12:59 and 13:00 that day.

(i) Complete the table below:

	Method 1	**Method 2**	**Method 3**
Number of bulbs tested			292
Number of defects	3		4
Proportion of defects		$\dfrac{2}{200}$ (= 1%)	
Total daily production:	140,000		

(ii) Does any method of testing provide some evidence that contradicts the company's claim? Say which method(s) and explain the evidence.

(iii) Which of the three methods is the only method that involves simple random sampling? Give reasons for your answer.

(iv) In your opinion, which method is most likely to generate a biased sample of daily production? Explain your answer.

(v) Excluding the method you outlined in part (iv) above, which of the remaining two methods would you choose as the most suitable method of testing to use? Why?

(vi) How could you adjust the method of testing you outlined in part (v) above so that the company's claim could be accepted/rejected with more certainty?

(vii) What disadvantages could such an adjustment lead to?

8.2 GRAPHS AND CHARTS

We display data using **charts** and **diagrams** so that we can see patterns, relationships and trends in the data. A display will reveal things that you are not likely to see in a table of numbers. On this course you need to be able to construct **bar charts**, **line plots**, **pie charts**, **stem-and-leaf plots** and **histograms**. However, you also need to develop the skill of interpreting many other types of display.

Displaying Categorical Data

Bar charts, pie charts and line plots are usually used to represent **categorical data**.

Bar charts show the count or frequency for each category next to each other for easy comparison. Bar charts can be either vertical or horizontal.

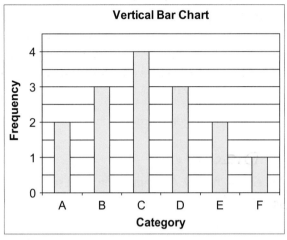

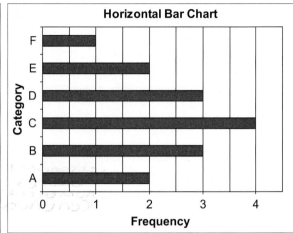

Pie charts show the proportion that each category makes of the total.

Line plots are similar to bar charts. A line plot uses symbols, usually *x*'s, or dots, to represent the count or frequency for each category.

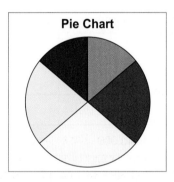

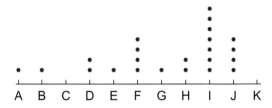

Worked Example 8.4

The table shows the number of passengers, by passenger category, who survived the sinking of the *Titanic*.

Passenger category	Number saved
Children, First Class	6
Children, Second Class	24
Women, First Class	140
Women, Crew	20
Women, Second Class	80
Women, Third Class	76
Children, Third Class	27
Men, First Class	57
Men, Crew	192
Men, Third Class	75
Men, Second Class	14

Source: British Parliamentary Papers, Shipping Casualties (Loss of Steamship, *Titanic*), 1912.

(i) Construct a horizontal bar chart displaying, by passenger category, the number of people saved from the sinking of the *Titanic*.

(ii) 'A male crew member had a better chance of survival than any other category of passenger and a First Class child had the least chance of survival.' Discuss the validity of this statement.

(iii) There were 885 male crew on board the *Titanic* and six First Class children. Use pie charts to display the survival rates for these two different passenger categories.

(iv) If a similar disaster were to take place today in exactly the same circumstances (i.e. same type of ship, same number of passengers, same weather conditions, same damage done to the ship, etc.), what would be the probability of survival for a male crew member? Answer as a percentage, correct to the nearest whole number.

Solution

(i)

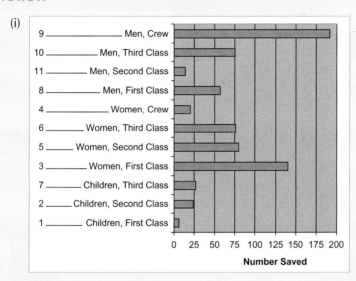

(ii) There were more male crew members saved than First Class children, but we cannot say that a male crew member had a better chance of survival than any other category of passenger, as the table does not give us the number of male crew members that were on board the ship. Similarly, we are not told the number of First Class children on board.

(iii) **Male Crew**

Angle for survival: $\dfrac{192}{885} \times 360°$

$\approx 78°$

First Class Children

Angle for survival: $\dfrac{6}{6} \times 360°$

$= 360°$

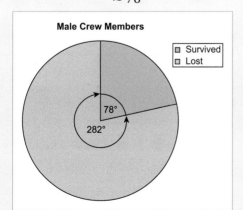

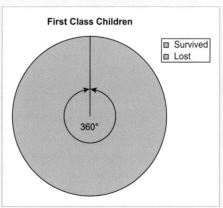

(iv) Probability of survival $= \dfrac{192}{885}$

$= \dfrac{64}{295}$

$\approx 22\%$

Displaying Numerical Data

When displaying **discrete numerical distributions**, we usually use bar charts, stem-and-leaf plots or line plots. Stem-and-leaf plots and histograms are used to display **continuous numerical distributions**.

> Outliers are extreme values that are not typical of the other values in the data set.

Histograms or stem-and-leaf plots that are symmetrical about the centre represent symmetric distributions. The distribution of heights of male third-year students in a school is generally a reasonably symmetric distribution.

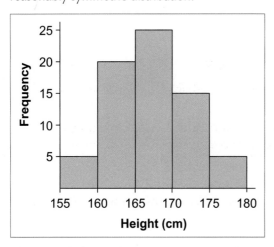

Distributions that tail to the right are called skewed right or positively skewed distributions. The distribution of total annual wages paid out by Premier League clubs is an example of a skewed right distribution.

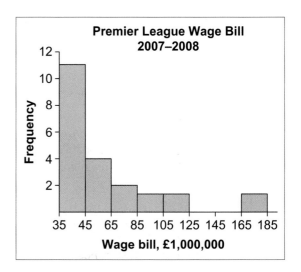

Distributions that tail to the left are called skewed left or negatively skewed distributions. An example of negatively skewed data would be age at retirement. Most people retire in their mid-sixties or older, with fewer retiring at younger ages. The histogram shows the retiring ages of 100 randomly selected retired people.

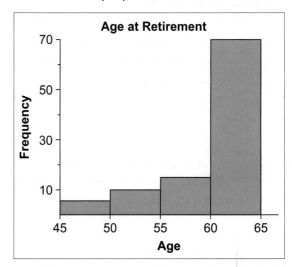

STATISTICS

Worked Example 8.5

The data below give the number of hurricanes that happened each year in the USA from 1944 to 2000, as reported by *Science* magazine.

3, 2, 1, 2, 4, 3, 7, 2, 3, 3, 2, 5, 2, 2, 4, 2, 2, 6, 0, 2, 5, 1, 3, 1, 0, 3, 2, 1, 0, 1, 2, 3, 2, 1, 2, 2, 2, 3, 1, 1, 1, 3, 0, 1, 3, 2, 1, 2, 1, 1, 0, 5, 6, 1, 3, 5, 3

(i)   Organise the data in a frequency table.

(ii) Display the data on a line plot.

(iii) Describe the distribution.

Solution

(i)

Number of hurricanes	0	1	2	3	4	5	6	7
Frequency	5	14	17	12	2	4	2	1

(ii)

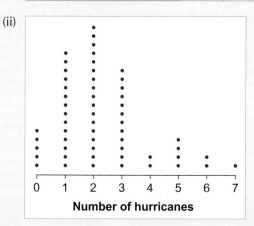

(iii) The most frequent number of hurricanes per year is two.

Most of the values are clustered around 2.

There is a tail to the right of the line plot, i.e. the distribution is skewed right. This suggests a large variation in the data.

Describing a distribution

When describing a distribution, make reference to each of the following:

1. **Shape** Is the distribution symmetric, skewed left, or skewed right?

2. **Centre of the distribution** Where is most of the data centred? If possible, give a measure of centre, such as the mean, median or mode.

3. **Spread of the distribution** Is there a large variation in the data? If possible, give a measure of spread, such as the range or interquartile range (IQR) (covered later in chapter).

4. **Outliers** Are there any outliers in the data?

Back-to-Back Stem-and-Leaf Plots

A back-to-back stem-and-leaf plot (or diagram) is a useful way of comparing data from two different sets of data. Both sets of data must be ordered, and there must be two keys.

Worked Example 8.6

Here is a back-to-back stem-and-leaf diagram showing the marks obtained by 30 girls and 30 boys in the same maths test. The girls' marks are on the left-hand side of the diagram.

Girls' marks	Stem	Boys' marks
9	0	7, 9
7, 2	1	3, 4
8	2	9
9, 6, 6	3	5, 7, 9
8, 8, 6, 6, 6, 4, 2, 2	4	3, 4, 4
8, 6, 0	5	2, 2, 3, 5, 7, 7, 8
8, 2	6	1, 2, 5, 8, 9
9, 6, 4	7	3, 4, 5, 9
8, 5, 2, 0	8	4, 7
Key: 4|7| = 74 marks 9, 8, 3	9	1 Key: |4|3 = 43 marks

(i) What was the highest mark achieved in the test?

(ii) What was the lowest mark achieved?

(iii) If 50 is the pass mark, did more boys or girls pass the test? Explain your answer.

(iv) The teacher decides to set a benchmark of X so that only the top 20% of students get a result of more than X. Calculate the value of X.

Solution

(i) The highest mark achieved was 99 (by a girl).

(ii) The lowest mark achieved was 7 (by a boy).

(iii) 19 boys passed the test and 15 girls passed. Therefore, more boys than girls passed the test.

(iv) 20% of 60 = 12. The 12th highest mark is 79, so X = 78.

Worked Example 8.7

The tables below give the arm span measurements for 10 boys and 10 girls. All measurements are given in centimetres.

Boys				
165	149	156	168	150
162	158	147	130	150

Girls				
150	160	156	147	148
132	158	157	172	153

Show these data on a back-to-back stem-and-leaf diagram.

Solution

Note: It is important to order the data before commencing with the ordered stem-and-leaf plot.

Girls		Boys
2	13	0
8, 7	14	7, 9
8, 7, 6, 3, 0	15	0, 0, 6, 8
0	16	2, 5, 8
2	17	

Key: 7|14| = 147 cm   Key: |14|9 = 149 cm

Note: Any piece of data from the question can be used as a key.

Exercise 8.2

1. The table shown details the number of each type of house on an estate. There are 360 houses in the estate.

Type of house	Number
Terraced	170
Semi-detached	
Detached	20
Bungalow	66

   (i) How many semi-detached houses are on the estate?

   (ii) Represent these data on a pie chart.

   (iii) What percentage of houses in the estate are detached?

   (iv) A bungalow on the estate has recently sold for €125,000. An estate agent has estimated the ratio of the selling price of a detached house to the selling price of a bungalow to be 3:2. Using the estate agent's estimate, find the selling price of a detached house.

2. The composite bar chart shows the nutritional content of broccoli and spinach.

(i) What percentage of broccoli is protein?

(ii) A head of broccoli weighs 560 g. Use the chart to estimate the number of grams of fat in the broccoli.

(iii) James says that a head of broccoli has more carbohydrates than a head of spinach. Explain why James may not be right.

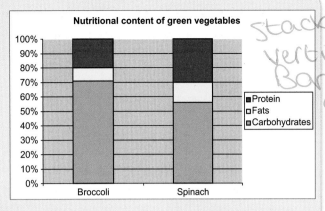

stacked verticle Bar chart

(iv) James has weighed a head of broccoli and a head of spinach. He has found that the spinach is 1.4 times heavier than the broccoli. If the spinach contains 180 g of protein, what is the weight of the head of broccoli?

3. The comparative pie charts show the changing proportions of passengers who left Ireland by sea and by air in 2000 and 2010.

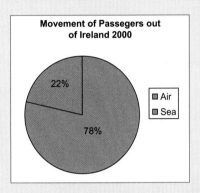
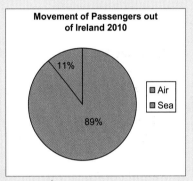

(i) 'Twice as many passengers left Ireland by sea in 2000 than left by sea in 2010.' Explain why this statement may not be right.

(ii) According to the CSO, 8,237,776 passengers left Ireland by air in 2000. How many passengers left by sea in 2000?

(iii) The radius length of the 2000 chart is 1 unit and the radius length of the 2010 chart is 1.08 units. How many times bigger is the area of the 2010 chart than the area of the 2000 chart?

(iv) In comparative pie charts, the areas of the circles are proportional to the totals they represent. How many passengers left Ireland in 2010?

4. The graph shows data collected at a school on the number of students in each year group who own a smartphone.

(i) How many students are in the school? *400*

(ii) How many students in the school own a smartphone? *310*

(iii) Which year group has the highest percentage of students with smartphones? *Fifth*

(iv) Identify a trend in the data shown in the graph. *Older you are more likely to have a phone*

(v) Two students are chosen at random, one from First Year and one from Third Year. Which is more likely to own a smartphone? Justify your answer with suitable calculations. *3rd.*

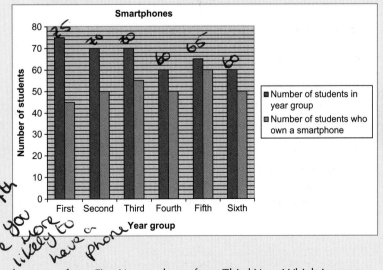

5. The chart shown is one developed by the world's most famous nurse, Florence Nightingale. Nightingale used the chart to illustrate that during the Crimean War, more soldiers died as a result of unsanitary conditions than were killed in combat. The area of each segment is proportional to the number that died during that month.

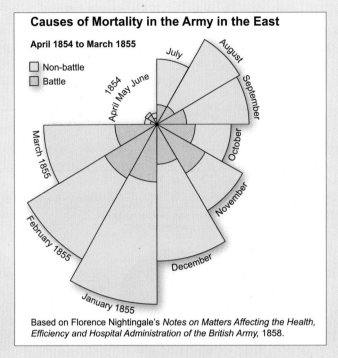

Causes of Mortality in the Army in the East

April 1854 to March 1855

☐ Non-battle
☐ Battle

Based on Florence Nightingale's *Notes on Matters Affecting the Health, Efficiency and Hospital Administration of the British Army*, 1858.

(i) During which month did the greatest number of soldiers die?

(ii) During which month did the smallest number of soldiers die?

(iii) What period of the war does the chart cover?

(iv) During which month were there proportionally more deaths due to battle rather than non-battle causes?

(v) The angle at the centre of each segment is the same for all segments of the chart. Find the size of this angle. Explain your reasoning.

(vi) Measure the radius length of the January 1855 segment and the radius length of the March 1855 segment. Hence, calculate the area of each segment.

(vii) Given that the number of soldiers who died during a particular month is proportional to the area of that month's segment, find the ratio of the number of soldiers who died during January 1855 to the number who died during March 1855.

6. A survey was carried out on 40 tourists who visited Galway last summer. Each person was asked a number of questions, including 'What age are you?' The data generated by that particular question was tabulated in a grouped frequency distribution.

Age	0–20	20–40	40–60	60–80	80–100
Frequency	9	12	8	8	3

Note: 0–20 means 0 is included but 20 is not, etc.

(i) What type of data was generated by the question?

(ii) Display the data in a suitable way.

(iii) Describe the distibution of ages.

(iv) The 40 people who participated in the survey are entered in a draw for two tickets to a concert in Galway. What is the probability that a person in the 20–40 age bracket will win the prize?

7. The following back-to-back stem-and-leaf diagram compares the pulse rates of 25 people before and after a 5-km run.

Before run		After run
7, 5, 2	5	
8, 6, 4, 2, 1, 1, 0	6	
8, 8, 8, 8, 6, 5, 3, 3, 1	7	
3, 2, 1	8	0, 2, 5
8, 5	9	6, 8
9	10	0, 0, 1, 5, 6, 6, 8, 9
	11	1, 2, 2, 6, 9
	12	7, 8, 8
	13	0, 1, 7
Key: 1|8| = 81 beats/min	14	2 Key: |11|1 = 111 beats/min

(i) How many people had pulse rates of more than 100 beats per minute after the run?

(ii) How many people had pulse rates of more than 100 beats per minute before the run?

(iii) What conclusions can you draw from the stem-and-leaf diagram?

8. Two classes took part in a fitness test. Each student did as many sit-ups as he or she could do in 1 minute. The results are shown below.

Class 1
32 33 35 35 40 42 43 45 46 46 47 48 48 50
50 52 53 53 54 55 55 55 56 57 59 60 61 63

Class 2
34 35 36 38 40 41 41 42 42 43 43 45 45
46 46 47 47 48 49 50 50 51 56 57 58 64

(i) Copy and complete the back-to-back stem-and-leaf plot below.

Class 1		Class 2
	3	
	3	
	4	
	4	
	5	
	5	
Key:	6	Key:

(ii) Describe both distributions.

(iii) Which class is better at sit-ups? Give a reason for your answer.

9. Draw a back-to-back stem-and-leaf diagram that will compare the heights (in centimetres) given below of a group of men and a group of women.

Men	179, 183, 181, 186, 185, 175, 191, 171, 174, 176, 179, 184, 159, 160, 166, 170, 178, 175, 170, 161, 168, 174, 183
Women	157, 155, 148, 171, 151, 157, 167, 162, 174, 166, 165, 149, 169, 178, 158, 154, 153, 152, 155, 150, 161, 158, 163

STATISTICS

10. Here is some random data from the CensusAtSchools site. All lengths are measured in centimetres.

Gender	Height	Foot length
Male	167	25
Female	151	22
Female	171	31
Male	151	24
Female	158	24
Male	158	24
Male	170	24
Female	149	21
Male	154	24
Female	150	22

Gender	Height	Foot length
Female	135	20
Male	164	31
Male	158	24
Male	147	24
Female	160	32
Female	156	24
Female	171	31
Male	118	23
Female	154	23
Male	148	22

(i) Draw a back-to-back stem-and-leaf diagram that will compare the heights of males and females in the group.

(ii) Draw a back-to-back stem-and-leaf diagram that will compare the foot lengths of males and females in the group.

11. Séamus and Aoife are sales representatives working for a pharmaceutical company. The table below shows the number of units of a particular headache tablet sold by each representative over a 30-week period.

Aoife	119, 126, 132, 148, 157, 168, 179, 186, 196, 208, 129, 135, 143, 159, 168, 175, 180, 193, 142, 152, 168, 178, 185, 158, 162, 172, 150, 166, 172, 176
Séamus	120, 131, 143, 151, 165, 178, 188, 120, 135, 147, 158, 169, 172, 183, 133, 148, 152, 164, 173, 184, 156, 165, 172, 181, 168, 173, 185, 177, 186, 187

(i) Display the information in a way that will allow you to compare both sets of data.

(ii) What was the greatest number of units sold in any one week by Aoife?

(iii) What was the least number of units sold in any one week by Séamus?

(iv) Compare and contrast both distributions.

12. Gardaí at a checkpoint measured the speed of passing cars in kilometres per hour. These are the results for the first 30 cars:

77.7	66.2	74.8	63.8	67.6
48.7	57.2	42.2	58.6	39.4
42.8	64.8	66.0	64.2	49.5
51.8	55.5	55.4	64.9	64.0
78.2	53.7	60.2	70.4	32.3
52.7	71.6	61.4	72.9	42.3

(i) Copy and complete the grouped frequency table shown below:

Speed km/h	32–40	40–48	48–56	56–64	64–72	72–80
Frequency						

Note: 32–40 means 32 or greater but less than 40.

(ii) Display the information in a suitable way.

(iii) Describe the distribution of these data.

8.3 MEASURES OF CENTRE

A measure of centre is a number that is representative of a data set, or in the case of categorical data, a member of a data set that is representative of the data. We study three measures of centre: the mean, the median and the mode. The measure of centre is also referred to as the average.

Average	When to use	Advantages/Disadvantages
Mode	■ If data is **categorical**, then the mode is the only sensible measure of centre to use. Therefore, for data on hair colour, eye colour, gender, etc. use only the mode. ■ It is sometimes appropriate to use the mode with **numerical** data.	*Advantages* ■ It can be used with any type of data. ■ It is easy to find. ■ It is not affected by extreme values or lack of symmetry *Disadvantages* ■ There is not always a mode or there may be more than one. ■ It does not use all the data.
Median	■ Used **only** with **numerical** data. ■ If there are **extreme values** in the data set or if the distribution is not (roughly) symmetric, then use the median.	*Advantages* ■ It is easy to calculate. ■ It is not heavily affected by extreme values or lack of symmetry. *Disadvantage* ■ It does not use all the data.
Mean	■ Used **only** with **numerical** data. ■ If the data set **does not have extreme values** and is (roughly) symmetric, then use the mean.	*Advantage* ■ It uses all the data. *Disadvantage* ■ It is affected by extreme values and lack of symmetry.

Worked Example 8.8

Two classes take part in a fitness test. Each student did as many push-ups as he or she could do in a minute. The results are shown in the back-to-back stem-and-leaf plot below.

Class 1		Class 2
4 1	3	3
6 6	3	6 7 8
4 2 1	4	0 1 1 2 2 4 4
9 9 8 8 6 5	4	5 5 6 6 7 7 9 9
4 3 3 2 0 0	5	1 1 2
8 6 6 5 5 5	5	6 7 8
3 1 0	6	4
Key: 2|4| = 42 push-ups 5	6	Key: |6|4 = 64 push-ups

Find an appropriate measure of centre that can be used to compare the ability of each class to do push-ups.

Solution

Both distributions are roughly symmetric, so the mean is the most appropriate measure of centre to use.

$$\text{Mean}_{\text{Class 1}} = \frac{1{,}445}{29} \approx 49.83$$

$$\text{Mean}_{\text{Class 2}} = \frac{1{,}201}{26} \approx 46.19$$

Therefore, in general, Class 1 are better at doing push-ups than Class 2.

Worked Example 8.9

Mr Grannell is writing up student reports and wishes to report to parents the average result of students in his class in their last exam.

The results (as percentages) were:

Aaron	86	Nico	73
Albert	78	Seán	80
Bilal	22	Stephen	70
James	67	Tom	80
Milo	82	Yousef	88

(i) Complete the grouped frequency table below:

Mark (%)	0–20	20–40	40–60	60–80	80–100
Frequency					

Note: 0–20 includes 0 and omits 20, etc.

(ii) What is the mean of the ten results?

What is the median?

What is the mode?

(iii) Which average should Mr Grannell report as the average result in his report to parents? Explain your choice.

Solution

(i) Your grouped frequency table should look like this:

Mark (%)	0–20	20–40	40–60	60–80	80–100
Frequency	0	1	0	4	5

(ii) $\text{Mean} = \dfrac{86 + 78 + 22 + 67 + 82 + 73 + 80 + 70 + 80 + 88}{10}$

$= \dfrac{726}{10} = 72.6\%$

Median: 22, 67, 70, 73, $\boxed{78, 80}$, 80, 82, 86, 88

$\therefore \text{Median} = \dfrac{78 + 80}{2} = \dfrac{158}{2} = 79\%$

Mode = 80%

(iii) Mr Grannell should use the median of 79% in his report.

The mean should not be used because the outlier (the extreme low) of 22% drags the mean down.

The mode will not provide parents with useful information in this instance.

Therefore, the median is the best measurement to use.

Mean of a Grouped Frequency Distribution

Consider the grouped frequency table below. The table summarises the time, in minutes, that it took 20 people to solve a problem.

Time (mins)	2–4	4–6	6–8	8–10
Frequency	4	9	6	1

Note: 2–4 means include 2 but omit 4, etc.

We can see from the table that four people spent between 2 and 4 minutes solving the problem. However, the table does not tell us the exact time that each person spent on the problem. To estimate the mean, we have to assign each person a time. We choose the mid-interval times as the times for each group.

Here is how we calculate the mid-interval values:

Time (mins)	2–4	4–6	6–8	8–10
Mid-interval value	$\dfrac{2+4}{2} = 3$	$\dfrac{4+6}{2} = 5$	$\dfrac{6+8}{2} = 7$	$\dfrac{8+10}{2} = 9$

We can now continue and estimate the mean:

Mid-interval value	3	5	7	9
Frequency	4	9	6	1

$$\text{Mean} = \frac{(4 \times 3) + (9 \times 5) + (6 \times 7) + (1 \times 9)}{4 + 9 + 6 + 1} = \frac{108}{20} = 5.4 \text{ minutes}$$

Exercise 8.3

1. The table shows the number of weddings held per week at a large hotel over a period of time.

Number	3	4	5	6	7
Frequency	20	64	50	12	6

   (i) Display the above data in a suitable way.

   (ii) How many weeks of data are given?

   (iii) Find the mean number of weddings and median number of weddings held per week.

   (iv) If each wedding brings in €10,000 in revenue for the hotel, how much revenue was generated for the hotel over the total period of time?

   (v) The Revenue Commissioners want to know what the average weekly revenue from weddings is at the hotel. What figure should the hotel provide? Show all calculations and explain your reasoning.

2. Lead is known to have serious effects on health. Lead in the air is measured in micrograms per cubic metre or $\mu g/m^3$. Following the destruction of the World Trade Center in New York, measurements were taken at the site on different days following the attack. The measurements in $\mu g/m^3$ are shown below.

5.40	1.10	0.42	0.73	0.48	1.10

   (i) Calculate the mean and median of the data.

   (ii) Which is the better measure of centre? Explain.

   (iii) One of the readings above was taken on the day immediately after the attack. Which reading? Suggest a reason for such a reading being recorded on that particular day.

STATISTICS

3. Listed below are intervals (in minutes) between eruptions of the Old Faithful geyser in Yellowstone National Park. The geyser is a major tourist attraction in the United States.

| 98 | 92 | 95 | 87 | 96 | 90 | 65 | 92 | 95 | 93 | 98 | 94 |

   (i)   Calculate the mean and median of these data.

   (ii) How many eruptions occurred to generate the above data?

   (iii) Which measure of centre do you think would be used to promote the attraction? Explain.

   (iv) Which is the *accurate* measure of centre? Explain.

4. The lengths (in minutes) of 20 phone calls made to a school switchboard are shown in the grouped frequency distribution below:

Length	0–2	2–4	4–6	6–8	8–10
Frequency	3	5	6	4	2

Note: 0–2 means 0 is included but 2 is not, etc.

   (i) Using mid-interval values, estimate the mean length.

   (ii) What is the maximum number of calls that could have been longer than 6.2 minutes?

5. The following frequency distribution shows the time (in minutes) taken by a group of people to complete a 5-mile run:

Time	30–35	35–40	40–45	45–50	50–55
Frequency	10	6	22	29	7

Note: 30–35 means 30 is included but 35 is not, etc.

   (i) Using mid-interval values, estimate the mean time.

   (ii) What is the maximum number of people who could have completed the run in less than 37 minutes?

6. The following frequency distribution shows the amounts spent by 30 customers in a shop:

Amount (€)	0–5	5–10	10–15	15–20
Frequency	12	8	8	2

Note: 0–5 means 0 is included but 5 is not, etc.

   (i) Using mid-interval values, estimate the mean amount spent.

   (ii) What percentage of the customers spent €10 or more?

7. The frequency distribution below shows the ages in years of people living on a particular street:

Age (years)	0–20	20–30	30–50	50–80
Frequency	24	16	41	15

Note: 0–20 means 0 is included but 20 is not, etc.

   (i)   How many people are living on the street?

   (ii) Estimate the mean age.

   (iii) What percentage of the residents are under 20 years of age?

   (iv) What is the largest number of residents who could fall into the 25–34 year old age category?

8. The heights of a random sample of 1,000 women are given in the frequency distribution below:

Height (cm)	140–145	145–150	150–155	155–160	160–165	165–170	170–175	175–180
Frequency	9	65	177	325	253	133	31	7

Note: 140–145 means 140 is included but 145 is not, etc.

(i) Display these data using a histogram.

(ii) Describe the distribution of these data.

(iii) Estimate the mean height.

(iv) In which interval would you find the median height?

(v) What measure of centre might be appropriate for these data?

9. The back-to-back stem-and-leaf plot below displays the scores by two clubs, Comaneci Gym Club and Hato Gym Club, for a gymnastics routine.

Comaneci		Hato
	3	2
4 1	4	3 3 7 7 9 9
3 1	5	1 4 4 6
8 7 6 2 1	6	1 7 7 8
8 6 5 4 3 2	7	1 2 5
7 6 5 1 1	8	2 2
Key: 1|4| = 4.1		Key: |3|2 = 3.2

Skewed left

Skewed Right

(i) Describe both distributions.

(ii) Find an appropriate measure of centre for each club. Explain your choice in each case.

(iii) From which club did the individual winner of the routine come?

10. A farmer has a mixed farm. The table shows how the farmer has divided his farm.

Land use	Hay	Vegetables	Wheat	Grazing
Number of acres	72	15	30	63

(i) Display the data in a suitable way.

(ii) Choose an appropriate measure of centre for these data.

(iii) What percentage of the farm is given over to wheat production?

8.4 MEASURES OF SPREAD

The concept of spread or variation is very important in statistics. A measure of centre such as the mean will not tell us everything about a distribution. In fact, the more the data varies, the less the mean alone can tell us. In this section we will look at measures of spread or variation. The most basic measure of spread is the **range**.

Worked Example 8.10

Five passengers on the 38A bus were asked how long they had been waiting for the bus. The results, in minutes, were {8, 8, 9, 11, 14}.

Five passengers on the 7A bus were asked how long they had been waiting for the bus. The results, in minutes, were {1, 3, 8, 17, 21}.

(i) Calculate the mean for each set.

(ii) Which mean is more representative of the waiting times of the passengers?

(iii) What is the range of the data for each set?

(iv) Compare the variation in waiting times between the passengers on the 38A with the waiting times of those on the 7A.

Solution

(i) $\text{Mean}_1 = \dfrac{8 + 8 + 9 + 11 + 14}{5}$

$= 10$ minutes

$$\text{Mean}_2 = \frac{1 + 3 + 8 + 17 + 21}{5}$$

$$= 10 \text{ minutes}$$

(ii) Both means are equal to 10 minutes. However, the mean waiting time of 10 minutes is more representative of the 38A passengers. All passengers on the 38A have waiting times within 4 minutes of the mean, whereas only one passenger on the 7A bus has a waiting time within 4 minutes of the mean.

(iii) $\text{Range}_1 = 14 - 8 = 6$ minutes

$\text{Range}_2 = 21 - 1 = 20$ minutes

> Range = Largest value – Smallest value

(iv) The variation in waiting times is greater on the 7A. There is a difference of 14 minutes between the two ranges.

Quartiles and the Interquartile Range

The quartiles of a set of values are the three values that divide the data set into four equal groups. There are three quartiles. The interquartile range is the difference between the first or **lower quartile** and the third or **upper quartile**. The **interquartile range** can be more reliable than the range as a measure of spread, as it is not affected by **outliers**.

Q_1, the **lower quartile** of a ranked set of data, is a value such that one-quarter of the values are less than or equal to it.

Q_2, the **second quartile**, is the median of the data.

Q_3, the **upper quartile** of a ranked set of data, is a value such that three-quarters of the values are less than or equal to it.

Interquartile range = $Q_3 - Q_1$

Outliers are extreme values that are not typical of the other values in the data set.

Worked Example 8.11

Using the stem-and-leaf plot shown, calculate:

(i) Q_1 (the lower quartile)

(ii) Q_3 (the upper quartile)

(iii) The interquartile range

Stem	Leaf
0	1, 3, 8, 8, 8, 9
1	1, 4, 7
2	0 Key: 1|7 = 17

Solution

Lower quartile

Stem	Leaf
0	1, 3, ⑧, 8, 8, 9
1	1, ④, 7
2	0 Key: 1|7 = 17

Upper quartile

(i) Count the number of leaves in the stem-and-leaf plot. There are 10 leaves.

Find $\frac{1}{4}$ of 10, which is 2.5. As this number is not a whole number, we round up to the nearest whole number

(always round **up**), which is 3. The third leaf on the plot is 8, so this is the lower quartile. $Q_1 = 8$.

(ii) Find $\frac{3}{4}$ of 10, which is 7.5. As 7.5 is not a whole number, round up to the nearest whole number, which is 8. The eighth value is 14, so this is the upper quartile. $Q_3 = 14$.

(iii) The interquartile range $= Q_3 - Q_1$

$= 14 - 8$

$= 6$

Worked Example 8.12

The set $B = \{6, 7, 8, 9, 9, 10, 11, 12, 14, 15, 15, 52\}$.

(a) Calculate for set B:

   (i) Q_2 (the median)

   (ii) Q_1 (the lower quartile)

   (iii) Q_3 (the upper quartile)

   (iv) The interquartile range

(b) Identify the outlier.

Solution

(a) (i) There are 12 data entries. The median is the mean of the sixth and seventh data entries.

$$Q_2 = \frac{10 + 11}{2} \Rightarrow Q_2 = 10.5$$

Alternatively, we could find the median by crossing out the smallest and the largest numbers in the set, then the second smallest and the second largest, and so on until we are left with the two numbers 10 and 11.

$$Q_2 = \frac{10 + 11}{2} = 10.5$$

(ii) Q_1 is the median of the first half of the data.

$$Q_1 = \frac{8 + 9}{2} = 8.5$$

(iii) Q_3 is the median of the second half of the data.

$$Q_3 = \frac{14 + 15}{2} = 14.5$$

> Note: This is an alternative method for finding the lower and upper quartiles.

(iv) The interquartile range is $14.5 - 8.5 = 6$

(b) The outlier is the data entry of 52.

ACTIVITY 8.2

Exercise 8.4

1. Represent the following sets on a stem-and-leaf plot, and then find the median, the lower quartile, the upper quartile and the interquartile range for each set:

   (i) $\{2, 15, 17, 23, 33, 42, 58\}$

   (ii) $\{5, 38, 26, 54, 25, 63, 54, 12\}$

   (iii) $\{28, 17, 36, 5, 44, 2, 1\}$

   (iv) $\{8, 7, 8, 7, 6, 5, 6, 5, 4, 3, 4, 3\}$

2. The ages of 45 people entering a shopping centre are summarised in the following stem-and-leaf plot:

Stem	Leaf
2	1, 2, 4
2	5, 5, 5, 5, 6, 7, 7, 8
3	0, 0, 1, 1, 1, 2, 2, 3, 3
3	6, 7, 8, 8
4	1, 1, 1, 2, 2, 3, 3, 4
4	8, 9
5	0, 1, 1, 2
5	7, 7
6	1, 2, 2
6	6, 6 Key: 4|1 = 41 years

(a) Calculate:

   (i) Q_2 (the median)

   (ii) Q_1 (the lower quartile)

   (iii) Q_3 (the upper quartile)

   (iv) The interquartile range

(b) What is the modal age of people entering the shopping centre?

3. The stem-and-leaf diagram shows the time (in seconds) it took contestants to answer a general knowledge question. All contestants answered in less than 7 seconds.

Stem	Leaf
2	1, 2, 2
3	2, 4, 8, 9
4	1, 3, 4, 6, 7
5	1, 5
6	8 Key: 5|1 = 5.1 seconds

Calculate:

(i) Q_1 (the lower quartile)

(ii) Q_3 (the upper quartile)

(iii) The interquartile range

(iv) The range

4. Twenty people attend a fancy dress party. Their ages are summarised in the following stem-and-leaf diagram:

Stem	Leaf
1	1, 3, 4, 5, 6, 9
2	1, 3, 5
3	3, 8
4	4, 5, 6, 7, 8
5	1, 6, 7
6	2 Key: 1|4 = 14 years

Using the stem-and-leaf diagram, calculate:

(i) Q_1 (the lower quartile)

(ii) Q_3 (the upper quartile)

(iii) The interquartile range

(iv) The range

5. Here is a back-to-back stem-and-leaf diagram showing the marks obtained by 30 girls and 30 boys in the same maths test. The girls' marks are on the left-hand side of the diagram:

Girls	Stem	Boys
9	0	7, 9
7, 2	1	3, 4
8	2	9
9, 6, 6	3	5, 7, 9
8, 8, 6, 6, 6, 4, 2, 2	4	3, 4, 4
8, 6, 4	5	2, 2, 3, 5, 7, 7, 8
8, 2	6	1, 2, 5, 8, 9
9, 6, 4	7	3, 4, 5, 9
8, 5, 2, 0	8	4, 7
Key: 6|3| = 36 marks 9, 8, 3	9	1 Key: |2|9 = 29 marks

(a) Calculate for both sets:

(i) The median mark

(ii) Q_1 (the lower quartile)

(iii) Q_3 (the upper quartile)

(iv) The interquartile range

(b) Write a short paragraph comparing the performance of girls and boys in the test. Make sure to make reference to measures of centre and measures of spread.

6. The table below gives the heights of 30 male and 30 female students aged 16 years. The data was obtained from the CensusAtSchools website. All heights are in centimetres.

Male	Female	Male	Female
171	168	180	168
172	160	184	160
173	165	172	164
180	174	178	169
172	174	170	160
178	160	178	156
174	164	209	173
167	160	182	168
174	170	171	177
200	150	160	153
176	176	163	158
165	150	170	173
190	171	184	171
178	167	175	173
190	153	179	167

(i) Copy and complete the **unordered** back-to-back stem-and-leaf plot.

Male	Stem	Female
	15	
	15	
	16	0 0
	16	8 5
2 3 2 1	17	4 4
8	17	
0	18	
	18	
	19	
	19	
	20	
Key:	20	Key:

(ii) Display the data in an **ordered** back-to-back stem-and-leaf plot.

(iii) Calculate the median height of the females in the sample and the median height of the males in the sample.

(iv) Find the upper and lower quartiles for both sets of data.

(v) Calculate the interquartile range for both sets of data. What does the interquartile range tell us about each set of data?

(vi) A male student is selected at random from the sample. Find the probability that the student has a height greater than 180 cm.

(vii) A female student is selected at random. Find the probability that the student's height lies between the lower quartile and the upper quartile of the female data.

7. A group of students sit a maths exam. The exam is marked out of 100. The summary statistics for the test are given below.

Count	48
Mean	68.35
Median	69.90
Minimum	43
Maximum	87
Lower quartile	59
Upper quartile	75

(i) How many students sat the test?

(ii) What is the range of the data?

(iii) What is the interquartile range?

(iv) Are there any outliers in the data? Explain.

8. Here are the summary statistics for the sizes (in acres) of farms in a region of south-west Cork.

Count	78
Mean	46.5
Median	34
Minimum	6
Maximum	250
Lower quartile	18.5
Upper quartile	55

(i) How many farms are in the region?

(ii) What is the range of the data?

(iii) What is the interquartile range?

(iv) Are there any outliers in the data? Explain.

(v) Write three sentences on farm sizes in this region.

9. One measure of difficulty of a golf course is its length. The length of a golf course is the total distance (in yards) from tee to hole for all 18 holes. The summary statistics for 45 randomly selected courses in the south-east of Ireland are shown.

Count	45
Mean	5870
Median	5920
Minimum	5150
Maximum	6760
Lower quartile	5580
Upper quartile	6120

(i) Describe one method for randomly selecting 45 courses in the south-east.

(ii) What is the range of the data?

(iii) Between what lengths do the central 50 per cent of these courses lie?

(iv) What is the interquartile range?

(v) Are there any outliers in the data? Explain.

(vi) Write three sentences on golf course sizes in this region.

10. A study on the weights of infants in different parts of the world is conducted by the World Health Organisation. They gather data on the weights of infants aged between 1 year 9 months and 2 years. A university researcher decides to use these data to compare infant weights across countries. He randomly selects ten pieces of data from four countries in different parts of the world. These data are presented below:

(All weights in kgs)

Australia		Chile		Egypt		Korea	
15.2	13.9	15.8	14.3	14.3	14.7	15.3	13.5
13.6	15.5	15.0	14.7	15.2	14.7	13.8	14.4
14.2	16.0	12.6	12.1	14.1	14.1	12.1	15.4
14.1	15.7	13.2	15.3	14.2	14.3	11.8	12.1
14.5	14.4	13.6	12.9	14.1	17.2	12.8	15.2

(i) Copy and complete the table below:

Country	Mean	Median	Range	IQR
Australia				
Chile				
Egypt				
Korea				

(ii) Which country should the researcher report as having the lightest infants (between 1 year 9 months and 2 years)? Explain your choice.

(iii) Which country should the researcher report as having the heaviest infants? Explain your choice.

(iv) Which of the four data sets shows the largest degree of variation? Explain your choice.

(v) One of the researcher's colleagues says: 'The Australian data set shows the least dispersion [variation].' Comment on the validity of this statement.

(vi) In order to draw inferences about the actual weights of infants in the four countries selected, what recommendations would you make to the researcher? Describe two such recommendations.

Revision Exercises

1. Give a reason why each of the following methods of sampling might not be very reliable.

(i) Find out how many people have computers in their home by interviewing people outside a computer shop.

(ii) Find out whether the potatoes are cooked by testing one with a fork.

(iii) Find out the most popular make of car by counting 100 cars in a five-star hotel car park.

(iv) You decide to do a survey on the amount of pocket money received by students in your school. You use your phone and ring 15 of your friends. All respond to the survey.

2. Stephen wishes to carry out a survey to see how much money people spend on entertainment each week.

Advise Stephen on the relative merits of conducting his survey by:

(i) Interview   (ii) Telephone

3. List one advantage and one disadvantage of a postal survey.

4. Give one reason why each of the following statements or graphs is misleading:

(i) 'In a recent survey, four out of every five teenagers said they preferred the channel JLS Music to any other music channel.'

Ten teenagers had been interviewed for the survey.

(ii) The chart below summarises the results of 500 throws of a die. The aim of the chart is to show that the die is biased.

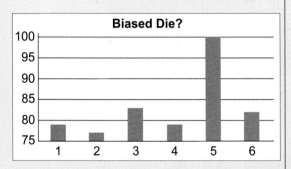

(iii) 'In a recent online survey, 10,000 out of 12,000 respondents believe that online shopping is a superior experience to conventional shopping.'

(iv) The graphic shows the amount of refuse (in tonnes) generated by a town in the years 1990, 2000 and 2010.

5. Liam wishes to compare the texting speed of students with that of teachers. He confines his study to his own school. He randomly selects 15 students and 15 teachers. Each is required to send a short message on a mobile phone. He times each of the participants. Here are the results:

Student times (seconds)	50	42	39	39	27	37	34	35	31	29	28	34	35	37	43
Teacher times (seconds)	29	61	56	45	43	42	41	38	36	44	43	45	42	35	45

(i) Display the results on a back-to-back stem-and-leaf plot.

(ii) Explain how Liam could have chosen his random samples.

(iii) Some teachers refused to take part in the study. Explain how this may affect the results.

6. Julie believes that men spend more money in shops than women. She stands outside her local hardware shop on a Saturday morning and asks each person who leaves the shop how much they have spent. Here are her results:

Men (€)	28	56	5	80	34	150	25	38	122	143	48	46
Women (€)	10	22	12	50	130	25	7	61				

(i) Display the results on a back-to-back stem-and-leaf diagram.

(ii) Why do you think there are more men than women in the sample? Give two reasons.

(iii) What do you think Julie will conclude from her survey?

(iv) Give three reasons why Julie's survey is biased.

(v) Suggest to Julie a better way of carrying out her survey.

7. The pulse rates in beats per minute of 20 adults are given in the table below:

68	64	88	72	64
72	60	88	76	60
96	72	56	64	60
64	84	76	84	88

(i) Calculate the mean pulse rate for the group.

(ii) Use your calculator to select 10 random samples of size five from the group, and show the samples on a table.

(iii) Calculate the mean of each sample.

(iv) Find the difference between the mean of each sample and the mean of the population (the 20 adults).

(v) How many of the sample means are within one beat per minute of the population mean?

8. One hundred randomly selected shoppers are asked the following question:

'If you do one main weekly shop, on which day of the week do you do it?'

The frequency table below shows the result of the survey.

Day	Mon.	Tue.	Wed.	Thur.	Fri.	Sat.	Sun.
Frequency	5	2	10	24	20	29	10

(i) Represent the data on a bar chart.

(ii) Which is the most popular shopping day?

(iii) Which is the least popular shopping day?

9. To study the eating habits of students at a local school, 30 randomly selected students were surveyed to determine the number of times they had eaten in the school canteen during the previous week.

The following results were obtained:

3, 4, 2, 3, 3, 4, 3, 2, 3, 4,
0, 0, 4, 4, 3, 2, 4, 1, 1, 1,
4, 3, 4, 5, 2, 5, 2, 3, 4, 4

(i) Organise the data by constructing a frequency table.

(ii) Construct a pie chart to represent the data.

(iii) Use a line plot to represent the data.

10. A gardener has measured the heights of the tulips from two different locations in his garden. The results are displayed in the back-to-back stem-and-leaf diagram below. All measurements are in centimetres.

Location 1	Stem	Location 2
2, 2, 1	1	
9, 9, 8, 5, 2, 1, 1, 0	2	1, 1, 2, 5
9, 4, 3, 2, 2, 1	3	3, 3, 4, 4, 6, 9
4, 3, 2	4	5, 6, 7, 8, 8, 8, 9
Key: 5|2| = 25 cm	5	1, 1, 2 Key: |3|4 = 34 cm

(i) How many tulips did the gardener measure?

(ii) What is the height of the smallest tulip?

(iii) What is the height of the tallest tulip?

(iv) What is the difference in height between the smallest and tallest tulips?

(v) Which is the better location for growing tulips? Explain your answer.

11. The tables below show measurements of the wrist circumferences of 15 randomly selected males and 15 randomly selected females. All subjects are adults and all measurements are in centimetres.

Table 1				
6.4	6.2	5.8	5.9	6.0
5.8	5.2	5.6	5.5	5.5
5.3	6.7	5.2	5.7	6.0

Table 2				
4.6	5.5	4.6	5.0	4.8
4.9	5.1	5.5	5.8	5.0
5.2	4.8	5.1	5.6	5.4

(i) Display the data on a back-to-back stem-and-leaf diagram.

(ii) From your stem-and-leaf diagram, can you tell which table contains the male measurements and which table contains the female measurements? Explain your answer.

(iii) What is the largest female measurement?

(iv) How many male measurements are greater than the largest female measurement?

(v) What is the smallest male measurement?

(vi) How many female measurements are smaller than the smallest male measurement?

12. Alice wishes to investigate the difference between adult male and adult female pulse rates. She randomly selects 20 males and 20 females from her street. She measures the pulse rates of each of the 40 individuals. All her subjects are aged 20 years or older. Here are her results:

Males				
68	64	88	72	64
72	60	88	76	60
96	72	56	64	60
64	84	76	84	88

Females				
76	72	88	60	72
68	80	64	68	68
80	76	68	72	96
72	68	72	64	80

(i) Represent the data on a back-to-back stem-and-leaf diagram.

(ii) By studying the stem-and-leaf diagram, would you say that the distribution (pattern) of pulse rates is similar for males and females? Explain your answer.

(iii) Describe how Alice might have selected the samples.

(iv) What is the range of pulse rates for men in the sample?

(v) What is the range of pulse rates for women in the sample?

(vi) Describe two possible sources of bias in the samples.

(vii) Calculate the interquartile range for the males.

13. An aircraft manufacturing company needs data on the heights of male adults and female adults. They hope to use this data to determine the seating capacity of a new aircraft that they are designing. They randomly select 20 male adults and 20 female adults from a passenger list they obtained from one of their customers. They then go to the airport and ask the selected people to participate. The measurements are given in the tables below. All measurements have been rounded to the nearest centimetre.

Females				
161	166	156	156	149
159	150	158	154	167
162	158	167	167	162
163	155	161	159	

Males				
177	166	179	172	169
173	166	168	170	164
158	183	170	178	153
181	166	174		

(i) Complete the following frequency distribution table for the female sample and then construct a histogram.

Height	145.5–155.5	155.5–165.5	165.5–175.5	175.5–185.5
Number				

Note: 145.5–155.5 means 145.5 is included but 155.5 is not, etc.

(ii) Complete the following frequency distribution table for the male sample and then construct a histogram.

Height	145.5–155.5	155.5–165.5	165.5–175.5	175.5–185.5
Number				

Note: 145.5–155.5 means 145.5 is included but 155.5 is not, etc.

(iii) Study the histograms you have constructed and state one similarity and one difference between the histograms.

(iv) Identify two problems with the method by which the samples were taken.

14. An orchard contains 100 apple trees. The weight of apples produced by each tree in one year was recorded. The results are given in the table below:

Weight (kg)	Frequency
50–60	6
60–70	6
70–80	14
80–90	9
90–100	21
100–110	21
110–120	19
120–130	3
130–140	1

Note: 50–60 means 50 is included but 60 is not, etc.

(i) Represent the data on a histogram.

(ii) Using mid-interval values, estimate the mean weight of apples produced by each tree.

(iii) If the weight of apples produced by one tree in the orchard is 50 kg and the weight of apples produced by another tree is 130 kg, calculate the range of weights for trees in this orchard.

15. The Health Service Executive is investigating the time spent by people exercising each day. It decides to survey 1,000 people in the Dublin area. The results are displayed in the frequency table below:

Time (min)	0–30	30–60	60–90	90–120	120–150	150–180
Number	100	170	500	110	85	35

Note: 0–30 means 0 is included but 30 is not, etc.

(i) Draw a histogram to represent the data.

(ii) Using mid-interval values, estimate the mean time these people spent exercising each day.

(iii) Comment on the estimate for the mean time.

(iv) The sample was taken using a list of all members of fitness clubs in Dublin. Explain why this sample is biased.

(v) Design a questionnaire that could be used in the survey. Include a total of five questions.

16. A group of students measured the reaction time of 25 other students. The times are given below correct to the nearest hundredth of a second.

0.44	0.31	0.47	0.19	0.28	0.26	0.46
0.33	0.28	0.29	0.26	0.29	0.41	0.47
0.36	0.21	0.43	0.36	0.37	0.27	0.16
0.30	0.27	0.28	0.49			

(i) Display the data on a stem-and-leaf diagram.

(ii) Calculate the mean reaction time.

(iii) Complete the grouped frequency table (reaction times are given correct to the nearest hundredth of a second):

Reaction time	0.15–0.20	0.20–0.25	0.25–0.30	0.30–0.35	0.35–0.40	0.40–0.45	0.45–0.50
Frequency							

Note: 0.15–0.20 means 0.15 is included but 0.20 is not, etc.

(iv) Represent the data on a histogram.

(v) Using mid-interval values, estimate the mean reaction time.

(vi) What is the difference between the mean reaction time and the estimated reaction time?

(vii) Write your answer to part (vi) as a percentage of the mean reaction time.

17. Alan claims that girls send more text messages than boys. He randomly selects 20 boys and 20 girls from his school, and asks each person how many text messages they had sent on the previous day. The results are displayed below in a back-to-back stem-and-leaf diagram:

Boys	Stem	Girls
9, 8, 8, 2, 2, 1, 0, 0, 0	0	0, 0, 1, 1, 3, 5, 7, 7, 8
4, 4, 4, 3, 3, 1, 1	1	0, 0, 2, 3, 3
5, 1, 0	2	1, 1, 2
	3	5, 8
	4	
Key: 5|2| = 25 texts 2	5	2 Key: |2|1 = 21 texts

(i) What is the least number of messages sent?

(ii) Calculate the mean number of text messages sent by the boys and the mean number of text messages sent by the girls.

(iii) Find the median number of text messages sent by the boys and the median number of text messages sent by the girls.

(iv) Which is the more appropriate average for each set, the median or the mean? Explain.

(v) Find the range and the interquartile range for both groups.

(vi) Alan has decided to use the range as a measure of spread for both groups. Comment on his choice.

(vii) Give a possible explanation for the outliers in both groups.

18. The table below shows the distances travelled by seven paper airplanes after they were thrown.

Airplane	A	B	C	D	E	F	G
Distance (cm)	188	200	250	30	380	330	302

(a) Find the median of the data.

(b) Find the mean of the data.

(c) Airplane D is thrown again and the distance it travels is measured and recorded in place of the original measurement. The median of the data remains unchanged and the mean is now equal to the median. How far did airplane D travel the second time?

(d) What is the minimum distance that airplane D would need to have travelled in order for the median to have changed?

SEC 2011, JCHL

19. Data on the type of broadband connection used by enterprises in Ireland for 2008 and 2009 is contained in the table below.

	2008	2009
	%	%
Broadband connection	84	84
By type of connection:		
DSL (<2 Mb/Second)	31	20
DSL (>2 Mb/Second)	41	45
Other fixed connection	31	20
Mobile broadband	24	21

Source: Central Statistics Office

(a) Display the data in a way that allows you to compare the data for the two years.

(b) Identify any trends that you think are shown by the data.

SEC 2011, JCHL

20. Morgan's Third Year Physical Education class did a fitness test. The number of sit-ups that each student did in one minute is recorded below:

59	48	27	53	36	29	52	46	45	37	49	51
33	45	38	52	40	51	37	44	47	45	60	41

The students practised this exercise for the next three weeks and then repeated the test in the same order. The data for the second test are as follows:

61	52	33	51	39	40	50	49	46	37	59	49
38	48	39	58	44	52	38	44	49	51	62	44

(a) Represent the data from the two tests on a back-to-back stem-and-leaf diagram.

Test 2	Stem	Test 1
	2	
	3	
	4	
	5	
Key:	6	Key:

(b) How many students are in the class?

(c) What is the range of sit-ups for each test for this class?

(d) Based on the data and the diagram, do you think that practice improves the ability to do sit-ups? Give a reason for your answer.

(e) Morgan did 41 sit-ups in Test 1 and 44 in Test 2. How did his performance compare with that of the rest of the class?

SEC 2011, JCHL

21. There are 24 students in a class. On a Friday, each student present in class is asked for the number of days they had been absent that week. The results are recorded in the table below.

Number of days absent	None	One	Two	Three	Four	Five
Number of students	9	2	3	4	1	0

(a) How many students were absent on that Friday?

(b) On the following Monday, all of the students were present in class and the table was updated to include the entire class. Which number(s) from the above table could not have changed? Give a reason for your answer.

(c) The total number of days that were missed during the week will depend on the answers given by the students who were absent on Friday. Complete the tables below to show how the largest possible and smallest possible number of days missed would arise.

Smallest possible number of days missed						
Number of days absent	None	One	Two	Three	Four	Five
Number of students						

Largest possible number of days missed						
Number of days absent	None	One	Two	Three	Four	Five
Number of students						

(d) Cathal decides to draw a pie chart of the actual data collected on Monday. He calculates the number of degrees for each sector of the pie chart. Use this data to calculate the mean number of absences per pupil for the previous week correct to one place of decimals.

Number of days absent	None	One	Two	Three	Four	Five
Number of students						
Number of degrees	135°	30°	75°	60°	45°	15°

SEC 2011, JCHL

22. The phase 9 *CensusAtSchool* questionnaire contained the question 'Approximately how long do you spend on social networking sites each week?' The histogram below illustrates the answers given by 100 students, randomly selected from those who completed the survey.

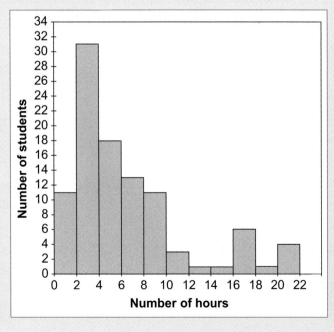

(a) Use the data from the histogram to complete the frequency table below.

No. of hours	0–2	2–4	4–6	6–8	8–10	10–12	12–14	14–16	16–18	18–20	20–22
No. of students											

[*Note:* 2–4 means 2 hours or more but less than 4 hours, etc.]

(b) What is the modal interval?

(c) Taking mid-interval values, find the mean amount of time spent on social networking sites.

(d) John is conducting a survey on computer usage by students at his school. His questionnaire asks the same question. He plans to carry out his survey by putting the question to twenty first year boys on the Monday after the mid-term break. Give some reasons why the results from John's question might not be as representative as those in the histogram.

SEC Sample Paper, JCHL

23. Students in a Third Year class were investigating how the number of jelly beans in a box varies for three different brands of jelly beans.

Each student counted the number of jelly beans in a box of brand A, B and C. The results are recorded in the tables below.

Brand A

23	25	25	26	26	26	26
27	27	27	27	28	29	29
29	30	30	31	31	31	32
32	32	33	34	35	35	39

Brand B

17	22	22	24	24	25	25
25	25	26	26	26	26	26
26	27	27	27	27	28	29
29	29	29	29	29	30	30

Brand C

25	25	25	26	26	26	26
26	27	27	27	28	28	28
28	28	28	28	28	28	29
29	29	30	30	31	32	32

(a) Display the data in a way that allows you to describe and compare the data for each brand.

(b) If you were to buy a box of jelly beans, which brand would you buy? Give a reason for your answer. In your explanation you should refer to the **mean** number of jelly beans per box and the **range** or **spread** of the number of jelly beans per box for each brand.

SEC Sample Paper, JCHL

24. The number of students attending primary and second level schools in Ireland in 2010 is illustrated in the pie-charts below.

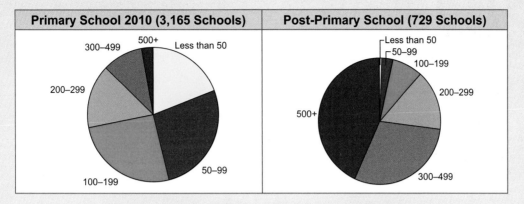

(a) The angle in the slice for Primary schools with between 100 and 199 pupils is 93.725°.
Calculate the number of schools in this category.

(b) Mary claims that the charts show that there is roughly the same number of post-primary schools as primary schools in the 200–299 range.
Do you agree with Mary? Give a reason for your answer.

SEC 2012, JCHL

25. The ages of the Academy Award winners for the best male actor and best female actor (at the time they won the award) from 1992 to 2011 are as follows:

Male actor	54, 52, 37, 38, 32, 45, 60, 46, 40, 36, 47, 29, 43, 37, 38, 45, 50, 48, 60, 50
Female actor	42, 29, 33, 36, 45, 49, 39, 26, 25, 33, 35, 35, 28, 30, 29, 61, 32, 33, 45, 29

(a) Represent the data on a back-to-back stem-and-leaf diagram.

Male actors		Female actors
	2	
	3	
	4	
	5	
Key:	6	Key:

(b) State one similarity and one difference that can be observed between the ages of the male and female winners.

(c) Mary says, 'The female winners were younger than the male winners.' Investigate this statement in relation to:

(i) The mean age of the male winners and mean age of the female winners.

(ii) The median age of the male winners and the median age of the female winners.

(d) Find the interquartile ranges of the ages of the male winners and of the female winners.

SEC 2012, JCHL

9

chapter

Indices

Learning Outcomes

In this chapter you will learn about:

⮑ **The Laws of Indices**

(1) $a^p \times a^q = a^{p+q}$

(2) $a^p \div a^q = a^{p-q}$

(3) $(a^p)^q = a^{pq}$

(4) $a^0 = 1$

(5) $a^{-p} = \dfrac{1}{a^p}$

(6) $a^{\frac{1}{q}} = \sqrt[q]{a}$

(7) $a^{\frac{p}{q}} = \sqrt[q]{a^p} = \left(\sqrt[q]{a}\right)^p$

(8) $(ab)^p = a^p b^p$

(9) $\left(\dfrac{a}{b}\right)^p = \dfrac{a^p}{b^p}$

⮑ **How to solve equations with x as an index**

⮑ **Working with numbers in scientific notation**

⮑ **Comparing numbers using orders of magnitude**

9.1 REVIEW

Pg 18 Tables

A number in index form is of the form b^n. We call b the **base** and n the **index, power** or **exponent**.

YOU SHOULD REMEMBER...

- Laws 1–3 of Indices
- How to express numbers greater than 1 in scientific notation
- Orders of magnitude
- Reciprocals

Negative Bases to Even and Odd Powers

Consider the number $(-3)^3$. Is this a positive or negative number?

$(-3)^3 = (-3) \times (-3) \times (-3) = -27$ (a negative number)

Is $(-1)^4$ positive or negative?

$(-1)^4 = (-1) \times (-1) \times (-1) \times (-1) = 1$ (a positive number)

In general:

- A negative number raised to an odd power is **negative**.
- A negative number raised to an even power is **positive**.

KEY WORDS

- **Index**
- **Power**
- **Exponent**
- **Base**
- **Index notation**
- **Scientific notation**
- **Order of magnitude**

Laws 1–4 of Indices

FORMULA

Law 1 $a^m \times a^n = a^{m+n}$
Law 2 $\dfrac{a^m}{a^n} = a^{m-n}$
Law 3 $(a^m)^n = a^{mn}$
Law 4 $a^0 = 1$

ACTIVITY 9.1

These formulae appear on page 21 of *Formulae and Tables*.

a^{pq} Worked Example 9.1

Simplify the following, giving the answers in index notation:

(i) $(-5)^3$

(ii) $(-4)^4$

Solution

(i) $(-5)^3 = -5^3$ $[(-)^{\text{odd power}} = -]$

(ii) $(-4)^4 = 4^4$ $[(-)^{\text{even power}} = +]$

a^{pq} Worked Example 9.2

Use the Laws of Indices to write each of the following in the form a^m, where a and $m \in N$.

(i) $3^4 \times 3^6$

(ii) $5^8 \div 5^3$

(iii) $(2^2)^5$

Solution

(i) $3^4 \times 3^6 = 3^{4+6}$ (Law 1)

         $= 3^{10}$

(ii) $5^8 \div 5^3 = 5^{8-3}$ (Law 2)

         $= 5^5$

(iii) $(2^2)^5 = 2^{10}$ (Law 3)

Exercise 9.1

1. Without using a calculator, evaluate each of the following:

    (i) 5^2 (iii) $(-3)^2$ (v) $(-1)^4$

    (ii) 2^3 (iv) $(-7)^3$ (vi) 4^0

2. Simplify the following, giving your answers in index notation:

    (i) $(4)^3$ (iv) $(-3)^3$ (vii) $-(7)^3$

    (ii) $(-2)^{20}$ (v) $(-5)^{12}$ (viii) $-(-11)^3$

    (iii) $(6)^{19}$ (vi) $-(-1)^{100}$ (ix) $(-1)^6$

3. Show that $-(-4)^7 = (4)^7$.

4. Use your calculator to evaluate the following to two decimal places where necessary:

    (i) 7.8^3 (v) $2.5^3 \times 3.8^4$

    (ii) $\dfrac{6.5^5}{2.3^2}$ (vi) $(5.1^2)^3 \times 2.8^2$

    (iii) $(2.5^3)^5$ (vii) $\dfrac{6.2^2}{5.8^3}$

    (iv) 12.45^0 (viii) $2.4^3 \times 3.7^2 \times 5.2^5$

5. Copy and complete the following tables:

(i)

Index notation	2	2^2	2^3	2^4	2^5	2^6	2^7
Whole number					32		

(ii)

Index notation	3	3^2	3^3	3^4	3^5	3^6
Whole number					243	

(iii)

Index notation	4	4^2	4^3	4^4	4^5	4^6
Whole number				256		

(iv)

Index notation	9	9^2	9^3	9^4	9^5	9^6
Whole number			729			

Using the tables above, find a value for x and a value for y, for each of the following equations:

    (a) $2^x = 4^y$ (b) $9^x = 3^y$ (c) $2(2^x) = 4^y$ (d) $3^{2x} = 9^y$

The answers you found for parts (a) to (d) are not unique. For example, in part (a), $2^4 = 16 = 4^2$ ($x = 4$, $y = 2$). But $2^6 = 64 = 4^3$ ($x = 6$, $y = 3$).

For each of parts (b), (c) and (d), find a second set of solutions.

6. Use the law $a^m \times a^n = a^{m+n}$ to write the following in index notation.

    (i) $5^3 \times 5^2$ (iv) $4^3 \times 4^5$

    (ii) $8^7 \times 8^3$ (v) $2^9 \times 2^{12}$

    (iii) 6×6^2 (vi) $(3)^3 \times (3)^4 \times (3)^0$

7. Use the law $a^m \times a^n = a^{m+n}$ to write the following in index notation. Simplify your answers.

    (i) $(-5)^3 \times (-5)^7$ (iv) $(-5)^3 \times (-5)^2$

    (ii) $(-2)^6 \times (-2)^3$ (v) $(-7)^3 \times (-7)^5$

    (iii) $(-3)^4 \times (-3)^3$ (vi) $(-4)^2 \times (-4)^3 \times (-4)^0$

8. Use the law $\dfrac{a^m}{a^n} = a^{m-n}$ to write the following in index notation.

    (i) $\dfrac{3^7}{3^6}$ (iii) $\dfrac{10^5}{10^2}$ (v) $\dfrac{10^8}{10^2}$

    (ii) $\dfrac{2^9}{2^3}$ (iv) $\dfrac{7^{12}}{7^5}$ (vi) $\dfrac{8^3}{8^9}$

9. Use the law $(a^m)^n = a^{mn}$ to simplify the following, giving your answers in index notation.

    (i) $(3^3)^5$ (iii) $(10^5)^5$ (v) $(7^6)^7$

    (ii) $(6^4)^5$ (iv) $(4^5)^6$ (vi) $(5^3)^{12}$

10. Copy and complete the following table:

Index notation	5	5^2	5^3	5^4	5^5	5^6
Whole number			125			

Using the table, write each of the following in the form 5^n, $n \in N$:

(i) 25×125

(ii) $3{,}125 \times 15{,}625$

(iii) 625×25

(iv) $15{,}625^{11}$

(v) $25^3 \times 625^5$

(vi) $\dfrac{15{,}625^4}{125^3}$

11. The number 64 can be written in index form as 8^2.

Write down four other ways in which it can be written in index form.

9.2 LAWS 5–9 OF INDICES

ACTIVITIES 9.2, 9.3, 9.4

In Activities 9.2 to 9.4 you derived Laws 5 to 7 of Indices.

> $\sqrt[q]{a}$ is called the qth root of a.
>
> b is the qth root of a if $b^q = a$.

$\sqrt[3]{27} = 3$, as $3^3 = 27$. Similarly, $\sqrt[6]{64} = 2$, as $2^6 = 64$.

FORMULA

Law 5 $a^{-p} = \dfrac{1}{a^p}$

Law 6 $a^{\frac{1}{q}} = \sqrt[q]{a}$

Law 7 $a^{\frac{p}{q}} = \sqrt[q]{a^p} = \left(\sqrt[q]{a}\right)^p$

These formulae appear on page 21 of *Formulae and Tables*.

Worked Example 9.3

Using the law $a^{-p} = \dfrac{1}{a^p}$, write each of the following in the form $\dfrac{1}{a^n}$, $n \in N$.

(i) 2^{-5} (ii) 3^{-6}

Solution

(i) $2^{-5} = \dfrac{1}{2^5}$ (ii) $3^{-6} = \dfrac{1}{3^6}$

Worked Example 9.4

Evaluate each of the following:

(i) $25^{\frac{1}{2}}$ (ii) $32^{\frac{1}{5}}$

Solution

(i) $25^{\frac{1}{2}} = \sqrt{25}$ (ii) $32^{\frac{1}{5}} = \sqrt[5]{32}$

    $= 5$ $= 2$

Worked Example 9.5

Evaluate each of the following using the law $a^{\frac{p}{q}} = \sqrt[q]{a^p} = \left(\sqrt[q]{a}\right)^p$.

(i) $32^{\frac{4}{5}}$ (ii) $81^{\frac{5}{4}}$

Solution

(i) $32^{\frac{4}{5}} = \left(\sqrt[5]{32}\right)^4$

    $= (2)^4$

    $= 16$

(ii) $81^{\frac{5}{4}} = \left(\sqrt[4]{81}\right)^5$

    $= (3)^5$

    $= 243$

INDICES

a^{pq} Worked Example 9.6

Evaluate each of the following:

(i) $64^{-\frac{4}{3}}$ (ii) $27^{-\frac{5}{3}}$

Solution

(i) $64^{-\frac{4}{3}} = \dfrac{1}{64^{\frac{4}{3}}}$ (Law 5)

$= \dfrac{1}{\left(\sqrt[3]{64}\right)^4}$ (Law 7)

$= \dfrac{1}{(4)^4}$

$= \dfrac{1}{256}$

(ii) $27^{-\frac{5}{3}} = \dfrac{1}{27^{\frac{5}{3}}}$ (Law 5)

$= \dfrac{1}{\left(\sqrt[3]{27}\right)^5}$ (Law 7)

$= \dfrac{1}{(3)^5}$

$= \dfrac{1}{243}$

a^{pq} Worked Example 9.7

Use your calculator to evaluate each of the following correct to two decimal places:

(i) $\sqrt[5]{122}$ (ii) $\sqrt[4]{17}$ (iii) $16^{\frac{2}{3}}$ (iv) $17^{-\frac{5}{3}}$

Solution

(i)

The answer 2.613797668 is displayed.

Answer = 2.61

(ii)

The answer 2.030543185 is displayed.

Answer = 2.03

(iii)

The answer 6.349604208 is displayed.

Answer = 6.35

(iv)

The answer 0.008897168 is displayed.

Answer = 0.01

Note that individual calculators may differ.

ACTIVITIES 9.5, 9.6

In Activities 9.5 and 9.6 you derived Laws 8 and 9 of Indices.

FORMULA

Law 8 $(ab)^p = a^p b^p$

Law 9 $\left(\dfrac{a}{b}\right)^p = \dfrac{a^p}{b^p}$

These formulae appear on page 21 of *Formulae and Tables*.

Worked Example 9.8

Use the law $(ab)^p = a^p b^p$ to show that $12^8 = 3^8 4^8$.

Solution

$12^8 = ((3)(4))^8$

$\quad = 3^8 4^8$ (Law 8)

Worked Example 9.9

Use the law $\left(\dfrac{a}{b}\right)^p = \dfrac{a^p}{b^p}$ to show that $(0.75)^9 = \dfrac{3^9}{4^9}$.

Solution

$0.75 = \dfrac{3}{4}$

$\therefore (0.75)^9 = \left(\dfrac{3}{4}\right)^9$

$\qquad = \dfrac{3^9}{4^9}$ (Law 9)

Worked Example 9.10

Evaluate $\left(\dfrac{27}{64}\right)^{-\frac{2}{3}}$

Solution

Method 1

$\left(\dfrac{27}{64}\right)^{-\frac{2}{3}} = \dfrac{1}{\left(\dfrac{27}{64}\right)^{\frac{2}{3}}}$ (Law 5)

$\quad = \dfrac{1}{\dfrac{27^{\frac{2}{3}}}{64^{\frac{2}{3}}}}$ (Law 9)

$\quad = \dfrac{1}{\dfrac{\left(\sqrt[3]{27}\right)^2}{\left(\sqrt[3]{64}\right)^2}}$ (Law 7)

$\quad = \dfrac{1}{\dfrac{(3)^2}{(4)^2}}$

$\quad = \dfrac{1}{\dfrac{9}{16}}$

$\quad = \dfrac{16}{9}$

Method 2

$\left(\dfrac{a}{b}\right)^{-p} = \dfrac{1}{\left(\dfrac{a}{b}\right)^p}$ (Law 5)

$\quad = \dfrac{1}{\dfrac{a^p}{b^p}}$ (Law 9)

$\quad = \dfrac{b^p}{a^p}$

$\quad = \left(\dfrac{b}{a}\right)^p$ (Law 9)

$\left(\dfrac{27}{64}\right)^{-\frac{2}{3}} = \left(\dfrac{64}{27}\right)^{\frac{2}{3}}$

$\quad = \dfrac{64^{\frac{2}{3}}}{27^{\frac{2}{3}}}$ (Law 9)

$\quad = \dfrac{\left(\sqrt[3]{64}\right)^2}{\left(\sqrt[3]{27}\right)^2}$ (Law 7)

$\quad = \dfrac{(4)^2}{(3)^2}$

$\quad = \dfrac{16}{9}$

Exercise 9.2

1. Using the law $a^{-p} = \dfrac{1}{a^p}$, write each of the following as fractions.

   (i) 3^{-3}

   (ii) 5^{-2}

   (iii) 9^{-2}

   (iv) 7^{-3}

   (v) 4^{-1}

   (vi) 2^{-5}

2. Using the law $a^{-p} = \dfrac{1}{a^p}$, write each of the following as fractions in their simplest form.

   (i) $6(4^{-3})$

   (ii) $2(7^{-2})$

   (iii) $6(3^{-2})$

   (iv) $5(2^{-4})$

   (v) $2(8^{-2})$

   (vi) $3(6^{-2})$

3. Without using a calculator, evaluate each of the following:

(i) $\sqrt{100}$ (iii) $\sqrt[3]{27}$ (v) $\sqrt[5]{32}$ (vii) $\sqrt[3]{1{,}000}$ (ix) $\sqrt[6]{64}$

(ii) $\sqrt{144}$ (iv) $\sqrt[4]{16}$ (vi) $\sqrt[10]{1}$ (viii) $\sqrt[4]{81}$ (x) $\sqrt[3]{125}$

4. Copy and complete the following tables:

x	1	2	3	4	5	6	7	8	9	10
x^2			9						81	

x	1	4	9	16	25	36	49	64	81	100
$\sqrt{x}$						6				

5. Copy and complete the following tables:

x	1	2	3	4	5	6	7	8	9	10
x^3			27							1,000

x	1	8	27	64	125	216	343	512	729	1,000
$\sqrt[3]{x}$							7			

6. Using the law $a^{\frac{1}{n}} = \sqrt[n]{a}$ and the completed tables from Questions 4 and 5, evaluate each of the following:

(i) $100^{\frac{1}{2}}$ (vi) $8^{\frac{1}{3}}$

(ii) $64^{\frac{1}{2}}$ (vii) $9^{\frac{1}{2}}$

(iii) $216^{\frac{1}{3}}$ (viii) $1000^{\frac{1}{3}}$

(iv) $512^{\frac{1}{3}}$ (ix) $64^{\frac{1}{3}}$

(v) $16^{\frac{1}{2}}$ (x) $36^{\frac{1}{2}}$

7. Using the law $a^{\frac{m}{n}} = (\sqrt[n]{a})^m$, evaluate each of the following:

(i) $16^{\frac{1}{4}}$ (vi) $125^{\frac{2}{3}}$

(ii) $27^{\frac{2}{3}}$ (vii) $16^{\frac{5}{4}}$

(iii) $64^{\frac{2}{3}}$ (viii) $81^{\frac{3}{4}}$

(iv) $16^{\frac{3}{4}}$ (ix) $9^{\frac{3}{2}}$

(v) $100^{\frac{3}{2}}$ (x) $64^{\frac{4}{3}}$

8. Using the laws $a^{-p} = \dfrac{1}{a^p}$ and $a^{\frac{m}{n}} = (\sqrt[n]{a})^m$, evaluate each of the following. Write your answers in the form $\dfrac{1}{p}$, $p \in N$:

(i) $100^{-\frac{1}{2}}$ (iii) $16^{-\frac{1}{4}}$

(ii) $36^{-\frac{1}{2}}$ (iv) $9^{-\frac{3}{2}}$

(v) $81^{-\frac{3}{4}}$ (viii) $125^{-\frac{2}{3}}$

(vi) $8^{-\frac{2}{3}}$ (ix) $16^{-\frac{5}{4}}$

(vii) $9^{-\frac{5}{2}}$ (x) $100^{-\frac{5}{2}}$

9. Using the law $(ab)^p = a^p b^p$, verify that each of the following is true.

(i) $20^4 = 5^4 4^4$ (iii) $36^{\frac{1}{2}} = 9^{\frac{1}{2}} 4^{\frac{1}{2}}$

(ii) $15^6 = 3^6 5^6$ (iv) $216^{\frac{1}{3}} = 8^{\frac{1}{3}} 27^{\frac{1}{3}}$

10. Using the law $\left(\dfrac{a}{b}\right)^p = \dfrac{a^p}{b^p}$, verify that each of the following is true:

(i) $\left(\dfrac{3}{4}\right)^8 = \dfrac{6^8}{8^8}$ (iii) $\left(\dfrac{9}{16}\right)^{\frac{1}{2}} = \dfrac{18^{\frac{1}{2}}}{32^{\frac{1}{2}}}$

(ii) $\left(\dfrac{3}{5}\right)^9 = \dfrac{9^9}{15^9}$ (iv) $\left(\dfrac{25}{64}\right)^{-\frac{1}{2}} = \dfrac{75^{-\frac{1}{2}}}{192^{-\frac{1}{2}}}$

11. Evaluate each of the following without using a calculator:

(i) $\left(\dfrac{1}{4}\right)^{\frac{1}{2}}$ (v) $\left(\dfrac{8}{27}\right)^{\frac{1}{3}}$

(ii) $\left(\dfrac{1}{25}\right)^{\frac{1}{2}}$ (vi) $\left(\dfrac{8}{125}\right)^{\frac{1}{3}}$

(iii) $\left(\dfrac{4}{9}\right)^{\frac{1}{2}}$ (vii) $\left(\dfrac{16}{81}\right)^{\frac{3}{4}}$

(iv) $\left(\dfrac{81}{25}\right)^{\frac{1}{2}}$ (viii) $\left(\dfrac{27}{64}\right)^{\frac{2}{3}}$

12. Evaluate each of the following without using a calculator:

(i) $\left(\dfrac{36}{25}\right)^{-\frac{1}{2}}$ (iv) $\left(\dfrac{27}{1000}\right)^{-\frac{2}{3}}$

(ii) $\left(\dfrac{4}{121}\right)^{-\frac{1}{2}}$ (v) $\left(\dfrac{125}{27}\right)^{-\frac{2}{3}}$

(iii) $\left(\dfrac{8}{125}\right)^{-\frac{1}{3}}$ (vi) $\left(\dfrac{4}{9}\right)^{-\frac{3}{2}}$

13. Use your calculator to evaluate each of the following to two decimal places.

(i) $\sqrt{19}$ (vi) $26^{\frac{3}{4}}$

(ii) 2.75^4 (vii) $42^{-\frac{7}{8}}$

(iii) $13^{\frac{1}{4}}$ (viii) $\sqrt[5]{34}$

(iv) $39^{\frac{3}{4}}$ (ix) $\sqrt[6]{100}$

(v) 3.42^{-3} (x) $\sqrt[3]{73}$

14. The laws $(a^p)^q = a^{pq}$ and $(ab)^p = a^p b^p$ can be used to write numbers of the form k^n as products of primes, where $k, n \in N$.

(i) Write 24 as a product of prime numbers.

(ii) Hence, write 24^3 as a product of primes.

15. Write 28^{2012} as a product of primes.

16. Write 100 as a product of prime factors, and hence, find the prime factorisation of 100^{1601}.

17. The set {1, 4, 9, 16, 25, 36, ...} is known as the set of square numbers. The square numbers can be written in the form a^2, where $a \in N$.

(i) Write each of the following square numbers as a product of prime factors:

144, 2500, 11025, 1002001

(ii) Copy and complete the following sentence:

'If a number is a square number, then the exponent (power) on each of its prime factors is always an _____ number.'

(iii) If $m = 3 \times 5^4 \times 23^5 \times 29^8$, what is the smallest natural number n, such that mn is a square number?
Explain your reasoning.

18. Write each of the following in the form 2^p.

(i) 4   (iv) 32   (vii) $\sqrt{2}$

(ii) 8   (v) $\dfrac{1}{2}$ (viii) $\sqrt[3]{2}$

(iii) 16   (vi) $\dfrac{1}{4}$ (ix) $\dfrac{1}{\sqrt{2}}$

19. Write each of the following in the form 3^p.

(i) 1   (iv) 81   (vii) $\sqrt{3}$

(ii) 9   (v) $\dfrac{1}{3}$ (viii) $\sqrt{27}$

(iii) 27   (vi) $\dfrac{1}{9}$ (ix) $\dfrac{1}{\sqrt{3}}$

20. Write each of the following in the form 5^p.

(i) 25   (vi) $\dfrac{1}{125}$

(ii) 125   (vii) $\sqrt{5}$

(iii) $\dfrac{1}{5}$ (viii) $\sqrt[5]{5}$

(iv) 1   (ix) $\dfrac{1}{\sqrt{5}}$

(v) $\dfrac{1}{25}$ (x) 0.2

21. Write each of the following in the form 10^p.

(i) 100   (vii) $\sqrt{10}$

(ii) 1,000   (viii) $100\sqrt{10}$

(iii) 0.01   (ix) $\dfrac{1}{\sqrt{10}}$

(iv) 10,000   (x) $\dfrac{\sqrt{10}}{\sqrt[3]{10}}$

(v) $\dfrac{1}{10}$ (xi) $\sqrt{1,000}$

(vi) $\dfrac{1}{10,000}$ (xii) $\dfrac{100}{\sqrt{10}}$

9.3 EQUATIONS WITH X AS AN INDEX

$$2^x = 64$$

Above is an example of an equation in which the unknown quantity x is an index or power. The laws of indices will help us to solve many equations where the unknown quantity is an index.

> If $a \in R$ and $a^x = a^y$, then $x = y$.

a^{pq} Worked Example 9.11

Solve each of the following equations:

(i) $2^x = 2^5$ (ii) $3^y = 3^{-2}$ (iii) $\left(\frac{1}{2}\right)^z = \left(\frac{1}{2}\right)^{\frac{1}{4}}$

Solution

(i) $2^x = 2^5$ (ii) $3^y = 3^{-2}$ (iii) $\left(\frac{1}{2}\right)^z = \left(\frac{1}{2}\right)^{\frac{1}{4}}$

$\therefore x = 5$ $\therefore y = -2$ $\therefore z = \frac{1}{4}$

a^{pq} Worked Example 9.12

Solve each of the following equations:

(i) $2^x = 16$

(ii) $3^x = 27$

Solution

(i) $2^x = 16$

     $2^x = 2^4$ (Express 16 as a power of 2)

     $\therefore x = 4$ (Equate the powers)

(ii) $3^x = 27$

     $3^x = 3^3$ (Express 27 as a power of 3)

     $\therefore x = 3$ (Equate the powers)

a^{pq} Worked Example 9.13

Find the value of n for which

$\dfrac{2^n \times 2^{3n+1}}{2^3 \times 2^{n-2}} = 64, \, n \in N.$

Solution

$\dfrac{2^n \times 2^{3n+1}}{2^3 \times 2^{n-2}} = 64$

$\dfrac{2^{4n+1}}{2^{n+1}} = 64$ (Law 1)

$2^{3n} = 64$ (Law 2)

$2^{3n} = 2^6$ (Express 64 as a power of 2)

$\therefore 3n = 6$ (Equate the powers)

$\therefore n = 2$

a^{pq} Worked Example 9.14

Solve $4^x = \dfrac{8}{\sqrt{2}}, \, x \in Q.$

Solution

All numbers in the equation can be written as powers of 2.

$2 = 2^1$

$4 = 2^2$

$8 = 2^3$

The equation can now be written as:

$(2^2)^x = \dfrac{2^3}{\sqrt{2}}$

$2^{2x} = \dfrac{2^3}{2^{\frac{1}{2}}}$ (Law 3 and Law 5)

$2^{2x} = 2^{2\frac{1}{2}}$ (Law 2)

$\therefore 2x = 2\frac{1}{2}$ (Equate the powers)

$\Rightarrow x = \dfrac{2\frac{1}{2}}{2}$

$\Rightarrow x = 1\frac{1}{4}$ $\left(\text{or} \quad \dfrac{5}{4}\right)$

1. Solve each of the following equations:

   (i) $2^x = 4$ (vi) $3^x = 81$

   (ii) $3^x = 27$ (vii) $10^x = 10{,}000$

   (iii) $5^x = 125$ (viii) $6^x = 216$

   (iv) $10^x = 1{,}000$ (ix) $7^x = 49$

   (v) $4^x = 64$ (x) $3^x = 729$

2. Solve each of the following equations:

   (i) $9^x = 3^4$ (vi) $2^x = 16^5$

   (ii) $4^x = 8^2$ (vii) $4^{2x} = 8^3$

   (iii) $5^x = 25^2$ (viii) $3^{3x} = 27^2$

   (iv) $10^x = 100^3$ (ix) $4^{5x} = 8^5$

   (v) $11^x = 121^5$ (x) $a^{2x} = (a^2)^3$

3. Using the Laws of Indices, solve each of the following equations:

   (i) $2^x = 2^7\sqrt{2}$ (vi) $7^x = \dfrac{49}{\sqrt[3]{7}}$

   (ii) $2^x = \dfrac{2^7}{4}$ (vii) $10^{2x-1} = \dfrac{\sqrt{1000}}{10}$

   (iii) $5^x = \dfrac{125}{\sqrt{5}}$ (viii) $4^x = \dfrac{32\sqrt{2}}{2}$

   (iv) $3^{x+1} = \dfrac{9}{\sqrt{3}}$ (ix) $49^x = \dfrac{49}{\sqrt{7}}$

   (v) $10^{x-3} = \dfrac{\sqrt{10}}{100}$ (x) $36^{x+2} = \dfrac{216}{\sqrt{6}}$

4. Write each of the following in the form 2^k, $k \in Q$.

   (i) 16 (ii) 8 (iii) $\sqrt{8}$ (iv) $\dfrac{16}{\sqrt{8}}$

   Hence, solve the equation $2^{2x-1} = \left(\dfrac{16}{\sqrt{8}}\right)^3$

5. Find the value of n for which

   $$\dfrac{9}{3^{1-n}} = 81, n \in N.$$

6. Find the value of n for which

   $$\dfrac{125 \times 5^{2n}}{5^{n+1}} = 625, n \in N.$$

7. Solve the equation

   $$\dfrac{7^2 \times 49^x}{7^{1+x}} = 343, x \in N.$$

8. Solve the simultaneous equations:

   $$p - q = 96$$
   $$p + q = 160$$

   Hence, solve the simultaneous equations:

   $$2^x - 2^y = 96$$
   $$2^x + 2^y = 160$$

9. Solve the simultaneous equations:

   $$5(3^x) - 2(3^y) = 387$$
   $$5(3^x) - 4(3^y) = 369$$

10. If $\sqrt{y-5} = 5$ and $2^x = 8$, find the value of $x + y$.

11. Each of the numbers 4, 5, 6, and 7 is assigned in some order to p, q, r and s.
    What is the largest possible value of $p^q + r^s$?

12. Write $\sqrt{244 + \sqrt{142 + \sqrt{4}}}$ in the form 2^n, where $n \in N$.

13. Find the prime factors of 75 and hence, solve the equation $\dfrac{5^x}{3} = \dfrac{5^6}{75}$.

14. Solve the equation $\left(a^{\frac{1}{3}}\right)\left(b^{\frac{1}{2}}\right) = c^{5-x}$, if

    (i) $a = 8$, $b = 4$ and $c = 2$

    (ii) $a = 27$, $b = 9$ and $c = 3$

15. Express 16 and $2\sqrt{2}$ as powers of 2. Hence, solve the equation:

    $$2^{2x-1} = \left(\dfrac{16}{2\sqrt{2}}\right)^3$$

16. Copy and complete the table below. Answers in the second row must be in index form.

$2^2 - 2$	$2^3 - 2^2$	$2^4 - 2^3$	$2^5 - 2^4$	$2^6 - 2^5$	$2^7 - 2^6$
2	2^2				

Hence, write $2^{p+1} - 2^p$ as a power of 2.

17. Using the results from Question 16, solve for x: $\left(\dfrac{2^{12}}{16}\right) = 2^{x+1} - 2^x$.

18. Solve for y: $\left(\dfrac{2^{16}}{8}\right) = 2^y - 2^{y-1}$.

9.4 SCIENTIFIC NOTATION

A number written in the form $a \times 10^n$, where $1 \leqslant a < 10$ and $n \in Z$ is said to be written in scientific notation or standard form.

Worked Example 9.15

Write the following numbers in scientific notation.

   (i) 24,000   (ii) 386,000,000   (iii) 5,300,000,000

Solution

   (i) $24{,}000 = 2.4 \times 10^4$

   (ii) $386{,}000{,}000 = 3.86 \times 10^8$

   (iii) $5{,}300{,}000{,}000 = 5.3 \times 10^9$

> $24{,}000 = 2.4 \times 10{,}000$
> Number between 1 and 10
> $= 2.4 \times 10^4$

When doing calculations, scientists also use very small numbers. For example, the time taken for light to travel a distance of 1 metre is 0.000000003 seconds. Very small numbers can also be expressed in scientific notation.

Worked Example 9.16

The radius of a hydrogen atom is 0.000000000025 metres. Express this number in scientific notation.

Solution

$$0.000000000025 = \frac{2.5}{100000000000}$$
$$= \frac{2.5}{10^{11}}$$
$$= 2.5 \times 10^{-11}$$

Worked Example 9.17

Use your calculator to simplify each of the following. Write each answer in scientific notation.

   (i) $2.5 \times 10^3 + 5.2 \times 10^4$

   (ii) $6.2 \times 10^7 - 2.3 \times 10^5$

   (iii) $(4.8 \times 10^9) \times (7.2 \times 10^{-13})$

   (iv) $\dfrac{8.6 \times 10^{11}}{4.3 \times 10^{-3}}$

INDICES

Solution

(i) 2.5 [Exp] 3 + 5.2 [Exp] 4 =

The answer 54,500 is displayed.

Answer = 5.45×10^4

(ii) 6.2 [Exp] 7 − 2.3 [Exp] 5 =

The answer 61,770,000 is displayed.

Answer = 6.177×10^7

(iii) 4.8 [Exp] 9 × 7.2 [Exp] −13 =

The answer 0.003456 is displayed.

Answer = 3.456×10^{-3}

(iv) 8.6 [Exp] 11 ÷ 4.3 [Exp] −3 =

The answer 2E14 is displayed.

Answer = 2×10^{14}

Orders of Magnitude

Orders of magnitude are generally used to make very approximate comparisons. If two numbers differ by one order of magnitude, one is about ten times larger than the other.

To compare two numbers using **order of magnitude**, we round each number to the nearest power of 10 and then subtract the powers. This difference in the powers of 10 is called the **order of magnitude**.

Worked Example 9.18

By how many orders of magnitude does 2,345 differ from 624,567,000?

Solution

Write both numbers in scientific notation:

$2,345 = 2.345 \times 10^3$ Rounded to the nearest power of 10 = $10^0 \times 10^3 = 10^3$

$624,567,000 = 6.24567 \times 10^8$ Rounded to the nearest power of 10 = $10^1 \times 10^8 = 10^9$

$\dfrac{10^9}{10^3} = 10^6$ (Divide the bigger value by the smaller value)

Note: $10^0 = 1$

Therefore, both numbers differ by six orders of magnitude.

Exercise 9.4

1. Write the following numbers in scientific notation:

   (i) 5,300
   (ii) 175,000
   (iii) 24,000
   (iv) 235,000,000
   (v) 7,376,000
   (vi) 0.02
   (vii) 0.0015
   (viii) 0.000167
   (ix) 0.00612
   (x) 0.000023

2. Write each of the following as decimal numbers:

   (i) 4×10^5
   (ii) 1.6×10^7
   (iii) 5.4×10^3
   (iv) 8.2×10^6
   (v) 9.4×10^2
   (vi) 1.9×10^{-3}
   (vii) 23.6×10^{-5}
   (viii) 2.6×10^{-2}
   (ix) 5.6×10^{-1}
   (x) 5.06×10^{-6}

INDICES

3. Write the answers to each of the following in scientific notation:

   (i) $3.4 \times 10^3 + 2.8 \times 10^3$

   (ii) $5.2 \times 10^3 - 3.8 \times 10^2$

   (iii) $(6.12 \times 10) \times (2.4 \times 10^7)$

   (iv) $8.2 \times 10^{13} \div 6.1 \times 10^2$

4. Write each of the following in the form $a \times 10^n$, where $1 \leqslant a < 10, n \in Z$:

   (i) 0.000036   (iv) 0.00063

   (ii) 0.0005613   (v) 0.0078

   (iii) 0.0345   (vi) 0.0404

5. By how many orders of magnitude do the following numbers differ?

   (i) 598,704 and 132

   (ii) 597,844,205 and 5672

   (iii) 240,926,000,000 and 85,000,000

   (iv) 48 and 7262

   (v) 7.5 and 922.89

   (vi) 6.2×10^{-5} and 8.15×10^{-2}

6. Light travels at a speed of approximately 2.9×10^8 ms^{-1}. It takes 8 minutes for light from the sun to reach Earth. Find the distance, in kilometres, between Earth and the sun. Give your answer in the form $a \times 10^n, 1 \leqslant a < 10, n \in Z$.

7. The average distance between two atoms is 1.6 angstroms, where 10^{10} angstroms are equal to 1 metre.

   Write 1.6 angstroms in metres in standard form.

8. A rectangle has length 1.6×10^4 metres and width 2.3×10^3 metres.

   Calculate:

   (i) The perimeter of the rectangle

   (ii) The area of the rectangle

   Write your answers in standard form.

9. Hugh saves some images onto a memory stick. Each image requires 32,000 bytes of memory.

   How many images can he save if the memory stick has a memory of 1.36×10^8 bytes? Give your answer in index form.

10. A company employs 3.8×10^3 workers. On average, the workers use 2.6×10^2 litres of water per year.

   How many litres of water does the company use in a year?

11. Dinosaurs roamed the earth about 140 million years ago.

   (i) Express 140 million in scientific notation.

   (ii) The average human life span is 72 years.

      How many average human life spans is 140 million years? Give your answer in index form, correct to three significant figures.

12. In 1950, China's population was approximately 5.6×10^8. By 2011, its population had increased by approximately 740 million.

   (i) What was the approximate population of China in 2011? Express your answer in the form $a \times 10^n, 1 \leqslant a < 10, n \in Z$.

   (ii) The world's population in 2011 was approximately 6.7×10^9. What percentage of the world's population was living in China at this time?

13. (i) The diameters of Venus and Saturn are 1.21×10^4 km and 1.21×10^5 km, respectively. What is the difference, in kilometres, between the diameter length of Venus and the diameter length of Saturn?

   (ii) By how many orders of magnitude do the equator lengths of Venus and Saturn differ?

   (iii) Can you answer part (ii) without having to do any calculations? Explain.

14. A sheet of gold leaf is one ten-millionth of a metre thick. The diameter of an atom of gold is approximately 0.26 nanometres (1 nanometre is 10^{-9} metres).

   Approximately how many atoms thick is the sheet of gold leaf?

15. A nanosecond is 0.000000001 of a second.

    (i) Write the number 0.000000001 in the form $a \times 10^n$, $1 \leqslant a < 10$, $n \in Z$.

    (ii) A computer does a calculation in 3 nanoseconds. How many such calculations can the computer do in 1 second?

16.

Planet	Radius length (km)	Mass (kg)
Jupiter	69,911	1.9×10^{27}
Saturn	58,232	5.7×10^{26}
Uranus	25,362	8.7×10^{25}
Neptune	24,622	1.0×10^{26}
Earth	6,371	6.0×10^{24}

    (i) Which planet has the greatest radius length?

    (ii) Which planet has approximately six times the mass of Neptune?

    (iii) What is the combined mass of Earth and Jupiter? Answer in scientific notation.

    (iv) What is the difference between the mass of Jupiter and the mass of Earth? Answer in scientific notation.

    (v) By how many orders of magnitude does the radius of Jupiter differ from the radius of Earth?

Revision Exercises

1. Write each of the following in index notation.

    (i) $7^3 \times 7^8$ (iii) $(2^2)^5$

    (ii) $\dfrac{4^5}{2^3}$ (iv) $\dfrac{11^{12}}{11^5}$

2. Write each of the following in the form a^p, $p \in Q$.

    (i) $\dfrac{1}{5^4}$ (iii) $\sqrt[5]{17^3}$

    (ii) $\sqrt[6]{12}$ (iv) $\dfrac{4^2}{\sqrt{4^5}}$

3. Use the Laws of Indices to simplify each of the following. Leave your answers in index notation.

    (i) $((6^5)(6^5))^2$ (iii) $\left(\dfrac{2^9}{2^5}\right)^6$

    (ii) $((8^6)(8^5))^2$ (iv) $\left(\dfrac{4^8}{4^3}\right)^7$

4. Write each of the following in the form a^n:

    (i) $p^3 \times p^6$ (iii) $\sqrt[4]{p^6}$

    (ii) $(p^4)^5$ (iv) $\sqrt[5]{p^7 \times p^9}$

5. (i) Evaluate $25^{\frac{1}{2}}$.

    (ii) Write 9 and $\sqrt{3}$ as powers of 3 and hence solve the equation $3^x = \dfrac{9}{\sqrt{3}}$.

6. Simplify $\dfrac{(4^{2012})(3^{2011})}{(6^{2011})(2^{2011})}$.

    Express your answer in the form 2^n, $n \in N$.

7. (i) Evaluate $64^{-\frac{1}{2}}$.

    (ii) Write 128 and $\sqrt{2}$ as a power of 2. Hence, solve the equation, $2^{2x+1} = \dfrac{128}{\sqrt{2}}$.

8. If $x + y = 0$ and $x \neq 0$, then simplify

$$\dfrac{x^{2012}}{y^{2012}} + 100.$$

9. Given that $x = 4 \times 10^{-5}$ and $y = 6 \times 10^{-7}$, evaluate $5x + 4y$. Give your answer in the form $a \times 10^n$, $1 \leqslant a < 10$, $n \in Z$.

INDICES

10. A googol is the large number 10^{100}. The term was coined in 1938 by 9-year-old Milton Sirotta, nephew of American mathematician Edward Kasner. Kasner used the term in his 1940 book, *Mathematics and the Imagination*.

    (i) Put the following list of numbers in order of increasing magnitude: googol^2, $100 \times$ googol, $3 \times$ googol, googol, googol^3.

    (ii) Which number on the list is $1{,}000^{100}$?

    (iii) By how many orders of magnitude do googol and googol^2 differ?

    (iv) Which of the following pairs of numbers differ by the larger order of magnitude?

    $100 \times$ googol and googol^2
    or
    googol^2 and googol^3.

11. Find the four solutions to the equation, $(n^2 - 5n + 5)^{n^2 + 2n - 24} = 1, n \in Z$.

12. (i) Simplify $a^4 + a^4 + a^4 + a^4$.

    Hence write $2^4 + 2^4 + 2^4 + 2^4$ as a power of 2.

    (ii) Write $2^{\frac{1}{4}} + 2^{\frac{1}{4}} + 2^{\frac{1}{4}} + 2^{\frac{1}{4}}$ as a power of 2.

    (iii) Simplify $3a^5 + 6a^5$.

    Hence, write $3(3^5) + 6(3^5)$ as a power of 3.

    (iv) Write $20(3^8) + 7(3^8)$ as a power of 3.

13. Joe says that $(3 \times 10^4) + (5 \times 10^4) = 8 \times 10^4$.

    Sarah says that $(3 \times 10^4) + (5 \times 10^4) = 8 \times 10^8$.

    Who is correct? Give a reason for your answer.

14. Which of these is the odd one out?

    $16^{-\frac{3}{4}}$ $64^{-\frac{1}{2}}$ $8^{-\frac{2}{3}}$

    Show how you decided.

15. The speed of sound (Mach 1) is 1,236 km/hr.

    A plane travelling at Mach 2 would be travelling at twice the speed of sound.

    How many kilometres would a plane travelling at Mach 3 travel in 5 minutes?

16. In 2011, 22.7 million passengers travelled through Dublin, Cork and Shannon airports.

    Dublin airport was the best performer with passenger numbers of 18.7 million.

    (i) What percentage of the total passenger numbers passed through Dublin airport? Answer in scientific notation correct to three significant figures.

    (ii) If each passenger using Dublin airport carried on average 15.6 kg of luggage, calculate the total mass of luggage carried by these passengers.

    (iii) Passenger numbers at Cork airport declined by 3% to 2.4 million between 2010 and 2011.

    Calculate the number of passengers who travelled through Cork airport in 2010. Answer in index form correct to four significant figures.

17. The radius of the Milky Way galaxy is 3.9×10^{20} m. The solar system has a radius of 5.9×10^{12} m. By how many orders of magnitude do the two radii differ?

18. One of the closest stars to our solar system is Alpha Centuri. It is 4.047×10^{13} km from Earth. A light year is the distance that light travels in one year, which is approximately 9.5×10^{12} km. How many light years from Earth is Alpha Centuri?

19. A computer is able to process 803,000 bits of data in 0.00000525 seconds. Find the rate of processing the data in bits/sec. Give your answer in scientific notation.

chapter 10

Applied Arithmetic

Learning Outcomes

In this chapter, you will:

⊃ Learn to solve problems that involve finding:

  ⊃ Income tax and net pay including deductions

  ⊃ Mark-up and margin

  ⊃ Compound interest exceeding three years

⊃ Revise applied arithmetic from the Junior Certificate Ordinary Level course

10.1 REVIEW

Income and Deductions

Employees expect to earn money for the work they carry out.

- If you are paid according to the number of hours worked or goods produced, this is called a **wage**.
- If you are paid the same amount regardless of the number of hours worked or goods produced, this is called a **salary**.

Most people cannot keep all the money they earn. Employees have several deductions made to their earnings before they receive their money.

Statutory and Non-Statutory Deductions

Deductions can be **statutory** or **non-statutory**.

> **Statutory deductions** are payments that must be made to the state. They are taken from gross pay by the employer.

Statutory deduction	What is it used for?
Income tax (PAYE – Pay As You Earn)	Payment of public services, e.g. Gardaí, health care, education, etc.
Pay-Related Social Insurance (PRSI)	Old-age pensions, jobseeker's benefit, jobseeker's allowance, child benefit, etc.
Universal social charge (USC)	Income for the state

The rates for the universal social charge (USC) are as follows (figures accurate for 2012):

- Zero, if total income is under €10,036

For people with an income of €10,036 or more, the rates are:

Rate of USC	Charged on income from
2%	€0 to €10,036
4%	€10,036.01 to €16,016
7%	Above €16,016

People over the age of 70 have a maximum USC rate of of 4% (even on incomes over €16,016).

Medical card holders also have a top USC rate of 4%.

> **Non-statutory deductions** are voluntary deductions. They are taken from gross pay by the employer at the request of the employee.

Examples of voluntary deductions include healthcare payments, union fees, pension payments, etc.

Income Tax (PAYE)

There are two rates of income tax in Ireland.

- The lower rate is called the **standard rate** of tax.
- The higher rate is called the **higher rate** of tax.

For example, the first €32,800 that a single person earns is taxed at 20%, and any income above this amount is taxed at 41% (figures accurate for 2012).

For a married couple or a couple in a civil partnership where both people are working, the first €65,600 is taxed at 20% and any additional income is taxed at 41%.

Every employee receives a **tax credit** certificate. This shows the employee's tax credit. This amount can change for individual employees.

> Note that these rates can vary from year to year.

> The amount up to which an employee is taxed at the standard rate is called the **standard rate cut-off point**.

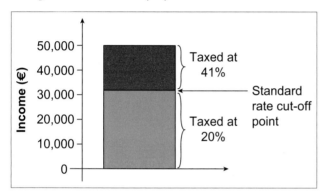

> **Gross tax** is the amount of income tax owed to the state before tax credits are deducted.

> The **tax credit** is a sum deducted from the total amount (gross tax) a taxpayer owes to the state.

> **Tax payable** is gross tax less the tax credit. This is the amount of income tax an employee actually pays to the state. So, gross tax – tax credit = tax payable.

 ## Worked Example 10.1

Albert earns €27,000 a year. He pays tax at a rate of 20%. He has instructed his employer to pay his annual health insurance premium of €550 directly from his salary. He pays no other deductions. He has a tax credit of €1,950. Find Albert's:

 (i) Tax payable   (ii) Total deductions   (iii) Net pay

Solution

(i) Gross tax = €27,000 × 20%

$\qquad$ = €27,000 × 0.2

$\qquad$ = €5,400

Tax payable = gross tax – tax credit

$\qquad$ = €5,400 – €1,950

$\qquad$ = €3,450

(ii) Total deductions = tax payable + health insurance

$\qquad$ = €3,450 + €550

$\qquad$ = €4,000

(iii) Net pay = gross pay – total deductions

$\qquad$ = €27,000 – €4,000

$\qquad$ = €23,000

Worked Example 10.2

The standard rate of income tax is 20% and the higher rate is 41%.

The standard rate cut-off point is €32,800.

Sandra has a gross income of €47,500 and total tax credits of €2,450.

Calculate Sandra's net income (ignore PRSI and USC).

Solution

Standard tax = €32,800 × 20%

$\qquad$ = €32,800 × 0.2

$\qquad$ = €6,560

Income liable for higher tax = €47,500 – €32,800

$\qquad$ = €14,700

Higher tax = €14,700 × 41%

$\qquad$ = €14,700 × 0.41

$\qquad$ = €6,027

Gross tax = standard tax + higher tax

$\qquad$ = €6,560 + €6,027

$\qquad$ = €12,587

Tax payable = gross tax – tax credit

$\qquad$ = €12,587 – €2,450

$\qquad$ = €10,137

Net pay = gross pay – tax payable

$\qquad$ = €47,500 – €10,137

$\qquad$ = €37,363

Worked Example 10.3

Sanabel earns €50,000 per annum.
Calculate the amount that will be deducted from her annual pay for the universal social charge.

Rate of USC	Charged on income from
2%	€0 to €10,036
4%	€10,036.01 to €16,016
7%	Above €16,016

Solution

Step 1

Break the salary down into the various threshold amounts.

€10,036 @ 2%

€16,016 – €10,036 = €5,980 @ 4%

€50,000 – €16,016 = €33,984 @ 7%

Step 2

Calculate the percentages.

First	Next	Remainder
€10,036	€5,980	€33,984
2%	4%	7%
€200.72	€239.20	€2,378.88

∴ The total USC = €200.72 + €239.20 + €2,378.88

$\qquad$ = €2,818.80.

APPLIED ARITHMETIC

Pay-Related Social Insurance (PRSI)

The amount of PRSI you pay depends on your earnings and the class under which you are insured.

For people in employment in Ireland, social insurance contributions are divided into different categories known as classes or rates of contribution. The type of class and rate of contribution you pay is determined by the nature of your work.

There are 11 different classes of social insurance in Ireland. The majority of people fall into Class A. The other classes are B, C, D, E, H, J, K, M, P and S. If you are insured under one of these classes, you are paying insurance at a lower rate than Class A contributors, which means that you are not entitled to the full range of social insurance payments.

Worked Example 10.4

Chloe earns €650 per week. She is in Class A1 for PRSI, which has the following rates:

	First €127	Balance
Employee %	0	4
Employer %	10.75	10.75

Calculate:

(i) Her PRSI payment this week

(ii) Her employer's PRSI payment this week

(iii) The total amount of PRSI that will be paid this week

Solution

(i) **Step 1**

Calculate the amount Chloe must pay PRSI on.

€650 − €127 = €523

Step 2

Calculate the PRSI.

€523 × 4%

= €523 × 0.04

= €20.92

∴ Chloe's PRSI payment is €20.92.

(ii) The employer must pay 10.75% on €650.

PRSI = €650 × 10.75%

= €650 × 0.1075

= €69.875

We round this amount to the nearest cent.

∴ PRSI payment = €69.88.

(iii) Total PRSI payment = €20.92 + €69.88

= €90.80

∴ Total PRSI payment is €90.80.

Worked Example 10.5

Derek has a gross annual income of €50,000. His standard rate cut-off point is €32,800. The standard rate of tax is 20%. The higher rate is 41%. His annual tax credit is €3,500. Derek is in Class A1 for PRSI, which has the weekly rates shown. He pays no other deductions. Assuming a 52-week year, calculate Derek's annual:

Weekly PRSI Rates		
	First €127	Balance
Employee %	0	4
Employer %	10.75	10.75

(i) Gross tax

(ii) Tax payable

(iii) Net income (ignoring PRSI)

(iv) PRSI payment

(v) Net income after PRSI has been paid

Solution

(i) Gross tax = standard tax + higher tax

Step 1

Standard tax = €32,800 × 0.2

= €6,560

Step 2

Income liable for higher tax = €50,000 − €32,800

$$= €17,200$$

Higher tax = €17,200 × 0.41

$$= €7,052$$

Step 3

Gross tax = €6,560 + €7,052

$$= €13,612$$

(ii) Tax payable = gross tax − tax credit

$$= €13,612 − €3,500$$

$$= €10,112$$

(iii) Net income (ignoring PRSI) = gross income − tax payable

$$= €50,000 − €10,112$$

$$= €39,888$$

(iv) **Step 1**

Derek pays no PRSI on the first €127 of his income each week.

There are 52 weeks in the year (assumed).

So, he pays no PRSI on the first €127 × 52 = €6,604 of his annual income.

Step 2

Income liable to PRSI = €50,000 − €6,604

$$= €43,396$$

Step 3

PRSI payment = €43,396 × 4%

$$= €43,396 × 0.04$$

$$= €1,735.84$$

(v) Net income − PRSI paid = €39,888 − €1,735.84

$$= €38,152.16$$

Exercise 10.1

For questions involving USC and/or PRSI, refer to the tables below:

Rate of USC	Charged on income
2%	On the first €10,036
4%	On the next €5,980
7%	On the balance

PRSI contribution rates from 1 January 2012					
Non-cumulative weekly earnings bands	PRSI Subclass	How much of weekly earnings	Employee	Employer	Employee & Employer
			%	%	%
More than €500	A1	First €127	0	10.75	10.75
		Balance	4.00	10.75	14.75

1. Ahmed earns €25,000 per annum. He pays tax at a standard rate of 20%. Calculate his tax payable (assume no tax credits).

2. Amelinda earns €46,000 per annum and pays tax at a rate of 22.5%. She has a tax credit of €2,500. Calculate her tax payable.

3. Shane earns €41,500 per annum. He pays tax at a rate of 22%. He has no other deductions. He has a tax credit of €2,340. Calculate his net income.

4. Natalie recently moved jobs. She is now earning €56,000 per annum. She has a standard rate cut-off point of €32,800. She pays tax at a standard rate of 20%. She pays 41% on the remainder of her earnings. She has no other deductions. She has no tax credits due to an underpayment of tax last year. Calculate her net income.

5. Professor Logan earns €94,500 per annum. She has a standard rate cut-off point of €33,000. She pays tax at a standard rate of 21% and a higher rate of 42%. She has no other deductions. Her tax credit is €3,450.

   Calculate:

   (i) Her tax payable   (ii) Her net pay

6. Ian earns €37,000 a year. His standard rate cut-off point is €37,400. The standard rate of tax is 21%. His tax credit is €2,100. His union fees are €450 and his annual health insurance is €350. He has no other deductions.

   What is Ian's annual take-home pay?

7. Neasa's tax bill for last year was €6,300. Her tax credit was €1,300. Her gross income was €38,000. She paid tax at the standard rate only.

   (i) How much was her gross tax?

   (ii) What rate did she pay tax at?

8. Bryan has a gross income of €50,000. He pays tax at 20% on the first €32,000 he earns and 42% on the remainder. His tax credit is €3,500. What is his tax payable?

9. Mark earns €35,000 a year. What is his annual USC charge?

10. Rian earns €46,500 a year. What is his annual USC charge?

11. Conor has an annual gross income of €72,000. His standard rate cut-off point is €34,600. The standard rate of tax is 20% and the higher rate is 41%. He has an annual tax credit of €3,000. He is in the class A1 for PRSI. (Assume a 52-week year.)

   (i) What is his PRSI contribution per week (2 d.p.)?

   (ii) What is his employer's PRSI contribution per week?

   (iii) Calculate his USC payment for the year.

   (iv) What is his weekly net income after all deductions?

12. Jamshaid has a gross income of €64,000 a year. His standard rate cut-off point is €32,400. The standard rate of tax is 20% and the higher rate is 41%. He has an annual tax credit of €2,400. He is in class A1 for PRSI. (Assume a 52-week year.)

   (i) What is his PRSI contribution per week?

   (ii) What is his employer's PRSI contribution per week?

   (iii) Calculate his USC payment for the year.

   (iv) What is his weekly net income after all deductions?

13. James and Celine have a combined annual income of €152,000. They pay tax at 20% on the first €65,600 they earn and 41% on the remainder. They have an annual tax credit of €3,400. They both pay PRSI at class A1 rates. Their total union fees amount to €704 each year and their total pension contributions are €5,063.

   (i) What is their total PRSI payment for the year? (Assume a 52-week year.)

   (ii) What is their combined USC for the year?

   (iii) Calculate their tax payable.

   (iv) What is their combined net income for the year?

14. Paula has a standard rate cut-off point of €35,400. The standard rate of tax is 20% and the higher rate is 41%. If Paula's gross tax is €12,396, what is her gross income (correct to the nearest cent)?

15. (i) Jenny has tax credits of €3,800 for the year and her standard rate cut-off point is €32,000. Her gross income is €45,000. The standard rate of income tax is 20% and the higher rate is 41%.

Calculate her total tax payable.

(ii) Chad pays tax at the same rate as Jenny. Chad's tax credits are €3,900, and he has the same standard cut-off point as Jenny. His total tax payable amounts to €13,680.

Calculate Chad's gross income.

(iii) Calculate the annual USC of the person with the higher gross income.

16. (a) The standard rate of income tax is 20% and the higher rate is 41%. The standard rate cut-off point is €32,800.

Chloe has a gross income of €57,500 and total tax credits of €2,830.

Calculate Chloe's net income. (Ignore all other deductions).

(b) The following year, Chloe's gross income increases.

The tax rates, cut-off point and tax credits remain unchanged.

Her net tax now amounts to €15,640.

What is her new gross income, correct to the nearest euro?

17. (i) Ciara is single, a PAYE worker and earned €42,000 this year. Ciara's tax credits are given in the table below.

Single person tax credit	€1,650
PAYE tax credit	€1,650
Trade union payment tax credit	€70

Calculate Ciara's total tax credits.

(ii) The standard rate cut-off point for a single person was €32,800. The standard rate of income tax is 20% and the higher rate is 41%.

Calculate the tax paid by Ciara on her income.

(iii) Ciara also had to pay the USC charge and PRSI. She is in the A1 PRSI subclass.

Calculate Ciara's net income after all deductions have been made.

18. Noel had a gross income of €50,000 last year. His total income tax payable amounted to €10,460.

The standard rate cut-off point was €32,800. The standard rate of tax was 20% and the higher rate was 41%.

Calculate Noel's tax credit for last year.

19. (a) The standard rate of income tax is 20% and the higher rate is 41%.

Shona has tax credits of €2,300 for the year and a standard rate cut-off point of €32,800. She has a gross income of €46,000 for the year.

Calculate the total tax payable by Shona for the year.

(b) Tony pays tax at the same rates as Shona. He has tax credits of €2,900 for the year and has the same standard rate cut-off point as Shona. His total tax payable amounts to €13,680 for the year.

Calculate Tony's gross income for the year.

10.2 PERCENTAGE PROFIT AND LOSS

Percentage Profit and Loss

> If a product or service is sold for more than it cost to buy or produce, then the seller has made a **profit**.

> If a product or service is sold for less than it cost to buy or produce, then the seller has made a **loss**.

> The **percentage profit mark-up** is the profit expressed as a percentage of the cost price: $\dfrac{\text{Profit}}{\text{Cost price}} \times 100\%$.

> The **selling price** is the cost price plus (minus) the profit (loss).

> The **percentage profit margin** is the profit expressed as a percentage of the selling price: $\dfrac{\text{Profit}}{\text{Selling price}} \times 100\%$.

Worked Example 10.6

Nick buys a DVD box set for €75 from an online retailer. He then sells it for €100.

(a) What is:

  (i) The cost price

  (ii) The selling price

  (iii) The profit made

  (iv) The percentage mark-up

  (v) The percentage margin

(b) Explain why, where a profit is made, the percentage mark-up is always greater than the percentage margin.

Solution

(a) (i) Cost price = €75 (the price Nick paid)

  (ii) Selling price = €100 (the price Nick sells for)

  (iii) Profit = selling price − cost price

$$= €100 - €75$$

$$= €25$$

(iv) Percentage mark-up $= \dfrac{\text{Profit}}{\text{Cost price}} \times 100\%$

$$= \frac{25}{75} \times 100\%$$

$$= 33\tfrac{1}{3}\%$$

(v) Percentage margin $= \dfrac{\text{Profit}}{\text{Selling price}} \times 100\%$

$$= \frac{25}{100} \times 100\%$$

$$= 25\%$$

(b) Compare $\dfrac{\text{Profit}}{\text{Cost price}}$ with $\dfrac{\text{Profit}}{\text{Selling price}}$.

Both numerators are the same. Therefore, the fraction with the smaller denominator will be the bigger quantity. As cost price < selling price, the percentage mark-up > percentage margin.

1. Copy the following table and fill in the missing figures:

	Cost price (€)	Selling price (€)	Profit (€)	% Mark-up (2 d.p.)	% Margin (2 d.p.)
(i)	25.00	30.00	5.00		
(ii)	31.00	36.00			
(iii)		20.00			25.00
(iv)	14.00		14.00		
(v)	12.00		6.00		
(vi)	18.00	18.90			
(vii)		4.00	3.00		
(viii)		2.80	0.70		
(ix)			2.00	20.00	
(x)	11.00		4.50		

2. Find the cost price of each of the following:

	Selling price (€)	% Margin
(i)	40	2
(ii)	85	5
(iii)	135	10
(iv)	100	0.5
(v)	1,565	3

3. A product costs a company €16,250 to produce. Find (a) the percentage mark-up and (b) the percentage margin if the company sells the product for €18,900. In each case answer correct to two decimal places.

4. A product costs a company €10,250 to produce. Find (a) the percentage mark-up and (b) the percentage margin if the company sells the product for €15,900. Answer correct to two decimal places in each case.

5. A retailer buys goods from a cash and carry outlet for €120. The recommended selling price is cost price plus 15%.

   (i) How much should she sell the goods for?

   (ii) What is her percentage margin (to the nearest percent)?

6. Derek bought a TV from a shop for €1,140. The percentage margin for the shop on this TV was 25%.

   (i) What was the original cost of the TV?

   (ii) In a sale, the shop manager decided to sell the TV at a mark-up of 15%. What is the new profit margin?

7. (i) Company A makes a 15% profit mark-up in a particular year. Calculate the percentage profit margin earned. (Answer to the nearest whole number.)

   (ii) Company B makes a 28.6% profit margin in a particular year. Express its profit performance as a percentage profit mark-up. (Answer to the nearest whole number.)

   (iii) Which is a company most likely to advertise – its percentage profit mark-up or its percentage profit margin? Explain your answer clearly.

   (iv) Which company would you prefer to buy shares in – one that earns a 43% mark-up on average each year or one that earns a 33% margin on average each year? Explain your answer clearly and make reference to appropriate calculations.

10.3 COMPOUND INTEREST: FUTURE VALUES

Individuals and businesses don't always have enough cash to buy what they want or to pay their bills. It is sometimes necessary for them to borrow money. Equally there are individuals and businesses that have large amounts of cash and who may like to invest some of it.

If you borrow money from a bank or financial institution, they will expect you to pay back the money you borrowed, but they will also charge you for the use of the money they loaned you. This is called **interest payable**.

When you invest money in an investment account or with a financial institution, you are giving the people who run the account or institution the use of your money. So they have to pay you a charge for the use of this money. This is called **investment interest**.

When a loan or an investment is paid back in full, the total amount is the sum borrowed or invested plus the interest that was paid.

When dealing with interest, we use the following symbols:

- F = Final value (amount borrowed or invested + interest)
- P = Principal (amount borrowed or invested)
- i = Rate of interest per annum (year) (always use decimal form)
- t = Time (usually in years)

This is a formula to be used when the interest rate remains unchanged.

FORMULA

$$F = P(1 + i)^t$$

This formula appears on page 30 of *Formulae and Tables*.

The rate of interest (i) that is used in the formula shown here is the Annual Percentage Rate (APR) or Annual Equivalent Rate (AER) as the formula $F = P(1 + i)^t$ assumes that compounding takes place once every year. The Annual Percentage Rate (APR) is used when dealing with loan and credit agreement calculations. The Annual Equivalent Rate (AER) is used when dealing with investments and savings; it can also be called the Annual Effective Rate or Effective Rate.

Worked Example 10.7

Niall borrows €100 for six years at an APR of 2% compounded annually. How much interest will he pay on the loan?

Solution

$F = P(1 + i)^t$

$P = €100$

$i = 2\% = 0.02$

$t = 6$ (years)

$F = €100 (1 + 0.02)^6$

$\quad = €100(1.02)^6$

$\quad \approx €112.62$

Interest = final value − principal

$\quad\quad\quad = €112.62 − €100$

$\quad\quad\quad = €12.62$

Worked Example 10.8

€10,000 is invested at 3% per annum. At the beginning of the second year, €1,450 is withdrawn from this amount. The interest rate for the second year rises to 3.5%.

Calculate:

(i) The value of the investment at the end of Year 1

(ii) The value of the investment at the end of Year 2

Solution

(i) Value of investment at end of Year 1:

$P_1 = €10,000$ $t = 1$ year $i = 0.03$

$F = P(1 + i)^t$

$= €10,000(1 + 0.03)^1$

$= €10,000(1.03)$

$= €10,300$

The value of the investment at the end of Year 1 is €10,300.

(ii) Value of investment at end of Year 2:

At the beginning of Year 2, €1,450 is withdrawn.

$\therefore P_2 = €10,300 - €1,450$

$= €8,850$ $t = 1$ year $i = 0.035$

$F = P(1 + i)^t$

$= €8,850(1 + 0.035)^1$

$= €8,850(1.035)$

$= €9,159.75$

The value of the investment at the end of Year 2 is €9,159.75.

Worked Example 10.9

A sum of €100 is invested in a three-year savings bond with an annual equivalent rate (AER) of 3.23%. Find the value of the investment when it matures in three years' time (to the nearest euro).

Solution

$F = P(1 + i)^t$

Method 1

	Principal	Rate of interest (i)	Amount at year end
Year 1	100	0.0323	$100(1.0323)^1$ = 103.23
Year 2	103.23	0.0323	$103.23(1.0323)^1$ = 106.5643
Year 3	106.5643	0.0323	$106.5643(1.0323)^1$ = 110.0064

The value of the investment at the end of three years is approximately €110.

Method 2

$P = €100$ $t = 3$ years $i = 0.0323$

$F = 100(1 + 0.0323)^3$

$= 100(1.0323)^3$

$= 110.0064$

$\approx €110$

1. €22,500 was invested at 5% for three years. Calculate the final value.

2. €16,000 was invested at 3% for six years. Calculate the total interest earned.

3. €10,200 was invested at 3.4% for eight years. Calculate the final value.

4. €1,500,000 was borrowed at 8% for three years. Calculate the final value.

5. €10,000 was borrowed at 6% for five years. Calculate the total interest accrued.

6. €25,400 was borrowed at 3% for ten years. Calculate the total interest accrued.

7. €200,500 was invested at 2.5% for eight years. Calculate the total interest earned.

8. €100,500 was borrowed at 5% for six years. Calculate the final value of the loan.

9. €1,000,000 was invested at 10.5% for three and a half years. Calculate the final value.

10. €9,600 was borrowed at 2% for four years. Calculate the total interest charged.

11. Find the amount, to the nearest cent, that needs to be invested at a rate of 6% to give €2,500 in five years' time.

12. Find the amount, to the nearest cent, that needs to be invested at a rate of 3.2% to give €12,500 in six years' time.

13. How much would Hannah need to invest, at a rate of 3.5%, to have €1,500 two years from now?

14. Mustafa borrows €16,000 at 3%. At the end of Year 1, he repays €2,000. The rate of interest is then lowered to 2%. How much will he owe at the end of the second year?

15. A country borrowed €1,500,000,000 to cover a budget deficit. The rate for the first year was 0.5% and the rate for the second year was 0.42%.

    Calculate the amount owing at the end of the second year.

16. A sum of €500 is invested in a three-year savings bond with an AER of 2.36%.

    Find the value of the investment when it matures in three years' time by completing the table below:

	Principal	Rate of interest	Amount at year end
Year 1			
Year 2			
Year 3			

17. Nicky invested €100,000 for four years in a variable-rate savings account. She was guaranteed an AER of 3% for the first year. At the start of the second year, the rate of interest changed to 3.25% and this rate was set for the remainder of the investment period.

    (i) Calculate the value of the investment at the end of Year 1.

    (ii) Nicky is advised to take out €5,000 at the end of Year 1 and that she will still have a final amount exceeding €108,000. Is this advice correct? Explain your answer clearly.

18. John invests €1,000 in a three-year savings account offering 4% annual interest. To calculate what his investment will amount to in three years' time, he calculates what 4% of €1,000 is, multiplies this amount by 3 and then adds this onto the €1,000 principal he originally invested.

    (i) What answer does John get for the final value of his investment?

    (ii) Was his method correct? Explain your answer.

1. Jarleth earns €27,000 a year. His standard rate cut-off point is €37,400. The standard rate of tax is 21%. His tax credit is €2,100. His union fees are €450 and his annual health insurance is €350. He has no other deductions. What is Jarleth's annual take-home pay?

2. Donna's tax bill for last year was €7,300. Her tax credit was €1,300. Her gross income was €37,000. She paid tax at the standard rate only.

   (i) How much was her gross tax?

   (ii) What rate did she pay tax at?

3. Gavin has a gross income of €45,000. He pays tax at 20% on the first €32,000 he earns and 42% on the remainder. His tax credit is €3,500. What is his tax payable?

4. Mark earns €35,800 a year. What is his USC charge?

Rate of USC	Charged on income from
2%	€0 to €10,036
4%	€10,036.01 to €16,016
7%	Above €16,016

5. Killian and his wife earn a combined salary of €79,000 per annum. They have a tax credit of €3,790 and pay tax at the standard rate of 20% on the first €72,000. Earnings above this amount are taxed at 41%. Every month they have deductions of €110 for VHI, €240 for pensions and €44 for union fees. They have no other deductions.

   How much is their fortnightly net pay? You may assume that 1 year = 52 weeks.

6. The USC is calculated on gross income. The rates of the USC are:

   ■ 2% on the first €10,036 of gross annual income

   ■ 4% on the next €5,980

   ■ 7% on the balance

   (a) Niamh earned €45,000 in 2011. Find her USC for that year.

   The table below shows a selection of the tax credits available in Ireland in 2011.

Individual's tax credits	Tax credit 2011
Single person	€1,650
Married or civil partner	€3,300
Widowed or surviving civil partner	€2,190
Home carer	€810
PAYE	€1,650
One-parent family	€1,650

   (b) Niamh is a single person who is a PAYE worker. Calculate her total tax credits for 2011.

   (c) The standard rate of tax is 20% and the higher rate is 41%. The standard rate cut-off point for a single person is €32,800. Calculate Niamh's tax bill for 2011.

   (d) Calculate Niamh's net pay for the year, after tax and USC are paid.

   SEC 2012, JCHL

7. A product costs a company €16,000 to produce. Find (a) the percentage mark-up and (b) the percentage margin if the company sells the product for €24,000.

8. A camera costs a retailer €120. The recommended selling price is cost price plus 15%.

   (i) How much should the retailer sell the camera for?

   (ii) What is the percentage margin (to the nearest per cent)?

9. Goods were sold to a customer for €3,750 at a profit margin of 25%.

   (i) What was the original cost of the goods?

   (ii) In a bid to attract more customers, it was decided to sell the goods at a mark-up of 15%. What is the new profit margin?

10. A meal in a restaurant cost Jerry €136.20. The price included VAT at 13.5%. Jerry wished to know the price of the meal before the VAT was included. He calculated 13.5% of €136.20 and subtracted it from the cost of the meal.

    (a) Explain why Jerry will not get the correct answer using this method.

    (b) From July 1, 2011, the VAT rate on food, in restaurants, was reduced to 9%. How much would Jerry have paid for the meal after this date if the VAT reduction was correctly applied?

    SEC Sample Paper, JCHL

11. A shop normally sells laptops at a profit margin of 60%. The manager decides to reduce prices in a sale, but still wishes to make 25% profit on the laptops sold in the sale.

    By what percentage of the normal selling price should the manager reduce prices in the sale?

12. A company has spent €35,000 on new equipment. The value of the equipment falls by 20% in the first year and by 15% in the second year after it was bought.

    (a) How much is the equipment worth when it is two years old?

    (b) The manager says that the value of the equipment has fallen by 35% in the two years.

    Is she correct? Explain your answer.

13. €1,500,000 was invested at 6.5% for three and a half years. Calculate the final value.

14. €18,600 was borrowed at 2% for four years. Calculate the interest payable.

15. Find the amount, to the nearest cent, that needs to be invested at a rate of 5% to give €20,500 in five years' time.

16. Find the amount, to the nearest cent, that needs to be invested at a rate of 4.2% to give €102,500 in six years' time.

17. Dermot has €5,000 and would like to invest it for two years. A special savings account is offering a rate of 3% for the first year and a higher rate for the second year, if the money is retained in the account. Tax of 27% will be deducted each year from the interest earned.

    (a) How much will the investment be worth at the end of one year, after tax is deducted?

    (b) Dermot calculates that, after tax has been deducted, his investment will be worth about €5,296 at the end of the second year. Calculate the rate of interest for the second year.

    SEC Sample Paper, JCHL

18. Norma has €7,290 in her bank account. This is after two years in which 8% was added to the account at the end of each year.

    How much did Norma have in the account two years ago?

19. Kevin found these exchange rates in a newspaper.

    - €1 was equivalent to 2.25 Swiss francs.
    - €1 was equivalent to 1.58 US dollars.

    Calculate the exchange rate between the Swiss Franc and the US Dollar in (a) francs per dollar and (b) dollars per franc.

20. The value of one euro against other currencies on a particular day is shown in the table below.

Currency	Rate
US Dollar	1.4045
Pound Sterling	0.87315
Lithuanian Litas	3.4528
Latvian Lats	0.7093
Polish Zloty	4.0440

    (a) Mary was going to the USA for a few months. She changed €1,200 into US Dollars using the exchange rate in the table.

       (i) How many dollars should she receive at this exchange rate?

       (ii) The bank charged 3% commission on the transaction. How many dollars did she receive?

APPLIED ARITHMETIC

(b) On returning to Ireland Mary had $3,060. She changed this amount into euro. The bank again charged her 3% commission on the transaction. She received €2,047.

Find the exchange rate on that day, correct to two decimal places.

(c) David changed a certain amount of sterling into euro at the exchange rate given in the table. A few days later he again changed the same amount of sterling into euro at a different exchange rate. He received fewer euro this time. No commission was charged on these transactions.

Write down one possible value for the exchange rate for the second transaction.

SEC 2012, JCHL

21. The number of children who can play safely in a schoolyard is directly proportional to the area of the yard.

A schoolyard with an area of 210 m² is safe for 610 children.

(a) How many children can safely play in a schoolyard of area 154 m²?

(b) A class has 24 children. What is the smallest area of the yard in which they can safely play?

22. The time taken to dig a hole is inversely proportional to the number of people doing the digging. It takes four people six hours to dig the hole.

(i) How long will it take eight people to dig the hole?

(ii) How long will it take six people to dig the hole?

23. A recipe to make lasagne for six people uses 300 g of minced beef. How much minced beef would be needed to serve eight people?

24. A 500 ml jug is filled with orange squash and water in the ratio 1 : 4.

Another 500 ml jug is filled with orange squash and water in the ratio 1 : 3.

Both jugs are poured into one large jug.

What is the ratio of orange squash to water in the large jug?

25. A soccer team has three strikers, John, Paul and Michael. The number of minutes each had played by the end of a particular season is shown on the table. The team divided a bonus of €150,000 between its strikers in proportion to the time each had played.

Name	Minutes played
John	2,250
Paul	2,600
Michael	150

(a) Calculate the amount each player received.

(b) At the end of the following season a larger total bonus was paid. At that time, John said: 'The bonus should be paid according to the number of goals scored by the striker. Paul scored 50% more goals than Michael. I scored as many as both of them together. I would get €140,000 if the team used this method.'

(i) Calculate the total bonus on offer that season.

(ii) How much each would Paul and Michael get under John's system?

SEC 2012, JCHL

26. Séamus is a car salesman. He earns a basic wage of €1,200 per month plus 15% commission on any sales he makes.

What value of cars does Séamus need to sell each year if he wishes to have an annual income of €60,000?

27. Cathal rents a house at a monthly rent of €620. The rent agreement states that the rent will be reviewed annually and will be increased by the annual inflation rate.

Assuming an annual inflation rate of 4%, find:

(a) The amount of rent paid in the first year

(b) The rent increase at the end of the first year

(c) The monthly rent paid during the second year

(d) The monthly rent to be paid during the seventh year

28. Before being fitted with a 'fuel-saver', John's car travelled 72 km on 9 litres of petrol. After the fuel-saver was fitted, it travelled 58.3 km on 5.5 litres of petrol.

Find the percentage increase in distance travelled per litre of petrol.

29. Alan pays income tax, a universal social charge (USC) and pay-related social insurance (PRSI) on his gross wages. His gross weekly wages are €510.

(a) Alan pays income tax at the rate of 20%. He has weekly tax credits of €63. How much income tax does he pay?

(b) Alan pays the USC at the rate of 2% on the first €193, 4% on the next €115 and 7% on the balance. Calculate the amount of USC Alan pays.

(c) Alan also pays PRSI. His total weekly deductions amount to €76.92. How much PRSI does Alan pay?

30. A sum of €2,500 was invested for three years at compound interest.

The rate of interest was 4% per annum for the first year and 3% per annum for the second year.

(i) Calculate the amount of the investment after two years.

(ii) If the investment amounted to €2,744.95 after three years, calculate the rate of interest per annum for the third year.

31. Aoife pays a fixed monthly charge of €15 for her mobile phone. This charge includes 100 free text messages and 50 minutes free call time each month. Further call time costs 28 cent per minute and additional text messages cost 11 cent each.

In one month Aoife sends 140 text messages and her call time is 2 hours.

(i) Find the total cost of her fixed charge, text messages and call time.

(ii) VAT is added to this cost at the rate of 23%. Find the amount paid, including VAT.

32. The standard rate of income tax is 20% and the higher rate is 42%.

Colm has weekly tax credits of €50 and a standard-rate cut-off point of €240. Until recently, he had a gross weekly income of €900.

(i) Calculate the tax Colm paid each week.

(ii) After he got a pay rise, Colm's weekly after-tax income increased by €20.30. Calculate the increase in his gross weekly income.

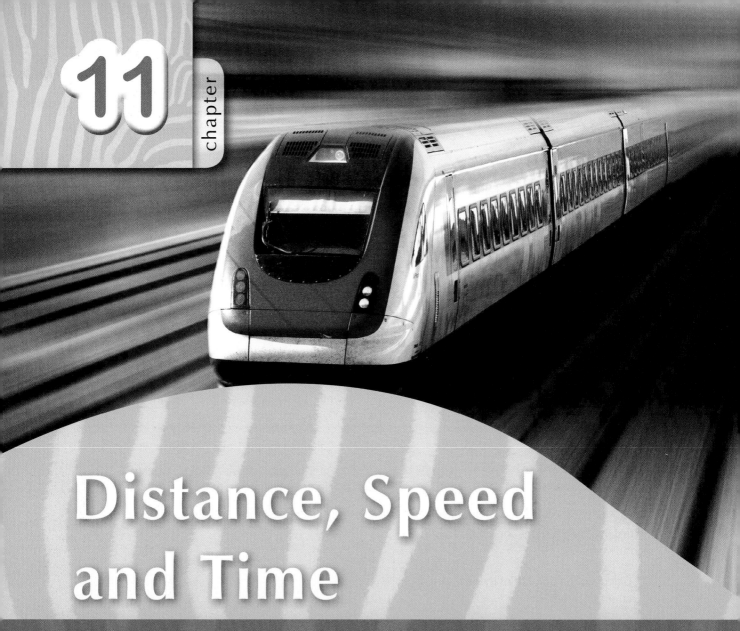

11 chapter

Distance, Speed and Time

Learning Outcomes

In this chapter you will learn to:

- Calculate, interpret and apply units of measure and time
- Solve problems that involve calculating average speed, distance and time
- Solve distance, speed and time problems involving graphs.

11.1 DISTANCE, SPEED AND TIME

DST Triangle

Problems which involve an object travelling at a constant speed or which involve average speed can often be answered with the aid of the following diagram, called the Distance–Speed–Time triangle, or DST triangle.

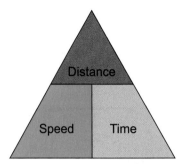

$$\text{Speed} = \frac{\text{Distance}}{\text{Time}}$$

$$\text{Distance} = \text{Speed} \times \text{Time}$$

$$\text{Time} = \frac{\text{Distance}}{\text{Speed}}$$

We can remember the DST triangle by using the following mnemonic:
Dad's **S**illy **T**riangle

YOU SHOULD REMEMBER...

■ How to work with distance, speed and time from *Active Maths 1*

■ How to construct and interpret graphs

KEY WORDS

■ DST Triangle
■ Average speed
■ Acceleration
■ Deceleration

When using the DST triangle, we must be careful to note which units of measurement are being used.

Commonly Used Units

Distance is often measured in kilometres (km) or metres (m).

Speed is often measured in kilometres per hour (km/hr or km/h) or metres per second (m/s).

Time is often measured in hours (hr), minutes (m) or seconds (s).

Worked Example 11.1

A car is involved in a two-legged journey. On the first stage of the journey the car travels at an average speed of 80 km/h for 4 hours and 10 minutes. On the next stage of its journey, the car travels 300 km in 5 hours.

  (i) What is the distance travelled by the car on the first stage of its journey?

  (ii) What is the average speed of the car for the second stage of its journey?

 (iii) What is the overall distance travelled by the car for the whole journey?

 (iv) How long does the whole journey take to complete? Answer in hours and minutes.

  (v) What is the car's overall average speed for the whole journey? Answer correct to the nearest km/hr.

Solution

  (i) 10 minutes $= \frac{10}{60}$ hour $= \frac{1}{6}$ of an hour

      Distance = Speed (km/h) × Time (hrs) $= 80 \times 4\frac{1}{6} = 333\frac{1}{3}$ km

  (ii) Speed $= \frac{\text{Distance (km)}}{\text{Time (h)}} = \frac{300}{5} = 60$ km/h

 (iii) Overall distance $= 333\frac{1}{3} + 300 = 633\frac{1}{3}$ km

 (iv) Total time $= 4\frac{1}{6}$ hrs + 5 hrs $= 9\frac{1}{6}$ hrs = 9 hrs 10 minutes

(v)   Overall average speed = $\dfrac{\text{Total distance (km)}}{\text{Total time (h)}} = \dfrac{633\frac{1}{3}}{9\frac{1}{6}} = 69\frac{1}{11}$ km/h

Overall average speed to the nearest km/h = 69 km/h.

Overall average speed = $\dfrac{\text{Overall or total distance}}{\text{Overall or total time}}$

Distance–Time and Speed–Time Graphs

We can use graphs to show the relationship between distance and time and between speed and time.

A tachograph is an example of a graph that shows the relationship between speed and time. It can also be used to express the relationship between distance and time. Tachographs are fitted to certain buses, lorries and other commercial vehicles.

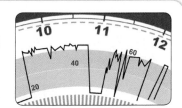

ACTIVITIES 11.1, 11.2

Features of a Distance–Time Graph

The horizontal axis is used to represent the time taken.

The vertical axis is used to represent the distance travelled.

Consider the graph shown, which relates distance travelled to time taken for a particular journey.

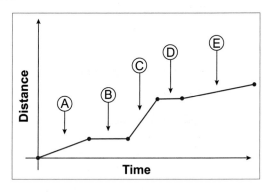

Consider the different stages of the journey:

Stage A   The graph is a straight upward-sloping line. This means that the object is travelling at a constant speed.

Stage B   The graph is a horizontal line (slope = 0). This means that the object is stationary.

Stage C   The graph is a straight upward-sloping line.
The slope for Stage C is greater than the slope for Stage A. So, for Stage C, the object is travelling at a faster constant speed than for Stage A.

Stage D   The object is stationary.

Stage E   The object is travelling at a slower constant speed than for Stages A or C.

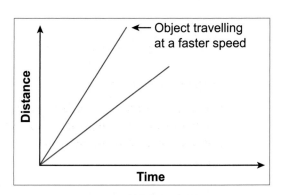

The steeper the gradient (slope) of the line, the faster the average speed it represents.

For a distance–time graph:

Slope = $\dfrac{\text{Rise}}{\text{Run}}$ = Speed

Worked Example 11.2

The graph below shows the distance travelled by Ellen when cycling from her home (*A*) to her friend's house (*F*).

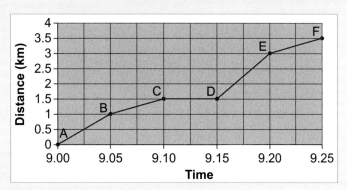

(i)   At what time did Ellen arrive at her friend's house?

(ii) Calculate (in km/hr) the average speed at which Ellen cycled between point *A* and point *B*.

(iii) Ellen stopped for a short rest. At what time did this occur?

(iv) Excluding the time that she stopped for a rest, what was Ellen's average speed for the whole journey?

(v)   Write a short paragraph describing the different stages of Ellen's journey to her friend's house after she stopped for her rest.

Solution

(i)   She arrived at 9.25 a.m.

(ii) **Method 1**

Find the slope of *AB*:

$$\text{Slope} = \frac{\text{Rise}}{\text{Run}} = \frac{1 \text{ (km)}}{5 \text{ (min)}}$$

∴ Speed = 0.2 km/min

0.2 km × 60 min = 12 km/hr

∴ Speed = 12 km/hr

Method 2

$$\text{Speed} = \frac{\text{Distance}}{\text{Time}} = \frac{1 \text{ (km)}}{\frac{1}{12}} \left[5 \text{ min} = \frac{1}{12} \text{ hr} \right]$$

∴ Speed = 12 km/hr

(iii) She stopped for a short rest between 9.10 and 9.15 a.m. This is represented by the horizontal line between the points *C* and *D*.

(iv) Overall distance = 3.5 km

Overall time = 20 min (25 min total – 5 min when she stopped for a rest)

$20 \text{ min} = \frac{1}{3}$ hr

∴ Overall average speed = $\dfrac{3.5}{\frac{1}{3}}$

= 10.5 km/hr

(v)   First, we work out the average speeds that are needed for writing the paragraph.

Slope of *DE* = $\dfrac{1.5}{5}$ km/min (18 km/hr)

Slope of *EF* = $\dfrac{0.5}{5}$ km/min (6 km/hr)

Now, write the paragraph:

Ellen starts to cycle to her friend's house again at 9.15 a.m. She travels at an average speed of 18 km/hr for 5 minutes. She then slows down for the last 5 minutes of her journey as she travels at an average speed of 6 km/hr. She reaches her friend's house at 9.25 a.m.

Worked Example 11.3

Consider the graph below, which relates distance travelled to time taken for a particular journey.

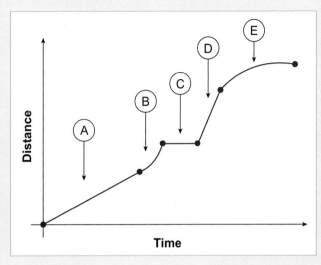

Solution

Consider the different stages of the journey:

Stage A The object is travelling at a constant speed.

Stage B The graph is a curve with increasing positive slope.

This means that the object is getting faster during Stage B. So, the object is accelerating.

Stage C The object is stationary.

Stage D The object is travelling at a faster constant speed than during Stage A.

Stage E The graph is a curve with decreasing positive slope.

This means that the object is getting slower during Stage E. So, the object is decelerating.

■ An object increasing in speed is **accelerating**. The slope of the distance–time graph is **positive** and **increasing**.

■ An object decreasing in speed is **decelerating**. The slope of the distance–time graph is **positive** and **decreasing**.

Features of a Speed–Time Graph

The vertical axis (y-axis) represents the speed of the object.

The horizontal axis (x-axis) represents the time taken.

An object moving at a constant speed is represented by a line drawn parallel to the x-axis (slope = 0).

An object increasing in speed (accelerating) is represented by a graph with a positive slope.

An object decreasing in speed (decelerating) is represented by a graph with a negative slope.

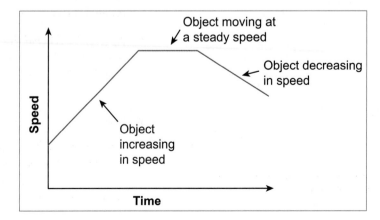

Worked Example 11.4

Consider the graph shown, which relates the speed of an object to the time taken for a particular journey.

Describe the speed of the object for each of the four stages of the journey.

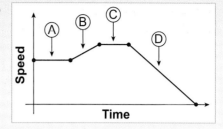

Solution

Consider the different stages of the journey:

Stage A   The slope is zero so the speed is neither increasing nor decreasing. So, the object is travelling at a constant speed.

Stage B   The slope is positive so the speed is increasing. The object is accelerating.

Stage C   The object is travelling at a higher constant speed than for Stage A.

Stage D   The slope is negative, so the speed is decreasing. The object is decelerating. The final speed is zero.

For a speed–time graph:

- Zero slope   ⇒ constant speed
- Positive slope   ⇒ accelerating
- Negative slope ⇒ decelerating

Distance From a Fixed Point

Sometimes we may be given questions that relate the distance from a fixed point to the time taken. Such questions will normally be given within very clear and specific contexts.

 Worked Example 11.5

Abby sets off for her local post office, posts a letter and then returns home by the same route. The diagram below shows a distance–time graph for her journey where 'distance' refers to 'distance from her home' rather than 'distance travelled'.

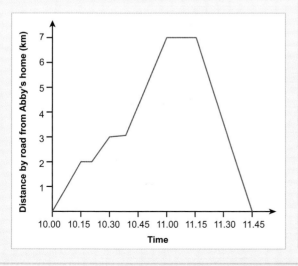

(i)   At what time does Abby leave home?

(ii)   At what time does she arrive at the post office?

(iii) Which is faster, her going to the post office or her return home?

(iv) What is her overall average speed for the entire journey?

(v)   Write a short paragraph describing the different stages of Abby's journey to and from the post office.

Solution

(i)   Abby leaves home at 10.00 a.m.

(ii)   Abby arrives at the post office at 11.00 a.m. We assume this, as 11.00 to 11.15 a.m. is the longest time that she remains at the same distance from her house.

(iii) It takes Abby 1 hour to reach the post office, whereas it takes her 30 minutes to return home. Her return journey is the faster.

(iv) Abby travels 14 km (7 km there and 7 km back) which takes her 1 hour and 45 minutes.

$$\text{Speed} = \frac{14}{1.75}$$

$$= 8 \text{ km/hr}$$

Note that question did not ask to exclude 'rest' times.

(v) Paragraph describing different stages in Abby's journey:

Abby leaves her house in her car at 10.00 a.m. On her journey to the post office she twice stops at a red light (10.15 and 10.30 a.m.). She arrives at her local post office at 11.00 a.m. She leaves the post office after 15 minutes and then returns home, arriving back home at 11.45. a.m.

Note: It is important to remember that a horizontal line on a 'distance from starting point vs. time graph' does not necessarily indicate a stationary object.

 Exercise 11.1

1. Copy and complete the following table.

Departure Time	Arrival Time	Time taken for journey
09:23	13:26	
09:05		6 hrs 52 mins
	21:35	6 hrs 48 mins
03:37		12 hrs 39 mins
	23:11	10 hrs 35 mins
00:29	18:14	
14:16	18:03	
07:25		14 hrs 53 mins

2. Copy and complete the following table.

Distance (km)	Speed (km/hr)	Time (hrs and minutes)
100	50	
75		$\frac{1}{2}$ hr
	62	3 hrs 15 mins
550	60	
10		20 minutes
350	80	
80	75	
	375	3 hrs 12 mins
90		16 hrs 40 minutes
	15	48 mins
650	60	
12.5	18	

3. Change the following speeds into the required units:

   (i) 12 km/h into m/s

   (ii) 800 m/s into km/h

   (iii) 63 km/h into m/s

   (iv) 5 cm/s into m/s

   (v) 18 cm/s into km/hr

4. A cyclist travels for 2 hours at an average speed of 11 km/hr. How far does the cyclist travel?

5. A car travels a total distance of 300 km in 5 hours. What is the average speed of the car?

6. The Belfast to Dublin rail timetable is shown.

Belfast Central - Portadown - Newry - Dundalk - Dublin • Table 5

Monday to Friday

See footnotes	⟠		1✕	1✕	1✕	1✕	1✕	1✕		1✕		1✕
Belfast Central Ⓜ		0600	**0650**	**0800**	**1035**	**1235**	**1410**	**1610**	1710	**1810**	1814	**2010**
Gt Victoria St		0610 0640	|	0750	| 1010	| 1210	| 1400	| 1540	| 1721	1801	| 1825 1915	|
Lisburn		0632 0651	|	0801	1032 *1047	1232 *1247	1410	| 1602	| 1732	1812	| 1836 1937	**2022***
Moira		0643 0701	|	0811	1043	1243	1421	| 1613	| 1743	1822	| 1847 1948	|
Lurgan		0651 0709	|	0819	1051	1251	1429	| 1621	| 1751	1830	| 1855 1956	|
Portadown	0615	0700 0716	**0721**	0826 **0831**	1058 **1108**	1258 **1308**	1436 **1441**	1630 **1641**	1800	1837 **1841**	1903 2005	**2043**
Scarva	0623	0708	|	|	|	|	|	|	1808	|	1911	|
Poyntzpass	0628	0713	|	|	|	|	|	|	1813	|	1916	|
Newry Ⓛ	0639 **0645** 0724		**0742**	**0852**	**1130**	**1330**	**1502**	**1702**	1825	**1902** 1928		**2105**
Dundalk		0710		0800	0910	1148	1348	1520	1720	1920		2123
Drogheda		0734		0823	|	1210	1410	1542	1742	1942		2145
Dublin Connolly		0831		0904	1000	1244	1444	1617	1815	2015		2218

✕ — Catering services available   1 — First Plus service available   * — Pick up only at Lisburn   *Light type denotes NIRailways Service providing connection opportunities with Enterprise*

Ⓜ — Free Metro bus between Belfast City Centre and Belfast Central for rail passengers

⟠ — Operated by Iarnrod Éireann (not Enterprise), serves main stations between Newry, Dublin Connolly and Bray arriving 0913.

Belfast First Plus Ticket & seat reservations 028 9066 6630
visit translink.co.uk

Dublin First Plus Ticket & seat reservations 01 70 34 070
Timetable information 01 83 66 222 or click www.irishrail.ie

Ⓛ — Free Ulsterbus Service 341 operates between Newry Buscentre, Newry city centre and Newry Rail Station for intending rail passengers
Rail Link bus from Newry Buscentre to Newry Rail Station (journey time approx 5 minutes)
• Monday-Friday 0825, 1035, 1115, 1205, 1315, 1420, 1445, 1615, 1645, 1745, 1805

(i) Name the Belfast to Dublin trains that stop at Lisburn.

(ii) What is the fastest time that any train takes to get from Belfast to Dublin?

(iii) William lives 15 minutes away from the train station in Moira. Write a short description of the trains he might take, and at what times, to ensure he arrives at Drogheda before 11:00.

(iv) If a passenger travelling from Lurgan to Poyntzpass takes the 16:21 train from Lurgan to Portadown and then travels by train from Portadown to Poyntzpass, what percentage of the journey is actually spent travelling by train?

   Assume that the journey starts at Lurgan station and ends at Poyntzpass station and that all trains run on time. Answer correct to the nearest whole number.

7. A train leaves a station at 19:12. The average speed of the train on its journey of 130 km is 75 km/hr. At what time did the train complete its journey?

8. (i) The speed of sound is approximately 340 m/s. Find the speed of sound in km/hr.

   (ii) The speed of an object is approximately 300,000 m/s. Find the speed of the object in km/hr.

9. Fiona cycles a distance of 6 km to school. She travels at an average speed of 18 km/h. If she leaves her home at 8.43 a.m., at what time will she arrive at school?

10. A section of a Bus Éireann timetable is shown.

Table No.

ATHLONE – SLIGO (summary timetable) 76

SERVICE NUMBER		MONDAY TO SATURDAY							SUNDAY	
		466	021	065	466	021	466		466	073
							FO			
Athlone (Bus Station)	dep.	0905	1105	1445	1630	1715	1920	....	....	1400	1615
Roscommon (Mart Road)			1135			1745		....	....		
Castlerea			1201			1815		....	....		
Ireland West Airport Knock	arr.		1255					....	....		
Knock (St. Anne's, Main St)	arr.					1847			....	....	
SERVICE NUMBER			**064**			**064**					
Knock (St. Anne's, Main St.)	dep.					1930					
Knock (Ballyhaunis Road)								....	....		
Ireland West Airport Knock			1340					....	....		
Longford (Rail Station)	arr.	1005		1535	1740		2010	....	....	1445	1700
SERVICE NUMBER		**023**		**023**	**023**		**023**			**023**	**023**
Longford (Rail Station)	dep.	1025		1550	1750		2100	....	....	1455	1705
Dromod		1045		1610	1808		2120	....	....	1516	1726
Carrick-on-Shannon		1103		1628	1823		2133	....	....	1533	1742
Boyle (King House)		1118		1643	1838**D**		2148	....	....	1548	1757
Collooney		R	1423	R		2025	R	....	....	1618**D**	1833**D**
Sligo (Bus Station)	arr.	1200	1445	1725	1915	2045	2235	....	....	1630	1845

D : – Drop–off stop only.

FO = Operates Friday only during College terms only.

(i) Which bus is the first to stop at Knock (Main St)?

(ii) What is the number of the bus that reaches Collooney at 14:23?

(iii) Padraig arrives in Knock at 15:05. How long will he have to wait before the next bus departs for Sligo?

(iv) Which two buses take the shortest time to reach Sligo from Athlone?

11. How many more minutes does it take to travel 500 km at 75 km/hr than at 80 km/hr?

12. Aga travels by car for 1 hour and 6 minutes to reach a railway station, which is 55 km away. She then takes a 110 km train journey at an average speed of 80 km/h.

(i) What was the average speed of her car journey?

(ii) How long did the train journey take?

(iii) What was the total distance travelled?

(iv) What was the overall time taken for the whole journey?

(v) What was the average speed for the whole journey?

(vi) The next day, Aga and her friend Peter travel to Rosslare harbour in separate cars. The ratio of the speeds of Aga's car to Peter's car is 8 : 9. If it takes Peter five hours to travel a distance of 270 km in his car, what is the average speed of Aga's car?

13. A car leaves a town at 12:35 and travels at 60 km/h for 1 hour 35 minutes. On the next stage of its journey, the car travels 180 km at an average speed of 80 km/h until it reaches its destination.

(i) What was the distance travelled for the first part of the journey?

(ii) How long did it take the car to complete the second part of its journey?

(iii) What was the overall distance travelled by the car?

(iv) What was the total time for the whole journey?

(v) At what time did the car reach its destination?

(vi) What was the car's overall average speed, to the nearest kilometre/hour?

(vii) Another car travels the first two hours of a journey at an average speed of 70 miles per hour (mph) and the remaining four hours at an average speed of 35 mph.

Using the relationship that 8 km is approximately equal to 5 miles, calculate the average speed of the car for the whole journey. Give your answer correct to the nearest kilometre per hour.

14. In a triathlon, an athlete swims 1.5 km at an average speed of 3 km/hr, cycles 40 km at a speed of 30 km/hr, and then runs 10 km in 42 minutes.

What was the athlete's average speed for the whole triathlon? Answer in km/hr correct to three significant figures.

15. Trevor took part in a triathlon consisting of a swim, followed by a cycle and ending in a run.

He completed the swim at an average speed of 2 metres/second in a total of 6 minutes.

He cycled a distance of 45 km in 1 hour 15 minutes.

He completed the run of 10 km running at an average speed of 12 km/hr.

(a) What was his average cycling speed? Answer in metres/second.

(b) For which portion of the race (swim, cycle or run) did he have the fastest average speed? You must provide evidence for your answer here.

(c) Calculate the total distance travelled, from start to finish, in the triathlon. Give your answer in metres.

(d) Calculate Trevor's average speed for the entire triathlon. Answer in metres/second correct to two places of decimals.

16. A competitor cycles at an average speed of 20 km/hr in a 175 km race. She decides that she will stop every 25 km for a rest of exactly 2 minutes duration. How long will it take her to complete the race?

17. Ellie and Daniel race each other in a swimming competition. The race is over two lengths of the pool.

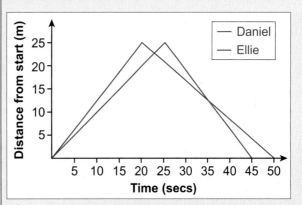

(i) Who completed the first length in the fastest time?

(ii) Who won the race?

(iii) What was the average speed of both swimmers for the first length?

(iv) What was the average speed of both swimmers for the second length?

(v) An Olympic swimming pool is 50 m in length. Is this pool 50 m in length? Explain your answer.

(vi) Estimate the time at which the swimmers passed by each other. Explain who was winning the race at both of these times.

18. For each of the following graphs, find the:

   (i) Distance travelled   (ii) Time taken   (iii) Overall average speed

Graph A   **Graph B**   **Graph C**   **Graph D**

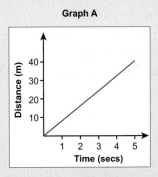 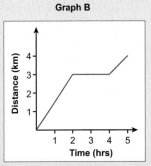 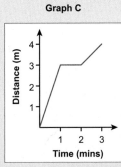 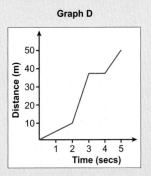

19. Joe leaves his house and walks to school. His journey, between the time he leaves his house and the time he arrives at school, is shown by the following graph.

   (i) At what time did Joe leave his house?

   (ii) At what time did he arrive in school?

   (iii) How far is the school from his house?

   (iv) Joe stops for a chat with his friends. At what points does this occur on the graph? Give a reason for your answer.

   (v) What is Joe's average speed, in km/hr, between the points B and C?

   (vi) Between what two points did Joe move the fastest? Give a reason for your answer and a possible explanation for this increase in speed.

   (vii) What is his average speed for the whole journey?

20. The distance–time graphs shown represent different parts of a car journey.

Graph A   **Graph B**   **Graph C**

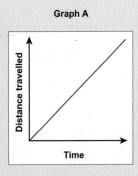 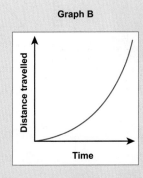 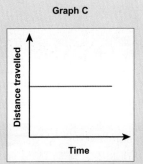

   (a) Which diagram represents the part of the journey where the car is:

      (i) Not moving

      (ii) Travelling at a constant speed

      (iii) Increasing in speed

   (b) A car reaches its destination and then returns home (to its starting point) along the exact same route. Draw a 'distance from starting point vs. time taken' graph to show how this journey could be represented.

21.

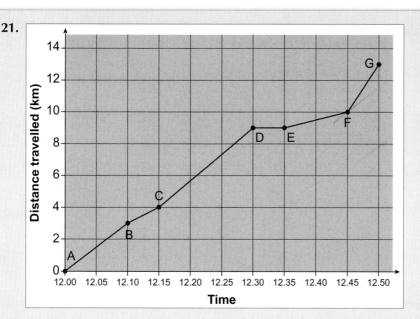

The graph shows the distance travelled by an object to the time taken for a particular journey.

Describe the average speed of the object between each point of the graph:

(a) In general (no calculation necessary)

(b) By calculating each average speed

22. A motorist travels a section of road in 20 minutes, at an average speed of 80 km/hr. The next day a new speed limit is imposed on this section of the motorway. Travelling at the maximum speed allowed, it takes 12 minutes longer to cover the same distance. What is the new speed limit for this section of road?

23. A person travels a distance of 150 km, at an average speed of 30 km/h. If they were to travel at an average speed that was two and a half times as fast, how much time would they have saved?

24. Write a report for each of the following graphs. Give a possible explanation for what is happening between each point.

(i)

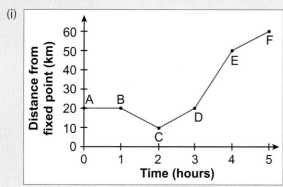

(iii)

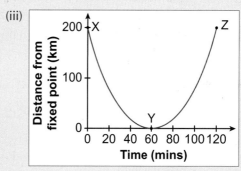

(ii)

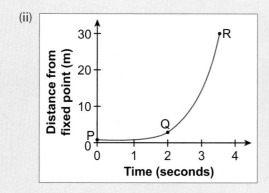

25. The speed–time graphs below represent the motion of four different particles.

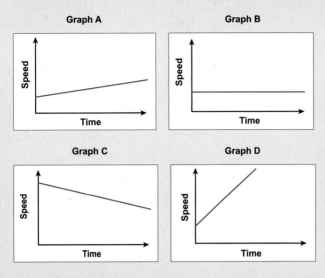

Graph A

Graph B

Graph C

Graph D

Which graph represents a particle that is:

(i) Travelling at a constant speed

(ii) Increasing in speed slowly

(iii) Increasing in speed quickly

(iv) Decreasing in speed

26. Draw separate distance–time graphs using each of the following race reports:

Race 1 Distance: 30 m. Winning time: 5 seconds.

Both runners run at constant speeds.

Both runners start at the same time, but runner A finishes one second before runner B.

Race 2 Distance: 50 m. Winning time: 8 seconds.

Runner B gets a 5 m head start so only runs 45 m, but both runners finish at the same time.

Both runners run at constant speeds.

Race 3 Distance: 25 m. Winning time: 4 seconds.

Runner A gets a 5 m head start. Both runners run at the same average speed.

Race 4 Distance: 40 m

Runner A runs at an average speed of 5 m/s.

Runner B runs at an average speed of 8 m/s.

27. A distance–time graph for three runners for a cross-country race is shown. 'Distance' refers to the distance from start, along the race route.

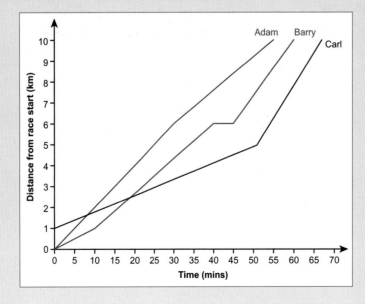

Write a report of this race. Make sure to include the following details:

(i) The winner of the race

(ii) The runner who was given a head start

(iii) The runner who had to stop for a rest

(iv) Which runner overtook whom and in what order

(v) The overall average speed for each runner

28. Draw a suitable graph for each of the following situations. The label for the vertical axis is given in brackets for each case.

(i) A child going on a Ferris wheel that completes one revolution at a constant speed (the child's distance from the ground)

(ii) Swimming four lengths of a swimming pool back and forth (the distance from the starting point)

(iii) A ball which is thrown vertically up in the air and then falls to the ground (the balls's distance from the ground)

(iv) A satellite orbiting the earth (distance from the earth's surface)

29. On a car journey on a motorway, Amir travels from junction 1 to junction 5.

From junction 1 to 2: travels at 20 km/hr for 30 mins

From junction 2 to 3: travels 10 km in 1 hour

From junction 3 to 4: travels at 60 km/hr for a quarter of an hour

From junction 4 to 5: travels 5 km at 15 km/hr

Draw a distance–time graph to illustrate this journey. Label each axis appropriately.

(i) What is the total distance of the car journey?

(ii) What is the total time taken to complete this journey?

(iii) What is the overall average speed of the car for this journey?

30.

(i) A train travelling at a speed of 60 km/hr passes a signal post in 15 seconds. How long is the train?

(ii) It takes this train 10 seconds to completely pass through a tunnel 80 m in length. Calculate the speed of the train as it passes through the tunnel.

(iii) Another train that is 120 metres long travels at a speed of 72 km/hr. How long will it take this train to pass a platform that is 80 metres long?

(iv) A train travelling at 60 km/hr takes 25 seconds to pass by an apartment block and 20 seconds to pass by a man standing in front of the apartment block. What is the length of the apartment block?

31. Chang sets off in his race car at an average speed of 20 m/s. Seven seconds later, Henry sets off at an average speed of 30 m/s.

(i) How long will it take Henry to overtake Chang?

(ii) In the next race, Chang races at average speed that is 20% faster than Henry. If Henry gets a 100-metre head start, the race will end in a dead heat.

What is the length of this race?

Area and Volume

Learning Outcomes

In this chapter you will:

⊃ Revise length, area and volume from *Active Maths 1*

⊃ Investigate nets of prisms (polygonal bases) cylinders and cones

⊃ Solve problems involving surface area of triangular base prisms (right angle, isosceles, equilateral), cylinders and cones

⊃ Solve problems involving curved surface area of cylinders, cones and spheres

⊃ Perform calculations to solve problems involving the volume of rectangular solids, cylinders, cones, triangular base prisms (right angle, isosceles, equilateral), spheres and combinations of these

12.1 TWO-DIMENSIONAL (2D) SHAPES

From determining the number of litres of paint needed to paint a room to working out the correct size wheel to fit a car, a knowledge of two-dimensional shapes is important.

On our course we need to be able to find the **area** and/or **perimeter** of certain shapes.

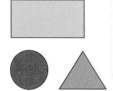

> **Area** is the amount of flat space that a shape occupies.
>
> **Perimeter** is the sum of the lengths of all the sides of a shape.

Perimeter is calculated by adding up various lengths of the shape's sides so the units will be in millimetres (mm), centimetres (cm), metres (m), or kilometres (km) usually.

The units of area will always be units², for example: mm², cm², m², km², etc.

When finding the area of a shape, make sure that you use the same units:

mm × mm, cm × cm, etc.

Rectangle	Square
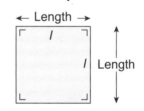 Area = length × width = $l \times w$ Perimeter = $2l + 2w$ **or** $2(l + w)$	Area = (length)² = l^2 Perimeter = $4l$
Triangle	**Parallelogram**
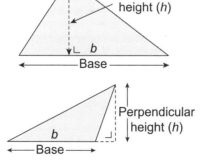 Area = $\frac{1}{2}$ × base × perpendicular height = $\frac{1}{2} bh$	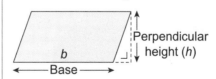 Area = base × perpendicular height = bh

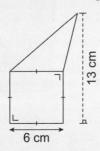

Worked Example 12.1

Calculate the area of the following shape:

13 cm

6 cm

Solution

We can see that this shape is made up of a square and a triangle.

Area of square:

Area $= l^2 = (6)^2 = 36$ cm^2

Area of triangle:

Perpendicular height $= 13 - 6$

$= 7$ cm

The base length of the triangle is the same as the side length of the square.

Area of triangle $= \frac{1}{2}bh$

$= \frac{1}{2} \times 6 \times 7$

$= 21$ cm^2

$\therefore$ Area of shape $= 36 + 21$

$= 57$ cm^2

Circles

Area and Circumference of a Circle

Another two-dimensional shape is that of a circle or disc.

In maths a circle refers to the curve, while a disc refers to the area within the curve. We find the area of a disc and the circumference of a circle. Commonly, it is acceptable to say that we find the area of a circle.

The circumference of any circle divided by the length of its diameter is always the same. This number is π (pronounced 'pi'). We use π when calculating the area and circumference (length) of a circle or sector of a circle.

$$\pi = \frac{\text{Circumference of a circle}}{\text{Length of diameter}}$$

FORMULA

Area of a disc $= \pi \times r^2$, usually written as πr^2.

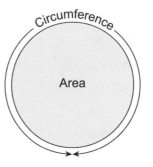

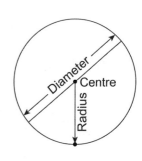

FORMULA

Circumference or length of a circle $= 2 \times \pi \times r$, usually written as $2\pi r$.

These formulae appear on page 8 of *Formulae and Tables*.

π is an irrational number. To eight decimal places, $\pi = 3.14159265$. As π is an infinite non-recurring decimal, we often use approximations of π in our calculations. In calculating the area or circumference of a circle, we may be told to use one of the following values for π:

- $\pi = 3.14$
- $\pi = \frac{22}{7}$
- The value of π from the calculator

We may also be asked to leave our answer in terms of π.

Worked Example 12.2

Find the area and perimeter of the following shape, taking $\pi = 3.14$. (Answer correct to one decimal place.)

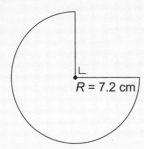

$R = 7.2$ cm

Solution

Area: The shape shown is $\frac{3}{4}$ of a full circle.

This shape is known as a **sector** of a circle.

> A **sector** of a circle is the portion of a circle bounded by two radii and the included arc.

Area of a full circle $= \pi r^2$

$$\therefore \text{ Area sector} = \frac{3}{4} \times 3.14 \times (7.2)^2$$

$$= \frac{3}{4} \times 3.14 \times 51.84$$

$$= 122.0832$$

$$= 122.1 \text{ cm}^2 \quad \text{(to one decimal place)}$$

Perimeter: Find the circumference of $\frac{3}{4}$ of the circle.

Circumference of a full circle $= 2\pi r$

$$\therefore \frac{3}{4} \text{ of circumference} = \frac{3}{4} \times 2 \times 3.14 \times 7.2$$

$$= 4.71 \times 7.2$$

$$= 33.912 \text{ cm}$$

This is the length of the arc within the shape.

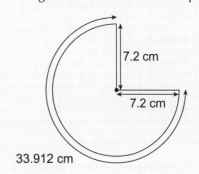

7.2 cm

7.2 cm

33.912 cm

$$\therefore \text{ Perimeter of shape} = 33.912 + 7.2 + 7.2$$

$$= 48.312$$

$$= 48.3 \text{ cm} \quad \text{(to one decimal place)}$$

Worked Example 12.3

A rectangular piece of card is shaded as shown. Find the area of the shaded part of the card, to the nearest cm^2. $\left(\pi = \frac{22}{7}\right)$

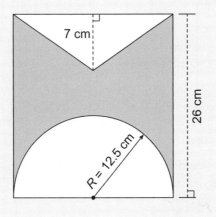

7 cm

26 cm

$R = 12.5$ cm

Solution

Area of shaded shape = total area – unshaded area.

Total area (rectangle):

length = 26 cm, breadth = 25 cm   (2 × 12.5)

∴ Total area = 26 × 25 = 650 cm²

Unshaded area:

Area of triangle + Area of half a circle

Area of triangle	Area of half a circle
$\frac{1}{2}bh = \frac{1}{2} \times 25 \times 7$	$\frac{1}{2}\pi r^2 = \frac{1}{2} \times \frac{22}{7} \times (12.5)^2$
$= 87.5 \text{ cm}^2$	$= 245\frac{15}{28} \text{ cm}^2$

∴ Unshaded area $= 87.5 + 245\frac{15}{28}$

$\qquad\qquad = 333\frac{1}{28} \text{ cm}^2$

∴ Area of shaded part $= 650 - 333\frac{1}{28}$

$\qquad\qquad\qquad = 316\frac{27}{28}$

$\qquad\qquad\qquad = 316.9642857$

$\qquad\qquad\qquad \approx 317 \text{ cm}^2$ (to the nearest unit)

Finding a Missing Dimension

Sometimes we may be given a shape's area or perimeter with an unknown side or radius. In this case we have to work backwards to find the unknown side or radius. There are several methods that we can follow to do this.

Worked Example 12.4

A plan for a garden is shown.

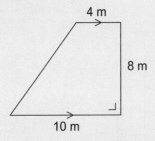

4 m

8 m

10 m

(i) Find the area of the garden.

(ii) The garden is to be enclosed by a fence.
A metre of fencing costs €5.60.

Find the cost of fencing this garden.

Solution

(i) Split the garden into two regular shapes.

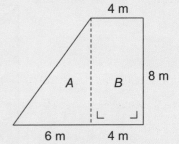

4 m

8 m

A   B

6 m   4 m

Triangle A (right-angled triangle)

Area $= \frac{1}{2}bh$

Area $= \frac{1}{2}(6)(8)$

$= 24 \text{ m}^2$

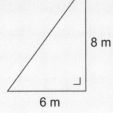

8 m

6 m

Rectangle B

Area $= lw$

Area $= (4)(8)$

$= 32 \text{ m}^2$

4 m

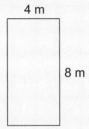

8 m

Area of garden $= 24 + 32$

$= 56 \text{ m}^2$

(ii) First find the perimeter of the garden.

In order to do so, we will need to find the length of the hypotenuse of triangle A.

$c^2 = a^2 + b^2$

$c^2 = (8)^2 + (6)^2$

$c^2 = 64 + 36$

$c^2 = 100$

$\therefore c = 10 \text{ m}$

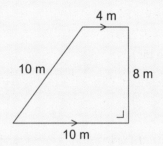

c

8 m

6 m

Now fill in all the necessary side lengths.

4 m

10 m

8 m

10 m

Perimeter $= 10 + 4 + 8 + 10$

$= 32 \text{ m}$

$\therefore$ Total cost $= 32 \times 5.60$

$= €179.20$

Worked Example 12.5

The circumference of a circle is 106.76 m. Calculate the length of the radius of the circle. ($\pi = 3.14$)

Solution

Method 1

Write down what we are given.	Circumference of the circle = 106.76
Write down the relevant formula.	$2\pi r = 106.76$
Fill in the known values.	$2(3.14)r = 106.76$ $6.28r = 106.76$
Solve for r.	$r = \dfrac{106.76}{6.28}$ $r = 17 \text{ m}$

Method 2 (Make r the subject of the formula)

Let C = Circumference of circle

$C = 2\pi r$

$\Rightarrow \dfrac{C}{2\pi} = r$

$\Rightarrow r = \dfrac{106.76}{2(3.14)}$

$\therefore r = 17 \text{ m}$

Worked Example 12.6

The area of a circle is $201\frac{1}{7}$ mm². Calculate the length of the radius of the circle $\left(\pi = \frac{22}{7}\right)$.

Solution

Method 1

Write down what we are given.	Area circle = $201\frac{1}{7}$
Write down the relevant formula.	$\pi r^2 = 201\frac{1}{7}$
Fill in the known values.	$\left(\frac{22}{7}\right)(r^2) = 201\frac{1}{7}$ $\frac{22}{7}r^2 = 201\frac{1}{7}$
Solve for r.	$r^2 = \dfrac{201\frac{1}{7}}{\frac{22}{7}}$ $= 64$ $\Rightarrow r = \sqrt{64}$ $r = 8$ mm

Method 2 (Make r the subject of the formula)

A = Area circle

$A = \pi r^2$

$\Rightarrow \dfrac{A}{\pi} = r^2$

$\Rightarrow \sqrt{\dfrac{A}{\pi}} = r$ (as $r > 0$)

$\Rightarrow r = \sqrt{\dfrac{201\frac{1}{7}}{\frac{22}{7}}}$

$\Rightarrow r = 8$ mm

Exercise 12.1

1. Calculate the area of each of the following shapes. All units are in metres.

(i)

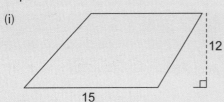

12

15

(ii)

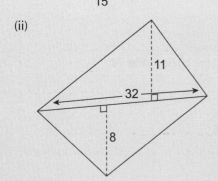

11

32

8

2. Find the area and perimeter of each of the following shapes. All units are in millimetres.

(i)

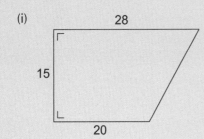

28

15

20

(ii)

26 15 13 12

3. Find the area, arc length and perimeter of each of the following sectors:

(i) $\pi = 3.14$

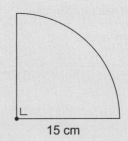

15 cm

(ii) $\pi = \frac{22}{7}$

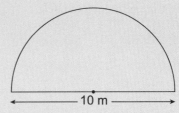

10 m

(iii) $\pi = 3.14$

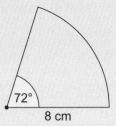

72°

8 cm

(iv) $\pi = 3.14$

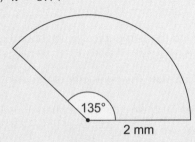

135°

2 mm

4. By using the information beside each diagram, find the value of x.

(i)

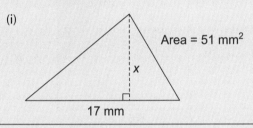

Area = 51 mm²

x

17 mm

(ii)

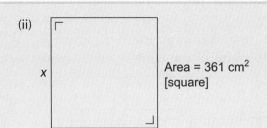

x

Area = 361 cm²
[square]

(iii)

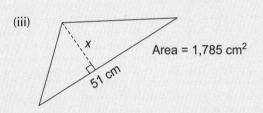

x

Area = 1,785 cm²

51 cm

(iv)

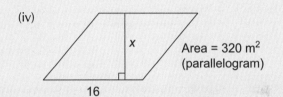

x

Area = 320 m²
(parallelogram)

16

5. Fill in the table below by first finding the radius of each of the circles.

π	r (cm)	Area (cm²)	Circumference (cm)
π		16π	
3.14			50.24
$\frac{22}{7}$		2,464	
π			24π
3.14		1,133.54	
$\frac{22}{7}$			180.4

6. Find the area and perimeter of each of the following shapes (correct to two decimal places where necessary).

All units are in centimetres. Each curve is a semicircle or quarter circle. Let $\pi = 3.14$.

(i)

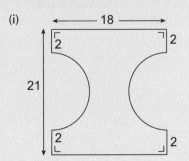

18

2   2

21

2   2

(ii)

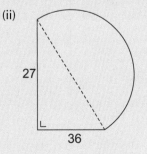

27

36

(iii)

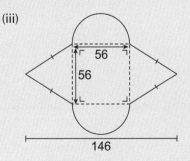

56

56

146

7. Find the area of the shaded regions of each of the following shapes (correct to one decimal place). All curves shown are sectors of circles.

(i)

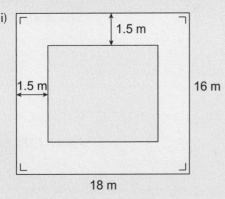

(ii) (*Note: π from calculator*)

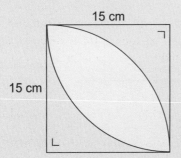

(iii) (*Note: π from calculator*)

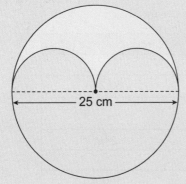

(iv)

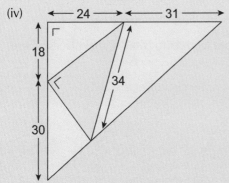

8. The area of the isosceles triangle shown is 168 cm² and its base length is 14 cm.

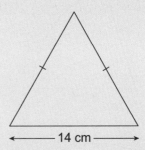

(i) Find the perpendicular height of the triangle.

(ii) Calculate the perimeter of the triangle.

9. An area of square tile with a quarter circle outlined on it is to be shaded blue as shown.

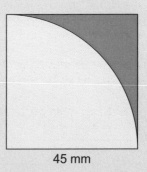

45 mm

(i) Find the area of the shaded region correct to two decimal places.

(ii) These tiles are used to tile the following wall space in a kitchen. Find how many tiles are needed to tile this space.

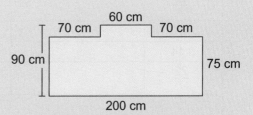

(iii) Each tile costs €2.50 and a tiler charges €50 per $\frac{1}{2}$ m² of tiling. VAT is added to the price of tiling this wall space at a rate of 21%. Calculate the total cost, to the nearest euro, to have this wall space tiled.

10. A satellite orbits the Earth at a distance of 1,250 km above the Earth's surface. The Earth has an approximate radius of 6,400 km.

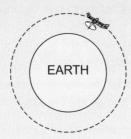

If it takes the satellite two hours to orbit the Earth:

(i) Calculate its orbital speed. Let $\pi = 3.14$.

Due to space debris the satellite is moved to a new orbit further away from the Earth. It now takes the satellite five hours 18 minutes more to orbit the Earth, travelling at a speed of 16,000 km/hr.

(ii) Calculate the change in height of the satellite (nearest km).

11. Calculate the shaded area of this shape.

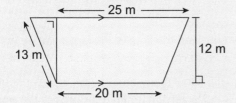

12. A rectangular floor tile is shaded as shown.

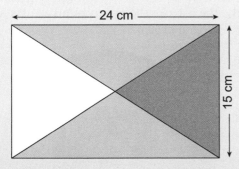

(i) Calculate the area covered by the pink part of the tile.

(ii) How many tiles will be needed to tile a floor measuring 10 m × 8 m?

(iii) What area of this floor will be white?

(iv) What percentage of the floor will be blue?

13. The semicircular end of a glass window is shown. Two sections of the window are tinted in a green colour.

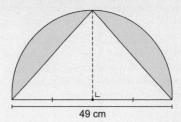

(i) Find the area of the green-tinted glass used in this window. Let $\pi = \frac{22}{7}$.

(ii) Express the area of the green-tinted glass as a percentage (to the nearest per cent) of the total glass used.

14. A map has a scale of 1 : 100,000. Calculate the scaled lengths that need to be drawn on the map to represent:

  (i) 1 km   (iii) 125 km

  (ii) 14 km   (iv) 600 m

15. A diagram has a scale of 1 : 2,500. Calculate the actual lengths of lines represented as:

  (i) 3 cm   (iii) 10 mm

  (ii) 12 cm   (iv) 0.45 m

16. A diagram of a human being 1.6 m tall is shown.

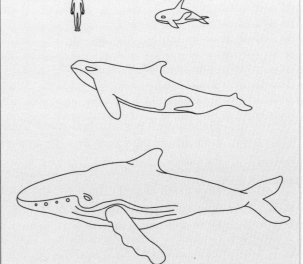

(a) Find the lengths of all the creatures shown. (Use a ruler to help you.)

(b) A blue whale can grow up to 27 m long. How long would a scaled drawing of this whale be, using the above scale?

17. A rectangular piece of plastic has six circular holes, each of radius r cm, bored into it as shown.

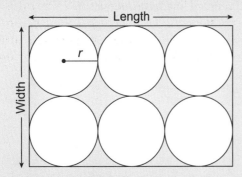

Find, in terms of r:

(i) The width of this piece of plastic

(ii) The length of this piece of plastic

(iii) The area of this piece of plastic after the six circular holes have been removed ($\pi = 3.14$)

(iv) Hence, express the area of the piece of plastic with the holes removed as a percentage of the area of the rectangle.

18. (i) Find the side length of the square shown in the diagram below if the area of the circle inscribed within the square is 81π cm².

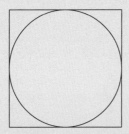

(ii) Write as a fraction, in terms of π:

$$\frac{\text{Area of circle}}{\text{Area of square}}$$

(iii) To the nearest per cent, how much bigger is the area of the square than the area of the circle?

19. (i) Find, to the nearest centimetre, the side length of a square that is inscribed in a circle of diameter 50 cm.

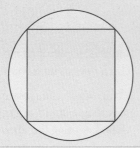

(ii) What percentage of the circle is covered by the square? Answer correct to one decimal place.

(iii) The drawing in part (i) represents a circular piece of wood. The square is to be cut out and three of the remaining parts to be laid out to form a wooden toy as shown.

Find, to the nearest centimetre, the height of the triangle enclosed by these three parts.

Hence, find the area of the triangle (nearest cm²).

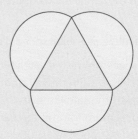

20. A square is to be constructed with a side length the same as the diagonal of a square of side length r cm.

(i) Find, in terms of r, the side length of the larger square.

(ii) Find the area of the larger square in terms of r.

(iii) How many times bigger is the area of the larger square than the area of the smaller square?

21. The diagram shown represents a target at a fairground game.

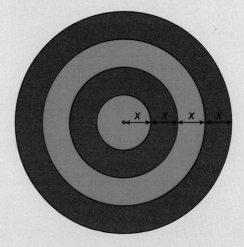

In the game, a dart lands on the target at a random location.

Find the percentage probability that the dart lands on the blue area of the target.

22. A circle of radius b units is cut from a circle of radius a units as shown in the diagram. Calculate the remaining area, given that $(a - b)(a + b) = 21$. Take $\pi = \frac{22}{7}$.

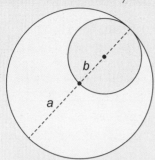

23. A round annulus is cut out of paper. The inner edge of the annulus is a circle of radius R. The width of the annulus is x.

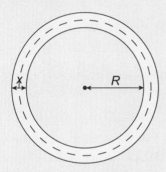

Prove that the area of the annulus is $2\pi Rx + \pi x^2$.

24. The diagram below shows the chain of a bicycle, passing over cogged wheels A and B, whose radii are 5 cm and 2 cm respectively. C is the wheel of the bicycle and has radius 21 cm. Wheel B turns the same number of times as wheel C. The bicycle travels a distance of 990 m.

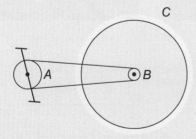

Find $\left(\text{taking } \pi = \frac{22}{7}\right)$:

(i) The circumference of wheel C

(ii) The number of times that wheel C turns

(iii) The number of times that wheel A turns

25. Pizzas come in two sizes: large ones with a radius of 11 cm and small ones with a radius of 6 cm. The large ones cost €6. The small ones cost €2. If Guiseppe has €6 to spend, should he buy one large pizza or three small ones in order to get the greatest possible area?

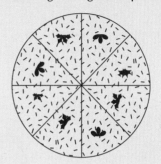

26. Three athletes A, B and C run around a track, as shown. The track is rectangular with semicircular ends. Each athlete runs in a lane which is 1 metre wide.

All measurement shown are in metres.
Let $\pi = 3.14$.

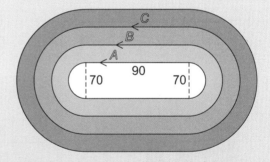

Answer these questions to the nearest metre:

(i) If A runs around the entire track once, how far does she travel?

(ii) If B travels around the entire track once in the next lane, how far does she travel?

(iii) The organisers want the three athletes to compete in a 400-metre race. How much 'stagger' must runners B and C be given (i.e. how far ahead of A should each start)?

27. (a) The diagram, not to scale, represents a shot-put zone in an athletics stadium. The area of *CDE* is a quarter of the area of a disc of centre *C* and of radius 100 m.

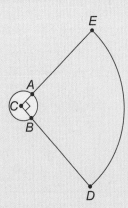

(i) Calculate the area of *CDE*, correct to two decimal places.

The shot-put zone consists of a throwing zone and a landing zone. The throwing zone (shaded yellow) is a disc of centre *C* and of radius 1 m.

(ii) Calculate the area of the throwing zone, correct to two decimal places.

The landing zone is the unshaded area *ABDE*, which is part of *CDE*.

(iii) Calculate the total area of the shot-put zone, correct to two decimal places.

(b) The diagram shows two pulley wheels of equal size, connected by a drive belt. The radius of each wheel is 7 cm and the distance between the centres is 28 cm.

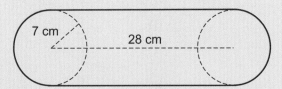

Calculate the length of the belt. Give your answer correct to the nearest whole number.

SEC 2011, JCHL

12.2 RECTANGULAR SOLIDS AND PRISMS

Rectangular Solids

One type of 3D object is the rectangular solid. To find the volume of a rectangular solid (cuboid), use the following formula.

Cuboid

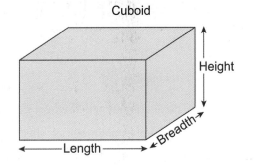

FORMULA

Volume of a cuboid = length × breadth × height
∴ Volume = *lbh*

If all sides of the rectangular solid are equal in length, then it can be referred to as a **cube**.

Cube

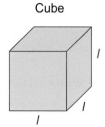

FORMULA

Volume of a cube = length × length × length

$$\therefore \text{Volume} = l^3$$

Surface Area and Nets

A cube or cuboid has six flat sides or faces.

The line where two faces meet is called an **edge**.

The corner where edges meet is called a **vertex**.

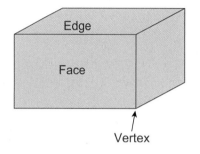

If we cut along the edges of a solid, we can create a **net** of that solid.

 ⇒ 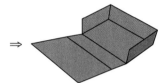 ⇒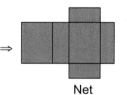

Net

A **net** is a 2D (flat) shape that folds up along its edges to make a 3D shape.

There can be many different nets for one rectangular solid. Both of the nets below are for a cube.

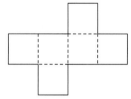   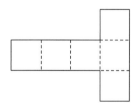

Nets can be used to help calculate the **surface area** of a 3D shape.

Surface area of a 3D shape = the sum of the area of all faces of its net.

> **Surface area of a cuboid** = the sum of the area of all six faces of its net.

Surface area = area of (top + base + front + back + side + side).

This can also be written as:

FORMULA

Surface area of a cuboid = $2lb + 2lh + 2bh$

FORMULA

Surface area of a cube = $6(\text{length})^2$ or $6l^2$

	Top 7	
	11	
	Back 10	
Side 7	Base 7	Side 7
10	11	10
	Front 10	
	11	

Prisms

> A **prism** is a 3D shape that has parallel congruent bases which are both polygons. It has the same cross-section along the whole length of its shape.

> A **right prism** is a prism that has two congruent bases, one directly above the other. Its side faces are rectangles.

The volume of a right prism is the area of its base multiplied by the prism's length.

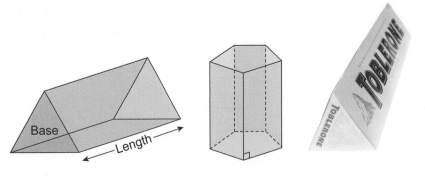

The surface area of a prism can be found by summing the area of all faces of its net.

FORMULA

Volume of a prism = area of base × length

Worked Example 12.7

A right prism is shown.
Draw an appropriate net for this prism.

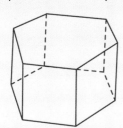

Solution

It can be helpful to count the number of faces the prism has. This prism has eight faces.

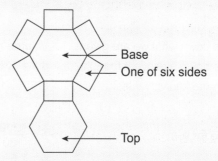

Base
One of six sides

Top

AREA AND VOLUME

Worked Example 12.8

A diagram of a container is shown. The container has no underside. Find the (i) volume and (ii) surface area of the container, given that it is a right prism.

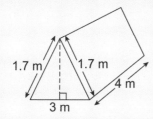

Solution

(i) Volume:

The base (front face) of the prism is an isosceles triangle.

Use the theorem of Pythagoras to find the perpendicular height (x) of the triangle.

The base length of 3 m is bisected.

$$h^2 = a^2 + b^2$$
$$(1.7)^2 = (1.5)^2 + x^2$$
$$2.89 = 2.25 + x^2$$
$$2.89 - 2.25 = x^2$$
$$0.64 = x^2$$
$$\sqrt{0.64} = x$$
$$0.8 \text{ m} = x$$

Now calculate the area of the base of the prism.

Area of base $= \frac{1}{2}(3)(0.8)$

$= 1.2 \text{ m}^2$

$\therefore$ Volume prism $=$ Area of base $\times$ length

$= (1.2)(4)$

$= 4.8 \text{ m}^3$

> It is important to remember that area will have units² while volume will have units³.

(ii) Surface area:

Draw out the net for the shape. As the shape has no underside, we shade that face orange to remind us not to include it in our calculations.

Remember that we have already worked out the area of the front and back of this shape.

Work out the area of each other face.

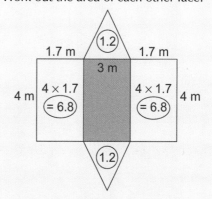

Surface area $= 2(6.8) + 2(1.2)$

$= 16 \text{ m}^2$

ACTIVITY 12.1

Worked Example 12.9

The volume of a cuboid is 1,350 cm³. Find the breadth of the cuboid if the length is 15 cm and the height is 12 cm.

Solution

Method 1

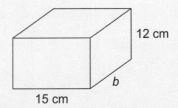

Write down what we are given.	Volume = 1350
Write down a relevant formula.	*lbh* = 1350
Fill in the known values.	(15)(*b*)(12) = 1350
	180*b* = 1350
Solve for *b*.	$b = \dfrac{1350}{180}$
	b = 7.5 cm
	∴ Breadth = 7.5 cm

Method 2 (Make breadth the subject of the formula)

V = Volume

$V = lbh$

$\Rightarrow \dfrac{V}{lh} = b$

$\Rightarrow b = \dfrac{1350}{(15)(12)}$

$\Rightarrow b = 7.5$ cm

∴ Breadth = 7.5 cm

Exercise 12.2

1. Calculate the volume and surface area of the following cuboids.

(i)

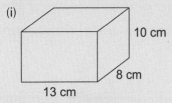

10 cm
8 cm
13 cm

(ii)

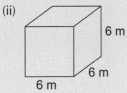

6 m
6 m
6 m

(iii)

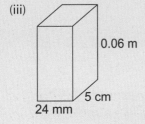

0.06 m
5 cm
24 mm

2. Find the volume and surface area of the following prisms.

(i)

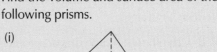

12 cm
105 cm
35 cm

(ii)

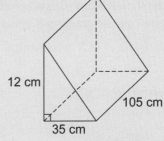

5 cm
6 cm
8 cm
10 cm

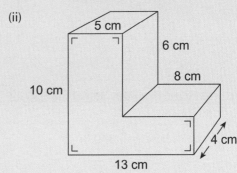

13 cm
4 cm

(iii) ($\pi = 3.14$)

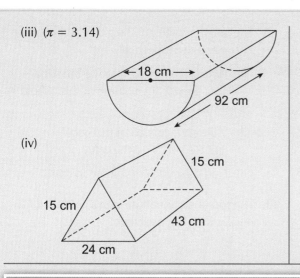

(iv)

(v)

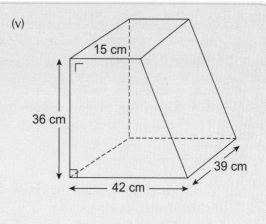

In Questions 3 and 4, copy and complete the tables. Make sure to show all work.

3. Cubes

Length (cm)	Volume (cm³)	Surface area (cm²)
	64	
		600
	3.375	
		45.375

4. Cuboids

Length (cm)	Breadth (cm)	Height (cm)	Volume (cm³)	Surface area (cm²)
	11	23	1,771	
9		9		486
12	14		6,720	
15	8.1			506.34
0.5		0.25		1.3

5. Draw nets for each of the following shapes. Include all known measurements on each net. In each case find the surface area of the shape, to two decimal places where necessary.

(i) Cylinder

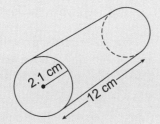

(ii) Cuboid

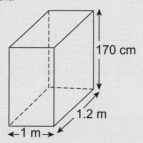

(iii) Prism

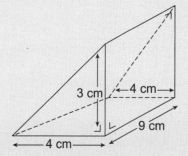

6. A cuboid has a volume of 18,000 cm³. It has a length of 36 cm and a width of 15 cm. Find its height.

7. A rectangular box has a surface area of 1,138 cm².

(i) Find its width, if it has a length of 19 cm and a height of 11 cm.

(ii) The box is to be used to hold a liquid. Find the capacity of this box in litres.

8. A cuboid has side length dimensions in the ratio 1 : 1.5 : 3.5. Find its dimensions if its volume is 2,688 cm³.

9. A box measuring 30 cm by 10 cm by 12 cm is gift-wrapped. If we assume that 10 per cent of the wrapping paper is wasted, what is the least amount of wrapping paper needed?

10. An ornamental pond is built from bricks in the shape of a cuboid, as shown.

The pond, when $\frac{3}{4}$ full, holds 240 litres of water. If the length of the pond is 1.2 m and its width is 80 cm, find the height of the pond.

11. A design for a concrete part of a bridge is shown.

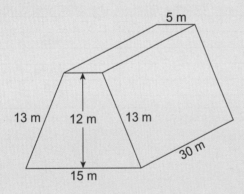

(i) How many litres of concrete are needed to make this part?

(ii) What is the weight in tonnes of this part if a litre of concrete weighs 2.4 kg?

(Note: 1 tonne = 1,000 kg)

(iii) This part is to be laid flat as shown and the exposed surfaces are to be painted. If 2 litres of paint cover 5 m², how many litres are required?

12. The length, width and height of a cuboid are 7y, 6y and 4y respectively.

(i) Write an expression for (a) the surface area and (b) the volume of this cuboid in terms of y.

(ii) If the surface area of this cuboid is 317.72 cm², find the value of y.

(iii) Find the cuboid's volume in cm³.

13. The top of an aquarium is in the shape of a regular hexagon as shown.

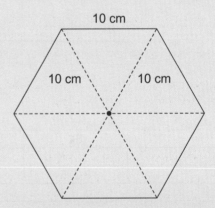

(i) Find, in surd form, the area of the top of this aquarium.

The aquarium has a height of 55 cm.

(ii) If the aquarium is recommended to be filled to $\frac{4}{5}$ of its total volume, how much water can it hold (nearest cm³)?

(iii) Due to a faulty panel, the aquarium starts leaking water at a rate of 5 cm³ per minute. How long will it take, to the nearest minute, for the aquarium to be half full if it is initially full (recommended capacity) when the leaking starts?

14. A rectangular tank with no lid has a surface area of 440 cm². It has a length of 15 cm and a width of x cm. The height of the tank is two and a half times its width.

Find the capacity of the tank in litres.

15. Three triangular based prisms are shown. The prisms represent the three different designs put forward for a new tent.

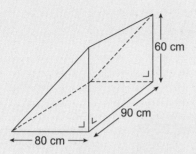 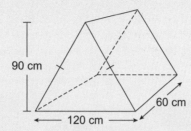 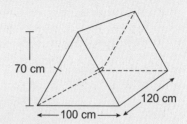

(i) Which tent has the greatest capacity?

(ii) The tents are to be covered in a material which costs €15 per square metre. The front and back of each tent are to be left open but the tent is to have a base made of this material. Find, to the nearest euro, the cost to cover each tent.

16. A blueprint for a garden shed made from wood is shown. A manufacturer is asked to build these sheds for a major garden supply retailer.

(i) Find the area of the front face of this shed.

(ii) Find the volume of this shed.

(iii) The wooden roof of this shed is to be covered in roofing felt which costs €12 per roll. Each roll is 4 m long by 1 m wide. The front face of the shed is to be constructed with a space for a door of dimensions 1.9 m by 90 cm. The shed will also have a wooden base. The timber needed to make this shed costs €14.20 per m². Find the cost to manufacture this shed (to the nearest euro).

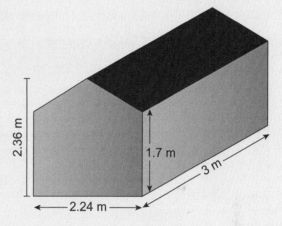

The company could also produce another type of shed whose blueprint is shown.

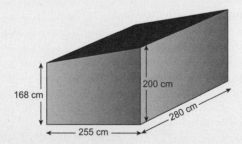

The same door dimensions and roofing felt are used.

(iv) Which shed has the greater capacity?

(v) Which shed costs the least to manufacture?

(vi) Using your answers from parts (iv) and (v), explain which shed you would advise the company to manufacture.

12.3 CYLINDERS, CONES, SPHERES AND HEMISPHERES

Cylinders

Volume of a Cylinder

The volume of a cylinder is:

FORMULA

Volume of cylinder = $\pi \times$ (radius)$^2 \times$ height

$\therefore$ Volume = $\pi r^2 h$

This formula appears on page 10 of *Formulae and Tables*.

Surface Area of a Cylinder

We can use a net to show how to calculate the two types of surface area of a cylinder.

Curved Surface Area (CSA) of a cylinder

This is the area of the curved part of the cylinder.

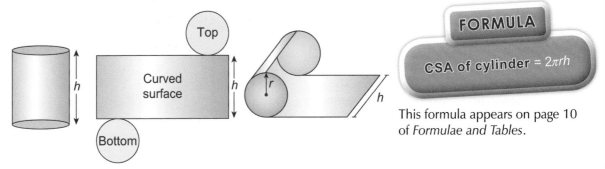

FORMULA

CSA of cylinder = $2\pi rh$

This formula appears on page 10 of *Formulae and Tables*.

Total Surface Area (TSA) of a Cylinder

There are three cases that must be considered:

Cylinder open at both ends   Cylinder closed at one end   Cylinder closed at both ends

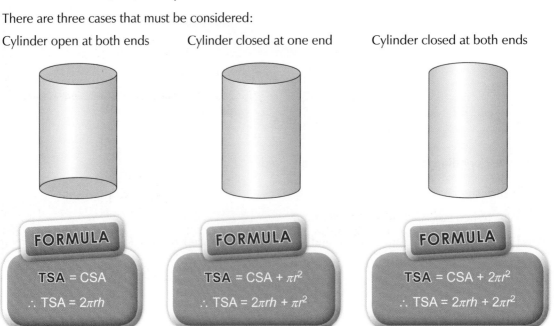

FORMULA

TSA = CSA

$\therefore$ TSA = $2\pi rh$

FORMULA

TSA = CSA + πr^2

$\therefore$ TSA = $2\pi rh + \pi r^2$

FORMULA

TSA = CSA + $2\pi r^2$

$\therefore$ TSA = $2\pi rh + 2\pi r^2$

Worked Example 12.10

Find the volume of the cylinder shown.
Take $\pi = 3.14$.

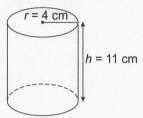

$r = 4$ cm

$h = 11$ cm

Solution

Volume $= \pi r^2 h$

$= 3.14 \times (4)^2 \times 11$

$= 3.14 \times 16 \times 11$

$= 552.64$ cm^3

Worked Example 12.11

Find (i) the curved surface area and (ii) the total surface area of the closed cylinder shown.
Take $\pi = \frac{22}{7}$.

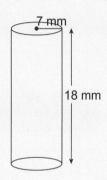

7 mm

18 mm

Solution

$h = 18, r = 7, \pi = \frac{22}{7}$

(i) CSA $= 2\pi rh$

$= 2 \times \frac{22}{7} \times 7 \times 18$

$= 792$ mm^2

(ii) TSA $= 2\pi rh + 2\pi r^2$

$= $ CSA $+ 2\pi r^2$

$= 792 + 2 \times \frac{22}{7} \times (7)^2$

$= 792 + 308$

$= 1{,}100$ mm^2

Cones

A **right circular cone** is a 3D shape formed by rotating a right-angled triangle 360° about one of the two shorter sides of the triangle.

Volume of a Cone

h

r

This formula appears on page 10 of *Formulae and Tables*.

FORMULA

Volume of cone $= \frac{1}{3} \times \pi \times $ (radius)$^2 \times$ height

$\therefore$ Volume $= \frac{1}{3}\pi r^2 h$

Surface Area of a Cone

There are two types of surface area of a cone.

Curved Surface Area (CSA) of a Cone

This is the area of just the curved part of the cone. To calculate the CSA, we must know the slant height (l) of the cone.

FORMULA

$l^2 = h^2 + r^2$

FORMULA

CSA of cone = πrl

This formula appears on page 10 of *Formulae and Tables*.

Total Surface Area (TSA) of a Cone

This is the area of the curved part of the cone **plus** the circular base.

The cone's surface is made up of two parts: its circular base and its curved circular area.

FORMULA

TSA of cone = CSA + πr^2

$\therefore$ TSA = $\pi rl + \pi r^2$

Worked Example 12.12

Find the volume of the following cones:

    (i) $r = 3$ m, $h = 12$ m, $\pi = 3.14$

    (ii) $r = 10$ cm, $h = 15$ cm, in terms of π

Solution

Volume = $\frac{1}{3}\pi r^2 h$

  (i) $= \frac{1}{3} \times 3.14 \times (3)^2 \times 12$

      $= 113.04$ m^3

  (ii) $= \frac{1}{3} \times \pi \times (10)^2 \times 15$

      $= 500\pi$ cm^3

Worked Example 12.13

Find the curved surface area and total surface area of the cone shown. Give both answers in terms of π:

2.4 cm 2.6 cm

Solution

To find the surface area of a cone, we must know the slant height (l) and radius (r).

$$l^2 = h^2 + r^2$$
$$(2.6)^2 = (2.4)^2 + r^2$$
$$6.76 = 5.76 + r^2$$
$$1 = r^2$$
$$1 = r$$

$\therefore$ radius = 1 cm

(i) CSA $= \pi r l$
$$= \pi \times 1 \times 2.6$$
$\therefore$ CSA $= 2.6\pi$ cm^2

(ii) TSA $=$ CSA $+ \pi r^2$
$$= 2.6\pi + \pi(1)^2$$
$$= 2.6\pi + \pi$$
$$= 3.6\pi \text{ cm}^2$$

ACTIVITY 12.2

Spheres

Volume of a Sphere

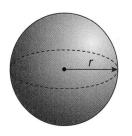

FORMULA

Volume of sphere $= \frac{4}{3} \times \pi \times (\text{radius})^3$

$\therefore$ Volume $= \frac{4}{3}\pi r^3$

This formula appears on page 10 of *Formulae and Tables*.

Surface Area of a Sphere

A sphere has no flat parts, so it can only have one type of surface area – a curved surface area.

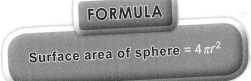

FORMULA

Surface area of sphere $= 4\pi r^2$

This formula appears on page 10 of *Formulae and Tables*.

Hemispheres

Volume of a Hemisphere

A hemisphere is **half** a sphere.

FORMULA

Volume of hemisphere $= \frac{2}{3}\pi r^3$

This formula is derived from that of a sphere:

Volume of hemisphere $= \frac{1}{2}\left(\frac{4}{3}\pi r^3\right)$
$$= \frac{2}{3}\pi r^3$$

Surface Area of a Hemisphere

A hemisphere has a flat circular part, so two types of surface area can be found.

Curved Surface Area (CSA) of a Hemisphere

The area of the curved part of the hemisphere is **half** that of the surface area of a sphere.

FORMULA

CSA of hemisphere = $2\pi r^2$

Total Surface Area (TSA) of a Hemisphere

This is the area of the curved part of the hemisphere **plus** the circular top.

FORMULA

TSA of hemisphere = $CSA + \pi r^2$

$\therefore$ TSA = $2\pi r^2 + \pi r^2 = 3\pi r^2$

Worked Example 12.14

Find the volume and surface area of the following sphere. Take $\pi = 3.14$.

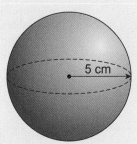
5 cm

Solution

Volume = $\frac{4}{3}\pi r^3$

$= \frac{4}{3} \times 3.14 \times (5)^3$

$= 523\frac{1}{3}$ cm^3

Surface area = $4\pi r^2$

$= 4 \times 3.14 \times (5)^2$

$= 314$ cm^2

Worked Example 12.15

Find:

  (i) The volume

  (ii) The curved surface area

  (iii) The total surface area

9 mm

of a solid hemisphere of radius 9 mm.

Give all answers in terms of π.

Solution

  (i) Volume = $\frac{2}{3}\pi r^3$

$= \frac{2}{3} \times \pi \times (9)^3$

$= 486\pi$ mm^3

  (ii) CSA = $2\pi r^2$

$= 2 \times \pi \times (9)^2$

$= 162\pi$ mm^2

  (iii) TSA = $CSA + \pi r^2$

$= 3\pi r^2$

$= 3 \times \pi \times (9)^2$

$= 243\pi$ mm^2

ACTIVITY 12.3

Exercise 12.3

Find the volume of each of the following cylinders:

1. $r = 11$ m, $h = 10$ m $(\pi = 3.14)$

2. $r = 8$ mm, $h = 14$ mm $\left(\pi = \frac{22}{7}\right)$

3. $r = 3$ cm, $h = 15$ mm   (in terms of π)

Find the curved surface area and the total surface area of each of the following solid cylinders:

4. $r = 1.5$ cm, $h = 4$ cm $(\pi = 3.14)$

5. $r = 80$ cm, $h = 1.25$ m   (in terms of π)

Find the volume of each of the following cones:

6. $r = 9$ cm, $h = 13$ cm   (in terms of π)

7. $r = 21$ mm, $h = 25$ mm $\left(\pi = \frac{22}{7}\right)$

8. $r = 40$ cm, $h = 3$ m $(\pi = 3.14)$

Find the curved surface area and the total surface area of each of the following solid cones:

9. $r = 6$ m, $l = 10$ m   (in terms of π)

10. $r = 160$ mm, $l = 34$ cm $(\pi = 3.14)$

11. $l = 40$ mm, $h = 32$ mm $\left(\pi = \frac{22}{7}\right)$

12. $r = 33$ cm, $h = 440$ mm   (in terms of π)

Find the volume of each of the following spheres or hemispheres:

13. Sphere: radius = 8 cm   (in terms of π)

14. Hemisphere: radius =10 mm $(\pi = 3.14)$

15. Sphere: diameter = 30 cm $\left(\pi = \frac{22}{7}\right)$

16. Hemisphere: radius = 2 cm   (in terms of π)

17. Sphere: radius = 12 m $(\pi = 3.14)$

18. Hemisphere: diameter = 14 m $\left(\pi = \frac{22}{7}\right)$

Find the curved surface area and the total surface area (where applicable) of each of the following spheres or hemispheres:

19. Sphere: radius = 4 m   (in terms of π)

20. Hemisphere: radius = 25 cm $(\pi = 3.14)$

21. Hemisphere: diameter = 1.2 m $(\pi = 3.14)$

22. Sphere: diameter = 3.6 mm $(\pi = 3.14)$

23. Using the following nets:

  (i) Identify the three-dimensional shape.

  (ii) Find the surface area of the shape. Take $\pi = 3.14$.

  (iii) Find the volume of the shape. Take $\pi = 3.14$.

Shape A

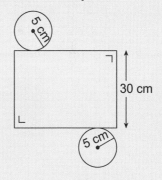

Shape B

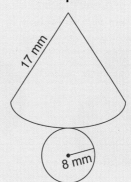

24. The graphs below show how the height of water in a container varies with time for four containers being filled at the same constant rate.

(i) Match each container with the correct graph.

(ii) Explain how you matched each container with its graph.

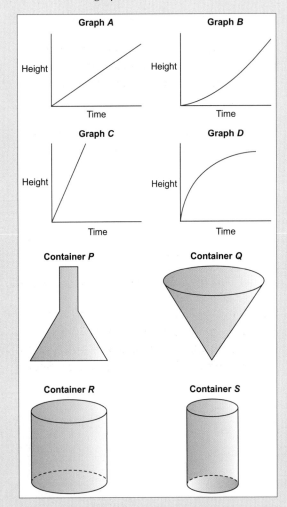

25. Each of the following shapes is filled with water flowing at a constant rate. Draw a graph of the depth of the water versus time for each shape.

(i)   (ii)

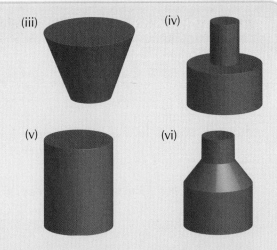

26. A buoy consists of a cone on a hemisphere. The diameter is 12 cm and the overall height of the buoy is 16 cm.

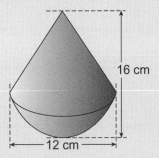

16 cm

12 cm

Calculate:

(i) The height of the conical part

(ii) The volume of the buoy in terms of π

(iii) The total surface area of the buoy in terms of π, to three significant figures

(iv) The buoy is to be covered in a special plastic to prevent rusting. The plastic coating costs €18.50 per m². How much would it cost to cover 150 such buoys?

27. A lighthouse consists of a hemisphere on a cylinder. The diameter is 14 m. The overall height is 37 m. Find, taking $\pi = \frac{22}{7}$, the external surface area of the lighthouse. (You may ignore the base area of the cylinder.)

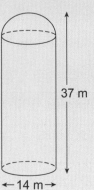

37 m

←14 m→

28. A rectangular box has length 10 cm, width 11 cm and height 6 cm.

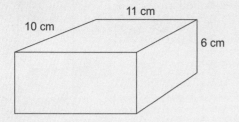

Find, in terms of π, the volume of:

(i) The largest sphere that will fit inside the box

(ii) The largest cylinder that will fit inside the box

(iii) The largest cone that will fit inside the box

29. (a) A tennis ball has radius 3 cm. Find its volume in terms of π.

(b) Three such tennis balls fit exactly into a cylindrical tube.

Find:

(i) The radius and height of the tube

(ii) The capacity (volume) of the tube in terms of π

(iii) The fraction of the volume of the tube that is taken up by the three tennis balls

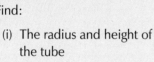

30. A candle consists of a cone on a cylinder. The diameter of the candle is 7 cm. The height of the cylindrical part is 8 cm. The height of the conical part is 3 cm.

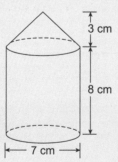

Find:

(i) The volume of each part $\left(\text{taking } \pi = \frac{22}{7}\right)$

(ii) The ratio of the volume of the cylindrical part to the volume of the conical part

(iii) The volume of the smallest rectangular box into which the candle will fit

31. A vitamin capsule is in the shape of a cylinder with hemispherical ends. The length of the capsule is 20 mm and the diameter is 6 mm.

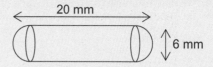

(i) Calculate the volume of the capsule, giving your answer correct to the nearest mm³.

A course of these vitamins consists of 24 capsules. The capsules are stacked in three rows of eight in a box, as shown in the diagram.

(ii) How much of the internal volume of the box is not occupied by the capsules?

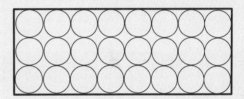

SEC Sample Paper, JCHL

32. The diagram shows a solid cylinder of diameter 54 cm and of height 70 cm. A cone, of the same diameter and height as the cylinder, is cut from inside the cylinder.

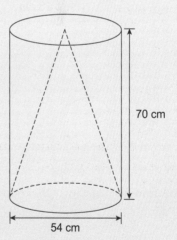

(i) Calculate the volume of the cylinder. Give your answer in terms of π.

(ii) Calculate the volume of the cone. Give your answer in terms of π.

(iii) What fraction of the cylinder remains after the cone is removed?

SEC 2011, JCHL

33. An ornament is carved from a rectangular block of wood which has a square base and a height of 24 cm. The ornament consists of two identical spheres and two identical cubes as illustrated in the diagram. The diameter of each sphere is equal to the length of the side of each cube. The ornament has the same width as the original block.

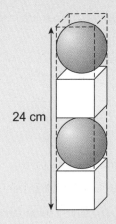

24 cm

(a) Find the length of a side of one of the cubes.

(b) Find the volume of the ornament.

(c) In making the ornament, what percentage of the original block of wood is carved away?

SEC 2012, JCHL

34. A soup tin in the form of a cylinder has a diameter of 7 cm and a height of 10 cm. The cylinder is constructed from pieces of metal cut from a thin sheet measuring 23 cm by 18 cm.

(a) Which one of the four diagrams A, B, C or D could represent the sheet of metal from which the cylinder has been cut?

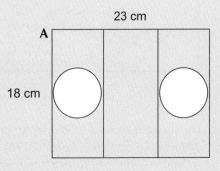

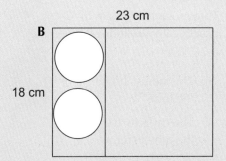

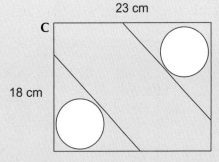

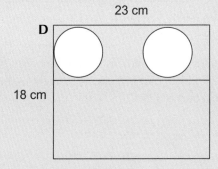

(b) Find the area of metal which remains after the pieces have been cut out.

(c) Find the capacity of the soup tin.

SEC 2012, JCHL

12.4 FINDING DIMENSIONS WHEN GIVEN VOLUME OR SURFACE AREA

We may encounter problems where we are given a shape's volume or surface area with an unknown side or radius which we have to calculate.

Worked Example 12.16

A solid metal sphere is made of lead. It is recast to form a cone of height 8.1 cm and radius 6 cm. Find the radius of the sphere. Give your answer correct to two decimal places.

Solution

Volume of the cone $= \frac{1}{3}\pi r^2 h = \frac{1}{3}\pi(6)^2(8.1) = 97.2\pi$ cm^3

Write down what is given.	Volume of cone = 97.2π cm^3
Write down the relevant formula. Volume of sphere = 97.2π	$\frac{4}{3}\pi r^3 = 97.2\pi$
Divide both sides by π.	$\frac{4}{3}r^3 = 97.2$
Solve for r.	$r^3 = \dfrac{97.2}{\frac{4}{3}}$ $r^3 = 72.9$ $r = \sqrt[3]{72.9}$ $r = 4.17742995$ $\therefore r = 4.18$ cm (to two decimal places)

Flow Problems

Problems involving the flow of a liquid are usually based on the speed or flow of a liquid through a cylindrical pipe. The flow speed through the pipe equals the height (length) of the column of water in the pipe for that particular time period.

A flow speed of 12 cm per second in a cylindrical pipe means that for every second of flow the water travels a distance of 12 cm.

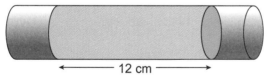

12 cm

Worked Example 12.17

Water is flowing through a cylindrical pipe at the speed of 35 cm/sec. The radius of the pipe is 5 cm. The water is poured into a cubic tank of side 100 cm. Find the rise in the depth of the water in the tank in 5 minutes. Use $\pi = \frac{22}{7}$.

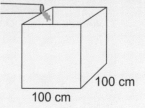

100 cm

100 cm

Solution

Calculate the amount of water that flows into the tank every second:

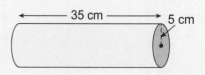

35 cm

5 cm

Volume $= \pi r^2 h = \frac{22}{7} \times 5^2 \times 35$

$= 2{,}750$ cm^3

There are 300 seconds in 5 minutes.

∴ The volume of water which flows into the tank in 5 minutes = 300 × 2,750

$$= 825,000 \text{ cm}^3$$

Let x = the increase in depth of the water in the tank.

$$(100)(100)(x) = 825,000$$

$$10,000x = 825,000$$

$$\therefore x = 82.5 \text{ cm}$$

∴ The rise in the depth of the water is 82.5 cm.

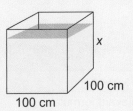

Displacement/Immersion Problems

Displacement/immersion problems are based on the following fact:

The volume of water displaced = the volume of the submerged object

This was first discovered by Archimedes of Syracuse (c. 287–c. 212 BC).

Volume of object = 50 cm³

Volume of water = 50 cm³

Worked Example 12.18

A cylindrical tank of radius 12 cm is partly filled with water. A sphere of radius 6 cm is then fully immersed in the water. By how much will the height of the water rise?

Solution

When the sphere is dropped in, the water level rises by h cm.

The volume of the sphere is equal to the volume of the displaced water in the cylinder.

Volume of sphere $= \frac{4}{3}\pi r^3 = \frac{4}{3} \times \pi \times (6)^3$

$$= 288\pi \text{ cm}^3$$

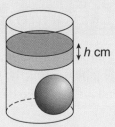

∴ Volume of displaced water (cylinder) $= 288\pi \text{ cm}^3$

$$\Rightarrow \pi r^2 h = 288\pi$$

$$r^2 h = 288$$

$$(12)^2 h = 288$$

$$144h = 288$$

$$h = \frac{288}{144}$$

$$\therefore h = 2 \text{ cm}$$

∴ The water rises by 2 cm.

Exercise 12.4

In Questions 1–4, copy and complete the tables. Make sure to show all work.

1. Cylinders (closed)

π	r (cm)	h (cm)	Volume (cm³)	CSA (cm²)	TSA (cm²)
π		3	12π		
3.14	13			81.64	
$\frac{22}{7}$		2.1		43.56	
3.14		12	5,425.92		
$\frac{22}{7}$	9				$1,046\frac{4}{7}$

2. Cones

π	r (cm)	h (cm)	l (cm)	Volume (cm³)	CSA (cm²)	TSA (cm²)
π		24		800π		
3.14		18		10,851.84		
$\frac{22}{7}$	72			$733,165\frac{5}{7}$		
3.14			145		39,611.1	
$\frac{22}{7}$	78					$50,989\frac{5}{7}$

3. Spheres

π	r (cm)	Volume (cm³)	TSA (cm²)
π		4,500π	
$\frac{22}{7}$			5,544
π		$1,774\frac{2}{3}π$	
3.14		7,234.56	

4. Hemispheres

π	r (cm)	Volume (cm³)	CSA (cm²)	TSA (cm²)
π		13,122π		
$\frac{22}{7}$			1,232	1,848
3.14			44,311.68	

5. A solid metal sphere of radius 18 cm is melted down and remoulded into a solid cone of radius 36 cm. (Diagram is not to scale.)

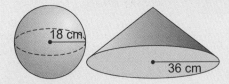

Find:

(i) The volume of the sphere in terms of π

(ii) The height of the cone

6. The radius of a cone is of length 9 cm. The curved surface area is 135π cm^2. Find:

(i) The slant height

(ii) The height

7. A solid cone of radius 8 cm and height 12 cm is made of wax. It is melted down and reformed to make a cylinder of height 16 cm. Find the radius of the cylinder.

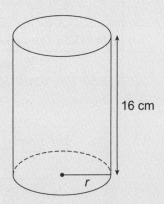

16 cm

r

8. A fishing buoy in the shape of a hemisphere has a volume of $32,708\frac{1}{3}$ cm^3. Find the radius of this buoy ($\pi = 3.14$).

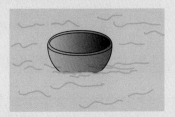

9. A cone of radius 10 cm has the same volume as a cylinder with height 8 cm and radius 4 cm. Find the height of the cone to the nearest millimetre.

10. A rectangular block of metal of volume 1,344 cm^3 is melted down into two identical metal spheres.

Ten per cent of the volume was lost in the melting of the block of metal. Find the radius of the spheres correct to two decimal places. ($\pi = 3.14$)

11. A solid metal sphere of radius 6 cm is melted down and remoulded into a solid cone of radius 3 cm.

Find:

(i) The volume of the sphere in terms of π

(ii) The height of the cone

12. The slant height of a solid cone is 5 cm. The total surface area is 14π cm^2. Find:

(i) The length of the radius of the cone

(ii) The height of the cone in surd form

13. A spinning top consists of a cone on a hemisphere, as shown. The radius of the hemisphere is of length 6 cm. The volume of the cone is one third of the volume of the hemisphere.

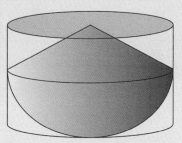

(a) Find:

    (i) The volume of the hemisphere in terms of π

    (ii) The height of the cone

    (iii) The overall height of the spinning top

(b) The spinning top fits exactly into a cylindrical container. Does it take up more or less than half of the capacity of the container?

14. The mass of a rectangular sheet of metal is 28,000 grams. The mass of 1 cm³ of this metal is 8 grams. The thickness of the metal is h cm, the length is 50 cm and the width is 20 cm.

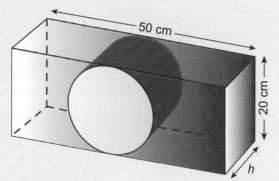

    (i) Calculate the value of h.

    (ii) A cylinder of radius 10 cm and height h is cut from the sheet of metal. Taking $\pi = \frac{22}{7}$, find the mass of the cylinder in kilograms.

15. A cylindrical tank of radius 4 cm is partly filled with water. A cone of radius 2 cm and height 3 cm is immersed in the water. By how much will the water rise?

16. Water flows through a cylindrical pipe at a rate of 35 cm per second. The pipe has diameter 4 cm. How long would it take to empty 22 litres of water? $\left(\text{Use } \pi = \frac{22}{7}\right)$
(1 litre = 1,000 cm³)

17. A closed plastic container is in the shape of a hollow cylinder on a hollow hemisphere, both of radius length 3 cm.

The container is partly filled with water, to a depth of 10 cm.

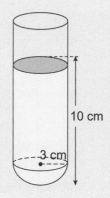

(i) Find the volume of the water, in terms of π.

(ii) If the container is turned upside-down, what will the depth of the water be in the cylindrical part?

18. A closed container consists of a cylinder joined to a cone. The height of the cylinder is 10 cm and its diameter is 7 cm.

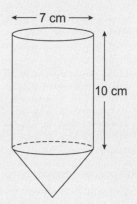

(a) Calculate:

    (i) The volume of the cylindrical part in terms of π

    (ii) The vertical height of the cone, given that its capacity is one fifth the capacity of the cylinder

    (iii) The volume of the water (in terms of π) in the container when its depth is 13 cm

(b) What would the height of the water in the cylinder be if the container were inverted?

19. Water is kept cool in a cylindrical container of diameter 28 cm and height 30 cm.

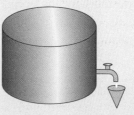

The water is poured into small conical cups, each of diameter 6 cm and height 7 cm.

When the cooler is full, how many cupfuls of water does it contain?

20. Water flows through a cylindrical pipe at a rate of 10 cm per second. The diameter of the pipe is 7 cm. The water is poured into an empty rectangular tank of length 55 cm and width 20 cm.

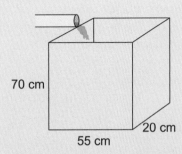

70 cm

20 cm

55 cm

(i) What is the depth of water after one minute? Answer correct to one decimal place.

(ii) To the nearest second, how long would it take to completely fill an empty tank?

21. Water pours through a pipe of radius 3 cm at a rate of 15 cm per second. It flows into a conical tank of height 0.9 metres and radius 0.6 metres.

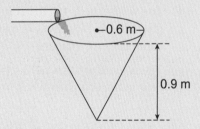

0.6 m

0.9 m

How long will it take to fill the tank?

22. A cone of height 6 cm and radius 2 cm is fully immersed in water in a cylinder of radius 4 cm. By how much will the level of the water drop when the cone is removed?

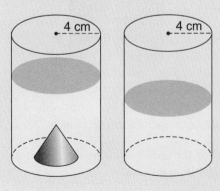

4 cm

4 cm

23. A cone has radius 2 cm and height $\frac{27}{8}$ cm. It is totally immersed in water inside a cylindrical tank of radius 6 cm.

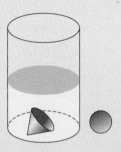

(i) When the cone is removed, calculate the drop in the depth of the water in the tank.

(ii) A sphere of radius r cm is then immersed in the water, which returns to its previous level. Find the value of r.

24. A flat roof on a garage is 11 m in length and 10 m in width.

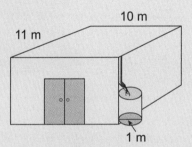

10 m

11 m

1 m

(i) Five millimetres of rain fall on the roof during a week. Find the volume of this rain in cm³.

(ii) The rain is caught by gutters and brought into a cylindrical barrel of diameter 1 metre. By how much will the depth of the water in the barrel rise during the week? $\left(\text{Use } \pi = \frac{22}{7}.\right)$

25. A test-tube consists of a hollow cylinder on a hollow hemisphere. Both have diameter 3 cm. The overall height of the test-tube is 8.5 cm.

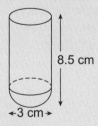

8.5 cm

3 cm

(i) Find the capacity of the test-tube (when full) in terms of π.

(ii) Find the depth of liquid in the test-tube, when it is half-full.

26. (a) A candle consists of a cone on a cylinder, as shown. The radius of both parts is 2 cm. The height of the conical part is 3 cm and the height of the cylindrical part is 9 cm. Find the volume of the candle in terms of π.

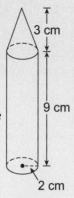

3 cm

9 cm

2 cm

(b) A taller candle is to be made in the shape of a cone of height 5 cm on a cylinder of height 10 cm. The radius of both is r cm. If the volume of this candle is 105π cm^3, calculate the value of r.

(c) Three of these taller candles are to be placed in the rectangular box below.

Find the volume of the box.

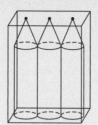

(d) Calculate the volume of empty space in this box to the nearest cubic centimetre, taking $\pi = 3.14$.

Revision Exercises

1. (a) Find the area of each of the figures below. All units are in centimetres.

(i)

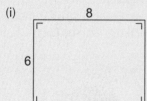

8

6

(ii)

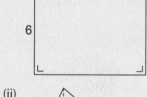

6

10

(iii)

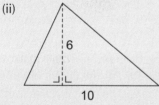

5

12

(iv)

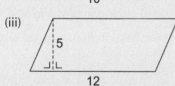

4

8

7

(v)

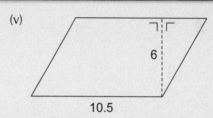

6

10.5

(b) Find the area and perimeter of each of the following shapes. $\left(\pi = \frac{22}{7}\right)$

All units are in centimetres.

(i)

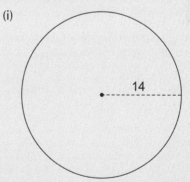

14

(ii)

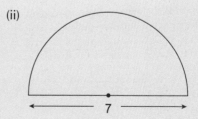

7

(c) Use $\pi = 3.14$ to find the area and perimeter of these sectors. All units are in centimetres.

(i)

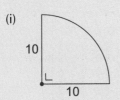

(ii)

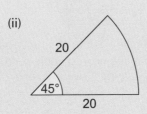

(iii)

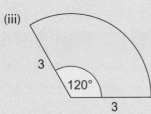

(iv)

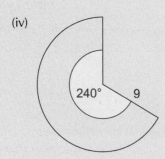

2. (a) Find the perimeter of the following shapes. All units are in centimetres.

(i)

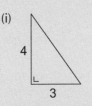

(ii)

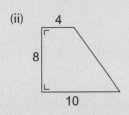

(iii)

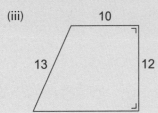

(b) Six small circles of radius r just fit inside a larger circle, as shown.

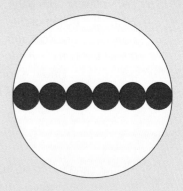

Write as a fraction in its lowest terms:

(i) $\dfrac{\text{Area of 6 small circles}}{\text{Area of large circle}}$

(ii) $\dfrac{\text{Area of region shaded yellow}}{\text{Area of large circle}}$

3. (a) A chain runs around two cogged wheels. The radii are 3 cm and 5 cm respectively. If the small wheel turns around 75 times, how many times will the large wheel turn?

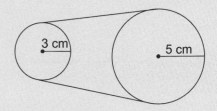

(b) The diagram shows a square ABCD of side 6x. P is the centre of symmetry of the square. The base is divided into three equal parts by the points M and N.

What fraction of the square is shaded?

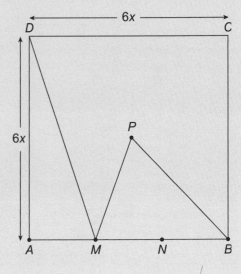

(c) A rectangular block has length 11 cm, width 4 cm and height 10 cm.

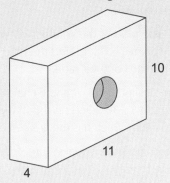

(i) Find its volume.

(ii) A cylindrical hole of radius r centimetres is drilled in the block, as shown. The volume of the remaining piece is $87\frac{1}{2}$ per cent of the original volume. Find r, correct to one decimal place. $\left(\text{Take } \pi = \frac{22}{7}.\right)$

4. (a) Water is kept cool in a cylindrical container of diameter 28 cm and height 30 cm.

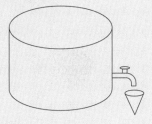

The water is poured into small conical cups, each of diameter 3 cm and height 3.5 cm.

When the container is full, how many cupfuls does it contain?

(b) A set of five equal steps is made out of concrete as shown.

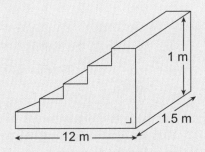

(i) Find the volume of concrete used (in cubic metres).

A thin strip of special coating, for added grip, is to be applied to the surface of the first three steps.

(ii) Find the area to be covered by this coating.

(c) A part of a child's toy is shown.

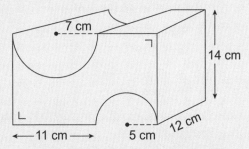

The toy is made from a cuboid with two half-cylinders removed. (Take $\pi = 3.14$.)

Find:

(i) The volume of the toy

(ii) The surface area of this toy

5. (a) A cone has radius of length 7 cm. The height is 24 cm. Using $\pi = \frac{22}{7}$, find:

(i) The volume of the cone

(ii) The curved surface area

(b) The diagram shows a plan for a playground. The two shaded rectangles are roofed areas for families to sit.

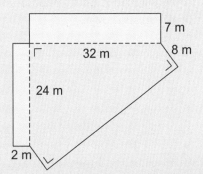

(i) What is the total area of the roofed part of the playground?

(ii) A raindrop falls at random onto the playground. What is the probability that it lands on a roof?

6. (a) Find the curved surface area and the total surface area (where applicable) of each of the following solid shapes:

  (i) Cylinder: $r = 14$ m, $h = 35$ m $\left(\pi = \frac{22}{7}\right)$

  (ii) Cone: $r = 18$ m, $h = 24$ m, $l = 30$ m (in terms of π)

  (iii) Sphere: diameter = 0.9 cm $(\pi = 3.14)$

  (iv) Hemisphere: radius = 5 cm (in terms of π)

 (b) The radius of a solid cone is 3 cm in length. The height is 4 cm.

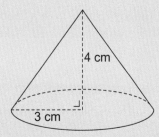

  (i) Find the slant height.

  (ii) Find the volume in terms of π.

  (iii) Find the curved surface area in terms of π.

  (iv) Find the total surface area in terms of π.

 (c) There is a path 2 metres wide around a small park as shown.

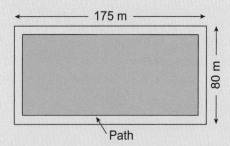

175 m

80 m

Path

Find:

  (i) The area of the park

  (ii) The area of the path

  (iii) The cost of replacing the path if 1 m² of path costs €10.20

 (d) (i) Two spheres have radii in the ratio 3 : 1. What is the ratio of their volumes?

  (ii) The ratio of the volumes of two spheres is 8 : 1. Find the ratio of the lengths of their radii.

 (e) Three cylinders (A, B and C) have radii in the ratio 5 : 3 : 2 and heights in the ratio 3 : 8 : 19. Which has the greatest volume?

 (f) Two cones have equal volume. Their radii are in the ratio 2 : 1. What is the ratio of their heights?

7. (a) A solid wax candle consists of a cone on a cylinder. It has dimensions as shown in the diagram.

  (i) Find, to the nearest cubic centimetre, the total volume of the candle.

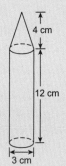

4 cm

12 cm

3 cm

  (ii) Find the volume of the smallest rectangular box into which the candle would just fit.

 (b) A test-tube consists of a hollow cylinder on a hollow hemisphere. The total height is 11 cm and the base has diameter 2 cm.

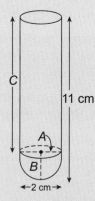

C

11 cm

A

B

←2 cm→

  (i) Write down the lengths A, B and C.

  (ii) Find the capacity of the test-tube in terms of π.

8. (a) The perimeter of a square is 20 cm. Find the length of a diagonal, correct to one decimal place.

(b) A toy consists of a cone on a hemisphere, as shown. The diameters of both the hemisphere and of the cone are 12 cm. The cone and the hemisphere have equal volumes.

← 12 cm →

(i) Find the total height of the toy.

(ii) The toy fits exactly into a cylindrical container. What fraction of the capacity of the container is taken up by the toy?

9. (a) A test-tube of diameter 3 cm, consists of a cylinder on a hemisphere. It is partly filled with water, to a depth of $7\frac{1}{2}$ cm, as shown.

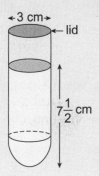

← 3 cm →
← lid

$7\frac{1}{2}$ cm

(i) Find the volume of the water in terms of π.

(ii) If the test-tube is inverted, find the height of the water in the cylindrical part.

(b) A candle is in the shape of a cone on a cylinder. The cylinder has radius 4 cm. The slant height of the cone is 5 cm.

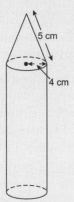

5 cm

4 cm

(i) Calculate the height of the cone.

(ii) Calculate the volume of the cone in terms of π.

(iii) If the volume of the cylinder is 10 times the volume of the cone, find the overall height of the candle.

10. (a) The area of the base of a cone is 66 cm² and its height is 10 cm. Find its volume.

(b) The slant height of a solid cone is 29 cm. The area of the base of the cone is 1,386 cm². Calculate $\left(\text{using } \pi = \frac{22}{7}\right)$:

(i) The radius length of the cone

(ii) The perpendicular height

(iii) The volume

11. (a) Two cylinders have radii in the ratio 5 : 2 and heights in the ratio 1 : 6. Which has the greater volume?

(b) (i) A sphere of radius 6 cm is totally immersed in water inside a cylindrical can of radius 8 cm. When the sphere is removed, calculate the drop in the depth of the water.

←8 cm→

6 cm

(ii) A cone of height 24 cm is now put into the water and the water returns to its original level. Find the radius of the cone.

12. (a) A cylinder of radius 6 cm is partly filled with water. A sphere of radius 3 cm is dropped in. By how much will the water rise?

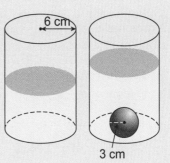

6 cm

3 cm

(b) Water flows through a cylindrical pipe of diameter 3.5 cm into a rectangular tank of length 1.1 metres, width 1.4 metres and height 1.5 metres. The tank is filled in 40 minutes. Find $\left(\text{using } \pi = \frac{22}{7}\right)$ the rate at which the water flows through the pipe (in cm/s).

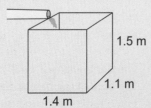

13. (a) A container in the shape of a cylinder has a capacity of 50 litres. The height of the cylinder is 0.7 m. Find the length of the diameter of the cylinder. Give your answer correct to the nearest whole number.

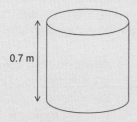

(b) A rectangular tank has a length of 0.6 m, a width of 0.35 m and its height measures 15 cm. Find the capacity of the rectangular tank.

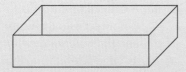

(c) The rectangular tank is full of water. This water is then poured into the cylindrical container in (a) above. Find the depth of water in the cylinder. Give your answer correct to one decimal place.

14. A cone has a slant height of 26 cm and a radius of 10 cm.

(i) Find the curved surface area of the cone, in terms of π.

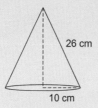

The curved surface area of the cone is doubled, while the slant height remains the same.

(ii) Find the radius and hence the vertical height of this cone, correct to the nearest centimetre.

(iii) Show that the volume of this cone is more than double the volume of the cone in part (i).

15. The height of a cone is twice its radius. If the volume of the cone is $341\frac{1}{3}\pi$ cm³, find the radius of this cone.

16. Three cones each have height 6 cm. Their radii are r, $2r$ and $3r$ respectively. Their total volume is 112π cm³. Find the value of r.

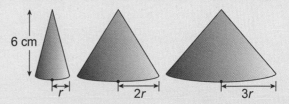

17. (a) A sphere of radius r cm is totally immersed in water which is in a cylindrical can of radius 4 cm. When the sphere is removed, the water level drops by 1 cm.

Find the radius of the sphere correct to two decimal places.

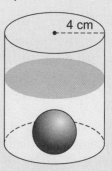

(b) (i) A sphere of ice has radius 3 cm. Find the volume of 12 such spheres in terms of π.

(ii) The spheres melt (without altering their volume) and the water is poured into a cylindrical can of internal radius r and height 6.75 cm. The can is then full.

Find the value of r.

18. Deirdre constructs a 'polytunnel' on a level part of her back garden. Five vertical semicircular metal hoops, each of radius 2 m, are attached to brackets at ground level and covered with a polythene sheet. The hoops are 2 m apart.

(i) Find the area of ground covered by the tunnel.

(ii) The hoops are also held in place by a straight piece of metal attached at the top of each hoop. Find, to the nearest centimetre, the total length of metal needed to construct the tunnel.

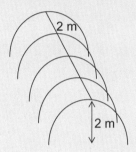

(iii) The polythene is buried in the ground to a depth of 25 cm all around the tunnel (including both ends). Find the dimensions and area of the smallest rectangular sheet of polythene that can be used.

(iv) Find the volume of air in the tunnel, to one decimal place.

(v) To finish, Deirdre constructs a rectangular raised bed of height 25 cm inside the tunnel. There is a space of 20 cm between the bed and each side of the tunnel. The bed is then filled with topsoil. Soil costs €80 per tonne and 1 m³ of soil weighs 0.75 tonnes. Find the cost of filling the bed with soil.

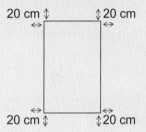

SEC Sample Paper, JCHL

Algebra III: Algebraic Fractions

Learning Outcomes

In this chapter you will learn how to:

- Add and subtract simple algebraic expressions of forms such as:
  - $$\frac{ax + b}{c} \pm \dots \pm \frac{dx + e}{f}$$
  - $$\frac{a}{bx + c} \pm \frac{d}{ex + f}$$
  where $a, b, c, d, e, f \in Z$

- Divide expressions of the form:
  - $$(ax^2 + bx + c) \div (dx + e)$$
  - $$(ax^3 + bx^2 + cx + d) \div (ex + f)$$
  where $a, b, c, d, e, f \in Z$

13.1 ADDING AND SUBTRACTING ALGEBRAIC FRACTIONS

To add or subtract two or more algebraic fractions, we first must first write each fraction in terms of a common denominator. To simplify the arithmetic involved, it is best to write each fraction in terms of a **lowest common denominator (LCD)**.

x^2 Worked Example 13.1

Write $\dfrac{3x + 2}{5} - \dfrac{x - 4}{2} - 3$ as a single fraction in its simplest form.

Solution

Rewrite as:

$\dfrac{3x + 2}{5} - \dfrac{x - 4}{2} - \dfrac{3}{1}$

The LCD of 5, 2 and 1 is 10:

$\therefore \dfrac{3x + 2}{5} - \dfrac{x - 4}{2} - \dfrac{3}{1}$

$= \dfrac{2(3x + 2) - 5(x - 4) - 10(3)}{10}$

$= \dfrac{6x + 4 - 5x + 20 - 30}{10}$

$= \dfrac{x - 6}{10}$

What did we actually do here?

- We multiplied $\dfrac{3x + 2}{5}$ by $\dfrac{2}{2} (= 1)$.
- We multiplied $\dfrac{x - 4}{2}$ by $\dfrac{5}{5} (= 1)$.
- We multiplied $\dfrac{3}{1}$ by $\dfrac{10}{10} (= 1)$.

Since we multiplied each of the three terms by 1, we did not change the value of the overall expression.

So, we got: $\dfrac{2}{2} \cdot \dfrac{(3x + 2)}{5} - \dfrac{5}{5} \cdot \dfrac{(x - 4)}{2} - \dfrac{10}{10} \cdot \dfrac{3}{1}$

$= \dfrac{2(3x + 2) - 5(x - 4) - 10(3)}{10}$

Etc.

Some algebraic fractions may have a variable (letter) in the denominator.

x^2 Worked Example 13.2

Express $\dfrac{2}{x - 3} + \dfrac{4}{x + 2}$ as a single fraction in its simplest form.

Solution

The denominators are $(x - 3)$ and $(x + 2)$.

So, the LCD $= (x - 3)(x + 2)$.

$\therefore \dfrac{2}{x - 3} + \dfrac{4}{x + 2} = \dfrac{2(x + 2) + 4(x - 3)}{(x - 3)(x + 2)}$

$= \dfrac{2x + 4 + 4x - 12}{(x - 3)(x + 2)}$

$= \dfrac{6x - 8}{(x - 3)(x + 2)}$

ACTIVITY 13.1

It is common practice not to expand the denominator unless required to do so.

x^2 **Worked Example 13.3**

Express $\dfrac{4}{x} - \dfrac{3}{4x + 1}$ as a single fraction in its simplest form.

Solution

The denominators are x and $(4x + 1)$.

So, the LCD $= x(4x + 1)$.

$$\therefore \frac{4}{x} - \frac{3}{4x + 1} = \frac{4(4x + 1) - 3(x)}{x(4x + 1)}$$

$$= \frac{16x + 4 - 3x}{x(4x + 1)}$$

$$= \frac{13x + 4}{x(4x + 1)}$$

x^2 **Worked Example 13.4**

Show that $\dfrac{3}{x - 4} - \dfrac{2}{4 - x}$ can be written in the form $\dfrac{a}{x - 4}$, where $a \in N$.

Solution

The denominators are $(x - 4)$ and $(4 - x)$.

These are the same expressions except for their signs. Rewrite the denominators as $(x - 4)$ and $-(x - 4)$.

$$\therefore \frac{3}{x - 4} - \frac{2}{4 - x} = \frac{3}{x - 4} - \frac{2}{-(x - 4)}$$

$$= \frac{3}{x - 4} + \frac{2}{x - 4}$$

$$= \frac{5}{x - 4}$$

Exercise 13.1

> Simplify each of the expressions in Questions 1–21.

1. $\dfrac{2x + 1}{3} + \dfrac{3x - 1}{2}$

2. $\dfrac{5p - 3}{2} - \dfrac{p + 2}{5}$

3. $\dfrac{y - 4}{4} - \dfrac{2y - 5}{3}$

4. $\dfrac{3y - 1}{3} + \dfrac{y - 1}{5} + 1$

5. $\dfrac{2x + 1}{7} - 2 + \dfrac{x + 2}{14}$

6. $\dfrac{1}{12} + \dfrac{4q - 2}{3} - \dfrac{7q - 2}{6}$

7. $\dfrac{5x - 1}{5} - \dfrac{x - 4}{3} + \dfrac{7}{15}$

8. $r - 3 - \dfrac{4r + 3}{5} - \dfrac{5r}{3}$

9. $\dfrac{2x - 9}{10} - \dfrac{2 - x}{2} - x$

10. $\dfrac{1}{5x} + \dfrac{3}{2x}$

11. $\dfrac{1}{3x} - \dfrac{2}{6x}$

12. $\dfrac{8}{x + 1} - \dfrac{1}{x}$

13. $\dfrac{3}{x + 4} - \dfrac{2}{x}$

14. $\dfrac{5}{2x - 1} + \dfrac{2}{3x - 1}$

15. $\dfrac{1}{x + 5} - \dfrac{3}{4x - 2}$

16. $\dfrac{1}{5x + 1} + \dfrac{2}{7 - x}$

17. $\dfrac{3}{2x - 1} - \dfrac{5}{4x - 3}$

18. $\dfrac{6}{5 - x} + \dfrac{2}{x + 2}$

19. $\dfrac{10}{2x - 5} - \dfrac{2}{3x - 2}$

20. $\dfrac{11}{x - 2} + \dfrac{2}{2 - x}$

21. $\dfrac{3}{3x - 4} - \dfrac{1}{4 - 3x}$

22. Write $\dfrac{7}{x - 3} + \dfrac{2}{3 - x}$ in the form $\dfrac{k}{x - 3}$, where $k \in R$.

23. (i) Evaluate $\dfrac{1}{x} - \dfrac{3}{2x+4}$ when $x = 2$.

   (ii) Write $\dfrac{1}{x} - \dfrac{3}{2x+4}$ as a single fraction in its simplest form.

   (iii) Evaluate your result in part (ii) for $x = 2$.

   (iv) What do you notice about your answers to parts (i) and (iii)?

24. (i) Evaluate $\dfrac{3}{2x-1} + \dfrac{2}{2x+4}$ when $x = -5$.

   (ii) Write $\dfrac{3}{2x-1} + \dfrac{2}{2x+4}$ as a single fraction in its simplest form.

   (iii) Evaluate your result in part (ii) for $x = -5$.

25. (i) Evaluate $\dfrac{4}{5x-2} + \dfrac{8}{x-3}$ when $x = \dfrac{1}{2}$.

   (ii) Write $\dfrac{4}{5x-2} + \dfrac{8}{x-3}$ as a single fraction in its simplest form.

   (iii) Evaluate your result in part (ii) for $x = \dfrac{1}{2}$.

26. (i) Evaluate $\dfrac{3}{x+1} + \dfrac{10}{x+2}$ when $x = \dfrac{1}{2}$.

   (ii) Write $\dfrac{3}{x+1} + \dfrac{10}{x+2}$ as a single fraction.

   (iii) Find the value of this single fraction when $x = \dfrac{1}{2}$.

13.2 REDUCING ALGEBRAIC FRACTIONS

Consider the fraction $\dfrac{3}{6}$.

To 'reduce' this fraction is to write it as $\dfrac{1}{2}$.

$\dfrac{1}{2}$ is the 'reduced' form of the fraction, since HCF$(1, 2) = 1$.

In other words, the numerator and the denominator share no common factor (except 1).

How did we reduce the fraction $\dfrac{3}{6}$?

We divided both the numerator and the denominator by their HCF. HCF$(3, 6) = 3$.

We follow the same approach when reducing algebraic fractions.

x^2 Worked Example 13.5

Simplify each of the following fractions:

  (i) $\dfrac{(x+2)(x-3)}{x+2}$ (ii) $\dfrac{x^2 - 14x + 48}{x-8}$ (iii) $\dfrac{4a^2 - 2a - 12}{2a^2 - 8}$ (iv) $\dfrac{50a^3 b^2}{15a^4 b}$

Solution

(i) Factors: Numerator $(x+2)$ and $(x-3)$

             Denominator $x+2$

$\therefore$ HCF $= x+2$

Divide the numerator and the denominator by $(x+2)$.

$\therefore \dfrac{^1(x+2)\,(x-3)}{x+2_1}$

$= \dfrac{x-3}{1}$

$= x - 3$

(ii) Factorise the numerator:

$x^2 - 14x + 48 = (x-8)(x-6)$

Factors: Numerator $(x-8)$ and $(x-6)$

            Denominator $x-8$

$\therefore$ HCF $= x-8$

Divide the numerator and the denominator by $(x-8)$.

$\therefore \dfrac{x^2 - 14x + 48}{x-8}$

$= \dfrac{^1(x-8)(x-6)}{_1x-8}$

$= \dfrac{x-6}{1}$

$= x - 6$

(iii) Factorise the numerator:

$$4a^2 - 2a - 12 = 2(2a^2 - a - 6)$$
$$= 2(2a + 3)(a - 2)$$

Factorise the denominator:

$$2a^2 - 8 = 2(a^2 - 4)$$
$$= 2(a - 2)(a + 2)$$

∴ HCF = $2(a - 2)$

Divide the numerator and the denominator by $2(a - 2)$.

$$\therefore \frac{4a^2 - 2a - 12}{2a^2 - 8}$$

$$= \frac{{}^1\!\cancel{2}(2a + 3)\,\cancel{(a - 2)}^1}{{}^1\!\cancel{2}\cancel{(a - 2)}_1\,(a + 2)}$$

$$= \frac{2a + 3}{a + 2}$$

(iv) $\dfrac{50a^3b^2}{15a^4b} = \dfrac{50}{15} \cdot \dfrac{a^3}{a^4} \cdot \dfrac{b^2}{b}$

$$= \frac{10}{3} \cdot \frac{1}{a} \cdot \frac{b}{1}$$

$$= \frac{10b}{3a}$$

x^2 Worked Example 13.6

(i) Factorise $x^2 + 3x - 10$.

(ii) Expand $(1 - 3x)(x^2 + 3x - 10)$.

(iii) Hence, simplify $\dfrac{-3x^3 - 8x^2 + 33x - 10}{x + 5}$.

(iv) Check your answer to part (iii) by letting $x = 1$.

Solution

(i) $x^2 + 3x - 10 = (x + 5)(x - 2)$

(ii) $(1 - 3x)(x^2 + 3x - 10)$

Method 1 (using properties)

$1(x^2 + 3x - 10) - 3x(x^2 + 3x - 10)$

$= x^2 + 3x - 10 - 3x^3 - 9x^2 + 30x$

$= -3x^3 - 8x^2 + 33x - 10$

Method 2 (using method based on area models)

	x^2	$3x$	-10
1	x^2	$3x$	-10
$-3x$	$-3x^3$	$-9x^2$	$30x$

∴ Answer: $-3x^3 - 8x^2 + 33x - 10$

(iii) $\dfrac{-3x^3 - 8x^2 + 33x - 10}{x + 5}$

$= \dfrac{(1 - 3x)(x^2 + 3x - 10)}{x + 5}$ (from part (ii))

$= \dfrac{(1 - 3x)\,(x + 5)\,(x - 2)}{x + 5}$ (from part (i))

$= (1 - 3x)(x - 2)$ (after dividing above and below by HCF)

$= x - 2 - 3x^2 + 6x$ (after expanding)

$= -3x^2 + 7x - 2$

(iv) Substitute $x = 1$ into $\dfrac{-3x^3 - 8x^2 + 33x - 10}{x + 5}$

$= \dfrac{-3(1)^3 - 8(1)^2 + 33(1) - 10}{1 + 5}$

$= \dfrac{-3 - 8 + 33 - 10}{6}$

$= \dfrac{12}{6}$

$= 2$

Now substitute $x = 1$ into $-3x^2 + 7x - 2$

$= -3(1)^2 + 7(1) - 2$

$= -3 + 7 - 2$

$= 2$

As both expressions give the same answer for $x = 1$, we have verified the answer to part (iii).

Exercise 13.2

Simplify each of the fractions in Questions 1–20.

1. $\dfrac{(x + 1)(x - 3)}{x + 1}$

2. $\dfrac{(x + 4)(x + 2)}{x + 2}$

3. $\dfrac{5x + 10}{x + 2}$

4. $\dfrac{4x + 2}{2}$

5. $\dfrac{3x - 1}{3x - 1}$

6. $\dfrac{5x + 15}{5}$

7. $\dfrac{18y - 4}{6y - 2}$

8. $\dfrac{x^2 - 16}{x - 4}$

9. $\dfrac{x^2 - 10x}{x - 10}$

10. $\dfrac{4x^2 - 64}{x - 4}$

11. $\dfrac{2y - 1}{1 - 2y}$

12. $\dfrac{x^2 + 6x + 8}{x + 4}$

13. $\dfrac{8p^3q^2}{2pq^2}$

14. $\dfrac{100a^2bc}{5ac^2}$

15. $\dfrac{x^2 - x - 6}{x + 2}$

16. $\dfrac{18p^3q^2r^2}{p^4q^2r}$

17. $\dfrac{2a^2 + 4a - 6}{2}$

18. $\dfrac{12x^3 + 18x^2 - 30x}{6x}$

19. $\dfrac{4x^2 + 7x - 2}{x + 2}$

20. $\dfrac{9x^2 - 3x - 2}{3x + 1}$

---

21. (i) Factorise fully $16x^2 - 16$.

    (ii) Factorise $x^2 + 2x + 1$.

    (iii) Hence, simplify $\dfrac{16x^2 - 16}{x^2 + 2x + 1}$.

22. (i) Factorise $x^2 + 9x + 20$.

    (ii) Expand $(x + 1)(x^2 + 9x + 20)$.

    (iii) Hence, simplify $\dfrac{x^3 + 10x^2 + 29x + 20}{x + 4}$.

    (iv) Check your answer to part (iii) by letting $x = 2$.

23. (i) Factorise $x^2 - 10x + 21$.

    (ii) Expand $(x - 5)(x^2 - 10x + 21)$.

    (iii) Hence, simplify $\dfrac{x^3 - 15x^2 + 71x - 105}{x - 3}$.

    (iv) Check your answer to part (iii) by letting $x = 4$.

24. (i) Factorise $3x^2 - 17x - 6$.

    (ii) Expand $(1 - x)(3x^2 - 17x - 6)$.

    (iii) Hence, reduce $\dfrac{-3x^3 + 20x^2 - 11x - 6}{3x + 1}$ to its lowest terms.

    (iv) Check your answer to part (iii) by letting $x = -1$.

In Questions 25–30, factorise the denominator and numerator of each fraction. Hence, simplify the fraction to its lowest terms.

25. $\dfrac{x^2 + 4x + 3}{x^2 - x - 12}$

26. $\dfrac{2x^2 + 9x + 4}{2x^2 + 11x + 5}$

27. $\dfrac{20x^2 - 8x - 12}{5x^2 - 2x - 3}$

28. $\dfrac{ax + ay - cx - cy}{ax + ay + cx + cy}$

29. $\dfrac{12x^2 - 2x - 24}{12x^2 + 52x + 48}$

30. $\dfrac{a - b}{b^2 - a^2}$

13.3 LONG DIVISION IN ALGEBRA

Another approach to dividing one algebraic expression by another is to use long division. We can use this method of long division when dividing an expression by an expression of lower degree.

Consider the following expressions and their corresponding degrees:

Expression	Degree	Reason
$x + 7$	1	Highest power is 1
$x^2 + 3x - 5$	2	Highest power is 2
$-x^3 + 11x + 7$	3	Highest power is 3

You should remember the method of long division from your primary school studies.

Example: Divide 312 by 24.

Solution:

$$\begin{array}{r} 1\ 3 \\ 24\,\overline{)3\,1\,2} \\ -(24)\downarrow \\ \hline 7\,2 \\ -(72) \\ \hline 0 \end{array}$$

Steps:
- ■ $31 \div 24 = 1$ Remainder 7
- ■ Bring down the 2
- ■ $72 \div 24 = 3$ Remainder 0

$$\therefore 312 \div 24 = 13$$

x^2 Worked Example 13.7

Divide $6x^2 + 11x + 3$ by $3x + 1$.

Solution

$$\begin{array}{r} 2x + 3 \\ 3x + 1\,\overline{)6x^2 + 11x + 3} \\ -(6x^2 + 2x) \\ \hline 9x + 3 \\ -(9x + 3) \\ \hline 0 \end{array}$$

Divide $6x^2$ by $3x$ to get $2x$.

Multiply $(3x + 1)$ by $2x$ to get $6x^2 + 2x$ and subtract to get $9x$.

Bring down the next term, which is 3. Divide $9x$ by $3x$ to get 3.

Multiply $(3x + 1)$ by 3 to get $9x + 3$ and subtract to get 0.

As the final remainder is 0, we know that $3x + 1$ divides 'evenly' into $6x^2 + 11x + 3$.

$\therefore$ Answer $= 2x + 3$

Note: It is good practice to check your work by expanding.

$(3x + 1)(2x + 3)$:

	$2x$	3
$3x$	$6x^2$	$9x$
1	$2x$	3

$\therefore (3x + 1)(2x + 3) = 6x^2 + 11x + 3$

x^2 Worked Example 13.8

Divide $2x^3 - 7x^2 + 5x - 1$ by $2x - 1$.

Solution

$$
\begin{array}{r}
x^2 - 3x + 1 \\
2x - 1 \overline{\big)\, 2x^3 - 7x^2 + 5x - 1} \\
-(2x^3 - x^2) \\
\hline
-6x^2 + 5x \\
-(-6x^2 + 3x) \\
\hline
2x - 1 \\
-(2x - 1) \\
\hline
0
\end{array}
$$

Divide $2x^3$ by $2x$ to get x^2.

Multiply $(2x - 1)$ by x^2 to get $2x^3 - x^2$ and subtract to get $-6x^2$.

Bring down the next term, which is $5x$. Divide $-6x^2$ by $2x$ to get $-3x$.

Multiply $(2x - 1)$ by $-3x$ to get $-6x^2 + 3x$ and subtract to get $2x$.

Bring down the next term, which is -1. Divide $2x$ by $2x$ to get 1.

Multiply $(2x - 1)$ by 1 to get $2x - 1$ and subtract to get 0.

As the final remainder is 0, we know that $2x - 1$ divides 'evenly' into $2x^3 - 7x^2 + 5x - 1$.

$\therefore$ Answer $= x^2 - 3x + 1$

Note: It is good practice to check your work by expanding.

$(2x - 1)(x^2 - 3x + 1)$:

	x^2	$-3x$	$+1$
$2x$	$2x^3$	$-6x^2$	$2x$
-1	$-x^2$	$3x$	-1

ACTIVITY 13.2

$\therefore (2x - 1)(x^2 - 3x + 1) = 2x^3 - 7x^2 + 5x - 1.$

x^2 Worked Example 13.9

Simplify $\dfrac{6x^3 - 26x^2 + 32}{3x - 4}$.

Solution

We can use long division to simplify this fraction.

Tip: As there is no x term, we write $6x^3 - 26x^2 + 32$ as $6x^3 - 26x^2 + 0x + 32$ before dividing.

$$
\begin{array}{r}
2x^2 - 6x - 8 \\
3x - 4 \overline{\big)\, 6x^3 - 26x^2 + 0x + 32} \\
-(6x^3 - 8x^2) \\
\hline
-18x^2 + 0x \\
-(-18x^2 + 24x) \\
\hline
-24x + 32 \\
-(-24x + 32) \\
\hline
0
\end{array}
$$

Divide $6x^3$ by $3x$ to get $2x^2$.

Multiply $(3x - 4)$ by $2x^2$ to get $6x^3 - 8x^2$ and subtract to get $-18x^2$.

Bring down the next term, which is $0x$. Divide $-18x^2$ by $3x$ to get $-6x$.

Multiply $(3x - 4)$ by $-6x$ to get $-18x^2 + 24x$ and subtract to get $-24x$.

Bring down the next term, which is 32. Divide $-24x$ by $3x$ to get -8.

Multiply $(3x - 4)$ by -8 to get $-24x + 32$ and subtract to get 0.

As the final remainder is 0, we know that $3x - 4$ divides 'evenly' into $6x^3 - 26x^2 + 32$.

$\therefore$ Answer $= 2x^2 - 6x - 8$

Now check your work by expanding:

$(3x - 4)(2x^2 - 6x - 8)$:

	$2x^2$	$-6x$	-8
$3x$	$6x^3$	$-18x^2$	$-24x$
-4	$-8x^2$	$24x$	32

$\therefore (3x - 4)(2x^2 - 6x - 8) = 6x^3 - 26x^2 + 32$

Exercise 13.3

1. (i) Factorise $x^2 + 7x + 12$.

   (ii) Hence, simplify $\dfrac{x^2 + 7x + 12}{x + 3}$.

   (iii) Use long division to divide $x^2 + 7x + 12$ by $x + 3$.

2. (i) Factorise $2x^2 + 11x + 5$.

   (ii) Hence, simplify $\dfrac{2x^2 + 11x + 5}{x + 5}$.

   (iii) Use long division to divide $2x^2 + 11x + 5$ by $x + 5$.

3. (i) Factorise $x^2 - 2x - 63$.

   (ii) Hence, simplify $\dfrac{x^2 - 2x - 63}{x - 9}$.

   (iii) Use long division to divide $x^2 - 2x - 63$ by $x - 9$.

4. (i) Factorise $6x^2 - 7x - 20$.

   (ii) Hence, simplify $\dfrac{6x^2 - 7x - 20}{2x - 5}$.

   (iii) Use long division to divide $6x^2 - 7x - 20$ by $2x - 5$.

Divide the following expressions (Questions 5–19).

---

5. $(8x^2 - 28x + 12) \div (x - 3)$

6. $(6x^2 - 11x - 35) \div (3x + 5)$

7. $(x^3 + 5x^2 + 7x + 3) \div (x + 3)$

8. $(x^3 + 2x^2 - 7x - 2) \div (x - 2)$

9. $(3x^2 + 8x + 5) \div (x + 1)$

10. $(16x^2 + 14x - 15) \div (2x + 3)$

11. $(2x^3 + 13x^2 + 2x - 72) \div (2x + 9)$

12. $(3x^3 - 26x^2 - 2x + 12) \div (3x - 2)$

13. $(4x^3 + 6x^2 + 8x + 3) \div (2x + 1)$

14. $(14x^3 + 43x^2 + 16x - 10) \div (2x + 5)$

15. $(35x^3 - 51x^2 + 74x - 48) \div (7x - 6)$

16. $(x^3 - 9x^2 + 8) \div (x - 1)$

17. $(x^2 - 4) \div (x + 2)$

18. $(4x^2 - 25) \div (2x - 5)$

19. $(9x^3 - 19x + 6) \div (3x - 1)$

20. (i) Expand $(x + 2)(x - 7)$.

    (ii) Expand $(2x - 1)(x^2 - 5x - 14)$.

    (iii) Simplify $\dfrac{2x^3 - 11x^2 - 23x + 14}{x - 7}$ without using long division.

    (iv) Divide $2x^3 - 11x^2 - 23x + 14$ by $2x - 1$ using long division.

21. (i) Expand $(2x + 3)(x - 4)$.

    (ii) Expand $(3x - 1)(2x^2 - 5x - 12)$.

    (iii) Simplify $\dfrac{6x^3 - 17x^2 - 31x + 12}{2x + 3}$ without using long division.

    (iv) Divide $6x^3 - 17x^2 - 31x + 12$ by $3x - 1$ using long division.

22. Simplify $\dfrac{2x^3 + 3x^2 - 23x - 12}{2x + 1}$ and factorise the simplified expression.

23. Simplify $\dfrac{x^3 - 13x - 12}{x + 1}$ and factorise the simplified expression.

24. Simplify $\dfrac{2k^3 + 9k^2 - 55k + 50}{2k - 5}$ and check your answer by letting $k = 3$.

25. (i) Expand $2a^2(2a + 3) - 27$.

    (ii) Simplify $\dfrac{2a^2(2a + 3) - 27}{2a - 3}$.

26. (i) Factorise $x^2 - 1$.

    (ii) Factorise $4x^2 - 7x + 3$.

    (iii) Expand $(x + 1)(4x^2 - 7x + 3)$.

    (iv) Simplify $\dfrac{4x^3 - 3x^2 - 4x + 3}{x^2 - 1}$ without using long division.

27. Divide $8x^3 - 1$ by $2x - 1$.

28. Simplify $(27x^3 + 64) \div (3x + 4)$.

1. (a) Write each of the following as a single fraction in its simplest form:

(i) $\dfrac{x+1}{3} + \dfrac{x+5}{2}$

(ii) $x + \dfrac{2x+3}{7}$

(iii) $\dfrac{5x-1}{2} - \dfrac{x-1}{3}$

(iv) $\dfrac{7x-2}{10} - \dfrac{2x-1}{5} + \dfrac{x+3}{2}$

(b) Simplify:

(i) $\dfrac{3a}{6a}$ (ii) $\dfrac{2a+2b}{3a+3b}$ (iii) $\dfrac{2x-4}{x^2-4}$

(c) Divide:

(i) $x^2 + 12x + 20$ by $x + 2$

(ii) $12a^2 + 14a + 4$ by $3a + 2$

(iii) $15c^2 + 11c - 14$ by $3c - 2$

2. (a) Simplify each of the following:

(i) $\dfrac{(x-3)(x+4)}{x+4}$

(ii) $\dfrac{4x+4}{x+1}$

(iii) $\dfrac{x^2+2x-15}{x+5}$

(iv) $\dfrac{4a^2b^3}{2ab}$

(v) $\dfrac{3x^2-2x-5}{x+1}$

(b) Write each of the following as a single fraction in its simplest form:

(i) $\dfrac{2x-1}{5} - \dfrac{3x-4}{2} + \dfrac{x+5}{3}$

(ii) $\dfrac{3}{x-5} + \dfrac{2}{3x-1}$

(iii) $\dfrac{4}{5x-2} - \dfrac{7}{2-5x}$

(c) (i) Factorise fully $2x^2 + 16x + 32$.

(ii) Hence, simplify $\dfrac{2x^2+16x+32}{(x+4)^2}$ to its lowest form.

(iii) Check your answer to part (ii) by letting $x = 5$.

3. (a) Simplify:

(i) $\dfrac{2x-6}{4x-12}$

(ii) $\dfrac{x^2-9}{x^2-4x+3}$

(iii) $\dfrac{x^2-7x+6}{2x-12}$

(iv) $\dfrac{2x^2+x-28}{2x+8}$

(b) Simplify each of the following:

(i) $(2x^2 + 7x - 4) \div (x + 4)$

(ii) $(2x^3 + 9x^2 - 55x + 50) \div (2x - 5)$

(iii) $(6x^3 - 14x^2 - 9x + 2) \div (3x + 2)$

(iv) $(8x^3 + 50x - 26) \div (2x - 1)$

(c) Write $\dfrac{8}{x-5} - \dfrac{12}{5-x}$ as a single fraction. Verify your answer by letting $x = 9$.

4. (a) Simplify each of the following:

(i) $\dfrac{4x^2-12x+9}{2x-3}$

(ii) $\dfrac{12x^3+13x^2-16x+3}{4x-1}$

(iii) $\dfrac{x^3-19x-30}{x-5}$

(iv) $\dfrac{3x^3+8x^2-1}{3x-1}$

(b) (i) Write $\dfrac{3}{x-1} - \dfrac{8}{1-x}$ as a single fraction.

(ii) Express $\dfrac{x+3}{x^2+2x-3}$ as a single fraction in its simplest form.

(iii) Hence, simplify $\dfrac{3}{x-1} - \dfrac{8}{1-x} + \dfrac{x+3}{x^2+2x-3}$.

5. (i) Consider the following sum: $10 \div 5 = 2$.

■ 5 is called the divisor.

■ 10 is called the dividend.

■ 2 is called the quotient.

Copy and complete the following table, by filling in the correct dividend, divisor or quotient for each question.

Divisor	Quotient	Dividend
	$x-5$	$6x^2-31x+5$
$4x-1$	$2x+1$	
$x-1$		x^3-4x^2-x+4
$2x-3$	$6x^2-3x+4$	

(ii) $x^2 - 16$ is the quotient when $3x^3 + 5x^2 - 48x - 80$ is divided by the divisor $px + q$. Find the value of p and the value of q.

Algebra IV: Manipulation of Formulae

Learning Outcomes

In this chapter you will learn:

➲ How to manipulate formulae

➲ How to use manipulated formulae to solve real-world problems

14.1 MANIPULATION OF FORMULAE

To calculate the distance travelled by an object, we can use the **formula**:

FORMULA

Distance = Speed × Time

OR

$D = S \times T$

A formula shows the relationship or link between two or more variables.

YOU SHOULD REMEMBER...

- How to use BIMDAS
- How to work with algebraic equations
- How to work with algebraic fractions

KEY WORDS

- **Manipulation**
- **Subject of a formula**

By rearranging or manipulating this formula, we can also calculate both the speed of an object and the time taken to travel a set distance.

Working with formulae and manipulation of formulae is often necessary to solve a range of real-world problems. To manipulate a formula, remember the order of operations (BIMDAS) and how to work with an equation – whatever is done to the left-hand side (LHS) must also be done to the right-hand side (RHS) to keep the equation in balance.

FORMULA

$S = \dfrac{D}{T}$ $T = \dfrac{D}{S}$

x^2 Worked Example 14.1

Make r the subject of the formula if $p + rs = q$.

Solution

Making r the subject of the formula means that the final formula must be in the form $r = ...$
In other words, we are being asked to express r in terms of all other variables.

$p + rs = q$

At the moment, on the LHS, p is being added to the product rs. The opposite of adding p is subtracting p. We subtract p from both sides of the equation.

$p + rs - p = q - p$

$\therefore rs = q - p$

At the moment, on the LHS, r is being multiplied by s. The opposite of multiplying by s is dividing by s. We divide both sides of the equation by s.

$\therefore \dfrac{rs}{s} = \dfrac{q - p}{s}$

$\Rightarrow r = \dfrac{q - p}{s}$

r is now the subject of the formula.

x^2 **Worked Example 14.2**

Express c in terms of a and b if:

$$\frac{a}{5} = \frac{b - 2c}{3}$$

Solution

The lowest common denominator (LCD) of 5 and 3 is 15. Multiply both sides of the equation by 15.

$$15\left(\frac{a}{5}\right) = 15\left(\frac{b - 2c}{3}\right)$$

$$\Rightarrow 3a = 5(b - 2c)$$

Expand the RHS:

$$3a = 5b - 10c$$

Method 1

On the RHS, $5b$ is being added to the product $-10c$. The opposite of adding $5b$ is subtracting $5b$. Subtract $5b$ from both sides.

$$\therefore 3a - 5b = -10c$$

Multiply both sides of the equation by -1:

$$\therefore 5b - 3a = 10c$$

On the RHS, c is being multiplied by 10. The opposite of multiplying by 10 is dividing by 10. Divide both sides of the equation by 10.

$$\therefore \frac{5b - 3a}{10} = c$$

Turning the equation around, we get:

$$c = \frac{5b - 3a}{10} \quad \text{or} \quad c = \frac{b}{2} - \frac{3a}{10}$$

Method 2

On the RHS, $10c$ is being subtracted from $5b$. The opposite of subtracting $10c$ is adding $10c$. Add $10c$ to both sides:

$$\therefore 3a + 10c = 5b$$

On the LHS, we are adding $3a$ to $10c$. The opposite of adding $3a$ is subtracting $3a$. Subtract $3a$ from both sides:

$$\therefore 10c = 5b - 3a$$

On the LHS, c is being multiplied by 10. The opposite of multiplying by 10 is dividing by 10. Divide both sides of the equation by 10:

$$\therefore c = \frac{5b - 3a}{10} \quad \text{or} \quad c = \frac{b}{2} - \frac{3a}{10}$$

ACTIVITY 14.1

x^2 **Worked Example 14.3**

Make q the subject of the following formula:

$$3pq - 2qr = 5rs$$

Solution

Look at the LHS of the given formula.

Both terms on the LHS contain the variable q.

We thus need to firstly factorise q out of both of these terms.

$$q(3p - 2r) = 5rs$$

On the LHS, q is being multiplied by $(3p - 2r)$.

The opposite of multiplying by $(3p - 2r)$ is dividing by $(3p - 2r)$.

Divide both sides of the formula by $(3p - 2r)$.

$$\therefore q = \frac{5rs}{3p - 2r}$$

Worked Example 14.4

If $\frac{2}{u} - \frac{1}{t} = \frac{3}{p}$, express t in terms of p and u.

Solution

The lowest common denominator (LCD) of p, t and u is ptu. Multiply both sides of the equation by ptu.

$$ptu\left(\frac{2}{u}\right) - ptu\left(\frac{1}{t}\right) = ptu\left(\frac{3}{p}\right)$$

$$\therefore 2pt - pu = 3tu$$

We need to have all terms containing t on the same side of the equation. To do this, first subtract $3tu$ from both sides:

$$2pt - pu - 3tu = 0$$

Add pu to both sides:

$$2pt - 3tu = pu$$

Factorise t out of both terms on the LHS:

$$t(2p - 3u) = pu$$

Divide both sides by $(2p - 3u)$:

$$\therefore t = \frac{pu}{2p - 3u}$$

Exercise 14.1

In Questions 1–20, express the variable in the square brackets in terms of the other variables.

1. $x + 2y = 3z$ [x]
2. $p + 4q = 2$ [p]
3. $2b - 5 = a$ [b]
4. $t = a + b + c$ [a]
5. $l + 2 = xy$ [y]
6. $r - 4u = pt$ [u]
7. $a - b = at$ [a]
8. $x = 2yz - z$ [z]
9. $3a = \frac{b + c}{2}$ [b]
10. $p = \frac{q - 3r}{4}$ [r]
11. $\frac{a}{2} = \frac{4b + c}{3}$ [b]
12. $\frac{p}{2} - \frac{3q}{5} = \frac{c}{10}$ [c]
13. $A = \frac{1}{2}(a + b)h$ [a]
14. $r - 2rs = q$ [r]
15. $pq = p - r$ [p]
16. $\frac{1}{u} + \frac{1}{v} = \frac{1}{f}$ [f]
17. $\frac{2}{a} - \frac{3}{b} = \frac{1}{c}$ [b]
18. $p = c + pq$ [p]
19. $a = \frac{bc - d}{3c}$ [c]
20. $a = \frac{p}{p + b}$ [p]

x^2 Worked Example 14.5

(i) Given that $a = bc^2$, write c in terms of a and b.

(ii) Given that $p = qr^3$, write r in terms of p and q.

Solution

(i) $a = bc^2$

On the RHS, c^2 is being multiplied by b. So divide both sides by b.

$$\therefore \frac{a}{b} = c^2$$

Turn the equation around:

$$c^2 = \frac{a}{b}$$
$$\therefore c = \pm\sqrt{\frac{a}{b}}$$

Note: If $x^2 = 9$
$\Rightarrow x = \pm\sqrt{9}$

(ii) $p = qr^3$

On the RHS, r^3 is being multiplied by q. So divide both sides by q.

$$\therefore \frac{p}{q} = r^3$$

Turn the equation around:

$$r^3 = \frac{p}{q}$$
$$\therefore r = \sqrt[3]{\frac{p}{q}}$$

x^2 **Worked Example 14.6**

Make p the subject of the following formula:

$$\sqrt{q + 2p} = 2r$$

Solution

$$\sqrt{q + 2p} = 2r$$

The LHS is equal to the RHS. Therefore, the square of the LHS is equal to the square of the RHS. To remove the square root on the LHS, square both sides.

$$(\sqrt{q + 2p})^2 = (2r)^2$$

$$\therefore q + 2p = 4r^2$$

> Remember that $(\sqrt{a})^2 = a$. Squaring removes the square root sign.

Subtract q from both sides:

$$2p = 4r^2 - q$$

Divide both sides by 2:

$$\therefore p = \frac{4r^2 - q}{2}$$

Note: We could also write the answer as $p = 2r^2 - \dfrac{q}{2}$.

x^2 **Worked Example 14.7**

If $y = ax + a$ and $x = 3a - 2$:

(i) Write y in terms of a.

(ii) Find the value of y when $a = 6$.

Solution

(i) $y = ax + a$ and $x = 3a - 2$

Substitute $3a - 2$ for x:

$$y = a(3a - 2) + a$$

$$y = 3a^2 - 2a + a$$

$$\therefore y = 3a^2 - a$$

(ii) Substitute $a = 6$ into $y = 3a^2 - a$:

$$\Rightarrow y = 3(6)^2 - (6)$$

$$= 3(36) - 6$$

$$= 108 - 6$$

$$\therefore y = 102$$

x^2 **Worked Example 14.8**

The total surface area of a closed cylinder is given by the formula $A = 2\pi r^2 + 2\pi rh$.

(i) What is the total surface area of a closed cylinder with $r = 3$ cm and $h = 4$ cm. Express your answer in terms of π.

(ii) Express h in terms of the other variables (A and r).

(iii) Hence, find the height of a closed cylinder with a total surface area of 345.4 cm^2 and a radius length of 5 cm. Take π to be equal to 3.14.

Solution

(i) Substitute $r = 3$ and $h = 4$ into the formula for A.

$$A = 2\pi(3)^2 + 2\pi(3)(4)$$
$$= 2\pi(9) + 2\pi(12)$$
$$= 18\pi + 24\pi$$
$$\therefore A = 42\pi \text{ cm}^2$$

(ii) $$A = 2\pi r^2 + 2\pi rh$$
$$A - 2\pi r^2 = 2\pi rh$$
$$2\pi rh = A - 2\pi r^2$$
$$\therefore h = \frac{A - 2\pi r^2}{2\pi r} \quad \textbf{or} \quad h = \frac{A}{2\pi r} - r$$

(iii) Substitute $A = 345.4$, $r = 5$ and $\pi = 3.14$ into the manipulated formula in part (ii).

$$h = \frac{345.4 - 2(3.14)(5)^2}{2(3.14)(5)}$$
$$= \frac{345.4 - 157}{31.4}$$
$$= \frac{188.4}{31.4}$$
$$\therefore h = 6 \text{ cm}$$

Exercise 14.2

In Questions 1–8 below, express the variable in the square brackets in terms of the other variables.

1. $c = \sqrt{a^2 + b^2}$ [a]

2. $3a^2 - 2b = c$ [a]

3. $r = \sqrt{pq + q}$ [q]

4. $\sqrt{\dfrac{a + b}{2}} = 3$ [b]

5. $\sqrt{\dfrac{p}{r - q}} = p$ [r]

6. $T = 2\pi\sqrt{\dfrac{l}{g}}$ [g]

7. $\dfrac{x}{b} = \dfrac{b^2}{a - d}$ [b]

8. $a = \dfrac{3\sqrt{rt}}{2}$ [t]

9. If $y = ax - 1$ and $x = 2a - 1$:

   (i) Write y as an expression in a.

   (ii) Factorise this expression.

10. Given that $x = ak + a^3$ and $k = 4 - 2a^2$:

   (i) Write x as an expression in a.

   (ii) Factorise fully this expression.

   (iii) Evaluate x when $a = 2$.

11. If $a + y = 2x$ and $2b - 2y = 5x$:

   (i) Show that $a + 10b = 27x + 9y$.

   If $3x + y = 4$:

   (ii) Show that $a + 10b = 36$.

12. The formula for the volume of a cone is $V = \dfrac{1}{3}\pi r^2 h$.

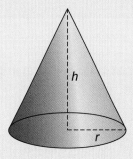

   (i) What is the volume of a cone with $h = 10$ cm, $r = 2$ cm and $\pi = 3.14$?

(ii) Write h in terms of the other variables, and hence, find the height of a cone where $r = 12$ mm, $\pi = \frac{22}{7}$ and $V = 2143.68$ mm^3.

(iii) Write r in terms of the other variables, and hence, find the radius of a cone where $h = 8$ cm, $\pi = 3.14$ and $V = 301.44$ cm^3.

13. A root (R) of the equation $ax^2 - c = 0$ can be found using the formula $R = \dfrac{\sqrt{-4ac}}{2a}$.

   (i) Express c in terms of a and R.

   (ii) Hence, find the value of c if $a = 13$ and $R = \sqrt{5}$.

14. Consider an object dropped from rest. If the object is dropped from a height h (metres), then its speed v (in metres per second) on hitting the ground is given by the formula $v = \sqrt{2gh}$, where g (on Earth) $= 9.8$.

   (i) What is the speed of an object when it hits the ground, if it is dropped from a height of 40 m?

   (ii) Write h in terms of v and hence, find the height from which an object was dropped, if its velocity when hitting the ground is 42 m/s.

   (iii) On another planet, an object dropped from a height of 117 m would hit the ground at a speed of 78 m/s. Find the value of g for this planet.

15. The kinetic energy of an object is the energy it has as a result of its motion. Kinetic energy is measured in joules. The formula for the kinetic energy of an object is $E = \frac{1}{2}mv^2$, where E is the kinetic energy (in joules), m is the mass of the object (in kilograms) and v is the speed of the object (in m/s).

(a) Which of the following objects has the greater kinetic energy?

   (i) An object of mass 10 kg travelling 5 m/s

   (ii) An object of mass 5 kg travelling at 7 m/s

   Show your calculations.

(b) The speed of a projectile is measured at a particular moment as being 4.9 m/s.

   If the projectile has a kinetic energy of 120.05 joules at this moment, then what is the mass of this projectile?

(c) Consider the formula $E = \frac{1}{2}mv^2$.

   (i) Make v the subject of this formula. (*Note:* $v \geqslant 0$)

   (ii) Hence, find the speed of an object that has a kinetic energy of 500 joules and a mass of 2 kg. Answer correct to two decimal places.

16. A bus is accelerating away from a bus stop at a constant rate. The distance travelled by the bus from the bus stop is given by the formula

$$s = ut + \frac{1}{2}at^2$$

where s is the distance travelled (in metres), u is the initial speed of the bus (in m/s), t is the time taken (in seconds) and a is the rate of acceleration (in m/s^2).

(a) By manipulating the above formula, express u in terms of a, s and t.

(b) By manipulating the original formula, express a in terms of s, t and u.

(c) Three seconds after leaving the bus stop, at which it had stopped, the bus has travelled a distance of 9 m.

   Given that the bus is accelerating at a constant rate, find this rate of acceleration of the bus.

17. A bank offers new customers a savings account in which interest will be paid at the end of one year, at which time the account will have to close.

If P is the principal sum saved, r is the interest rate (e.g. a 5% interest rate implies $r = 5$) and A is the final amount with interest, then A, P and r are related by the formula $A = P\left(1 + \dfrac{r}{100}\right)$.

(a) Using the above formula, express r in terms of A and P.

(b) A new customer opens a savings account with the bank. She lodges €3,500 into the account. One year later, the account has a value of €3,727.15.

Using your answer from part (a), find the exact rate of interest that the bank must have been offering.

A second bank is offering a savings account in which interest is compounded on an annual basis. Once an account is opened, customers cannot make any lodgements or withdrawals. They can close their account and withdraw the total amount in the account at any time.

If P is the principal sum saved, i is the interest rate as a decimal (e.g. a 5% interest rate implies that $i = 0.05$) and A is the final amount with interest, then A, P and i are related by the formula $A = P(1 + i)^T$, where T is the time (in years) for which the account has been open.

(c) Write down the formula that relates A, P and i for a customer who closes their account after two years.

(d) Using your answer for part (c) above, express i in terms of A and P for a customer with a two-year account.

(e) Salvador opens a two-year savings account with this bank. He lodges €38,000 on 11 September 2011 and withdraws €40,470.91 on 11 September 2013. Using your result in part (d) above, calculate the rate of interest that the bank was offering him on his savings. Answer, as a percentage, correct to two significant figures.

18. In Ireland, meteorologists generally report temperatures in degrees Celsius (°C). In other countries, such as the USA, temperatures are usually reported in degrees Fahrenheit (°F). The following formula can be used to convert from degrees Fahrenheit to degrees Celsius:

$$C = \frac{5}{9}(F - 32)$$

(a) On a particular day, the *San Francisco Chronicle* reports that the afternoon high temperature in the San Francisco Bay area will be 77°F. On the same day, the *Irish Independent* reports that the afternoon high temperature in the Greater Dublin area will be 24°C.

Which city is predicted to have the higher maximum temperature on this day?

(b) Using the formula given above, derive the conversion formula for Celsius to Fahrenheit.

(c) Absolute zero is a theoretical temperature defined as 0 degrees Kelvin, where the conversion formula from Celsius to Kelvin is $K = C + 273.15$.

What is the value of absolute zero in degrees Fahrenheit?

19. Doctors sometimes need to work out how much medicine to give a child, based on the correct dose for an adult. There are different ways of doing this, based on the child's age, weight, height, or some other measure.

(a) One rule for working out the child's dose from the adult dose is called Clark's rule. It is:

$$C = \left(\frac{W}{68}\right) \times A$$

where C is the child's dose, A is the adult's dose and W is the child's weight in kilograms.

The adult dose of a certain medicine is 125 mg per day. Calculate the correct dose for a child weighing 30 kg, using Clark's rule. Give the answer correct to the nearest 5 mg.

(b) Another rule for working out the child's dose is called Young's rule. Below are three different descriptions of Young's rule, taken from the internet. In each case, write down a formula that **exactly** matches the description in words. State clearly the meaning of any letters you use in your formulae.

(i) **Young's rule:** A mathematical expression used to determine a drug dosage for children. The correct dosage is calculated by dividing the child's age by an amount equal to the child's age plus 12 and then multiplying by the usual adult dose.

Mosby's Dental Dictionary, 2nd edition

(ii) **Young's rule:** A rule for calculating the dose of medicine correct for a child by adding 12 to the child's age, dividing the sum by the child's age, then dividing the adult dose by the figure obtained.

The American Heritage Medical Dictionary

(iii) **Young's rule:** The dose of a drug for a child is obtained by multiplying the adult dose by the child's age in years and dividing the result by the sum of the child's age plus 12.

Miller-Keane Encyclopedia and Dictionary of Medicine, Nursing, and Allied Health, 7th edition

(c) Explain why the three formulae in part (b) above all give the same result.

(d) The adult dose of a certain medicine is 150 mg per day. According to Young's rule, what is the correct dose for a six-year-old child?

(e) Young's rule results in a certain child being given one-fifth of the adult dose of a medicine. How old is this child?

SEC 2012, LCOL

chapter 15

Algebra V: Linear Equations

Learning Outcomes

In this chapter you will learn how to:

- ⊃ Solve linear equations in one variable
- ⊃ Solve linear equations in two variables
- ⊃ Find the values of unknown coefficients using linear equations
- ⊃ Use linear equations to solve problems

15.1 SOLVING LINEAR EQUATIONS IN ONE VARIABLE

Linear equations are algebraic equations of the form:

$ax + b = 0$ (in x)   **or** $y = ax + b$ (in x and y)

where x and y are variables and a and b are constants.

An equation is 'linear' because, when graphed, it forms a straight line.

Linear equations are polynomial equations of the first degree. This means that the variable(s) have a highest power of 1 (so a linear equation cannot contain terms such as x^2 or y^3).

When solving an equation in one variable/unknown, we are being asked to find the value of the unknown that satisfies the equation. In many cases, this unknown is represented by the letter x, although any letter can be used.

For example, consider the equation $5x + 2 = 12$.

Here, $x = 2$ is the solution: $5(2) + 2 = 10 + 2$

$$= 12$$

While there are different approaches to solving an equation (graphical, trial and error, algebraic), in this chapter we will look at algebraic approaches.

YOU SHOULD REMEMBER...

- How to solve linear equations from *Active Maths 1*

- How to solve a system of linear equations simultaneously from *Active Maths 1*

KEY WORDS

- **Linear equation**

- **Lowest common denominator (LCD)**

- **Simultaneous equations**

x^2 Worked Example 15.1

Solve $5x + 1 = 2(x - 4)$ and verify your solution.

Solution

$5x + 1 = 2(x - 4)$

$5x + 1 = 2x - 8$ (Expand the RHS)

$5x - 2x = -8 - 1$ (Subtract $2x$ from both sides; subtract 1 from both sides)

$\quad 3x = -9$

$\quad \dfrac{3x}{3} = -\dfrac{9}{3}$ (Divide both sides by 3)

$\quad \therefore x = -3$

Verifying the solution means checking to see if the answer we found is correct.

We do this by substituting the value that we got for x back into the original equation.

$$5x + 1 = 2(x - 4)$$

For $x = -3$: $5(-3) + 1 = 2((-3) - 4)$

$$-15 + 1 = 2(-7)$$

$$-14 = -14$$

TRUE

$\therefore x = -3$ is the correct solution.

x^2 Worked Example 15.2

Solve $5(2x - 1) = 2(6x - 3) + 4x - 2$.

Solution

$5(2x - 1) = 2(6x - 3) + 4x - 2$

$10x - 5 = 12x - 6 + 4x - 2$

$10x - 5 = 16x - 8$

$10x - 16x = -8 + 5$

$-6x = -3$

$6x = 3$

$\dfrac{6x}{6} = \dfrac{3}{6}$

$\therefore x = \dfrac{1}{2}$

Alternatively, we could have brought the x terms to the RHS:

$5(2x - 1) = 2(6x - 3) + 4x - 2$

$10x - 5 = 12x - 6 + 4x - 2$

$10x - 5 = 16x - 8$

$-5 + 8 = 16x - 10x$

$3 = 6x$

$\dfrac{3}{6} = x$

$\therefore x = \dfrac{1}{2}$

Note: It is good practice to check your solution.

Use rough work if you are not asked explicitly to check your solution.

$5\left(2\left(\dfrac{1}{2}\right) - 1\right) = 2\left(6\left(\dfrac{1}{2}\right) - 3\right) + 4\left(\dfrac{1}{2}\right) - 2$

$5(1 - 1) = 2(3 - 3) + 4\left(\dfrac{1}{2}\right) - 2$

$5(0) = 2(0) + 4\left(\dfrac{1}{2}\right) - 2$

$0 = 0 + 2 - 2$

$0 = 0 + 0$

$0 = 0$

TRUE

$\therefore x = \dfrac{1}{2}$ is the correct solution.

x^2 Worked Example 15.3

Solve for x: $\quad \dfrac{1}{3}(3x + 2) - \dfrac{4x - 2}{5} = \dfrac{3}{2}$

Solution

$\dfrac{1}{3}(3x + 2)$ can be written as $\dfrac{3x + 2}{3}$.

$\therefore \dfrac{3x + 2}{3} - \dfrac{4x - 2}{5} = \dfrac{3}{2}$

The LCD of 3, 5 and 2 is 30.

Multiply both sides of the equation by the LCD. This removes all denominators.

$\dfrac{30(3x + 2)}{3} - \dfrac{30(4x - 2)}{5} = 30\left(\dfrac{3}{2}\right)$

$\dfrac{^{10}\cancel{30}(3x + 2)}{\cancel{3}_1} - \dfrac{^{6}\cancel{30}(4x - 2)}{\cancel{5}_1} = {}^{15}\cancel{30}\left(\dfrac{3}{\cancel{2}_1}\right)$

$10(3x + 2) - 6(4x - 2) = 15(3)$

$30x + 20 - 24x + 12 = 45$

$6x + 32 = 45$

$6x = 13$

$\therefore x = \dfrac{13}{6} \quad \left(\text{or } 2\dfrac{1}{6}\right)$

A linear equation in one variable will always have one solution only.

Consider the general linear equation in x, $ax + b = 0$, where $a, b \in R$, $a \neq 0$:

$ax + b = 0$

$\quad ax = -b \quad$ (Subtract b from both sides)

$\quad x = -\dfrac{b}{a} \quad$ (Divide both sides by a)

The **unique** solution of this equation is $-\dfrac{b}{a}$.

ACTIVITIES 15.1, 15.2

Exercise 15.1

Solve the following equations
(Questions 1–22).

1. $2x + 3 = 7 - x$

2. $5x - 3 = 4x + 3$

3. $10(x + 5) - 4(x + 2) = 6$

4. $5(y - 3) = 2y - (y + 4)$

5. $4x + 3(x + 2) = 11x + 2(3 - x)$

6. $5[2 - (x + 3)] = 1 + 3x$

7. $2(t + 1) - 3(t - 1) - 12 = 0$

8. $9(x - 3) - 5(x - 1) + 5 = -9$

9. $2x - 4 - 2(x + 2) + 8 = x$

10. $-(p - 2) = 2(p + 5) - 13$

11. $\dfrac{3}{4} = 2x$

12. $\dfrac{2x + 5}{8} = \dfrac{1}{2}$

13. $\dfrac{3x - 1}{2} = 7$

14. $\dfrac{2x + 3}{3} - \dfrac{4x}{5} = 1$

15. $\dfrac{5y - 2}{4} + \dfrac{2y - 1}{3} = \dfrac{13}{12}$

16. $x - \dfrac{4x - 7}{2} = 1\dfrac{1}{2}$

17. $\dfrac{2x - 11}{6} + \dfrac{5x - 1}{3} = 2$

18. $\dfrac{-x - 1}{4} + \dfrac{1 - x}{7} = \dfrac{1}{28}$

19. $\dfrac{2x - 2}{3} - \dfrac{3x - 1}{5} = 0$

20. $\dfrac{7t - 1}{3} - \dfrac{2t + 5}{6} = -\dfrac{3}{2}$

21. $\dfrac{13x - 3}{8} + \dfrac{6 - 5x}{4} = \dfrac{1}{2}$

22. $\dfrac{2x + 1}{6} - \dfrac{2x + 1}{10} = \dfrac{4}{5}$

Solve the following equations and
verify your answer in each case
(Questions 23–25).

23. $3(2x + 1) + \dfrac{1}{4}(3x) = 9$

24. $\dfrac{1}{3}(x + 4) - \dfrac{2}{5}(x + 1) = 2$

25. $\dfrac{3}{7}(2x + 1) - \dfrac{1}{2}(3x - 1) = \dfrac{1}{5}$

15.2 SOLVING LINEAR EQUATIONS IN TWO VARIABLES

The equation $y = 2x + 5$ is a linear equation since it represents the equation of a line with a slope of 2 and a y-intercept of 5.

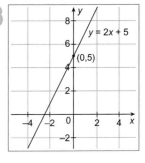

This equation could also have been written as:

$y = 2x + 5$

$0 = 2x - y + 5$ (Subtract y from both sides)

$-5 = 2x - y$ (Subtract 5 from both sides)

$2x - y = -5$ (Turn the equation around)

In this section we will examine how to solve a system of linear equations simultaneously. We will be working with 2 × 2 ('two-by-two') systems; that is, systems with two equations in two unknowns. When finding a solution to such a system, we are actually finding the point of intersection (POI) of the two lines that make up the system.

Here are some possibilities:

Two non-parallel lines	Two parallel (and not identical) lines	Two identical lines
One solution	No solution	Infinite number of solutions
(One POI)	(No POI)	(Infinitely many POIs)

We will generally be working with systems that have one solution only.

x^2 Worked Example 15.4

Solve for x and y:

$5x - 3y = 7$

$-3 + 2x = y$

Solution

Method 1 (By elimination)

Step 1 Write each equation in the form $ax + by = c$:

$5x - 3y = 7$ (A)

$2x - y = 3$ (B)

Step 2 Make all x-coefficients (or all y-coefficients) the same in each equation.

$5x - 3y = 7$ (× 2) → $10x - 6y = 14$

$2x - y = 3$ (× 5) → $10x - 5y = 15$

Step 3 The x-coefficients are the same sign, so we will subtract the second equation from the first:

$10x - 6y = 14$

$- (10x - 5y = 15)$

$\underline{}$

$10x - 6y = 14$

$\underline{-10x + 5y = -15}$

$-y = -1$

$\therefore y = 1$

Step 4 Substitute $y = 1$ into either the first or second equation to find x:

$$2x - y = 3 \quad \text{(B)}$$
$$\therefore 2x - (1) = 3$$
$$2x - 1 = 3$$
$$2x = 4$$
$$x = 2$$

Step 5 $\therefore$ Solution is $x = 2$, $y = 1$.

Method 2 (By substitution)

Step 1 Make y the subject of each equation:

$$-3y = -5x + 7 \quad \text{(A)}$$
$$3y = 5x - 7$$
$$\therefore \boxed{y = \frac{5x - 7}{3}}$$
$$\therefore \boxed{y = 2x - 3} \quad \text{(B)}$$

Step 2 Let $y = y$.

$$\therefore \frac{5x - 7}{3} = 2x - 3$$
$$5x - 7 = 3(2x - 3)$$
$$5x - 7 = 6x - 9$$
$$9 - 7 = 6x - 5x$$
$$2 = x$$
$$\therefore x = 2$$

Step 3 Solve for y using the first or second equation.

$$y = 2(2) - 3 \quad \text{(B)}$$
$$y = 4 - 3$$
$$\therefore y = 1$$

Step 4 $\therefore$ Solution is $x = 2$, $y = 1$.

Note: It is good practice to check your work.

$5x - 3y = 7$	$2x - y = 3$
$5(2) - 3(1) = 7$	$2(2) - (1) = 3$
$10 - 3 = 7$	$4 - 1 = 3$
$7 = 7$	$3 = 3$
TRUE	TRUE

As $(2,1)$ satisfies both equations, $(x,y) = (2,1)$ is a solution.

ACTIVITY 15.3

x^2 **Worked Example 15.5**

Solve the simultaneous equations:

$$\frac{5x}{3} - \frac{y}{2} = 7 \qquad \frac{x + 2y}{5} = -1$$

Solution

The first thing we need to do is eliminate the denominators from each equation.

$$\frac{5x}{3} - \frac{y}{2} = 7$$

The LCD is 6.

$$\frac{6(5x)}{3} - \frac{6(y)}{2} = 6(7)$$
$$10x - 3y = 42 \quad \text{(A)}$$

$$\frac{x + 2y}{5} = -1$$

The LCD is 5.

$$\frac{5(x + 2y)}{5} = 5(-1)$$
$$x + 2y = -5 \quad \text{(B)}$$

We now proceed, as before, using either Method 1 (by elimination) or Method 2 (by substitution).

Method 1   (by elimination)

Step 1   Write each equation in the form $ax + by = c$:

$$10x - 3y = 42$$
$$x + 2y = -5$$

Step 2   Make all x-coefficients (or all y-coefficients) the same in each equation:

$$10x - 3y = 42$$
$$10x + 20y = -50$$

Step 3   The x-coefficients are the same sign, so we will subtract the second equation from the first:

$$10x - 3y = 42$$
$$\underline{-(10x + 20y = -50)}$$
$$10x - 3y = 42$$
$$\underline{-10x - 20y = 50}$$
$$-23y = 92$$
$$23y = -92$$
$$\therefore y = -4$$

Step 4   Substitute $y = -4$ into either the first or second equation to find x:

$$x + 2y = -5 \quad \text{(B)}$$
$$\therefore x + 2(-4) = -5$$
$$x - 8 = -5$$
$$x = 3$$

Step 5 $\therefore$ Solution is $x = 3$, $y = -4$.

   (Remember to check your solution.)

> Note: The method of substitution could also be used here.

x^2 Worked Example 15.6

Solve for x and y:

$$2x - y = 0$$
$$10x + 5y = 6$$

Solution

Method 1   (By elimination)

Eliminate y:

$$2x - y = 0 \;(\times 5) \;\rightarrow\; 10x - 5y = 0$$
$$10x + 5y = 6 \;(\times 1) \;\rightarrow\; 10x + 5y = 6$$

Add the two equations:

$$10x - 5y = 0$$
$$\underline{10x + 5y = 6}$$
$$20x = 6$$
$$x = \frac{6}{20}$$
$$\therefore x = \frac{3}{10}$$

Solve for y:

$$2\left(\frac{3}{10}\right) - y = 0$$
$$\frac{6}{10} - y = 0$$
$$\frac{3}{5} - y = 0$$
$$\therefore y = \frac{3}{5}$$

Solution is (x, y) is $\left(\frac{3}{10}, \frac{3}{5}\right)$.

(Remember to check your solution.)

> Note: The method of substitution could also be used here.

Exercise 15.2

Solve each of the following systems of simultaneous equations. (You may use either the 'method of elimination' or the 'method of substitution'.)

1. $x + y = 4$
$x + 7y = 10$

2. $x - y = -2$
$x + 9y = 8$

3. $4x + y = 3$
$2x + y = 1$

4. $p - 2q = 0$
$2p - 9q = 10$

5. $3a - 2b = 19$
$2a + 5b = 0$

6. $4m + 5n = 32$
$2m - 3n = -6$

7. $3r + 2s = -6$
$5r + 4s = -8$

8. $3u + 2v = -21$
$u + v = -8$

9. $5x - 3y + 9 = 0$
$3x - 7y = 5$

10. $3x = 4y + 13$
$3y = 3 - 2x$

11. $6x + 3y - 21 = 0$
$2x - 5y + 11 = 0$

12. $2x + 3y + 26 = 12$
$3x - 2 = 2y - 24$

13. $14 = 9x - 2y$
$0 = 3y + x - 8$

14. $\frac{1}{2}x + \frac{2}{3}y = 6$
$\frac{1}{8}x + \frac{5}{4}y = 8$

15. $2x + y = 3$
$y = 0.2x + 0.8$

16. $6x - 8y = 1$
$7x + 2y = 4$

17. $9x + 5y = 5$
$3x + 5y = 3$

18. $5x - 6y = -4$
$x - 3y = -1$

19. $\frac{x+1}{4} + \frac{y-1}{2} = 3$; $x + y = 10$

20. $3x + 2y + 1 = 0$; $\frac{x}{2} + \frac{y+8}{4} = 2$

21. $\frac{x+2y}{6} = 2$; $\frac{x}{5} + 3y = 5$

22. $\frac{4x-y}{5} = 3$; $\frac{2x}{7} - \frac{y+5}{2} = -1$

23. $2p + 3q = 7p + 10q = 1$

24. $\frac{3x-2}{4} - \frac{y-3}{2} = -\frac{1}{2}$
$\frac{2x+4}{3} + \frac{y+1}{4} = \frac{1}{4}$

15.3 UNKNOWN COEFFICIENTS

$x^2 = 16$ is an example of an equation. In this equation, there are only two values of x where x^2 will be equal to 16: $x = 4$ or $x = -4$.

An equation that is true for every value of the variable is called an **identity**. For example, $(x - 2)^2 = x^2 - 4x + 4$ is an example of an identity. This identity will be true for all values of $x \in R$. This is because the LHS will always be equal to the RHS. We can use this property of identities to find the value of unknown coefficients.

x^2 Worked Example 15.7

If $3px + q = 6x + 5$ for all values of x, find the value of p and the value of q.

Solution

Compare the LHS with the RHS of the identity. Equate like terms from each side:

x-terms	Constants
$3px = 6x$	$q = 5$
$\therefore\ 3p = 6$	
$\Rightarrow p = 2$	

Answer: $p = 2$, $q = 5$

Worked Example 15.8

If $a(x + 3) + b(x - 1) = 20x - 4$ for all values of x, solve for a and b.

Solution

$a(x + 3) + b(x - 1) = 20x - 4$

$ax + 3a + bx - b = 20x - 4$ (Expanding brackets)

$ax + bx + 3a - b = 20x - 4$ (Grouping like terms)

$(a + b)x + 3a - b = 20x - 4$

Equate like terms from each side:

x-terms	Constants
$(a + b)x = 20x$	$3a - b = -4$
$\therefore\ a + b = 20$	

As there are two unknowns in each equation, solve using simultaneous equations.

Here, the method of elimination is used, but the method of substitution could also be used.

$$\begin{array}{l} a + b = 20 \\ \underline{3a - b = -4} \\ \quad 4a = 16 \\ \quad \therefore a = 4 \end{array}$$

Solve for b: $a + b = 20$

$\quad\quad\quad\quad\quad 4 + b = 20$

$\quad\quad\quad\quad\quad \therefore b = 16$

Exercise 15.3

1. If $10(ax + b) = 50x + 30$ for all values of x, find the value of a and the value of b.

2. If $3(bx - 2dy) = 9x + 12y$ for all values of x and y, solve for b and d.

3. If $(x + 5)(x - 3) = ax^2 + bx + c$ for all values of x, solve for a and b.

4. If $(x + b)^2 = x^2 - 8x + c$ for all values of x, find the value of b and the value of c.

5. If $(ax - 2)(x - b) = 2x^2 + 6x - 8$ for all values of x, find the value of a and the value of b.

6. If $p(2x - 3) - q(3x - 1) = 9x - 10$ for all values of x, find the value of p and the value of q.

7. If $3(x^2 + 2cx) - b(2x + 1) + c = 3x^2 - 2x + 1$ for all values of x, solve for b and c.

8. If $2(x - p)(x - 4) + q(x + 5) = 2x^2 - 8x + 1$ for all values of x, find the value of p and the value of q.

9. Given that $p(x + 2)(x + 1) - q(x - 3)(x - 1) = 5x^2 + x + 12$ for all values of x, solve for p and q.

15.4 SOLVING PROBLEMS INVOLVING LINEAR EQUATIONS

Using a Single Linear Equation

When solving a problem using algebra, it is often useful to follow the steps below:

1. Identify an unknown value and represent it with a letter (say x).

2. Most problems will consist of several unknown values, so let your letter (say x) represent the simplest of these.

3. Express all other unknown values in terms of this simplest value.

4. Convert the word equation into a mathematical equation.

5. Solve this mathematical equation for the variable in which it has been written (x).

6. Then, answer the question which was asked.

x^2 Worked Example 15.9

Aidan has x euro. Bashir has four and a half times as much money as Aidan. Charlie has €20 more than Aidan and Bashir combined. They have €130 altogether. How much money does each boy have?

Solution

Let Aidan's amount of money = €x.

Let Bashir's amount = €$4.5x$.

Let Charlie's amount = €$(x + 4.5x + 20)$

$$= €(5.5x + 20)$$

Word equation: All three sums of money add up to €130.

Maths equation: $x + 4.5x + (5.5x + 20) = 130$

$$\text{Solve for } x: \qquad 11x + 20 = 130$$
$$11x = 110$$
$$\therefore x = 10$$

Now write down each boy's sum of money.

Aidan = €x = €10

Bashir = €$4.5x$ = €45

Charlie = €$(5.5x + 20)$ = €$(55 + 20)$ = €75

Check the answer using the word equation:

€10 + €45 + €75 = €130

$$€130 = €130$$

TRUE

x^2 Worked Example 15.10

Róisín has y stickers in her collection. Her brother Zack has three times as many. She gives five stickers to Zack. Now he has four times as many as his sister.

How many stickers do they each have now?

Solution

Start: Róisín = y **Present:** Róisín (gives Zack five stickers): $y - 5$

         Zack = $3y$ Zack: $3y + 5$

 Word equation: Zack **now** has four times as many stickers as Róisín.

                   So, Zack's amount equals four times Róisín's amount.

Maths equation: $3y + 5 = 4(y - 5)$

   Solve for y: $3y + 5 = 4y - 20$

                         $25 = y$

                        $\therefore y = 25$

Write down how many stickers each has **now**:

Róisín: $y - 5 = 25 - 5$ $= 20$ stickers

Zack: $3y + 5 = 3(25) + 5 = 80$ stickers

Check the answer using the word equation:

$80 = 4(20)$

$80 = 80$

TRUE

x^2 Worked Example 15.11

The groundsman of an athletics club is given three lengths of tape, each 100 m long. He is told to form three rectangular enclosures using each of the three lengths of tape.
Each enclosure should have a perimeter of 100 m.

- For the first enclosure, the length and width should be the same.
- For the second enclosure, the length should be three times the width.
- For the third enclosure, the length should be 11.5 m shorter than the width.

For each enclosure:

(i) Draw a diagram showing the dimensions.

Write each dimension in terms of x, where x is the smaller dimension. Diagrams need not be to scale.

(ii) Form a mathematical equation in terms of x.

(iii) Solve this equation for x.

(iv) Write down the length and width.

(v) Check your answers to part (iv).

(vi) Also, for which enclosures could you have drawn a scaled diagram prior to answering part (iii)? Explain.

Solution

| | 1st enclosure | 2nd enclosure | 3rd enclosure |

1st enclosure

(i)

Width = x

Length = x

(ii) 4x = 100

(iii) x = 25

(iv) Length = 25 m

Width = 25 m

(v) 4(25) = 100

100 = 100

TRUE

2nd enclosure

(i)

Width = x

Length = 3x

(ii) 2(3x) + 2x = 100

(iii) 6x + 2x = 100

8x = 100

x = 12.5

(iv) Length = 3(12.5) = 37.5 m

Width = 12.5 m

(v) 2(37.5) + 2(12.5) = 100

75 + 25 = 100

TRUE

3rd enclosure

(i)

Width = x + 11.5

Length = x

(ii) 2x + 2(x + 11.5) = 100

(iii) 2x + 2x + 23 = 100

4x = 77

x = 19.25

(iv) Length = 19.25 m

Width = 19.25 + 11.5

= 30.75 m

(v) 2(19.25) + 2(30.75) = 100

38.5 + 61.5 = 100

TRUE

(vi) We could have drawn a scaled diagram for the first and second enclosures.

Reason: Ratio $x : x = 1 : 1$ is independent of x.

Ratio $3x : x = 3 : 1$ is independent of x.

Ratio $x : (x + 11.5)$ is **not** independent of x.

x^2 Worked Example 15.12

An aeroplane flying from Buenos Aires to Paris makes a stopover in Madrid.

- The plane flies at an average speed of 750 km/hr on the leg from Buenos Aires to Madrid.
- The stopover in Madrid lasts 45 minutes.
- The plane then continues on its journey from Madrid to Paris. The average speed for this leg of the journey is 650 km/hr.
- The flight distance from Buenos Aires to Madrid is 8,000 km longer than from Madrid to Paris.
- The total time taken for the whole journey is 13 hours 45 minutes.

(i) Letting x represent the flight distance (in km) from Madrid to Paris, form an equation in x.

(ii) Solve this equation for x.

(iii) How long is the flight distance from Buenos Aires to Madrid?

(iv) How long did the flight from Madrid to Paris take?

(v) Why do you think the average speed of the Madrid–Paris flight was less than the average speed of the Buenos Aires–Madrid flight?

Solution

(i)

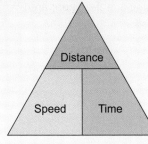

$$\text{Time} = \frac{\text{Distance}}{\text{(Average) speed}}$$

$$\underbrace{\frac{x + 8,000}{750}}_{\text{Buenos Aires to Madrid}} + \underbrace{\frac{x}{650}}_{\text{Madrid to Paris}} = \underbrace{13}_{\text{Total time (flying)}}$$

(ii) The LCD of 750, 650 and 1 is 9,750.

$$\frac{9,750(x + 8,000)}{750} + \frac{9,750(x)}{650} = 9,750(13)$$

$$13(x + 8,000) + 15(x) = 126,750$$

$$13x + 104,000 + 15x = 126,750$$

$$28x = 22,750$$

$$x = 812.5$$

(iii) $x + 8,000 = 812.5 + 8,000$

$\qquad = 8,812.5$ km

(iv) $\dfrac{x}{650} = \dfrac{812.5}{650}$

$\qquad = 1.25$ hrs

$\qquad = 1$ hr 15 mins

(v) The distance travelled is less on the Madrid–Paris flight so a greater percentage of the flight time is spent taking off and landing. Take-off and landing are done at slower speeds.

Using Simultaneous Linear Equations

We may also encounter problems where there are two unknowns. We can use simultaneous linear equations to solve such problems.

x^2 **Worked Example 15.13**

A company manufactures two types of sofa: leather and fabric. During a single day the factory produces 50 sofas. A leather sofa costs €500 to make; a fabric sofa costs €350 to make. The total amount spent on manufacturing sofas per day is €22,000.

Calculate the number of each type of sofa produced in a single day.

Solution

It may be easier to set up the simultaneous equations for this question using a table. There are two limiting factors: the number of sofas produced and the manufacturing costs.

Let x = number of leather sofas produced.

Let y = number of fabric sofas produced.

Sofa type	Leather		Fabric		Day
Number of sofas produced	x	+	y	=	50
Manufacturing costs	$500x$	+	$350y$	=	22,000

Maths equation (1): $x + y = 50$

Maths equation (2): $500x + 350y = 22,000$

Solve for x and y. We will use the method of elimination.

$$x + y = 50 \qquad (\times 500) \rightarrow \quad 500x + 500y = 25,000$$
$$500x + 350y = 22,000 \ (\times 1) \quad \rightarrow \quad \underline{500x + 350y = 22,000}$$

$$500x + 500y = 25,000$$
$$\underline{-(500x + 350y = 22,000)}$$

$$500x + 500y = 25,000$$
$$\underline{-500x - 350y = -22,000}$$

$$150y = 3,000$$
$$\therefore y = 20$$

$$x + y = 50$$
$$y = 20 \Rightarrow x + 20 = 50$$
$$\therefore x = 30$$

Answer: Number of leather sofas produced = x = 30.

Number of fabric sofas produced = y = 20.

Note: Remember to check your solution.

Also, we could have used the 'method of substitution' to solve this question.

Exercise 15.4

1. Find the length of all three sides of each triangle.

(i)
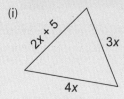
Perimeter = 23

(ii)
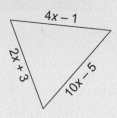
Perimeter = 21

(iii)
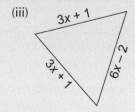
Perimeter = 42

2. There are 100 seats in a theatre. Some are ordinary seats, which cost €20 each. The rest are deluxe seats, which cost €30 each.

  (i) If x is the number of ordinary seats, how many deluxe seats are there in terms of x?

  (ii) Write an expression in terms of x for the amount of money taken in when all the ordinary seats are sold.

  (iii) Write an expression in terms of x for the amount of money taken in when all the deluxe seats are sold.

When all seats are sold, the theatre takes in €2,350.

  (iv) Write an equation in x to represent the above information.

  (v) Using this equation, calculate how many ordinary seats and how many deluxe seats there are in the theatre.

3. The sum of two numbers is 7. If you subtract five times the second number from twice the first number, you get 28.

Let x be equal to the value of the first number and let y be equal to the value of the second number.

  (i) Write an equation, in terms of x and y, which shows that the two numbers added together sum to 7.

  (ii) Write an equation, in terms of x and y, which shows that if you subtract five times the second number from twice the first number, you get 28.

  (iii) Use these two equations to find the value of x and the value of y.

4. Paul has 30 coins in his piggy bank. Some of these coins are 50c and the rest are €2. The total amount in the piggy bank is €33.

Let x equal the number of 50c coins.

  (i) Express, in terms of x, the number of €2 coins that Paul has.

  (ii) Write an equation which shows that the total value of 50c and €2 coins is €33.

  (iii) Solve this equation to find how many coins of each type Paul has.

5. A school concert charged €1 for children and €3 for adults. One hundred people attended the concert and the takings at the door amounted to €158.

How many adults were there?

6. Forty people attended a show in a small theatre. Some paid the full price of €10 to attend; the rest paid the concession price of €5. If the takings totalled €340, how many paid the full price?

7. An uncle divides up €57 into two parts so that one part is equal to $\frac{2}{3}$ of the other. How much is each part worth?

8. There are 70 animals on a farm. All of them are either ducks or sheep. Altogether, the animals have 232 legs. How many ducks are on the farm, and how many sheep?

9. One-sixth of a number, when subtracted from one-half of the same number, is equal to two-thirds the number plus 4. What is the number?

10. A woman is 41 years old and her daughter is 15. In how many years will the mother be twice as old as her daughter?

11. Lana's monthly salary is 75 per cent of Carla's. Both of them save €80 per month and spend the rest. Lana spends €1,500 less per year than Carla. How much does Lana spend per month?

12. A motorist completed a journey of 100 kilometres in 3.5 hours. She went part of the way at a steady 32 km/hr and the rest at a steady 24 km/hr. How far did she travel at each speed?

13. A family hostel has two kinds of rooms, double and single. A double room and three single rooms cost €59. Two double rooms and one single room cost €53. Find the cost of each kind of room.

14. Harry invests a total of €9,000 in two investment funds. The first fund pays 5% per annum and the second pays 6%. At the end of one year, his income from the first fund is €180 more than his income from the second.

(i) If Harry invests x amount in the first fund, how much, in terms of x, does he invest in the second fund?

(ii) How much, in terms of x, does the first fund earn per annum?

(iii) How much, in terms of x, does the second fund earn per annum?

(iv) Write an equation in x to represent a situation in which the first fund earns €180 more than the second fund.

(v) Hence, solve this equation to find the amount of money invested in each fund.

15. A creamery operator wants to mix milk (which contains 4 per cent fat) and cream (which contains 40 per cent fat) to make 90 litres of a mixture that will contain 20 per cent fat. How many litres of milk and how many litres of cream are required?

16. A man invested a total of €1,000 in two companies. He made a profit of 20 per cent through the first company, but lost 30 per cent on the second. Overall, he made a profit of 5 per cent. How much did he invest in each company?

17. Seán drives his car from home to work at a speed of 80 km/hr. He drives home at a speed of 60 km/hr.

Let x represent the distance in kilometres from his home to his workplace.

(i) Write an expression for the time taken for the journey to work.

(ii) Write an expression for the time taken for the journey home.

The total driving time for his day is 84 minutes.

(iii) Write an equation to show this information. Hence, find the distance between his home and his workplace.

18. There are x tents and y caravans on a campsite. Each tent can hold three people and each caravan holds eight. There are 180 people altogether.

(i) Write an equation, in x and y, to show this information.

Each tent requires an area of 40 m² and each caravan requires 100 m². The campsite is just big enough, having an area of 2,300 m².

(ii) Write an equation, in x and y, to show this information.

(iii) Using your equations from parts (i) and (ii), find the total number of tents and the total number of caravans on the campsite.

(iv) If the campsite charges €10 per day for a tent and €18 per day for a caravan, what is the amount of money collected per day?

19. A train leaves a station at 11.00 a.m., heading north. Another train, 320 km away, leaves at the same time, heading south. The average speed of the train heading north is 20 km/hr faster than that of the train heading south. If the trains pass each other at 1.30 p.m., what was the average speed of the southbound train?

20: Joe trains each day by running to a certain spot on a beach and back. Today it took him 6 minutes to run to the spot and back. His average speed running to the spot was 4 m/s and his average speed on the way back was 5 m/s.

Let x represent the distance from Joe's starting point to the spot on the beach.

(i) Write an expression in x to show the time it took Joe to run to the spot on the beach.

(ii) Write an expression in x to show the time it took Joe to run back from the spot to his starting position.

(iii) Calculate the total distance he ran.

(iv) Joe then increases the total distance run by a further y metres without changing his average speed. It now takes him an extra $1\frac{1}{2}$ minutes to run this distance. Calculate the percentage increase in his running distance.

21. A factory makes plastic and metal parts for a kitchen manufacturer. Each plastic part takes three working hours to make; each metal part takes two working hours. Each plastic part costs €10 to produce; metal parts cost €15 to produce.

(i) A certain order took 90 working hours and cost €600 to produce. How many parts of each type were supplied on the order?

(ii) A single plastic part yields a profit of €8. A single metal part yields a profit of €6. How much profit is made on the order?

22. An examination paper consists of 30 questions. For every correct answer, four marks are given. For every incorrect answer, three marks are deducted. A student answers all 30 questions, getting a total score for the examination of 71 marks.

How many questions did the student answer incorrectly?

23. Jan takes a trip from Town A to Town B. She travels this journey at an average speed of 50 km/hr. She then stops for a 5-minute break before continuing her journey to Town C, travelling at a rate of 60 km/hr.

The distance from Town B to Town C is 10 km more than the distance from Town A to Town B. The total travelling time for the whole journey is 3 hours.

Let x represent the distance from Town A to Town B.

(i) Write an expression in x for the time taken to travel from Town A to Town B.

(ii) Write an expression in x for the time taken to travel from Town B to Town C.

(iii) Using parts (i) and (ii), form an equation in x that represents the total time taken for the journey.

Using the equation from part (iii):

(iv) Find the distance from Town A to Town B.

(v) Find the time taken to travel from Town B to Town C.

24. A landlord buys a house with nine rooms. He can convert them into offices or flats. To convert a room into an office costs €3,000, while to convert a room into a flat costs €7,000.

(i) If the landlord spent €39,000 on the conversion, how many rooms of each type does the house have?

(ii) The rent per office is €150 per week, while the rent per flat is €275 per week. After how many weeks will the landlord have recouped his conversion costs?

25. A building contractor installs x compact radiators and y flat panel radiators in an apartment block. A compact radiator costs €100 each and a flat panel radiator costs €120 each. The total cost of the installation is €4,660. The contractor spent €860 more on the flat panel radiators than on the compact radiators. Find the total number of each type of radiator installed in the apartment block.

26. On a journey, a car travels at an average speed of *s* km/hr covering a distance of *d* km in 3 hours. The next day, the car travels 20 km less than on the previous day. The journey takes 2 hours but with an average speed 10 km faster than on the previous journey.

    (i) Express the time taken for the first journey in terms of *s* and *d*.

    (ii) Express the time taken for the second journey in terms of *s* and *d*.

    (iii) Hence, calculate (a) the distance travelled for each journey and (b) the speed for the second journey.

 Revision Exercises

1. (a) Solve the following equations:

    (i) $2(x - 2) = 6(x - 8)$

    (ii) $16(x + 1) = 12(x + 4)$

    (iii) $2(1 - x) = 3(-1 - x)$

  (b) Solve the following simultaneous equations:

    (i) $2x - y = 7$

      $3x + 2y = 21$

    (ii) $x + y = 2$

      $4x - 3y = 15$

    (iii) $7x - 3y = 26$

      $x + 5y = 1$

  (c) Solve the following equations:

    (i) $\dfrac{5(x - 1) + 2}{11} = 2$

    (ii) $\dfrac{7(x - 1)}{10} = x - 4$

    (iii) $\dfrac{x}{6} + \dfrac{x}{3} = 6$

    (iv) $\dfrac{x}{4} + \dfrac{x}{5} = 2$

2. (a) Solve the following simultaneous equations:

    (i) $x - 3y = 9$

      $5x - 11y = 35$

    (ii) $a = b - 1$

      $4a = 3b$

  (b) Solve the following equations:

    (i) $\dfrac{7x + 1}{5} = 3$

    (ii) $\dfrac{11x - 3}{7} = 9$

    (iii) $\dfrac{5x - 1}{7} = 7$

  (c) Solve the following equations:

    (i) $\dfrac{x + 1}{3} + \dfrac{3x + 1}{5} = x$

    (ii) $\dfrac{9 - x}{6} - \dfrac{x + 1}{2} + x = 0$

3. (a) Solve the following simultaneous equations:

    (i) $2x = 6 + 3y$

      $2y = 3x - 4$

    (ii) $0 = 5 - 2p - 5q$

      $23 + q = 6p$

  (b) Solve the following equations:

    (i) $\dfrac{4(6x - 1)}{7} - \dfrac{3(2x + 3)}{4} = \dfrac{2x - 1}{2}$

    (ii) $\dfrac{5(x - 1) + 6}{9} = \dfrac{3x + 7}{7}$

  (c) Solve the following simultaneous equations:

    (i) $\dfrac{3x + 1}{2} - \dfrac{y - 1}{5} = 6; \; x + y + 1 = 0$

    (ii) $\dfrac{x + y + 1}{4} - \dfrac{y}{3} + 1 = 0; \; 9x + 2y = 0$

4. (a) Find two consecutive natural numbers such that one third of the first added to one quarter of the second gives a total of 9.

  (b) (i) If $2(ax - 4by) = 6x + 8y$ for all values of *x* and *y*, solve for *a* and *b*.

    (ii) If $2(3x^2 - c) - 2b(4x - 5) - cx = 6x^2 + 19x - 40$ for all values of *x*, solve for *b* and *c*.

    (iii) Given that $p(2x - 1)(x + 3) + q(3x - 5)(2x - 7) = 12x^2 - 16x + 26$ for all values of *x*, solve for *p* and *q*.

  (c) If $a(x + 1)(x - 4) - b(x - 2)(x - 3) = \dfrac{-3x^2 + 25x - 68}{40}$ for all values of *x*, solve for *a* and *b*.

5. A bus and a car leave a town at 10.30 a.m. and travel in opposite directions. The bus travels at an average speed of 50 km/hr and the car travels at an average speed of 55 km/hr.

Let t equal the time taken for the journey.

   (i) Write an expression in t for the distance travelled by the bus.

   (ii) Write an expression in t for the distance travelled by the car.

   (iii) Write an equation in t to show the time at which the bus and the car are 140 km apart.

   (iv) Solve for t.

   (v) If the car and bus had travelled in the same direction, at what time would the car be 30 km in front of the bus?

6. (a) Divide 31 into two parts such that one quarter of one part is one more than one-fifth of the other.

   (b) Find three consecutive natural numbers so that the sum of $\frac{1}{7}$ of the first number and $\frac{1}{5}$ of the second number is equal to $\frac{1}{3}$ of the third number.

   (c) Divide €60 into two unequal parts such that a quarter of the bigger part is €1 more than one third of the smaller part. (Let x = the bigger part, $\therefore$ $60 - x$ = the smaller part).

7. A freight train leaves Seattle and heads to the next town at an average speed of 61 km/hr. One and a half hours later, a passenger train leaves Seattle, travelling at an average speed of 70 km/hr.

   Let x equal the time taken for the passenger train to pass the freight train.

   (i) Write an expression for the distance travelled by the passenger train.

   (ii) Write an expression for the distance travelled by the freight train.

   (iii) How long will it take the passenger train to pass the freight train?

   (iv) If the passenger train had left 20 minutes after the freight train and travelled 11 km/hr faster, how long would it have taken to pass the freight train?

8. (a) A hurling team scored on 15 occasions during a match (including goals and points). At the end of match their total score was worth 23 points. (A goal is worth 3 points).

   Let x = the number of goals and y = the number of points. Write down two equations in x and y and hence find their values.

   (b) There are eight times as many 10c coins as there are 5c coins in a money box. The value of all the 10c coins is €4.50 more than the value of the 5c coins.

   How many 5c and 10c coins are there in the money box?

   (c) Abdul can paint a room in six hours, while Ben can paint the same room in four hours.

      (i) How much of the room will Abdul paint in x hours?

      (ii) How much of the room will Ben paint in x hours?

      (iii) How long will it take to paint the room if they work together?

9. (a) Travelling at a steady speed of x km/h, a cyclist did a journey in 15 hours. If she had travelled 7 km/h faster, she would have finished the journey in 8 hours. What was her actual speed?

   (b) 100 tickets are sold for a school play. Tickets for a child cost €1.50 each. Tickets for an adult cost €2.50 each. If the organisers had charged €1 each for a child's ticket and €5 each for an adult's ticket, they would have made €10 more. How many children and how many adults came to the play?

(c) Edward can wallpaper a room in six hours and Zack can wallpaper the same room in nine hours.

Edward starts wallpapering the room at 9:00 and Zack joins him an hour later. They both work together to finish the room.

At what time will they finish wallpapering the room?

10. (a) A man buys a turkey and a ham for Christmas. The total cost is €33. A year later, the cost of a turkey has gone up by 10% and the cost of a ham has gone up by 8%. The same turkey and ham now cost a total of €36.

What was the cost of a turkey and the cost of a ham in the first year?

(b) The hot water tap of a bath takes 22 minutes to fill up the bath, while the cold water tap takes 38 minutes.

(i) How much of the bath will be filled in x minutes using the cold tap only?

(ii) How much of the bath will be filled in x minutes using the hot tap only?

(iii) How long will it take to fill the bath if both taps are used together?

If the plug is not inserted in the drain, the bath will empty in 15 minutes.

(iv) How long will it take to fill the bath if both taps are running and the plug is not inserted?

11. A boat takes 15 hours to travel a distance of 150 km upstream (against the current). The return trip takes 8 hours (with the current).

(i) Calculate the speed of the boat travelling upstream.

(ii) Calculate the speed of the boat travelling downstream.

Let x represent the speed of the boat by itself and let y represent the speed of the current.

(iii) Write an equation, in x and y, that represents the speed of the boat travelling upstream.

(iv) Write an equation, in x and y, that represents the speed of the boat travelling downstream.

(v) Calculate the speed of the boat without the current.

(vi) Calculate the speed of the current.

12. Ann is thinking of changing her natural gas supplier. She compares the price of two companies.

	Company A	Company B
Fixed quarterly charge	€23.83	€20.67
Charge per kWh	5.187 cent	5.432 cent

(kWh stands for kilowatt-hours, a unit used by energy suppliers to calculate the amount of energy used by a home or business.)

Let x represent the number of kilowatt-hours.

(i) Write an expression in x to show the total quarterly bill for Company A.

(ii) Write an expression in x to show the total quarterly bill for Company B.

(iii) If Ann calculates that she used 5,500 kWh of gas per quarter, which option is the cheapest and by how much? (Answer to the nearest cent.)

(iv) How many kWh would need to be used for the quarterly bill to cost the same from both companies? (Answer to two decimal places.)

(v) Explain how your answer from part (iv) could be used to advise customers wishing to choose between Company A and Company B.

Another company offers a reduced night rate as shown.

	Company C
Fixed quarterly charge	€22.35
Charge per kWh (day)	5.631c
Charge per kWh (night)	4.83c

Ann determines that her night-time usage would amount to $\frac{2}{7}$ of her total gas consumption.

(vi) Write an expression in x to show the total quarterly bill for Company C.

(vii) Calculate to the nearest cent Ann's quarterly bill if she uses 5,500 kWh of gas.

(viii) How many kWh would need to be used for the quarterly bill to cost the same as Company A? (Answer to two decimal places).

Algebra VI: Solving Inequalities

Learning Outcomes

In this chapter you will learn:

- To solve linear inequalities in one variable of the form $g(x) \leqslant k$, where $g(x) = ax + b$, $a \in N$ and $b, k \in Z$

- To solve compound linear inequalities of the form $k \leqslant g(x) \leqslant h$, where $g(x) = ax + b$ and $k, h, a, b \in Z$ and $x \in R$

16.1 INEQUALITIES

Sometimes, when we solve for an unknown, we do not find an exact value of x. Instead, we find a range of values. This occurs when we are dealing with an **inequality**.

In an equation, one side of the equation = the other side of the equation.

In an **inequality**, one side of the inequality is:

- greater than,
- greater than or equal to,
- less than
- less than or equal to

the other side.

KEY WORDS

- **Inequality**
- **Natural number**
- **Integer**
- **Real number**
- **Compound inequality**

We are often asked to graph the solution set of an inequality on a numberline. To do this, we must first understand the three different types of number we may meet when solving inequalities.

Natural Numbers – N

A **natural number** is any positive whole number (i.e. any whole number greater than 0).

$N = \{1, 2, 3, 4, ...\}$

The set of natural numbers is denoted by the letter N.

$x \in N$ means x is a natural number.

As natural numbers are whole numbers, in order to graph them on the numberline, we use shaded dots.

The set of naturals

Integers – Z

An **integer** is any whole number: positive, negative and zero.

$Z = \{0, 1, -1, 2, -2, 3, -3, ...\}$

The set of integers is denoted by the letter Z.

$x \in Z$ means x is an integer.

As integers are also whole numbers, in order to graph them on the numberline, we use shaded dots.

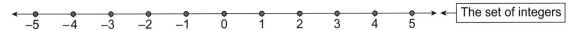

The set of integers

Real Numbers – R

A **real number** is any number whose square is non-negative. Real numbers are all the numbers on the numberline: naturals, integers, rationals and irrationals.

The set of real numbers is denoted by the letter R.

$x \in R$ means x is a real number.

As real numbers can be any number, in order to graph them on the numberline, we use a solid/shaded line.

The set of reals

 **Worked Example 16.1**

Solve $6x + 1 \leqslant 5x + 3$, $x \in N$, and show the solution set on the number line.

Solution

$6x + 1 \leqslant 5x + 3$

$6x - 5x \leqslant 3 - 1$

$x \leqslant 2, x \in N$

> Do not put an arrow at either end of the numberline, as we are only including the numbers 1 and 2.

Multiplying/Dividing an Inequality by a Negative Number

Is $5 > 4$?   TRUE

Now, multiply both sides by –1.

Is $-5 > -4$?   FALSE

Is $-5 < -4$?   TRUE

Is $-10 \leqslant 4$?   TRUE

Now, divide both sides by –2.

Is $5 \leqslant -2$?   FALSE

Is $5 \geqslant -2$?   TRUE

> When we multiply or divide both sides of an inequality by a negative number we **flip** or **reverse** the inequality sign, as well as changing the sign of each term.

 **ACTIVITY 16.1**

Consider the inequality $-2x \leqslant 10$, $x \in Z$.

■ Multiplying both sides by –1, we get: $2x \geqslant -10$, $x \in Z$
■ Dividing both sides by 2, we get: $x \geqslant -5$, $x \in Z$

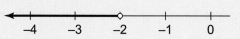 **Worked Example 16.2**

Solve $2(2x - 4) > 3(3x + 1) - 1$, $x \in R$, and show the solution set on the numberline.

Solution

$2(2x - 4) > 3(3x + 1) - 1$

$4x - 8 > 9x + 3 - 1$

$4x - 8 > 9x + 2$

$4x - 9x > 2 + 8$

$-5x > 10$

Multiply both sides by –1. Remember to change the signs and flip the inequality sign.

$5x < -10$

$x < -2, x \in R$

We do not shade in –2, as $x \neq -2$.

We use a shaded line to the left of –2, as $x \in R$ and $x < -2$.

The arrow on the left indicates that the solution set continues indefinitely (forever) in this direction.

x^2 Worked Example 16.3

Solve $5x + 6 \leqslant 8x - 6$, $x \in R$, and graph the solution set on the numberline.

Solution

Method 1

$5x + 6 \leqslant 8x - 6$

$5x - 8x \leqslant -6 - 6$

$\quad -3x \leqslant -12$

Divide both sides by -3.

$\dfrac{-3x}{-3} \geqslant \dfrac{-12}{-3}$

$\quad x \geqslant 4$

Method 2

$5x + 6 \leqslant 8x - 6$

$\quad 6 + 6 \leqslant 8x - 5x$

$\quad\quad 12 \leqslant 3x$

$\quad\quad\; 4 \leqslant x$

This is the same as $x \geqslant 4$, because if 4 is less than or equal to x, then x must be greater than or equal to 4.

We shade in 4, since $x = 4$.

We use a shaded line to the right of 4, as $x \in R$ and $x \geqslant 4$.

The arrow on the right indicates that the solution set continues indefinitely (forever) in this direction.

x^2 Worked Example 16.4

A cab company has a call-out charge of €5 and then charges €3 per kilometre. Kate has only €20 for her fare home. Let x represent the number of kilometres she travels.

    (i) Write an inequality in x to represent the above situation.

   (ii) Solve the inequality to find out how many kilometres Kate can travel.

Solution

    (i) We first write an equation for the cost of a fare, using x to represent the number of kilometres travelled.

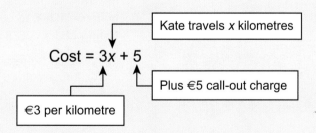

        Kate has only €20 to spend on the fare. The cost of the fare must be less than or equal to €20.

        $\therefore 3x + 5 \leqslant 20$

   (ii) We now solve this inequality.

        $3x + 5 \leqslant 20$

          $3x \leqslant 20 - 5$

          $3x \leqslant 15$

           $x \leqslant 5$ (x is less than or equal to 5 km)

        Kate can travel up to 5 km with €20.

Exercise 16.1

1. Draw separate numberlines to show the following inequalities.

   (i) $x \leqslant 2, x \in Z$

   (ii) $x > 1, x \in N$

   (iii) $x \geqslant -4, x \in R$

   (iv) $1 > x, x \in R$

   (v) $x < -6, x \in Z$

   (vi) $x < 5, x \in N$

   (vii) $-x \geqslant 3, x \in Z$

   (viii) $-x < -5, x \in Z$

   (ix) $-5 > -x, x \in R$

   (x) $0 < -x, x \in R$

2. Write down an inequality represented by each of the following diagrams:

   (i) $x \in N$

   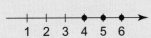

   (ii) $x \in Z$

   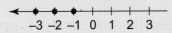

   (iii) $x \in R$

   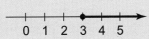

   (iv) $x \in R$

   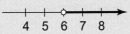

   (v) $x \in Z$

   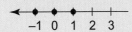

   (vi) $x \in N$

   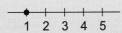

Solve each of the linear inequalities in Questions 3–18, and in each case, show the solution set on the numberline.

3. $4x > 8, x \in N$

4. $10x - 4 \geqslant 6, x \in R$

5. $8 < 2 + x, x \in N$

6. $3x + 8 \leqslant x - 4, x \in Z$

7. $2x + 3 > 6 + x, x \in Z$

8. $2x - 5 \geqslant 4x + 3, x \in R$

9. $x + 4 < 2x - 2, x \in R$

10. $4x - 3 \leqslant 6x - 5, x \in N$

11. $2x - 5 < 3x, x \in Z$

12. $8x - 5 > 9x - 5, x \in Z$

13. $3x - 6 < 10x + 1, x \in R$

14. $3(2x - 1) \geqslant 5(3x + 5) - 1, x \in R$

15. $4(x - 2) > 3(2x - 5), x \in R$

16. $3(7x - 4) - 2(x + 4) + x > 0, x \in N$

17. $3(2x - 10) \leqslant 6x - 5(2x + 2), x \in Z$

18. $x - 2(6x - 1) < 4(x + 1) - 2, x \in R$

19. Kellie is being charged €400, plus €35 per person, for her wedding meal. She has budgeted €3,750 for this meal.

    (i) Write an inequality to represent this information. Let p equal the number of people attending the meal.

    (ii) What is the largest number of guests she can afford to invite to her wedding meal?

20. Siobhán has €1,000 in her bank account for her overseas trekking tour. She will return home once her account drops below €400. If she withdraws €75 per week:

    (i) Write an expression in x for money withdrawn after x weeks.

    (ii) How much is left in her account after 4 weeks?

    (iii) How much is left in her account after x weeks?

    (iv) Form an inequality in x given that she will return home once she has less than €400 left in her account.

    (v) Solve this inequality to find out how long her tour will last.

21. A car rental firm offers two payment options:

Option A: €100 initial charge, then €45 per day

Option B: €76 initial charge, then €47 per day

Write down and solve an inequality to find out for how many days Option B will be cheaper than Option A.

22. Evan wants to order books over the internet for his new bookshop. Each book costs €4.99 to buy and then each order includes €50 for post and packaging. Evan does not want to spend more than €200.

(i) Write an inequality in x to represent the above situation.

(ii) Solve the inequality to find out how many books Evan can buy.

23. Company A charges €115, plus an additional €31 per day, to rent out a mini-digger.

Company B charges €65, plus an additional €38 per day, to rent out the same mini-digger.

(i) Construct an inequality to find out for how many days it will be cheaper to rent from Company B than Company A.

(ii) Show in a table the charge per company for renting a mini-digger for each of the first 10 days.

Day	Company A (€)	Company B (€)
1		
2		
3		
4		
5		
6		
7		
8		
9		
10		

(iii) Graph the charge for each company for renting a mini-digger for the first 10 days. Use the same scales and axes, representing number of days on the horizontal axis.

(iv) Use your graph to find out for how many days it will be cheaper to rent from Company B than Company A.

24. For real numbers a, b and c, complete the table below. Indicate whether each statement is always true, never true or sometimes true.

Statement	Always true	Never true	Sometimes true
If $a > b$ and $b > c$, then $a > c$	✓		
If $-a < 4$ and $b < -4$, then $a < b$		✓	
If $a > b$, then $-a > -b$		✓	
If $a > b$ and $b < c$, then $a < c$		✓	
If $3a + 1 > 2$, then $a > 0$	✓		
If $2b - 4 < 3b - 8$, then $b > 4$	✓		
If a and b are both positive and $a < b$, then $\frac{1}{a} < \frac{1}{b}$		✓	

SEC 2012, JCHL

16.2 COMPOUND INEQUALITIES

We may also be asked to solve **compound inequalities**, where two inequalities are linked.

A compound inequality means that the variable lies between two known values.

x^2 Worked Example 16.5

Solve $-14 < 5x + 1 \leqslant 11$, $x \in R$, and show the solution set on the numberline.

Solution

$-14 < 5x + 1 \leqslant 11$

First ensure that the middle term of the inequality has an x-term only. To do this, subtract 1 from each part.

$-14 - 1 < 5x + 1 - 1 \leqslant 11 - 1$

$-15 < 5x \leqslant 10$

Now divide each term by the coefficient of x.

$-\dfrac{15}{5} < \dfrac{5x}{5} \leqslant \dfrac{10}{5}$

$\therefore -3 < x \leqslant 2$, $x \in R$

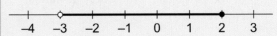

Do not shade in -3, as $x \neq -3$.

Shade in 2, as $x = 2$.

Then shade in every number bigger than -3 up to and including 2. Use a shaded line, since $x \in R$.

x^2 Worked Example 16.6

(i) $A = \{x \mid 2x - 1 \leqslant 9, x \in Z\}$. List the elements of set A.

(ii) $B = \{x \mid 1 - 2x < 3, x \in Z\}$. List the elements of set B.

(iii) List the elements of $A \cap B$.

(iv) Graph on a numberline the elements of the set $A \cap B$.

Solution

(i) $2x - 1 \leqslant 9$
$2x \leqslant 9 + 1$
$2x \leqslant 10$
$\therefore x \leqslant 5$, $x \in Z$ \quad $A = \{..., 3, 4, 5\}$

(ii) $1 - 2x < 3$
$-2x < 3 - 1$
$-2x < 2$
$\therefore x > -1$, $x \in Z$ \quad $B = \{0, 1, 2, 3, ...\}$

ACTIVITY 16.2

(iii) $A \cap B = \{0, 1, 2, 3, 4, 5\}$

(iv)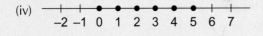

x^2 Worked Example 16.7

A car sales firm must sell more than five cars a week to ensure its survival. The firm can have at most 30 cars on the premises for any given week. Let x equal the number of cars sold per week.

Write down a compound inequality that shows the above information.

Solution

We identify the lowest (minimum) and highest (maximum) values:

Lowest: Firm must sell more than five cars a week. $\therefore x > 5$ **or** $5 < x$

Highest: Firm can have at most 30 cars. $\therefore x \leqslant 30$

We now write down a compound inequality that shows this information:

Answer: $5 < x \leqslant 30, x \in N$

Exercise 16.2

1. Write down an inequality shown in each of the following diagrams:

   (i) $x \in Z$

   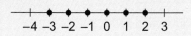
   $$-4 \ -3 \ -2 \ -1 \ \ 0 \ \ 1 \ \ 2 \ \ 3$$

   (ii) $x \in N$

   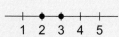
   $$1 \ \ 2 \ \ 3 \ \ 4 \ \ 5$$

   (iii) $x \in Z$

   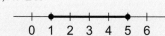
   $$-1 \ \ 0 \ \ 1 \ \ 2 \ \ 3$$

   (iv) $x \in R$

   $$0 \ \ 1 \ \ 2 \ \ 3 \ \ 4 \ \ 5 \ \ 6$$

   (v) $x \in R$

   $$-9 \ -8 \ -7 \ -6 \ -5 \ -4 \ -3$$

   (vi) $x \in R$

   $$-1 \ \ 0 \ \ 1 \ \ 2 \ \ 3 \ \ 4 \ \ 5$$

   (vii) $x \in R$

   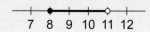
   $$7 \ \ 8 \ \ 9 \ \ 10 \ \ 11 \ \ 12$$

> Solve each of the inequalities in Questions 2–16, and in each case, graph the solution on the numberline.

2. $4 < x < 8, x \in N$

3. $-3 \leqslant x \leqslant 1, x \in Z$

4. $-2 \leqslant 2x \leqslant 2, x \in R$

5. $5 \leqslant 5x < 10, x \in R$

6. $2 < x + 1 \leqslant 5, x \in N$

7. $-4 < 2x - 2 < 0, x \in Z$

8. $-7 \leqslant 3x - 1 \leqslant 2, x \in R$

9. $9 \leqslant 5x + 4 < 19, x \in R$

10. $-2 < -3 + x < 1, x \in R$

11. $10 < 8x + 2 \leqslant 18, x \in N$

12. $3 > -x > 1, x \in R$

13. $2 \geqslant -x \geqslant -1, x \in Z$

14. $10 \geqslant -2x + 4 \geqslant 2, x \in R$

15. $20 \geqslant 6 - 7x > 6, x \in R$

16. $-12 > -2 - 5x \geqslant -27, x \in N$

17. (i) List the elements of set
    $A = \{x \mid 3x - 6 < 9, x \in Z\}$.

    (ii) List the elements of set
    $B = \{x \mid 5x + 3 \geqslant -2, x \in Z\}$.

(iii) List the elements of A ∩ B.

(iv) Graph on a numberline the elements of the set A ∩ B.

18. (i) List the elements of set
C = {x | 2x − 8 ⩽ 6, x ∈ N}.

(ii) List the elements of set
D = {x | 3x − 2 ⩾ 4, x ∈ N}.

(iii) List the elements of C ∩ D.

(iv) Graph on a numberline the elements of the set C ∩ D.

19. (i) Graph the solution set E of:
x + 3 > −4, x ∈ R

(ii) Graph the solution set F of:
2x + 1 > 3x + 2, x ∈ R

(iii) Graph the solution set of E ∩ F.

20. (i) Graph the solution set G of:
3(2x + 1) > −(x − 3), x ∈ R

(ii) Graph the solution set H of:
3(x + 2) ⩾ 4(x − 1), x ∈ R

(iii) Graph the solution set of G ∩ H.

21. Solve each of the following inequalities:

(i) −2 < x −3, x ∈ R

(ii) 4x − 9 ⩽ 7, x ∈ R

List the integer values of x which satisfy both inequalities.

22. The water temperature for a tropical fish must be between 20°C and 27°C, inclusive. The water was heated by 9°C to reach the correct temperature.

(i) Write an inequality that shows this information. Let t represent the temperature of the water before it was heated.

(ii) What was the range of temperatures that the water could have been at before heating?

23. The start heights of different ecological zones that can be found on a mountain are shown below. The mountain has a height of 4,100 metres.

(*Note:* Height refers to height above sea level.)

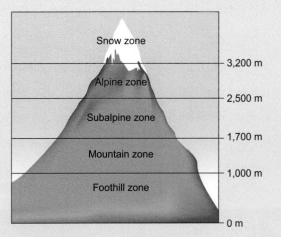

Let x represent height in metres.

Write down an inequality in x that represents each of the following regions:

(i) Foothill zone

(ii) Subalpine zone

(iii) Snow zone

24. Golf balls have dimples on their surface to increase the distance the ball can be hit. Even if a smooth golf ball is hit with the same force, it will travel only half as far as a dimpled ball.

Josh knows he can hit a dimpled golf ball between 70 and 120 metres.

Let x represent the distance the golf ball travels.

Write down an inequality that shows how far Josh can hit:

(i) A dimpled golf ball

(ii) A smooth golf ball

Manufacturers usually put between 300 and 450 dimples on the surface of a golf ball.

Let y represent the number of dimples on a golf ball.

(iii) Write down an inequality that shows the range of values for the number of dimples on a golf ball.

A manufacturer decides never to have 400 or more dimples on the surface of its golf balls.

(iv) Write down an inequality that shows this situation. Let y represent the number of dimples.

25. The speed of an object when fired vertically upwards is given by the formula

$$V = 58 - 10t$$

where t is the time, in seconds, from firing. At what times will the speed of the object be between 10 and 40 metres per second? (*Note*: $V \neq 10, 40$)

26. An integer p is doubled and then added to 5. The answer must be more than 12 but less than 49.

(i) Write down an inequality that shows this information.

(ii) Find the range of values of p.

27. A marketing company charges a fee of €500 upfront to conduct a marketing campaign. It then charges €220 per day thereafter. The manager of a waste disposal firm has been allocated between €5,000 and €9,500 to launch a marketing campaign for their new services.

(i) Write down an inequality that shows this information. Let x represent the length of the marketing campaign in days.

(ii) What is the least and most number of days for which the firm can hire the marketing company?

28. Shokri and Amy both work in the same office. Shokri lives 6 km from the office. Amy lives 10 km from the office.

(i) What is the smallest distance they may live from each other?

(ii) What is the greatest distance they may live from each other?

(iii) Write down an inequality that shows the range of distances between their homes.

(iv) Hence, illustrate the above situation geometrically, using two circles with the office as the centre for both circles.

29. Zara sells handmade candles at her local market every Saturday. She notices that she sells eight candles less each week. On the sixth Saturday, she sells 24 candles.

(i) How many candles did she sell on the first Saturday?

(ii) Let c equal the number of candles sold each week and let n equal the number of weeks after the first Saturday.

Write an equation that shows the number of candles sold on a Saturday after n weeks.

(iii) Zara would be content to sell between 15 and 40 candles per week.

Write an inequality in n to represent this information.

(iv) For how many Saturdays was Zara content with her sales?

30. (a) (i) Solve the inequality $-2 < 5x + 3 \leqslant 18, x \in R$.

(ii) Graph your solution on the numberline below.

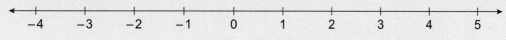

(b) Niamh is in a clothes shop and has a voucher which she must use. The voucher gives a €10 reduction when more than €35 is spent. She also has €50 cash.

Write down an inequality in x to show the range of money she could spend in the shop.

Write down an inequality in y to show the total price of all articles bought.

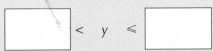

SEC Sample Paper, JCHL (amended)

31. In order to win a school quiz, Joseph must score at least 250 points. He calculates that he does not need to score more than 322 points to win the quiz. However, he is caught cheating and has 30 points deducted from his score.

If each question is worth 8 points:

(i) Write down a compound inequality that shows the lowest and highest number of correctly answered questions needed for a possible victory.

(ii) Solve this inequality to find the number of questions needed to guarantee victory.

Revision Exercises

1. Solve each inequality and graph the solution set on the numberline in each case:

  (i) $3x - 1 \leq x + 3, x \in Z$

  (ii) $4x + 1 \leq 13, x \in R$

  (iii) $2x + 1 < 10, x \in N$

  (iv) $x + 3 \leq 5x - 17, x \in R$

  (v) $1 + x \geq 3x - 1, x \in N$

  (vi) $1 - 5x > -29, x \in R$

  (vii) $4 < 1 - x, x \in R$

2. Solve each inequality and graph the solution set on the numberline in each case:

  (i) $5 \leq 2x + 1 \leq 11, x \in N$

  (ii) $-3 < 2x - 1 \leq 13, x \in Z$

  (iii) $-1 < 3x + 2 \leq 17, x \in R$

  (iv) $-9 \leq 4x - 1 \leq 11, x \in Z$

  (v) $1 < 2x - 7 < 5, x \in N$

3. List the elements in these sets:

  (i) A: $1 - 3x \geq -8, x \in N$

  (ii) B: $-11 \leq 3 + 7x < 31, x \in Z$

  (iii) C: $-14 < 5x + 1 < 26, x \in Z$

  (iv) D: $-8 \leq 7x - 1 \leq 20, x \in Z$

  (v) E: $-5 < 1 - 2x \leq 3, x \in Z$

4. Solve the following inequalities. In each case, write a sentence that describes the solution set.

  (i) $2x + 4 < 12, x \in N$

  (ii) $-3x + 1 \leq 4, x \in Z$

  (iii) $1 < 2x + 3 < 13, x \in R$

  (iv) $-3 \leq 3 - 2x < 2, x \in R$

  (v) $-50 < 15x - 200 \leq 520, x \in N$

5. List the elements of $E \cap F$ where:

$$E = \{x \mid 2x - 1 \leq 7, x \in N\}$$
and
$$F = \{x \mid 5 - 4x \leq 1, x \in N\}$$

6. Show each of these sets on separate number lines:

  (i) $P = \{x \mid 1 - 6x < 16, x \in R\}$

  (ii) $Q = \{x \mid 23 - 4x \geq 3, x \in R\}$

  (iii) $P \cap Q$

7. If $x \leqslant y$, which one of the following is not true? (x and y are real numbers.)

  (i) $x - 5 \leqslant y - 5$

  (ii) $5x \leqslant 5y$

  (iii) $\dfrac{x}{-5} \leqslant \dfrac{y}{-5}$

  (iv) $\dfrac{x}{5} \leqslant \dfrac{y}{5}$

8. If $x > y$, state whether each of the following is true or false. (x and y are real numbers.)

  (i) $x + 3 > y + 3$

  (ii) $x - 3 > y - 3$

  (iii) $\dfrac{x}{3} > \dfrac{y}{3}$

  (iv) $-3x > -3y$

  If $x > y$, is $x^2 > y^2$ always? Explain.

9. Explain why it is incorrect to write $5 < x < -4$, $x \in R$.

10. Samir gets €10 a week in pocket money. Samir asks Hamza how much he gets each week. Hamza says, 'I get more than €5 but less than you.' Hamza's pocket money is made up of €1 coins and 50c coins.

  List the possible amounts Hamza might get.

11. Séamus is 178 cm tall. Nóirín is 167 cm tall. Susie is taller than Nóirín but shorter than Séamus.

  (a) Show Susie's possible height on a numberline.

  (b) Explain why you cannot make a list of possible heights for Susie.

12. Rachel is 16 years old. She says to her uncle Bill, 'How old are you?' He says, 'In 11 years time, I shall be more than twice as old as I was when you were born.'

  Write down an inequality and solve it to find the greatest age Bill could be.

13. The perimeter of this rectangle is greater than 10 but less than 16. What are the limits of the area?

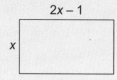

14. Sheena went to a local shop with €20. She wanted to buy two CDs costing €x each and a DVD costing €9. When she went to pay she found she didn't have enough money. She left the DVD and paid for the two CDs. On her way home, she had enough change to buy perfume for €7.

  (i) Explain why $2x + 9 > 20$ and solve the inequality.

  (ii) Explain why $2x + 7 \leqslant 20$ and solve the inequality.

  (iii) If the price of a CD is a whole number of euros, how much does it cost?

15. Three sides of a triangle are x, $x + 3$ and 12 cm.

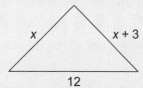

  x is a whole number. What is the smallest value x can have?

16.

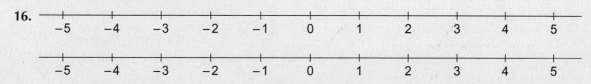

  (i) On copies of the numberlines above, draw two different compound inequalities so that only the integers $\{-2, -1, 0, 1\}$ are common to both inequalities.

  (ii) Write down the two inequalities that you have drawn.

17. The length of a rectangle is 4 cm longer than the width.

  If the perimeter is less than 30 cm, form and solve a suitable inequality to find the range of possible values for the width.

18. Fionn has exactly €12 more than Sid. They have less than €60 altogether.

  Form and solve a suitable inequality to find the maximum amount Sid can have.

Algebra VII: Quadratic Equations

Learning Outcomes

In this chapter you will learn how to:

- Solve quadratic equations using:
  - Factors
  - The quadratic formula
- Form quadratic equations given whole number roots
- Solve problems using quadratic equations

17.1 SOLVING QUADRATIC EQUATIONS BY FACTORISING

Quadratic equations in x are equations of the form:

$$ax^2 + bx + c = 0$$

where x is the unknown (variable) and $a, b, c \in R$, $a \neq 0$.

When solving a quadratic equation, we are finding the values of the unknown (of x) that satisfy the equation.

One of the most common methods of solving a quadratic equation is to:

- Find the factors of the quadratic expression.
- Use these factors to find the solutions of the equation.

Note: It is sometimes not possible to solve by first factorising.

Quadratic equations can come in a variety of forms. To solve any quadratic equation, we usually ensure that:

- All the terms of the equation are on the same side of the equals sign.
- The coefficient of the squared term (the x^2 term) is positive.

In other words, we write the quadratic equation in the form $ax^2 + bx + c = 0$, where $a > 0$, $a, b, c \in R$.

Note: From here on, we will use the letter x to represent the unknown (variable). However, any letter could be used.

YOU SHOULD REMEMBER...

- How to solve linear equations
- How to find the factors of quadratic expressions
- How to simplify surds

KEY WORDS

- Solve
- Solution
- Roots
- Factors
- Highest common factor (HCF)
- Difference of two squares
- Quadratic trinomials
- Quadratic formula
- Discriminant
- Surd form

ALGEBRA VII: QUADRATIC EQUATIONS

Highest Common Factor

Any quadratic equation of the form $ax^2 + bx = 0$, where $a, b \in R$, $a \neq 0$, can be solved by taking out the **highest common factor (HCF)** as follows:

$$x^2 + \frac{b}{a}x = 0$$
$$x\left(x + \frac{b}{a}\right) = 0$$
$$x = 0 \quad \textbf{or} \quad x + \frac{b}{a} = 0$$
$$x = 0 \quad \textbf{or} \quad x = -\frac{b}{a}$$

For example: $x^2 - 3x = 0$. The HCF is x. So, we get:

$$x(x - 3) = 0$$
$$x = 0 \quad \textbf{or} \quad x - 3 = 0$$
$$x = 0 \quad \textbf{or} \quad x = 3$$

These two solutions can be checked by substituting back into the original equation.

Solve for x:

(i) $4x^2 + 10x = 0$ (ii) $5x^2 = 7x$

Solution

(i) $4x^2 + 10x = 0$

$\Rightarrow \quad 2x^2 + 5x = 0$ (Divide the whole equation by 2)

$\Rightarrow \quad x(2x + 5) = 0$ (HCF = x)

$\Rightarrow \quad x = 0 \quad \textbf{or} \quad 2x + 5 = 0$ (*Note:* If AB = 0, then A = 0 or B = 0.)

$$2x = -5$$

$$\therefore x = 0 \quad \textbf{or} \qquad x = -\frac{5}{2}$$

It is good practice to check the solutions:

$4x^2 + 10x = 0$	$4x^2 + 10x = 0$
$x = 0 \Rightarrow \quad 4(0)^2 + 10(0) = 0$	$x = -\frac{5}{2} \Rightarrow \quad 4\left(-\frac{5}{2}\right)^2 + 10\left(-\frac{5}{2}\right) = 0$
$4(0) + 10(0) = 0$	$4\left(\frac{25}{4}\right) + 10\left(-\frac{5}{2}\right) = 0$
$0 + 0 = 0$	$25 - \frac{50}{2} = 0$
TRUE	$25 - 25 = 0$
$\therefore x = 0$ is a solution.	$0 = 0$
	TRUE
	$\therefore x = -\frac{5}{2}$ is a solution.

(ii) $5x^2 = 7x$

$\Rightarrow \quad 5x^2 - 7x = 0$ (Subtract $7x$ from both sides.)

$\Rightarrow \quad x(5x - 7) = 0$ (HCF = x)

$\Rightarrow \quad x = 0 \quad \textbf{or} \quad 5x - 7 = 0$ (*Note:* If AB = 0, then A = 0 or B = 0.)

$$5x = 7$$

$$\therefore x = 0 \quad \textbf{or} \qquad x = \frac{7}{5}$$

You can check these solutions by substituting back into the original equation.

Difference of Two Squares

Any quadratic equation of the form $ax^2 + c = 0$, where $a, c \in R$, $a \neq 0$, can be solved as follows:

$$x^2 + \frac{c}{a} = 0$$

$$x^2 = -\frac{c}{a}$$

$$x = \pm\sqrt{-\frac{c}{a}}$$

This method is equivalent to solving by taking the **difference of two squares**.

For example: $x^2 - 100 = 0$.

We note that this equation has an x^2 term and a constant term only. So, we write the equation as:

$$x^2 = 100$$
$$x = \pm\sqrt{100}$$
$$x = \pm 10$$

The solutions can be checked by substituting back into the original equation.

Alternatively, we could have solved the original equation by using the method of difference of two squares directly:

$$x^2 - 100 = 0$$

becomes

$$(x)^2 - (10)^2 = 0$$
$$\Rightarrow \quad (x - 10)(x + 10) = 0$$
$$\Rightarrow \quad x - 10 = 0 \quad \textbf{or} \quad x + 10 = 0$$
$$\Rightarrow \quad x = 10 \quad \textbf{or} \quad x = -10$$
$$\therefore x = \pm 10$$

x^2 Worked Example 17.2

Solve for the unknown in each case:

(i) $y^2 - 81 = 0$ (ii) $25x^2 - 256 = 0$

Solution

(i) $y^2 - 81 = 0$

Method 1	Method 2
$y^2 - 81 = 0$	$y^2 - 81 = 0$
$y^2 = 81$	$(y)^2 - (9)^2 = 0$
$y = \pm\sqrt{81}$	$(y - 9)(y + 9) = 0$
$y = \pm 9$	$y - 9 = 0 \quad \textbf{or} \quad y + 9 = 0$
	$y = 9 \quad \textbf{or} \quad y = -9$

You can check these solutions by substituting back into the original equation.

(ii) $25x^2 - 256 = 0$

Method 1	Method 2
$25x^2 - 256 = 0$	$25x^2 - 256 = 0$
$25x^2 = 256$	$(5x)^2 - (16)^2 = 0$
$x^2 = \dfrac{256}{25}$	$(5x - 16)(5x + 16) = 0$
$x = \pm\sqrt{\dfrac{256}{25}}$	$5x - 16 = 0 \quad \textbf{or} \quad 5x + 16 = 0$
$x = \pm\dfrac{16}{5}$	$5x = 16 \quad \textbf{or} \quad 5x = -16$
	$x = \dfrac{16}{5} \quad \textbf{or} \quad x = -\dfrac{16}{5}$

You can check these solutions by substituting back into the original equation.

Quadratic Trinomials

A quadratic trinomial in x has an x^2 term, an x term and a non-zero constant. So, any equation of the form $ax^2 + bx + c = 0$, where none of a, b, c are equal to 0, involves a quadratic trinomial.

For example: $2x^2 + x - 15 = 0$.

In a previous chapter on factorising, we examined different methods of factorising a quadratic trinomial.

So, $2x^2 + x - 15 = 0$ becomes:

$(2x - 5)(x + 3) = 0$

$$\Rightarrow \quad 2x - 5 = 0 \quad \textbf{or} \quad x + 3 = 0$$

$$\Rightarrow \quad 2x = 5 \quad \textbf{or} \quad x = -3$$

$$\Rightarrow \quad x = \frac{5}{2} \quad \textbf{or} \quad x = -3$$

These two solutions can be checked by substituting back into the original equation.

Note: Not all quadratic trinomials can be (easily) factorised.

x^2 Worked Example 17.3

Solve $3x^2 + 7x - 20 = 0$.

Solution

$$3x^2 + 7x - 20 = 0$$

$$\Rightarrow \quad (3x - 5)(x + 4) = 0$$

$$\Rightarrow \quad 3x - 5 = 0 \quad \textbf{or} \quad x + 4 = 0$$

$$3x = 5 \quad \textbf{or} \quad x = -4$$

$$\therefore x = \frac{5}{3} \quad \textbf{or} \quad x = -4$$

You can check these solutions by substituting back into the original equation.

x^2 Worked Example 17.4

Solve $4x^2 - 18x - 36 = 0$.

Solution

While we can factorise $4x^2 - 18x - 36$, it may be easier to factorise if we first divide every term by 2.

$$\Rightarrow \quad 2x^2 - 9x - 18 = 0$$

Now factorise.

$$\Rightarrow \quad (2x + 3)(x - 6) = 0$$

$$\Rightarrow \quad 2x + 3 = 0 \quad \textbf{or} \quad x - 6 = 0$$

$$2x = -3 \quad \textbf{or} \quad x = 6$$

$$\therefore x = -\frac{3}{2} \quad \textbf{or} \quad x = 6$$

You can check these solutions by substituting back into the original equation.

x^2 Worked Example 17.5

Solve $\frac{5}{3}x^2 - \frac{21}{2}x - 15 = 0$.

Solution

The LCD of 3 and 2 is 6.

Multiply every term in the equation by 6.

$$6\left(\frac{5}{3}x^2\right) - 6\left(\frac{21}{2}x\right) - 6(15) = 0$$

$$10x^2 - 63x - 90 = 0$$

Now factorise.

$$\Rightarrow \quad (5x + 6)(2x - 15) = 0$$

$$\Rightarrow \quad 5x + 6 = 0 \quad \textbf{or} \quad 2x - 15 = 0$$

$$5x = -6 \quad \textbf{or} \quad 2x = 15$$

$$x = -\frac{6}{5} \quad \textbf{or} \quad x = \frac{15}{2}$$

You can check these solutions by substituting back into the original equation.

Exercise 17.1

Solve the following quadratic equations. You should check your solutions in each case.

1. $x^2 + 10x + 21 = 0$

2. $x^2 - 3x + 2 = 0$

3. $x^2 - 5x = 0$

4. $x^2 - x - 20 = 0$

5. $x^2 - 15x + 56 = 0$

6. $x^2 - 64 = 0$

7. $3x^2 + 8x + 5 = 0$

8. $4p^2 - 16 = 0$

9. $7q^2 + 8q + 1 = 0$

10. $4x^2 - 16x = 0$

11. $3y^2 - 2y - 1 = 0$

12. $3x^2 + 20x - 7 = 0$

13. $3x^2 + 19x + 6 = 0$

14. $-2x^2 + 11x = 0$

15. $81 - 4x^2 = 0$

16. $5a^2 = 2a$

17. $100x^2 - 25 = 0$

18. $2x^2 + 2x - 12 = 0$

19. $25x^2 - 25 = 0$

20. $2b^2 - b = 10$

21. $2x^2 - 3x = 0$

22. $(3x + 4)(x - 3) = 10$

23. $625x^2 - 196 = 0$

24. $5y^2 = 7y$

25. $3x^2 - 24x + 36 = 0$

26. $5y^2 - 125 = 0$

27. $(2x + 1)(x - 3) - 4 = 0$

28. $4x^2 + 8x + 3 = 0$

29. $6x^2 + 7x + 2 = 0$

30. $9x^2 - 7x - 2 = 0$

31. $-6x^2 + 5x + 1 = 0$

32. $4x^2 - 13x + 3 = 0$

33. $10x^2 - 37x + 7 = 0$

34. $80a^2 - 245 = 0$

35. $4b^2 + 16b + 15 = 0$

36. $8c^2 - 6 + 13c = 0$

37. $21 = 10m^2 + 29m$

38. $\frac{1}{4}x^2 + 3x + 5 = 0$

39. $x^2 - 2.4x - 6.4 = 0$

40. $\frac{x^2}{3} + \frac{x}{2} - \frac{5}{6} = 0$

41. $\frac{3x^2}{5} - \frac{11x}{10} - 1 = 0$

42. $\frac{1}{2}x^2 - \frac{17}{8}x + \frac{1}{2} = 0$

17.2 SOLVING QUADRATIC EQUATIONS BY FORMULA I

Another approach to solving a quadratic equation is to use the quadratic formula (or '–b formula'). This method can always be used to solve a quadratic equation.

The solution(s) to the equation $ax^2 + bx + c = 0$, where $a, b, c \in R$ ($a \neq 0$) is (are) given by:

FORMULA

$$x = \frac{-b \pm \sqrt{b^2 - 4ac}}{2a}$$

This formula appears on page 20 of *Formulae and Tables*.

When using the quadratic formula, we should ensure that:

- All the terms of the equation are on the same side of the equals sign.
- The equation is in the form $ax^2 + bx + c = 0$.
- The a-value is positive.

In the quadratic formula, $b^2 - 4ac$ is called the **discriminant**.

- If $b^2 - 4ac \geqslant 0$, then the equation has real solutions (real roots).
- If $b^2 - 4ac < 0$, then the equation has no real solutions (no real roots).

When using the quadratic formula, it is important to note that in, for example, the equation $x^2 - 3x - 6 = 0$:

$a = 1$ (the coefficient of x^2)

$b = -3$ (the coefficient of x)

$c = -6$ (the constant)

x^2 Worked Example 17.6

Solve $x^2 - 4x - 5 = 0$ using the quadratic formula.

Solution

Using the quadratic formula:

$a = 1$ $b = -4$ $c = -5$

$b^2 - 4ac = (-4)^2 - 4(1)(-5)$

$\qquad = 16 + 20$

$\qquad = 36$

$\therefore x = \dfrac{-(-4) \pm \sqrt{36}}{2(1)}$

$\qquad = \dfrac{4 \pm 6}{2}$

$x = \dfrac{4 + 6}{2}$ **or** $x = \dfrac{4 - 6}{2}$

$\qquad = \dfrac{10}{2}$ **or** $\qquad = \dfrac{-2}{2}$

$\therefore x = 5$ **or** $x = -1$

You can check these solutions by substituting back into the original equation.

x^2 Worked Example 17.7

Solve x $4x^2 = -12x - 5$.

Solution

To solve the equation, first make sure that all terms are on the same side of the equals sign and that the x^2 term has a positive coefficient.

$4x^2 = -12x - 5$

$\Rightarrow \quad 4x^2 + 12x + 5 = 0$

Using the quadratic formula:

$a = 4$ $b = 12$ $c = 5$

Discriminant $= b^2 - 4ac$

$\qquad = (12)^2 - 4(4)(5)$

$\qquad = 144 - 80$

$\qquad = 64$

$\therefore x = \dfrac{-12 \pm \sqrt{64}}{2(4)}$

$\qquad = \dfrac{-12 \pm 8}{8}$

$x = \dfrac{-12 + 8}{8}$ **or** $x = \dfrac{-12 - 8}{8}$

$\qquad = -\dfrac{4}{8}$ **or** $\qquad = -\dfrac{20}{8}$

$\qquad = -\dfrac{1}{2}$ **or** $\qquad = -\dfrac{5}{2}$

$\therefore x = -\dfrac{1}{2}$ **or** $x = -\dfrac{5}{2}$

You can check these solutions by substituting back into the original equation.

 ACTIVITY 17.1

Exercise 17.2

Use the quadratic formula to solve each of the following equations.

1. $x^2 + 8x + 15 = 0$

2. $x^2 + 7x + 10 = 0$

3. $x^2 + x - 6 = 0$

4. $2x^2 - 13x + 20 = 0$

5. $2x^2 - 7x + 5 = 0$

6. $4x^2 - 17x + 13 = 0$

7. $5x^2 - 18x + 9 = 0$

8. $7x^2 + 25x + 12 = 0$

9. $3x^2 = 4x + 7$

10. $4x^2 = 4x + 8$

11. $23x + 20 = -6x^2$

12. $x^2 + \frac{7}{2}x = 2$

17.3 SOLVING QUADRATIC EQUATIONS BY FORMULA II

One of the main reasons why we may have to use the quadratic formula instead of factorising and then solving is that the roots of some quadratic equations are decimals or surds.

We can usually spot when we have to use the quadratic formula. The question will ask for the solution to be given correct to a certain number of decimal places **or** in surd form. Otherwise, if we try to factorise and solve, and run into difficulty, we can go back and use the quadratic formula to solve.

x^2 Worked Example 17.8

Solve, correct to two decimal places, $2x^2 + x - 5 = 0$.

Solution

Using the quadratic formula:

$$x = \frac{-b \pm \sqrt{b^2 - 4ac}}{2a}.$$

$a = 2 \qquad b = 1 \qquad c = -5$

$b^2 - 4ac = (1)^2 - 4(2)(-5)$

$\qquad = 1 + 40$

$\qquad = 41$

$\therefore x = \frac{-1 \pm \sqrt{41}}{4}$

$x \approx 1.35 \quad \text{or} \quad x \approx -1.85$

x^2 Worked Example 17.9

Find the roots, in surd form, of the equation $3x^2 - 12x + 7 = 0$.

Solution

Using the quadratic formula:

$a = 3 \qquad b = -12 \qquad c = 7$

$b^2 - 4ac = (-12)^2 - 4(3)(7)$

$\qquad = 144 - 84$

$\qquad = 60$

Now, $\sqrt{60} = \sqrt{(4)(15)}$

$\qquad = \sqrt{4}\,\sqrt{15}$

$\qquad = 2\sqrt{15}$

$\therefore x = \frac{12 \pm 2\sqrt{15}}{6}$

$x = \frac{6 \pm \sqrt{15}}{3}$ (Divide all terms by 2)

$x = \frac{6 + \sqrt{15}}{3} \quad \text{or} \quad x = \frac{6 - \sqrt{15}}{3}$

 ACTIVITY 17.2

Exercise 17.3

Use the quadratic formula to solve each of the following equations.

1 d.p. = Answer to one decimal place.

2 d.p. = Answer to two decimal places.

3 d.p. = Answer to three decimal places.

Surd = Answer in surd form.

1. $x^2 + 6x + 1 = 0$	[Surd]	**15.** $4x^2 + 10x + 5 = 0$ [Surd]
2. $x^2 + 8x + 5 = 0$	[3 d.p.]	**16.** $x^2 - 12x + 14 = 0$ [Surd]
3. $y^2 - 2y - 29 = 0$	[2 d.p.]	**17.** $5x^2 - 16x + 9 = 0$ [1 d.p.]
4. $x^2 - 5x - 28 = 0$	[1 d.p.]	**18.** $15x^2 - 21x + 1 = 0$ [2 d.p.]
5. $2x^2 - 11x - 9 = 0$	[3 d.p.]	**19.** $4x^2 = 1 - 2x$ [Surd]
6. $3x^2 - 10x + 4 = 0$	[Surd]	**20.** $2 - 10x + 9x^2 = 0$ [Surd]
7. $2x^2 - 5x - 21 = 0$	[3 d.p.]	**21.** $3x = 20 - 8x^2$ [3 d.p.]
8. $4q^2 - q - 13 = 0$	[1 d.p.]	**22.** $15x^2 - 14x = 9$ [Surd]
9. $5x^2 + 4x - 5 = 0$	[2 d.p.]	**23.** $8x^2 = 3 - 8x$ [Surd]
10. $8x^2 - 5x - 11 = 0$	[3 d.p.]	**24.** $5x^2 = 2x + 11$ [2 d.p.]
11. $9a^2 - 8a - 24 = 0$	[2 d.p.]	**25.** $2x^2 + 5x + \frac{3}{8} = 0$ [2 d.p.]
12. $3x^2 - 9x + 5 = 0$	[1 d.p.]	**26.** $\frac{x^2}{3} + \frac{2x}{5} - 4 = 0$ [3 d.p.]
13. $11b^2 - 3b - 7 = 0$	[3 d.p.]	**27.** $\frac{4}{9}x^2 = \frac{3}{2}x + \frac{1}{5}$ [2 d.p.]
14. $2x^2 + 4x + 1 = 0$	[Surd]	**28.** $(x + 2)^2 - 2(2x - 3)^2 = 10$ [Surd]

17.4 LINKED QUADRATIC EQUATIONS

Two quadratic equations may be linked by the fact that the solutions of one equation can be used to find the solutions of the other equation.

x^2 Worked Example 17.10

Solve $x^2 - 18x + 45 = 0$ and hence solve $(y^2 + 2y)^2 - 18(y^2 + 2y) + 45 = 0$.

Solution

$x^2 - 18x + 45 = 0$

Factorise to get:

$(x - 15)(x - 3) = 0$

$\Rightarrow \quad x - 15 = 0 \quad$ **or** $\quad x - 3 = 0$

$\therefore x = 15 \quad$ **or** $\quad x = 3$

To solve $(y^2 + 2y)^2 - 18(y^2 + 2y) + 45 = 0$, we must realise that this equation has the same structure as the original equation. That is: $A^2 - 18A + 45 = 0$.

In the first equation, $A = x$.

In the second equation, $A = y^2 + 2y$.

So, $\quad y^2 + 2y = 15$ **or** $\quad y^2 + 2y = 3$

$\quad y^2 + 2y - 15 = 0 \quad$ **or** $\quad y^2 + 2y - 3 = 0$

$\quad (y + 5)(y - 3) = 0 \quad$ **or** $\quad (y + 3)(y - 1) = 0$

$\quad y = -5$ **or** $y = 3 \quad$ **or** $\quad y = -3$ **or** $y = 1$

$\therefore y = -5, 3, 1$ or -3

 ACTIVITY 17.3

 ## Exercise 17.4

1. Solve $x^2 + 9x + 20 = 0$, and hence, solve $(y + 1)^2 + 9(y + 1) + 20 = 0$.

2. Solve $x^2 - 4x - 32 = 0$, and hence, solve $(4t)^2 - 4(4t) - 32 = 0$.

3. Solve $x^2 - 2x - 3 = 0$, and hence, solve $(t + 1)^2 - 2(t + 1) - 3 = 0$.

4. (i) Solve $x^2 - 2x - 15 = 0$.
   (ii) Hence, solve $(3a - 1)^2 - 2(3a - 1) - 15 = 0$.

5. Solve $2x^2 + 7x - 4 = 0$, and hence, solve $2\left(2p - \dfrac{1}{2}\right)^2 + 7\left(2p - \dfrac{1}{2}\right) - 4 = 0$.

6. Solve $x^2 + 2x - 24 = 0$, and hence, solve $24 - 2(2y + 2) - (2y + 2)^2 = 0$.

7. (i) Solve $2x^2 - 9x - 18 = 0$.
   (ii) Hence, solve $2(2a^2 - 2)^2 - 9(2a^2 - 2) - 18 = 0$.

8. Solve $x^2 - 6x - 16 = 0$, and hence, solve $(3q^2 - 5q)^2 - 6(3q^2 - 5q) - 16 = 0$.

9. Solve, correct to two decimal places, $x^2 - 2x - 7 = 0$. Hence, solve $(2p - 5)^2 - 2(2p - 5) - 7 = 0$.

10. (i) Solve $5x^2 - 2x - 15 = 0$, correct to one decimal place.
    (ii) Hence, solve $5\left(\dfrac{a}{2} + 1\right)^2 - 2\left(\dfrac{a}{2} + 1\right) - 15 = 0$.

11. Solve $12x^2 - 11x + 2 = 0$, and hence, solve $12(3y^2 + y)^2 - 11(3y^2 + y) + 2 = 0$.

17.5 FORMING QUADRATIC EQUATIONS

If we are given the roots of a quadratic equation, it is possible to work backwards to form a quadratic equation that has these roots. This process involves (1) changing the roots into factors and (2) using these factors to form the equation.

Roots	→	Factors	→	Equation
$x = 6$ **or** $x = -2$		$x - 6 = 0$ **or** $x + 2 = 0$		$(x - 6)(x + 2) = 0$ $x(x + 2) - 6(x + 2) = 0$ $x^2 + 2x - 6x - 12 = 0$ $x^2 - 4x - 12 = 0$

x^2 Worked Example 17.11

Form a quadratic equation with the following roots:

    (i) 5, 4

    (ii) −2, 8

    (iii) $\frac{2}{5}$, $1\frac{1}{2}$

    (iv) a, b

Solution

    (i) 5, 4

$$x = 5 \quad \text{or} \quad x = 4$$
$$x - 5 = 0 \quad \text{or} \quad x - 4 = 0$$
$$(x - 5)(x - 4) = 0$$
$$x(x - 4) - 5(x - 4) = 0$$
$$x^2 - 4x - 5x + 20 = 0$$
$$x^2 - 9x + 20 = 0$$

    (ii) −2, 8

$$x = -2 \quad \text{or} \quad x = 8$$
$$x + 2 = 0 \quad \text{or} \quad x - 8 = 0$$
$$(x + 2)(x - 8) = 0$$
$$x(x - 8) + 2(x - 8) = 0$$
$$x^2 - 8x + 2x - 16 = 0$$
$$x^2 - 6x - 16 = 0$$

    (iii) $\frac{2}{5}$, $1\frac{1}{2}$

$$x = \frac{2}{5} \quad \text{or} \quad x = 1\frac{1}{2}$$
$$5x = 2 \quad \text{or} \quad x = \frac{3}{2}$$
$$\Rightarrow 2x = 3$$
$$5x - 2 = 0 \quad \text{or} \quad 2x - 3 = 0$$
$$(5x - 2)(2x - 3) = 0$$
$$5x(2x - 3) - 2(2x - 3) = 0$$
$$10x^2 - 15x - 4x + 6 = 0$$
$$10x^2 - 19x + 6 = 0$$

    (iv) a, b

$$x = a \quad \text{or} \quad x = b$$
$$x - a = 0 \quad \text{or} \quad x - b = 0$$
$$(x - a)(x - b) = 0$$
$$x(x - b) - a(x - b) = 0$$
$$x^2 - bx - ax + ab = 0$$
$$x^2 - (a + b)x + ab = 0$$

If $x = a$ and $x = b$ are the roots of a quadratic equation, then that equation can be written as:

$$x^2 - (a + b)x + ab = 0$$

i.e. $x^2 - $ (SUM OF ROOTS)$x + $ (PRODUCT OF ROOTS) $= 0$

So, for example, in part (i) above:

Sum of roots $= 5 + 4 = 9$

Product of roots $= (5)(4) = 20$

Equation: $x^2 - 9x + 20 = 0$

Exercise 17.5

In Questions 1–10, form a quadratic equation with the given pair of roots.

1. 1, 2   **3.** 4, −2   **5.** −11, 11   **7.** −5, −4   **9.** ± 5

2. 5, 6   **4.** 7, −5   **6.** 8, 0   **8.** 0, −6   **10.** $-\frac{1}{3}, \frac{2}{7}$

11. The roots of a quadratic equation $x^2 + px + q = 0$ are 3 and −2.

   Find the value of p and the value of q.

12. The roots of a quadratic equation $x^2 + bx + c = 0$ are 0 and −4.

   Find the value of b and and the value of c.

13. The roots of a quadratic equation $x^2 - 8x + c = 0$ are the same.

   Find the value of c.

17.6 SOLVING PROBLEMS INVOLVING QUADRATIC EQUATIONS

In this section we examine how the knowledge of quadratic equations developed so far in this chapter can be used to answer an array of real-world problems and applications.

x^2 Worked Example 17.12

The product of two consecutive even natural numbers is equal to 288. Find both numbers.

Solution

First number = x.

Second number = $x + 2$.

Word equation: One number multiplied by the other number is equal to 288.

Maths equation:

$$x(x + 2) = 288$$

$$x^2 + 2x = 288$$

$$x^2 + 2x - 288 = 0$$

$$(x - 16)(x + 18) = 0$$

$$x - 16 = 0 \quad \textbf{or} \quad x + 18 = 0$$

$$x = 16 \quad \textbf{or} \quad x = -18$$

First number = x = 16.   (We reject $x = -18$, as $-18 \notin N$).

Second number = $x + 2$ = 18.

x^2 Worked Example 17.13

The height (h) in metres of a firework above the ground, when fired from the top of an apartment block, is given by the formula:

$$h = 32 + 12t - 5t^2$$

where t is the time in seconds after the firework is fired.

   (i) What is the height of the firework after 2 seconds?

   (ii) What is the height of the firework when fired?

   (ii) Find the time it takes the firework to strike the ground.

Solution

   (i) The height of the firework after 2 seconds

   Substitute $t = 2$ into the formula.

   $$h = 32 + 12t - 5t^2$$

   $$= 32 + 12(2) - 5(2)^2$$

   $$= 32 + 24 - 20$$

   $$\therefore h = 36 \text{ m}$$

(ii) The height of the firework when fired

The firework is fired at $t = 0$ seconds.

$\therefore h = 32 + 12(0) - 5(0)^2$

$\qquad = 32$ m

(iii) The time it takes the firework to strike the ground

Height of firework when it strikes the ground $= 0$

$\therefore 32 + 12t - 5t^2 = 0$

Now solve this equation:

$5t^2 - 12t - 32 = 0$

$(5t + 8)(t - 4) = 0$

$5t + 8 = 0 \quad$ **or** $\quad t - 4 = 0$

$\qquad 5t = -8$

$\therefore t = -\dfrac{8}{5} \quad$ **or** $\qquad t = 4$

We reject $t = -\dfrac{8}{5}$, as time starts at 0.

$\therefore$ The firework strikes the ground after 4 seconds.

x^2 Worked Example 17.14

The number of bacteria (millions) counted in a sample of food is given by the formula:

$$N(C) = C^2 - 6C + 9$$

where C is the temperature of the food in degrees Celsius.

(i) How many bacteria are present at a temperature of 5°C?

(ii) At what temperature will no bacteria be present in the sample?

Solution

(i) Substitute $C = 5$ into the formula.

$N(C) = C^2 - 6C + 9$

$\therefore N(5) = (5)^2 - 6(5) + 9$

$\qquad = 25 - 30 + 9$

$\qquad = 4$

$\therefore$ Four million bacteria are present.

(ii) No bacteria means that the number of bacteria $= 0$.

$\therefore C^2 - 6C + 9 = 0$

$(C - 3)(C - 3) = 0$

$C - 3 = 0$

$C = 3$

$\therefore$ The temperature is 3°C.

Exercise 17.6

1. A positive number is squared and three times the number is then added. The result is 88. Find the number.

2. Find two consecutive odd natural numbers whose product is 399.

3. When 15 is added to the square of a number, the result is equal to eight times the number. Find two possible values for the number.

4. The sum of the areas of these three rectangles is 189 cm². Find the value of x.

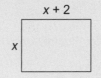
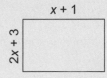

5. The perimeter of a rectangle is 160 metres.

   (i) If $x = $ the length, write down (in terms of x) an expression for the width.

   (ii) If the area of this rectangle is 1,536 m², find its dimensions.

6. The dimensions for each of the following shapes are shown. Find the value of x for each shape.

(i)

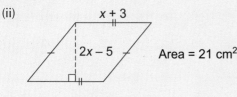

x cm

$(x + 5)$ cm

Area = 14 cm²

(ii)

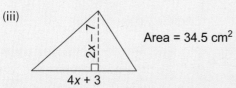

$x + 3$

$2x - 5$

Area = 21 cm²

(iii)

$2x - 7$

$4x + 3$

Area = 34.5 cm²

7. A rectangular garden has dimensions $(x + 5)$ metres by $(16 - 2x)$ metres. It is surrounded by a path of constant width of x metres. The area of the path is 67.5 m².

 (i) Find the area of the garden in terms of x.

 (ii) Find the area covered by the path in terms of x.

 (iii) Find the value of x.

8. For the years between 1990 and 1999, the number of computer games sold (in thousands) per annum by a company can be estimated by the formula $g = -2t^2 + 20t + 7$, where t represents the year (for example, $t = 5$ represents 1995).

 (i) How many games were sold in 1997?

 (ii) In which half of the decade were more games sold: 1990 to 1994 **or** 1995 to 1999?

 (iii) In which years were 25,000 games sold?

 (iv) After the year 2000, this formula was no longer valid. Give a reason why this was the case.

9. A wholesaler sold n bars for $(n + 1)$ cents each. On the following day, she doubled the price but sold two bars less. The amount of the money taken on each day was the same. Find the value of n.

10. A rectangular swimming pool has a perimeter of 46 metres. The length of the pool is x metres.

 (i) Write an expression for the width of the pool in terms of x.

 A path of width $(x - 8)$ metres is to be built around the pool as shown.

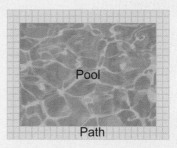

Pool

Path

 (ii) If the area of the path is 140 m², find the dimensions of the pool.

11. A manufacturer of office chairs estimates the daily cost of manufacturing using the formula $C(x) = 9 + 16x - 0.5x^2$, where C is the cost in euros and x is the number of chairs produced. The factory produces a maximum of 17 chairs per day.

 (i) How much does it cost to produce 10 chairs?

 (ii) How many chairs can be produced for €135 in one day?

 (iii) The chairs are to be sold at a price of €30 per chair. How much profit will be made if 15 chairs are sold?

12. The height h in metres of an object fired vertically upwards from the balcony of an apartment complex is given by the formula $h(t) = -5t^2 + 18t + 8$.

 (i) From what height is the object fired?

 (ii) What is the average speed of the object in the first second of flight?

 (iii) How long will it take for the object to hit the ground?

13. A laboratory is testing a particular fungicide to check its effectiveness in killing fungal spores. The number of fungal spores in a Petri dish is given by the formula $N(t) = 16t^2 - 200t + 625$, where t is the is the time in minutes after a fungicide has been added to the Petri dish.

 (i) How many spores were present when the fungicide was applied?

(ii) How many spores were present after 3 minutes?

(iii) The laboratory technician is testing the fungicide for commercial use. To be successful, the fungicide must kill 84% of all the spores initially present. What is the shortest time in which this percentage can be achieved?

(iv) The laboratory technician recommends that this fungicide should not be released for commercial use. She does this by looking at her answer from part (iii). Explain why she has made this recommendation.

14. The dimensions of a field are shown below. A farmer wished to build a barn on the parcel of land shown.

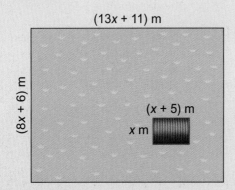

(13x + 11) m

(8x + 6) m

(x + 5) m

x m

(i) Find the area of the field in terms of x.

(ii) Find the area covered by the barn in terms of x.

(iii) If the area of unbuilt land is equal to 1,476 m², find the length and width of the field.

15. The height of a ball when hit with a baseball bat is given by the equation $y = -2x^2 + 9x + 1$ where y is the height in metres above the ground and x is the horizontal distance from the home plate in metres.

(i) What is the height of the ball when hit by the bat?

(ii) What is the height of the ball after 2 metres?

(iii) At what distance did the ball land from the batter? Give your answer to the nearest centimetre.

(iv) Do you think the batter was pleased with how he hit the ball? Give a reason for your answer.

16. Abdul copies a diagram of a right-angled triangle from his maths book, as shown.

8x − 21

6x

3x − 7

(i) Find the value of x.

(ii) He draws another right-angled triangle but, this time, he thinks he has made an error in the diagram. Explain why he thinks he has made an error.

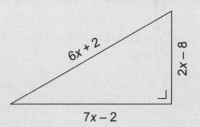

6x + 2

2x − 8

7x − 2

17. Ann is solving a quadratic equation using the quadratic formula. She writes down the following:

$$x = \frac{4 \pm \sqrt{76}}{6}$$

(i) Write down the quadratic equation that Ann is trying to solve.

Bob is trying to solve the quadratic equation $2x^2 - 5x + 9 = 0$. Ann checks his equation and explains that he must have made an error when taking down the question.

(ii) Explain why Ann thinks Bob has made an error.

(iii) Suggest one possible correction that could be made to Bob's equation.

18. A car and a motorbike leave a house at 08:50. The motorbike travels due north at an average speed of 27 km/hr. The car travels due east at an average speed of 36 km/hr.
At what time will the two be exactly 60 km apart?

19. The path of a pebble thrown off a cliff is given by the formula $y = -\frac{9}{20}x^2 + \frac{5}{2}x + 11$, where y is the height in metres above sea level and x is the horizontal distance from the cliff face in metres.

(i) What is the height of the pebble when thrown?

(ii) What is the height of the pebble after travelling 3 metres horizontally?

(iii) How far is the pebble from the cliff face when it hits the water? Answer correct to two decimal places.

20. On a dry road, the approximate stopping distance of a car (d) in metres, travelling at a speed of v in kilometres per hour is given by the formula $d = 0.0058v^2 + 0.20v$.

(i) What would be the stopping distance of a car travelling at 70 km/hr?

(ii) If a car takes 100 m to stop, what was its speed, to the nearest km/hr?

21. Two equal rectangular fields are to be fenced using 200 metres of fencing as shown below.

Each field has an area of $833\frac{1}{3}$ m². Let x represent the length of one of the shorter field sides to be fenced and let y represent the total length of the field side to be fenced.

(i) Show that $y = \frac{200 - 3x}{2}$.

(ii) Write an expression for the area of one of the fields in terms of x.

(iii) Hence, find the value of x and the value of y.

22. A company's revenue from sales of certain furniture units is given by the equation $R(x) = 80x - \frac{1}{2}x^2$, where x is the number of furniture units produced.

(i) Calculate the revenue on selling 50 units.

(ii) What is the minimum number of units that must be sold in order to have revenue of €3,000?

The company calculates the cost (c) of manufacturing x amount of furniture units by the equation $c(x) = 10x + 50$.

(iii) Calculate the cost of producing 25 units.

(iv) If the total cost of production for a day is €750, how many units were manufactured that day?

The profit is determined by subtracting the cost of the manufacture from the sales revenue.

(v) What is the minimum number of furniture units that must be manufactured and sold to net a profit of €1,950?

23. The height of a cannonball as it is fired from a cannon on top of a castle is given by the formula $h = 22 + 60t - 10t^2$, where t is the time in seconds after the cannonball is fired from the cannon and h is the height of the cannonball in metres.

(i) At what time does the cannonball hit the ground? Answer correct to one decimal place.

(ii) From what height was the cannonball fired?

(iii) The cannonball never reaches a height of 120 m above the ground.

Give a reason why.

Revision Exercises

1. (a) Solve the following quadratic equations:

   (i) $x^2 + x - 20 = 0$

   (ii) $x^2 + 3x - 70 = 0$

   (iii) $x^2 - 25 = 0$

   (iv) $x^2 - 7x = 0$

   (b) Use the quadratic formula to solve these equations, giving your answer correct to two decimal places:

   (i) $x^2 + 5x - 3 = 0$

   (ii) $x^2 - 7x - 1 = 0$

   (iii) $x^2 - 4x - 2 = 0$

   (c) Solve $x^2 - 10x + 21 = 0$ and hence solve $(2t + 1)^2 - 10(2t + 1) + 21 = 0$.

2. (a) Solve the following quadratic equations:

   (i) $2x^2 - 3x = 0$

   (ii) $10x^2 + x - 2 = 0$

   (iii) $9x^2 - 4 = 0$

   (b) Use the quadratic formula to solve these equations, giving your answers in surd form:

   (i) $2x^2 + 8x - 3 = 0$

   (ii) $5x^2 - 11x + 1 = 0$

   (iii) $6x^2 - x - 3 = 0$

3. (a) Form a quadratic equation with the following pairs of roots:

   (i) 2 and 3   (iii) 3 and −5

   (ii) −4 and 2   (iv) 2 and 0

   (b) Solve, correct to three decimal places:

   (i) $x^2 = 5x + 7$

   (ii) $2x^2 + 1 = 10x$

   (iii) $3 - x - 3x^2 = 0$

   (c) Solve the following quadratic equations:

   (i) $21x^2 + 2x - 3 = 0$

   (ii) $5x^2 + 6 = 13x$

   (iii) $5(x^2 - 4) = 2(x - 10)$

4. (a) (i) The roots of $x^2 - ax - b = 0$ are 7 and −2. Find the values of a and b.

   (ii) The roots of $x^2 + ax + b =$ are −8 and −2. Find the values of a and b.

   (b) Solve $x^2 - 10x - 11 = 0$ and hence solve $(3t - 1)^2 - 10(3t - 1) - 11 = 0$.

   (c) (i) Find, correct to one decimal place, the values of x that satisfy $x^2 + 2x - 10 = 0$.

   (ii) Hence, find (correct to one decimal place), the values of t that satisfy $(t + 1)^2 + 2(t + 1) - 10 = 0$.

5. The number of bacteria (thousands) counted in a container of spoiled food is given by $N(t) = -2t^2 + 11t + 13$, where t is the time in hours.

   (i) How many bacteria were initially present in the food?

   (ii) At what times will there be an estimated 25,000 bacteria in the food?

   (iii) At what time will there be no bacteria in the food?

   (iv) This formula will only give valid values between two times. Explain why this is the case.

6. One metre is divided into two parts such that the area of the square on the larger part is twice the area of the square on the smaller part. Find the length of each part, correct to three decimal places.

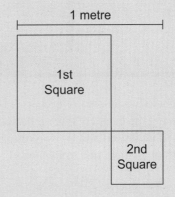

7. The length of a rectangle is 3 metres more than twice its width. Let x equal the width of the rectangle.

   (i) Write an expression in x for the length of the rectangle.

   (ii) Write an expression in x for the area of this rectangle

   (iii) If the area of this rectangle is 27 m², find its length and width.

8. A piece of wire 20 metres in length is cut to form the sides of two squares. One square has a side length of $(x + 0.5)$ metres.

   (i) Write an expression for the side length of the other square.

   (ii) The sum of the areas of these two squares equals 14.33 m². Find the side length of each square correct to two decimal places.

9. The value of a investment is given by the formula $v(t) = 10 + 36t - 5t^2$, where v is the value of the investment (in thousands) and t is the time in months.

   (i) What was the original value of the investment?

   (ii) After three months, by how much has the value of the investment increased?

   (iii) After how many months is the value of the investment worth €52,750?

   (iv) The investor decides to cash in on the investment after four months. Based on the formula given, give a reason why the investor chooses to cash in at this time.

10. A garden has an area of $(6x^2 + 11x - 10)$ m². The length of the garden is to be increased by 2 metres and the width is to be decreased by 2 metres. This results in a decrease of 10 m² in the overall area of the garden. Find the two possible values for the length and width of the garden.

11. A boulder ball rolls down a hill and travels a distance d metres according to the equation $d = 3t + \dfrac{t^2}{4}$, where t is the number of seconds the boulder is rolling.

   (i) Find the distance travelled in one second.

   (ii) Find the time at which the boulder is 14 metres away from its starting point.

   (iii) Find the average speed of the boulder over the first 32 metres.

12. The length of the hypotenuse of a right-angled triangle is 193 cm. The sum of the other two side lengths is 263 cm. Find the lengths of all three sides.

13. The height in metres of a small rocket when launched is given by $h(t) = 54t - 5t^2$, where t is the time in seconds.

   (i) What will the rocket's height be after 3 seconds?

   (ii) What was the height of the rocket when launched?

   (iii) How long will it take for the rocket to return to the ground?

14. Arthur wants to fence three sides of his rectangular garden. The fourth side of the garden faces onto the back of his house. He has 80 metres of fencing. Let x represent the width of his garden and let y represent the length of his garden.

   (i) Show that $y = 80 - 2x$.

   (ii) Write an expression for the area of the garden in terms of x.

   (iii) If the garden has an area of 487.5 m², find two possible values for the width and length of the garden.

15. Three identical rectangular plots of land are to be made from 800 metres of fencing as shown. Find two possible values for the length and width of each plot if the total area to be fenced is 10,200 m².

16. A plot consists of a garden measuring 8 m by 10 m surrounded by a path. The total area of the plot is 143 m². Three students, Kevin, Elaine and Tony, have been given the problem of trying to find the width of the path. Each of them is using a different method, but all of them are using x to represent the width of the path.

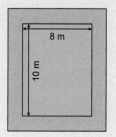

Kevin divides the path into eight pieces. He writes down the area of each piece in terms of x. He then forms an equation by setting the area of the path plus the area of the garden equal to the total area of the plot.

(a) Copy Kevin's diagram into your copybook. Write, in terms of x, the area of each section into Kevin's diagram.

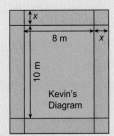

(b) Write down and simplify the equation which you think Kevin got. Give your answer in the form $ax^2 + bx + c = 0$.

Elaine writes down the length and width of the plot in terms of x. She multiplies these and sets the answer equal to the total area of the plot.

(c) Copy Elaine's diagram into your copybook.

Write, in terms of x, the length and width of the plot on Elaine's diagram.

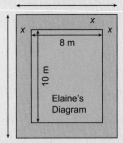

(d) Write down and simplify the equation which you think Elaine got. Give your answer in the form $ax^2 + bx + c = 0$.

(e) Solve an equation to find the width of the path.

(f) Tony does not answer the problem by solving an equation. Instead, he does it by trying out different values for x. Show some calculations that Tony might have used to solve the problem.

(g) Which of the three methods do you think is best? Give a reason for your answer.

SEC Sample Paper, JCHL

17. The golden ratio has played an important role historically in art, engineering and theology, among other areas.

Two lengths, p and q, are said to be in golden ratio (to each other) if the ratio of the larger length to the smaller is the same as the ratio of the sum of the two lengths to the larger length.

Let p and q be in golden ratio to each other, where $p > q$.

(a) Copy and complete the table below, writing your answers in terms of p and q:

Larger length : Shorter length	Sum of lengths : Larger length

(b) Let x be the golden ratio. Express x in terms of p and q.

Hint: Remember, $x = \dfrac{\text{Larger Length}}{\text{Shorter Length}}$

(c) As $\dfrac{p+q}{p} = 1 + \dfrac{q}{p}$, write $\dfrac{p+q}{p}$ in terms of x.

(d) Hence, form a quadratic equation in terms of x. Write your answer in the form $ax^2 + bx + c = 0, x \neq 0$.

(e) Solve the equation in part (d), giving your answers correct to three decimal places.

(f) (i) What is x_1, the negative solution in part (e)?

    (ii) What is x_2, the positive solution in part (e)?

(g) Since the golden ratio is a positive number, which solution, x_1 or x_2, is equal to the golden ratio?

(h) Hence, complete this statement:

'Correct to the nearest thousandth, the golden ratio is equal to _____. So, if one quantity is _____ % larger than another quantity, then the two quantities are in golden ratio to each other.'

(i) Evaluate $-\dfrac{1}{x_1}$ correct to three decimal places. What do you notice?

(j) Describe in words the relationship between the golden ratio and its reciprocal.

(k) The Fibonacci sequence is defined as follows:

- The first term is 1.
- The second term is 1.
- For every other term in the sequence, the term is equal to the sum of the two previous terms.

Complete the sequence, showing the first 12 Fibonacci terms, below:

1, 1, 2, ____, ____, ____, ____, ____, ____, ____, ____, ____,

(l) Complete the table below. Answer correct to three decimal places in each case.

(Term 2) ÷ (Term 1)	
(Term 3) ÷ (Term 2)	
(Term 4) ÷ (Term 3)	
(Term 5) ÷ (Term 4)	
(Term 6) ÷ (Term 5)	
(Term 7) ÷ (Term 6)	
(Term 8) ÷ (Term 7)	
(Term 9) ÷ (Term 8)	
(Term 10) ÷ (Term 9)	

(m) Describe in words your result in part (l) above.

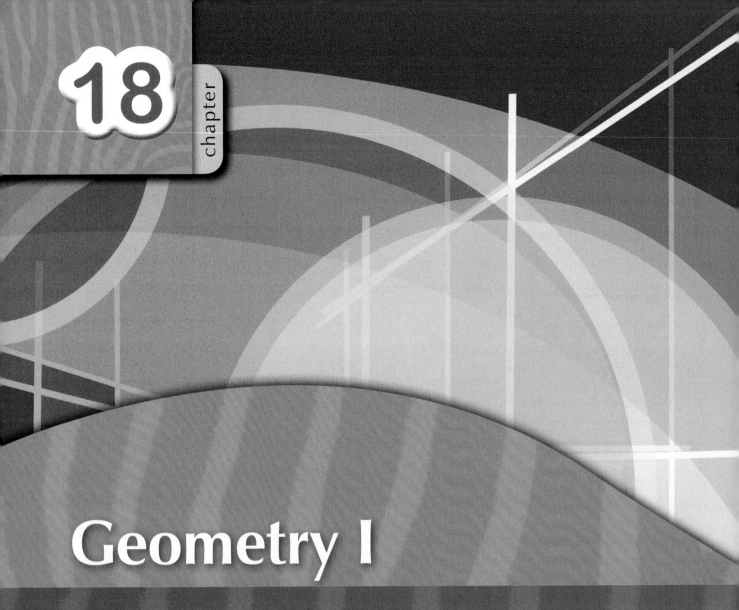

Geometry I

Learning Outcomes

In this chapter you will:

- Revise topics in geometry from the Ordinary Level course

You will learn about and apply the following theorems and corollaries:

- Theorem 11. If three parallel lines cut off equal segments on some transversal line, then they will cut off equal segments on any other transversal.

- Theorem 12. Let ABC be a triangle. If a line l is parallel to BC and cuts [AB] in the ratio m : n, then it also cuts [AC] in the same ratio (and converse).

- Theorem 13. If two triangles are similar, then their sides are proportional, in order (and converse).

- Theorem 19. The angle at the centre of a circle standing on a given arc is twice the angle at any point of the circle standing on the same arc.

- Corollary 2. All angles at points of a circle, standing on the same arc, are equal (and converse).

- Corollary 5. If ABCD is a cyclic quadrilateral, then opposite angles sum to 180° (and converse).

18.1 REVISION OF GEOMETRY

In this section we will revise some of the theorems covered on the ordinary level course. This section also covers axioms and transformations.

The Plane

Points and lines are shown on a plane.

If two points lie on the same plane, they are said to be **coplanar**.

> A **plane** is a flat two-dimensional surface. It has length and width, but it has no thickness.

KEY WORDS

■ **Axiom**

■ **Theorem**

■ **Corollary**

■ **Converse**

■ **Transversal**

■ **Similar triangles**

■ **Congruent triangles**

■ **Cyclic quadrilateral**

Lines and Angles

A **line** is a straight curve that goes on forever in both directions – it has **no endpoints**. A line can be named by any two points on the line or by a lowercase letter. It has an infinite number of points on it.

This line can be named the line *AB* or the line *l*.

This is the line segment [*AB*].

> A **line segment** is part of a straight line. It has two endpoints and can be measured using a ruler.

> A **ray** is part of a line that originates at a point and goes on forever in only one direction.

This is the ray [*AB*.

> **Perpendicular lines** are lines that are at right angles or 90° to each other.

> **Parallel lines** are lines that are always the same distance apart. They never meet.

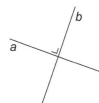

The line *a* is **perpendicular** to the line *b*. We denote this as *a* ⊥ *b*.

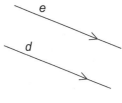

The line *d* is **parallel** to the line *e*. We denote this as *d* ∥ *e*.

> Points that lie on the same line are called **collinear points**.

The points *X*, *Y* and *Z* are collinear.

Angle Notation

There are many different ways to label an angle:

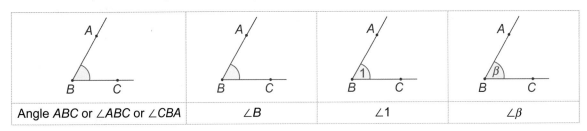

Angle *ABC* or ∠*ABC* or ∠*CBA*	∠*B*	∠1	∠*β*

Identifying Different Types of Angles

Angles can be divided into many different types.

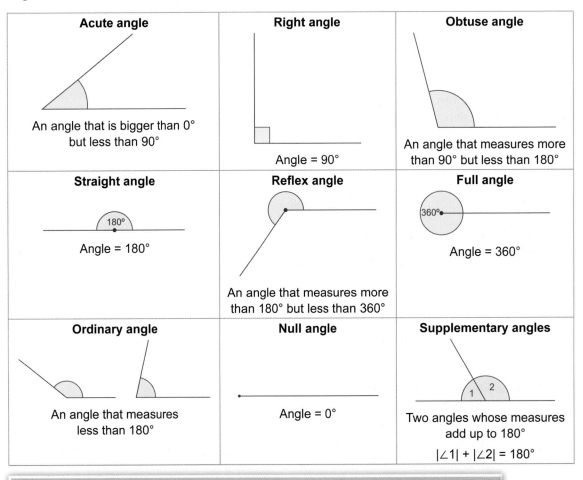

Acute angle	Right angle	Obtuse angle
An angle that is bigger than 0° but less than 90°	Angle = 90°	An angle that measures more than 90° but less than 180°
Straight angle	**Reflex angle**	**Full angle**
180° Angle = 180°	An angle that measures more than 180° but less than 360°	360° Angle = 360°
Ordinary angle	**Null angle**	**Supplementary angles**
An angle that measures less than 180°	Angle = 0°	Two angles whose measures add up to 180°
		|∠1| + |∠2| = 180°

> Supplementary angles do not need to be beside or adjacent to each other.
> Their measures just need to add to 180°.

Axioms

An axiom is a statement we accept as true without proof. There are five axioms on our course that we need to know and understand.

Axiom 1 (Two Points Axiom)

There is exactly one line through any two given points.

We can draw only one line through the points *A* and *B*.

Axiom 2 (Ruler Axiom)

The properties of the distance between points.

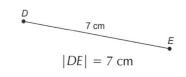

$|DE| = 7$ cm

Axiom 3 (Protractor Axiom)

The properties of the degree measure of an angle.

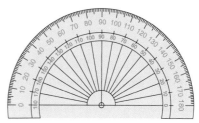

Axiom 4

Congruent triangles (SSS, SAS, ASA and RHS).

Congruent Triangles: Side, Side, Side (SSS)

$\triangle ABC$ is congruent to $\triangle XYZ$ **or** $\triangle ABC \equiv \triangle XYZ$.

The side lengths in $\triangle ABC$ are the same as the side lengths in $\triangle XYZ$.

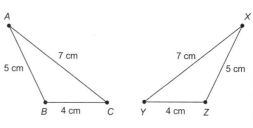

Congruent Triangles: Side, Angle, Side (SAS)

$\triangle DEF$ is congruent to $\triangle PQR$ **or** $\triangle DEF \equiv \triangle PQR$.

Two sides and the angle in between them are equal.

> The **in–between** angle can also be called the **included angle**.

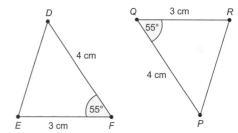

Congruent Triangles: Angle, Side, Angle (ASA)

$\triangle PQR$ is congruent to $\triangle MNO$ **or** $\triangle PQR \equiv \triangle MNO$.

Two angles and the corresponding side are equal.

> The corresponding side is the side between the two given angles.

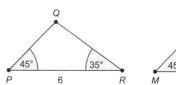 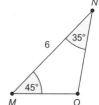

Congruent Triangles: Right Angle, Hypotenuse, One Other Side (RHS)

> The **hypotenuse** is the side opposite the right angle; it is also the longest side in the right-angled triangle.

$\triangle RST$ is congruent to $\triangle UVW$ **or** $\triangle RST \equiv \triangle UVW$.

Both of these triangles are right-angled, their hypotenuses are the same length, and they have one other side that is equal in length.

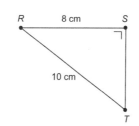 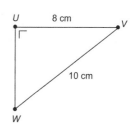

> As congruent triangles have the same shape and size, the area of the congruent triangles are equal as well.

GEOMETRY I

Axiom 5 (Axiom of Parallels)

Given any line *l* and a point *P*, there is exactly one line through *P* that is parallel to *l*.

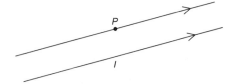

Theorems

A theorem is a rule that you can prove by following a certain number of logical steps or by using a previous theorem or axiom that you already know.

We studied a number of theorems on the ordinary level geometry course:

Angle Theorems

Theorem 1

Vertically opposite angles are equal in measure.

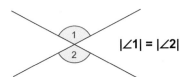

$|\angle 1| = |\angle 2|$

A way to spot **vertically opposite angles** is to look for the X shape.

Theorem 3

If a transversal makes equal alternate angles on two lines, then the lines are **parallel**.

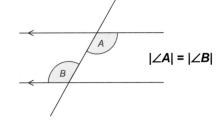

$|\angle A| = |\angle B|$

Conversely, if two lines are parallel, the alternate angles formed by a transversal are equal.

An easy way to remember which angles are **alternate** is to look for the **Z shape**.

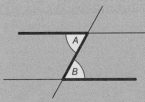
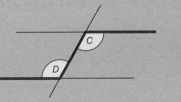

Theorem 5

Two lines are parallel if, and only if, for any transversal, the corresponding angles are equal in measure.

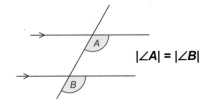

$|\angle A| = |\angle B|$

An easy way to remember which angles are **corresponding** is to look for the **F shape**.

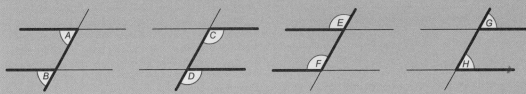

Triangle Theorems

Types of Triangle

Triangles are usually divided into three types according to its sides and angles.

The different triangles and their properties are:

Equilateral	Isosceles	Scalene
All sides the same length	At least two sides the same length	Three sides different in length
All angles the same size (60°)	At least two angles the same size	Three angles different in measure

Isosceles Triangle

Theorem 2

In an isosceles triangle the angles opposite the equal sides are equal in measure. Conversely, if two angles in a triangle are equal in measure, then the triangle is isosceles.

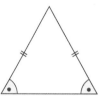

Angles in a Triangle

Theorem 4

The angles in any triangle add to 180°.

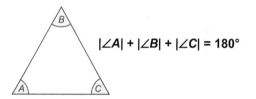

$|\angle A| + |\angle B| + |\angle C| = 180°$

Exterior Angles of a Triangle

Theorem 6

Each exterior angle of a triangle is equal in measure to the sum of the measures of the two interior opposite angles.

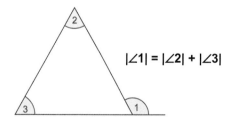

$|\angle 1| = |\angle 2| + |\angle 3|$

ACTIVE MATHS 2

Parallelogram Theorems

> A parallelogram is a quadrilateral that has two pairs of parallel sides.

There are four types of quadrilateral which can be considered parallelograms.

Type of quadrilateral	Sides	Parallel sides	Angles	Diagonals
Square	Four sides of equal length	Opposite sides are parallel	All angles the same size (90°)	Bisect each other – angle of 90° formed
Rectangle	Opposite sides of equal length	Opposite sides are parallel	All angles the same size (90°)	Bisect each other
Parallelogram	Opposite sides of equal length	Opposite sides are parallel	Opposite angles of equal measure	Bisect each other
Rhombus	Four sides of equal length	Opposite sides are parallel	Opposite angles of equal measure	Bisect each other – angle of 90° formed

A square, rectangle and rhombus are three specific types of parallelogram.

Theorem 9

In a parallelogram, opposite sides are equal in measure and opposite angles are equal in measure.

Conversely, for a quadrilateral, if opposite sides or opposite angles are equal in measure, the quadrilateral is a parallelogram.

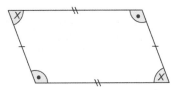

We also know that:

Theorem 10

The diagonals of a parallelogram bisect each other.

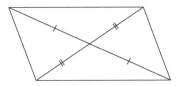

Transformations

A **transformation** changes the position and/or orientation of an object. The point or shape we start with is called the **object**. The transformed point or shape is called the **image**.

There are many different types of transformation.

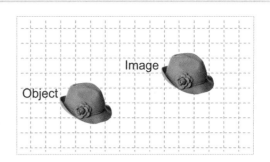

Translation

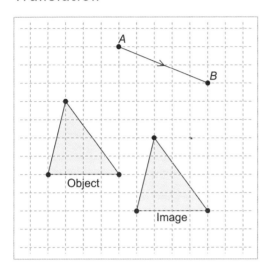

> A **translation** moves every point the same distance and in the same direction without changing the orientation.

Each point in the object shape has been moved the same distance as $|AB|$, parallel to AB and in the direction of A to B.

> Under a translation, the image shape has the same size and orientation as the object shape.

Central Symmetry (In a Point)

In a **central symmetry**, each point is mapped through some point (here O) and reflected the same distance out the other side. $|AO| = |OA'|$, $|BO| = |OB'|$ and $|CO| = |OC'|$.

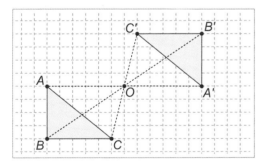

> A **central symmetry** is a reflection through a point.

Note how the image triangle $A'B'C'$ is upside-down and back-to-front when compared to the object triangle ABC.

> In a central symmetry, the image will be upside down and back-to-front in relation to the object.

Axis of Symmetry

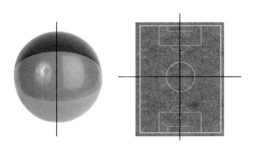

> If an imaginary line can be drawn through a shape that divides the shape into two halves that are reflections or mirror images of each other, then the shape is **symmetrical**. This imaginary line is called an **axis of symmetry**.

GEOMETRY I

Axial Symmetry (Symmetry in a Line)

In an **axial symmetry**, each point is mapped through a line (axis) at right angles and reflected the same distance out the other side.

> An **axial symmetry** is a reflection in a line or axis. The line acts as a mirror.

> In an axial symmetry, the image and object are the same distance from the axis used, and one is a mirror image of the other.

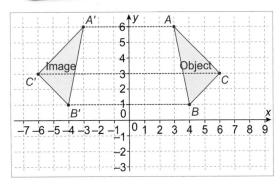

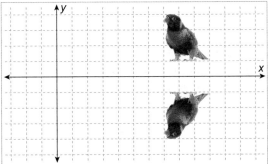

In an axial symmetry in the y-axis, each point is mapped through the y-axis and reflected out the same distance on the other side. The diagram above left shows an axial symmetry in the y-axis on object *ABC*. The diagram above right shows an axial symmetry in the x-axis.

Centre of Symmetry

Certain shapes can be mapped onto themselves under a central symmetry in a point. This point is called the **centre of symmetry**.

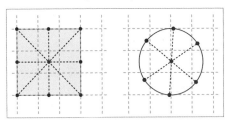

> If a shape can be mapped onto itself under a central symmetry in a point, this point is called a **centre of symmetry**.

To check if an object has a centre of symmetry, we rotate the object around a fixed point exactly 180°. If the image lands exactly on the object, then the point used is a centre of symmetry.

Not all shapes have a centre of symmetry.

These shapes have a centre of symmetry. → **S H** | **F U** ← These shapes do not have a centre of symmetry.

Exercise 18.1

1. Find the value of x and/or y in each of the following without measuring:

(i)

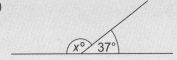

(ii)

(iii)

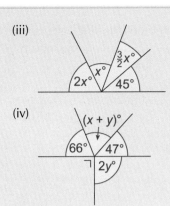

(iv)

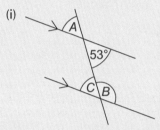

2. Find the size of each angle marked with a letter in the following diagrams. Provide reasons for your answers.

(i)

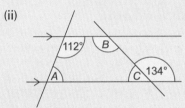

(ii)

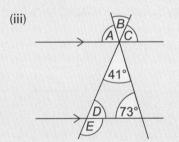

(iii)

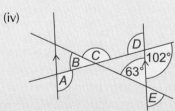

(iv)

(v)

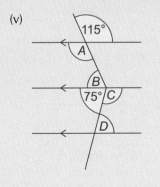

3. In your own words, explain the difference between each of the terms that follow.

Use diagrams to help your explanations where necessary.

(i) A line and a ray

(ii) Coplanar and collinear

(iii) Acute and ordinary angles

(iv) Theorem and axiom

4. Find the measure of the angles marked with letters in the following diagrams. Show as much work as possible.

(i)

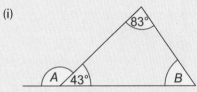

(ii)

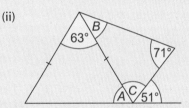

(iii)

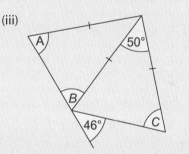

(iv)

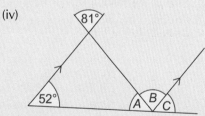

5. Find the measure of the angles A, B and C in each of the following. Show as much work as possible.

(i)

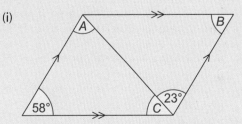

(ii)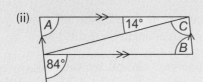

(iii)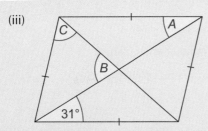

(iv)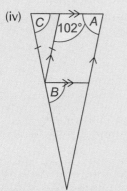

6. Consider the diagram shown:

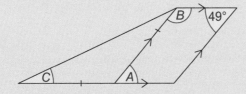

Showing all your work, calculate:

(i) $|\angle A|$ (ii) $|\angle B|$ (iii) $|\angle C|$

7. Classify each of the following pairs of angles using the diagram below. The first pair has been done for you.

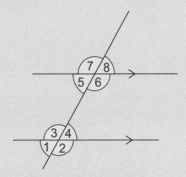

(i) $\angle 1$ and $\angle 4$: *Vertically opposite*

(ii) $\angle 3$ and $\angle 7$:

(iii) $\angle 8$ and $\angle 7$:

(iv) $\angle 5$ and $\angle 4$:

8. (a) State whether the following pairs of triangles are congruent or not. Explain your answers fully.

(i)

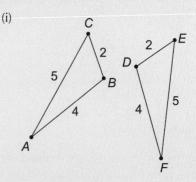

(ii) $\triangle PQT$ and $\triangle PST$

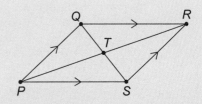

(iii) $\triangle ABF$ and $\triangle DEF$

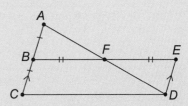

(iv) $\triangle ABE$ and $\triangle ADE$

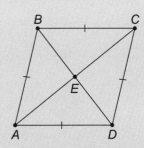

(b) Reconsider the diagrams in parts (ii) and (iv). For each diagram, write down **all** the pairs of congruent triangles you can find.

9. Identify **all** the pairs of parallel lines in the diagram below. Explain your answers fully.

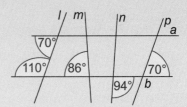

10. Draw a shape that has exactly:

   (i) two

  (ii) three

 (iii) four

axes of symmetry.

Show the axes on each of your diagrams.

11. In each of parts (i) to (vi) given on the right-hand side, show:

  (a) An axis of symmetry

  (b) The centre of symmetry (label with the letter C)

Note that some shapes may not have an axis of symmetry or a centre of symmetry.

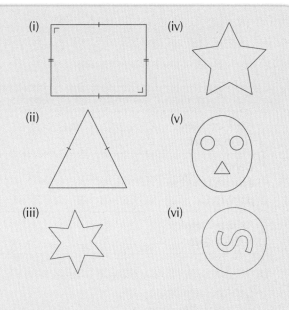

12. In each question below, three images labelled A, B and C are the images of the object under a transformation. The transformations could be a translation, an axial symmetry or a central symmetry.

For each image, state which transformation has been used.

  (i)

 (ii)

 (iii)

13. The diagram shows a rectangle *A* on the co-ordinate plane.

  (a) Copy this diagram and draw the image of rectangle *A* under the following transformations:

     (i) Axial symmetry in the x-axis

    (ii) Central symmetry in the point (0,0)

    (iii) Axial symmetry in the y-axis

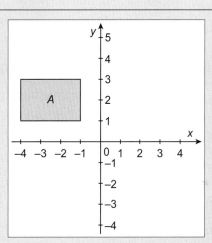

(b) Hence, write down the co-ordinates of the images of the vertices of *A* under each of the transformations.

Transformation	Co-ordinates of vertices
Axial symmetry in the *x*-axis	(,), (,), (,), (,)
Central symmetry in the point (0,0)	
Axial symmetry in the *y*-axis	

14. The diagram below shows a triangle *B* on the co-ordinate plane.

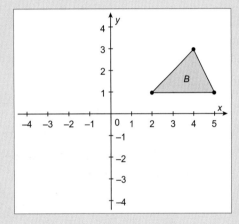

(a) Copy this diagram and draw the image of triangle *B* under the following transformations:

   (i) Axial symmetry in the *y*-axis

   (ii) Central symmetry in the point (0,0)

   (iii) A translation which maps the point (2,1) onto (0,1)

(b) Hence, write down the co-ordinates of the images of the vertices of *B* under each of the transformations.

Transformation	Co-ordinates of vertices
Axial symmetry in the *y*-axis	(,), (,), (,)
Central symmetry in the point (0,0)	
A translation which maps the point (2,1) onto (0,1)	

15. The diagram below shows parallelogram *C* on the co-ordinate plane.

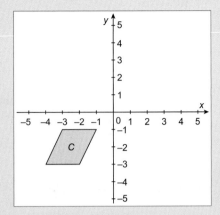

(a) Copy this diagram and draw the image of parallelogram *C* under the following transformations:

   (i) Axial symmetry in the *x*-axis

   (ii) Central symmetry in the point (–1,1)

   (iii) Axial symmetry in the *y*-axis

(b) Hence, write down the co-ordinates of the images of the vertices of *C* under each of the transformations.

Transformation	Co-ordinates of vertices
Axial symmetry in the *x*-axis	(,), (,), (,), (,)
Central symmetry in the point (–1,1)	
Axial symmetry in the *y*-axis	

16. The diagram below shows the triangle *ABC* on the co-ordinate plane.

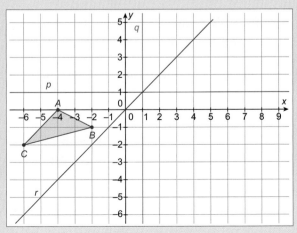

(a) Copy this diagram and draw the image of triangle *ABC* under a number of transformations:

   (i) Axial symmetry in the line *q*

   (ii) Axial symmetry in the line *p*

   (iii) Axial symmetry in the line *r*

(b) Hence, write down the co-ordinates of the images of the vertices of the triangle *ABC* under each of the transformations.

Transformation	Co-ordinates of vertices
Axial symmetry in the line *q*	
Axial symmetry in the line *p*	
Axial symmetry in the line *r*	

17. *PQRS* is a parallelogram. Find the measure of the following line segments, giving a reason in each case:

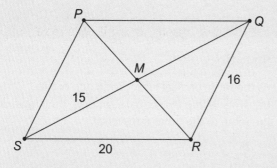

   (i) $|QP|$

   (ii) $|PS|$

   (iii) $|MQ|$

   (iv) $|SQ|$

18. Find the value of *x* and *y* in each of the following diagrams:

(i)

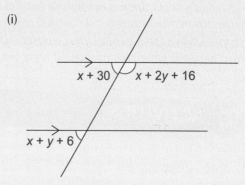

(ii)

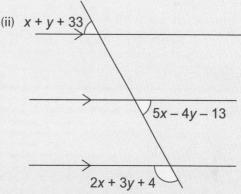

19. Find the value of *a* and *b* in each of the following parallelograms:

(i)

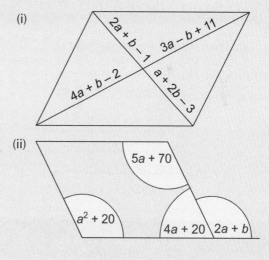

(ii)

18.2 PARALLEL LINES

We already know some properties of parallel lines that deal with the angles formed by a transversal. We will now consider (a) what happens when three parallel lines intersect a transversal and (b) what happens when that transversal is cut into two equal segments.

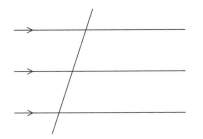

ACTIVITIES 18.1, 18.2, 18.3

From our investigations, we can determine that:

> If a transversal is cut into two equal parts by three parallel lines, then any other transversal drawn across these parallel lines will also be cut into two equal parts.

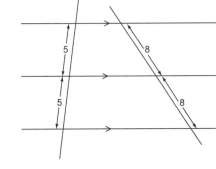

We can now state this as a theorem.

Theorem 11

If three parallel lines cut off equal segments on some transversal line, then they will cut off equal segments on any other transversal.

Worked Example 18.1

Find the length of the line segment [AB].

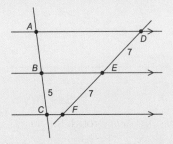

Solution

As the three parallel lines divide one of the transversals into two equal segments, they must do the same to the other transversal.

$$|BC| = 5$$
$$\therefore |AB| = 5$$

Worked Example 18.2

Find the value of a, if $|XZ| + |PR| = 24$ cm.

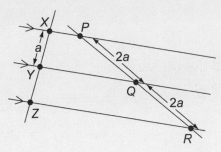

Solution

We can see that the transversal PR is cut into two equal segments. So the transversal XZ is also cut into two equal segments.

As $|XY| = a$, then $|YZ| = a$.

We can now form an equation:

$$a + a + 2a + 2a = 24$$
$$6a = 24$$
$$\therefore a = 4$$

Exercise 18.2

1. In each of the following diagrams, find the value of *x*.

(i)

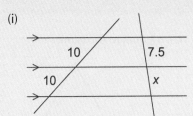

(ii)

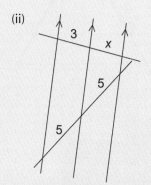

2. In each of the following diagrams, the three parallel lines cut any transversal into equal segments. Find the value of *x* and *y*.

(i)

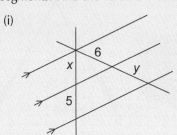

(ii)

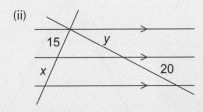

(iii)

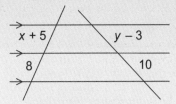

3. (i) Find the value of *x* given that $|AB| + |CD| = 56$ cm.

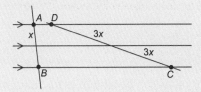

(ii) Find the value of *x* if $|DE| + |GH| = 40$ cm.

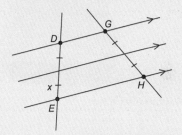

4. In the following diagram $|PS| = 9$ cm and $|TV| = 8$ cm.

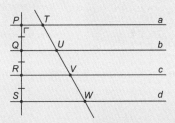

A line is drawn through the point *T*, perpendicular to the line *a*. This line intersects the lines *b*, *c* and *d* at the points *X*, *Y* and *Z* respectively. Find:

(i) $|XU|$ (ii) $|YV|$ (iii) $|ZW|$

18.3 PARALLEL LINES AND TRIANGLES

We will now investigate what happens when a line that is parallel to one side of a triangle divides another side of the triangle into a certain ratio.

ACTIVITY 18.4

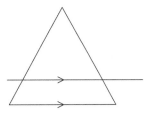

From our investigations, we know that:

> A line that is parallel to one side of a triangle cuts the other two sides of the triangle in the same ratio.

We know that if $|AX| : |XB|$ is equal to a certain ratio, then $|AY| : |YC|$ is equal to the same ratio.

This can be written more formally as:

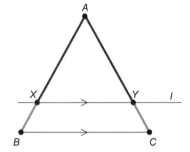

Theorem 12

Let ABC be a triangle. If a line l is parallel to BC and cuts $[AB]$ in the ratio $m : n$, then it also cuts $[AC]$ in the same ratio.

As ratios can be written as fractions, it is more common to write:

FORMULA

$$\frac{|AX|}{|XB|} = \frac{|AY|}{|YC|}$$

or

FORMULA

$$\frac{\text{Top length}}{\text{Bottom length}} = \frac{\text{Top length}}{\text{Bottom length}}$$

We can also state:

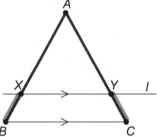

FORMULA

$$\frac{|AB|}{|XB|} = \frac{|AC|}{|YC|}$$

or

FORMULA

$$\frac{\text{Overall length}}{\text{Bottom length}} = \frac{\text{Overall length}}{\text{Bottom length}}$$

This means that the following is also true:

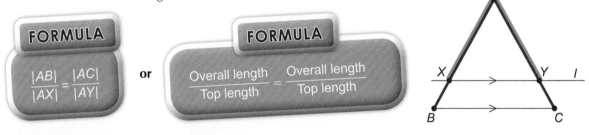

FORMULA

$$\frac{|AB|}{|AX|} = \frac{|AC|}{|AY|}$$

or

FORMULA

$$\frac{\text{Overall length}}{\text{Top length}} = \frac{\text{Overall length}}{\text{Top length}}$$

It is important to realise that all of these ratios can be inverted or turned upside down. In other words, taking the last set of ratios as an example:

$$\frac{|AX|}{|AB|} = \frac{|AY|}{|AC|}$$

$$\frac{\text{Top length}}{\text{Overall length}} = \frac{\text{Top length}}{\text{Overall length}}$$

The converse of Theorem 12 can be used to show that two lines are parallel:

> If a line cuts two sides of a triangle in the same ratio, then this line is parallel to the side not cut by the line.

Worked Example 18.3

Find the length of [PQ], given that QS ∥ RT.

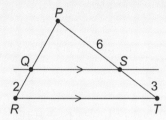

Solution

We need to find |PQ|, so we must identify what ratio to use:

> When writing the ratio, start with the side you are looking for, as this makes your calculations easier.

$$\frac{\text{Top length}}{\text{Bottom length}} = \frac{\text{Top length}}{\text{Bottom length}}$$

$$\frac{|PQ|}{2} = \frac{6}{3}$$

Cross-multiply to eliminate fractions:

$$3|PQ| = 12$$

$$\therefore |PQ| = 4$$

Worked Example 18.4

In the triangle DFH, |DH| = 12.
Find the length of [DG].

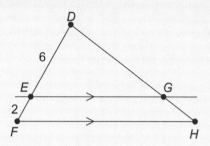

Solution

We need to find |DG|, so again we must identify which ratio we are using.

> We are looking for the top length, and we have been given the overall length of one side.

$$|DF| = |DE| + |EF|$$

$$= 6 + 2$$

$$\therefore |DF| = 8$$

$$\frac{\text{Top length}}{\text{Overall length}} = \frac{\text{Top length}}{\text{Overall length}}$$

$$\frac{|DG|}{12} = \frac{6}{8}$$

Cross-multiply: $8|DG| = 6 \times 12$

$$8|DG| = 72$$

$$\therefore |DG| = 9$$

Worked Example 18.5

Investigate if AB ∥ CD.

Solution

We will use the converse of Theorem 12:

'If a line cuts two sides of a triangle in the same ratio, then this line is parallel to the side not cut by the line.'

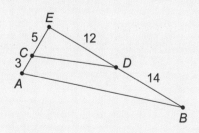

If $AB \parallel CD \Rightarrow \dfrac{\text{Top length}}{\text{Bottom length}} = \dfrac{\text{Top length}}{\text{Bottom length}}$.

But $\dfrac{5}{3} \neq \dfrac{12}{14}$, as $\dfrac{5}{3} = 1\dfrac{2}{3}$ and $\dfrac{12}{14} = \dfrac{6}{7}$.

$\therefore$ AB is not parallel to CD.

1. Find the value of x in each case.

(i)

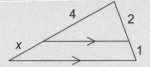

(ii)

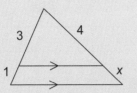

(iii)

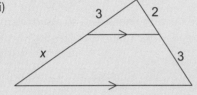

(iv)

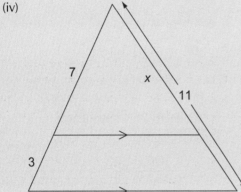

2. Find the value of y in each case.

(i)

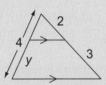

(ii)

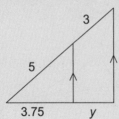

(iii)

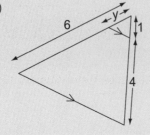

(iv)

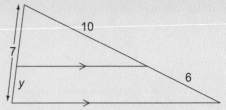

3. In the triangle PRT, $QS \parallel RT$ and $|PT| = 22.5$.

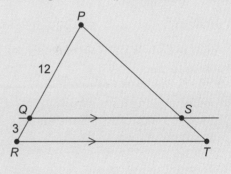

(i) $|PS|$

(ii) $|ST|$

(iii) The ratio $|PS| : |ST|$

4. In the diagram, $BC \parallel DE$ and $|AD| : |BD| = 5 : 2$.

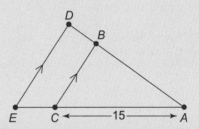

(a) If $|AC| = 15$, find:

(i) $|AB| : |BD|$ (ii) $|CE|$

(b) Is $|AD| = 5$? Explain your answer.

5. In the triangle shown, $CE \parallel BF \parallel AG$.

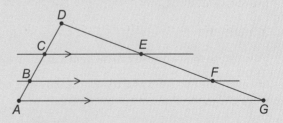

$|AB| = 2$, $|AC| = 6$ and $|AD| = 9.5$.
If $|DG| = 23.75$, find:

(i) $|DE|$ (ii) $|FG|$

6. In the diagram below, $DE \parallel BC$.
Also, $|AD| : |DB| = 5 : 2$.

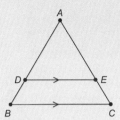

Write down the following ratios:

(i) $|AE| : |EC|$ (iii) $|EC| : |AC|$

(ii) $|AC| : |AE|$ (iv) $|AB| : |AD|$

7. In the diagram below, $XY \parallel BC$.
Also, $|AX| : |AB| = 3 : 7$.

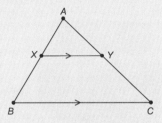

Write down the following ratios:

(i) $\dfrac{|AX|}{|XB|}$ (ii) $\dfrac{|AY|}{|YC|}$ (iii) $\dfrac{|YC|}{|AC|}$

8. Investigate if $ED \parallel BC$.

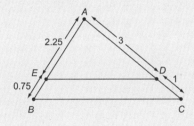

9. Investigate if $XY \parallel BC$.

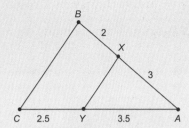

10. Earl wants to row across a lake in his dinghy from point A to point B.

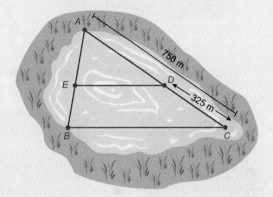

The points E, D and C represent navigation buoys placed on the lake. Earl knows that point A is 250 metres from point E. He has calculated other distances as shown on the diagram.

(i) Assuming that ED is parallel to BC, calculate the distance he rowed across the lake correct to the nearest metre.

(ii) If he rowed at an average rate of 30 metres per minute, how long did it take him to row from A to B?

18.4 FURTHER SIMILAR TRIANGLES

Two triangles are similar if they have the same angle measurements.

We have already encountered some of the properties that similar or equiangular triangles have.

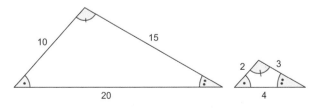

The two triangles above are similar. When we measure the corresponding sides, we discover that:

$$\frac{10}{2} = \frac{15}{3} = \frac{20}{4} = 5$$

GEOMETRY I

From this, we can state the following theorem:

Theorem 13

If two triangles are similar, then their sides are proportional, in order.

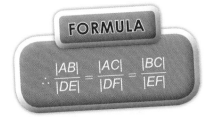

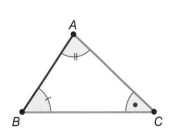

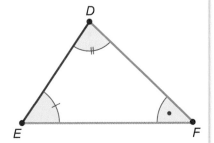

In practice, we only need to use two of the ratios to determine a missing side:

or

or

As before, these ratios can be inverted or turned upside down.

One way of showing that two triangles are similar is to show that two angles in one triangle are equal to two angles in another triangle.

For example, the two triangles shown are similar since they both contain angles of measure 50° and 60°. With only 180° in any triangle, $|\angle A| = |\angle B| = 70°$.

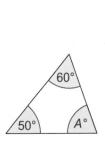

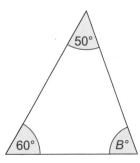

Another way of showing similarity is to use the converse of Theorem 13 which says:

If, in any two triangles, the sides (in order) are in proportion, i.e. if
$$\frac{|AB|}{|DE|} = \frac{|AC|}{|DF|} = \frac{|BC|}{|EF|}$$
then the two triangles are similar (equiangular) to each other.

Finally, it is also apparent that:

> If a triangle is cut by a line parallel to one of its sides, this line divides the triangle into two similar triangles.

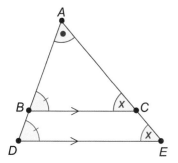
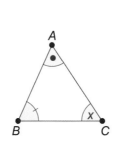
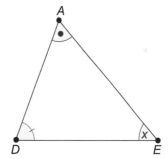

The triangle ABC is similar to the triangle ADE.

Worked Example 18.6

Given the two triangles below, find the value of x.

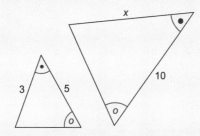

Solution

> It is always a good idea to redraw the triangles so that the corresponding sides match on the diagram.

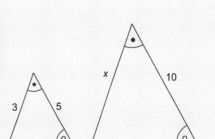

Start with our unknown and put it over the corresponding side, which we know:

$$\frac{x}{3} = \frac{10}{5}$$

Cross-multiply:

$5x = 30$

$\therefore x = 6$

Note: We could also have written:

$$\frac{x}{10} = \frac{3}{5}$$

$5x = 30$

$\therefore x = 6$

Sometimes the similar triangles are drawn one inside the other.

Worked Example 18.7

If $\triangle AEB$ is similar to $\triangle ADC$, find the value of:

    (i) $|AE|$ (ii) $|AC|$

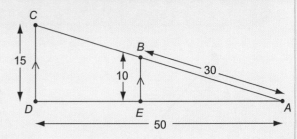

Solution

Redraw the triangles as two separate similar triangles.

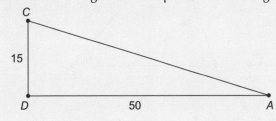
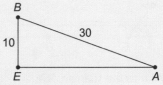

(i) $\dfrac{|AE|}{50} = \dfrac{10}{15}$

$\dfrac{|AE|}{50} = \dfrac{2}{3}$

Cross-multiply:

$3|AE| = 100$

$|AE| = \dfrac{100}{3}$

$\therefore |AE| = 33\dfrac{1}{3}$

(ii) $\dfrac{|AC|}{30} = \dfrac{15}{10}$

$\dfrac{|AC|}{30} = \dfrac{3}{2}$

Cross-multiply:

$2|AC| = 90$

$\therefore |AC| = 45$

Worked Example 18.8

Is $\triangle PQR$ similar to $\triangle PST$?

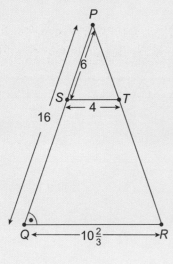

Solution

Use the converse of Theorem 13:
'If, in any two triangles, the sides (in order) are in proportion, then the two triangles are similar to each other.'

If $\triangle PQR$ is similar to $\triangle PST$, then the sides (in order) will be in proportion.

Redraw the triangles into two separate triangles.

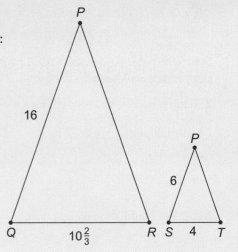

$\dfrac{|PQ|}{|PS|} = \dfrac{16}{6} = \dfrac{8}{3}$

$\dfrac{|QR|}{|ST|} = \dfrac{10\frac{2}{3}}{4} = \dfrac{8}{3}$

$\therefore \triangle PQR$ is similar to $\triangle PST$.

Worked Example 18.9

The diagram shows a person who is 1.8 m tall. Her shadow length is 5.6 m.
Find the height of the nearby tree if the person is standing 16.8 m away from the tree.

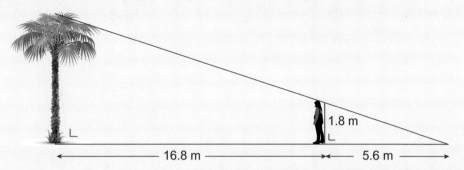

1.8 m

← 16.8 m → ← 5.6 m →

Solution

Assume that both the tree and person are standing perpendicular to the ground. We can label the unknown height of the tree as x. Use the properties of similar triangles to find the height of the tree.

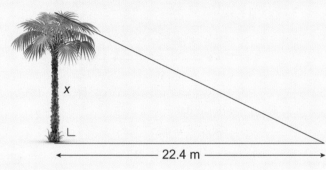

x

← 22.4 m →

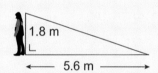

1.8 m

← 5.6 m →

$\dfrac{x}{1.8} = \dfrac{22.4}{5.6}$

$5.6x = 40.32$

$x = \dfrac{40.32}{5.6}$

$\quad = 7.2 \text{ m}$

$\therefore$ Height of tree $= 7.2$ m

 Exercise 18.4

1. Find the value of x in each case.

(i)

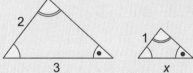

2

3

1

x

(ii)

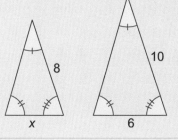

8

10

x

6

(iii)

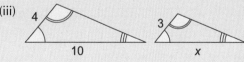

4

10

3

x

(iv)

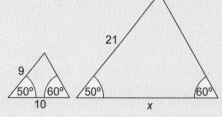

21

9

50° 60°

10

50°

x

60°

GEOMETRY I

2. Find the value of *y* in each case.

(i)

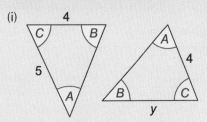

(ii)

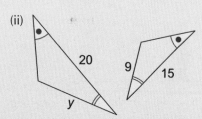

(iii)

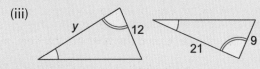

(iv)

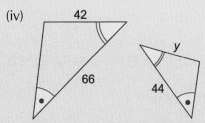

3. For each question, the triangles *ABC* and *ADE* are similar. Find the value of *x* and *y* in each case.

> We can also use Theorem 12 to help us find the required sides.

(i)

(ii)

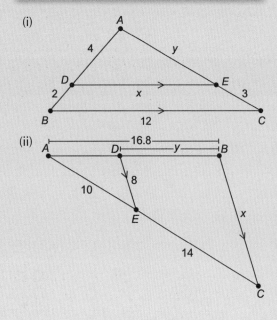

(iii)

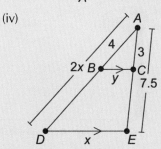

(iv)

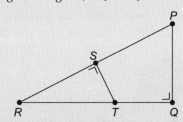

4. In the given diagram, $PQ \perp RQ$ and $ST \perp PR$.

(i) Show that the two triangles *RST* and *PQR* are similar.

Given that $|ST| = 6$, $|PQ| = 12$ and $|RT| = 10$, find:

(ii) $|PR|$ (iii) $|RQ|$ (iv) $|RS|$

5. In the given diagram, $EF \parallel GH$, $|EF| = \frac{7}{8}|DF|$.

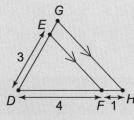

Find:

(i) $|EG|$

(ii) $|GH|$

6. In the given diagram, $|\angle ABC|$ and $|\angle EDC| = 90°$.

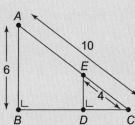

(i) Find $|BC|$.

(ii) Find $|ED|$.

(iii) Find $|DC|$.

(iv) Calculate the ratio Area $\triangle ABC$: Area $\triangle EDC$.

7. Investigate if the following triangles are similar to each other. Explain your answers.

    (i) Is △ABC similar to △ADE?

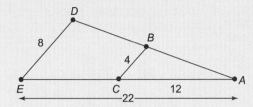

    (ii) Is △PST similar to △PQR?

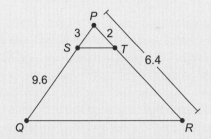

8. What value of y will make the two triangles shown similar, if x < 21 and z < y?

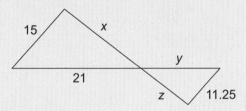

9. A building casts a shadow of length 2.1 m. At the same time, a 1 m high pole casts a shadow of length 0.75 m. How tall is the building?

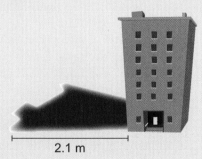

2.1 m

10. A student is 1.72 m tall and has a shadow that is 2.5 m long. A nearby tree has a shadow that is 10.5 m long.
What is the height of the tree?

11. A model for a triangular timber frame is shown.

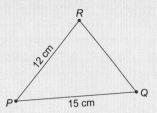

The distance between the points P and Q on the actual frame is 3 m. Find |PR| on the actual frame.

12. A girl 1.45 m tall, stands at a distance of 4.2 m from a flagpole. Her shadow is 1.2 m long. The end of her shadow and the flagpole's shadow coincide on the ground.

    (i) Draw a diagram to show this information.

    (ii) How tall is the flagpole (to the nearest cm)?

13. Abby wants to measure the height of her school building. She notices that she can see the top of her building reflected in a puddle on the ground. This puddle is 22 m away from the school building. Abby is 1.45 m tall and she is 5 m away from the puddle as shown.

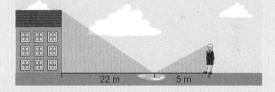

Find the height of the school building.

14. Conor wishes to measure the width of a local river. From his observations he knows that a river which is 25 m wide will carry an object 12 m downstream across to the opposite bank as shown.

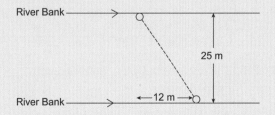

How wide is a river which will carry the same object downstream 28 m to the opposite bank?

Assume that both rivers carry the object at the same speed.

15. Harry is flying his kite and wishes to calculate how high the kite is flying. He asks his friend Paul to measure the height of the kite string when he is 1 m away from him. Paul tells Harry that the kite string is 2 m above the ground at this point. Paul then measures the distance from where Harry is standing to directly underneath the kite. If this distance is 60 m and Harry is 1.7 m tall, find:

(i) The height at which the kite is flying

(ii) The string length of the kite (to the nearest centimetre).

16. Tommy cycles from his home to his school as shown on the diagram. The journey has a total distance of 9 km. Two kilometres into his journey, he passes his local shop.

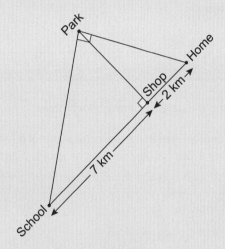

Find, to the nearest metre:

(i) The distance between the shop and the park

(ii) The distance between the school and the park

17. James is 1.85 m tall. He stands in front of a road sign that is 2.15 m high. When he stands 12 m away from the road sign, he can see that the top of the road sign just lines up with the top of his house. From where he is standing, the road sign is 38 m away from his house.

(i) Draw a suitable diagram to show the above information. (Include the fact that James is 1.85 m tall.)

(ii) Hence, find the height of his house.

18. A group of students were trying to find the distance between two trees on opposite sides of a river using pegs, a measuring tape and a large amount of string. They align the pegs in a particular way, take several measurements and sketch this diagram. On the diagram, A and B are the trees and C, D and E are the pegs.

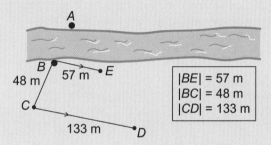

(i) In what way must the pegs and the trees be aligned if the students are to use these measurements to calculate |AB|?

(ii) Calculate the distance between the trees.

(iii) Another group of students repeats the activity. They have a similar diagram but different measurements. Their measurements are |BE| = 40 m and |BC| = 9 m. Based on the value of |AB| that the first group got, what measurement will this second group have for |CD|?

(iv) Suggest how the group of students might have ensured that [BE] was parallel to [CD].

SEC 2011, JCHL

18.5 FURTHER PYTHAGORAS' THEOREM

We have already encountered two theorems concerning right-angled triangles.

> ### Theorem 14: The theorem of Pythagoras
> In a right–angled triangle the square of the hypotenuse is equal to the sum of the squares of the other two sides.

This formula appears on page 16 of *Formulae and Tables*

$c^2 = a^2 + b^2$

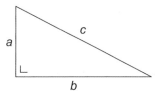

The converse of Pythagoras' theorem is also true:

> ### Theorem 15
> If the square of one side of a triangle is equal to the sum of the squares of the other two sides, then the angle opposite the first side is a right angle.

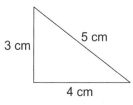

$5^2 = 3^2 + 4^2$

⇒ The angle opposite the side of 5 cm is a right angle.

 Worked Example 18.10

Find the value of x and the value of y in the diagram shown.

Solution

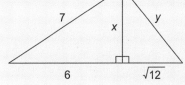

(i) Value of x

Write Pythagoras' theorem.	$h^2 = a^2 + b^2$
Write down the value of h, a and b.	$h = 7$, $a = x$, $b = 6$
Put these values into the equation.	$7^2 = x^2 + 6^2$
	$49 = x^2 + 36$
Put the unknown value on one side and everything else on the other side.	$49 - 36 = x^2$
	$13 = x^2$
Leave x in surd form.	$x = \sqrt{13}$

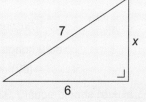

(ii) Value of y

Write Pythagoras' theorem.	$h^2 = a^2 + b^2$
Write down the value of h, a and b.	$a = \sqrt{13}$, $b = \sqrt{12}$, $h = y$
Put these values into the equation and simplify the right-hand side.	$y^2 = (\sqrt{13})^2 + (\sqrt{12})^2$
	$y^2 = 13 + 12$
	$y^2 = 25$
Solve for y.	$y = \sqrt{25}$
	$\therefore y = 5$

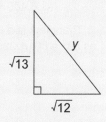

ACTIVE MATHS 2   **363**

Worked Example 18.11

Find the value of x in the following diagram.

Solution

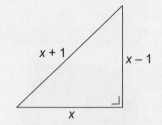

Write Pythagoras' theorem.	$h^2 = a^2 + b^2$
Fill in the values of a, b and h.	$a = x$, $b = x - 1$, $h = x + 1$
Put these values into the equation and bring all terms to one side.	$(x + 1)^2 = x^2 + (x - 1)^2$ $x^2 + 2x + 1 = x^2 + x^2 - 2x + 1$ $x^2 - 4x = 0$
Solve the equation.	$x(x - 4) = 0$ $x = 0$ **or** $x - 4 = 0$ $x = 0$ **or** $x = 4$
x cannot be equal to 0, as we would get sides of 0, 1 and –1.	$\therefore x = 4$

Worked Example 18.12

Which of the following triangles are right-angled triangles? (Triangles are not drawn to scale.)

Triangle 1

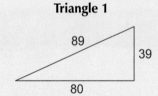

Triangle 2

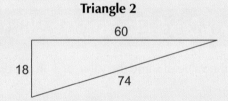

Solution

If a triangle is right-angled, then $c^2 = a^2 + b^2$.

First identify which side is the hypotenuse. The hypotenuse is always the longest side.

Triangle 1	**Triangle 2**
$c = 89$ (longest side) $\therefore c^2 = (89)^2 = 7{,}921$	$c = 74$ (longest side) $\therefore c^2 = (74)^2 = 5{,}476$
$a^2 + b^2$ should equal 7,921 if the triangle has a right angle: $a = 80 \rightarrow a^2 = (80)^2 = 6{,}400$ $b = 39 \rightarrow b^2 = (39)^2 = 1{,}521$	$a^2 + b^2$ should equal 5,476 if the triangle has a right angle: $a = 60 \rightarrow a^2 = (60)^2 = 3{,}600$ $b = 18 \rightarrow b^2 = (18)^2 = 324$
$6{,}400 + 1521 = 7{,}921$ $\therefore$ Triangle 1 is a right-angled triangle, as $89^2 = 80^2 + 39^2$.	$3{,}600 + 324 = 3{,}924$ $3{,}924 \neq 5{,}476$ $\therefore$ Triangle 2 is **NOT** a right-angled triangle, as $74^2 \neq 60^2 + 18^2$.

Worked Example 18.13

A shed roof has sloping sides at a pitch of $\theta°$. Each edge is 3 m long.

(i) Calculate the height of the shed correct to two decimal places.

(ii) Calculate the pitch of the roof correct to the nearest degree.

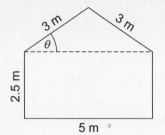

Solution

(i) Consider the roof:

$$(3)^2 = h^2 + (2.5)^2$$
$$(3)^2 - (2.5)^2 = h^2$$
$$2.75 = h^2$$
$$1.66 \approx h$$

∴ Height of shed = 1.66 + 2.5

= 4.16 m

(ii)

$$\cos\theta = \frac{2.5}{3}$$
$$\theta = \cos^{-1}\left(\frac{2.5}{3}\right)$$
$$\theta \approx 34°$$

∴ Pitch of roof = 34°

 Exercise 18.5

1. Find the value of x in each of the following triangles.
   (Answer in surd form where necessary.)

(i)

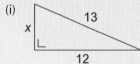

(ii)

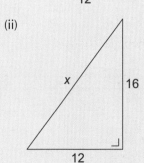

(iii)

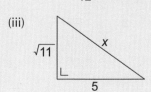

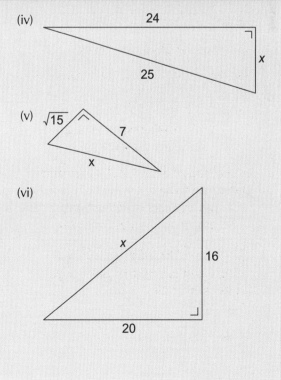

(iv)

(v)

(vi)

(vii)

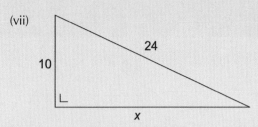

(viii)

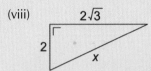

2. Find the value of *x* and *y* in each of the following triangles.
(Answer in surd form where necessary.)

(i)

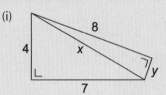

(ii)

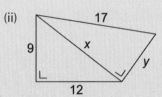

(iii)

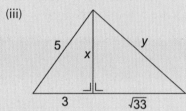

(iv)

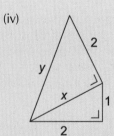

3. Find the value of *x* in each of the following shapes (to three significant figures where necessary).

(i)

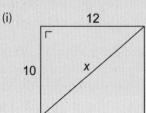

(ii)

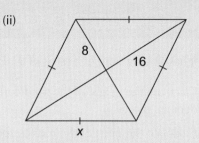

(iii)

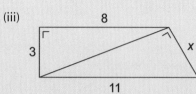

(iv)

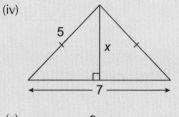

(v)

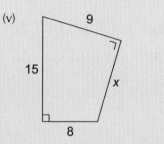

(vi)

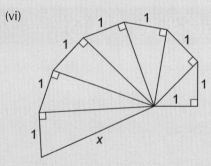

4. Four triangles are shown (not to scale). Which triangles are right-angled triangles?

(i)

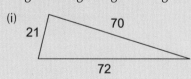

(ii)

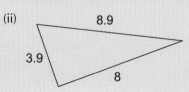

(iii)
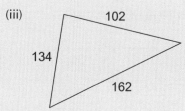

(iv)
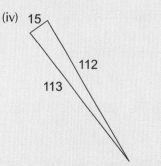

5. The side lengths of triangles are shown.
Which lengths will form right-angled triangles?

(i) 60, 63, 87   (iii) 55, 130, 148

(ii) 39, 80, 89   (iv) 64, 120, 136

6. Find the distance *AB* in each of the following
diagrams.

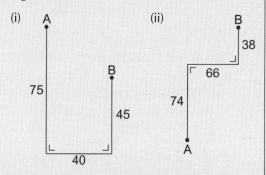

7. Using the theorem of Pythagoras, find the
value of *x* in each of the following right-angled
triangles (to two decimal places where
necessary).

(i)
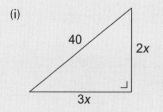

(ii)
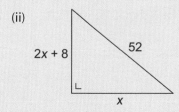

(iii)
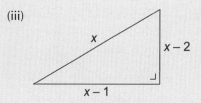

(iv)
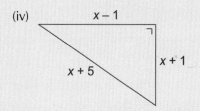

8. A ladder 2.25 m long stands on level ground
so that the top end of the ladder just reaches
the top of a wall 1.6 m high.

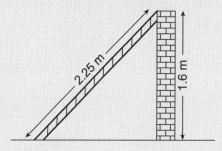

(i) How far is the foot of the ladder from the
wall to the nearest centimetre?

The ladder slips down so that its base is now
190 cm away from the wall.

(ii) How far did the ladder slip to the nearest
centimetre?

9. A Pythagorean triple is a set of three positive
integers *a*, *b* and *c* such that $a^2 + b^2 = c^2$.

(i) For what value of *p* does the set
$\{p + 4, p - 2, p + 1\}$ form a
Pythagorean triple?

(ii) Show that $\{p + 1, p + 6, p - 3\}$ does
not form a Pythagorean triple.

10. A reinforcing steel wire is designed to fit inside
a cylindrical drum with a height of 80 cm
and radius 39 cm. What is the length of the
longest wire that will fit inside the drum?

11. Two insects set off from the same position.
After two minutes one insect has crawled
40 cm due north and the other insect has
crawled 12 cm due east. To the nearest
centimetre, how far apart are the insects from
each other?

12. A cube has a side length of 3 cm. Find the length of a diagonal of the cube.

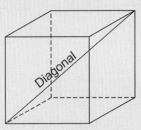

13. A rectangular garden has a length of 4.8 m and a diagonal measuring 6 m. Find:

(i) The width of the garden

(ii) The perimeter of the garden

Another rectangular garden is shown.

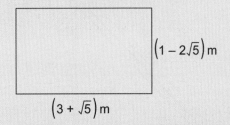

$(1 - 2\sqrt{5})$ m

$(3 + \sqrt{5})$ m

A drainage pipe is to be laid between the two opposite corners of the garden.

(iii) Find, to the nearest centimetre, the length of this pipe.

14. A cube has side lengths of 12 cm. Find, to the nearest millimetre, the radius, height and slant height of a cone that will fit exactly in this cube.

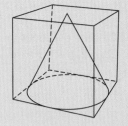

15. A truncated right-circular cone is shown.

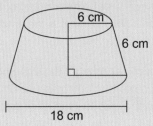

6 cm

6 cm

18 cm

Find the height of the original cone, to the nearest millimetre.

16. A room is 10 m by 8 m by 3 m.

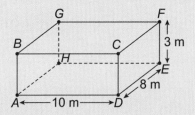

3 m

8 m

10 m

Find, to the nearest centimetre:

(i) $|AE|$　　　(ii) $|AF|$

The point P is the midpoint of $[FG]$. Find

(iii) $|BP|$　　　(iv) $|AP|$

17. A wire frame model of a pyramid, of height 30 cm, is shown.

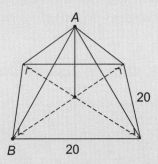

20

20

The pyramid has a square base with a side length of 20 cm. Find the length of wire needed to connect point A to point B, correct to the nearest centimetre.

18. Two ships leave a harbour at the same time. Ship A sails 9 km due west and then 18 km due north. Ship B sails 5 km due east and then 12 km north. To two significant figures:

(i) How far is ship A from the harbour?

(ii) How far is ship B from the harbour?

(iii) How far apart are the ships?

Another ship, ship C, also left the harbour at the same time and sailed 4 km due east and then 8 km due south.

(iv) How far is ship C from ship B?

(v) How far is ship C from ship A?

18.6 FURTHER CIRCLES

In *Active Maths 1*, we investigated some properties of circles:

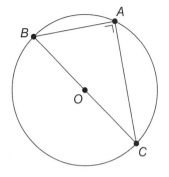

Corollary 3
Each angle in a semicircle is a right angle.

Corollary 4
If the angle standing on a chord [BC] at some point of the circle is a right angle, then [BC] is a diameter.

Using this knowledge, we can now investigate some further properties of circles.

(a) Angle at the Centre of a Circle Compared with the Angle at Any Point of the Circle

ACTIVITIES 18.6, 18.7

The circle in the diagram shown contains the angles BOC (angle at the centre) and BAC (angle at the circle):

From our investigations, we can see that:

The angle at the centre of the circle is twice the measure of the angle at the circle.

FORMULA

$$|\angle BOC| = 2|\angle BAC|$$

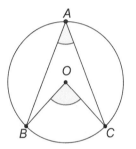

This leads us to state the following theorem:

Theorem 19
The angle at the centre of a circle standing on a given arc is twice the angle at any point of the circle standing on the same arc.

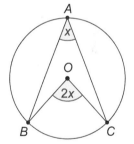

(b) Two Angles on a Circle Standing on the Same Arc

We can use Theorem 19 to explore what happens when we compare two angles on a circle standing on the same arc.

In the diagram, both angles at B and D are on the same arc, AC.

From our investigations, we can see that:

Corollary 2
All angles at points of a circle, standing on the same arc, are equal in measure.

Note: Corollary 2 is a corollary of Theorem 19.

ACTIVITIES 18.8, 18.9

GEOMETRY I

18

The converse of this corollary also applies:

> If the angles at points of the circle are equal, then they must be standing on the same arc.

(c) Cyclic Quadrilaterals

In our work with circles, we will sometimes meet a shape called a cyclic quadrilateral.

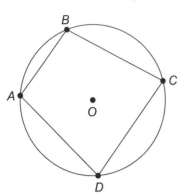

> A quadrilateral in which all four vertices (corners) are points on a circle is referred to as a **cyclic quadrilateral**.

We can now explore the special property that the angles in a cyclic quadrilateral have.

From these investigations, we know that:

ACTIVITY 18.10

> The **opposite angles** in a cyclic quadrilateral add up to 180°.

FORMULA

$|\angle A| + |\angle C| = 180°$. Also, $|\angle B| + |\angle D| = 180°$.

From this, we can now state the following corollary of Theorem 19:

Corollary 5

If *ABCD* is a cyclic quadrilateral, then opposite angles sum to 180°.

The converse of this corollary is also true and states:

> If the opposite angles of a quadrilateral sum to 180°, then it is cyclic, i.e. the vertices of the quadrilateral will lie on a circle.

> This corollary sometimes gets confused with the theorem on opposite angles in a parallelogram (Theorem 9). Remember that in a cyclic quadrilateral, the opposite angles add up to 180°. In a parallelogram, opposite angles are equal.

Worked Example 18.14

In the following circle with centre O, find:

(i) $|\angle A|$ (ii) $|\angle B|$

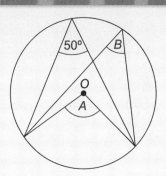

Solution

(i) $|\angle A| = 2 \times 50°$ (angle at the centre)

    $\therefore |\angle A| = 100°$

(ii) $|\angle B| = 50°$ (angles standing on the same arc)

Worked Example 18.15

Work out the measure of $\angle 1$ and of $\angle 2$ in the following circle with centre O.

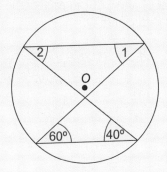

Solution

If you are not sure which arc to use, try colouring in the arc to make it easier to identify.

$|\angle 1| = 40°$
(angles standing on the same arc [red])

$|\angle 2| = 60°$
(angles standing on the same arc [blue])

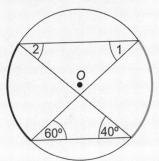

Worked Example 18.16

Find $|\angle ABC|$ and $|\angle ADC|$ in the following circle with centre O.

Solution

(i) $|\angle ABC| = 120° \div 2$ (angle at the centre)

    $\therefore |\angle ABC| = 60°$

(ii) $|\angle ABC| + |\angle ADC| = 180°$ (cyclic quadrilateral)

    $|\angle ADC| = 180° - 60°$

    $\therefore |\angle ADC| = 120°$

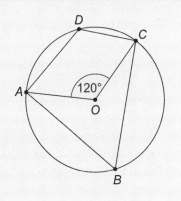

GEOMETRY I

1. Find the measure of ∠A in each of the following circles with centre O.

(i)

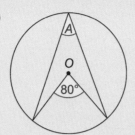

(ii)

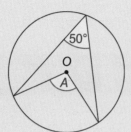

(iii)

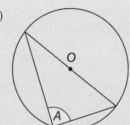

(iv)

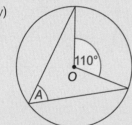

(v)

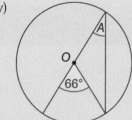

(vi)

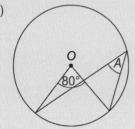

(vii)

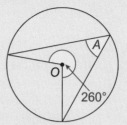

(viii)

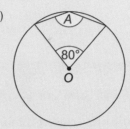

2. Find |∠A| and |∠B| in each of the following circles with centre O.

(i)

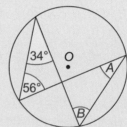

(ii)

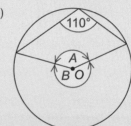

(iii)

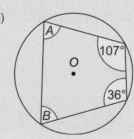

(iv)

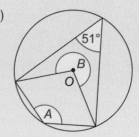

(v)

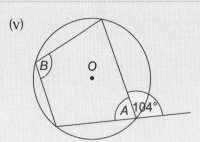

(v)

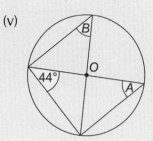

(vi)

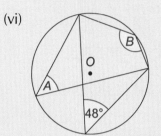

(vi)

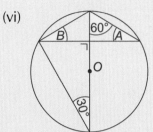

3. Find $|\angle A|$ and $|\angle B|$ in each of the following circles with centre O.

(i)

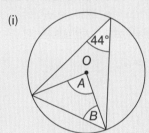

(ii)

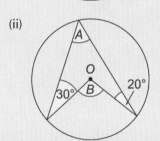

(iii)

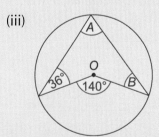

(iv)

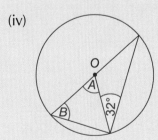

4. Find the measure of each angle labelled in the following diagrams. Remember to show as much work as possible. O is the centre in each case.

(i)

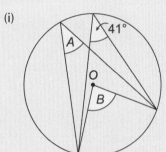

(ii)

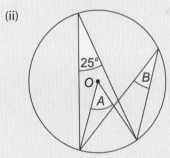

(iii)

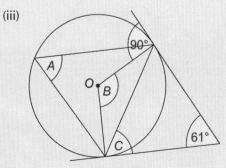

(iv)

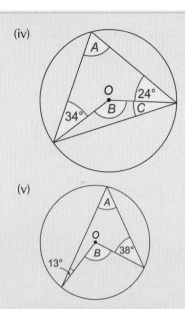

(v)

5. Identify which of the following quadrilaterals could be inscribed in a circle. In case case, give a reason for your answer.

(i)

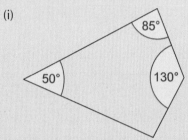

(ii)

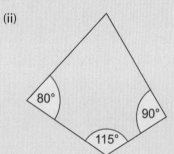

(iii)

(iv)

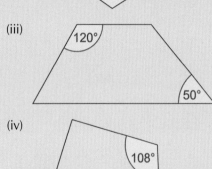

6. In the diagram shown, O is the centre of the circle.

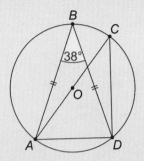

$|AB| = |BD|$ and $|\angle ABD| = 38°$

Find:

(i) $|\angle ACD|$ (iii) $|\angle ADB|$

(ii) $|\angle CDA|$ (iv) $|\angle DAC|$

7. Consider the following circle, in which O is the centre. C, O, D and E are collinear.

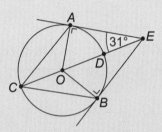

Find:

(i) $|\angle AOB|$ (obtuse) (iii) $|\angle OBC|$

(ii) $|\angle ACO|$ (iv) $|\angle ADB|$ (obtuse)

8. Consider the following diagram, in which O is the centre of the circle. P, O and R are collinear.

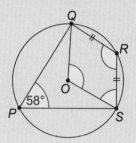

Find:

(i) $|\angle QOS|$ (iii) $|\angle RSO|$

(ii) $|\angle QRS|$ (iv) $|\angle PQO|$

9. Explain what type of parallelogram can be inscribed in a circle.

10. A design for a flag with a five-pointed star inscribed in a circle is shown. All sides of the star are of equal length.

What is the measure of the angle *A* in each point of this star?

11. Daniel attends a school musical. The stage and the first six rows of seats are shown in a diagram.

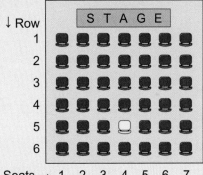

Daniel decides that the best place to sit is in Row 5 Seat 4, as this gives the best viewing angle. Unfortunately, someone has already taken this seat.

Explain where else Daniel could sit to have the same viewing angle.

Revision Exercises

1. (a) Find the value of *x* and *y* in the following diagrams.

(i)

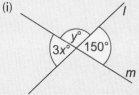

(ii)

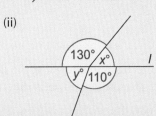

(iii)

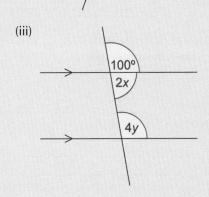

(iv)

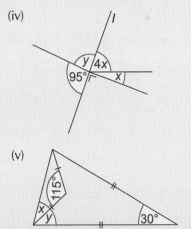

(v)

(b) In the diagram $XY \parallel BC$.

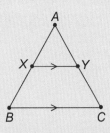

If $|AX| : |XB| = 3 : 5$,
find the ratio $|AC| : |YC|$.

2. (a) In each of the following diagrams, write down two equations in x and y. Using these equations, find the value of x and the value of y.

(i)

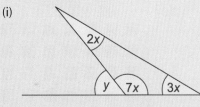

(ii)

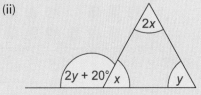

(iii)

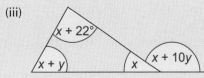

(iv)

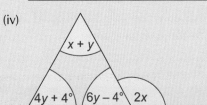

(b) In each of the following diagrams, find the value of a and the value of b.

(i)

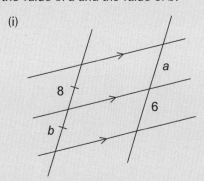

(ii)

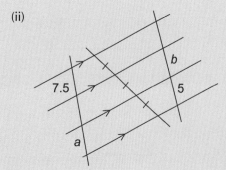

3. (a) In each of the following diagrams, write down two equations in x and y. Using these equations, find the value of x and the value of y.

(i)

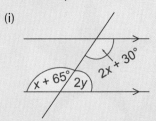

(ii)

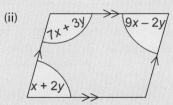

(iii)

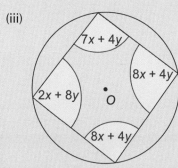

(b) A flag is lowered to half-mast.

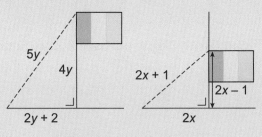

(i) Calculate the height of the flagpole.

(ii) Calculate the height of the flag at half-mast (as shown in diagram).

(iii) Was the flag correctly lowered to half-mast? Explain your answer.

4. (a) Find $|\angle A|$, $|\angle B|$ and $|\angle C|$ in each of the following diagrams.

(i)

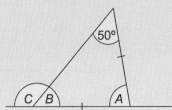

(ii)

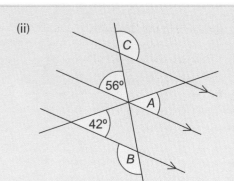

(iii)

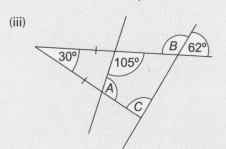

(iv)

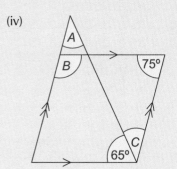

(v)

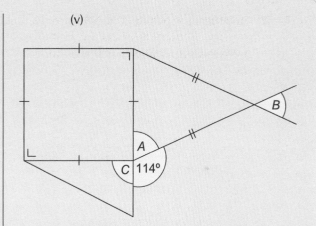

(b) In the triangle ABC, $[DE]$ is parallel to $[BC]$.

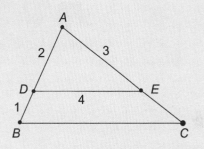

(i) Draw $\triangle ABC$ and $\triangle ADE$ separately.

(ii) Show that $\triangle ABC$ and $\triangle ADE$ are equiangular.

(iii) Find $|EC|$.

(iv) Find $|BC|$.

5. (a) Find the value of x and y in each of the following triangles.

(i)

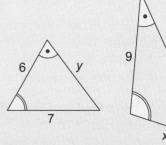

(iii)

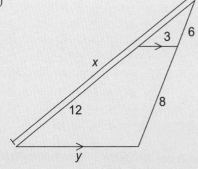

(ii)

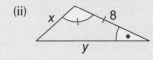 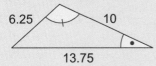

(iv)

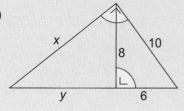

(b) An antenna is placed 20 m away from a building as shown in the diagram.

Calculate the height of the building.

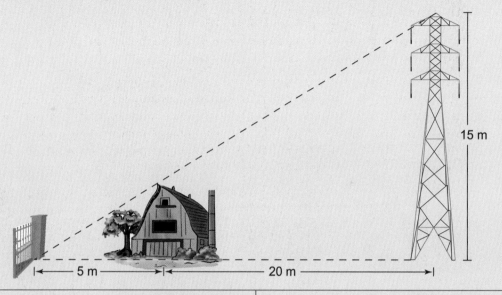

5 m   20 m   15 m

6. (a) Investigate if the following lines are parallel:

(i) Is BC ∥ DE?

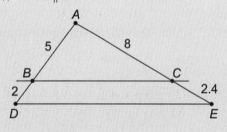

(ii) Is RQ ∥ TS?

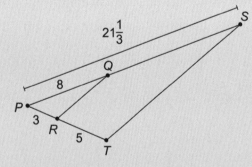

(b) Investigate if the following triangles are similar:

(i) Is △ECD similar to △ABE?

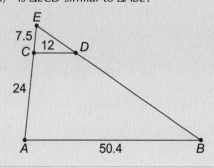

(ii) Is △FGH similar to △DEH?

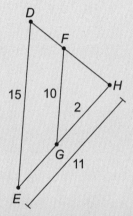

(c) Sinéad takes her homework down from the board. When she starts her homework, she realises that she must have taken one of the questions down incorrectly.

Question 1

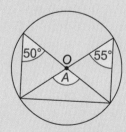

Question 2

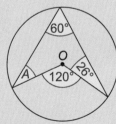

(i) Which question did Sinéad take down incorrectly? Give a reason for your answer.

(ii) Find the value of A in the correct question.

7. (a) Calculate $|\angle A|$ and $|\angle B|$ in each of the following circles with centre O.

(i)

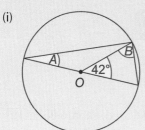

(ii)

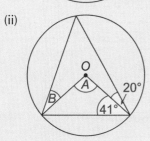

(iii) Note: $|XY| = |XZ|$.

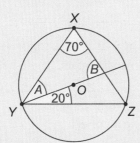

(iv)

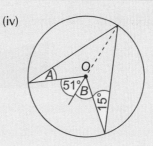

(b) Sharon measures the shadow of a tree and notices that it is 10 m long. She then measures the shadow of her friend and notices that it is 4 m long.

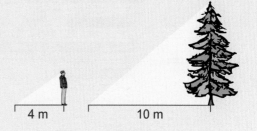

If her friend is 1.6 m tall, how tall is the tree?

8. (a) In each of the following diagrams, find the value of x and the value of y. (Answer in surd form where necessary.)

(i)

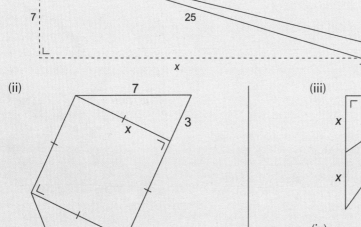

(ii)

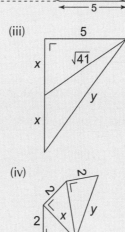

(iii)

(iv)

(b) A car drives up a hill with a gradient or slope of 1 : 5 or $\frac{1}{5}$.

The car travels a distance of 650 m.

Find the height (h) of the hill, correct to the nearest metre.

9. (a) Monica has a set of nine coloured plastic strips (long red, middle red, short red, etc.) as shown below. The strips can be joined together by pins through small holes at their ends.

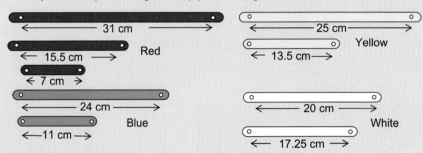

(i) Is it possible to make an isosceles triangle using any three of the nine strips? Explain your answer.

(ii) Monica would like to join four strips together to form a parallelogram. Explain why it is not possible to do this.

(iii) The long yellow, long blue and short red strips are used to form a triangle. Monica thinks that this might be a right-angled triangle. Investigate if she is correct.

(iv) Monica uses the long blue and the long white strips to form the arms of a right angle. Find the length of a strip that would be needed to complete this triangle. Give your answer correct to two places of decimals.

(b) A surveyor wants to calculate the distance across a lake. The lake is surrounded by woods. Three paths have been constructed to provide access to the lake from a road AC as shown in the diagram.

The lengths of the paths from the road to the lake are as follows:

$|AE| = 120$ m

$|BE| = 80$ m

$|CD| = 200$ m

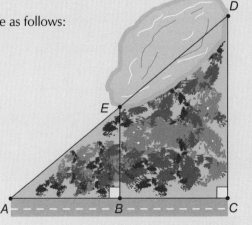

(i) Explain how these measurements can be used to find $|ED|$.

(ii) Calculate $|ED|$, the distance across the lake.

SEC Sample Paper, JCHL

10. (a) A barrel of oil is tipped onto its side as shown. Calculate the depth (*d*) of the oil.

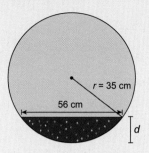

r = 35 cm

56 cm

d

(b) Mary is thinking of buying a new television. The television is advertised as having a '40-inch' screen. This refers to the diagonal measurement of the screen. The *aspect ratio* of a television screen is the ratio of its width to its height. For this television, the aspect ratio is 16 : 9 (sixteen units wide for every nine units in height).

(i) Convert 40 inches to centimetres if 1 inch = 2.54 cm.

(ii) Find the width and the height of the screen, in centimetres. Give your answers correct to the nearest cm.

(iii) A different 40-inch television screen has an aspect ratio of 4 : 3. Which of the two television screens has the greatest area, and by how much?

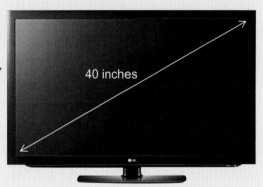

40 inches

SEC 2011, JCHL

11. (a) (i) Draw a shape that has exactly two axes of symmetry. Show the axes on the diagram.

(ii) Draw a shape that has exactly three axes of symmetry. Show the axes on the diagram.

(iii) Draw a shape that has exactly four axes of symmetry. Show the axes on the diagram.

(b) Each of the four diagrams A, B, C and D show the object in **Figure 1** and its image under a transformation. For each of A, B, C and D, state one transformation (translation, axial symmetry or central symmetry) that will map the object onto that image.

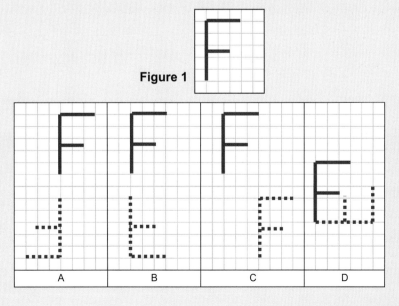

Figure 1

| A | B | C | D |

SEC Sample Paper, JCHL

(c) If $l_1 \parallel l_2$, find the angles α, β and γ in the following diagram.

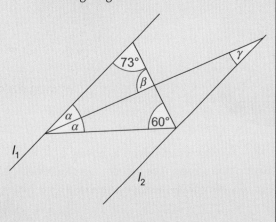

SEC Sample Paper, JCHL

(d) (i) Find $|AB|$ in surd form in the following diagram.

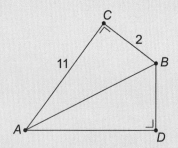

(ii) If $|AD| = 2|BD|$, find $|BD|$. (Let $|BD| = x$.)

chapter 19

Geometry II: Proofs

Learning Outcomes

In this chapter you will:

- Learn about and be able to use the following terms: *axiom*, *theorem*, *proof*, *corollary*, *converse* and *implies*

- Answer questions that concern proofs based on theorems 4, 6, 9, 14 and 19

- Learn the formal proofs of Theorems 4, 6, 9, 14 and 19

- Learn about Corollary 1: A diagonal divides a parallelogram into two congruent triangles

19.1 FORMAL PROOFS

When studying geometry, we must be able to understand and use certain terms: **axiom**, **theorem**, **proof**, **corollary**, **converse** and **implies**.

An **axiom** is a rule or statement that we accept as true without any proof.

KEY WORDS
- Axiom
- Theorem
- Proof
- Corollary
- Converse
- Implies

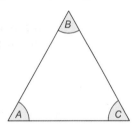 180°

Example:
There are 180 degrees in a straight angle.

A **theorem** is a rule or statement that you may be able to prove by following a certain number of logical steps or by using a previous theorem or axiom that you already know.

Example:
The angles in any triangle add to 180°.

$|\angle A| + |\angle B| + |\angle C| = 180°$

The Greek mathematician Euclid (fl. 300 BC) is known as the 'Father of Geometry'.

A **proof** is a series of logical steps that we use to show that a theorem is true.

To prove:

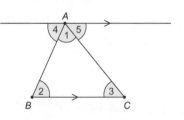

Statement	Reason
$|\angle 4| + |\angle 1| + |\angle 5| = 180°$	Straight angle
$|\angle 4| = |\angle 2|$	Alternate angles
$|\angle 5| = |\angle 3|$	Alternate angles
$\Rightarrow |\angle 4| + |\angle 1| + |\angle 5| = |\angle 2| + |\angle 1| + |\angle 3|$	As $|\angle 4| = |\angle 2|$ and $|\angle 5| = |\angle 3|$
$\therefore |\angle 1| + |\angle 2| + |\angle 3| = 180°$	

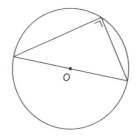

A **corollary** is a statement that follows readily from a previous theorem. Often, a corollary is a statement of a theorem in a more specific context.

Example:
In the previous chapter, we studied the theorem that in a circle, the angle at the centre, standing on a given arc, is twice the angle at any point of the circle, standing on the same arc. A corollary of this theorem is that each angle in a semicircle is a right angle.

The **converse** of a statement is formed by reversing the order in which the statement is made. For example: Statement: If P, then Q.

Converse: If Q, then P.

Statement: If a triangle is a right-angled triangle, **then** the square of the hypotenuse is equal to the sum of the squares of the other two sides.

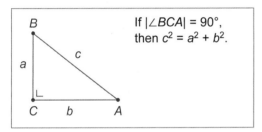

If $|\angle BCA| = 90°$, then $c^2 = a^2 + b^2$.

Converse: If the sum of the squares of the two shortest sides in a triangle is equal to the square of the longest side, **then** the triangle is right-angled.

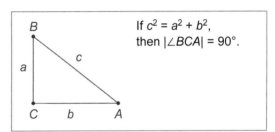

If $c^2 = a^2 + b^2$, then $|\angle BCA| = 90°$.

The converse of Pythagoras' theorem (shown above) is true.

However, the converse of a statement may not be true.

Example:
Statement – If a figure is a square then it is a quadrilateral. (True)
Converse – If a figure is a quadrilateral then it is a square. (False)

ACTIVITY 19.1

'Implies' is a term we can use in a proof when we write down a fact or conclusion that follows from previous statements.

$\Rightarrow$ is the symbol for 'implies'.

Example:
A car of type A breaks down less often than a car of type B.
$\Rightarrow$ Type A is a more reliable car.

Proofs

When you are asked for a proof in geometry, there are certain steps that you should follow.

Theorem: If asked to prove a certain theorem, write down its title.

Given: Write down the information that has been given in the question. Also draw any diagrams that are given in the question.

To prove: Write down what you need to prove. It helps to know the properties of what you are trying to prove. If you need to prove that a figure is a square, then it is necessary to know the properties of a square.

Construction: You may need extra lines or angles to help you to prove the theorem. Construct these lines or angles and label them clearly in your diagram.

Proof: Write down one reason or statement per line which will go towards proving what you have been asked to prove.

When writing down statements in the proof section, you should always try to give a reason for the statement, whether you have been given this information or whether you have used some theorem or corollary or earlier statement.

Statement	Reason
$|\angle A| = |\angle B|$	Vertically opposite angles

You can finish your proof by writing **Q.E.D.**

> **Q.E.D.** stands for the Latin phrase *Quod erat demonstrandum*, which means 'what was to be proved'. It is a short-hand way of saying 'it has been shown' and signals the successful end of the proof.

Worked Example 19.1

Prove that △*ABC* is congruent to △*DEF*.

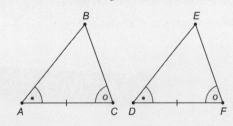

Solution

Given: Triangle *ABC* and triangle *DEF* with $|\angle A| = |\angle D|$, $|\angle C| = |\angle F|$ and $|AC| = |DF|$.

> Draw the diagram that is given in the question.

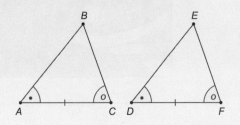

To prove: Triangle *ABC* is congruent to triangle *DEF*.

> This can also be written as △*ABC* ≡ △*DEF*.

Construction: None.

Proof:

Statement	Reason
$|\angle A| = |\angle D|$	Given
$|\angle C| = |\angle F|$	Given
$|AC| = |DF|$	Given
⇒ △*ABC* ≡ △*DEF*	ASA
Q.E.D.	

ACTIVITY 19.2

GEOMETRY II: PROOFS

Worked Example 19.2

Prove that △PQR is similar to △RST.

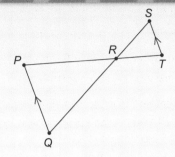

Solution

Given: Triangle PQR and triangle RST with PQ ∥ ST.

To prove: △PQR is similar to △RST.

Construction: Label angles 1, 2, 3 and 4.

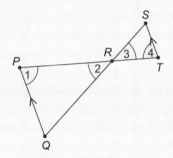

> It is sometimes easier to use |∠1| instead of |∠QPR|. You must put these labels onto the diagram you have drawn.

Proof:

Statement	Reason
|∠2| = |∠3|	Vertically opposite angles
|∠1| = |∠4|	Alternate angles
⇒ △PQR is similar to △RST	Two pairs of angles equal ⇒ equiangular triangles
Q.E.D.	

Exercise 19.1

1. In your own words, write down what each of the following terms mean. Give an example in each case.

    (i) Axiom   (iii) Proof   (v) Converse

    (ii) Theorem   (iv) Corollary

2. Give an example of:

    (i) A statement that is true and of which the converse is also true.

    (ii) A statement that is true and of which the converse is false.

3. Copy and complete the following table. One answer has been done for you.

Statement	Converse	Converse is True/False
If the largest angle in a triangle is obtuse, then the two smaller angles are acute.	If the two smaller angles in a triangle are acute, then the largest angle is obtuse.	False
If two triangles are congruent, then they are similar.		
If a triangle is equilateral, then it is also isosceles.		
If a number is divisible by 6, then it is also divisible by 3.		

4. *l* and *m* are two parallel lines. |AC| = |DE|.
Prove that △ABC ≡ △DBE.

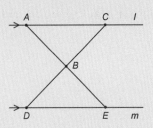

5. Consider the following circle of centre *R* with
the chords [PQ] and [ST].

  (i) Prove that △PQR and
      △SRT are congruent.

  (ii) Prove that |PT| = |QS|.

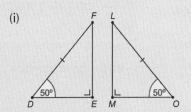

6. Prove that the following pairs of triangles are
congruent to each other.

  (i)

  (ii)

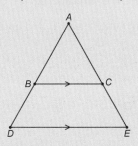

(iii)

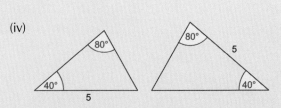

(iv)

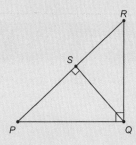

7. (i) Is △ABC similar to △ADE?

   Explain your answer clearly.

  (ii) Is △PQS similar to △RSQ?

   Explain your answer clearly.

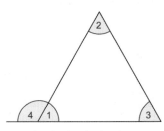

19.2 THEOREMS 4 AND 6

Theorem 4
The angles in any triangle add to 180°.

Theorem 6
Each exterior angle of a triangle is equal to
the sum of the interior opposite angles.

|∠1| + |∠2| + |∠3| = 180°
and
|∠4| = |∠2| + |∠3|

ACTIVITIES 19.3, 19.4

Worked Example 19.3

Prove that $|BC| = |DC|$.

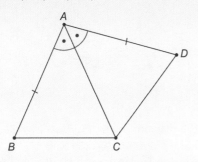

Construction: Label angles 1 and 2.

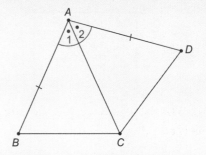

Solution

Given: A quadrilateral $ABCD$ as shown.

> **'As shown'** is a good phrase to use rather than writing out all the other bits of information present on the diagram.

To prove: $|BC| = |DC|$.

Proof: Consider $\triangle ABC$ and $\triangle ACD$.

Statement	Reason
$|AB| = |AD|$	Given
$|\angle 1| = |\angle 2|$	Given
$|AC| = |AC|$	Common side
$\Rightarrow \triangle ABC \equiv \triangle ADC$	SAS
$\Rightarrow |BC| = |CD|$	Corresponding sides
Q.E.D.	

Worked Example 19.4

The triangle ABC is an isosceles triangle, such that $|AB| = |AC|$. X is any point on $[AC]$, $X \neq A, C$.

Prove that $|\angle AXB| > |\angle ABC|$.

Solution

Given: Triangle ABC as shown.

To prove: $|\angle AXB| > |\angle ABC|$.

Construction: Label angles 1, 2, 3 and 4.

Proof:

Statement	Reason
$|\angle 2| = |\angle 4|$	Isosceles triangle
$|\angle 1| = |\angle 2| + |\angle 3|$	Exterior angle
$\Rightarrow |\angle 1| = |\angle 4| + |\angle 3|$	As $|\angle 2| = |\angle 4|$
$\Rightarrow |\angle 1| > |\angle 4|$	Since $|\angle 1| = |\angle 4| +$ more
Q.E.D.	

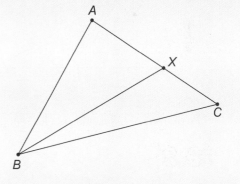

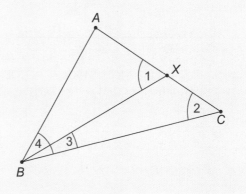

Exercise 19.2

1. *ABCD* is a square. Prove that $|\angle ACB| = 45°$.

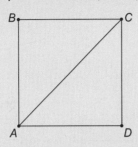

2. In the diagram below, $|XY| = |XZ| = |XW|$.
Prove that $|\angle YZW| = 90°$.

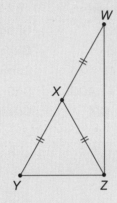

3. Prove that $|\angle ABC| > |\angle CDB|$.

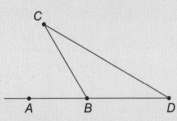

4. *PQS* is a triangle.
Prove that $\triangle PQR$ is an isosceles triangle.

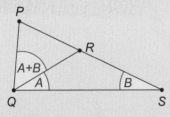

5. *BCD* is a triangle. $|\angle ABC| = |\angle CDE|$.
Prove that $|\angle CBD| = |\angle CDB|$.

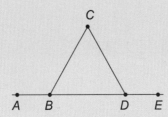

6. Prove that $|\angle BCE| = |\angle CED| + |\angle ABC|$.

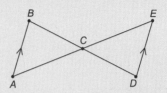

7. In the diagram below, *PQR* is a triangle.
X is any point on [*PR*], $X \neq R$, *P*.
Prove that $|\angle PXQ| > |\angle PRQ|$.

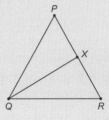

8. Prove that $|\angle DCB| = 90° + \dfrac{|\angle ABC|}{2}$.

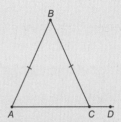

9. Consider the following diagram.
$|AE| = |AD|$ and $|AB| = |AC|$.
Prove that $\triangle ABE \equiv \triangle ACD$.

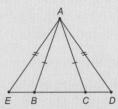

10. $\triangle ABC$ is an isosceles triangle, such that
$|AB| = |AC|$. Also, *M* is the midpoint of [*BC*].

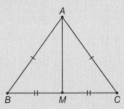

   (i) Prove that $\triangle ABM$ and $\triangle ACM$ are congruent.

   (ii) Show that $|\angle AMB| = |\angle AMC|$.

   (iii) Prove that $AM \perp BC$.

11. Prove that $|\angle 1| + |\angle 2| + |\angle 3| = 360°$.

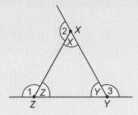

12. $\triangle PQR$ is an isosceles triangle. $|PQ| = |PR|$. $SY \perp QR$.

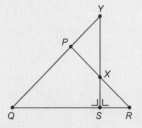

   (i) Prove that $\triangle XYP$ is also an isosceles triangle.

   (ii) Find a value for $\angle PQR$ that would make $\triangle PXY$ equilateral.

13. In the diagram below, $|AB| = |AC|$ and $|BC| = |CD|$. Prove that $|\angle ABC| = 2|\angle CDB|$.

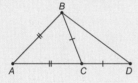

14. Prove that $|\angle PSQ| + |\angle QSR| = 90°$.

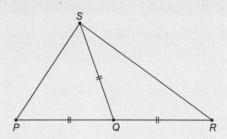

15. ABC is an isosceles triangle with $|AB| = |AC|$. $[BA]$ is produced to D. AE is parallel to BC.

   (a) Prove that $[AE$ bisects $\angle DAC$.

   (b) Would the result in part (a) still apply if $|AB|$ and $|AC|$ were not equal? Give a reason for your answer.

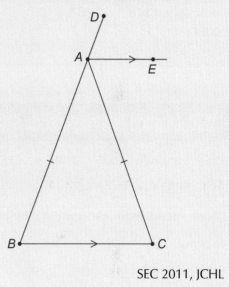

SEC 2011, JCHL

19.3 THEOREM 9

ACTIVITY 19.5

Theorem 9

In a parallelogram, opposite sides are equal in length and opposite angles are equal in measure.

In the parallelogram, $|\angle A| = |\angle C|$ and $|\angle B| = |\angle D|$.
Also, $|AB| = |CD|$ and $|BC| = |AD|$.

Corollary 1

A diagonal divides a parallelogram into two congruent triangles.

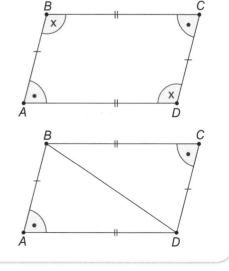

In the diagram shown $\triangle ABD \equiv \triangle BCD$ Reason: (SAS)

Worked Example 19.5

Prove that in the parallelogram *PQRS*, Δ*PXQ* ≡ Δ*SXR*.

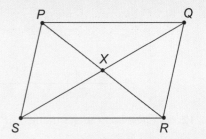

Solution

Given: A parallelogram *PQRS* as shown.

To prove: Δ*PXQ* ≡ Δ*SXR*.

Construction: Label angles 1, 2, 3 and 4.

Proof:

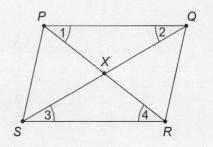

Statement	Reason
|∠1| = |∠4|	Alternate angles
|∠2| = |∠3|	Alternate angles
|*PQ*| = |*SR*|	Opposite sides in a parallelogram
⇒ Δ*PXQ* ≡ Δ*SXR*	ASA
Q.E.D.	

Worked Example 19.6

ABCD is a parallelogram. \|∠*BAE*\| = \|∠*FCD*\|. Prove that \|*FB*\| = \|*DE*\|.

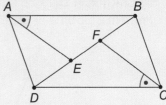

Solution

Given: Parallelogram *ABCD* with \|∠*BAE*\| = \|∠*FCD*\|.

To prove: \|*FB*\| = \|*DE*\|.

Construction: Label angles 1, 2, 3 and 4.

Proof:

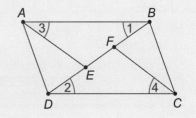

Statement	Reason
|∠1| = |∠2|	Alternate angles
|*AB*| = |*DC*|	Opposite sides in a parallelogram
|∠3| = |∠4|	Given
⇒ Δ*ABE* ≡ Δ*DFC*	ASA
|*EB*| = |*DF*|	Corresponding sides
|*EB*| = |*EF*| + |*FB*|	Obviously (Axiom)
|*DF*| = |*DE*| + |*EF*|	Obviously (Axiom)
⇒ |*EF*| + |*FB*| = |*DE*| + |*EF*|	Since |*EB*| = |*DF*|
⇒ |*FB*| = |*DE*|	Subtracting |*EF*| from both sides
Q.E.D.	

1. *ABCD* is a parallelogram.
   Prove that △*ADY* is similar to △*BXY*.

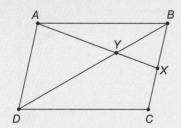

2. *PQRS* is a rhombus.
   Prove that [*PR*] bisects the angle *QPS*.

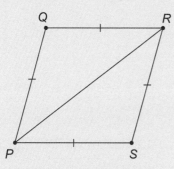

3. *ABCD* and *ABEC* are two parallelograms.
   Prove that △*ADC* ≡ △*BCE*.

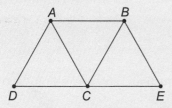

4. Prove that the diagonals of any rectangle are
   equal in length. *DEFG* below is a rectangle.

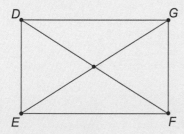

5. *LMOP* is a parallelogram.
   Prove that |∠1| + |∠2| = 180°.

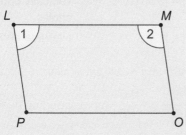

6. *ABCD* is a parallelogram. |*AD*| = 2|*AB*|.
   M is the midpoint of [*BC*].
   Prove that |∠*AMD*| = 90°.

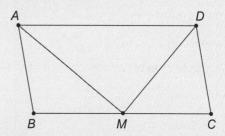

7. In the following diagram, *PQRS* is a
   parallelogram.

   (a) Prove that △*RSY* and △*PXQ* are congruent.

   (b) Prove that |*SY*| = |*QX*|.

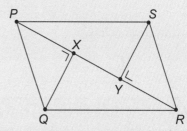

8. *ABCD* is a parallelogram. *M* is the midpoint of
   [*AC*]. Prove that |*MX*| = |*MY*|.

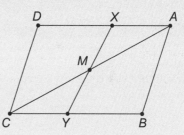

9. Consider the parallelogram *PQRS*. *T* is the
   midpoint of [*SR*].

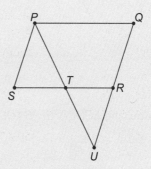

   (i) Prove that △*PST* ≡ △*RTU*.

   Hence prove that:

   (ii) |*RU*| = |*PS*|

   (iii) |*QU*| = 2|*PS*|

10. *DEFG* is a square. The midpoints of the sides are *P*, *Q*, *R* and *S*. The diagonals intersect at *O*.

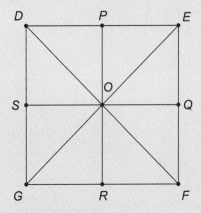

(i) Prove that $\Delta DOS \equiv \Delta GRO$.

(ii) Prove that $\Delta DOG \equiv \Delta DOE$.

(iii) If the area of $\Delta ROF = 8$ cm², calculate the area of *DEFG*.

11. *ABCD* is a parallelogram with $AX \perp BC$ and $CY \perp AD$.

Prove that $|BP| = |DQ|$.

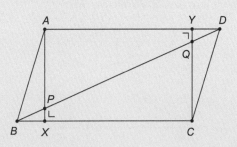

19.4 SIMILAR TRIANGLES

Worked Example 19.7

Prove that $\dfrac{|AC|}{|CE|} = \dfrac{|BC|}{|CD|}$.

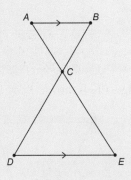

Construction: Label angles 1, 2, 3 and 4.

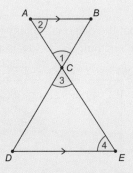

Solution

Given: ΔABC and ΔCDE with $AB \parallel DE$.

To prove: $\dfrac{|AC|}{|CE|} = \dfrac{|BC|}{|CD|}$.

Proof:

Statement	Reason
$|\angle 1| = |\angle 3|$	vertically opposite angles
$|\angle 2| = |\angle 4|$	alternate angles

∴ ΔABC and ΔCDE are similar.

$\Rightarrow \dfrac{|AC|}{|CE|} = \dfrac{|BC|}{|CD|}$ (corresponding sides)

Worked Example 19.8

$\triangle ABC$ is right-angled at C. $CD \perp AB$.

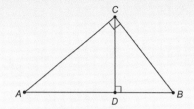

(i) Show that $\triangle ABC$ and $\triangle BDC$ are similar.

(ii) Prove that $|BC|^2 = |AB|.|BD|$.

Solution

(i) **Given:** Right-angled $\triangle ABC$ with $CD \perp AB$.

To prove: $\triangle ABC$ and $\triangle BDC$ are similar.

Construction: Draw triangles ABC and BDC separately:

Proof:

Statement	Reason
$\|\angle ACB\| = \|\angle CDB\|$	Given
$\|\angle ABC\| = \|\angle CBD\|$	Common angle
$\therefore \triangle ABC$ and $\triangle BDC$ are similar.	
Q.E.D.	

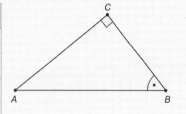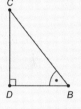

(ii) $\dfrac{|BC|}{|BD|} = \dfrac{|AB|}{|BC|}$ (sides are proportional, in order)

$|BC|.|BC| = |AB|.|BD|$ (cross multiply)

$\therefore |BC|^2 = |AB|.|BD|$

 Exercise 19.4

1. Consider the parallelogram $ABCD$.

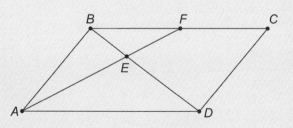

Show that $|DE|.|EF| = |BE|.|AE|$

2. The triangle PTS is shown. $RQ \parallel TS$.

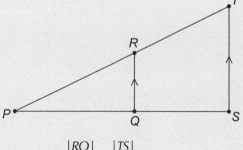

Prove that $\dfrac{|RQ|}{|PR|} = \dfrac{|TS|}{|PT|}$.

3. Consider the following diagram:

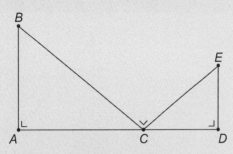

   (i) Prove that $\triangle ABC$ is similar to $\triangle CDE$.

  (ii) Prove that $\dfrac{|AC|}{|DE|} = \dfrac{|BC|}{|CE|}$.

4. In the diagram, $BD \parallel CE$ and $DF \parallel EG$.

    Prove that $|AC|.|FG| = |AG|.|BC|$

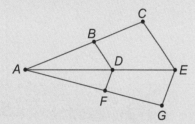

5. Consider the parallelogram $ABCD$.

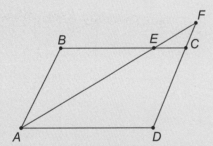

   (i) Prove that $\dfrac{|AE|}{|EF|} = \dfrac{|BE|}{|CE|}$.

  (ii) Prove that $|CD|.|CE| = |BE|.|FC|$

6. The triangle RTS is shown. $QS \perp RT$.

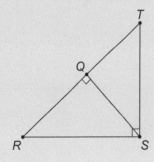

Let $|RQ| = x$ and $|QS| = y$.

Show that $|QT| = \dfrac{y^2}{x}$.

7. ABC is a triangle as shown.
$EF \parallel BC$ and $DF \parallel EC$.

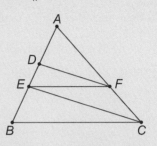

Prove that $\dfrac{|AD|}{|DE|} = \dfrac{|AE|}{|EB|}$.

8. The triangle PRT is shown. $QT \perp PR$ and $QS \perp RT$. $PT \parallel QS$.

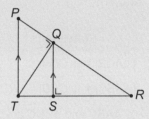

   (i) Prove that $\triangle QTS$ is similar to $\triangle QTP$.

  (ii) Prove that $|QT|^2 = |PT|.|QS|$

9. The right-angled triangle ABC is shown. $BD \perp AC$.

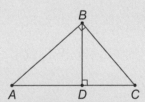

Prove that $|AB|^2 = |AD|.|AC|$

10. A, B, C and D are four points on a circle as shown. $[AD]$ bisects $\angle BAC$.
P is the point of intersection of AD and BC.

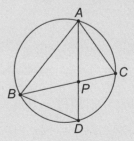

  (a) Show that $\triangle ADB$ and $\triangle APC$ are similar.

  (b) Show that $|AC|.|BD| = |AD|.|PC|$

SEC Sample Paper, JCHL

11. *PQRS* is a parallelogram as shown.

    (i) Prove that $\triangle PQT$ and $\triangle RWQ$ are similar triangles.

    (ii) If $|PT| = 2|TS|$, find the ratio $|RS| : |RW|$.

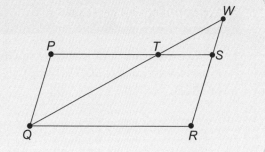

19.5 THEOREM 14

Theorem 14: Theorem of Pythagoras

In a right-angled triangle, the square of the hypotenuse is equal to the sum of the squares of the other two sides.

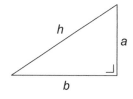

FORMULA

$$h^2 = a^2 + b^2$$

ACTIVITIES 19.6, 19.7

Worked Example 19.9

Consider the triangle *ABC*. $BD \perp AC$.

Prove that $|AB|^2 - |AD|^2 = |BC|^2 - |DC|^2$

Solution

Given: $\triangle ABC$ with $BD \perp AC$.

To prove: $|AB|^2 - |AD|^2 = |BC|^2 - |DC|^2$

Construction: None needed

Proof:

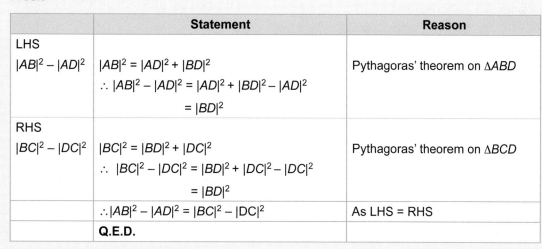

Statement		Reason
LHS $|AB|^2 - |AD|^2$	$|AB|^2 = |AD|^2 + |BD|^2$ $\therefore |AB|^2 - |AD|^2 = |AD|^2 + |BD|^2 - |AD|^2$ $\qquad\qquad = |BD|^2$	Pythagoras' theorem on $\triangle ABD$
RHS $|BC|^2 - |DC|^2$	$|BC|^2 = |BD|^2 + |DC|^2$ $\therefore |BC|^2 - |DC|^2 = |BD|^2 + |DC|^2 - |DC|^2$ $\qquad\qquad = |BD|^2$	Pythagoras' theorem on $\triangle BCD$
	$\therefore |AB|^2 - |AD|^2 = |BC|^2 - |DC|^2$	As LHS = RHS
	Q.E.D.	

1. *ABCD* is a square. *BDEF* is another square. Prove that the area of *BDEF* is twice the area of *ABCD*.

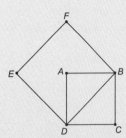

   (*Hint:* let x = length of side of the smaller square.)

2. *PQR* is a triangle such that $|PQ| = |QR|$ and $QS \perp PR$.

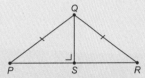

   Using the theorem of Pythagoras, prove that $|PS|^2 = |RS|^2$.

3. *ABC* is a triangle. Prove that:
   $$|AB|^2 + |DC|^2 = |BD|^2 + |AC|^2$$

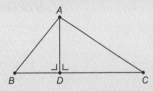

4. *ABC* is a triangle. *APQ* is another triangle. Prove that $|BQ|^2 + |CP|^2 = |PQ|^2 + |BC|^2$.

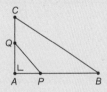

5. *O* is the centre of a circle. *AB* and *AC* are tangents to the circle.
   Prove that $|AB| = |AC|$.

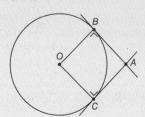

6. The triangle *ABC* has semicircles constructed on each of its sides as shown.

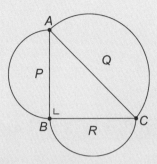

   Prove that:
   Area of semicircle *P* + area of semicircle *R* = area of semicircle *Q*

7. The triangle *ABC* is shown.

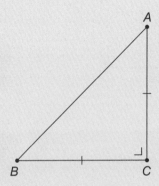

   Show that $|AB| = \sqrt{2} \cdot |BC|$

8. The equilateral triangle *POR* is shown.

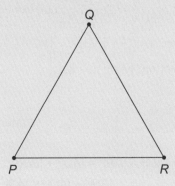

   Show that the perpendicular height of the triangle $PQR = \dfrac{\sqrt{3}}{2} \cdot |PR|$

9. The rectangle *PQRS* with the point *T* is shown.

Prove that $|PT|^2 + |TR|^2 = |TS|^2 + |TQ|^2$.

10. A regular rectangular solid is shown.

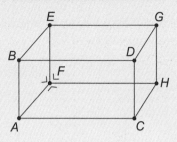

Prove that $|EC|^2 = |AF|^2 + |AC|^2 + |AB|^2$.

19.6 THEOREM 19

Theorem 19
The angle at the centre of a circle standing on a given arc is twice the angle at any point of the circle standing on the same arc.

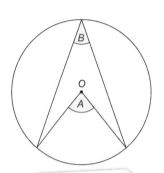

ACTIVITY 19.8

FORMULA

$$|\angle A| = 2\,|\angle B|$$

Worked Example 19.10

Prove that in the following circle with centre *O*, $|LS| = |PS|$.

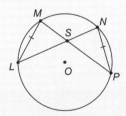

Solution

Given: Circle as shown. $|LM| = |NP|$

To prove: $|LS| = |PS|$.

Construction: Label angles as shown:

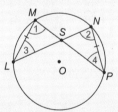

Proof:

Statement	Reason
$|\angle 1| = |\angle 2|$	Angles on the arc *LP*
$|LM| = |NP|$	Given
$|\angle 3| = |\angle 4|$	Angles on the arc *MN*
$\Rightarrow \triangle LMS \equiv \triangle NPS$	ASA
$\Rightarrow |LS| = |PS|$	Corresponding sides
Q.E.D.	

1. *E*, *D* and *F* are points on a circle with centre *O*. Prove that Δ*DEO* ≡ Δ*EFO*.

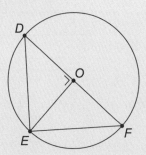

2. Consider the diagram as shown. Prove that $|\angle 1| = |\angle 2|$.

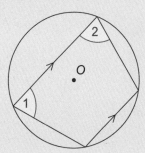

3. [*BD*] is the diameter of a circle with centre *O*. Prove that $|\angle 1| + |\angle 2| = 90°$.

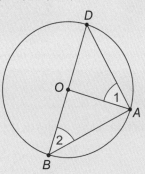

4. [*PQ*] and [*RS*] are chords of a circle. Prove that Δ*PXS* and Δ*RXQ* are similar.

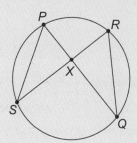

5. *A*, *B*, *C* and *D* are points on a circle. *E* is on *AD*. Prove that $|\angle CDE| = |\angle CBA|$.

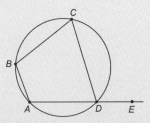

6. [*AB*] and [*PQ*] are diameters of a circle with centre *C*.

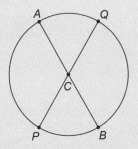

Prove that:

(i) $|\angle APQ| = |\angle PQB|$ (ii) $AP \parallel BQ$

7. A circle with centre *O* is shown. *A*, *B* and *C* are points on the circle with $|AB| = |BC|$.

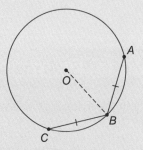

Prove that *OB* bisects the angle *ABC*, i.e. $|\angle ABO| = |\angle CBO|$.

8. Consider the following circle with centre *O*. [*DB*] is a diameter of the circle.

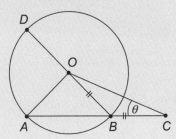

(i) Prove that $|\angle ABO| = 2\theta$.

(ii) Prove that $|\angle AOD| = 4\theta$.

9. *O* is the centre of a circle. The point *M* is the midpoint of [AB]. Prove that |∠AOM| = |∠APB|.

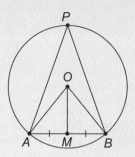

10. [AB] is the diameter of a circle with centre *C*. |BQ| = |AB|.

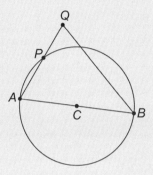

Prove that:

(i) |∠BPQ| = 90°

(ii) *P* is the midpoint of [AQ]

11. *ABCD* is a quadrilateral. Prove that it is possible to draw a single circle that contains points *A*, *B*, *C* and *D*.

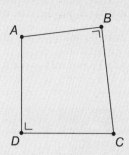

12. [AB] is the diameter of a circle with centre *C*. A smaller circle has [AC] as its diameter. A line is drawn through *A* which meets the circles at *P* and *Q*.

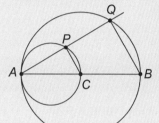

Prove that:

(i) *PC* ∥ *QB*

(ii) |AP| = |PQ|

19.7 FORMAL PROOFS OF THEOREMS

Theorem 4

The angles in any triangle add up to 180°.

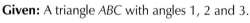

Given: A triangle *ABC* with angles 1, 2 and 3.

To prove: |∠1| + |∠2| + |∠3| = 180°.

Construction: Draw a line through *A*, parallel to *BC*. Label angles 4 and 5.

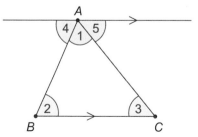

Proof:

Statement	Reason
|∠4| + |∠1| + |∠5| = 180°	Straight angle
|∠4| = |∠2|	Alternate angles
|∠5| = |∠3|	Alternate angles
⇒ |∠4| + |∠1| + |∠5| = |∠2| + |∠1| + |∠3|	As |∠4| = |∠2| and |∠5| = |∠3|
⇒ |∠1| + |∠2| + |∠3| = 180°	
Q.E.D.	

Theorem 6

Each exterior angle of a triangle is equal to the sum of the interior opposite angles.

Given: A triangle with interior angles 1, 2 and 3, and an exterior angle 4.

To prove: $|\angle 1| + |\angle 2| = |\angle 4|$.

Proof:

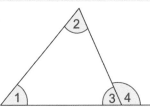

Statement	Reason
$|\angle 3| + |\angle 4| = 180°$	Straight angle
$|\angle 1| + |\angle 2| + |\angle 3| = 180°$	Angles in a triangle
$\Rightarrow |\angle 1| + |\angle 2| + |\angle 3| = |\angle 3| + |\angle 4|$	Both = 180°
$\Rightarrow |\angle 1| + |\angle 2| = |\angle 4|$	Subtracting $|\angle 3|$ from both sides
Q.E.D.	

Theorem 9

In a parallelogram, opposite sides are equal and opposite angles are equal.

Given: A parallelogram *ABCD*.

To prove:

   (i) $|AB| = |CD|$ and $|BC| = |AD|$ (opposite sides are equal)

   (ii) $|\angle ABC| = |\angle ADC|$, $|\angle BAD| = |\angle BCD|$ (opposite angles are equal)

Construction: Draw the diagonal [*AC*].   **Proof:**

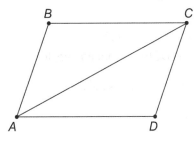

Statement	Reason
$|\angle BCA| = |\angle CAD|$	Alternate angles
$|AC| = |AC|$	Common side
$|\angle BAC| = |\angle ACD|$	Alternate angles
$\Rightarrow \triangle BAC \equiv \triangle ADC$	ASA
$\Rightarrow |AB| = |CD|$ and $|BC| = |AD|$	Corresponding sides
Also, $|\angle ABC| = |\angle ADC|$	Corresponding angle
Similarly, $|\angle BAD| = |\angle BCD|$	
Q.E.D.	

Theorem 14: Theorem of Pythagoras

In a right-angled triangle, the square of the hypotenuse is equal to the sum of the squares of the other two sides.

Given: A right-angled triangle *ABC* with $|\angle ABC| = 90°$.

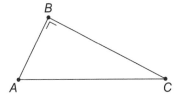

To prove: $|AC|^2 = |AB|^2 + |BC|^2$.

Construction: Draw $BD \perp AC$.

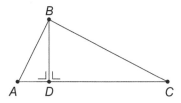

Proof:

Step 1

Consider the triangles ABC and ABD.

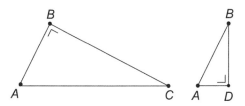

$|\angle ABC| = |\angle ADB|$	90°
$|\angle BAC| = |\angle BAD|$	Common angle

$\therefore \triangle ABC$ and $\triangle ABD$ are similar.

Statement	Reason
$\triangle ABC$ and $\triangle ABD$ are similar.	Construction
$\Rightarrow \dfrac{|AC|}{|AB|} = \dfrac{|AB|}{|AD|}$	Sides are proportional in order
$\Rightarrow |AB|.|AB| = |AC|.|AD|$	
$\Rightarrow |AB|^2 = |AC|.|AD|$	

Step 2

Consider the triangles ABC and BCD.

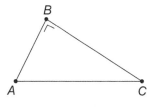 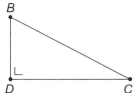

$|\angle ABC| = |\angle BDC|$	90°
$|\angle ACB| = |\angle DCB|$	Common angle

$\therefore \triangle ABC$ and $\triangle BCD$ are similar.

Statement	Reason
$\triangle ABC$ and $\triangle BCD$ are similar.	Construction
$\Rightarrow \dfrac{|AC|}{|BC|} = \dfrac{|BC|}{|DC|}$	Sides are proportional in order
$\Rightarrow |BC|.|BC| = |AC|.|DC|$	
$\Rightarrow |BC|^2 = |AC|.|DC|$	

Step 3

$\begin{aligned}|AB|^2 + |BC|^2 &= |AC|.|AD| + |AC|.|DC| \\ &= |AC|.(|AD| + |DC|)\end{aligned}$
$\Rightarrow |AB|^2 + |BC|^2 = |AC|.|AC|$ (Since $|AD| + |DC| = |AC|$)
$\therefore |AB|^2 + |BC|^2 = |AC|^2$
Q.E.D.

Theorem 19

The angle at the centre of a circle standing on a given arc is twice the angle at any point of the circle standing on the same arc.

Given: A circle with centre O and an arc AC.
A point B on the circle. Angles ABC and AOC formed.

To prove: $|\angle AOC| = 2|\angle ABC|$.

Construction: Join B to O and continue to a point D.
Label angles 1, 2, 3, 4, 5 and 6 as shown.

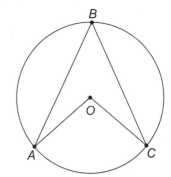

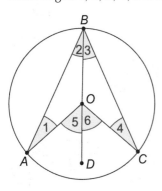

$|\angle AOC| = |\angle 5| + |\angle 6|$

$|\angle ABC| = |\angle 2| + |\angle 3|$

Proof:

Statement	Reason
$|OA| = |OB|$	Radii
$|\angle 1| = |\angle 2|$	Isosceles triangle
$|\angle 5| = |\angle 1| + |\angle 2|$	Exterior angle
$\Rightarrow |\angle 5| = 2|\angle 2|$	Since $|\angle 1| = |\angle 2|$
Similarly, $|\angle 6| = 2|\angle 3|$	
$\Rightarrow |\angle 5| + |\angle 6| = 2|\angle 2| + 2|\angle 3|$	
$\Rightarrow |\angle 5| + |\angle 6| = 2(|\angle 2| + |\angle 3|)$	
$\therefore |\angle AOC| = 2|\angle ABC|$	
Q.E.D.	

chapter 20

Co-ordinate Geometry

Learning Outcomes

In this chapter you will:

- ➲ Review Co-ordinate Geometry specified for Ordinary Level
- ➲ Learn how to find the slopes of parallel and perpendicular lines
- ➲ Examine the relationships between the slopes of parallel and perpendicular lines

20.1 REVISION OF FORMULAE

Given the points A and B:

1. **Distance between two points**

   Finding the distance between two points A and B is the equivalent of finding the length of the line segment $[AB]$. Therefore, the distance formula will also be used to find the length of a line segment.

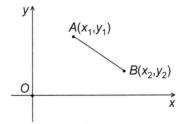

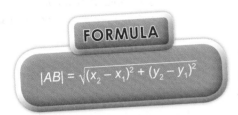

FORMULA

$$|AB| = \sqrt{(x_2 - x_1)^2 + (y_2 - y_1)^2}$$

This formula appears on page 18 of *Formulae and Tables*.

2. **Midpoint of a line segment**

   The point that bisects a line segment is called the midpoint of the line segment. If C is the midpoint of $[AB]$, then $|AC| = |CB|$.

FORMULA

$$\text{Midpoint} = \left(\frac{x_1 + x_2}{2}, \frac{y_1 + y_2}{2} \right)$$

This formula appears on page 18 of *Formulae and Tables*.

3. **Slope of a line given two points**

   The slope of a line is a measure of the 'steepness' of the line. We calculate the slope of a line by finding how much the line rises or falls as we move from left to right along it.

   Consider the line l, which contains the points $A(1,1)$ and $B(4,3)$.

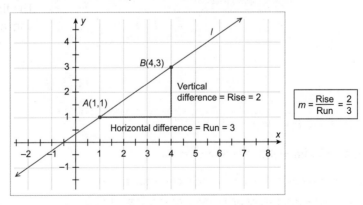

- The horizontal difference between A and B is 3. We sometimes call this number the **run**.
- The vertical difference between A and B is 2. This number is called the **rise**.
- The slope of l is $\dfrac{\text{Rise}}{\text{Run}} = \dfrac{2}{3}$. We can use the letter m to denote slope; therefore, $m = \dfrac{2}{3}$ for our line l.

Consider the line *k*, which contains the points C(−2,3) and D(2,1).

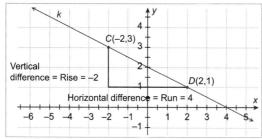

$m = \dfrac{\text{Rise}}{\text{Run}} = \dfrac{-2}{4} = -\dfrac{1}{2}$

FORMULA

$\text{Slope} = m = \dfrac{y_2 - y_1}{x_2 - x_1}$

This formula appears on page 18 of *Formulae and Tables*.

- The horizontal difference (the run) between C and D is 4.
  The vertical difference (the rise) between C and D is −2.
  The rise is negative here, as we are dropping down from C to D.

- The slope of *k* is: $m = \dfrac{\text{Rise}}{\text{Run}} = \dfrac{-2}{4} = -\dfrac{1}{2}$.

- The slope is negative because the line goes down from left to right.

4. Equation of a line

The equation of a line tells us how the *x* co-ordinate and the *y* co-ordinate of every point on the line are related to each other.

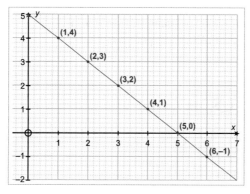

For example, consider the equation *x* + *y* = 5. This equation tells us that, for every point on this line, the *x* co-ordinate added to the *y* co-ordinate equals 5. Therefore, points on this line would include (0,5), (5,0), (1,4), (4,1), (2,3), (3,2), (6,−1), (−1,6), and so on.

FORMULA

Equations are written in three main forms:

(i) $y - y_1 = m(x - x_1)$
(ii) $y = mx + c$ [*m* = slope; *c* is called the *y*-intercept; this is where the line cuts the *y*-axis]

(iii) $ax + by + c = 0$

The first two formulae appear on page 18 of *Formulae and Tables*.

5. Point of intersection of a line with the *x*- and *y*-axes

- When a line cuts the *x*-axis, the value of the *y* co-ordinate is 0.
- When a line cuts the *y*-axis, the value of the *x* co-ordinate is 0.

6. Point of intersection of two lines

There are two main methods for finding where two lines intersect.

(a) Graph the two lines, and read the point of intersection from the graph.
(b) Use the method of solving simultaneous equations to find the point of intersection.

CO-ORDINATE GEOMETRY

(i) Plot the points $A(-1,7)$, $B(4,2)$, $C(-3,-1)$ and $D(6,8)$ on the co-ordinate plane.

(ii) Graph the lines AB and CD.

(iii) Find $|AB|$.

(iv) Find the midpoint of $[CD]$.

(v) Find the slope of AB and the slope of CD.

(vi) Find the equation of AB and the equation of CD.

(vii) Using your graphs, write down the point of intersection of the lines AB and CD.

(viii) Verify your answer to part (vii) by solving an appropriate set of simultaneous equations.

Solution

(i) and (ii)

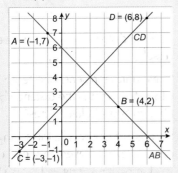

(iii) $A(-1,7)$ $B(4,2)$
       x_1,y_1 x_2,y_2

$$|AB| = \sqrt{(x_2 - x_1)^2 + (y_2 - y_1)^2}$$
$$|AB| = \sqrt{(4 + 1)^2 + (2 - 7)^2}$$
$$= \sqrt{(5)^2 + (-5)^2}$$
$$= \sqrt{50} \quad \textbf{(or } 5\sqrt{2})$$

(iv) $C(-3,-1)$ $D(6,8)$
      x_1,y_1 x_2,y_2

$$\text{Midpoint} = \left(\frac{x_1 + x_2}{2}, \frac{y_1 + y_2}{2} \right)$$
$$= \left(\frac{-3 + 6}{2}, \frac{-1 + 8}{2} \right)$$
$$= \left(\frac{3}{2}, \frac{7}{2} \right)$$

(v) Slope of AB $A(-1,7)$ $B(4,2)$
                         x_1,y_1 x_2,y_2

$$m = \frac{y_2 - y_1}{x_2 - x_1}$$
$$= \frac{2 - 7}{4 + 1}$$
$$= \frac{-5}{5}$$

$\therefore$ Slope $AB = -1$

Slope of CD $C(-3,-1)$ $D(6,8)$
                    x_1, y_1 x_2,y_2

$$m = \frac{8 + 1}{6 + 3}$$
$$= \frac{9}{9}$$

$\therefore$ Slope $CD = 1$

(vi) To find the equation of a line, you need:

1. The slope of the line

2. A point on the line

Eq. AB: $m = -1$ (from part (v))

   Point $B(4,2)$
         x_1,y_1

Equation: $y - y_1 = m(x - x_1)$
$$y - 2 = -1(x - 4)$$
$$y - 2 = -x + 4$$

Eq. AB: $x + y - 6 = 0$

Eq. CD: $m = 1$ (from part (v))

   Point $D(6,8)$
         x_1,y_1

Equation: $y - y_1 = m(x - x_1)$
$$y - 8 = 1(x - 6)$$
$$y - 8 = x - 6$$

Eq. CD: $x - y + 2 = 0$

(vii) From the graph, the point of intersection is $(2,4)$.

(viii) Solve for x and y using simultaneous equations:

$$x + y - 6 = 0 \quad \text{①}$$
$$x - y + 2 = 0 \quad \text{②}$$
$$2x \qquad - 4 = 0$$
$$2x = 4$$
$$x = 2$$

Substitute $x = 2$ into either ① or ② to find the y co-ordinate:

① $x = 2 \Rightarrow$ $2 + y - 6 = 0$
$$y - 4 = 0$$
$$y = 4$$

The point of intersection is $(2,4)$.

This verifies the answer to part (vii).

Exercise 20.1

1. $A(2,2)$ and $B(-4,6)$ are two points.

   (i) Plot the points A and B.

   (ii) Find C, the midpoint of $[AB]$.

   (iii) Verify that $|AC| = |CB|$.

   (iv) Find the equation of AB.

   (v) Find the co-ordinates of the point where AB cuts the y-axis.

   (vi) Find the co-ordinates of the point where AB cuts the x-axis.

2. $A(2,4)$, $B(6,0)$ and $C(-2,0)$ are three points.

   (i) Plot the points A, B and C.

   (ii) Find M, the midpoint of $[BC]$.

   (iii) Find the slope of AB.

   (iv) Find the equation of AB.

   (v) Given that the equation of AC is $x - y + 2 = 0$, verify that the point of intersection of AB and AC is $(2,4)$.

   (vi) Using your graph, find the area of the triangle ABC.

3. m is the line $x + 4y - 8 = 0$ and n is the line $x - y - 3 = 0$.

   (i) Using the same axes and scales, draw the lines m and n.

   (ii) Use your graphs to find the point of intersection of m and n.

   (iii) Check your answer to part (ii) by solving the equations for m and n simultaneously.

   (iv) Use algebra to find the point where the line m crosses the y-axis.

4. r is the line $2x - y + 3 = 0$ and s is the line $5x + y - 10 = 0$.

   (i) Using the same axes and scales, draw the lines r and s.

   (ii) Use your graphs to find the point of intersection of r and s.

   (iii) Check your answer to part (ii) by solving the equations for r and s simultaneously.

   (iv) Use algebra to find the co-ordinates of the point where line r crosses the x-axis.

5. p is the line $3x + 2y = 18$ and q is the line $y = 3x$.

   (i) Using the same axes and scales, draw the lines p and q.

   (ii) Use your graphs to find the point of intersection of p and q.

   (iii) Check your answer to part (ii) by solving the equations for p and q simultaneously.

6. A cruiser hits rocks. Its co-ordinates are given as $(-3,-2)$. The nearest boat is a sailing boat at co-ordinates $(5,4)$.

   (i) Find the distance in units between the two vessels.

   (ii) If one unit represents one-tenth of a kilometre, what is the distance between the two boats in kilometres?

   (iii) Because of low winds, the sailing boat can only travel at an average speed of 2.5 km/hr. How long will it take the sailing boat to reach the cruiser?

7. h is a line with equation $3x + y = 5$.

   (i) Verify that the point $(1,2)$ lies on this line.

   (ii) $(k,0)$ is another point on this line. Find the value of k.

   (iii) Write down three other points on the line h.

   (iv) Find the slope of h using the slope formula.

   (v) Find the slope of h by writing the equation of h in the form $y = mx + c$.

8. Write down the equation of a line that has:

   (i) Gradient 4 and y-intercept -3

   (ii) Gradient -3 and y-intercept 5

   Graph each of the lines defined in parts (i) and (ii).

9. The midpoint of the line joining (a,b) and $(2,4)$ has co-ordinates $(3,-1)$.

   Find the value of a and the value of b.

10. The points A and B have co-ordinates $(4,6)$ and $(12,2)$ respectively.

The line l_1 passes through A and B.

(i) Find the equation of l_1 in the form $ax + by = c$, where $a, b, c \in Z$.

The line l_2 passes through the origin and has a slope of -4.

(ii) Write down the equation of l_2.

The lines l_1 and l_2 intersect at the point C.

(iii) Find the co-ordinates of the midpoint of $[AC]$.

11. (a) Write down the co-ordinates of point A and point B on the diagram.

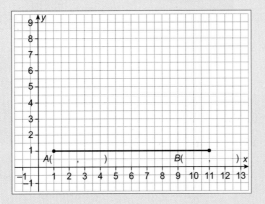

(b) Mark in the point $D(6,8)$ on the diagram.

(c) Find the co-ordinates of C, the midpoint of $[AB]$.

(d) Join A to D. Join B to D. Join C to D.

(e) Use the distance formula to find $|AD|$ and $|BD|$.

(f) What type of triangle is ABD? Give a reason for your answer.

(g) State whether the triangles ACD and BCD are congruent. Give a reason for your answer.

SEC 2012, JCOL

12. $A(2,3)$, $B(10,4)$, $C(12,9)$ and $D(4,8)$ are four points.

(i) Plot the points on the co-ordinate plane below and join them to form the quadrilateral $ABCD$.

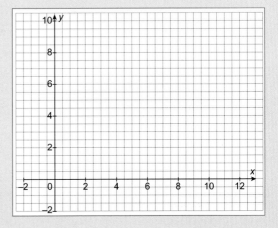

(ii) Verify that one pair of opposite sides of $ABCD$ are equal in length.

(iii) By finding E and F, the midpoints of $[AC]$ and $[BD]$ respectively, verify that the diagonals of $ABCD$ bisect each other.

(iv) Can you now conclude that $ABCD$ is a parallelogram? Give a reason for your answer.

SEC Sample Paper, JCHL

20.2 PARALLEL AND PERPENDICULAR LINES

ACTIVITIES 20.1, 20.2

FORMULA

If two lines l and k have slopes m_1 and m_2 respectively, then:

- l is parallel to k (written $l \parallel k$) if and only if $m_1 = m_2$

- l is perpendicular to k (written $l \perp k$) if and only if $m_1 \times m_2 = -1$

There is an exception to $l \perp k \Leftrightarrow m_1 \times m_2 = -1$. That is, if l is horizontal and k is vertical (or vice versa).

We need to be able to get the slope of a line when given its equation.

Method 1   Write in the form $y = mx + c$, and the coefficient of x is the slope.

Method 2   Write in the form $ax + by + c = 0$, and the slope $= -\dfrac{a}{b}$.

 Worked Example 20.2

Find the slope of the following lines:

      (i) $7x - 3y + 6 = 0$ (ii) $4x = 3 - 5y$

Solution

(i) **Method 1**

$$7x - 3y + 6 = 0$$
$$-3y = -7x - 6$$
$$3y = 7x + 6$$
$$y = \frac{7}{3}x + 2$$
$$\therefore \text{Slope} = \frac{7}{3}$$

Method 2

$$7x - 3y + 6 = 0$$
$$a = 7 \quad b = -3$$
$$\text{Slope} = -\frac{a}{b}$$
$$= -\frac{7}{-3}$$
$$\therefore \text{Slope} = \frac{7}{3}$$

(ii) **Method 1**

$$4x = 3 - 5y$$
$$5y = -4x + 3$$
$$y = -\frac{4}{5}x + \frac{3}{5}$$
$$\therefore \text{Slope} = -\frac{4}{5}$$

Method 2

First bring all terms to one side.

$$4x + 5y - 3 = 0$$
$$a = 4 \quad b = 5$$
$$\text{Slope} = -\frac{a}{b}$$
$$\therefore \text{Slope} = -\frac{4}{5}$$

 Worked Example 20.3

l is the line $2x + 4y - 6 = 0$. Which of the following lines are:

(a)   perpendicular to *l*   (b)   parallel to *l*

j: $2x + 4y - 12 = 0$ *k*: $3x + 6y = 7$ *m*: $x - 2y + 4 = 0$ *n*: $y = 2x + 4$

Solution

Step 1   Find the slope of line *l*.
$$2x + 4y - 6 = 0$$
$$4y = -2x + 6$$
$$y = -\frac{x}{2} + \frac{3}{2}$$
$$\therefore \text{Slope of } l = -\frac{1}{2}$$

Alternative method

$$2x + 4y - 6 = 0$$
$$a = 2 \quad b = 4$$
$$\text{Slope} = -\frac{2}{4}$$
$$\therefore \text{Slope of } l = -\frac{1}{2}$$

Step 2 Find the slope of each of the lines we are investigating.

Line	Slope
j: $2x + 4y - 12 = 0$	$-\frac{2}{4} = -\frac{1}{2}$
k: $3x + 6y = 7$	$-\frac{3}{6} = -\frac{1}{2}$
m: $x - 2y + 4 = 0$	$-\frac{1}{-2} = \frac{1}{2}$
n: $y = 2x + 4$	2

Step 3

Line	Slope	Slope of l × slope of given line	Perpendicular $(m_1 \times m_2 = -1)$	Parallel $(m_1 = m_2)$
j: $2x + 4y - 12 = 0$	$-\frac{1}{2}$	$-\frac{1}{2} \times -\frac{1}{2} = \frac{1}{4}$	No	Yes
k: $3x + 6y = 7$	$-\frac{1}{2}$	$-\frac{1}{2} \times -\frac{1}{2} = \frac{1}{4}$	No	Yes
m: $x - 2y + 4 = 0$	$\frac{1}{2}$	$-\frac{1}{2} \times \frac{1}{2} = -\frac{1}{4}$	No	No
n: $y = 2x + 4$	2	$-\frac{1}{2} \times 2 = -1$	Yes	No

Conclusion: n is the only line that is perpendicular to l.

j and k are parallel to l.

Equation of a Line Parallel or Perpendicular to a Given Line

To find the equation of a line **parallel** to a given line through a given point:

(1) Find the slope of the given line.

(2) The slope of the parallel line will be the same as the slope of the given line.

(3) Using the slope in Step 2 and the given point, substitute into the formula $y - y_1 = m(x - x_1)$.

To find the equation of a line **perpendicular** to a given line through a given point:

(1) Find the slope of the given line.

(2) Turn this slope upside down and change the sign to get the slope of the perpendicular line.

(3) Using this new slope and the given point, substitute into the formula $y - y_1 = m(x - x_1)$.

 Worked Example 20.4

l is the line $4x - 3y = 4$. The line k contains the point $(3, -5)$ and is perpendicular to l.

Find the equation of k.

Solution

To find the equation of k, we need:

1. The slope of k

2. A point on k

As $k \perp l$, we can find the slope of k from the slope of l.

Slope of *l*	Equation of *k*
Write the equation in the form $y = mx + c$.	1. $m = -\dfrac{3}{4}$
l: $4x - 3y = 4$	2. Point $(3,-5)$
$-3y = -4x + 4$	$\quad\quad\; \underset{x_1,y_1}{}$
$3y = 4x - 4$	$y - y_1 = m(x - x_1)$
$y = \dfrac{4}{3}x - \dfrac{4}{3}$	$y + 5 = -\dfrac{3}{4}(x - 3)$
Slope of $l = \dfrac{4}{3}$	$4(y + 5) = -3(x - 3)$
As $k \perp l \Rightarrow$ Slope of $k = -\dfrac{3}{4}$	$4y + 20 = -3x + 9$
	k: $3x + 4y + 11 = 0$

 ## Worked Example 20.5

t is the line $y = 4x + 7$.

Write down the equation of the line *s* that is perpendicular to *t* and passes through the same *y*-intercept as *t*.

Solution

t: $y = 4x + 7$

Comparing with $y = mx + c$, we can see that $m = 4$ and that the *y*-intercept is 7.

The slope of *t* is 4, so the slope of *s* is $-\dfrac{1}{4}$ (as $s \perp t$).

Therefore, the equation of the line *s* is $y = -\dfrac{1}{4}x + 7$ (using $y = mx + c$).

 ## Exercise 20.2

1. Copy and complete the following table.

Slope	Slope of parallel line	Slope of perpendicular line
$-\dfrac{1}{2}$	$-\dfrac{1}{2}$	2
$\dfrac{3}{4}$		
$-\dfrac{1}{3}$		
$-\dfrac{8}{11}$		
13		

2. The line *k* has a slope of $\dfrac{5}{4}$.
   Find the slope of *m* if $m \parallel k$.

3. The line *m* has a slope of $-\dfrac{3}{4}$.
   Find the slope of *l* if $l \perp m$.

4. The line *k* has a slope of 2.
   Find the slope of *m* if $m \perp k$.

5. The line *k* has a slope of 0.25.
   Find the slope of *l* if $l \perp k$.

6. The line *k* has a slope of $\dfrac{1}{3}$.
   Find the slope of *m* if $m \parallel k$.

7. Find the slopes of the following lines:

   (i) $2x + y - 8 = 0$

   (ii) $3x - y + 6 = 0$

   (iii) $2x - 2y = 9$

   (iv) $3(x - y) = 4$

   (v) $2x - 3(y - 2) = 0$

   (vi) $4x = 6 - 5y$

8. Find the equation of the line that is perpendicular to $3x + y = 6$ and has the same *y*-intercept.

9. Find the equation of the line that is perpendicular to $2x - y = 3$ and has the same *y*-intercept.

10. Find the equation of the line that is perpendicular to $x + 2y = 4$ and has the same *y*-intercept.

11. Find the equation of the line that is parallel to the line $x - 3y + 6 = 0$ and passes through the point (2,4).

12. Find the equation of the line that is perpendicular to the line $2x + 3y + 6 = 0$ and passes through the point (1,–6).

13. For each of the given parts, investigate if $a \perp b$:

   (i) a: $2x + 3y - 8 = 0$ b: $2x - 3y + 6 = 0$ (iv) a: $2x - 4y - 3 = 0$ b: $y = -2x + 10$

   (ii) a: $-2x + 3y - 8 = 0$ b: $2x - 3y + 14 = 0$ (v) a: $-2x + 3y - 3 = 0$ b: $3y = -2x + 10$

   (iii) a: $2x - 6y - 8 = 0$ b: $x - 3y + 1 = 0$ (vi) a: $y = 2x - 7$ b: $x + 2y = 3$

14. A line a passes through (1,2) and is perpendicular to $y = 3$.

   (i) What is the equation of this line?

   (ii) Explain why it is not possible to verify that the line a is perpendicular to $y = 3$, using the formula $m_1 \times m_2 = -1$.

15. l is the line $5x - y + 4 = 0$. The line k contains the point (4,–3) and is parallel to l. Find the equation of k.

16. m is the line $3x - 6y + 11 = 0$. The line n contains the point (–4,2) and is perpendicular to m. Find the equation of n.

17. p is the line $7x - y + 14 = 0$. The line q contains the point (–1,3) and is parallel to p. Find the equation of q.

18. l is the line $x - y + 4 = 0$. The line k contains the point (2,2) and is perpendicular to l. Find the equation of k.

Revision Exercises

1.

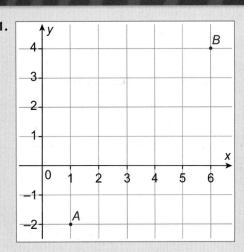

(i) Find the slope of the line AB.

(ii) Find C, the midpoint of the line segment $[AB]$.

(iii) Find the distance between A and B.

(iv) Find the equation of the line k that passes through the point C and is perpendicular to AB.

(v) Find the points at which the line k cuts the x- and y-axes.

2. l is the line $3x - 4y + 7 = 0$ and contains the point $P(-1,h)$.

   m is the line $4x + 3y - 24 = 0$ and contains the point $Q(k,0)$.

(i) Find the values of h and k.

(ii) l and m intersect at the point R. Find the co-ordinates of R.

(iii) Show P, Q, R, l and m on a co-ordinate diagram on graph paper.

(iv) Prove that $\angle PRQ$ is a right angle.

3. $P(-1,2)$ and $R(3,4)$ are two points.

    (i) Find M, the midpoint of $[PR]$.

    (ii) Find the slope of PR.

    (iii) Find the equation of the line l, the perpendicular bisector of $[PR]$.

    (iv) The equation of the line k is $x - 2y = 0$.

        Find N, the point of intersection of l and k.

4. The line k passes through the point $P(3,2)$.

    k is perpendicular to the line l: $2x + 3y = -1$.

    (i) Find the equation of k.

    (ii) Find the co-ordinates of the image of P by an axial symmetry in l.

                     SEC 2011, JCHL

5. A is the point $(1,-3)$, B is the point $(-2,1)$ and C is the point $(4,-2)$.

    $D(2,-1)$ is a point on the line BC.

    (i) Show that AD is perpendicular to BC.

    (ii) Find $|BC|$.

    (iii) Given that $|AD| = \sqrt{5}$, find the area of the triangle ABC.

6. The line l: $3x - 5y + 15 = 0$ and the line m: $3x + 4y - 12 = 0$ cut the x-axis at the points C and D, respectively.

    (i) Find the co-ordinates of C and D.

    (ii) Find E, the point of intersection of l and m.

    (iii) Show the lines l and m on a co-ordinate diagram on graph paper.

    (iv) Find the area of $\triangle CDE$.

7. P is the point $(2,-3)$ and Q is the point $(-2,1)$.

    (i) Find R, the midpoint of $[PQ]$.

    k is the line through R, perpendicular to $[PQ]$.

    (ii) Find the equation of k.

    (iii) Show that $S(3,2)$ is on the line k.

    (iv) Prove that the triangle $\triangle PQS$ is isosceles.

8. The graphs below show the relationship between distances travelled and fuel consumption for John's car. The segments l_1 and l_2 represent the fuel consumption at steady speeds of 60 km/h and 100 km/h, respectively.

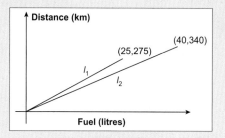

    (a) Find the slopes of l_1 and l_2.

    (b) What do these slopes tell you about the fuel consumption of the car at these speeds?

    (c) Fuel costs 149.9 cent per litre. John drives a distance of 200 km at a steady speed. How much cheaper is the journey at 60 km/h than at 100 km/h?

                     SEC 2011, JCHL

9. The table below gives the equations of six lines.

Line 1	$y = 3x - 6$
Line 2	$y = 3x + 12$
Line 3	$y = 5x + 20$
Line 4	$y = x - 7$
Line 5	$y = -2x + 4$
Line 6	$y = 4x - 16$

    (a) Which line has the greatest slope? Give a reason for your answer.

    (b) Which lines are parallel? Give a reason for your answer.

    (c) Draw a sketch of Line 1 on the axes shown.

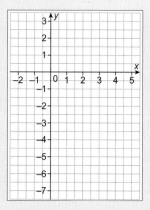

CO-ORDINATE GEOMETRY

(d) The diagram below represents one of the given lines. Which line does it represent?

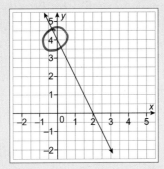

(e) The table shows some values of x and y for the equation of one of the lines.

Which equation do they satisfy?

x	y
7	12
9	20
10	24

(f) There is one value of x which will give the same value of y for Line 4 as it will for Line 6.

Find, using algebra, this value of x and the corresponding value of y.

(g) Verify your answer to (f) above.

SEC 2012, JCHL

10. The point A is shown on the diagram.

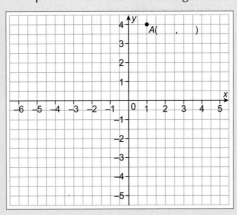

(a) Write down the co-ordinates of A.

(b) Plot the following points on the diagram above.

B	C	D	E	F
(2,0)	(−4,−4)	(0,4)	(−6,0)	(4,−4)

(c) Calculate the midpoint of [DF].

(d) Write down the equation of the line BF in the form y = mx + c.

(e) Find the slope of the line CE.

(f) Write the equation of the line CE in the form of ax + by + c = 0.

(g) What is the ratio of the area of the triangle BCE to the area of the triangle BCF?

(h) State whether the two triangles in part (g) above are congruent.
Give a reason for your answer.

SEC 2012, JCHL

11. k is the line 4x − 3y + 12 = 0. k intersects the x-axis at A and the y-axis at B.

(i) Find the co-ordinates of A and the co-ordinates of B.

(ii) m is the line that passes through B and is perpendicular to k. Show m and k on a diagram.

(iii) Find the equation of m.

12. l is the line x + 2y − 10 = 0.

k is the line x − y + 2 = 0.

Q is the point (3,5).

(i) Find the co-ordinates of the point R, the point of intersection of l and k.

(ii) Show that k contains the point Q.

(iii) Find |QR|.

13. a is the line x + y − 8 = 0 and b is the line x − 2y + 10 = 0.

(i) Find R, the point of intersection of a and b.

(ii) Find the co-ordinates of Q, the point where a intersects the x-axis.

(iii) Find the co-ordinates of P, the point where b intersects the y-axis.

(iv) Show a and b on a co-ordinated plane.

(v) Now find the midpoint, T, of [PQ].

(vi) Find the equation of PT.

14. For each of the lines in the diagram below, state whether the slope is positive, negative, zero or undefined:

Line	Slope
p	
q	
r	
s	
t	

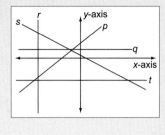

15. A (−1,−3) and B (5,−7) are the co-ordinates of two points.

(i) Find C, the midpoint of [AB].

(ii) What is the slope of AB?

(iii) Write down the equation of the line p through C that is perpendicular to AB.

(iv) Write the equation of p in the form $y = mx + c$.

(v) Now write down the co-ordinates of the point where p intersects the y-axis.

16. The line l_1 in the diagram below has slope 3 and y-intercept 2.

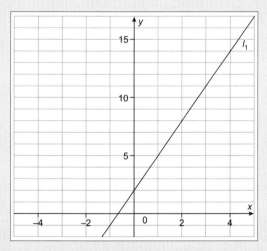

(a) Write down the equation of this line in the form $y = mx + c$.

(b) On the diagram, draw and label the lines l_2 and l_3, where:

l_2 has slope 3 and y-intercept 7

l_3 has slope 1 and y-intercept 8

(c) On the diagram, draw and label the line l_4, which is perpendicular to l_1 and passes through the point (0,4).

(d) Determine whether l_4 passes through the point (27,−4).

17. The points A(3,0) and B(0,4) are two vertices of the rectangle ABCD, as shown in the diagram below.

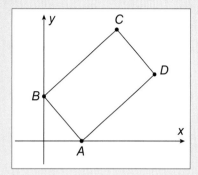

(i) Find the slope of AB, and hence, find the slope of BC.

(ii) The point C has co-ordinates (8,k), where k is a positive constant. Find the length of BC in terms of k.

(iii) Given that the length of BC is 10, and using your answer to part (ii), find the value of k.

(iv) Calculate the area of ABCD.

18. The points A, B and C have co-ordinates (1,2), (3,4) and (9,−2), respectively.

(i) Calculate the slope of AB.

(ii) Show that BC ⊥ AB.

(iii) Find the equation of BC.

(iv) The length of [AB] may be written in the form $p\sqrt{2}$.

Find the value of the constant p.

(v) Find the area of triangle ABC.

19. The map below shows part of a town containing a park and some streets. Distances are measured (in kilometres) horizontally and vertically from the Town Hall and shown in co-ordinate form.

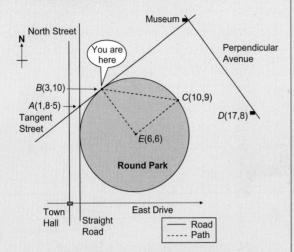

(a) How long is the path from $B(3,10)$ to $C(10,9)$? Give your answer correct to three significant figures.

(b) $E(6,6)$ is the centre of Round Park. How much shorter is it to walk directly from B to C rather than take the path to E and then on to C? Give your answer correct to the nearest kilometre.

(c) The points $A(1,8.5)$ and $B(3,10)$ are on Tangent Street. Find the equation of Tangent Street.

(d) Perpendicular Avenue is perpendicular to Tangent Street and passes through $D(17,8)$. Find its equation.

(e) The museum is located at the intersection of Tangent Street and Perpendicular Avenue. Find the co-ordinates of the museum.

(f) John is at the Town Hall and wants to get to the museum. Give one possible route he might take, and calculate the total distance he must travel if he takes that route.

SEC 2011, JCHL

20. The points $A(6,1)$ and $B(2,-1)$ are shown on the diagram.

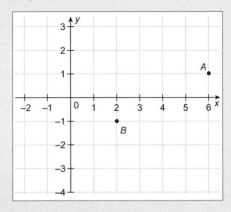

(a) Find the equation of the line AB.

(b) The line AB crosses the y-axis at C. Find the co-ordinates of C.

(c) Find the ratio $\dfrac{|AB|}{|AC|}$, giving your answer in the form $\dfrac{p}{q}$, where p and q are whole numbers.

SEC 2011, LCOL

21. Five lines j, k, l, m, and n in the co-ordinate plane are shown in the diagram.

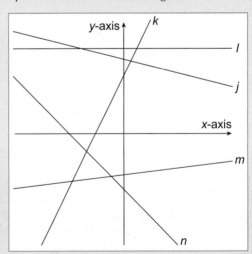

The slopes of the five lines are in the table below. Complete the table, matching the lines to their slopes.

Slope	Line
2	
$\dfrac{1}{8}$	
0	
$-\dfrac{1}{4}$	
-1	

SEC Sample Paper, LCOL

chapter 21

Trigonometry

Learning Outcomes

In this chapter you will learn about:

➲ The theorem of Pythagoras

➲ The trigonometric ratios: sin, cos and tan

➲ Manipulating measure of angles in both decimal and DMS (degrees, minutes, seconds) forms

➲ Trigonometric ratios in surd form for angles: 30°, 45° and 60°

➲ Using the trigonometric ratios to solve problems

21.1 REVIEW

The Theorem of Pythagoras

The Theorem of Pythogoras

In a right-angled triangle, the area of the square on the hypotenuse is equal to the sum of the areas of the squares on the other two sides.

The side opposite the right angle in a right-angled triangle is called the **hypotenuse.**

FORMULA

$$c^2 = a^2 + b^2$$

c^2

a^2

b^2

c a

b

ACTIVITY 21.1

Worked Example 21.1

A steel pipe is being carried down a hallway that is 2 m wide. At the end of the hall there is a right-angled turn into a wider hallway that is 4 m wide. When the pipe is in the position shown in the diagram, the corner at *A* bisects the length of the pipe. The distance from one end of the pipe to the point *B* is 8 m.

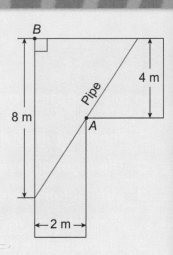

(i) Find, to the nearest centimetre, the length of the steel pipe.

(ii) Calculate the distance of the other end of the pipe from *B*.

Solution

(i) Mark points *C* and *D* as shown in the diagram on the next page.

$|AC|^2 = (4)^2 + (2)^2$ (Theorem of Pythagoras)

$|AC|^2 = 20$

$|AC| = \sqrt{20}$

$= 2\sqrt{5}$

$\therefore |CD| = 4\sqrt{5}$

≈ 8.94 m

The length of the pipe is 8 m 94 cm.

(ii) $|CD|^2 = |BC|^2 + |BD|^2$

$(4\sqrt{5})^2 = (8)^2 + |BD|^2$

$80 = 64 + |BD|^2$

$|BD|^2 = 80 - 64$

$= 16$

$\therefore |BD| = \sqrt{16}$

$= 4\ m$

The distance of the other end of the pipe from B is 4 m.

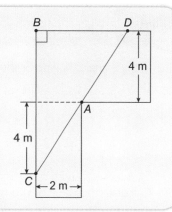

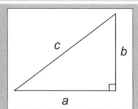

$a^2 + b^2 = c^2$

So: ▪ $c = \sqrt{a^2 + b^2}$

▪ $a = \sqrt{c^2 - b^2}$

▪ $b = \sqrt{c^2 - a^2}$

This approach can be useful when answering questions.

21.2 RIGHT-ANGLED TRIANGLES AND THE TRIGONOMETRIC RATIOS

In a right-angled triangle we have the following special ratios:

These ratios appear on page 16 of *Formulae and Tables*.

$$\sin A = \frac{\text{opposite}}{\text{hypotenuse}}$$

$$\cos A = \frac{\text{adjacent}}{\text{hypotenuse}}$$

$$\tan A = \frac{\text{opposite}}{\text{adjacent}}$$

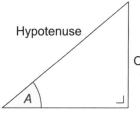

ACTIVITY 21.2

Worked Example 21.2

A girl is standing 10 m away from the foot of a radio mast. Using a clinometer, she measures the angle of elevation to the top of the mast to be 70°. Find, to the nearest metre, the height of the mast.

You may assume that the angle of elevation is taken from ground level.

Solution

Let h = the height of the mast.

$\tan 70° = \dfrac{h}{10}$

$h = 10 \tan 70°$

$= 27.474...$

$\therefore h \approx 27\ m$

Note: Make sure your calculator is in degree mode.

Worked Example 21.3

In the triangle shown, x is the length of the hypotenuse.

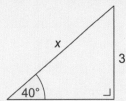

Calculate the value of x to two decimal places.

Solution

$$\sin 40° = \frac{3}{x}$$

$$\Rightarrow x \sin 40° = 3$$

$$x = \frac{3}{\sin 40°}$$

$$\therefore x \approx 4.67$$

Worked Example 21.4

A coastguard standing on a clifftop at a point C sees a boat S in the sea below. The cliff is 88 m high and the boat is 100 m away from the cliff.

Calculate, to the nearest degree, the angle of depression α of the boat from the top of the cliff.

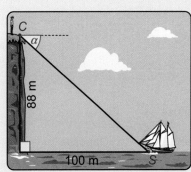

Solution

Consider the angle θ in the diagram shown.

$\theta = \alpha$ (alternate angles)

$$\tan \theta = \frac{88}{100}$$

$$\tan \theta = 0.88$$

$$\theta = \tan^{-1}(0.88)$$

On a calculator, key in the following:

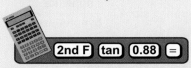

$\therefore \theta = 41°$ (to the nearest degree)

Therefore, the angle of depression α is 41°.

Exercise 21.1

1. Find the value of x in each case:

(i)
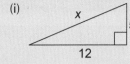

(ii)
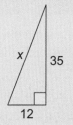

(iii)
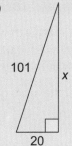

(iv)
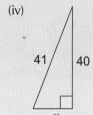

(v)
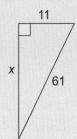

(vi)
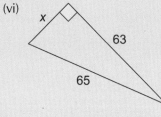

2. In each of the following triangles, find, correct to one decimal place, the value of *x*.

(i)

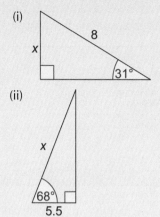

(ii)

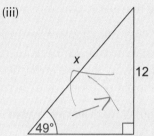

(iii)

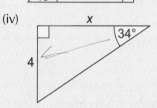

(iv)

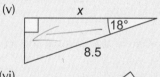

(v)

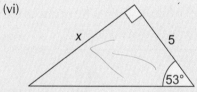

(vi)

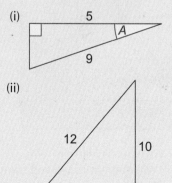

3. Find the size of the angle *A* in each of the following triangles. Give your answers correct to the nearest degree.

(i)

(ii)

(iii)

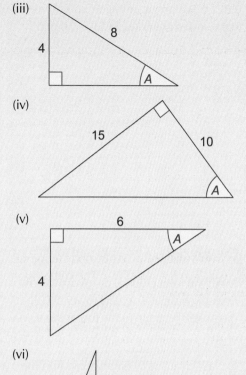

(iv)

(v)

(vi)

4. Find the value of *x* and the value of *y*, correct to one decimal place.

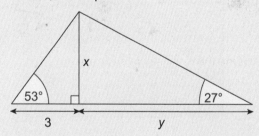

5. In the given triangle find:

(i) The value of *y*

(ii) The measure of the angle *A*, to the nearest degree

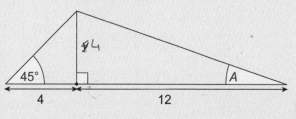

6. *ABCDE* is a pentagon made up of three similar right-angled triangles. |*AB*| = 10 cm.

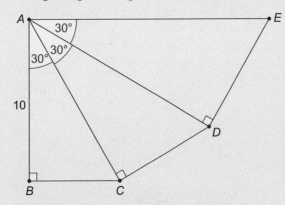

Calculate |*AE*|. Answer in surd form.

7. Sarah, on level ground, paces out 100 m from the base of a vertical tower. She then measures the angle to the top of the tower as 27°.

Explain clearly how Sarah could find the height of the tower.

8. A boy is flying a kite on a string 33 m long. The string, which is being held at 1.5 m above the ground, makes an angle of 39° with the horizontal.

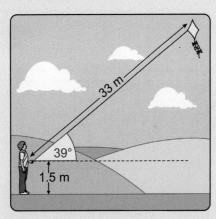

How high is the kite above the ground? Answer correct to the nearest centimetre.

9. A falcon flies from the top of a 14 m tall tree, at an angle of depression of 32°, to catch a rabbit on the ground.

(i) How far does the falcon actually fly? Answer in metres correct to two decimal places.

(ii) How far was the rabbit from the base of the tree? Answer correct to the nearest metre.

10. Brian and Yasmin are standing on opposite sides of a tree. Brian measures the angle of elevation of the tree with a clinometer, held at a height of 1.4 m above the horizontal.

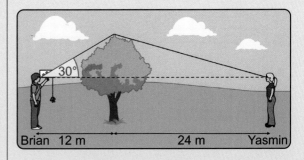

Brian is 12 m away, and the angle of elevation to the top of the tree is 30°.

Yasmin is 24 m away. She says that the angle of elevation for her must be 15° because she is twice as far away. She also holds the clinometer at a height of 1.4 m.

(i) Is Yasmin correct? Explain clearly your thinking.

(ii) Calculate the height of the tree. Give your answer in metres, correct to two decimal places.

11. The angle of elevation of the top of a building, as viewed from a point *a*, 81 m from the base of the building, is 27°.

(i) Find the height of the building correct to the nearest metre.

The bottom of a balloon is 62 m above the top of the building, as shown.

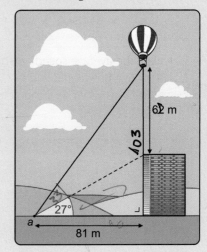

(ii) Find the angle of elevation of the bottom of the balloon as viewed from the point *a*. Give your answer correct to the nearest degree.

12. A builder wants to construct a roof with a pitch of 30°. The height of the apex above the ceiling level is 2 m, as shown in the diagram.

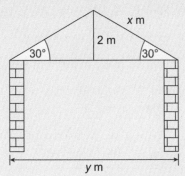

(i) Calculate x, the length of the rafter.

(ii) Calculate y, the length of the ceiling joist, correct to two decimal places.

13. A boat sails due east from the base A of a 30 m high lighthouse, [AD]. At the point B, the angle of elevation of the boat to the top of the lighthouse is 68°.

Ten seconds later, the boat is at the point C and the angle of depression from the top of the lighthouse to the boat is 33°.

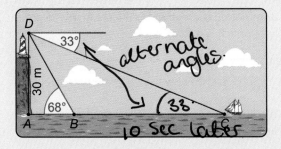

(i) Find |BC|, the distance the boat has travelled in this time.

(ii) Calculate the average speed at which the boat is sailing between B and C. Give your answer in metres per second, correct to one decimal place.

14. 6 tan A = 8, 0° ≤ A < 90°. Without using a calculator:

(i) Construct the angle A.

(ii) Calculate sin A and cos A.

15. Tan A = $\frac{3}{4}$, 0° ≤ A < 90°. Without using a calculator:

(i) Construct the angle A.

(ii) Calculate sin A and cos A.

16. Two pedestrian lights A and B, each of height h, are standing on opposite sides of a narrow street. M is a point between the two lights and N is a point on the base of B. The angle of elevation to the top of B from M is 42°. The lights are 7 m apart.

(i) Find θ, the angle of elevation to the top of A from M.

(ii) If |MN| = x, then find, in terms of x, the distance from M to the base of A.

(iii) Write h in terms of x in two different ways.

(iv) Hence, show that $x = \dfrac{7 \tan 48°}{\tan 48° + \tan 42°}$.

(v) Find h, the height of the pedestrian lights.

Answer correct to the nearest centimetre.

17. A rain gutter is to be constructed from a metal sheet of width 30 cm by bending up one-third of the sheet on each side by an angle θ.

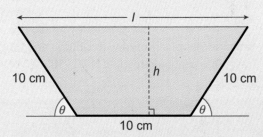

(i) Find h in terms of θ.

Divide the cross-sectional area of the gutter into a rectangle and two right-angled triangles.

(ii) Show that the width l of the top of the gutter is given by l = 10 + 20 cos θ.

(iii) Show that the cross-sectional area A of the gutter is given by:

A = 100 sin θ + 100 sin θ cos θ

(iv) Find A if θ = 60°. Answer in surd form.

(v) Find A if θ = 45°. Answer in surd form.

18. The diagram shows a unit circle (a circle of radius length 1).

- $|\angle SOW| = 90°$
- SW is a tangent to the circle at U
- $[OC$ intersects SW at W
- $|\angle UCO| = 90°$
- $|\angle UOW| = \theta$

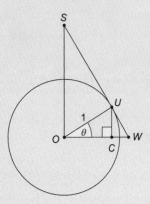

(i) Explain why SU is perpendicular to $[OU]$.

(ii) Find, in terms of θ, $|\angle SOU|$.

(iii) Hence, explain why $|\angle OSU| = \theta$.

(iv) Express $|UC|$ in terms of θ.

(v) Express $|OC|$ in terms of θ.

(vi) $(\sin \theta)^2$ is written as $\sin^2 \theta$ and $(\cos \theta)^2$ is written as $\cos^2 \theta$.

Use your answers for parts (iv) and (v) to evaluate the following:

$$\sin^2 \theta + \cos^2 \theta$$

(vii) Express $|SU|$ in terms of θ.

21.3 DEGREES, MINUTES AND SECONDS

In our course, we measure angles in units called degrees. One degree is $\frac{1}{360}$ of the angle in a full circle. A degree can be subdivided into smaller units known as minutes. There are 60 minutes in one degree. We write $60' = 1°$.

Therefore, if we wish to change degrees to minutes, we multiply the number of degrees by 60.

A minute can be subdivided into 60 seconds. We write $60'' = 1'$.

Seconds are usually used with latitude and longtitude readings. For example, Ballyjamesduff in County Cavan has a latitude reading of 53° 50' 34″ N and a longitude reading of 7° 11' 6″ W.

Worked Example 21.5

(i) Using your calculator, convert 12.4° to degrees and minutes.

(ii) Using your calculator convert 12° 44′ to decimal form.

(iii) Using your calculator, find the angle A in degrees and minutes, if $\tan A = 0.7638$. Give your answer to the nearest minute.

Solution

(i)

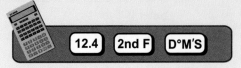

| 12.4 | 2nd F | D°M'S |

Note: Individual calculators may differ.

The answer 12° 24' 0″ is displayed.

So, the required answer is 12° 24'.

(ii)

The answer 12.73̇ is displayed.

So, the required answer is 12.73̇°.

(iii)

The answer 37.37259114 is displayed.

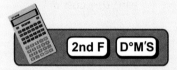

The answer 37° 22′ 21.33″ is displayed.

So, the required answer is 37° 22′.

> Remember to round up only if the display shows 30 minutes or more.

Worked Example 21.6

Using your calculator, find the measure of the angle A.

Solution

From geometry, we know that the angles in a triangle sum to 180°. Therefore, we add 52°48′ and 82°30′. Then we subtract this answer from 180°.

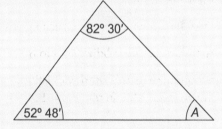

52° 48′ + 82° 30′ = 135° 18′ 0″. Now subtract this answer from 180°.

180° − 135° 18′ = 44° 42′

Exercise 21.2

1. Change each of the following to degrees and minutes. Give your answers to the nearest minute.

   (i)   2.5°   (vii)   24.75°

   (ii) 2.25°   (viii) 36.25°

   (iii) 2.75°   (ix)   55.125°

   (iv) 25.4°   (x) $\frac{1}{3}$ of a degree

   (v)   4.2°   (xi) $\frac{3}{4}$ of a degree

   (vi) 15.5°   (xii) $\frac{2}{5}$ of a degree

2. Change the following to decimal form. Give your answers correct to two decimal places where necessary.

   (i)   2° 30′   (vi)   33° 33′

   (ii) 10° 40′   (vii)   42° 10′

   (iii) 25° 50′   (viii) 58° 45′

   (iv) 70° 22′   (ix)   56° 30′

   (v)   11° 36′   (x)   82° 12′

3. Using your calculator, do the following additions (and subtractions), giving your answers in degrees and minutes.

   (i)   2° 30′ + 4° 15′

   (ii)   6° 12′ + 10° 40′

   (iii) 25° 50′ + 42° 20′

   (iv)   61° 55′ + 70° 22′

   (v)   11° 37′ + 24° 38′

   (vi)   48° 19′ − 41° 41′

   (vii) 10° 8′ − 2° 30′

   (viii) 19° 50′ − 6° 10′

   (ix)   10° 10′ − 2° 40′

   (x)   90° − 33° 33′

4. Find the measure of missing angles A, B, C and D.

   (i)

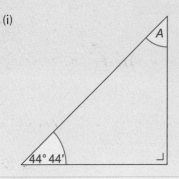

   (ii)

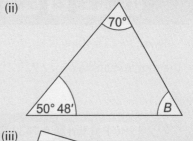

   (iii)

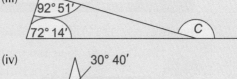

   (iv)

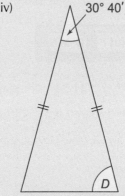

5. In the diagram below, ABCD represents the course in a triathlon. Competitors must swim the 9 km from A to B, then run the 12 km from B to C and cycle from C to D and back to A.

   $|\angle ADC| = 36.87°$

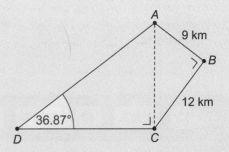

   (i)   Find the straight distance from A to C.

   (ii) Find the shortest distance from C to D, correct to the nearest kilometre.

   (iii) Find the total length of the course.

6. *ABC* is a right-angled triangle with $|\angle C| = \alpha$.

   (i) Explain why $0° < \alpha < 90°$.

  (ii) For what range of values of α is $\tan \alpha > 1$? Explain your answer.

 (iii) Explain why $\sin \alpha$ and $\cos \alpha$ must always be less than 1.

 (iv) By choosing an appropriate value for α, show that the following statement is false:

       $\sin 2\alpha = 2\sin \alpha$, for all α, $0° < \alpha < 90°$

7. When the moon is exactly half full, Earth, the moon and the sun form a right-angled triangle. At that time the angle formed by the sun, Earth and the moon is measured to be 89° 50′ 58″. The distance from Earth to the moon is 3.84×10^8 m.

   (i) Find the measure of the angle formed by Earth, the sun and the moon, when the moon is exactly half full.

  (ii) Find the distance from Earth to the sun in metres. Give your answer in the form $a \times 10^n$, $1 \leqslant a < 10$, $n \in N$.

 (iii) Light travels at a speed of 3.0×10^8 m/s. Find the time taken for light from the sun to reach Earth. Answer correct to the nearest second.

 (iv) Assuming Earth's orbit around the sun to be circular, find the distance travelled by Earth in one year. Give your answer in scientific notation.

  (v) Convert $365\frac{1}{4}$ days to seconds.

 (vi) Find the speed, in m/s, at which Earth travels around the sun. Give your answer to the nearest whole number. (*Note:* 1 year = $365\frac{1}{4}$ days)

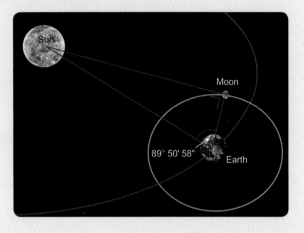

8. From a satellite 960 km above Earth, it is observed that the angle formed by a point *A* on Earth's surface, the satellite and the centre *O* of Earth is 60° 16′ 34″.

   (i) Find the measure of $\angle AOB$.

  (ii) Let $|OA|$, the length of Earth's radius, be *r*. Find, in terms of *r*, $|OB|$, the distance from the satellite to the centre of Earth.

 (iii) Hence, find $|OA|$, the radius length of Earth. Give your answer to the nearest kilometre.

 (iv) Find $|OB|$, the distance from the satellite to the centre of Earth.

  (v) All satellites travel in a circular orbit around the centre of Earth. This satellite has an orbit radius $|OB|$. Find, to the nearest kilometre, the length of one complete orbit for the satellite.

 (vi) If the satellite is travelling at a speed of 27,000 km/h, find the time taken to complete one full orbit. Answer correct to the nearest minute.

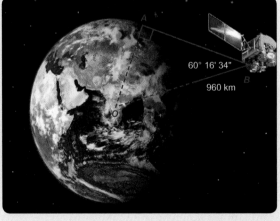

21.4 SPECIAL ANGLES 30°, 60° AND 45°

Special Angles 30° and 60°

A 60° angle can be constructed as follows, with just a ruler and compass:

(a) Construct an equilateral triangle with sides of length 2 units.

(b) Bisect one of the angles in the triangle.

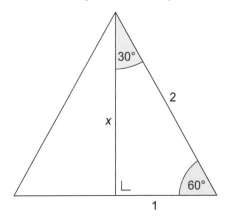

(c) Let x be the perpendicular distance from the vertex of the bisected angle to the opposite side.

(d) Use the theorem of Pythagoras to find x.

$$x^2 + 1^2 = 2^2$$

$$x^2 = 4 - 1$$

$$x^2 = 3$$

$$x = \sqrt{3}$$

From the triangle, we have:

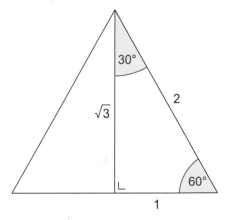

- $\sin 60° = \dfrac{\sqrt{3}}{2}$

- $\cos 60° = \dfrac{1}{2}$

- $\tan 60° = \sqrt{3}$

- $\sin 30° = \dfrac{1}{2}$

- $\cos 30° = \dfrac{\sqrt{3}}{2}$

- $\tan 30° = \dfrac{1}{\sqrt{3}}$

All these ratios appear on page 13 of *Formulae and Tables*.

Special Angle 45°

A 45° angle can also be constructed with just a ruler and compass.

(a) Construct a right-angled isosceles triangle with the equal sides being 1 unit in length.

(b) Let x be the the length of the hypotenuse.

(c) Use the theorem of Pythagoras to find x.

$$1^2 + 1^2 = x^2$$

$$2 = x^2$$

$$x = \sqrt{2}$$

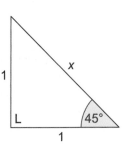

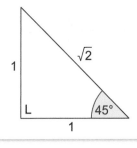

From the triangle, we have:

- $\sin 45° = \dfrac{1}{\sqrt{2}}$

- $\cos 45° = \dfrac{1}{\sqrt{2}}$

- $\tan 45° = 1$

> The ratios $\dfrac{\sqrt{3}}{2}$, $\sqrt{3}$, $\dfrac{1}{\sqrt{3}}$ and $\dfrac{1}{\sqrt{2}}$ are in surd form, i.e. they cannot be written in the form $\dfrac{p}{q}$, where $p, q \in Z$, $q \neq 0$.
>
> All these ratios appear on page 13 of *Formulae and Tables*.

 Worked Example 21.7

A thin rod, of length $3\sqrt{3}$ units, just fits diagonally inside a cylinder. The rod makes an angle of $60°$ with the base of the cylinder.

(i) Find h, the height of the cylinder.

(ii) Find r, the radius length of the cylinder. Answer in surd form.

(iii) Find, in terms of π, the capacity of the cylinder.

(iv) The rod is placed upright and water is poured into the cylinder. The water covers one-third of the length of the rod. Find the volume of water in the cylinder.

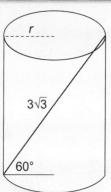

Solution

(i) $\sin 60° = \dfrac{h}{3\sqrt{3}}$

$\qquad h = 3\sqrt{3} \sin 60°$

$\qquad h = 3\sqrt{3}\left(\dfrac{\sqrt{3}}{2}\right)$

$\qquad h = \dfrac{9}{2}$ units

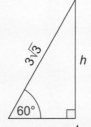

(ii) If d is the length of the diameter, then:

$\cos 60° = \dfrac{d}{3\sqrt{3}}$.

$\qquad d = 3\sqrt{3} \cos 60°$

$\qquad d = 3\sqrt{3}\left(\dfrac{1}{2}\right)$

$\qquad d = \dfrac{3\sqrt{3}}{2}$

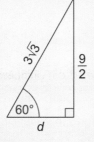

Diameter length $= \dfrac{3\sqrt{3}}{2}$ units

$\therefore$ Radius length $(r) = \dfrac{3\sqrt{3}}{2} \div 2$

$\qquad\qquad\qquad\quad = \dfrac{3\sqrt{3}}{4}$ units

(iii) $V = \pi r^2 h$ (page 10 of *Formulae and Tables*)

$\qquad V = \pi\left(\dfrac{3\sqrt{3}}{4}\right)^2\left(\dfrac{9}{2}\right)$

$\qquad\quad = \pi \dfrac{27}{16} \cdot \dfrac{9}{2}$

$\qquad \therefore V = \dfrac{243\pi}{32}$ units^3

(iv) Height of water in cylinder $= \dfrac{1}{3}(3\sqrt{3})$

$\qquad\qquad\qquad\qquad\qquad\quad = \sqrt{3}$

$\qquad\qquad \therefore V = \pi r^2 h$

$\qquad\qquad\qquad = \pi\left(\dfrac{3\sqrt{3}}{4}\right)^2 \sqrt{3}$

$\qquad\qquad\qquad = \pi \cdot \dfrac{27}{16} \cdot \sqrt{3}$

$\qquad\qquad\qquad = \dfrac{27\sqrt{3}\pi}{16}$ units^3

Worked Example 21.8

A man standing on top of a flat-roofed building uses a clinometer to measure the angle of depression of an object on the ground.

The object is located 10 m from the foot of the building and the angle of depression measured by the man is 50°.

If the man's height is 180 cm, calculate the height of the building to the nearest centimetre.

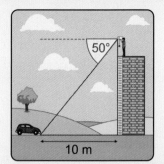

Solution

$\tan 50 = \dfrac{y}{10}$

$y = 10 \tan 50$

$y = 11.9175$

∴ Height of the building = 11.9175 – 1.8

$\approx 10 \text{ m } 12 \text{ cm}$

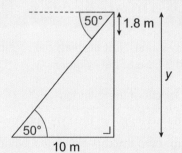

Exercise 21.3

1. (i) By using appropriate constructions, copy and complete the following table. Give your answers in surd form.

A	30°	45°	60°
sin A	$\frac{1}{2}$	$\frac{1}{\sqrt{2}}$	$\frac{\sqrt{3}}{2}$
cos A	$\frac{\sqrt{3}}{2}$	$\frac{1}{\sqrt{2}}$	$\frac{1}{2}$
tan A	$\frac{1}{\sqrt{3}}$	1	$\sqrt{3}$

(ii) Find x, y and z in surd form.

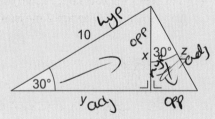

(iii) Find the value of x, the value of y and the value of z, in surd form.

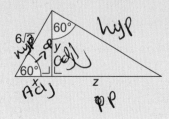

2.

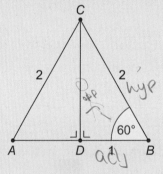

(i) What is the measure of ∠CAB? Explain your answer.

(ii) Explain why ΔCAD ≡ ΔCDB.

(iii) Find |CD| in surd form.

(iv) Hence, find the area of ΔCAD

3. A vertical flagpole [AC] stands on horizontal ground. From a point B on the ground, the angle of elevation to the top of the pole is 30°. From a point D, 4 m nearer the pole, the angle of elevation to the top of the pole is 45°.

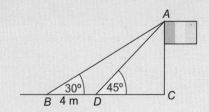

(i) Express $|DC|$ in terms of h, where h is the height of the flagpole.

(ii) Use $\triangle ABC$ to form an equation in h.

(iii) Solve the equation formed in part (ii) to find the height h of the flagpole. Answer in surd form.

4. Find the value of x and the value of y, in surd form.

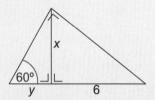

5. A man standing on a hilltop observes a flagpole that he knows is $8\sqrt{6}$ metres tall. He measures the angle of depression to the bottom of the flagpole to be $45°$ and the angle of elevation to the top of the pole to be $30°$. x is the horizontal distance from the man to the flagpole.

(*Note:* Diagram is not to scale.)

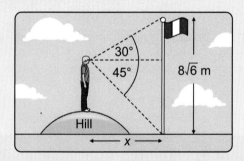

(i) Show that there is one isosceles triangle in the diagram.

(ii) Find, in terms of x, the length of each side in this isosceles triangle.

(iii) Show that there is a triangle containing an angle that measures $60°$ in the diagram.

(iv) Find, in terms of x, the length of each side in this triangle.

(v) Evaluate $(1 + \sqrt{3})(1 - \sqrt{3})$.

(vi) Find the value of x, correct to three significant figures.

(vii) If the man's eye level is 1.7 metres above the ground on which he stands, how high is the hilltop? Answer in metres, correct to one decimal place.

6. Two students, Thomas and Hannah, are investigating some properties of the sine and tangent functions.

Thomas is trying to show that for any angle, α, $0° < \alpha < 90°$, $\sin \alpha$ is unique.

Hannah is investigating the behaviour of $\tan \alpha$ as α increases.

(i) Which one of the two diagrams has Hannah drawn? Explain your answer.

Diagram 1

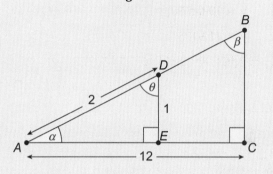

Diagram 2

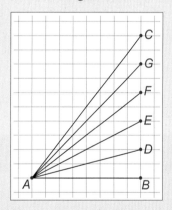

(ii) Find $|AE|$ in Diagram 2 in surd form. Each square in Diagram 2 measures 1 unit by 1 unit.

(iii) Write θ and β, in terms of α.

(iv) Hence, explain why triangles ABC and ADE in Diagram 1 are equiangular.

(v) Using a theorem from geometry, show that $|BC|$ in Diagram 1 can be written in the form $c\sqrt{d}$, where c and d are positive integers.

(vi) Use the theorem of Pythagoras to find $|AB|$ in Diagram 1 and write the answer in the form $a\sqrt{b}$, where a and b are positive integers.

(vii) Do you think sin α is unique for this particular value of α? Explain your answer clearly.

(viii) What is the length of [AB] and [BC] in Diagram 2 in grid units?

(ix) Use the theorem of Pythagoras to find in grid units the lengths of [AD], [AE], [AF] and [AG] in Diagram 2.

(x) Thomas and Hannah feel that Diagram 2 can be used to investigate the behaviour of cos α as α increases. Explain why they think that cos α decreases as α increases, using evidence from Diagram 2.

7. Evaluate $\sin^2 45° + \cos^2 45°$.
Note: $\sin^2 45° = (\sin 45°)^2$.

8. Evaluate:

$$\sin^2 60° + \cos^2 60° + \tan^2 60°$$

9. Evaluate:

$$\tan^2 30° + \sin^2 30° + \cos^2 30°$$

10. Show that:

$$\frac{\sin 30°}{\cos 30°} = \tan 30°$$

11. The diagram below shows an equilateral triangle and the incircle of the triangle with centre o.

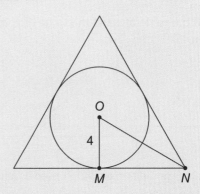

(i) Given that $|OM| = 4$, find $|MN|$, giving your answer in surd form.

(ii) Find $|ON|$.

(iii) Write down the height of the equilateral triangle.

(iv) Calculate the area of the equilateral triangle, giving your answer in surd form.

Revision Exercises

1. In each of the following triangles, find the value of x.
Give your answers to one decimal place where necessary.

(i)

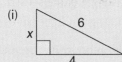

(ii)

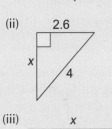

(iii)

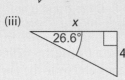

(iv)

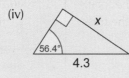

(v)

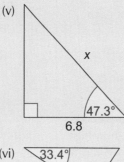

(vi)

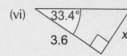

(vii) (viii)

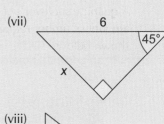

2. Find the size of the angle *A* in each of the following triangles. Give your answers correct to the nearest degree.

(i)

(ii)

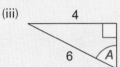

(iii)

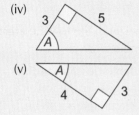

(iv)

(v)

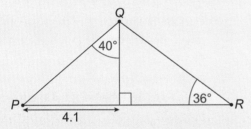

3. Find the area of triangle *PQR* in the diagram below. Answer correct to one decimal place.

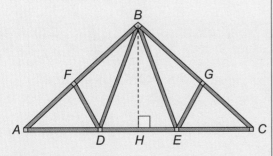

4. Roof buildings are often supported by frameworks of timber called roof trusses. A quantity surveyor needs to know the total amount of timber required to make the truss shown below.

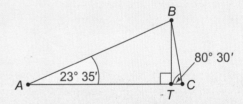

The quantity surveyor has been given the following information:

■ $|\angle ABC| = 90°$

■ The height, $|BH|$, of the truss is 3 metres.

■ $|AD| = |DE| = |EC|$

■ $|BF| = |BG|$

■ $|FD| = |GE|$

■ $|BD| = |BE| = 2|FD|$

(i) Prove that $\triangle ABH \equiv \triangle CBH$.

(ii) Find the length of [*AB*] in metres, correct to two decimal places.

(iii) Find the length of [*BD*] in metres, correct to two decimal places.

(iv) Calculate the total length of timber required to make the truss, correct to two decimal places.

(v) The timber used to make the truss costs €3.40 per metre. Assuming 10 per cent wastage in the manufacture of the trusses, calculate the cost of making 36 such trusses.

5. (i) If tan *B* = 0.2908, find tan 2*B* correct to three decimal places.

A vertical pole [*BT*] stands on horizontal ground. It is kept in position by two wires [*AB*] and [*BC*], which make angles of 23° 35′ and 80° 30′ respectively with the ground. |*AT*| = 97 m.

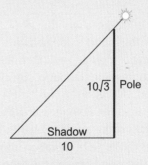

(ii) Find the height of the pole [*BT*] in metres, correct to two decimal places.

(iii) Hence, find the length of the shorter wire [*BC*].

6. A vertical pole stands on horizontal ground. The height of the pole is $10\sqrt{3}$ m. It casts a shadow of length 10 m on the ground.

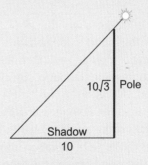

Find the angle of elevation of the sun.

7. A clock is designed to have a circular face on a triangular surround. The triangle is equilateral.

The face extends to the edge of the triangle.

The diameter of the clock face is 18 cm.

What is the perimeter of the triangle? Answer in surd form.

8. Find the area of trapezium *ABCD*. Answer correct to five significant figures.

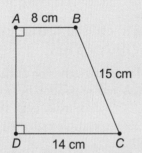

9.

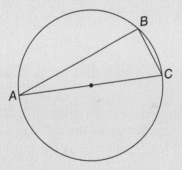

|*BC*| = 14 cm

The area of △*ABC* is 140 cm².

Calculate the radius length of the circle.

10. A group of students wish to calculate the height of the round tower shown. The tower stands on flat level ground. Dermot and Eoin decide to measure the angle of elevation, from ground level, from two different points outside the tower. Eoin measures the angle of elevation of the tower to be 30°. Dermot measures the angle of elevation from a point that lies between Eoin and the tower to be 51°. The distance between these points is 14.75 m.

Let *x* represent the distance from the centre of the tower to the point nearest the tower.

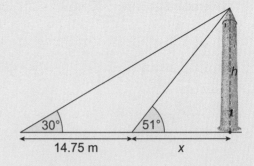

(i) Write *h* in terms of *x* in two different ways.

(ii) Hence, show that

$$x = \frac{14.75 \tan 30°}{\tan 51° - \tan 30°}$$

(iii) Evaluate *x* to four decimal places.

(iv) Find *h*, the height of the tower correct to the nearest metre.

Ethna, another student, measures the circumference of the base of the tower. She measured the circumference to be 25.13 m. She then measures the distance from the base of the tower to the point where Dermot calculated the angle of elevation.

(v) Find the radius length of the base of the tower. Answer correct to the nearest metre.

(vi) Explain how Ethna's measurement could be used to find the height of the tower.

(vii) Use the method you outlined in part (vi) to find the height of the tower, correct to the nearest metre.

11. A vertical mast [*AB*] stands on level ground. A straight wire joins *B*, the top of the mast, to *C*, a point on the ground, such that |*CA*| = 30 m.

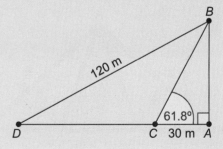

(i) If |∠*BCA*| = 61.8°, find |*AB*|, the height of the mast, correct to the nearest degree.

(ii) A second wire joins *B* to *D*, another point on the ground. If |*BD*| = 120 m, find |∠*BDA*| correct to the nearest degree.

12. A mobile phone mast is held upright by two cables. The cables are held in place by two stakes in the ground at P and Q. The angle of elevation from P to the top of the mast is 51° 36′, and the angle of elevation from Q to the top of the mast is 28° 30′.

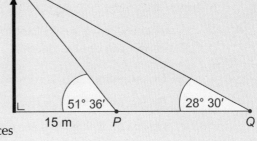

If the distance from P to the base of the mast is 15 m, calculate:

   (i) The height of the mast, correct to two decimal places

  (ii) The distance from P to Q, correct to two decimal places

13. Given that $\tan A = 4$, write $\cos A$ in the form $\dfrac{1}{\sqrt{x}}$, $x \in N$, where A is acute.

14. From the top of a cliff 20 m above sea level, the angles of depression of two boats are 45° and 30° 15′. Find d, the distance between the two boats, correct to the nearest metre.

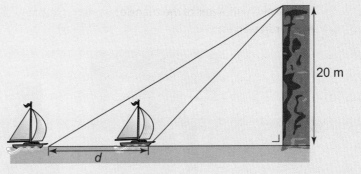

15. In the diagram below, $\tan\big(|\angle ACD|\big) = 0.30573$ and $|\angle BCD| = 58°\ 30′$. $|DC| = 10$ cm.

   Find:

   (i) $|\angle ACD|$, to the nearest degree

  (ii) $|AD|$, to the nearest centimetre

 (iii) $|AB|$, to the nearest centimetre

 (iv) $|BD|$, to the nearest centimetre

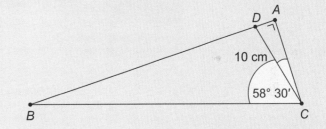

16. In the diagram below, $\tan\big(|\angle DAC|\big) = \sqrt{3}$. $|\angle ADC| = |\angle BAC| = 90°$. $|AC| = 4$ m, and $|BD| = \dfrac{1}{2}|AC|$.

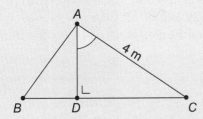

   Find:

   (i) $|\angle DAC|$

  (ii) $|BD|$

 (iii) $|BC|$, correct to two decimal places

 (iv) $|AB|$, correct to two decimal places

17. During a trigonometry lesson, a group of students wrote down some statements about what they expected to happen when they looked at the values of trigonometric functions of some angles. They then found the sin, cos and tan of some angles, correct to three decimal places, to test their ideas. Here are some of the things they wrote down.

   (i) The value from any of these trigonometric functions will **always** be less than 1.

  (ii) If the size of the angle is doubled, then the value from the trigonometric functions will not double.

(iii) The value from all of the trigonometric functions will increase if the size of the angle is increased.

(iv) I do not need to use a calculator to find sin 60°. I can do it by drawing an equilateral triangle. The answer will be in surd form.

    (a) Do you think that (i) is correct? Give an example to justify your answer.

    (b) Do you think that (ii) is correct? Give an example to justify your answer.

    (c) Do you think that (iii) is correct? Give an example to justify your answer.

    (d) Show how an equilateral triangle of side 2 cm can be used to find sin 60° in surd form.

SEC Sample Paper, JCHL

18. The Leaning Tower of Pisa is 55.863 m tall and leans 3.9 m from the perpendicular, as shown below. The Suurhusen church tower in northwestern Germany is 27.37 m tall and leans 2.47 m from the perpendicular.

The Leaning Tower of Pisa

The Suurhusen church tower

By providing diagrams and suitable calculations and explanations, decide which tower should enter the *Guinness Book of Records* as the 'Most Tilted Tower in the World'.

SEC Sample Paper, JCHL

19. A group of students wish to calculate the height of the Millennium Spire in Dublin. The Spire stands on flat level ground. Maria, who is 1.72 m tall, looks up at the top of the Spire using a clinometer and records an angle of elevation of 60°. Her feet are 70 m from the base of the Spire. Ultan measures the circumference of the base of the Spire as 7.07 m.

    (a) Explain how Ultan's measurement will be used in the calculation of the height of the Spire.

    (b) Draw a suitable diagram and calculate the height of the Spire, to the nearest metre, using the measurements obtained by the students.

SEC 2011, JCHL

20. (a) A homeowner wishes to replace the three identical steps leading to her front door with a ramp. Each step is 10 cm high and 35 cm long. Find the length of the ramp. Give your answer correct to one decimal place.

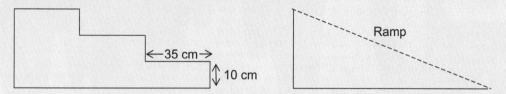

(b) Two vertical poles *A* and *B*, each of height *h*, are standing on opposite sides of a level road. They are 24 m apart. The point *P*, on the road directly between the two poles, is a distance *x* from pole *A*. The angle of elevation from *P* to the top of pole *A* is 60°.

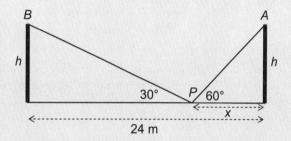

   (i) Write *h* in terms of *x*.

   (ii) From *P*, the angle of elevation to the top of pole *B* is 30°. Find *h*, the height of the two poles.

SEC 2012, JCHL

21. The Titanium Building in Santiago, Chile, was completed in 2009 and is the fourth tallest building in South America.

Two engineering students from the Universidad de Chile, Fernando and Alejandra, were asked to use a clinometer, tape measure and calculator to estimate the height of the tower to the nearest centimetre, as the first part of their final exam in trigonometry.

They decided to take three measurements at different times on the same day and to use the average of these as their estimate of the buildings's height.

The method they decided to use was to measure the length of the shadow of the building on the ground in the afternoon sun, along with the corresponding angle of inclination from the end of the shadow to the top of the building. The building is situated in a very flat part of the city, so the two students were able to neglect changes in elevation as they took their measurements.

Fernando measured the shadow lengths while Alejandra measured the angles of inclination. These measurements are presented here.

Fernando determined that Alejandra held the clinometer 1.62 m above the ground when taking each clinometer reading.

Time	Shadow length	Angle of inclination
12:07	56.38 m	73.68°
13:25	72.07 m	69.47°
15:56	164.29 m	49.52°

(a) Draw a suitable diagram representing the taking of the first reading. (The diagram should include the unknown building height, the measured shadow length, the measured angle of inclination and the measured height above the ground of the clinometer.)

(b) With the aid of this diagram, calculate the first estimate of the building's height of the two students. Give your answer in metres, correct to four decimal places.

(c) Calculate the second estimate and the third estimate of the building's height. Give your answers in metres, correct to four decimal places.

(d) What was the final estimate of the building's height that the students arrived at? Give your answer correct to the nearest centimetre.

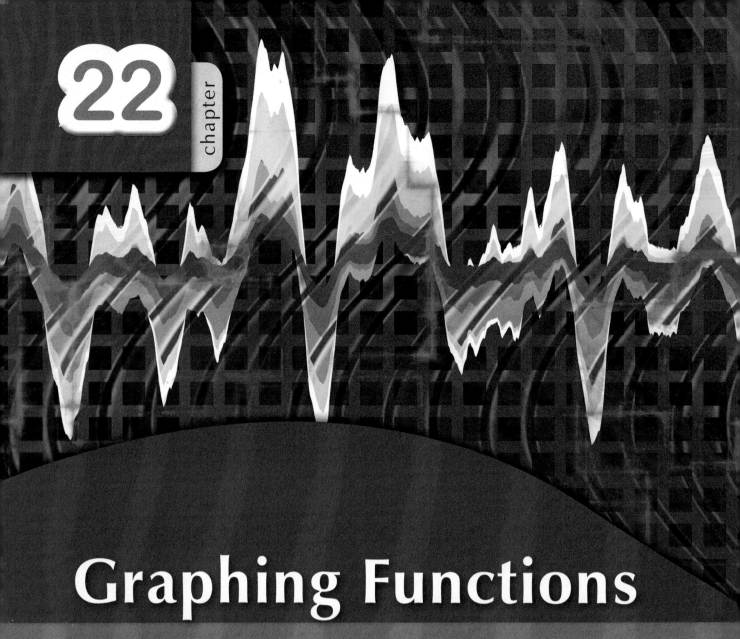

22 chapter

Graphing Functions

Learning Outcomes

In this chapter you will learn to:

○ Graph functions of the form

  ○ $f(x) = ax^2 + bx + c$, where $a, b, c \in Z, x \in R$

  ○ $f(x) = a.2^x$ and $f(x) = a.3^x$, where $a \in N, x \in R$

○ Find maximum and minimum values of quadratic functions from a graph

○ Interpret inequalities of the form $f(x) \leq g(x)$ as a comparison of the above functions, including linear functions

○ Use graphical methods to find approximate solution sets of these inequalities and interpret the results

○ Perform transformations of exponential functions

22.1 LINEAR FUNCTIONS

A **linear function** f in x is a function of the form $f(x) = ax + b$, where a and b are constants and x is a variable.

YOU SHOULD REMEMBER...

■ How to graph linear functions

■ How to graph quadratic functions of the form $ax^2 + bx + c$, where $a \in N$; $b, c \in Z$; $x \in R$

■ Transformations of the above functions

■ The Laws of Indices

A constant is a value that does not vary.

A variable can change depending on the value we give it. Variables are represented by letters.

Example: For the function f defined by $f(x) = 2x + 1$, x is variable while 1 is constant. 2 is the coefficient of x.

A graph is a pictorial representation of information showing how one quantity varies with respect to another quantity. The graph of a linear function is a straight line. The graph of $f(x) = 2x + 1$ is shown below.

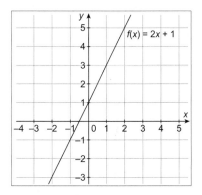

KEY WORDS

■ **Linear functions**

■ **Quadratic functions**

■ **U-shaped graph**

■ **∩-shaped graph**

■ **Exponential functions**

■ **Coefficient**

ACTIVITY 22.1

22.2 QUADRATIC FUNCTIONS

A **quadratic function** f in x is a function of the form $f(x) = ax^2 + bx + c$, where a, b and c are constants ($a \neq 0$) and x is a variable.

The graph of a quadratic function takes the form of a curve, known as a parabola. The graph of a quadratic function can be drawn by making a table of input values (for x) and finding the corresponding output values (for y). Then plot the resultant couples and connect these together with a smooth curve.

The graph can be ∪-shaped or ∩-shaped, depending on the coefficient of the squared variable.

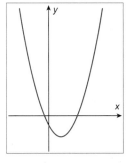

$y = ax^2 + bx + c$
Here, a is **positive**.

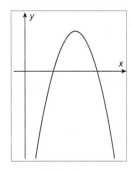

$y = ax^2 + bx + c$
Here, a is **negative**.

Worked Example 22.1

Graph the function $f: x \rightarrow 3x^2 - 2x - 7$ in the domain $-2 \leqslant x \leqslant 3$, $x \in R$.

(a) Estimate from your graph:

   (i) The value of $f(2.5)$

   (ii) The values of x for which $f(x) = 3$

   (iii) The minimum value of $f(x)$ and the x-value at which it occurs

   (iv) The range of values of x for which $3x^2 - 2x - 7 \geqslant 0$

(b) Use algebra to answer parts (i) and (ii) accurately.

Solution

x (input)	$3x^2 - 2x - 7$	y (output)	Couples to graph
−2	3(4) + 4 − 7	9	(−2,9)
−1	3(1) + 2 − 7	−2	(−1,−2)
0	3(0) − 0 − 7	−7	(0,−7)
1	3(1) − 2 − 7	−6	(1,−6)
2	3(4) − 4 − 7	1	(2,1)
3	3(9) − 6 − 7	14	(3,14)

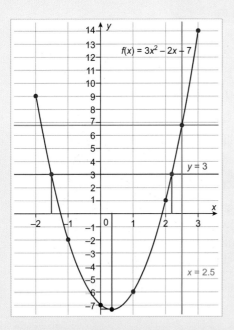

Note: It is important to draw an accurate graph if estimates are to be reliable.

(a) (i) Draw a line from $x = 2.5$ on the x-axis up to the graph (this is the vertical green line on the diagram). Then draw a line from here across to the y-axis. The reading is 6.7. Therefore, $f(2.5) \approx 6.7$.

   (ii) Draw the line $y = 3$ (this is the horizontal red line on the diagram). Where this line cuts the graph of the function, drop perpendicular lines down to the x-axis.

     This gives the corresponding x-values: $x = -1.5$ and $x = 2.2$.

   (iii) The minimum value of $f(x)$ is approximately −7.3 at $x = 0.3$.

   (iv) The values of x for which $3x^2 - 2x - 7 \geqslant 0$:

     This means the values of x for which the graph is on or above the x-axis.

     The graph is on the x-axis at $x = -1.2$ and $x = 1.9$.

     $\therefore f(x) \geqslant 0$ for $-2 \leqslant x \leqslant -1.2$
          or $1.9 \leqslant x \leqslant 3$

(b) Checking (i):

$$f(2.5) = 3(2.5)^2 - 2(2.5) - 7$$
$$= 6.75$$

Checking (ii):

$$f(x) = 3$$
$$\therefore 3x^2 - 2x - 7 = 3$$

$$\boxed{3}x^2 \; \boxed{-2}x \; \boxed{-10} = 0$$
$$\;\;a\;\;\;\;\;\;\;b\;\;\;\;\;\;\;c$$

$$x = \frac{-b \pm \sqrt{b^2 - 4ac}}{2a}$$

$$x = \frac{2 + \sqrt{124}}{6} \quad \text{or} \quad x = \frac{2 - \sqrt{124}}{6}$$

$$\approx 2.19 \qquad\qquad \approx -1.52$$

Worked Example 22.2

Using the same scales and axes, graph the functions g and h defined by $g(x) = -x^2 + 6x$ and $h(x) = \frac{2}{3}x + 1$, respectively, in the domain $0 \leqslant x \leqslant 6, x \in R$.

Use your graphs to estimate the values of x where:

 (i) $g(x) = 5.5$ (ii) $h(x) = 3.5$ (iii) $g(x) = h(x)$ (iv) $\frac{2}{3}x - 1 = 0$

Solution

Set up an input–output table for each function to find the couples that need to be graphed.

	$g(x)$		
x	$-x^2 + 6x$	y	(x,y)
0	0 + 0	0	(0,0)
1	−1 + 6	5	(1,5)
2	−4 + 12	8	(2,8)
3	−9 + 18	9	(3,9)
4	−16 + 24	8	(4,8)
5	−25 + 30	5	(5,5)
6	−36 + 36	0	(6,0)

h is a linear function, so three points will be sufficient to graph it.

	$h(x)$		
x	$\frac{2}{3}x + 1$	y	(x,y)
0	0 + 1	1	(0,1)
3	2 + 1	3	(3,3)
6	4 + 1	5	(6,5)

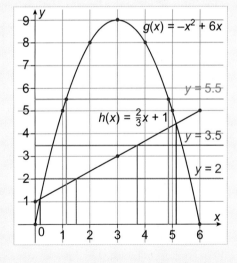

 (i) Draw the line $y = 5.5$ (green line on graph)

 Where this line cuts the graph of $g(x)$, drop perpendiculars to the x-axis and read off the x-values: $x = 1.2$ and $x = 4.8$.

 (ii) Draw the line $y = 3.5$ (red line on graph).

 Where this line cuts the graph of $h(x)$, drop a perpendicular to the x-axis and read off the x-value: $x = 3.7$.

 (iii) These are the two x-values where the graphs of the functions intersect: $x = 0.2$ and $x = 5.2$.

 (iv) $\frac{2}{3}x - 1 = 0$

 $\Rightarrow \frac{2}{3}x + 1 - 2 = 0$

 $\frac{2}{3}x + 1 = 2$

 $\therefore h(x) = 2$

Draw the line $y = 2$ (blue line on graph). Where this line cuts the graph of $h(x)$, drop a perpendicular to the x-axis and read off the x-value: $x = 1.5$.

Exercise 22.1

1. Draw a graph of the following functions with the given domains:

	Function	Domain
(i)	$h(x) = 2 - 3x$	$0 \leqslant x \leqslant 5, x \in R$
(ii)	$f: x \to x + 6$	$6 \leqslant x \leqslant 12, x \in R$
(iii)	$g: x \to 2x + \frac{3}{4}$	$-8 \leqslant x \leqslant -2, x \in R$
(iv)	$h: x \to \frac{1}{5} - x$	$-2 \leqslant x \leqslant 2, x \in R$

2. Draw a graph of the following functions with the given domains:

	Function	Domain
(i)	$f(x) = \frac{2}{3}x - 2$	$-2 \leqslant x \leqslant 2, x \in R$
(ii)	$g(x) = -\frac{4}{3}x$	$-3 \leqslant x \leqslant 1, x \in R$
(iii)	$h(x) = \frac{x}{2} + \frac{3}{2}$	$0 \leqslant x \leqslant 5, x \in R$
(iv)	$i(x) = 3x + \frac{1}{2}$	$6 \leqslant x \leqslant 12, x \in R$

3. Draw the graph of the linear function
$f: x \to 4x - 3$ in the domain $-3 \leqslant x \leqslant 4, x \in R$.

Use your graph to estimate:

(i) The value of $f(x)$, when $x = 2.5$

(ii) The value of x for which $4x - 3 = 6$

(iii) The value of x for which $4x - 3 = -7$

(iv) The range of values of x for which $f(x) \geqslant 1$

4. A car passes a point P, after which its speed v (in m/s) is given by the function $v = 15 - 3t$, where t is the time in seconds.

Draw a graph of v for $0 \leqslant t \leqslant 5$.
Use your graph to estimate:

(i) The speed of the car at $t = 2.3$

(ii) The time at which the speed is 10 m/s

(iii) The speed as the car passes P

(iv) The time taken by the car to stop after it passes the point P

5. By completing the following input–output table, graph the function $f(x) = x^2 + 3x - 4$ in the domain $-4 \leqslant x \leqslant 1, x \in R$.

x	$x^2 + 3x - 4$	y	(x,y)
-4	$(-4)^2 + 3(-4) - 4$	0	$(-4,0)$
-3			
-2			
-1			
0			
1			

(i) What is the minimum value of $f(x)$?

(ii) From your graph, find the value(s) of x where $f(x) = -6$.

(iii) Verify your answer to part (ii) algebraically.

6. Graph the following functions in the domain $-2 \leqslant x \leqslant 3, x \in R$:

(i) $f(x) = x^2 - 2x + 4$

(ii) $g(x) = 4 + 2x - 2x^2$

(iii) $h(x) = -x^2 - 3x + 7$

(iv) $j: x \to -3x^2 + 2x + 12$

(v) $k: x \to x^2 + 1$

7. A tennis ball machine is malfunctioning and shoots out a tennis ball so that its height y (in metres) is given by the function $f(x) = 6x - x^2$, where x is the horizontal distance in metres travelled by the tennis ball.

(i) Complete a table of values relating x to y for the domain $0 \leqslant x \leqslant 6, x \in R$.

(ii) Draw the graph of y against x.

(iii) What is the maximum height reached by the tennis ball?

(iv) If the player hits the ball when it is at a height of 2 metres, estimate the two possible horizontal distances the ball had travelled up to then.

8. Graph the function $f(x) = x^2 - x - 4$ in the domain $-2 \leqslant x \leqslant 4, x \in R$.

Find from your graph:

(i) The value of $f(1.5)$

(ii) The values of x for which $x^2 - x - 4 = 0$

(iii) The values of x for which $x^2 - x - 4 \leqslant 0$

(iv) The minimum value of $f(x)$

9. A water skier hits the wake wave created by a passing boat when out skiing. The height of the jump that he makes is modelled by the function $f(x) = -x^2 + 15x - 5$, where x is the time passed in tenths of a second.

   (i) Using a suitable domain, graph this function.

   (ii) At 0.7 seconds, what height is the skier above the water?

   (iii) What is the maximum height he reaches?

   (iv) At what time does he land back down on the water?

10. Graph the function $f: x \rightarrow x^2 + 6x - 3$ in the domain $-8 \leqslant x \leqslant 2, x \in R$.

    Estimate from your graph:

    (i) The value of $f(x)$ if $x = -4.5$

    (ii) The values of x for which $x^2 + 6x - 3 = 0$

    (iii) The values of x for which $x^2 + 6x - 3 = 2$

    (iv) The values of x for which $x^2 + 6x - 8 = 0$

    (v) The minimum value of $f(x)$

11. A ball is thrown in the air so that t seconds after it is thrown, its height h (in metres) above the ground is given by $h(t) = 25t - 5t^2$.

    Another ball is fired from a machine, and its height above the ground is given by $g(t) = 5 + 3t$, where g is height (in metres) and t is time (in seconds) after it is fired.

    (*Note:* Ignore effects of gravity.)

    (i) Using the same axes and scales, graph the two functions.

    (ii) Use your graphs to estimate the time(s) at which the two balls will be at the same height.

    (iii) What is the maximum height reached by each ball in the first 5 seconds?

   (iv) At what time does each ball reach its maximum height?

   (v) For how long is the first ball above the second ball if they are both fired/thrown at the same time?

12. The functions $f(x) = 0.25x + 4$ and $g(x) = 7x - x^2$ are graphed below on the domain $0 \leqslant x \leqslant 7$.

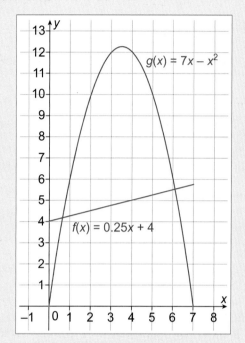

   (i) What is the maximum value of $f(x)$?

   (ii) Use the graphs to estimate the values of x for which $f(x) = g(x)$.

   (iii) Use the graphs to estimate the values of x for which $f(x) \geqslant g(x)$.

   (iv) Use the graphs to estimate the values of x for which $f(x) \leqslant g(x)$.

13. Draw the graph of the function $f: x \rightarrow 5 - 2x - x^2$ in the domain $-3 \leqslant x \leqslant 3, x \in R$.

    Find from your graph:

    (i) The value of $f(-1.5)$

    (ii) The values of x for which $f(x) = 2$

    (iii) The maximum value of $f(x)$

    (iv) The range of values of k for which $5 - 2x - x^2 = k$ has two solutions, where $k \in R$

14. Use the same scales and axes to draw the graphs of the two functions $f(x) = 2 + 2x + x^2$ and $g(x) = 6 - 2x - x^2$ in the domain $-3 \leqslant x \leqslant 2, x \in R$.

  (i) Use your graphs to estimate the values of x for which $f(x) = g(x)$.

  (ii) Use your graphs to estimate the values of x for which $f(x) \geqslant g(x)$.

15. A missile is launched into the air following the trajectory mapped out by the quadratic function $h(t) = 6t - t^2$, where h is the height in metres above the ground and t is the time in seconds.

  (i) Graph the trajectory of the missile for 0–6 seconds.

  (ii) At what times is the missile 8 metres above the ground?

A counter-attack missile is launched at the same time from a height one metre above the ground. The trajectory of this missile is given by the function $j(t) = 1.2t + 1$, where t is time in seconds.

  (iii) Graph the trajectory of the counter-attack missile.

  (iv) At what time will the two missiles collide?

  (v) At what height will this collision take place?

16. The owner of a manufacturing company pays his workers on a piece rate basis. The owner uses a quadratic function to determine the pay each employee will receive each month. He has determined that above a certain level of production by each employee, he encounters a problem with wastage. To eliminate wastage, he has told his employees that above a given level of production, their pay will decline.

The quadratic function he uses for calculating pay is defined as $P = 10Q - Q^2$, where P is monthly pay in €100s and Q is quantity produced in 100s.

  (i) Graph the function for pay, with quantity produced on the horizontal axis and monthly pay on the vertical axis. Use the domain $0 \leqslant Q \leqslant 10$.

  (ii) What is the optimal amount for an employee to produce?

  (iii) If the optimal amount is produced, what pay will the employee receive that month?

  (iv) If a worker receives monthly pay of €2,400, what are the two possible levels of production she has reached?

  (v) Is it more lucrative for an employee to produce 250 units or 725 units? Explain how you came to your decision.

22.3 EXPONENTIAL FUNCTIONS

An **exponential function** f in x is a function of the form $f(x) = a.b^x$, where a and b are constants and x is variable. x is called the exponent (or index or power).

When dealing with exponential functions, we take a number, called the base, and raise it to a power called the exponent.

$$y = ab^x$$

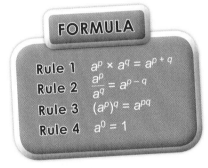

The **exponent**: For our course, this can be any real number.

The **base**: For our course, this can be any real number.

We may also be asked to multiply the exponential function by any natural number.

The base and exponent make up the exponential function.

Before dealing with exponential functions, it is essential that you know the rules for working with indices. Some key rules are shown below.

FORMULA

Rule 1 $a^p \times a^q = a^{p+q}$

Rule 2 $\dfrac{a^p}{a^q} = a^{p-q}$

Rule 3 $(a^p)^q = a^{pq}$

Rule 4 $a^0 = 1$

These formulae appear on page 21 of *Formulae and Tables*.

ACTIVITY 22.2

Graphs of Exponential Functions

The graph of an exponential function has a very distinctive shape.

The graph of the function $a.b^x$ will pass through the point $(0,a)$.

Reason: At $x = 0$, $y = ab^0$ Note: $b \neq 0$

$\qquad\qquad\qquad = a(1)$

$\qquad\qquad\qquad = a$

The graph of an exponential function will never touch or cross the x-axis.

Exponential functions are often used to model growth and decay in nature. They are also used in economic and financial models. We are going to examine the distinctive shape and properties of exponential functions in the following worked examples.

 Worked Example 22.3

Graph the function $y = 2^x$ in the domain $-2 \leqslant x \leqslant 2$, $x \in R$.

Describe in your own words some characteristics of this graph.

Solution

x	2^x	y	(x,y)
−2	$2^{-2} = \dfrac{1}{2^2}$	$\dfrac{1}{4}$	$\left(-2, \dfrac{1}{4}\right)$
−1	$2^{-1} = \dfrac{1}{2^1}$	$\dfrac{1}{2}$	$\left(-1, \dfrac{1}{2}\right)$
0	2^0	1	(0,1)
1	2^1	2	(1,2)
2	2^2	4	(2,4)

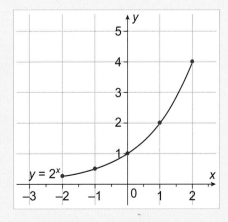

The graph is upward-sloping. It passes through the point $(0,1)$. It is above the x-axis.

Worked Example 22.4

Graph the function f defined by $f(x) = 2(3^x)$ in the domain $-2 \leqslant x \leqslant 2, x \in R$.

Describe in your own words some characteristics of this graph.

Solution

x	$2(3^x)$	y	(x,y)
−2	$2(3^{-2})$	$\frac{2}{9}$	$\left(-2, \frac{2}{9}\right)$
−1	$2(3^{-1})$	$\frac{2}{3}$	$\left(-1, \frac{2}{3}\right)$
0	$2(3^0)$	2	$(0,2)$
1	$2(3^1)$	6	$(1,6)$
2	$2(3^2)$	18	$(2,18)$

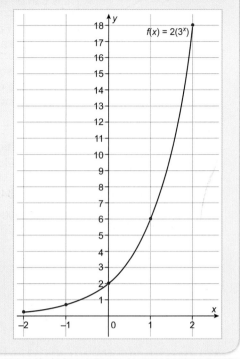

The graph is upward-sloping. It passes through the point $(0,2)$. It is above the x-axis.

 Worked Example 22.5

Find the value of a, given the graph of the function f defined by $f(x) = ab^x$, $b > 0$.

Solution

$(0,3)$ lies on the graph of f.

$\Rightarrow f(0) = 3$

But $f(0) = a.b^0$

$\qquad = a(1)$

$\qquad = a$

$\therefore a = 3$

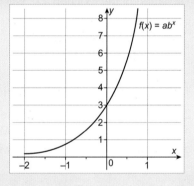

 Worked Example 22.6

Bacterial growth can be modelled using exponential functions.

The population of a particular bacteria is given by the function $p(x) = 150,000(2^x)$, where x is time in hours.

    (i)   Graph this population function for the first four hours of growth.

   (ii)   Estimate the population size after 2.5 hours of growth by taking a suitable reading from your graph.

  (iii)   Find the exact population size after 2.5 hours of growth using algebra. Answer correct to the nearest whole number.

  (iv)   Calculate the percentage error in your estimate in part (ii) by using your answer from part (iii). Answer correct to one decimal place.

Solution

(i)

x	150,000(2^x)	y
0	150,000(1)	150,000
1	150,000(2)	300,000
2	150,000(4)	600,000
3	150,000(8)	1,200,000
4	150,000(16)	2,400,000

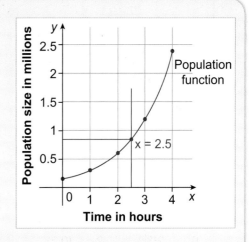

(ii) Draw the vertical line $x = 2.5$ and read off the y-value where it crosses the graph of the population function.

Answer: $\approx 850,000$

(iii) $p(2.5) = 150,000(2^{2.5}) = 848,528.1374 \approx 848,528.$

(iv) Percentage error $= \dfrac{850,000 - 848,528}{848,528} \times 100 \approx 0.2\%$

Note

For a function f where $f(x) = a.2^x$ (or $a.3^x$), where $a \in N$:

- The graph of f is upward-sloping.
- The graph of f passes through the point $(0,a)$.
- The graph of f is above the x-axis.

 Exercise 22.2

In Questions 1–8, graph each function in the domain $-2 \leqslant x \leqslant 3$, $x \in R$.

1. $y = 2^x$ **4.** $y = 4(2^x)$ **7.** $y = 2(2^x)$

2. $y = 3^x$ **5.** $y = 2(3^x)$ **8.** $y = 4(3^x)$

3. $y = 3(2^x)$ **6.** $y = 3(3^x)$

---

9. Find the value of a given the graph of the function $f(x) = a.2^x$.

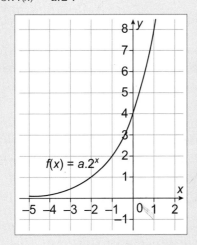

10. Find the value of a given the graph of the function $f(x) = a.2^x$.

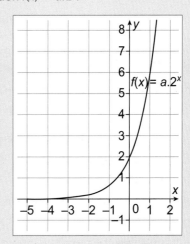

11.

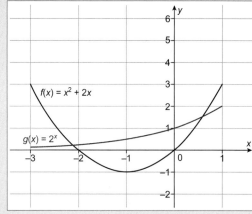

Using the above graphs, estimate:

(i) The range of values of x for which $f(x) > g(x)$

(ii) The range of values of x for which $g(x) \geqslant f(x)$

12.

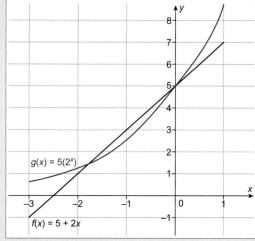

Using the above graphs, estimate:

(i) The range of values of x for which $f(x) > g(x)$

(ii) The range of values of x for which $g(x) \geqslant f(x)$

13. Graph the following functions in the domain $-2 \leqslant x \leqslant 1, x \in R$:

$f(x) = 5(2^x)$ and $g(x) = 3 + \dfrac{x}{4}$

Use your graph to give the range of values of x for which $f(x) > g(x)$.

14. Graph the following functions in the domain $-2 \leqslant x \leqslant 3, x \in R$:

$f(x) = 2.2^x$ and $g(x) = 2x^2 - 3x + 1$

Use your graph to give the range of values of x for which $g(x) \leqslant f(x)$.

15. A population of bacteria has a growth model given by the function $f(x) = 2^x$, where x is the number of days passed. On Day 1, there are two bacteria in a Petri dish.

(i) What will the population of bacteria in the dish be on Day 6?

(ii) Using suitable scales and axes, draw a graph to represent the population of the bacteria over a week-long period.

(iii) Use your graph to estimate the population at midweek.

(iv) From your graph, estimate to the nearest day the time taken for the population to reach 70.

16. On 1 June, a type of algae was introduced to Lough Arrow. The algae grew and spread so that after t days the volume of water containing the algae was given by $A(t) = 2^t$, where A is the volume in m³.

(i) Draw a graph to show the volume of algae in the lake for the first six days.

On the same date, a pollutant began to seep into the lake. The pollutant spread so that after t days the volume of water containing pollutant was given by $P(t) = 30 + 4t$, where P is the volume in m³.

(ii) Using the same axes and scales as for part (i) above, draw the graph of P.

(iii) After how much time will the volume of water containing the algae equal the volume of water containing the pollutant? Answer correct to the nearest six hours.

22.4 TRANSFORMATIONS OF EXPONENTIAL FUNCTIONS

Consider the function $y = 2^x$ in the domain $-2 \leqslant x \leqslant 2, x \in R$.

x	2^x	y	(x,y)
-2	$2^{-2} = \frac{1}{2^2}$	$\frac{1}{4}$	$\left(-2, \frac{1}{4}\right)$
-1	$2^{-1} = \frac{1}{2^1}$	$\frac{1}{2}$	$\left(-1, \frac{1}{2}\right)$
0	2^0	1	$(0,1)$
1	2^1	2	$(1,2)$
2	2^2	4	$(2,4)$

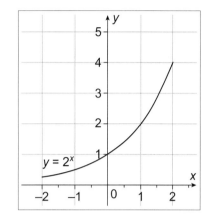

The graph of $y = 2^x$ is upward sloping and passes through the point $(0,1)$.

Graphs of Functions of the Form $y = ak^x$, $a > 0$

Consider the function $y = 2(2^x)$ in the same domain.

x	$2(2^x)$	y	(x,y)
-2	$2(2^{-2}) = 2\left(\frac{1}{2^2}\right)$	$\frac{1}{2}$	$\left(-2, \frac{1}{2}\right)$
-1	$2(2^{-1}) = 2\left(\frac{1}{2^1}\right)$	1	$(-1,1)$
0	$2(2^0) = 2(1)$	2	$(0,2)$
1	$2(2^1) = 2(2)$	4	$(1,4)$
2	$2(2^2) = 2(4)$	8	$(2,8)$

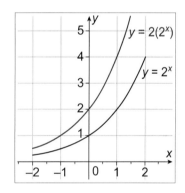

Note: For a given x-value, the y-value has been multiplied by 2.

What do you notice about the graph of $y = 2(2^x)$?

- The graph of $y = 2(2^x)$ is upward sloping.
- The graph passes through the point $(0,2)$.
- The graph of $y = 2(2^x)$ lies above the graph of $y = 2^x$. This is because, compared with $y = 2^x$, for a given x-value, each y-value has been multiplied by 2.

- The graph of $f(x) = a.k^x$, $a > 0$, lies above the graph of $y = k^x$ if $a > 1$.
- The graph of $f(x) = a.k^x$, $a > 0$, lies below the graph of $y = k^x$ if $a < 1$.
- The graph of $f(x) = a.k^x$ contains the point $(0,a)$.

Graphs of Functions of the Form $y = k^x + b$

Consider the function $y = 2^x + 1$ in the same domain as before.

x	2ˣ + 1	y	(x,y)
−2	$2^{-2} + 1 = \frac{1}{2^2} + 1$	1.25	(−2,1.25)
−1	$2^{-1} + 1 = \frac{1}{2^1} + 1$	1.5	(−1,1.5)
0	$2^0 + 1 = 1 + 1$	2	(0,2)
1	$2^1 + 1 = 2 + 1$	3	(1,3)
2	$2^2 + 1 = 4 + 1$	5	(2,5)

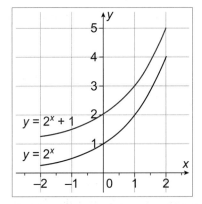

We can see that the graph of $y = 2^x + 1$ is the graph of $y = 2^x$ shifted (translated) one unit upwards.

> The graph of $f(x) = k^x + b$ is the graph of $y = k^x$ shifted b units upwards if $b > 0$ **or** shifted $-b$ units downwards if $b < 0$.

Graphs of Functions of the Form $y = k^{x + h}$

Consider the function $y = 2^{x + 1}$ in the same domain as before.

x	2ˣ⁺¹	y	(x,y)
−2	2^{-1}	$\frac{1}{2}$	$\left(-2, \frac{1}{2}\right)$
−1	2^0	1	(−1,1)
0	2^1	2	(0,2)
1	2^2	4	(1,4)
2	2^3	8	(2,8)

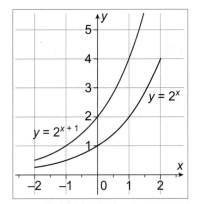

Note the position of the graph of $y = 2^{x + 1}$. There are two ways of thinking about this graph:

(1) The graph of $y = 2^{x + 1}$ ($= 2(2^x)$) lies above the graph of $y = 2^x$.

(2) The graph of $y = 2^{x + 1}$ is the graph of $y = 2^x$ shifted one unit to the left.

Consider the function $y = 2^{x - 1}$ in the same domain.

x	2ˣ⁻¹	y	(x,y)
−2	$2^{-3} = \frac{1}{2^3}$	$\frac{1}{8}$	$\left(-2, \frac{1}{8}\right)$
−1	$2^{-2} = \frac{1}{2^2}$	$\frac{1}{4}$	$\left(-1, \frac{1}{4}\right)$
0	$2^{-1} = \frac{1}{2^1}$	$\frac{1}{2}$	$\left(0, \frac{1}{2}\right)$
1	$2^0 = 1$	1	(1,1)
2	$2^1 = 2$	2	(2,2)

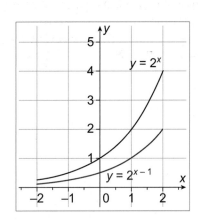

Note the position of the graph of $y = 2^{x-1}$. Again, there are two ways of thinking about this graph:

(1) The graph of $y = 2^{x-1}$ ($= 2^{-1}.2^x = \frac{1}{2}(2^x)$) lies below the graph of $y = 2^x$.

(2) The graph of $y = 2^{x-1}$ is the graph of $y = 2^x$ shifted one unit to the right.

> The graph of $f(x) = k^{x+h}$ is the graph of $y = k^x$ shifted h units to the left if $h > 0$ **or** $-h$ units to the right if $h < 0$.

Worked Example 22.7

Graph the function $y = 3(3^x)$ in the domain $-3 \leqslant x \leqslant 2, x \in R$.

Hence, sketch the functions:

    (i) $f(x) = 3^x$ (ii) $g(x) = 3^{x-1}$ (iii) $h(x) = 3^x + 4$

Solution

x	$3(3^x)$	y	(x,y)
-3	$3(3^{-3})$	0.11	$(-3, 0.11)$
-2	$3(3^{-2})$	0.33	$(-2, 0.33)$
-1	$3(3^{-1})$	1	$(-1, 1)$
0	$3(3^0)$	3	$(0, 3)$
1	$3(3^1)$	9	$(1, 9)$
2	$3(3^2)$	27	$(2, 27)$

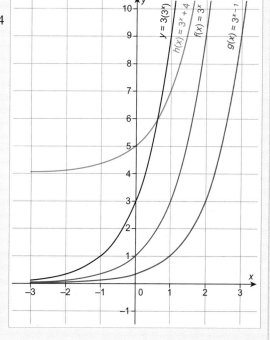

    (i) $y = 3(3^x) \Rightarrow y = 3^{x+1}$
            Therefore, the graph of $f(x) = 3^x$ is the
            graph of $y = 3^{x+1}$ shifted one unit to the right.

    (ii)   The graph of $g(x) = 3^{x-1}$ is the graph of $y = 3^x$
            shifted one unit to the right.

    (iii)   The graph of $h(x) = 3^x + 4$ is the graph of $y = 3^x$
            shifted four units upwards.

Exercise 22.3

1. Shown on the right is the graph of the function $f(x) = 3(2^x)$
   on the domain $-3 \leqslant x \leqslant 2, x \in R$.
   Use the graph to match the following functions with those
   graphed.

       (i) $g(x) = 2^x$

       (ii) $h(x) = 2^{x-1}$

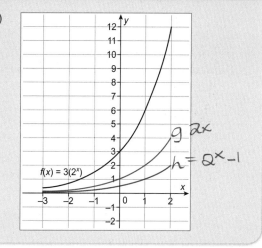

2. Shown below is the graph of the function $h(x) = 2.2^x$. Use the graph to match the following functions with those graphed below.

   (i) $f(x) = 4.2^x$ (ii) $g(x) = 3.2^x$

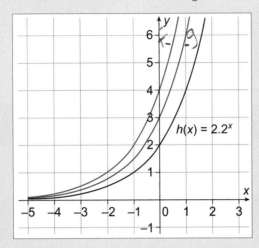

3. Shown below is the graph of the function $h(x) = 3^x$. Use the graph to match the following functions with those graphed below:

   (i) $g(x) = 3.3^x$ (ii) $f(x) = 3^x + 1$

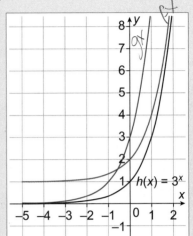

4. Graph the function $y = 2^x$ over the domain $-2 \leqslant x \leqslant 2, x \in R$.

   Hence, sketch the functions:

   (i) $f(x) = 2^{x+1}$ (ii) $g(x) = 2^x + 2$ (iii) $h(x) = 3(2^x)$

5. The graph of the function $y = 3^x$ is shifted three units to the right. What is the new functional form?

6. The graph of the function $y = 2^x$ is shifted to the left by two units and is shifted upwards by three units. What is the new functional form?

Revision Exercises

1. Draw a graph of the following functions on the given domains:

	Function	Domain
(i)	$f(x) = 6x - 2$	$-2 \leqslant x \leqslant 2, x \in R$
(ii)	$g(x) = 2 - 4x$	$-3 \leqslant x \leqslant 1, x \in R$

2. The variable cost per unit of a product is €5. Fixed costs are €45,000 (these costs are incurred regardless of the quantity produced). [Use the same axes and scales in parts (i)–(vi).]

   (i) Write an expression for variable costs in terms of x, where x is units produced.

   (ii) Graph the variable costs for this product for a range of production from 0 units to 50,000 units.

   (iii) Write an expression for fixed costs.

   (iv) Graph the fixed costs for this product for the same range of production as in part (ii).

   (v) If total costs = fixed costs + variable costs, write a function in terms of x (quantity produced) to represent total costs.

   (vi) Graph the function for total costs using the same range of production as before.

   (vii) If the selling price per unit is €6, write a function in terms of x to represent sales revenue for the same range of production (assuming all goods produced are sold).

   (viii) Graph this function using the same scales and axes as in part (vi).

   (ix) The break-even point is the number of units at which sales revenue and total costs are equal – that is to say, neither a profit nor a loss is made. From your graph, estimate what this level of production is.

   (x) Use algebra to answer part (ix) accurately.

3. Graph the following functions in the domain $-3 \leqslant x \leqslant 2$, $x \in R$:

   (i) $f(x) = x^2 + 3x - 4$

   (ii) $g(x) = 2x^2 - 2x - 1$

   (iii) $h(x) = 4 - 3x - x^2$

   (iv) $j(x) = -2x^2 - 3x + 4$

4. Graph the function $f(x) = x^2 - 2x - 4$ in the domain $-2 \leqslant x \leqslant 4$, $x \in R$.

  Find from your graph:

   (i) The value of $f(1.5)$

   (ii) The values of x for which $x^2 - 2x - 4 = 0$

   (iii) The values of x for which $x^2 - 2x - 3 \leqslant 0$.

   (iv) The minimum value of $f(x)$

5. Graph each of the following functions in the domain $-2 \leqslant x \leqslant 2$, $x \in R$.

   (i) $y = 3(3^x)$ (iv) $y = 2(3^x)$

   (ii) $y = 3(2^x)$ (v) $y = 5(2^x)$

   (iii) $y = 4(2^x)$

6. The graphs of the functions $f(x) = 2^x$ and $g(x)$ are given.

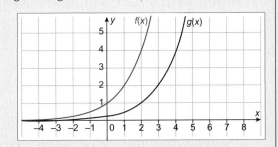

   (i) Describe in your own words a transformation that would map the graph of $f(x)$ to the graph of $g(x)$.

   (ii) What is the functional form of $g(x)$?

7. Charlie puts a proposal to his parents. He asks for his pocket money to be paid in the following way:

  Week 1: he will receive €1;

  Week 2: he will receive €2;

  Week 3: he will receive €4, and so on.

   (i) Set up a table to show the amount of pocket money Charlie will receive each week for the first eight weeks.

   (ii) Graph the data in the table, placing the week number on the x-axis.

   (iii) What type of function is this? Explain your answer.

   (iv) Is it possible that the pattern of payments is different to the pattern you described in part (i)? Explain your answer.

8. Label each function in the diagram below.

   (i) $f(x) = 2^x$ (ii) $g(x) = x^2 + 3x - 4$

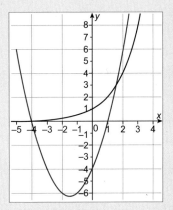

9. Graph the following functions in the domain $0 \leqslant x \leqslant 6$, $x \in R$:

   (i) $f(x) = x^2 - 7x + 10$

   (ii) $g(x) = x + 3$

  Use your graphs to give the range of values of x for which $f(x) \geqslant g(x)$.

10. Graph the following functions in the domain $-2 \leqslant x \leqslant 3$, $x \in R$:

   (i) $f(x) = 2(2^x)$

   (ii) $g(x) = -x^2 - 6x + 4$

  Use your graph to give the range of values of x for which $g(x) < f(x)$.

11. Ahmad was given a sketch of the graph of $y = x^2 + 3x + 5$ and asked to draw an appropriate straight line to solve $x^2 + x - 2 = 0$.

  Here are Ahmad's workings:

  Old $y = x^2 + 3x + 5$

$$\text{New} \quad \frac{0 = x^2 + x - 2}{y = \quad\quad 2x - 7}$$

When Ahmad drew the line $y = 2x - 7$, it did not intersect with the parabola $y = x^2 + 3x + 5$.

He concluded that the equation $x^2 + x - 2 = 0$ did not have any real solutions.

(a) Show that the equation $x^2 + x - 2 = 0$ has two real solutions.

(b) Explain the error that Ahmad made.

(c) What line should Ahmad have drawn?

(d) Graph $y = x^2 + 3x + 5$ and the line you have named in part (c).

Use the domain $-4 \leqslant x \leqslant 2, x \in R$.

(e) Use your graph to verify the solution to part (a).

12. A group of four students is studying graphs of functions of the form $f: x \rightarrow x^2 + 2x + k, x \in R$.

Each takes an integer value of k and draws the graph of their function in a suitable domain.

Maria took $k = -8$ and drew the graph below.

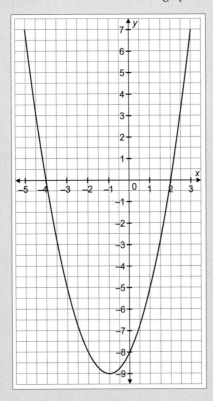

(a) Use the graph to write down the roots of the equation $x^2 + 2x - 8 = 0$.

(b) Keith's graph passes through the point $(3,2)$. Find the value of k that Keith used.

(c) On Alice's graph, the two roots of the function are the same.

Find the value of k that Alice used.

(d) Draw a sketch of Alice's function on the diagram shown in part (a).

(e) Emma's graph shows that the roots of her function are -5 and 3.

Find the value of k that she used.

SEC 2012, JCHL

13. The time taken in hours to manufacture a single unit of a product is modelled by the function $f(x) = x^2 - 6x + 22$, where x is the number of units (in tens) of the product produced to date.

Using appropriate scales and axes, graph the function in the domain $0 \leqslant x \leqslant 4$.

(i) After producing 10 units, how long should it take a worker to produce a unit of the product?

(ii) After producing 20 units, how long should it take a worker to produce a unit of the product?

(iii) What is the minimum time taken to produce a unit of the product?

(iv) The production line manager states that once production exceeds 30 units, the process becomes inefficient. Does the graph of the function support this claim?

14. A square of side x cm is removed from a triangle of card as shown.

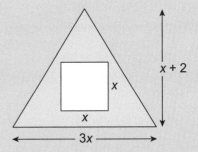

(a) Express the area of the shaded region in terms of x.

The remaining area of card (shaded in the diagram) is 3.5 cm².

(b) By letting the expression from part (a) equal 3.5, form a quadratic equation in the form $ax^2 + bx + c = 0$, where $a, b, c \in Z$.

(c) Draw the graph of the quadratic function $ax^2 + bx + c$ found in part (b).

(d) Use your graph to find the x-value that satisfies the equation in part (b).

(e) What are the dimensions of the triangle?

(f) By solving the equation in part (b) using algebra methods, verify your answer to part (e).

15. Myles the electrician uses this formula to work out how much to charge for a job:

$$C = 25 + 30H$$

where C is the charge and H is how long the job takes in hours.

Sarah the electrician uses this formula:

$$C = 35 + 27.5H$$

(a) Graph the charge for Myles and the charge for Sarah for $0 \leqslant H \leqslant 8, H \in R$, using the same scales and axes.

(b) Who would you hire for a job that takes 5 hours to complete?

(c) For what value of H is the charge the same for both electricians (use your graph)?

(d) Verify your answer to part (c) using algebra methods.

16. The graph of $y = x^2 + 4x + 2$ has a minimum point at $(-2, -2)$.

Write down the minimum point of the graph of $y = x^2 + 4x - 5$.

Answers

Chapter 1

Exercise 1.1

1. (i) Not well defined   (ii) Well defined
(iii) Not well defined   (iv) Well defined
2. (i) $\{0, 2, 3, 4, 5, 6, 7, 8\}$ (ii) $\{2\}$
(iii) $\{0, 1, 4, 6, 8\}$ (iv) $\{1, 3, 5, 7\}$ (v) $\{3, 5, 7\}$
(vi) $\{0, 4, 6, 8\}$ (vii) $\{1\}$ (viii) $\{0, 1, 2, 4, 6, 8\}$
3. (b) (i) $\{21, 23, 25\}$ (ii) $\{23\}$ (iii) $\{20, 22, 24\}$
(iv) $\{20, 21, 22, 24, 25\}$ (v) $\{20, 21, 22, 24, 25\}$
(vi) $\{20, 21, 22, 24, 25\}$ (vii) $\{\}$ or $\varnothing$
(viii) $\{21, 25\}$ (c) Yes   (d) $B \subset A$ **4.** (i) 8
(ii) $\{\}, \{x\}, \{y\}, \{z\}, \{x, y\}, \{x, z\}, \{y, z\}, \{x, y, z\}$
(iii) $\{x, y, z\}$ **5.** (i) $A \cup B$ (ii) $A \cap B$ (iii) $(A \cap B)'$
(iv) $B \backslash A$ **7.** (a) $U = \{1, 2, 3, 4, 5, 6, 7, 8\}$
$O = \{1, 3, 5, 7\}$ $P = \{3, 5, 7\}$ (c) (i) 4   (ii) 3
(iii) 3   (iv) 1   (v) 4   (vi) 4   (d) =; =
8. (ii) 41.8%   **9.** (ii) 20   (iii) 20%   (iv) 52.5%
11. (a) A   (b) $A \cap B$ (c) $A \cup B$ (d) $\varnothing$
12. (c) $D = (A \backslash B) \cup (B \backslash A) = (A \cup B) \backslash (A \cap B)$
13. (a) 4, 8, 12, 16, 20   (b) A_5
14. (ii) Total Number $= 490 - 2x$ (iii) 30

Exercise 1.2

2. (i) $A \cap B \cap C$ (ii) $A \backslash (B \cup C)$ (iii) $(B \cap C) \backslash A$
(iv) $(A \cup B \cup C)'$ **3.** (i) $\{4, 5\}$ (ii) $\{2, 8\}$
(iii) $\{8\}$ (iv) $\{2\}$ (v) $\{2, 3, 4, 5, 6, 8, 9\}$
(vi) $\{7\}$ **4.** (i) $\{0, 1, 2, 3, 5, 6, 8, 9\}$ (ii) $\{0\}$
(iii) $\{9\}$ (iv) $\{6\}$ (v) $\{0, 6, 9\}$ (vi) $\{4, 7\}$
5. (i) $(X \cap Y) \backslash Z$ (ii) $X \backslash Y$ (iii) $Z \backslash (X \cup Y)$
(iv) $(X \cup Y \cup Z)'$ **7.** (b) (i) $\{1\}$ (ii) $\{5, 6\}$
(iii) $\{1, 2, 3, 4, 5, 6, 7\}$ (iv) $\{6\}$ (v) $\{3, 4, 5, 7, 8\}$
(vi) $\{8\}$ (vii) $\{1\}$ (viii) $\varnothing$ (ix) $\{1, 7, 8\}$
(x) $\{1, 5, 6, 7\}$ (xi) $\{1, 6\}$ (xii) $\{1\}$ **8.** (ii) $\{b, c\}$
(iii) $\{d\}$ (iv) 6   (v) $(Y \cap Z) \backslash X$ **9.** (ii) $\{3, 5, 7\}$
(iii) $\{2\}$ (iv) $\#(A \cup B \cup C) = 9 = \#U$
(v) $A \backslash (B \cup C)$; $A \cap B \cap C$; $(B \cap C) \backslash A$; $U \backslash (A \cup B \cup C)$
10. (i) $A = \{2, 3\}$ $B = \{1, 2, 3, 4, 6, 12\}$
$C = \{1, 2, 4, 8\}$ (iii) $\{1, 2, 4\}$ (iv) $\{2\}$ (v) 7
(vi) $A \backslash (B \cup C)$ $(A \cap C) \backslash B$ **11.** (i) $P \cap Q \cap R$

(ii) $P \cup Q \cup R$ (iii) Q   (iv) $Q \backslash (P \cup R)$ (v) $P \cap R$
(vi) $(P \cap Q) \backslash R$ (vii) R' (viii) $(P \cup Q \cup R)'$
12. (ii) $N \backslash Z$ and $P \backslash N$ (iii) (a) $P \subset N$ (b) $N \subset Z$
13. (a) $\{5, 11, 17\}$ (b) $\{2, 8, 14, 20\}$
(c) $\{3, 7, 9, 13, 15, 19\}$

Exercise 1.3

1. (i) 2   (ii) 6   (iii) 15   (iv) 5   (v) 19   (vi) 23
(vii) 21   **2.** (ii) 3   **3.** (ii) 6   **4.** (ii) 5   (iii) 2
(iv) $\frac{1}{30}$ **5.** (ii) 15   **6.** (i) 4   (ii) 7   **7.** (i) 2
(ii) 20   **8.** (ii) 7   (iii) 4   (iv) $\frac{1}{20}$ (v) $\frac{13}{20}$ (vi) $\frac{17}{40}$
9. (ii) 2   (iii) 46   (iv) 52   (v) 43   (vi) 93%
(vii) 57%   **10.** (ii) 3   (iii) Two   (iv) Six
11. (ii) $\frac{17}{20}$ (iii) $\frac{3}{40}$ **12.** (ii) $\frac{1}{7}$ (iii) $\frac{9}{35}$ (iv) $\frac{5}{7}$

Exercise 1.4

6. $M \cup (N \cap O)$ **7.** $(T \cap R) \cup (T \cap S)$ **8.** (i) A'
(ii) B' (iii) Region 1   (iv) $(A \cup B)' = A' \cap B'$
(v) $(A \cap B)'$ (vi) $(A \cap B)' = A' \cup B'$ **10.** (i) $\{2, 3\}$
(ii) $\{1, 4, 5, 6, 7, 8, 9, 10\}$

Revision Exercises

1. (b) (i) $\{1, 2, 4, 5, 6, 8, 10, 12, 14, 16, 18, 20\}$
(ii) $\{2, 4, 10, 20\}$ (iii) $\{3, 6, 7, 8, 9, 11, 12, 13, 14,$
$15, 16, 17, 18, 19\}$ (iv) $\{1, 3, 5, 7, 9, 11, 13, 15,$
$17, 19\}$ (v) $\{1, 3, 5, 6, 7, 8, 9, 11, 12, 13, 14, 15,$
$16, 17, 18, 19\}$ (vi) $\{1, 3, 5, 6, 7, 8, 9, 11, 12, 13,$
$14, 15, 16, 17, 18, 19\}$ (vii) $\{1, 5, 6, 8, 12, 14,$
$16, 18\}$ (viii) $\varnothing$ **2.** (i) 4   (ii) 4   (iii) 2   (iv) 2
(v) 6   (vi) 2   **3.** (ii) $\{w, y, z\}$ (iii) $\varnothing$ (iv) 8
(v) $\{X \backslash (Y \cup Z)\}$ (vi) $\{Y \backslash (X \cup Z), (X \cap Y) \backslash Z,$
$(X \cap Z) \backslash Y, (Y \cap Z) \backslash X\}$ **4.** (ii) 3,060   (iii) 66.47%
(iv) 27.97%   (v) 51%   (vi) JLS   **6.** (ii) 7
(iii) 35%   **7.** (i) 8   (ii) 14   **8.** (ii) 45   (iii) 58%
(iv) 42%   **9.** (a) (i) $\{1, 2, 3, 4, 5, 6\}$ (ii) $\{5, 6\}$
(iii) $\{1, 2, 4, 5, 6\}$ (b) $(P \cup Q) \cap (P \cup R)$
10. (a) 7   (b) One   (c) Prime   **11.** (b) 68%

(c) 3%   **12.** (i) (A\B) ∪ (C ∩ B) = {1, 3, 4, 5}
(A ∪ B) ∩ (C\B) = {1, 4}   (ii) 12
13. (b) (i) U = a + b − x + y

Chapter 2

Exercise 2.1

1. (i) Z   (ii) N   (iii) Q   (iv) Z   (v) N   (vi) N
2. (a) {2, 3, 5, 7, 11, 13, 17, 19, 23, 29, 31, 37, 41,
43, 47}   (b) (i) $2^3 \times 3 \times 5 \times 11$ (ii) $2^4 \times 5^2 \times 13$
(iii) $2^2 \times 3 \times 11^2$ (iv) $2 \times 3 \times 5 \times 7 \times 11$
(v) $2^5 \times 3^5$ (vi) $2 \times 31 \times 43$ **3.** (a) (i) 4 × 3 = 12
(ii) 3 × 5 = 15   (iii) 8 × 3 = 24
(iv) 2 × 6 = 12   (b) (i) 1,008   (ii) 2,356
(iii) 2,982   (iv) 51,460   (v) 55,022   110,080
4. (i) 2   (ii) −2   (iii) −8   (iv) −4   (v) −11
(vi) −3   **5.** (i) $\frac{9}{10}$ (ii) $\frac{15}{16}$ (iii) $\frac{7}{6}$ (iv) $\frac{11}{8}$
(b) (i) $\frac{4}{5}$ (ii) $\frac{3}{8}$ (iii) $\frac{3}{10}$ **7.** (i) HCF = 3;
LCM = 2,829   (ii) HCF = 23;   LCM = 9,936
(iii) HCF = 8;   LCM = 97,240   (iv) HCF = 9;
LCM = 2,063,205   (v) HCF = 96;   LCM = 24,288
(vi) HCF = 3;   LCM = 430,005
8. (i) Commutative property of addition
(ii) Commutative property of multiplication
(iii) Associative property of addition
(iv) Associative property of multiplication
(v) Distributive property of multiplication over
addition   **9.** (i) 320   (ii) 16   (iii) $4\frac{59}{64}$ (iv) $34\frac{1}{2}$
10. 6,272   **11.** 212   **12.** Largest: $15\frac{1}{3}$
Smallest: $\frac{199}{252}$ **13.** 16 : 9   **14.** 121 : 25

Exercise 2.2

1. $\sqrt{7}$, $3 − \sqrt{9}$ **2.** (i) Yes   (ii) No   (iii) Yes   (iv) Yes
(v) Yes   (vi) No   (vii) No   (viii) No   (ix) No
3. (i) 5   (ii) 11   (iii) 17   (iv) 27   (v) 34   (vi) 27
(vii) 250   (viii) $\frac{29}{9}$ (ix) $\frac{65}{16}$ (x) $\frac{171}{64}$ **4.** (i) False
(ii) False   (iii) True   (iv) True   **5.** (i) Commutative
property of addition   (ii) Associative property
of multiplication   (iii) Distributive property of
multiplication over addition   **7.** (i) 6   (ii) 10
(iii) 4   (iv) 8   (v) 10   (vi) 12   **8.** (i) 3   (ii) 5
(iii) 2   (iv) 3   (v) 5   (vi) 10   **9.** (i) $2\sqrt{2}$ (ii) $3\sqrt{5}$
(iii) $10\sqrt{3}$ (iv) $2\sqrt{3}$ (v) $4\sqrt{2}$ (vi) $10\sqrt{5}$ (vii) $3\sqrt{3}$
(viii) $3\sqrt{6}$ (ix) $5\sqrt{3}$ (x) $7\sqrt{2}$ **10.** $7\sqrt{2}$ **11.** $5\sqrt{3}$
12. $7\sqrt{5}$ **13.** 1   **14.** $10\sqrt{2}$ **15.** $6\sqrt{3}$ **16.** (i) $\sqrt{2}$
and $\sqrt{8}$ (ii) $\sqrt{2}$ and $\sqrt{3}$ **17.** (i) $5\frac{1}{3}$ (ii) $\sqrt{5\frac{1}{2}}$

(iii) 16   (iv) 5   **18.** $\sqrt{1.1}, \sqrt{1.2}, \sqrt{1.3}$
19. (i) $\sqrt{10}$ sq. units   (ii) 2   **21.** $3\sqrt{2}$ sq. units
23. $\sqrt{3}$ is between 1 and 2 so $2 + \sqrt{3}$ is between
3 and 4.   **24.** He does not have enough cable.

Exercise 2.3

1. (i) $\sqrt{2} + \sqrt{10}$ (ii) $11 + 5\sqrt{5}$ (iii) $15 + 6\sqrt{6}$
(iv) $3 + 2\sqrt{2}$; $6 + 4\sqrt{2}$ **2.** (i) $\sqrt{26} + \sqrt{13}$
(ii) $\sqrt{5} − 5$ (iii) $2 − \sqrt{2}$ (iv) $8 + 2\sqrt{7}$
3. (i) $−1 + \sqrt{3}$ (ii) $1 + \sqrt{7}$ (iii) $27 + 10\sqrt{2}$
(iv) $a^2 + 2ab + b^2$ **4.** (i) $6 + 11\sqrt{2}$ (ii) $10 + 2\sqrt{5}$
5. (i) $\frac{\sqrt{3}}{3}$ (ii) $\frac{2\sqrt{5}}{5}$ (iii) $\sqrt{2}$ (iv) $\sqrt{7}$ (v) $\frac{3\sqrt{21}}{7}$
(vi) $\frac{2\sqrt{6}}{9}$ (vii) $\frac{\sqrt{15}}{15}$ (viii) $\frac{1}{4}\sqrt{2}$ **6.** (i) $−\frac{1}{2} + \frac{1}{2}\sqrt{5}$
(ii) $−\frac{5}{2} − \frac{5}{2}\sqrt{3}$ (iii) $\frac{60}{23} + \frac{12}{23}\sqrt{2}$ (iv) $−\frac{3}{2} − \frac{1}{2}\sqrt{3}$
(v) $−\frac{3}{2} − \frac{1}{2}\sqrt{5}$ (vi) $2 − \sqrt{3}$ **7.** $−\sqrt{6} + 2\sqrt{3} + \sqrt{2}$
8. (i) $\frac{6}{5}\sqrt{5}$ (ii) $−1 − \sqrt{3}$ (iii) $−\frac{6}{13} + \frac{5}{13}\sqrt{3}$
9. $1 + 4\sqrt{2}$ sq. units   **10.** $−6 + 6\sqrt{5}$ (m)
11. (a) $\sqrt{2}$ sq. units   (b) $2\sqrt{3} + \sqrt{21}$ sq. units
12. (i) 20 units   (ii) 22 sq. units   (iii) $2\sqrt{14}$ units
13. (a) 1.5 sq. units   (b) $\sqrt{22}$ units

Revision Exercises

2. (a) (i) $\frac{1}{2}$ (ii) $\frac{1}{4}$ (iii) $\frac{13}{8}$ (iv) $\frac{7}{10}$ (b) (i) 600
(ii) 1,312   (iii) 2,728   (iv) 27,520   **3.** (i) HCF = 3;
LCM = 5,382   (ii) HCF = 17;   LCM = 26,520
(iii) HCF = 22;   LCM = 11,286   (iv) HCF = 4;
LCM = 203,320   **4.** (i) 12   (ii) $5\sqrt{10}$ (iii) 4
(iv) 36   (v) 30   (vi) $4\sqrt{7}$ **5.** $ab\sqrt{b}$ **6.** (i) 7
(ii) 9   (iii) 8   (iv) 2   **7.** (i) $3\sqrt{10}$ (ii) $3\sqrt{5}$
(iii) $20\sqrt{2}$ (iv) $8\sqrt{3}$ (v) $4\sqrt{10}$ (vi) $15\sqrt{10}$
8. (i) Multiplication is commutative   (ii) Addition
is associative   (iii) Multiplication is distributive
over addition   (iv) Addition is commutative
(v) Multiplication is associative   **9.** (i) 93   (ii) 6
(iii) $15\frac{67}{70}$ (iv) −1   **10.** (i) $4 = 2^2$; $9 = 3^2$;
$16 = 2^4$; $25 = 5^2$ (ii) $5,929 = 7^2 \times 11^2$
(iii) Even numbers   (iv) 44,100   **11.** (i) $−4 + \sqrt{6}$
(ii) $10 − 30\sqrt{3} + 12\sqrt{5} − 5\sqrt{15}$ (iii) $38 + 12\sqrt{2}$
12. (i) $3 − \sqrt{7}$ (ii) $\frac{12}{13} + \frac{13}{13}\sqrt{3}$ (iii) $\frac{11}{10} + \frac{1}{10}\sqrt{11}$
(iv) $\frac{1}{2} + \frac{1}{2}\sqrt{3}$ (v) $−\frac{7}{6} − \frac{1}{6}\sqrt{13}$ (vi) $5\sqrt{3} − 5\sqrt{2}$
13. (b) π or $\sqrt{\sqrt{2}}$ **14.** $\frac{1}{\sqrt{2}} = \frac{\sqrt{8}}{4}$; $6 = 3\sqrt{4}$;
$\sqrt{8} \times \sqrt{5} = \sqrt{40}$; $\frac{\sqrt{40}}{\sqrt{10}} = 2$ **15.** (ii) a = 2 and
b = 5   **16.** 36 cans   **17.** 8 girls   **18.** (a) 25 cm²

(b) 5 cm   **19.** (a) 4   (b) $4\sqrt{10}$ (c) $83\frac{1}{3}\%$
20. (a) $a = 16$ $b = 30, c = 34$ **21.** (i) 14
(ii) $2{,}520 = 2^3 \times 3^2 \times 5 \times 7$; $154 = 2 \times 7 \times 11$

Chapter 3

Exercise 3.1

1. 160   **2.** (i) Christmas Day is on the 10th November   (ii) The sun rises in the east
(iii) Rolling a number greater than 1 on a die
(iv) Winning the Lotto   (v) Rolling an odd number
on a die   **3.** (i) 2   (ii) 6   (iii) 24   (iv) 120
4. (i) 120   (ii) 360   (iii) 720   (iv) 30   **5.** (i) 5,040
(ii) 10,000   (iii) 2,016   **6.** 64   **7.** 6,760   **8.** 500,
e.g. 1, 3, 3, H, H   **9.** (i) 1   (ii) $\frac{1}{6}$ (iii) $\frac{1}{2}$ (iv) $\frac{1}{6}$
10. (i) 35%   (ii) 65%   **11.** $\frac{3}{11}$ **12.** $\frac{6}{50} \approx 0.12$;
the die could be unfair   **13.** (i) 43%   (ii) 57%;
the coin appears to be biased   **14.** (i) $66\frac{2}{3}\%$
(ii) 16   **15.** (i) 16%   (ii) Yes   **16.** (i) $\frac{5}{40}$ or 12.5%;
$\frac{7}{30}$ or $23\frac{1}{3}\%$; $\frac{3}{16}$ or $18\frac{3}{4}\%$; $\frac{6}{25}$ or 24%
(ii) 100 rolls   (iii) Yes   **17.** 5   **18.** (i) $\frac{12}{23}$
(ii) $\frac{11}{23}$ **19.** (i) $\frac{1}{2}$ (ii) $\frac{2}{9}$ (iii) $\frac{13}{18}$ (iv) $\frac{5}{18}, \frac{13}{18}$
(v) $\frac{7}{9}$ **20.** (i) $\frac{1}{6}$ (ii) 0   (iii) $\frac{1}{2}$ (iv) $\frac{1}{2}$ (v) $\frac{1}{2}$
(vi) $\frac{1}{6}$ **21.** (i) $\frac{5}{13}$ (ii) $\frac{2}{13}$ (iii) $\frac{2}{13}$ (iv) $\frac{11}{13}$
22. (i) $\frac{1}{2}$ (ii) $\frac{1}{2}$ (iii) 1   (iv) $\frac{1}{26}$ (v) $\frac{7}{13}$ (vi) $\frac{3}{13}$
23. (i) $\frac{1}{2}$ (ii) 20 times

24. (i)

Sector	R.F.
P	0.18
Q	0.18
R	0.27

(ii) Not fair   (iii) 180 times   **25.** (i) 260
(ii) 120   (iii) 40   (iv) 20   **26.** 8%   **27.** (a) (i) $\frac{2}{3}$
(ii) $\frac{1}{3}$ (iii) $\frac{7}{10}$ (iv) $\frac{1}{6}$ (b) $\frac{2}{15}$ (c) 90 days
28. (i) $\frac{1}{20}$ (ii) $\frac{1}{2}$ (iii) $\frac{9}{20}$ (iv) $\frac{1}{5}$ (v) $\frac{1}{10}$
(vi) $\frac{1}{2}$ or 0.5   (vii) $\frac{3}{20}$ or 0.15

29.

	1	2	3	4	5	6
1	1,1	1,2	1,3	1,4	1,5	1,6
2	2,1	2,2	2,3	2,4	2,5	2,6
3	3,1	3,2	3,3	3,4	3,5	3,6
4	4,1	4,2	4,3	4,4	4,5	4,6
5	5,1	5,2	5,3	5,4	5,5	5,6
6	6,1	6,2	6,3	6,4	6,5	6,6

(i) $\frac{1}{4}$ (ii) $\frac{1}{6}$ (iii) $\frac{5}{6}$ (iv) $\frac{1}{4}$ **30.** (i) $\frac{1}{8}$
(ii) $\frac{1}{8}$ (iii) $\frac{3}{8}$ (iv) $\frac{1}{2}$

31.

		Red					
		1	2	3	4	5	6
Black	1	2	3	4	5	6	7
	2	3	4	5	6	7	8
	3	4	5	6	7	8	9
	4	5	6	7	8	9	10
	5	6	7	8	9	10	11
	6	7	8	9	10	11	12

(i) $\frac{5}{36}$ (ii) $\frac{1}{2}$ (iii) $\frac{5}{12}$ (iv) $\frac{11}{18}$ (v) $\frac{1}{12}$ (vi) $\frac{2}{9}$

32. (i)

	Ford	Honda	Nissan	Volvo	Total
Petrol	11	7	11	13	42
Diesel	17	20	12	9	58
Total	28	27	23	22	100

(ii) Diesel   (iii) $\frac{27}{100}$ or 27%   (iv) $\frac{11}{50}$ or 22%
(v) $\frac{29}{50}$ or 58%   (vi) $\frac{11}{100}$ or 11%   (vii) $\frac{17}{58}$ or 29%
(viii) $\frac{20}{29}$ or 79%

33.

	1	2	3	4	5	6
1	1	2	3	4	5	6
2	2	4	6	8	10	12
3	3	6	9	12	15	18
4	4	8	12	16	20	24
5	5	10	15	20	25	30
6	6	12	18	24	30	36

(i) $\frac{1}{18}$ (ii) $\frac{4}{9}$ (iii) $\frac{1}{6}$ (iv) $\frac{8}{9}$ (v) $\frac{5}{12}$ (vi) $\frac{1}{6}$
34. (i) $\frac{1}{9}$ (ii) $\frac{4}{9}$ (iii) $\frac{5}{9}$ (iv) $\frac{1}{3}$ (v) $\frac{2}{3}$
35. (i) $\frac{12}{25}$ (ii) $\frac{26}{125}$ (iii) $\frac{2}{25}$ (iv) $\frac{22}{25}$
(v) $\frac{1}{12}$ (vi) $\frac{13}{15}$ (vii) $\frac{10}{13}$

36. (a)

8	0	2	3	4	7	8				
9	0	2	3	5	5	6	9			
10	0	1	1	1	2	3	3	5	5	9	9
11	1	4	5	8	8					

(b) (i) $\frac{23}{30}$ (ii) $\frac{13}{30}$ (iii) $\frac{8}{15}$ (c) 500 apples

37. (i)

Combined score	2	3	4	5	6	7	8	9	10	11	12
Frequency	4	6	4	1	5	3	4	2	3	1	3

(ii) $\frac{5}{36}$ (iv)

	1	2	3	4	5	6
1	2	3	4	5	6	7
2	3	4	5	6	7	8
3	4	5	6	7	8	9
4	5	6	7	8	9	10
5	6	7	8	9	10	11
6	7	8	9	10	11	12

(v) $\frac{5}{36}$ (viii) Do many more rolls of the dice
(ix) No

38. (a)

Category \ Version	Hardback	Softback	Totals
Fiction	124	1,820	1,944
Non-fiction	341	239	580
Classics	155	21	176
Totals	620	2,080	2,700

(b) (i) $\frac{239}{2,700}$ (ii) $\frac{859}{2,700}$ (iii) $\frac{7}{8}$ (c) 11 **39.** (i) $\frac{9}{20}$
(ii) $\frac{11}{20}$ (iii) 10 marbles **40.** (ii) 0.5 (iv) 0.5
(vi) 0.5 (vii) 0.125 (viii) 0.125 (ix) 0.375
(x) 0.375

Exercise 3.2

1. $\frac{3}{16}$ **2.** (i) 0.3 (ii) 0.09 **3.** $\frac{9}{64}$ **4.** $\frac{12}{49}$ **5.** 0.04
6. $\frac{1}{25}$ **7.** 0.16 **8.** $\frac{1}{9}$ **9.** (i) $\frac{49}{100}$ (ii) $\frac{21}{100}$ (iii) $\frac{42}{100}$
10. (i) $\frac{6}{25}$ (ii) $\frac{6}{25}$ (iii) $\frac{4}{25}$ (iv) $\frac{13}{25}$ (v) $\frac{12}{25}$ **11.** $\frac{16}{121}$
(ii) $\frac{49}{121}$ (iii) $\frac{65}{121}$ (iv) $\frac{56}{121}$ (v) $\frac{105}{121}$ **12.** (i) 0.24
(ii) 0.76 (iii) 0.52 **13.** $\frac{1}{2}$ (ii) $\frac{1}{4}$ (iii) $\frac{1}{4}$;
probability player does not win = $\frac{1}{8}$
14. (i) 0.0025 (ii) 0.9025 (iii) 0.0975
15. (i) $\frac{1}{6}$ (ii) $\frac{5}{36}$ (iii) $\frac{25}{216}$; probability player
does not win = $\frac{125}{216}$ **16.** (i) $\frac{5}{21}$ (ii) $\frac{16}{21}$;
the game is not fair **17.** (ii) 0.971 **18.** (ii) 0.045
(iii) 0.8615 (iv) 0.8781 **19.** (ii) $\frac{23}{60}$ (iii) $\frac{15}{23}$
20. (i) $\frac{3}{10}$ (ii) $\frac{1}{6}$ (iii) $\frac{7}{15}$ (iv) $\frac{8}{15}$

Exercise 3.3

1. (i) $\frac{12}{30}$ (ii) $\frac{1}{2}$ (iii) $\frac{7}{30}$ (iv) $\frac{1}{3}$ **2.** (i) $\frac{11}{15}$ (ii) $\frac{2}{5}$
(iii) $\frac{2}{15}$ **3.** (a) (i) $\frac{12}{13}$ (ii) $\frac{3}{13}$ (iii) $\frac{4}{13}$ (iv) $\frac{1}{13}$
(b) (i) $\frac{8}{13}$ (ii) $\frac{0}{13}$ (iii) $\frac{1}{13}$ (iv) $\frac{5}{13}$ **4.** (i) $\frac{17}{45}$
(ii) $\frac{28}{45}$ (iii) $\frac{1}{9}$ **5.** (i) $\frac{2}{3}$ (ii) $\frac{1}{2}$ (iii) $\frac{13}{15}$ (iv) $\frac{2}{25}$
6. (a) (i) 7 (ii) 2 (iii) 3 (iv) $\frac{7}{12}$ (v) $\frac{1}{6}$

(vi) $\frac{1}{4}$ **7.** (ii) 0.6 **8.** (ii) 0.2 **9.** (ii) 0.3 (iii) 0.2
10. (i) $\frac{1}{2}$ (ii) $\frac{3}{10}$ (iii) $\frac{1}{20}$ (iv) $\frac{4}{5}$ **11.** (i) 0.54
(ii) 0.68 (iii) $\frac{7}{25}$ (iv) $\frac{13}{50}$ **12.** (i) $\frac{1}{2}$ (ii) $\frac{1}{6}$
(iii) $\frac{1}{30}$ (iv) $\frac{2}{15}$ (v) $\frac{1}{10}$ (vi) $\frac{1}{15}$ **13.** (i) $\frac{2}{3}$ (ii) $\frac{2}{11}$
(iii) $\frac{2}{33}$ (iv) $\frac{2}{3}$ **14.** (ii) $\frac{10}{17}$ (iii) $\frac{2}{17}$ (iv) $\frac{81}{85}$
(v) $\frac{4}{85}$ **15.** (ii) $\frac{32}{45}$ (iii) $\frac{19}{45}$ (iv) $\frac{13}{45}$ **16.** (b) $\frac{3}{25}$
(c) $\frac{14}{25}$ **17.** (i) $\frac{1}{7}$ (ii) $\frac{5}{14}$ (iii) $\frac{5}{14}$

Revision Exercises

1. (a) (ii) 36 (iii) $\frac{1}{36}$ (iv) $\frac{1}{36}$ (v) $\frac{1}{12}$ (vi) $\frac{1}{4}$
(vii) $\frac{1}{4}$ (b) (ii) P(B, B) = $\frac{8}{49}$; P(Y, Y) = $\frac{15}{49}$;
P(B, Y) = $\frac{20}{49}$; P(BB or YY) = $\frac{23}{49}$ (c) $\frac{1}{36}$
3. (a) (i) 4 (ii) 128 (b) (i) $\frac{1}{100}$ or 0.01
(ii) $\frac{1}{10}$ or 0.1 (iii) $\frac{21}{25}$ or 0.84 (iv) O⁻
4. (a) (i) 90 (iv) $\frac{7}{50}$ or 0.14 (vi) No
(b) (i) 89 times (iii) 152 times **5.** (a) 0.466
6. (i) $\frac{1}{8}$ (ii) $\frac{1}{4}$ (iii) $\frac{1}{4}$ (iv) $\frac{7}{8}$ (b) (ii) P(pass on
1st attempt) = 0.4; P(fail on both attempts) = 0.36;
P(pass on 2nd attempt) = 0.24 (c) (i) $\frac{2}{5}$ (ii) $\frac{1}{5}$
(iii) 3 more red marbles added **7.** (a) (i) $\frac{3}{4}$
(ii) $\frac{1}{4}$ (iii) $\frac{5}{24}$ (iv) $\frac{2}{3}$ (v) $\frac{1}{4}$ (vi) $\frac{1}{8}$ (b) (i) 0.105
(ii) 0.105 (iii) 0.105 (c) (i) 4 (ii) 1 (iii) 0.16
(iv) 0.04 **8.** (a) (i) $\frac{1}{8}$ (ii) $\frac{1}{4}$ (b) (i) (a) E.g. Italy,
Iceland, Norway (b) E.g. Spain, Cyprus,
Turkey (ii) 300 (c) (iii) No **9.** (a) (ii) 82
(b) (ii) $\frac{1}{18}$ (iii) 18 goes (iv) 2 wins (v) 0.00017
(vi) 0.158 (vii) 0.0089 **10.** (a) (i) $\frac{3}{10}$ (2) $\frac{19}{30}$
(3) $\frac{11}{75}$ (4) $\frac{59}{150}$ (ii) $\frac{11}{69}$ (iii) (1) Discrete
(2) Continuous (b) x = 0.2, y = 0.2,
z = 0.05 **11.** (i) $\frac{1}{18}$ (ii) $\frac{1}{3}$ (iii) $\frac{2}{3}$ (b) (i) $\frac{1}{40}$
(ii) $\frac{13}{20}$ (iii) $\frac{2}{5}$ (iv) $\frac{9}{40}$ (c) (i) 0.4 (ii) 0.3
13. (a) (i) $\frac{1}{16}$ (ii) $\frac{1}{4}$ (iii) $\frac{11}{16}$ (iv) $\frac{5}{16}$ (v) $\frac{1}{16}$
(b) (ii) $\frac{1}{50}$ (iii) No (iv) $\frac{1}{10}$ (c) (i) $\frac{1}{6}$ (ii) $\frac{5}{18}$
(iii) $\frac{5}{18}$ (iv) $\frac{5}{9}$ **14.** (a) $\frac{2}{3}$ (b) $\frac{1}{6}$ (c) $\frac{1}{3}$
15. (a) $\frac{1}{6} = 0.1\dot{6}$ (b) 86

Chapter 4

Exercise 4.1

1. (i) Square (ii) Circle (iii) Circle (iv) Triangle
2. (i) Green (ii) Red (iii) 10 times

3. (i) 13 matchsticks   (ii) 16 matchsticks
(iii) ▢▢▢▢   ▢▢▢▢▢   (iv) 91 matchsticks
4. (i) (a) 2   (b) +4   (c) 18, 22, 26   (d) Start with
2 and then add 4 to every term   (ii) (a) 7
(b) +12   (c) 55, 67, 79   (d) Start with 7 and
then add 12 to every term   (iii) (a) 9   (b) +15
(c) 69, 84, 99   (d) Start with 9 and then add 15 to
every term   (iv) (a) 3   (b) −8   (c) −29, −37, −45
(d) Start with 3 and then subtract 8 every term
(v) (a) 1   (b) −11   (c) −43, −54, −65
(d) Start with 1 and then subtract 11 every term
5. (i) (a) 6   (b) +3   (c) $T_n = 3n + 3$ (d) 30
(ii) (a) 9   (b) +5   (c) $T_n = 5n + 4$ (d) 69
(iii) (a) 0   (b) −3   (c) $T_n = -3n + 3$ (d) −54
(iv) (a) −10   (b) +3   (c) $T_n = 3n - 13$ (d) 143
(v) (a) 1000   (b) −252   (c) $T_n = -252n + 1252$
(d) −23,948   **6.** (i) (a) 3   (b) 9   (c) 135
(ii) (a) 7   (b) 11   (c) 95   (iii) (a) −2   (b) 0
(c) 42   (iv) (a) 3   (b) 1   (c) −41   (v) (a) 8   (b) 26
(c) 404   (vi) (a) 1   (b) −3   (c) −87
7. (i)

	Student A	Student B	Student C
Start amount	€10	€0	€90
End amount	€130	€600	€180

(ii) Student A: $m = 20t + 10$; Student B: $m = 100t$;
Student C: $m = 15t + 90$ (iii) Student A has
€250; Student B has €1,200; Student C has
€270   (iv) The graph for Student B is directly
proportional, as the line goes through the
origin.   (v) Constant of proportionality = 100
8. (i) 32   (ii) $m = 5n + 2$ (iv) 127 matches
(v) Pattern 36   **9.** (i) 18 marbles
(ii) $3n + 3$ marbles   (iv) 30th pattern
10. (i) 22 coins   (iii) Five complete patterns
11. (ii) Cost for 1 minute = €0.035   (iii) Cost for
1 minute = €0.025   (iv) Company B; 8 cents
(v) Company A costs an initial 30 cent (€0.30) to
make a phone call plus an additional 3.5 cent
(€0.035) per minute. Company B costs an initial
38 cent (€0.38) to make a phone call plus an
additional 2.5 cent (€0.025) per minute
(vi) Company A: $c = 0.035m + 0.3$;
Company B: $c = 0.025m + 0.38$
(vii) 8-minute call   (ix) Company A: €1.105;
Company B: €0.955   **12.** (i) Company A: €5/km;
Company B: €3/km   (ii) Company B has a
standing charge of €50.   (iii) The trip would cost
€5 per km with Company A. The trip would cost
€50 plus €3 per km with Company B

(iv) Company A: $c = 5d$; Company B: $c = 3d + 50$
(v) Approx. 25 km   (vii) Company B, 150 km
(viii) Company A   **13.** (iii) $V = -2.5t + 50$
(iv) The formula means that you start with
50 (litres) of water and subtract 2.5 (litres) every
hour. The subtraction describes the leak from
the water storage tank.   (v) $V = 35$ litres
(vi) 20 hours   **14.** (ii) 2.5   (iii) For every tonne
of metal, 2.5 cars are produced.   (iv) $m = 2.5 c$
(v) $c = 0.4 m$ (vi) 210 cars   (vii) 312.5 tonnes
of metal   **15.** (ii) Graph B is directly proportional,
as it passes through the origin and the equation
of this line would be in the form $y = mx$, where
m (the slope) is 60.   (iii) $40t + 50$, $c = 60t$
16. (ii) Carla: $s = 25t + 150$; Alvaro: $s = 40t + 60$
(s = amount saved; t = time in weeks)
(iii) 6 weeks   (iv) 3 weeks   (v) $s = 65t + 210$
17. (iii) Siobhán   (iv) Máire: 50 m/min; Siobhán:
100 m/min   (v) Siobhán lives further from school
because she had the greater distance to travel
(500 m) compared with Máire (300 m).
(vi) 4 minutes   (vii) $d = -50t + 300$,
$d = -100t + 500$ (viii) $3\frac{1}{2}$ minutes, $4\frac{1}{2}$ minutes
18. 1,000th letter is X   **19.** (a) 9th term   (b) 39
20. (iii) 75   (iv) $C = 75A$ (v) €900   (vi) 60 m²
(vii) 1 m² = €65   (viii) Company B; €300
21. (i) 6 blue   (ii) 22 red   (iii) 37 counters
(iv) $4n + 1$ (v) $3n + 1$ (vi) n counters
(vii)(a) The number of red counters in the pattern is
calculated by 3 times the pattern number plus 1.
(b) The number of blue counters in the pattern is
the same as the pattern number.   **22.** (i) 21 blue
(ii) 58 tiles   (iii)(a) $T_n = n - 1$ (b) $T_n = 2n - 1$
(c) $T_n = 3n - 2$ (iv) The decorator can only
make five complete patterns using 35 of the
tiles.   **23.** (iii) $d = 1.25e$ (iv) 1.25
(v) The constant of proportionality represents the
exchange rate, i.e. €1 = $1.25.   (vi) $1,000
24. (ii) $25t + 75$, $c = 50t$ (iii) Mechanic A: €75;
Mechanic B: €0   (iv) Mechanic A is cheaper.
25. (i) Decreased by 70   (ii) 780 houses built
(iii) 4,650   **26.** (c) 5 seconds   (d) After 9 seconds
Jenny is furthest from Tina and 4 m ahead of
Bill.   (e) $d = 2t + 7$ (f) $d = 3t + 2$
(h) $27\frac{1}{2}$ seconds   (i) 105 seconds   **27.** (a) From
the data in the table there is a common difference
of €18 for every 100 units used.   (c) €20
(e) $C = 0.18u + 20$ (f) 13.5%   (h) Plan B is
cheaper only if Lisa uses more than approx.
650 units of electricity.   (j) 640 units

Exercise 4.2

1. (i) (a) 14   (b) 1st differences: 1, 6, 11 …;
2nd difference: +5   (c) 48, 69, 95
(ii) (b) 1st differences: 10, 16, 22; 2nd difference: +6
(iii) (b) 1st differences: 4, 7, 10; 2nd difference: +3
(c) 34, 50, 69   (iv) (b) 1st differences: 2, −1, −4;
2nd difference: −3   (v) (a) $T_1 = -8$
(b) 1st differences: −4, 2, 8; 2nd difference: +6
(c) 12, 32, 58   **2.** (i) (a) Sequence doubles
(b) Next 3 terms: 48, 96, 192   (ii) (a) Sequence
triples   (b) 1053, 3159, 9477   (iii) (a) Sequence
doubles   (b) Next 3 terms: 2, 4, 8
(iv) (a) Sequence triples   (b) Next 3 terms: 1, 3, 9
(v) (a) Sequence triples   **3.** (i) The sequence is
quadratic, as the 2nd difference is constant.
(ii) The sequence is linear, as the 1st difference
is constant.   (iii) Quadratic; 2nd difference is
constant   (iv) Exponential, as each term is
double the previous term.   **4.** (i) 8 blocks
(ii) 16 blocks   (iii) 512 blocks   (iv) 7 blocks
(v) 11 blocks   **5.** (i) (a) 2   (b) 5   (c) 10; General
term: Square the number and add 1.   (ii) (a) 1
(b) 8   (c) 19   (iii) (a) −4   (b) −10   (c) −18
(iv) (a) −4   (b) −11   (c) −20   (v) (a) 3
(b) 9   (c) 27   **6.** (i) $T_n = 2n^2 - 3n + 19$
(ii) $T_n = 2.5n^2 - 2.5n + 2$ (iii) $T_n = 3.5n^2 - 8.5n + 5$
(iv) $T_n = 1.5n^2 - 8.5n + 8$ (v) $T_n = -3n^2 + 10n - 17$
7. (iii) $n^2 + n$ blocks   (iv) $T_{10} = 110$
(v) The number of blocks needed for the
nth pattern is obtained by squaring the number
and then adding the number to this.
8. (ii) $3n^2 - 6n + 12$ tiles needed   (iii) 372 tiles
(iv) Pattern 9   **9.** (ii) Quadratic   (iii) 85 red discs
(iv) $T_n = 2n^2 - 2n + 1$ **10.** (i) $h = -5t^2 + 25t$
(iii) 26.25 m   (iv) 0 seconds and 5 seconds
11. (ii) Exponential   (iii) 88,573.5 m²
12. (i) Quadratic   (iii) Approx. 12,000
(iv) $T_n = -n^2 + 7n$ (v) 0 weeks, 7 weeks
13. (ii) Quadratic   (iii) $v = -2t^2 + 12t + 1$
(iv) $v = 18.5$ m/s   (v) 0 seconds and 6 seconds
14. (iii) Approx. 22–23 amoebas   (iv) 22.6 amoebas
(to 1 d.p.)   (v) 16 hours   **15.** (ii) 28 green tiles
(iii) 49 red tiles   (iv) 100 tiles in total
(v) $4n + 4$ tiles in the nth green pattern
(vi) n^2 tiles in the nth red pattern   (vii) $n^2 + 4n + 4$ or
$(n + 2)^2$ tiles in the nth pattern   **16.** (i) $T_n = n^2 + n$
(ii) 110 blue tiles   (iii) $T_n = n + 1$ (iv) 18 red tiles
needed   (ix) $T_n = n^2 + 2n + 1$ or $(n + 1)^2$
(iv) 11 patterns in total can be made.
17. Graph A: linear; Graph B: exponential;

Graph C: quadratic   **18.** (i) Yes   (ii) Between 2
and 4 seconds   (iii) $h = t^2 - 6t + 8$ (iv) 8 m
(v) 288 m   (vi) Barry has assumed that the paper
aeroplane will continue to fly in a quadratic pattern.
(vii) No   **19.** (a)(i) Quadratic   (ii) Not quadratic
(iii) Quadratic   (b) $T_n = \frac{1}{2}n^2 + 3.5n + 7$ **20.** (b) No
21. (i) €956   (ii) $v = -4m^2 + 72m + 732$
(iii) €732   (iv) 9 months   (v) The shares increase
in value until reaching their peak in the ninth
month and then start to fall in value in the 10th
month.   **22.** (i) Yes   (ii) 80 m (iii) $f = 5t^2$
(iv) $t = 6.3$ seconds (to 1 d.p.)   (vi) $h = 200 - 5t^2$
(vii) At 5.5 seconds   (viii) 2,000 m
(ix) 45 seconds

Chapter 5

Exercise 5.1

1. (i) 1   (ii) 8   (iii) −6   (iv) 8   (v) 2   (vi) 4
2. (i) −7   (ii) 1   (iii) 10   (iv) $-\frac{2}{5}$ (v) −12
(vi) $1\frac{5}{8}$ **3.** (i) 0   (ii) 7   (iii) 23   (iv) −17   (v) 25
(vi) 14   **4.** (i) =   (ii) <   (iii) >   (iv) =   (v) <
(vi) =   **5.** (i) $1\frac{1}{3}$ (ii) $-\frac{1}{2}$ (iii) $-\frac{4}{5}$ (iv) $\frac{14}{9}$
6. (i) 9   (ii) 20   (iii) 16   (iv) $6\sqrt{2}$ **7.** (i) $3\frac{7}{10}$
(ii) $27\frac{3}{10}$ (iii) $-4\frac{9}{10}$ (iv) $8\frac{7}{10}$ **8.** Cone 1: 2,198 cm²;
Cone 2: 5,581.7 m²;   Cone 3: 12,858.3 cm²;
Cone 4: $5,107\frac{1}{7}$ mm²   **9.** Triangle 1: 2.90 cm²;
Triangle 2: 48.08 cm²;   Triangle 3: 0.08 cm²

Exercise 5.2

1. (i) $4x$ (ii) $3a - 3b$ (iii) $x^2 + 2x - 1$
(iv) $5c - 1$ (v) $2x^2 - x$ **2.** (i) $12a - b + 22$
(ii) $4p + 28q - 68$ (iii) $-11x - 5$
(iv) $32x^2 - 12x + 8$ (v) $10x^3 - 20x$
(vi) $-55a^3 - 11a$ **3.** (i) $-11a + 3b + 5$
(ii) $8x^2 + 12x$ (iii) $-p$ (iv) $2x - 15y + 35$
4. (i) $x^2 + 3x + 2$ (ii) $2x^2 + 5x - 3$
(iii) $6x^2 - 7x + 2$ (iv) $2a^2 - a - 10$
(v) $6a^2 - 10a + 4$ (vi) $x^2 - y^2$ (vii) $m^2 - 2mn + n^2$
(viii) $10a^2 - 23a + 12$ (ix) $1 - 4a^2$
(x) $9a^2 + 15a - 14$ **5.** (i) $x^2 - 6x + 9$
(ii) $25x^2 + 10x + 1$ (iii) $9y^2 - 12y + 4$
(iv) $16y^2 + 40y + 25$ (v) $16x^2 - 48x + 36$
6. (i) $x^3 + 3x^2 + 5x + 3$ (ii) $2x^3 + 7x^2 + 5x - 2$
(iii) $6x^3 + 10x^2 - 2x - 6$ (iv) $2a^3 + a^2 - 10a + 6$
(v) $9a^3 - 15a^2 + a + 1$ (vi) $a^3 + 2a^2 - 7a + 4$
7. (i) $x^3 + 4x^2 + 3x$ (ii) $-4a^3 + 2a^2 + 6a$
(iii) $-p^3 + p$

8.

	7x − 11		
	x − 8	6x − 3	
	−2x − 3	3x − 5	3x + 2
−3x + 1	x − 4	2x − 1	x + 3

9. (i) $4x^2 + 34x + 60$ (ii) $4x^2 + 34x$
10. (i) $(2x^2 − 10x)$ m²   (ii) $(6x − 10)$ metres
(iii) $(x^2 − 5x)$ m²   **11.** (i) $(x^2 + 6x − 71)$ cm²
(ii) $(4x^2 − 40x + 36)$ cm³   **12.** (i) Area $= 3x^2 + 4x − 9$,
Perimeter $= 6x + 12$ (ii) Area $= 10.28x^2 − 8x$,
Perimeter $= 9.28x − 1$
(iii) Area $= 0.215x^2 + 1.72x + 3.44$,
Perimeter $= 3.57x + 14.28$ **13.** (a) $4x^2$ units²
(b) (i) $4x^2 − 6x$ units²   (ii) 9 units²
14. (a) (i) $−4x + 1$ (ii) $−13x^2 + 16x − 17$
(iii) $−30x^3 + 139x^2 − 111x − 28$ (c) $A − B + C$
15. $4(3x^2 + 4x); 4x(3x + 4); 2(6x^2 + 8x); 2x(6x + 8)$

Revision Exercises

1. (a) (i) 24   (ii) 25   (iii) 41   (iv) 11   (v) $\frac{6}{7}$
(b) (i) $6a + 15b$ (ii) $24b − 4c$ (iii) $21x − 14y$
(iv) $−4x − 14y$ (v) $−3x + 3y$ (c) (i) $7x^2 − x − 2$
(ii) $2x^2 − 2x + 4$ (iii) $10a^2 − 3a + 3$
(iv) $3b^2 − 10b + 6$ (d) (i) $x^2 + 7x + 12$
(ii) $x^2 + 7x + 10$ (iii) $x^2 + 13x + 30$
(iv) $y^2 + 9y + 14$ (v) $2y^2 + 7y + 3$ **2.** (a) (i) $−9$
(ii) $6\frac{1}{2}$ (iii) 4   (iv) $−3$ (v) $−1\frac{3}{8}$ (b) (i) $−20x + 50y$
(ii) $−x + y − z$ (iii) $2x^2 + 5x$ (iv) $12a^2 − 4a$
(v) $21a^2 − 6ab$ (c) (i) $6x^2 − 11x − 7$
(ii) $6a^2 − 22a + 20$ (iii) $9y^2 + 12y + 4$
(iv) $64x^2 − 16x + 1$ (v) $x^2 − 20x + 100$
3. (i) $x^3 + 9x^2 + 20x$ (ii) $x^3 + 5x^2 − 24x$
(iii) $x^3 + 5x^2 − x − 5$ (iv) $x^2 + 2x + 1$
(v) $x^3 + 3x^2 + 3x + 1$ (vi) $4x^2 − 4x + 1$
(vii) $8x^3 − 12x^2 + 6x − 1$ **4.** (a) (i) $9a − 5b$
(ii) $2x + 11y + 14$ (iii) $−10x^3 + 20x$
(iv) $5x + 3y − 1\frac{1}{3}$ (v) 0   (b) (i) $x^3 − x^2 + 3x − 10$
(ii) $2x^3 + 5x^2 − 4x − 3$ (iii) $x^3 − 8$
(iv) $8x^3 + 27$ (v) $x^4 + 4x^3y + 6x^2y^2 + 4xy^3 + y^4$
5. (a) (i) $−3$ (ii) 0   (iii) 10   (iv) $−11$
(b) (i) $16a^3 − 32a − 14$ (ii) $12y^3 − 20y^2 − 27y + 5$
(iii) $−2y^3 + 2y^2 + 10y + 6$ (iv) $2x^3 + 3x^2 − 5x − 3$
6. (a) (i) $=$ (ii) $>$ (iii) $=$ (iv) $=$ (v) $<$
(b) (i) $2x^2 + 2x − 1$ (ii) $−4x + 5$
(iii) $4x^2 + 3$ (iv) $x^2 − 9x + 12$
(c) (i) $x^2 + 2x + 4$ (ii) $2x^3 − x^2 + 10x − 5$
(iii) $4x^4 − 4x^3 + 21x^2 − 20x + 5$ **7.** (i) $x + 4$
(ii) $x + 3$ (iii) $4x + 14$ (iv) $4x^2 + 28x + 48$

8. (a)

Rectangle	Length	Width	Area
A	x − 2	x − 3	(x − 2)(x − 3)
B	2	x − 3	(2)(x − 3)
C	2	3	(2)(3)
D	x − 2	3	(x − 2)(3)

(b) $5x − 6$ **9.** (a) $14f + 24s$ (b) $420f + 720s$
(c) €46,520

Chapter 6

Exercise 6.1

1. $5(a + 2)$ **2.** $x(x + 4)$ **3.** $y(y − 7)$ **4.** $y(x − 5)$
5. $x(x − 3)$ **6.** $−2p(q − 2)$ **7.** $2y(2x − 1)$
8. $3b(a − 4d)$ **9.** $x(1 − 4x)$ **10.** $7ab(3b + 2)$
11. $−xy(9y + 1)$ **12.** $6p(1 − 2pq)$
13. $−2ab(4 − 5b)$ **14.** $2x(x^2 + 3x − 1)$
15. $b(a^2 + ab − 3c)$ **16.** $−5x^2y(4yz − x − 2y)$
17. $3(xy − x − 2)$

Exercise 6.2

1. $(a + b)(d + c)$ **2.** $(a + b)(p + q)$
3. $(x + 3)(y − 4)$ **4.** $(a − 2)(b + 4)$
5. $(w − 3)(r + 2)$ **6.** $(x + y)(a + 2b)$
7. $(r − 5p)(2q − s)$ **8.** $(3a + b)(2d − e)$
9. $(2x − y)(3x − z)$ **10.** $(4a − 7b)(10c − 3a)$
11. $(p + q)(m + n)$ **12.** $(3 + x)(a + b)$
13. $(c − d)(a + b)$ **14.** $(m − 12b)(x − 2y)$
15. $(2x − 5y)(x + 2a)$ **16.** $(x + y)(x − 2)$
17. $(a + 3c)(3a − b)$ **18.** $(2y + 1)(5x + z)$
19. $(3p − 1)(p − 2q)$ **20.** $(b − 1)(a + 1)$
21. $(x − y)(1 − 2y)$ **22.** $(p − 1)(q − r)$

Exercise 6.3

1. $(x + 3)(x + 1)$ **2.** $(x + 2)(x − 6)$
3. $(x + 1)(x + 4)$ **4.** $(x + 3)(x + 2)$
5. $(x − 1)(x − 2)$ **6.** $(x − 1)(x − 4)$
7. $(x − 2)(x − 4)$ **8.** $(x + 4)(x + 4)$
9. $(x + 4)(x − 3)$ **10.** $(x − 7)(x + 5)$
11. $(x + 7)(x − 2)$ **12.** $(x + 6)(x + 1)$
13. $(x − 9)(x + 2)$ **14.** $(x − 7)(x − 4)$
15. $(x + 7)(x − 3)$ **16.** $(x − 5)(x − 3)$
17. $(x + 7)(x − 5)$ **18.** $(x + 7)(x + 1)$
19. $(x − 6)(x − 7)$ **20.** $(x − 1)(x − 7)$
21. $(x + 3)(x − 7)$ **22.** $(x + 3)(x + 9)$
23. $(x − 2)(x − 9)$ **24.** $(x + 6)(x − 2)$
25. $(x + 8)(x − 7)$ **26.** $(x + 18)(x + 6)$
27. $(x + 11)(x − 12)$

Exercise 6.4

1. $(x + 3)(2x + 1)$ **2.** $(x + 3)(3x - 1)$
3. $(11x - 1)(x - 1)$ **4.** $(2x + 3)(x - 1)$
5. $(2x - 5)(x - 1)$ **6.** $(3x - 2)(x + 1)$
7. $(2x - 3)(x - 1)$ **8.** $(5x + 2)(x + 1)$
9. $(2x - 1)(x - 4)$ **10.** $(5x + 1)(x - 1)$
11. $(5x - 2)(x + 3)$ **12.** $(7x + 3)(x - 3)$
13. $(5x - 2)(x - 1)$ **14.** $(3x + 4)(x - 1)$
15. $(2x + 3)(x + 4)$ **16.** $(2x + 3)(x + 3)$
17. $(5x + 3)(x - 2)$ **18.** $(3x + 2)(x + 4)$
19. $(3x + 4)(x - 4)$ **20.** $(5x + 2)(x - 3)$
21. $(3x + 1)(x - 1)$ **22.** $(13x + 4)(x - 3)$
23. $(2x + 5)(x - 4)$ **24.** $(4x - 1)(x + 1)$
25. $(8x + 1)(x + 7)$ **26.** $(2x - 5)(2x - 1)$
27. $(8x + 3)(x - 1)$ **28.** $(6x - 1)(3x - 4)$
29. $(4x + 3)(x - 3)$ **30.** $(4x + 3)(x + 4)$
31. $(4x + 1)(x - 16)$ **32.** $(4x - 7)(3x - 10)$
33. $(5x - 2)(x - 2)$

Exercise 6.5

1. $(x + 13)(x - 13)$ **2.** $(x + 10)(x - 10)$
3. $(x + 12)(x - 12)$ **4.** $(6 + x)(6 - x)$
5. $(x + 9)(x - 9)$ **6.** $(p + 11)(p - 11)$
7. $(14 + a)(14 - a)$ **8.** $(3x - 17)(3x + 17)$
9. $(4x - 9)(4x + 9)$ **10.** $(6x + 5)(6x - 5)$
11. $(9y + 8)(9y - 8)$ **12.** $(12x + 7)(12x - 7)$
13. $(9 + 2x)(9 - 2x)$ **14.** $(14q + 1)(14q - 1)$
15. $(11x + 5y)(11x - 5y)$ **16.** $(13a + 9b)(13a - 9b)$
17. $(10x + 7y)(10x - 7y)$ **18.** $(11a + 5b)(11a - 5b)$
19. $(4x + 3y)(4x - 3y)$ **20.** $(7x + 2y)(7x - 2y)$
21. $(16x + 25y)(16x - 25y)$ **22.** $(3q + 5p)(3q - 5p)$
23. $(30x + 14y)(30x - 14y)$ **24.** $(4b + a)(4b - a)$
25. $(x + 21y)(x - 21y)$ **26.** $(19x + 17y)(19x - 17y)$
27. $(2a - b)(2a + b)(4a^2 + b^2)$ **28.** $2,000$
29. 96 **30.** $(a + 2b)(a - 2b)$

Exercise 6.6

1. $2(x + 2)(x - 2)$ **2.** $3(y + 10)(y - 10)$
3. $2(a + b)(c - d)$ **4.** $5(2x + 1)^2$
5. $4(x + 1)(x - 3)$ **6.** $y(y + 5)(y - 5)$
7. $3a(x - 2)(x + 4)$ **8.** $5x(x - 4)(x + 4)$
9. $5(x + 2p)(x - 2q)$ **10.** $5a^2(a + 3)(a - 3)$
11. $x(2x - 5)(x + 3)$ **12.** $3a(a - 2b)(a - 3c)$
13. $3(p + 2)(p - 3)$ **14.** $4(9x - 1)(x + 2)$
15. $2(3x + 2)(3x - 2)$ **16.** $4(2q - 1)(q - 5)$
17. $a^2(a + 5b)(a - 5b)$ **18.** $10y(3y + 1)(2y - 3)$
19. $5p(2p + q)(4r - 3s)$ **20.** $2(5y - 3)(4y + 1)$

21. $2(2x + 3y)(2x - 3y)$ **22.** $x(x + 5)(x - 5)$
23. $3(2a + c)(2a - c)$ **24.** $(x + 5)(x - 5)$
$(x + 2)(x - 2)$

Revision Exercises

1. $x(y + 2)$ **2.** $3(x + 1)$ **3.** $2x(5x + 1)$
4. $a(5a - 1)$ **5.** $(a + c)(d + c)$ **6.** $(y + 7)(y - 7)$
7. $(x + 7)(x + 1)$ **8.** $(x + 10)(x + 3)$
9. $(m + n)(p - q)$ **10.** $(g + 6)(g - 2)$
11. $(p + 4)(p - 4)$ **12.** $(k + 4)(k - 25)$
13. $(m - 12b)(x - 2y)$ **14.** $(x + 4)(x - 5)$
15. $(c + 5)(c - 5)$ **16.** $7xy(2x - 3y)$
17. $(a - 2)(a + 4)$ **18.** $(m - 3)(m - 2)$
19. $(7x + 2)(x + 1)$ **20.** $(a - 5b)(x + 2y)$
21. $(2x - 1)(x - 1)$ **22.** $(3x - 1)(x + 5)$
23. $(12r + 11s)(12r - 11s)$ **24.** $(7x - 9)(x + 5)$
25. $(5x - 2)(x + 3)$ **26.** $(6y + z)(6y - z)$
27. $(5m - 2n)(3k - 1)$ **28.** $(3x - 5)(x + 2)$
29. $(r - s)(p - q)$ **30.** $(ab + 2xy)(ab - 2xy)$
31. $(5x + 4)(x - 1)$ **32.** $(a - b)(c - d)$
33. $(2x - 3a)(3x - 5b)$ **34.** $(2x + 1)(2x + 3)$
35. $(10x + 1)(x + 5)$ **36.** $(a - c)(x - y)$
37. $(4x - 15)(2x + 1)$ **38.** $(10y + 9x)(10y - 9x)$
39. $2(3x - 2)(x + 5)$ **40.** $x(x - 3)(x + 1)$
41. $2, (a + 3b), (a - 3b)$ **42.** $2, (x - 2), (x + 7)$
43. $x, (x + 8), (x - 7)$ **44.** Factors: $p, (q + r), (s - t)$
45. Factors: $2, (3x - 4), (5x - 1)$ **46.** Factors: x,
$(1 + x), (3 - a)$ **47.** Factors: $(x^2 + 4), (x + 2)$,
$(x - 2)$ **48.** 1, 12; 2, 6 or 3, 4
49. (i) $x^2 + ax + bx + ab$ (ii) (a) 8 (b) 15
50. (i) $2x + 5$ (ii) $(a + b)(a - b)$ (iii) $2x + 5$
(v) $3(2x + 5)$ **51.** (i) Yes (iii) $6(x + 1)(x + 5)$
52. $k = 9$ $k = 6$ **53.** $k = 7$ $k = -7$ $k = 2$
$k = -2$ **54.** $k = -12$ **55.** $\frac{2}{5}$

Chapter 8

Exercise 8.1

1. (i) Discrete numerical (ii) Nominal categorical
(iii) Continuous (iv) Sample **2.** (i) Time (quicker),
Economy (cheaper) (ii) Biased question
(iii) Biased – not a random sample **3.** (i) Time
(quicker), Economy (cheaper), Practicality
(not possible to survey all customers)
(ii) Only representing a single route; Only on
a Monday (iii) Only represents customers
who listen to the radio; Only represents
customers who are willing to speak on radio

(iv) Take a sample from each of its bus routes each day of the week at both peak and off-peak times. **4.** (i) The selection of each student is not influenced by anything (all names selected without looking). (ii) Every possible sample within the population cannot occur, e.g. we cannot get a sample with all eight being girls. (iii) Put all the names (girls and boys) into a single hat and select eight. **6.** (i) Registered voters who have phones and are in the telephone directory (ii) People may not answer or may not be willing to take part in the survey. (iii) Answers are likely to be estimated and hence subject to bias and error. **7.** (i) Male First Year students who play PlayStation (ii) Only boys, only First Years were sampled. (iii) Take a sample from all the students in the school. **8.** No **10.** (i) 78 (seconds) (ii) Sample 1: 73.66, Sample 2: 75, Sample 3: 76.66, Sample 4: 76, Sample 5: 77.66, Sample 6: 79, Sample 7: 78.33, Sample 8: 80, Sample 9: 81.33, Sample 10: 82.33 (iii) 78 (same as the mean estimated time for the 5 girls) (iv) 0.3 (v) 0.1 **11.** (ii) Method 3 suggests that 1.37% of bulbs have defects, which is greater than the company's claim of < 1%. (iii) Method 2 is the only method that gives every possible sample of the population the same chance of being selected. (iv) Method 3: The sample only considers a very small part of the whole population and hence is biased. (v) Method 2 (vi) Increase the size of the sample taken (vii) Takes more time; Costs more money; Wastes produce (bulbs)

Exercise 8.2

1. (i) 104 (iii) 5.56% (iv) €187,500 **2.** (i) 20% (ii) 56 g (iii) A head of broccoli has a greater percentage of carbohydrate but one cannot say it has more carbohydrates than spinach, as this depends on the size of each. (iv) 428.6 g **3.** (i) We only know the percentage of passengers left by sea; we do not know the number of passengers. (ii) 2,323,475 (iii) 1.166 (iv) 12,314,419 **4.** (i) 400 (ii) 310 (iii) 5th Year (v) 3rd Year **5.** (i) January (ii) June (iii) April 1854 to March 1855 (One year) (iv) May (v) 30° (vi) January 1855: $1,849\pi$ mm²; March 1855: 784π mm² (vii) 1,849 : 784 **6.** (i) Continuous numerical data (iii) The most frequent age bracket is 20–40; There is a tail to the right, and

hence, we have a positively skewed/skewed right distribution. (iv) 30% **7.** (i) 18 (ii) 1 (iii) People had higher pulse rates after the run. **8.** (ii) Class 1 has a tail to the left, meaning that it is skewed left; Class 2 has a more symmetrical distribution. (iii) Class 1 has a greater mean (49.0 vs 45.92), a greater median and a greater mode campared with Class 2. **11.** (ii) 208 (iii) 120 (iv) Aoife's sales have a symmetrical distribution, whereas Séamus has a distribution that is skewed left. **12.** (iii) There is a tail to the left, so data is skewed left.

Exercise 8.3

1. (ii) 152 (iii) Mean = 4.47; Median = 4 (iv) €680,000 (v) €44,700 **2.** (i) Mean = 1.54; Median = 0.915 (ii) Median (iii) 5.4 **3.** (i) Mean = 91.25 mins (91 mins 15 secs); Median = 93.5 mins (93 mins 30 secs) (ii) 13 (iii) Mean (iv) Median **4.** (i) 4.7 mins (ii) 6 **5.** (i) 43.65 mins (ii) 16 **6.** (i) 7.5 (ii) $33\frac{1}{3}$% **7.** (i) 96 (ii) 33.9 years (iii) 25% (iv) 57 **8.** (ii) Distribution is roughly symmetrical (iii) 159.03 cm (iv) 155–160 cm interval (v) Mean **9.** (i) Comaneci: skewed left, Hato: skewed right (ii) Comaneci: 7.25; Hato: 5.5 (iii) Comaneci **10.** (ii) Mode (iii) 16.67%

Exercise 8.4

1. (i) Median = 23; Q_1 = 15; Q_3 = 42; IQR = 27 (ii) Median = 32; Q_1 = 18.5; Q_3 = 54; IQR = 35.5 (iii) Median = 17; Q_1 = 2; Q_3 = 36; IQR = 34 (iv) Median = 5.5; Q_1 = 4; Q_3 = 7; IQR = 3 **2.** (a) (i) 38 (ii) 30 (iii) 49 (iv) 19 (b) 25 **3.** (i) 3.2 (ii) 4.7 (iii) 1.5 (iv) 4.7 **4.** (i) 17.5 (ii) 47.5 (iii) 30 (iv) 51 **5.** (a) (i) Girls: 51; Boys: 56 (ii) Girls: 42; Boys: 39 (iii) Girls: 79; Boys: 69 (iv) Girls: 37; Boys: 30 **6.** (iii) Females: 167; Males: 175.5 (iv) Females: Q_3 = 171, Q_1 = 160; Males: Q_3 = 180, Q_1 = 171 (v) Females: 11; Males: 9 (vi) 0.233 (vii) 0.566 **7.** (i) 48 (ii) 44 (iii) 16 (iv) No **8.** (i) 78 (ii) 244 (iii) 36.5 (iv) Yes **9.** (ii) 1,610 (iii) Between 5,580 and 6,120 yards (iv) 540 (v) No **10.** (ii) Korea (iii) Australia (iv) Korea

Revision Exercises

1. (i) Biased (towards people with an interest in computers) (ii) Sample size too small (only one potato) (iii) Biased (towards wealthier people and hence more expensive cars (iv) Not a random sample **6.** (ii) Men take a greater interest in hardware/DIY than women (in general); A lot of male-dominated occupations (plumber, carpenter) would require them to go to hardware shops. (iii) Julie concluded that men spend more than women in shops **7.** (i) 72.8 beats/min
8. (ii) Saturday (iii) Tuesday **10.** (i) 40
(ii) 11 cm (iii) 52 cm (iv) 41 cm (v) Location 2
11. (ii) Table 1 is Male, as it contains the larger wrist data (iii) 5.8 cm (iv) 6 (v) 5.2 cm
(vi) 9 **12.** (ii) No (iv) 40 (v) 36 **14.** (ii) 94.3 kg
(iii) 80 kg **15.** (ii) 75.45 mins **16.** (ii) 0.3296 secs
(v) 0.333 secs (vi) 0.0034 secs (vii) 1.03%
17. (i) 0 (ii) Boys: 11.9; Girls: 13.95 (iii) Boys: 11; Girls: 10 (iv) Median (v) Boys: Range = 52, ICQ = 12; Girls: Range = 52, ICQ = 17
18. (a) 250 cm (b) 240 cm (c) 100 cm
(d) A distance greater than 250 cm **20.** (b) 24
(c) Test 1: 33; Test 2: 29 (d) Yes (e) Slightly better than class average **21.** (a) 5 (b) 9 (no days absent) (d) 1.7 days **22.** (b) 4–6 hours
(c) 6.5 hrs **23.** (b) Brand A **24.** (a) 824
(b) No **25.** (c) (i) True (ii) True
(d) Male: 12.5; Female: 11.5

Chapter 9

Exercise 9.1

1. (i) 25 (ii) 8 (iii) 9 (iv) −343 (v) 1 (vi) 1
2. (i) 2^6 (ii) 2^{20} (iii) 6^{19} (iv) -3^3 (v) 5^{12}
(vi) -1^{100} (vii) -7^3 (viii) 11^3 (ix) 1^6 **3.** 4^7
4. (i) 474.55 (ii) 2,193.37 (iii) 931,322.57
(iv) 1 (v) 3,258.03 (vi) 137,954.9 (vii) 0.2
(viii) 719,538.26 **5.** (i) Whole number: 2, 4, 8, 16, 32, 64, 128 (ii) Whole number: 3, 9, 27, 81, 243, 729 (iii) Whole number: 4, 16, 64, 256, 1,024, 4,096 (iv) 9, 81, 729, 6,561, 59,049, 531,441 (a) $x = 2, y = 1$ (b) $x = 1, y = 2$
(c) $x = 1, y = 1$ (d) $x = 1, y = 1$ **6.** (i) 5^5
(ii) 8^{10} (iii) 6^3 (iv) 4^8 (v) 2^{21} (vi) 3^7 **7.** (i) 5^{10}
(ii) -2^9 (iii) -3^7 (iv) -5^5 (v) -7^8 (vi) -4^5
8. (i) 3^1 (ii) 2^6 (iii) 10^3 (iv) 7^7 (v) 10^6 (vi) 8^{-6}
9. (i) 3^{15} (ii) 6^{20} (iii) 10^{25} (iv) 4^{30} (v) 7^{42}
(vi) 5^{36} **10.** Whole number: 5, 25, 125, 625,

3,125, 15,625 (i) 5^5 (ii) 5^{11} (iii) 5^6 (iv) 5^{66}
(v) 5^{26} (vi) 5^{15} **11.** (i) 2^6 (ii) 4^3 (iii) 64^1
(iv) $4,096^{\frac{1}{2}}$

Exercise 9.2

1. (i) $\frac{1}{27}$ (ii) $\frac{1}{25}$ (iii) $\frac{1}{81}$ (iv) $\frac{1}{343}$ (v) $\frac{1}{4}$
(vi) $\frac{1}{32}$ **2.** (i) $\frac{3}{32}$ (ii) $\frac{2}{49}$ (iii) $\frac{2}{3}$ (iv) $\frac{5}{16}$ (v) $\frac{1}{32}$
(vi) $\frac{1}{12}$ **3.** (i) 10 (ii) 12 (iii) 3 (iv) 2 (v) 2
(vi) 1 (vii) 10 (viii) 3 (ix) 2 (x) 5 **4.** x^2: 1, 4, 9, 16, 25, 36, 49, 64, 81, 100; $\sqrt{x}$: 1, 2, 3, 4, 5, 6, 7, 8, 9, 10 **5.** x^3: 1, 8, 27, 64, 125, 216, 343, 512, 729, 1,000; $\sqrt[3]{x}$: 1, 2, 3, 4, 5, 6, 7, 8, 9, 10
6. (i) 10 (ii) 8 (iii) 6 (iv) 8 (v) 4 (vi) 2
(vii) 3 (viii) 10 (ix) 4 (x) 6 **7.** (i) 2
(ii) 9 (iii) 16 (iv) 8 (v) 1,000 (vi) 25
(vii) 32 (viii) 27 (ix) 27 (x) 256 **8.** (i) $\frac{1}{10}$
(ii) $\frac{1}{6}$ (iii) $\frac{1}{2}$ (iv) $\frac{1}{27}$ (v) $\frac{1}{27}$ (vi) $\frac{1}{4}$ (vii) $\frac{1}{243}$
(viii) $\frac{1}{25}$ (ix) $\frac{1}{32}$ (x) $\frac{1}{100,000}$ **11.** (i) $\frac{1}{2}$ (ii) $\frac{1}{5}$
(iii) $\frac{2}{3}$ (iv) $\frac{9}{5}$ (v) $\frac{2}{3}$ (vi) $\frac{2}{5}$ (vii) $\frac{8}{27}$ (viii) $\frac{9}{16}$
12. (i) $\frac{5}{6}$ (ii) $\frac{11}{2}$ (iii) $\frac{5}{2}$ (iv) $\frac{100}{9}$ (v) $\frac{9}{25}$
(vi) $\frac{27}{8}$ **13.** (i) 4.36 (ii) 57.19 (iii) 1.9
(iv) 15.61 (v) 0.02 (vi) 11.51 (vii) 0.04
(viii) 2.02 (ix) 2.15 (x) 4.18 **14.** (i) $2^3.3$
(ii) $2^9.3^3$ **15.** $2^{4048}.7^{2012}$ **16.** $2^{3202}.5^{3202}$
17. (i) $144 = 2^4.3^2$; $2,500 = 2^2.5^4$;
$11,025 = 3^2.5^2.7^2$; $1,002,001 = 7^2.11^2.13^2$
(ii) Missing word: even (iii) 69 **18.** (i) 2
(ii) 2^3 (iii) 2^4 (iv) 2^5 (v) 2^{-1} (vi) 2^{-2} (vii) $2^{\frac{1}{2}}$
(viii) $2^{\frac{1}{3}}$ (ix) $2^{-\frac{1}{2}}$ **19.** (i) 3^0 (ii) 3^2 (iii) 3^3 (iv) 3^4
(v) 3^{-1} (vi) 3^{-2} (vii) $3^{\frac{1}{2}}$ (viii) $3^{\frac{3}{2}}$ (ix) $3^{-\frac{1}{2}}$
20. (i) 5^2 (ii) 5^3 (iii) 5^{-1} (iv) 5^0 (v) 5^{-2}
(vi) 5^{-3} (vii) $5^{\frac{1}{2}}$ (viii) $5^{\frac{1}{5}}$ (ix) $5^{-\frac{1}{2}}$ (x) 5^{-1}
21. (i) 10^2 (ii) 10^3 (iii) 10^{-2} (iv) 10^4
(v) 10^{-1} (vi) 10^{-4} (vii) $10^{\frac{1}{2}}$ (viii) $10^{2.5}$
(ix) $10^{-\frac{1}{2}}$ (x) $10^{\frac{1}{6}}$ (xi) $10^{\frac{3}{2}}$ (xii) $10^{1.5}$

Exercise 9.3

1. (i) $x = 2$ (ii) $x = 3$ (iii) $x = 3$ (iv) $x = 3$
(v) $x = 3$ (vi) $x = 4$ (vii) $x = 4$ (viii) $x = 3$
(ix) $x = 2$ (x) $x = 6$ **2.** (i) $x = 2$ (ii) $x = 3$
(iii) $x = 4$ (iv) $x = 6$ (v) $x = 10$ (vi) $x = 20$
(vii) $x = \frac{9}{4}$ (viii) $x = 2$ (ix) $x = \frac{3}{2}$ (x) $x = 3$
3. (i) $x = 7\frac{1}{2}$ (ii) $x = 5$ (iii) $x = 2.5$ (iv) $x = \frac{1}{2}$
(v) $x = 1.5$ (vi) $x = 1\frac{2}{3}$ (vii) $x = \frac{3}{4}$ (viii) $x = 2\frac{1}{4}$

(ix) $x = \frac{3}{4}$　(x) $x = -\frac{3}{4}$　**4.** (i) 2^4　(ii) 2^3　(iii) $2^{\frac{3}{2}}$
(iv) $2^{2.5}$; $x = 4.25$　**5.** $n = 3$　**6.** $n = 2$　**7.** $x = 4$
8. $p = 128$, $q = 32$; $x = 7$, $y = 5$　**9.** $x = 4$, $y = 2$
10. 33　**11.** 280,960　**12.** 2^4　**13.** $75 = 3 \times 5^2$;
$x = 4$　**14.** (i) $x = 3$　(ii) $x = 3$　**15.** $x = 4\frac{1}{4}$
16. 2nd row: 2, 2^2, 2^3, 2^4, 2^5, 2^6; $2^{p+1} - 2^p = 2^p$
17. $x = 8$　**18.** $y = 14$

Exercise 9.4

1. (i) 5.3×10^3　(ii) 1.75×10^5　(iii) 2.4×10^4
(iv) 2.35×10^8　(v) 7.376×10^6　(vi) 2.0×10^{-2}
(vii) 1.5×10^{-3}　(viii) 1.67×10^{-4}　(ix) 6.12×10^{-3}
(x) 2.3×10^{-5}　**2.** (i) 400,000　(ii) 16,000,000
(iii) 5,400　(iv) 8,200,000　(v) 940　(vi) 0.0019
(vii) 0.000236　(viii) 0.026　(ix) 0.56
(x) 0.00000506　**3.** (i) 6.2×10^3　(ii) 5.162×10^4
(iii) 1.4688×10^9　(iv) 1.344×10^{11}
4. (i) 3.6×10^{-5}　(ii) 5.613×10^{-4}
(iii) 3.45×10^{-2}　(iv) 6.3×10^{-4}　(v) 7.8×10^{-3}
(vi) 4.04×10^{-2}　**5.** (i) 4　(ii) 5　(iii) 3
(iv) 3　(v) 2　(vi) 3　**6.** 1.392×10^8 km
7. 1.6×10^{-10} m　**8.** (i) 3.66×10^4 m
(ii) 3.68×10^7 m^2　**9.** 4.25×10^3 images
10. 988,000 litres　**11.** (i) 1.4×10^8
(ii) 1.94×10^6　**12.** (i) 1.3×10^9　(ii) 19.4%
13. (i) 108,900 km　(ii) 6 orders of magnitude
(iii) Yes　**14.** Approx. 38 atoms
15. (i) 1.0×10^{-9} seconds　(ii) 333,333,333
calculations　**16.** (i) Jupiter　(ii) Saturn
(iii) 1.906×10^{27} kg　(iv) 1.894×10^{27} kg
(v) 1 order of magnitude

Revision Exercises

1. (i) 7^{11}　(ii) 2^7　(iii) 2^{10}　(iv) 11^7　**2.** (i) 5^{-4}
(ii) $12^{\frac{1}{6}}$　(iii) $17^{\frac{3}{5}}$　(iv) $4^{-\frac{1}{2}}$　**3.** (i) 6^{20}　(ii) 8^{22}
(iii) 2^{24}　(iv) 4^{35}　**4.** (i) p^9　(ii) p^{20}　(iii) $p^{\frac{3}{2}}$
(iv) $p^{\frac{16}{5}}$　**5.** (i) 5　(ii) $9 = 3^2$; $\sqrt{3} = 3^{\frac{1}{2}}$; $x = 1\frac{1}{2}$
6. 2^2　**7.** (i) $\frac{1}{8}$　(ii) $\frac{11}{4}$　**8.** 101　**9.** 2.024×10^{-4}
10. (i) googol; $3 \times$ googol; $100 \times$ googol;
googol^2; googol^3　(ii) googol^3　(iii) 100 orders
of magnitude　(iv) googol^2 and googol^3
11. $n = -6$, $n = -2$, $n = 1$, $n = 4$　**12.** (i) 2^6
(ii) $2^{\frac{9}{4}}$　(iii) 3^7　(iv) 3^{11}　**13.** Joe is correct.
14. $8^{-\frac{2}{3}}$　**15.** 309 km　**16.** (i) 8.24×10^1%
(ii) 291,720,000 kg　(iii) 2.474×10^6
17. 7 orders of magnitude　**18.** 4.26 light years
19. 1.53×10^{11} bits/sec

Chapter 10

Exercise 10.1

1. €5,000　**2.** €7,850　**3.** €34,710　**4.** €39,928
5. (i) €29,310　(ii) €65,190　**6.** €30,530
7. (i) €7,600　(ii) 20%　**8.** €10,460　**9.** €1,768.80
10. €2,573.80　**11.** (i) €50.30　(ii) €148.85
(iii) €4,358.80　(iv) €880.22　**12.** (i) €44.15
(ii) €132.31　(iii) €3,798.80　(iv) €785.95
13. (i) €5,551.68　(ii) €9,277.60　(iii) €45,144
(iv) €92,026.72　**14.** €48,365.85　**15.** (i) €7,930
(ii) €59,268.29　(iii) €3,467.58　**16.** (a) €43,643
(b) €61,848.78　**17.** (i) €3,370　(ii) €6,962
(iii) €31,363.36　**18.** €3,152　**19.** (a) €9,672
(b) €57,239.02

Exercise 10.2

1. (i) % Mark-up = 20.00%; % Margin = 16.67%
(ii) Profit = €5.00; % Mark-up = 16.13%;
% Margin = 13.89%　(iii) Cost price = €15.00;
Profit = €5.00; % Mark-up = 33.33%
(iv) Selling price = €28.00; % Mark-up = 100.00%;
% Margin = 50.00%　(v) Selling price = €18.00;
% Mark-up = 50.00%; % Margin = 33.33%
(vi) Profit = €0.90; % Mark-up = 5.00%;
% Margin = 4.76%　(vii) Cost price = €1.00;
% Mark-up = 300.00%; % Margin = 75.00%
(viii) Cost price = €2.10; % Mark-up = 33.33%;
% Margin = 25.00%　(ix) Cost price = €10.00;
Selling price = €12.00; % Margin = 16.67%
(x) Selling price = €15.50; % Mark-up = 40.91%;
% Margin = €29.03%　**2.** (i) €39.20　(ii) €80.75
(iii) €121.50　(iv) €99.50　(v) €1,518.05
3. (a) 16.31%　(b) 14.02%　**4.** (a) 55.12%
(b) 35.53%　**5.** (i) €138　(ii) 13%　**6.** (i) €855
(ii) 13.04%　**7.** (i) 13.04%　(ii) 40.06%
(iii) Percentage profit mark-up　(iv) It is better to
buy shares in a company with a 33% profit margin.

Exercise 10.3

1. 26,046.56　**2.** €3,104.84　**3.** €13,327.98
4. €1,889,568　**5.** €3,382.26　**6.** €8,735.48
7. €43,789.78　**8.** €134,679.61　**9.** €1,418,299.58
10. €791.35　**11.** €1,868.15　**12.** €10,347.41
13. €1,400.27　**14.** €14,769.60　**15.** €1,513,831,500
16. Year 1: Principal = €500; Interest rate = 2.36%;
Amount at year end = €511.80;
Year 2: Principal = €511.80; Interest rate = 2.36%;

Amount at year end = €523.88; Year 3: Principal = €523.88; Interest rate = 2.36%;
Amount at year end = €536.24 **17.** (i) €103,000
(ii) No **18.** (i) €1,120 (ii) No

Revision Exercises

1. €22,630 **2.** (i) €8,600 (ii) 23.24%
3. €8,360 **4.** €1,824.80 **5.** €2,338.15
6. (a) €2,468.80 (b) €3,300 (c) €8,262
(d) €34,269.20 **7.** (a) 50% (b) 33.33%
8. (i) €138 (ii) 13% **9.** (i) €2,812.50 (ii) 13.04%
10. (a) He got the wrong answer because he
calculated 13.5% of the meal price + VAT,
not 13.5% of the original cost of the meal.
(b) €130.80 **11.** 50% **12.** (a) €23,800
(b) No **13.** €1,869,884.95 **14.** €1,533.24
15. €16,062.29 **16.** €80,078.80
17. (a) €5,109.50 (b) 5% **18.** €6,250
19. US$1 = 1.42 Swiss Francs
(b) 1 Swiss Franc = US$0.70
20. (a) (i) US$1,685.40 (ii) US$1,634.84
(b) €1 = US$1.45 (c) €1 = £0.89
21. (a) 447 children (b) 8.26 m² **22.** (i) 3 hours
(ii) 4 hours **23.** 400 g **24.** 9 : 31
25. (a) John: €67,500; Paul: €78,000;
Michael: €4,500 (b) (i) €280,000
(ii) Paul: €84,000; Michael: €56,000
26. €304,000 **27.** (a) €7,440 (b) €297.60 or
€24.80 per month (c) €644.80 (d) €784.50
28. 32.5% **29.** (a) €39 (b) €22.60 (c) €15.32
30. (i) €2,678 (ii) 2.5% **31.** (i) €39.00
(ii) €47.97 **32.** (i) €275.20 (ii) €35

Chapter 11

Exercise 11.1

1.

Departure Time	Arrival Time	Time taken for journey
09:23	13:26	4 hrs 03 mins
09:05	15:57	6 hrs 52 mins
14:47	21:35	6 hrs 48 mins
03:37	16:16	12 hrs 39 mins
12:36	23:11	10 hrs 35 mins
00:29	18:14	17 hrs 45 mins
14:16	18:03	3 hrs 47 mins
07:25	22:18	14 hrs 53 mins

2.

Distance (km)	Speed (km/hr)	Time (hrs and minutes)
100	50	2 hrs
75	150	$\frac{1}{2}$ hr
201.5	62	3 hrs 15 mins
550	60	9 hrs 10 mins
10	30	20 mins
350	80	4 hrs 22.5 mins
80	75	1 hr 4 mins
1200	375	3 hrs 12 mins
90	5.4	16 hrs 40 mins
12	15	48 mins
650	60	10 hrs 50 mins
12.5	18	$41\frac{2}{3}$ mins

3. (i) $3\frac{1}{3}$ m/s (ii) 2,880 km/hr (iii) 17.5 m/s
(iv) 0.05 m/s (v) 0.648 km/hr **4.** 22 km
5. 60 km/hr **6.** (i) 10:35, 12:35, 20:10
(ii) 2 hrs (iv) 20% **7.** 20:56 **8.** (i) 1,224 km/hr
(ii) 1,080,000 km/hr **9.** 9:03 a.m. **10.** (i) 17:15
(ii) 064 (iii) 4 hrs 25 mins **11.** 25 mins
12. (i) 50 km/hr (ii) 1 hr 22.5 mins (iii) 165 km
(iv) 2 hrs 28.5 mins (v) $66\frac{2}{3}$ km/hr (vi) 48 km/hr
13. (i) 95 km (ii) 2 hrs 15 mins (iii) 275 km
(iv) 3 hrs 50 mins (v) 16:25 (vi) 71 km/hr
(vii) 75 km/hr **14.** 20.3 km/hr **15.** (a) 36 km/hr
(b) Trevor's fastest speed was in the cycling portion
of the triathlon. (c) 55,720 m (d) 7.09 m/s
16. 8 hrs 57 mins **17.** (i) Daniel (ii) Ellie
(iii) 1.25 m/s; 1 m/s (iv) $\frac{5}{6}$ m/s; 1.25 m/s
(v) No (vi) 22.5 seconds (Daniel winning) and
35 seconds (Ellie winning)

18.

	Graph A	Graph B	Graph C	Graph D
(i)	40 m	4 km	4 m	50 m
(ii)	5 s	5 hrs	3 mins	5 s
(iii)	8 m/s	0.8 km/hr	$1\frac{1}{3}$ m/min or 0.02$\dot{2}$ m/s	10 m/s

19. (i) 8:00 (ii) 8:50 (iii) 2.5 km (iv) C and D
(v) 1.5 km/hr (vii) 3 km/hr **20.** (a) (i) Graph C
(ii) Graph A (iii) Graph B **21.** (a) A to B – upward
sloping ⇒ constant speed.
B to C – A slower constant speed than A to B.
C to D – A faster constant speed than A to B and
A to C.
D to E – The object is stationary – slope = 0.

E to F – The object has started travelling at a constant speed – slower than previously.
F to G – The object is travelling at its fastest constant speed. **21.** (b) Between A and B: Constant speed of 18 km/hr.
B and C: Constant speed of 12 km/hr.
C and D: Constant speed of 20 km/hr
D and E: Object is not moving.
E and F: Constant speed of 6 km/hr.
F and G: Constant speed of 36 km/hr.
22. 50 km/hr   **23.** 3 hours   **25.** (i) Graph B
(ii) Graph A (iii) Graph D (iv) Graph C
27. (i) Adam (ii) Carl (iii) Barry (iv) First Adam, then Barry overtook Carl (v) Adam 11km/hr, Barry 10km/hr, Carl 9km/hr **30.** (i) 250 m
(ii) 33 m/s (iii) 10 seconds (iv) $83\frac{1}{3}$ m
31. (i) Henry will overtake Chang after 14 seconds.
(ii) 600 m

Chapter 12

Exercise 12.1

1. (i) 180 m² (ii) 304 m²   **2.** (i) $A = 360$ mm², $P = 80$ mm   (ii) $A = 280$ mm², $P = 94$ mm
3. (i) Area = 176.625 cm², arc length = 23.55 cm, perimeter = 53.55 cm   (ii) Area = $39\frac{2}{7}$ m², arc length = $15\frac{5}{7}$ m, perimeter = $25\frac{5}{7}$ m
(iii) Area = 40.192 cm², arc length = 10.048 cm, perimeter = 26.048 cm   (iv) Area = 4.71 mm², arc length = 4.71 mm, perimeter = 8.71 mm
4. (i) $x = 6$ (ii) $x = 19$ (iii) $x = 70$ (iv) $x = 20$
6. (i) Area = 151.14 cm², perimeter = 93.38 cm
(ii) Area = 1,280.81 cm², perimeter = 133.65 cm
(iii) Area = 8,117.76 cm², perimeter = 387.84 cm
7. (i) 93 m² (ii) 128.4 cm² (iii) 122.7 cm²
(iv) 1,080 cm²   **8.** (i) 24 cm   (ii) 64 cm
9. (i) 4.35 cm² (ii) 786 tiles (iii) €2,570
10. (i) 24,021 km/hr (ii) 10,949 km   **11.** 270 m²
12. (i) 90 cm² (ii) 2,223 tiles (iii) 20 m²
(iv) 50%   **13.** (i) 343 cm² (ii) 36%   **14.** (i) 1 cm
(ii) 14 cm (iii) 125 cm (iv) 0.6 cm   **15.** (i) 75 m
(ii) 300 m (iii) 25 m (iv) 1.125 km
16. (a) Creature 1: 2.08 m; Creature 2: 7.2 m; Creature 3: 10.88 m (b) 16.875 cm   **17.** (i) $4r$
(ii) $6r$ (iii) $5.16r^2$ (iv) 21.5%   **18.** (i) 18 cm   (ii) $\frac{\pi}{4}$
(iii) ≈27%   **19.** (i) 35 cm (ii) 62.3%
(iii) Height: ≈30 cm; area: 525 cm²   **20.** (i) $\sqrt{2}r$
(ii) $2r^2$ (iii) Two times bigger   **21.** 37.5%
22. 66 units²   **24.** (i) 132 cm (ii) 750 times
(iii) 300 times   **25.** One large pizza   **26.** (i) ≈400 m
(ii) ≈406 m (iii) Runner B: 6 m ahead;

Runner C: 12 m ahead   **27.** (a)(i) 7,853.98 m²   (ii) 3.14 m²   (iii) 7,856.34 m²   (b) 100 m

Exercise 12.2

1. (i) $V = 1,040$ cm³, SA = 628 cm   (ii) $V = 216$ m³, 216 m² (iii) $V = 72$ cm³, SA = 112.8 cm²
2. (i) $V = 22,050$ cm³, SA = 9,240 cm²
(ii) $V = 328$ cm³, SA = 348 cm²
(iii) $V = 11,699.64$ cm³, SA = 4,510.26 cm²
(iv) $V = 4,644$ cm³, SA = 2,538 cm²
(v) $V = 40,014$ cm³, SA = 7,434 cm²
5. (i) 186.05 cm² (ii) 9.88 m² (iii) 120 cm²
6. $33\frac{1}{3}$ cm   **7.** (i) 12 cm   (ii) 2.508 litres
8. 8 cm, 12 cm, 28 cm   **9.** 1,716 cm²
10. $33\frac{1}{3}$ cm   **11.** (i) 3,600,000 litres
(ii) 8,640 tonnes (iii) 468 litres   **12.** (i) (a) 188 y^2
(b) 168 y^3 (ii) $y = 1.3$ (iii) 369.096 cm³
13. (i) $25\sqrt{3}$ cm² (ii) 1,905 cm³ (iii) 191 mins
14. 0.6 litres   **15.** (i) The third tent
(ii) Tent 1: €32.40, Tent 2: €30.27, Tent 3: €48.97
16. (i) 4.5472 m² (ii) 13.6416 m³ (iii) €480
(iv) The first shed   (v) The first shed
(vi) The company should manufacture the first shed.

Exercise 12.3

1. 3,799.4 m³   **2.** 2,816 mm³   **3.** 13.5π cm³
4. CSA = 37.68 cm², TSA = 51.81 cm²
5. CSA = 2π m² or $20,000\pi$ cm², TSA = 3.28π m² or $32,800\pi$ cm²   **6.** 351π cm³   **7.** 11,550 mm³
8. 0.5024 m³   **9.** CSA = 60π m², TSA = 96π m²
10. CSA = 1,708.16 cm², TSA = 2,512 cm²
11. CSA = $3,017\frac{1}{7}$ mm², TSA = $4,827\frac{3}{7}$ mm²
12. CSA = $1,815\pi$ cm², TSA = $2,904\pi$ cm²
13. $682\frac{2}{3}\pi$ cm³   **14.** $2,093\frac{1}{3}$ mm³   **15.** $14,142\frac{6}{7}$ cm³
16. $\frac{16}{3}\pi$ cm³   **17.** 7,234.56 m³   **18.** $718\frac{2}{3}$ m³
19. CSA = 64π m²   **20.** CSA = 3,925 cm², TSA = 5,887.5 cm²   **21.** CSA = 2.2608 m², TSA = 3.3912 m²   **22.** CSA = 40.6944 mm²
23. Shape A: (i) Cylinder (ii) 1,099 cm²
(iii) 2,355 cm³   Shape B: (i) Cone (ii) 628 mm²
(iii) 1,570 mm³   **24.** (i) Graph A: Container R; Graph B: Container P; Graph C: Container S, Graph D: Container Q   **26.** (i) 10 cm
(ii) 264π cm³ (iii) ≈446 cm² (iv) €123.77
27. 1,364 m²   **28.** (i) 36π cm³ (ii) 150π cm³
(iii) 50π cm³   **29.** (a) 36π cm³ (b) (i) $r = 3$ cm, $h = 18$ cm (ii) 162π cm³ (iii) $\frac{2}{3}$
30. (i) Cone: 38.5 cm³, cylinder: 308 cm³

(ii) 8 : 1   (iii) 539 cm³   **31.** (i) 509 mm³
(ii) 5,064 mm³   **32.** (i) 51,030π cm³   (ii) 17,010π cm³
(iii) $\frac{2}{3}$ **33.** (a) 6 cm   (b) 658.19 cm³   (c) 23.82%
34. (a) Diagram D   (b) 117.03 cm²   (c) 384.85 cm³

Exercise 12.4

5. 7,776π cm³   (ii) 18 cm   **6.** (i) 15 cm   (ii) 12 cm
7. 4 cm   **8.** 25 cm   **9.** ≈38 mm   **10.** ≈5.25 cm
11. (i) 288π cm³   (ii) 96 cm   **12.** (i) 2 cm
(ii) $\sqrt{21}$ cm   **13.** (a)(i) 144π cm³   (ii) 4 cm
(iii) 10 cm   (b) More than half   **14.** (i) 3.5 cm
(ii) 8.8 kg   **15.** $\frac{1}{4}$ cm   **16.** 50 seconds
17. (i) 81π cm³   (ii) 9 cm   **18.** (i) 122.5π cm³
(ii) 6 cm   (iii) 110.25π cm³   (iv) 9 cm
19. 280 cupfuls   **20.** (i) 21 cm   (ii) 3 mins 20 secs
21. 13 mins 20 secs   **22.** 0.5 cm   **23.** (i) 0.125 cm
(ii) 1.5 cm   **24.** (i) 550,000 cm³   (ii) 70 cm
25. (i) 18π cm³   (ii) 4.5 cm   **26.** (a) 40π cm³
(b) 3 cm   (c) 1,620 cm³   (d) 631 cm³

Revision Exercises

1. (a) (i) 48 cm²   (ii) 30 cm²   (iii) 60 cm²
(iv) 44 cm²   (v) 63 cm²   (b) (i) Area = 616 cm²,
perimeter = 88 cm   (ii) Area = 19.25 cm²,
perimeter = 18 cm   (c) (i) Area = 78.5 cm²,
perimeter = 35.7 cm   (ii) Area = 157 cm²,
perimeter = 55.7 cm   (iii) Area = 9.42 cm²,
perimeter = 12.28 cm   (iv) Area = 169.56 cm²,
perimeter = 55.68 cm   **2.** (a) (i) 12 cm
(ii) 32 cm   (iii) 50 cm   (b) (i) $\frac{1}{6}$ (ii) $\frac{5}{6}$
3. (a) 45 times   (b) $\frac{1}{3}$ (c) (i) 440 cm³   (ii) 2.1 cm
4. (a) 2,240 cupfuls   (b) (i) 10.8 m³   (ii) 10.8 m²
(c) (i) 2,133.84 cm³   (ii) 1,359.8 cm²
5. (a) (i) 1,232 cm³   (ii) 550 cm²   (b) (i) 272 m²
(ii) $\frac{17}{61}$ **6.** (a) (i) CSA = 3,080 m², TSA = 4,312 m²
(ii) CSA = 540π m², TSA = 864π m²
(iii) CSA = 2.5434 cm²   (iv) 50π cm²,
TSA = 75π cm²   (b) (i) 5 cm   (ii) 12π cm³
(iii) 15π cm²   (iv) 24π cm²   (c) (i) 12,996 m²
(ii) 1,004 m²   (iii) €10,240.80   (d) (i) 27 : 1
(ii) 2 : 1   (e) Cylinder C   (f) 1 : 4   **7.** (a) (i) 94 cm³
(ii) 144 cm³   (b) (i) A = 1 cm, B = 1 cm,
C = 10 cm   (ii) $10\frac{2}{3}\pi$ cm³   **8.** (a) 7.1 cm
(b) (i) 18 cm   (ii) $\frac{4}{9}$ **9.** (a) (i) $15\frac{3}{4}\pi$ cm³   (ii) 7 cm
(b) (i) 3 cm   (ii) 16π cm³   (iii) 13 cm
10. (a) 220 cm³   (b) (i) 21 cm   (ii) 20 cm
(iii) 9,240 cm³   **11.** (a) (i) Cylinder with radii in
ratio 5 : 2   (b) (i) 4.5 cm   (ii) 6 cm   **12.** (a) 1 cm

(b) 25 cm/s   **13.** (a) 30 cm   (b) 31.5 litres
(c) 44.6 cm   **14.** (i) 260π cm²   (ii) Radius = 20 cm,
height = 17 cm   **15.** 8 cm   **16.** 2 cm
17. (a) 2.29 cm   (b) (i) 432π cm³   (ii) 8 cm
18. (i) 32 m²   (ii) 39.42 m   (iii) Dimensions: 6.8 m,
12.5 m; Area: 85 m²   (iv) 50.3 m³   (v) €410.40

Chapter 13

Exercise 13.1

1. $\frac{13x - 1}{6}$ **2.** $\frac{23p - 19}{10}$ **3.** $\frac{-5y + 8}{12}$
4. $\frac{18y + 7}{15}$ **5.** $\frac{5x - 24}{14}$ **6.** $\frac{2q - 3}{12}$ **7.** $\frac{10x + 24}{15}$
8. $\frac{-22r - 54}{15}$ **9.** $\frac{-3x - 19}{10}$ **10.** $\frac{17}{10x}$ **11.** 0
12. $\frac{7x - 1}{(x + 1) \cdot x}$ **13.** $\frac{x - 8}{(x + 4) \cdot x}$ **14.** $\frac{19x - 7}{(2x - 1)(3x - 1)}$
15. $\frac{x - 17}{(x + 5)(4x - 2)}$ **16.** $\frac{9x + 9}{(5x + 1)(7 - x)}$
17. $\frac{2x - 4}{(2x - 1)(4x - 3)}$ **18.** $\frac{4x + 22}{(5 - x)(x + 2)}$
19. $\frac{26x - 10}{(2x - 5)(3x - 2)}$ **20.** $\frac{9}{x - 2}$ **21.** $\frac{4}{3x - 4}$
22. $\frac{5}{x - 3}$ **23.** (i) $\frac{1}{8}$ (ii) $\frac{-x + 4}{x(2x + 4)}$ (iii) $\frac{1}{8}$

(iv) The answers to parts (i) and (iii) are the same.
24. (i) $\frac{-20}{33}$ (ii) $\frac{10(x + 1)}{(2x - 1)(2x + 4)}$ (iii) $\frac{-20}{33}$
25. (i) $\frac{24}{5}$ (ii) $\frac{44x - 28}{(5x - 2)(x - 3)}$ (iii) $\frac{24}{5}$ **26.** (i) 6
(ii) $\frac{13x + 16}{(x + 1)(x + 2)}$ (iii) 6

Exercise 13.2

1. $(x - 3)$ **2.** $x + 4$ **3.** 5   **4.** $2x + 1$ **5.** 1
6. $x + 3$ **7.** $\frac{9y - 2}{3y - 1}$ **8.** $x + 4$ **9.** x
10. $4x + 16$ or $4(x + 4)$ **11.** −1   **12.** $x + 2$
13. $4p^2$ **14.** $\frac{20ab}{c}$ **15.** $x - 3$ **16.** $\frac{18 \cdot r}{p}$
17. $a^2 + 2a - 3$ **18.** $2x^2 + 3x - 5$ **19.** $4x - 1$
20. $3x - 2$ **21.** (i) $16(x - 1)(x + 1)$ (ii) $(x + 1)(x + 1)$
(iii) $\frac{16(x - 1)}{x + 1}$ **22.** (i) $(x + 5)(x + 4)$
(ii) $x^3 + 10x^2 + 29x + 20$ (iii) $(x + 1)(x + 5)$
23. (i) $(x - 7)(x - 3)$ (ii) $x^3 - 15x^2 + 71x - 105$
(iii) $(x - 5)(x - 7)$ (iv) 3   **24.** (i) $(3x + 1)(x - 6)$
(ii) $-3x^3 + 20x^2 - 11x - 6$ (iii) $(1 - x)(x - 6)$
(iv) −14   **25.** $\frac{x + 1}{x - 4}$ **26.** $\frac{x + 4}{x + 5}$ **27.** 4
28. $\frac{a - c}{a + c}$ **29.** $\frac{2x - 3}{2(x + 3)}$ **30.** $\frac{-1}{b + a}$

Exercise 13.3

1. (i) $(x + 4)(x + 3)$ (ii) $x + 4$ (iii) $x + 4$
2. (i) $(2x + 1)(x + 5)$ (ii) $2x + 1$ (iii) $2x + 1$
3. (i) $(x - 9)(x + 7)$ (ii) $x + 7$ (iii) $x + 7$
4. (i) $(3x + 4)(2x - 5)$ (ii) $3x + 4$ (iii) $3x + 4$
5. $8x - 4$ **6.** $2x - 7$ **7.** $x^2 + 2x + 1$
8. $x^2 + 4x + 1$ **9.** $3x + 5$ **10.** $8x - 5$
11. $x^2 + 2x - 8$ **12.** $x^2 - 8x - 6$
13. $2x^2 + 2x + 3$ **14.** $7x^2 + 4x - 2$
15. $5x^2 - 3x + 8$ **16.** $x^2 - 8x - 8$ **17.** $x - 2$
18. $2x + 5$ **19.** $3x^2 + x - 6$ **20.** (i) $x^2 - 5x - 14$
(ii) $2x^3 - 11x^2 - 23x + 14$ (iii) $(2x - 1)(x + 2)$
(iv) $x^2 - 5x - 14$ **21.** (i) $2x^2 - 5x - 12$
(ii) $6x^3 - 17x^2 - 31x + 12$ (iii) $(3x - 1)(x - 4)$
(iv) $2x^2 - 5x - 12$ **22.** $(x + 4)(x - 3)$
23. $(x - 4)(x + 3)$ **24.** $k^2 + 7k - 10$
25. (i) $4a^3 + 6a^2 - 27$ (ii) $2a^2 + 6a + 19$
26. (i) $(x - 1)(x + 1)$ (ii) $(4x - 3)(x - 1)$
(iii) $4x^3 - 3x^2 - 4x + 3$ (iv) $4x - 3$
27. $4x^2 + 2x + 1$ **28.** $9x^2 - 12x + 16$

Revision Exercises

1. (a) (i) $\dfrac{5x + 17}{6}$ (ii) $\dfrac{9x + 3}{7}$ (iii) $\dfrac{13x - 1}{6}$
(iv) $\dfrac{8x + 15}{10}$ (b) (i) $\dfrac{1}{2}$ (ii) $\dfrac{2}{3}$ (iii) $\dfrac{2}{x + 2}$
(c) (i) $x + 10$ (ii) $4a + 2$ (iii) $5c + 7$ **2.** (a) (i) $x - 3$
(ii) 4 (iii) $x - 3$ (iv) $2ab^2$ (v) $3x - 5$
(b) (i) $\dfrac{-23x + 104}{30}$ (ii) $\dfrac{11x - 13}{(x - 5)(3x - 1)}$ (iii) $\dfrac{11}{5x - 2}$
(c) (i) $2(x + 4)(x + 4)$ (ii) 2 (iii) 2 **3.** (a) (i) $\dfrac{1}{2}$
(ii) $\dfrac{x + 3}{x - 1}$ (iii) $\dfrac{x - 1}{2}$ (iv) $\dfrac{2x - 7}{2}$ (b) (i) $2x - 1$
(ii) $x^2 + 7x - 10$ (iii) $2x^2 - 6x + 1$
(iv) $4x^2 + 2x + 26$ (c) $\dfrac{20}{x - 5}$ **4.** (a) (i) $2x - 3$
(ii) $3x^2 + 4x - 3$ (iii) $x^2 + 5x + 6$ (iv) $x^2 + 3x + 1$
(b) (i) $\dfrac{11}{x - 1}$ (ii) $\dfrac{1}{x - 1}$ (iii) $\dfrac{12}{x - 1}$
5. (i)

Divisor	Quotient	Dividend
$6x - 1$	$x - 5$	$6x^2 - 31x + 5$
$4x - 1$	$2x + 1$	$8x^2 + 2x - 1$
$x - 1$	$x^2 - 3x - 4$	$x^3 - 4x^2 - x + 4$
$2x - 3$	$6x^2 - 3x + 4$	$12x^3 - 24x^2 + 17x - 12$

(ii) $p = 3, q = 5$

Chapter 14

Exercise 14.1

1. $x = 3z - 2y$ **2.** $p = 2 - 4q$ **3.** $b = \dfrac{a + 5}{2}$
4. $a = t - b - c$ **5.** $y = \dfrac{l + 2}{x}$ **6.** $u = \dfrac{r - pt}{4}$

7. $a = \dfrac{b}{1 - t}$ **8.** $z = \dfrac{x}{2y - 1}$ **9.** $b = 6a - c$
10. $r = \dfrac{q - 4p}{3}$ **11.** $b = \dfrac{3a - 2c}{8}$
12. $c = 5p - 6q$ **13.** $a = \dfrac{2A}{h} - b$
14. $r = \dfrac{q}{1 - 2s}$ **15.** $p = \dfrac{r}{1 - q}$ **16.** $f = \dfrac{uv}{u + v}$
17. $b = \dfrac{3ac}{2 - a}$ **18.** $p = \dfrac{c}{1 - q}$ **19.** $c = \dfrac{d}{b - 3a}$
20. $p = \dfrac{ab}{1 - a}$

Exercise 14.2

1. $a = \pm\sqrt{c^2 - b^2}$ **2.** $a = \pm\sqrt{\dfrac{2b + c}{3}}$
3. $q = \dfrac{r^2}{p + 1}$ **4.** $b = 18 - a$ **5.** $r = \dfrac{1}{p} + q$
6. $g = \dfrac{4\pi^2 l}{T^2}$ **7.** $b = \sqrt[3]{ax - dx}$ **8.** $t = \dfrac{4a^2}{9r}$
9. (i) $y = 2a^2 - a - 1$ (ii) $y = (2a + 1)(a - 1)$
10. (i) $x = 4a - a^3$ (ii) $a(2 - a)(2 + a)$
(iii) 0 **11.** (i) $a + 10b = 27x + 9y$
(ii) $a + 10b = 36$ **12.** (i) $V = 41.87$ cm^3
(ii) $h = \dfrac{3V}{\pi r^2}; h = 14.21$ mm (iii) $r = \sqrt{\dfrac{3V}{\pi h}}; r = 6$ cm
13. (i) $c = -R^2 a$ (ii) $c = -65$ **14.** (i) 28 m/s
(ii) $h = \dfrac{V^2}{2g}, h = 90$ m (iii) $g = \dfrac{V^2}{2h}, g = 26$
15. (a) (i) Object of mass 10 kg travelling at 5 m/s
has greater kinetic energy. (b) $m = 10$ kg
(c) (i) $V = \sqrt{\dfrac{2E}{m}}$ (ii) $V = 22.36$ m/s
16. (a) $u = \dfrac{s}{t} - \dfrac{1}{2}at$ (b) $a = \dfrac{2(s - ut)}{t^2}$ (c) 2 m/s^2
17. (a) $r = 100\left(\dfrac{A}{p} - 1\right)$ (b) $r = 6.49\%$
(c) $A = p(1 + i)^2$ (d) $i = \sqrt{\dfrac{A}{p}} - 1$ (e) $i = 3.2\%$
18. (a) San Francisco (b) $F = \dfrac{9}{5}c + 32$
(c) $-459.67°F$ **19.** (a) $c = 55$ mg
(b) (i) $c = \left(\dfrac{x}{x + 12}\right) \times A$ (ii) $c = \dfrac{A}{\left(\frac{x + 12}{x}\right)}$
(iii) $c = \dfrac{Ax}{x + 12}$ (d) $c = 50$ mg per day (e) 3

Chapter 15

Exercise 15.1

1. $x = \dfrac{4}{3}$ **2.** $x = 6$ **3.** $x = -6$ **4.** $y = \dfrac{11}{4}$
5. $x = 0$ **6.** $x = -\dfrac{3}{4}$ **7.** $t = -7$ **8.** $x = 2$
9. $x = 0$ **10.** $p = \dfrac{5}{3}$ **11.** $x = \dfrac{3}{8}$ **12.** $x = -\dfrac{1}{2}$
13. $x = 5$ **14.** $x = 0$ **15.** $y = 1$ **16.** $x = 2$
17. $x = \dfrac{25}{12}$ (or $2\frac{1}{12}$) **18.** $x = -\dfrac{4}{11}$ **19.** $x = 7$

20. $-\frac{1}{6}$ **21.** $x = -\frac{5}{3}$ **22.** $x = \frac{11}{2}$ **23.** $x = \frac{8}{9}$

24. $x = -16$ **25.** $x = \frac{17}{15}$

Exercise 15.2

1. $x = 3, y = -1$ **2.** $x = -1, y = 1$
3. $x = 1, y = -1$ **4.** $p = -4, q = -2$
5. $a = 5, b = -2$ **6.** $m = 3, n = 4$
7. $r = -4, s = 3$ **8.** $u = -5, v = -3$
9. $x = -3, y = -2$ **10.** $x = 3, y = -1$
11. $x = 2, y = 3$ **12.** $x = -4, y = -2$
13. $x = 2, y = 2$ **14.** $x = 4, y = 6$
15. $x = 1, y = 1$ **16.** $x = \frac{1}{2}, y = \frac{1}{4}$
17. $x = \frac{1}{3}, y = \frac{2}{5}$ **18.** $x = -\frac{2}{3}, y = \frac{1}{9}$
19. $x = 7, y = 3$ **20.** $x = 1, y = -2$
21. $x = 10, y = 1$ **22.** $x = \frac{7}{2}, y = -1$
23. $p = -7, q = 5$ **24.** $x = -2, y = 0$

Exercise 15.3

1. $a = 5, b = 3$ **2.** $b = 3, d = -2$
3. $a = 1, b = 2, c = -15$ **4.** $b = -4, c = 16$
5. $a = 2, b = -4$ **6.** $p = 3, q = -1$
7. $b = -2, c = -1$ **8.** $p = \frac{1}{18}, q = \frac{1}{9}$
9. $p = 3, q = -2$

Exercise 15.4

1. (i) 9, 6, 8   (ii) 5, 6, 10   (iii) 11.5, 11.5, 19
2. (i) $100 - x$ (ii) $20x$ (iii) $30(100 - x)$
(iv) $20x + 30(100 - x) = 2,350$
(v) 65 ordinary seats 35 deluxe seats
3. (i) $x + y = 7$ (ii) $2x - 5y = 28$
(iii) $x = 9, y = -2$ **4.** (i) $(30 - x)$
(ii) $x(0.50) + (30 - x)(2) = 33$ (iii) 18 50c coins,
12 €2 coins   **5.** 29   **6.** 28   **7.** €34.20,
€22.80   **8.** 24 ducks, 46 sheep   **9.** $x = -12$
10. 11   **11.** €500   **12.** 64 km at 36 km/hr;
36 km at 24 km/hr   **13.** Double = €20,
single = €13   **14.** (i) $9,000 - x$ euros
(ii) $(0.05)x$ euros   (iii) $(0.06)(9,000 - x)$
(iv) $0.05x = (0.06)(9,000 - x) + 180$
(v) First: €6,545.45, Second: €2,454.55
15. 50 litres milk, 40 litres cream
16. 1st company: €700; 2nd company: €300
17. (i) $\frac{x}{80}$ hrs   (ii) $\frac{x}{60}$ hrs   (iii) $\frac{x}{80} + \frac{x}{60} = \frac{7}{5}$, 48 km
18. (i) $3x + 8y = 180$ (ii) $40x + 100y = 2,300$
(iii) 20 tents, 15 caravans   (iv) €470
19. 54 km/hr   **20.** (i) $\frac{x}{4}$ seconds   (ii) $\frac{x}{5}$ seconds

(iii) 1,600 m   (iv) 25%   **21.** (i) 6 plastic parts,
36 metal parts   (ii) €264   **22.** 7 incorrect answers
23. (i) Time $= \frac{x}{50}$ hrs   (ii) Time $= \frac{x + 10}{60}$ hrs
(iii) $\frac{x}{50} + \frac{x + 10}{60} + \frac{1}{12} = 3$ (iv) 75 km   (v) 85 km
24. (i) 6 offices, 3 flats   (ii) 23   **25.** 19 compact
radiators; 23 flat-panel radiators   **26.** (i) $\frac{d}{s} = 3$
(ii) $\frac{d - 20}{s + 10} = 2$ (iii) (a) 1st journey: 120 km;
2nd journey: 100 km   (b) 50 km/hr

Revision Exercises

1. (a) (i) $x = 11$ (ii) $x = 8$ (iii) $x = -5$
(b) (i) $x = 5, y = 3$ (ii) $x = 3, y = -1$
(iii) $x = \frac{7}{2}, y = -\frac{1}{2}$ (c) (i) $x = 5$
(ii) $x = 11$ (iii) $x = 12$ (iv) $x = \frac{40}{9}$
2. (a) (i) $x = \frac{3}{2}, y = -\frac{5}{2}$ (ii) $a = 3, b = 4$
(b) (i) $x = 2$ (ii) $x = 6$ (iii) $x = 10$
(c) (i) $x = 8$ (ii) $x = -3$ **3.** (a) (i) $x = 0, y = -2$
(ii) $p = \frac{15}{4}, q = -\frac{1}{2}$ (b) (i) $\frac{5}{2}$ (ii) $x = 7$
(c) (i) $x = 3, y = -4$ (ii) $x = -2, y = 9$
4. (a) 15, 16   (b) (i) $a = 3, b = -1$
(ii) $b = -3, c = 5$ (iii) $p = 3, q = 1$
(c) $a = \frac{1}{8}, b = \frac{1}{5}$ **5.** (i) $50t$ (ii) $55t$
(iii) $50t + 55t = 140$ (iv) 1 hr 20 mins
(v) 16:30 pm   **6.** (a) 16, 15   (b) 49, 50, 51
(c) 36, 24   **7.** (i) $70(x)$ (ii) $61\left(x + \frac{3}{2}\right)$
(iii) $\frac{61}{6}$ hrs   (iv) 1 hr 1 min   **8.** (a) $x = 4, y = 11$
(b) 6 5c coins, 48 10c coins   (c) (i) $\frac{x}{6}$ (ii) $\frac{x}{4}$
(iii) $\frac{12}{5}$ hrs   **9.** (a) 8 km/hr   (b) 80 children,
20 adults   (c) 1 pm   **10.** (a) Turkey = €18,
ham = €15   (b) (i) $\frac{x}{38}$ (ii) $\frac{x}{22}$ (iii) 13 mins
56 secs   (iv) 195 mins 56.25 secs
11. (i) 10 km/hr   (ii) 18.75 km/hr
(iii) $x - y = 10$ (iv) $x + y = 18.75$ (v) 14.375
(vi) $y = 4.375$ **12.** (i) $23.83 + (0.05187)(x)$
(ii) $20.67 + (0.05432)(x)$ (iii) Company A is
cheaper by €10.32   (iv) 1,289.80 kWh
(vi) $22.35 + (0.05631)\left(\frac{5x}{7}\right) + (0.0483)\left(\frac{2x}{7}\right)$
(vii) €319.47   (viii) 688.37 kWh

Chapter 16

Exercise 16.1

1. (i)   (ii)

(iii)   (iv)

(v) ◄—●—●—●—●   −8 −7 −6 −5   (vi) —●—●—●—●—●→   1 2 3 4 5

(vii) ◄—●—●—●—●   −5 −4 −3 −2   (viii) —+—+—●—●—●   4 5 6 7

(ix) —+—○—●—●—→   4 5 6 7   (x) ◄—+—+—○—+   −2 −1 0 1

2. (i) $x \geqslant 4, x \in N$ (ii) $x \leqslant -1, x \in Z$
(iii) $x \geqslant 3, x \in R$ (iv) $x > 6, x \in R$
(v) $x \leqslant 1, x \in Z$ (vi) $x \leqslant 1, x \in N$

3. $x > 2, x \in N$, —+—+—●—●—→   1 2 3 4

4. $x \geqslant 1, x \in R$, —+—+—●—●—→   −1 0 1 2

5. $x > 6, x \in N$, —+—+—●—●—→   5 6 7 8

6. $x \leqslant -6, x \in Z$, ◄—●—●—+—+   −8 −7 −6 −5

7. $x > 3, x \in z$, —+—+—●—→   2 3 4 5

8. $x \leqslant -4, x \in R$, ◄—+—●—+—+   −6 −5 −4 −3

9. $x > 6, x \in R$, —+—○—+—→   5 6 7 8

10. $x \geqslant 1, x \in N$, —●—●—●—●—→   1 2 3 4

11. $x > -5, x \in Z$, —+—+—●—●—→   −6 −5 −4 −3

12. $x < 0, x \in Z$, ◄—●—●—+—+   −2 −1 0 1

13. $x > -1, x \in R$, —+—○——●—→   −2 −1 0 1

14. $x \leqslant -3, x \in R$, ◄———●—+—+   −5 −4 −3 −2

15. $x < 3\frac{1}{2}, x \in R$, ◄———○—+   1 2 3 4 $3\frac{1}{2}$

16. $x > 1, x \in N$, —+—●—●—●—→   1 2 3 4

17. $x \leqslant 2, x \in Z$, ◄—●—●—●—+   0 1 2 3

18. $x > 0, x \in R$, —+—○——●—→   −1 0 1 2

19. (i) $35p + 400 \leqslant 3{,}750$ (ii) The maximum number of guests possible is 95.   **20.** (i) $75x$
(ii) €700   (iii) $1{,}000 - 75x$ (iv) $1{,}000 - 75x < 400$
(v) 8 weeks   **21.** $x < 12$, 11 days
22. (ii) $x \leqslant 30.06$, 30 books
23. (i) $38x + 65 < 31x + 115$; 7 days
24. (iv) Seven days

Exercise 16.2

1. (i) $-3 \leqslant x \leqslant 2$ (ii) $1 \leqslant x \leqslant 3$
(iii) $0 \leqslant x \leqslant 1$ (iv) $1 \leqslant x \leqslant 5$
(v) $-8 < x < -4$ (vi) $0 < x \leqslant 4$ (vii) $8 \leqslant x < 11$

2. $4 < x < 8, x \in N$, —+—●—●—●—+   4 5 6 7 8

3. $-3 \leqslant x \leqslant 1, x \in Z$, —●—●—●—●—●—   −3 −2 −1 0 1

4. $-1 \leqslant x \leqslant 1, x \in R$, —●——●—+   −1 0 1

5. $1 \leqslant x < 2, x \in R$, —●——○—+   0 1 2

6. $1 < x \leqslant 4, x \in N$, —+—●—●—●—   1 2 3 4

7. $-1 < x < 1, x \in Z$, —+—●—+—   −1 0 1

8. $-2 \leqslant x \leqslant 1, x \in R$, —●———●—   −2 −1 0 1

9. $1 \leqslant x < 3, x \in R$, —●——○—   1 2 3

10. $1 < x < 4, x \in R$, —○———○—   1 2 3 4

11. $1 < x \leqslant 2, x \in N$, —+—●—+—   1 2 3

12. $-3 < x < -1, x \in R$, —○——○—   −3 −2 −1

13. $-2 \leqslant x \leqslant 1, x \in Z$, —●—●—●—●—   −2 −1 0 1

14. $-3 \leqslant x \leqslant 1, x \in R$, —●————●—   −3 −2 −1 0 1

15. $-2 \leqslant x < 0, x \in R$, —●——○—   −2 −1 0

16. $2 < x \leqslant 5, x \in N$, —+—●—●—●—   2 3 4 5

17. (i) $x < 5, x \in Z$, $A = \{\ldots, 2, 3, 4\}$
(ii) $x \geqslant -1, x \in Z$, $B = \{-1, 0, 1, 2 \ldots\}$
(iii) —●—●—●—●—●—●—   −1 0 1 2 3 4
(iv) $A \cap B = \{-1, 0, 1, 2, 3, 4\}$
18. (i) $C = \{1, 2, 3, 4, 5, 6, 7\}$ (ii) $D = \{2, 3, 4 \ldots\}$
(iii) —●—●—●—●—●—●—   2 3 4 5 6 7
(iv) $C \cap D = \{2, 3, 4, 5, 6, 7\}$

19. (i) —○—+—+—→   −7 −6 −5   (ii) ◄—+—○—+   −2 −1 0
(iii) —○—+—+—+—+—+—○—   −7 −6 −5 −4 −3 −2 −1   **20.** (i) —○—+—→   0 1
(ii) ◄—+—●—   9 10   (iii) ○———●   0 10   **21.** (i) $x > 1$

(ii) $x \leqslant 4$; $\{2, 3, 4\}$ **22.** (i) $20 \leqslant x + 9 \leqslant 27$
(ii) 11°C to 18°C   **23.** (i) $0 < x \leqslant 1{,}000$
(ii) $1{,}700 < x \leqslant 2{,}500$ (iii) $3{,}200 < x \leqslant 4{,}100$
24. (i) $70 \leqslant x \leqslant 120$ (ii) $35 \leqslant x \leqslant 60$
(iii) $300 \leqslant y \leqslant 450$ (iv) $300 \leqslant y < 400$
25. Between 1.8 and 4.8 seconds
26. (i) $12 < 2p + 5 < 49, x \in Z$
(ii) $3.5 < p < 22, x \in Z$, p can range from 4 to 21
27. (i) $5{,}000 \leqslant 220x + 500 \leqslant 9{,}500$
(ii) The least number of days is 21 and the most is 40.   **28.** (i) 4 km   (ii) 16 km   (iii) $4 \leqslant x \leqslant 16$

29. (i) 64 candles (ii) $C = 64 - 8n$
(iii) $15 \leqslant 64 - 8n \leqslant 40$
30. (a) $-1 < x \leqslant 3, x \in R$
(b)
(c) $35 < x \leqslant 50, 35 < y \leqslant 60$
31. (i) $250 \leqslant 8x - 30 \leqslant 322$ (ii) 44 questions
needed to guarantee victory

Revision Exercises

1. (i) $x \leqslant 2, x \in Z$,

(ii) $x \leqslant 3, x \in R$,

(iii) $x < 4\frac{1}{2}, x \in N$,

(iv) $x \geqslant 5, x \in R$,

(v) $x \leqslant 1, x \in N$,

(vi) $x < 6, x \in R$,

(vii) $x < -3, x \in R$,

2. (i) $2 \leqslant x \leqslant 5, x \in N$,

(ii) $-1 < x \leqslant 7, x \in Z$,

(iii) $-1 < x \leqslant 5, x \in R$,

(iv) $-2 \leqslant x \leqslant 3, x \in Z$,

(v) $4 < x < 6, x \in N$,

3. (i) $A = \{1, 2, 3\}$ (ii) $B = \{-2, -1, 0, 1, 2, 3\}$
(iii) $C = \{-2, -1, 0, 1, 2, 3, 4\}$
(v) $D = \{-1, 0, 1, 2, 3\}$ (vi) $E = \{-1, 0, 1, 2\}$
4. (i) $x < 4$; the set of values less than four
(ii) $x \geqslant -1$; the set of values greater than or equal
to negative one (iii) $-1 < x < 5$; the set of values
greater than negative one but less than five
(iv) $\frac{1}{2} < x \leqslant 3$; the set of values greater than a half
but less than or equal to three
(v) $10 < x \leqslant 48$; the set of values greater than
10 but less than or equal to 48 **5.** $\{1, 2, 3, 4\}$
6. (i) (ii)

(iii)

7. (i) True (ii) True (iii) Not True (iv) True
8. (i) True (ii) True (iii) True (iv) Not True; No
10. €5.50, €6.00, €6.50, €7.00, €7.50, €8.00,
€8.50, €9.00, €9.50

11. (a)

12. $x < 43$; Bill must be younger than 43
13. The area is greater than 6 but less than
15 square units. **14.** (i) $x > 5.50$ (ii) $x \leqslant 6.50$
(iii) €6.00 **15.** $x = 5$ or more
16. (ii) $-4 \leqslant x \leqslant 1, x \in Z, -2 \leqslant x \leqslant 2, x \in Z$
17. $0 < x < 5.5$; the width is greater than 0 but less
than 5.5 cm **18.** Sid has less than € 24.

Chapter 17

Exercise 17.1

1. $x = -3$ or 7 **2.** $x = 1$ or 2 **3.** $x = 0$ or 5
4. $x = -4$ or 5 **5.** $x = 7$ or 8 **6.** $x = \pm8$
7. $x = -\frac{5}{3}$ or -1 **8.** $p = \pm2$ **9.** $q = -\frac{1}{7}$ or -1
10. $x = 0$ or 4 **11.** $y = -\frac{1}{3}$ or 1
12. $x = \frac{1}{3}$ or -7 **13.** $x = -\frac{1}{3}$ or -6
14. $x = 0$ or $\frac{11}{2}$ **15.** $x = \pm\frac{9}{2}$ **16.** $a = 0$ or $\frac{2}{5}$
17. $x = \pm\frac{1}{2}$ **18.** $x = 2$ or -3 **19.** $x = \pm1$
20. $b = \frac{5}{2}$ or -2 **21.** $x = 0$ or $\frac{3}{2}$ **22.** $x = \frac{11}{3}$ or -2
23. $x = \pm\frac{14}{25}$ **24.** $y = 0$ or $\frac{7}{5}$ **25.** $x = 2$ or 6
26. $y = \pm5$ **27.** $x = \frac{7}{2}$ or -1 **28.** $x = -\frac{1}{2}$ or $-\frac{3}{2}$
29. $x = -\frac{1}{2}$ or $-\frac{2}{3}$ **30.** $x = -\frac{2}{9}$ or 1 **31.** $x = -\frac{1}{6}$
or 1 **32.** $x = \frac{1}{4}$ or 3 **33.** $x = \frac{1}{5}$ or $\frac{7}{2}$
34. $a = \pm\frac{7}{4}$ **35.** $b = -\frac{3}{2}$ or $-\frac{5}{2}$ **36.** $c = \frac{3}{8}$ or -2
37. $m = \frac{3}{5}$ or $-\frac{7}{2}$ **38.** $x = -2$ or -10
39. $x = -\frac{8}{5}$ or 4 **40.** $x = -\frac{5}{2}$ or 1
41. $x = -\frac{2}{3}$ or $\frac{5}{2}$ **42.** $x = \frac{1}{4}$ or 4

Exercise 17.2

1. $x = -3$ or -5 **2.** $x = -2$ or -5 **3.** $x = 2$ or -3
4. $x = 4$ or $\frac{5}{2}$ **5.** $x = \frac{5}{2}$ or 1 **6.** $x = \frac{13}{4}$ or 1
7. $x = 3$ or $\frac{3}{5}$ **8.** $x = -\frac{4}{7}$ or -3 **9.** $x = \frac{7}{3}$ or -1
10. $x = 2$ or -1 **11.** $x = -\frac{4}{3}$ or $-\frac{5}{2}$
12. $x = \frac{1}{2}$ or -4

Exercise 17.3

1. $x = -3 + 2\sqrt{2}$ or $-3 - 2\sqrt{2}$
2. $x = -0.683$ or -7.317 **3.** $y = 6.48$ or -4.48
4. $x = 8.4$ or -3.4 **5.** $x = 6.223$ or -0.723

6. $x = \frac{5 + \sqrt{13}}{3}$ or $\frac{5 - \sqrt{13}}{3}$ **7.** $x = 4.723$ or -2.223

8. $q = 1.9$ or -1.7 **9.** $x = 0.68$ or -1.48

10. $x = 1.526$ or -0.901 **11.** $a = 2.14$ or -1.25

12. $x = 2.3$ or 0.7 **13.** $b = 0.946$ or -0.673

14. $x = \frac{-2 + \sqrt{2}}{2}$ or $\frac{-2 - \sqrt{2}}{2}$ **15.** $x = \frac{-5 + \sqrt{5}}{4}$ or $\frac{-5 - \sqrt{5}}{4}$

16. $x = 6 + \sqrt{22}$ or $6 - \sqrt{22}$ **17.** $x = 2.5$ or 0.7

18. $x = 1.35$ or 0.05 **19.** $x = \frac{-1 + \sqrt{5}}{4}$ or $\frac{-1 - \sqrt{5}}{4}$

20. $x = \frac{5 + \sqrt{7}}{9}$ or $\frac{5 - \sqrt{7}}{9}$ **21.** $x = 1.405$ or -1.780

22. $x = \frac{7 + 2\sqrt{46}}{15}$ or $x = \frac{7 - 2\sqrt{46}}{15}$

23. $x = \frac{-2 + \sqrt{10}}{4}$ or $\frac{-2 - \sqrt{10}}{4}$ **24.** $x = 1.70$ or -1.30

25. $x = -0.08$ or -2.42 **26.** $x = 2.916$ or -4.116

27. $x = 3.50$ or -0.13 **28.** $x = \frac{14 + 2\sqrt{7}}{7}$ or $\frac{14 - 2\sqrt{7}}{7}$

Exercise 17.4

1. $y = -5$ or -6 **2.** $t = -1$ or 2 **3.** $t = -2$ or 2

4. (i) $x = -3$ or 5 (ii) $a = -\frac{2}{3}$ or 2 **5.** $x = \frac{1}{2}$ or -4;

$p = \frac{1}{2}$ or $-\frac{7}{4}$ **6.** $x = 4$ or -6; $y = 1$ or -4

7. (i) $x = -\frac{3}{2}$ or 6 (ii) $a = \frac{1}{2}, -\frac{1}{2}, 2$ or -2

8. $x = -2$ or 8; $q = \frac{2}{3}, 1, \frac{8}{3}$ or -1 **9.** $x = 3.83$ or

-1.83; $p = 4.415$ or 1.585 **10.** (i) $x = 1.9$

or -1.5; $a = 1.8$ or -5 **11.** $x = \frac{2}{3}$ or $\frac{1}{4}$; $y = \frac{1}{3}, -\frac{2}{3},$

$\frac{1}{6}$ or $-\frac{1}{2}$

Exercise 17.5

1. $x^2 - 3x + 2 = 0$ **2.** $x^2 - 11x + 30 = 0$

3. $x^2 - 2x - 8 = 0$ **4.** $x^2 - 2x - 35 = 0$

5. $x^2 - 121 = 0$ **6.** $x^2 - 8x = 0$

7. $x^2 + 9x + 20 = 0$ **8.** $x^2 + 6x = 0$

9. $x^2 - 25 = 0$ **10.** $21x^2 + x - 2 = 0$

11. $p = -1, q = -6$ **12.** $b = -4, c = 0$

13. $c = 16$

Exercise 17.6

1. 8   **2.** 19 and 21   **3.** 3 or 5   **4.** $x = 6$

5. Width $= 80 - x$ (ii) 23 m, 48 m

6. (i) $x = 2$ cm   (ii) $x = 4$ cm   (iii) $x = 5$ cm

7. (i) $-2x^2 + 6x + 80$ (m²)   (ii) $2x^2 + 42x$ (m²)

(iii) $x = 1.5$ m   **8.** (i) 49,000   (ii) More games

were sold from 1995 to 1999.   (iii) 1991 and 1999

(iv) After 2000, the formula gives a negative answer

for the number of games sold.   **9.** $n = 4$

10. (i) $23 - x$ (metres)   (ii) Length: 10.5 m,

width: 12.5 m   **11.** (i) €119   (ii) 14 chairs

(iii) €313.50   **12.** (i) 8 m   (ii) 13 m/s

(iii) 4 seconds   **13.** (i) 625   (ii) 169

(iii) $3\frac{3}{4}$ minutes   (iv) The time of $3\frac{3}{4}$ minutes is

too long to wait to kill 84% of the spores initially

present.   **14.** (i) $104x^2 + 166x + 66$ (m²)

(ii) $x^2 + 5x$ (m²)   (iii) Length 50 m, width 30 m

15. (i) 1 metre   (ii) 11 m   (iii) 461 cm

(iv) No, as 461 cm is a very short distance to hit

the ball.   **16.** $x = 14$ **17.** (i) $3x^2 - 4x - 5 = 0$

(ii) The discriminant is negative, so the equation

has no real solutions.   (iii) Possible change to

equation: Change $+9$ to -9 **18.** At 10:10

19. (i) 11 m   (ii) $14\frac{9}{20}$ m or 14.45 m   (iii) 8.45 m

20. (i) 42.42 m   (ii) 115 km/hr   **21.** (ii) $\frac{200x - 3x^2}{4}$ m²

(iii) $x = 33\frac{1}{3}$ m, $y = 50$ m   **22.** (i) €2,750

(ii) 60 units   (iii) €300   (iv) 70 units   (v) 40 units

23. (i) 6.3 seconds   (ii) 22 m   (iii) From the

formula, the maximum height reached by the

cannonball is 112 m.

Revision Exercises

1. (a) (i) $x = 4$ or -5 (ii) $x = 7$ or -10 (iii) $x = \pm5$

(iv) $x = 0$ or 7 (b) (i) $x = 0.54$ or -5.54

(ii) $x = 7.14$ or -0.14 (iii) $x = 4.45$ or -0.45

(c) $x = 3$ or 7; $t = 1$ or 3 **2.** (a) (i) $x = 0$ or $\frac{3}{2}$

(ii) $x = -\frac{1}{2}$ or $\frac{2}{5}$ (iii) $x = \pm\frac{2}{3}$ (b) $x = \frac{-4 + \sqrt{22}}{2}$

or $\frac{-4 - \sqrt{22}}{2}$ (ii) $x = \frac{11 + \sqrt{101}}{10}$ or $\frac{11 - \sqrt{101}}{10}$

(iii) $x = \frac{1 + \sqrt{73}}{12}$ or $\frac{1 - \sqrt{73}}{12}$ **3.** (a) (i) $x^2 - 5x + 6 = 0$

(ii) $x^2 + 2x - 8 = 0$ (iii) $x^2 + 2x - 15 = 0$

(iv) $x^2 - 2x = 0$ (b) (i) $x = 6.140$ or -1.140

(ii) $x = 4.898$ or 0.102 (iii) $x = 0.847$ or -1.180

(c) (i) $x = -\frac{3}{7}$ or $\frac{1}{3}$ (ii) $x = \frac{3}{5}$ or 2 (iii) $x = 0$ or $\frac{2}{5}$

4. (a) (i) $a = 5, b = 14$ (ii) $a = 10, b = 16$

(b) $x = -1$ or 11; $t = 0$ or 4 (c) (i) $x = 2.3$ or -4.3

(ii) $t = 1.3$ or -5.3 **5.** (i) 13,000   (ii) At $1\frac{1}{2}$ hours

and 4 hours   (iii) At $6\frac{1}{2}$ hours   (iv) The formula

only gives valid values between $t = 0$ and $t = 6\frac{1}{2}$.

Outside these times, negative answers are given.

6. Small square: 0.414 m; large square: 0.586 m

7. (i) $2x + 3$ (ii) $2x^2 + 3x$ (iii) Width: 3 m;

length: 9 m   **8.** (i) $4.5 - x$ (metres)   (ii) 1.54 m

and 3.46 m   **9.** (i) €10,000   (ii) €63,000

(iii) 5.7 months   (iv) After four months, the value of the investment starts to decline.   **10.** 25 m by 28 m OR 10 m by 13 m   **11.** (i) 3.25 m (ii) $t = 3.6$ seconds   (iii) 4.7 m/s   **12.** 95 cm, 168 cm, 193 cm   **13.** (i) 117 m   (ii) 0 m (iii) 10.8 seconds   **14.** (ii) $80x - 2x^2$ (m²) (iii) Width 32.5 m, length 15 m; width 7.5 m, length 65 m   **15.** Width 20 m, length 170 m; width 30 m, length $113\frac{1}{3}$ m

16. (b) $4x^2 + 36x - 63 = 0$ (d) $4x^2 + 36x - 63 = 0$ (e) 1.5 m   (f) For simple whole numbers (e.g. a path of 1 m or 2 m), Tony's method is quick and easy; for larger numbers or decimal lengths, Elaine's method is the most direct.   **17.** (b) $x = \frac{p}{q}$ (c) $1 + \frac{1}{x}$ (d) $x^2 - x - 1 = 0$ (e) $x \approx -0.618$ or 1.618 (f) $x_1 = -0.618$; $x_2 = 1.618$ (g) x_2 (h) 1.618; 61.8 (%)   (i) 1.618; This is equal to x_2. (j) The golden ratio minus its reciprocal equals 1. (k) 1, 1, 2, 3, 5, 8, 13, 21, 34, 55, 89, 144   (l) 2nd column: 1.000, 2.000, 1.500, 1.667, 1.600, 1.625, 1.615, 1.619, 1.618   (m) Consecutive terms in the Fibonacci sequence are approximately in golden ratio to each other the further we move into the sequence.

Chapter 18

Exercise 18.1

1. (i) 143°   (ii) 90°   (iii) 30°   (iv) $x + y = 67$°; $2y = 90$°   **2.** (i) $A = 53$°, $B = 127$°, $C = 53$° (ii) $A = 68$°, $B = 134$°, $C = 46$°   (iii) $A = 73$°, $B = 41$°, $C = 66$°, $D = 66$°, $E = 114$°   (iv) $A = 102$°, $B = 39$°, $C = 141$°, $D = 102$°, $E = 63$° (v) $A = 115$°, $B = 65$°, $C = 105$°, $D = 66$°, $E = 75$° **4.** (i) $A = 137$°, $B = 54$°   (ii) $A = 58.5$°, $B = 38.5$°, $C = 70.5$°   (iii) $A = 69$°, $B = 69$°, $C = 65$° (iv) $A = 47$°, $B = 81$°, $C = 52$°   **5.** (i) $A = 23$°, $B = 58$°, $C = 99$°   (ii) $A = 84$°, $B = 84$°, $C = 82$°   (iii) $A = 31$°, $B = 90$°, $C = 59$° (iv) $A = 78$°, $B = 78$°, $C = 78$°   **6.** (i) 49° (ii) 131°   (iii) 24.5°   **7.** (ii) Corresponding (iii) Straight line   (iv) Alternate angles **8.** (a) (i) Congruent; SSS   (ii) Not congruent (iii) Congruent; SAS or ASA   (iv) Congruent; SSS or SAS or ASA   (b) Diagram (ii): $\triangle PQT \equiv \triangle STR$, $\triangle QTR \equiv \triangle PTS$; Diagram (iv): all triangles are congruent   **9.** line $a \parallel$ line b; line $l \parallel$ line p **12.** (i) A = translation, B = central symmetry,

C = axial symmetry   (ii) A = axial symmetry, B = axial symmetry, C = translation   (iii) A = axial symmetry, B = translation, C = central symmetry **13.** (b) (i) $(-1,-1)$, $(-4,-1)$, $(-4,-3)$, $(-1,-3)$ (ii) $(1,-1)$, $(4,-1)$, $(4,-3)$, $(4,-3)$, $(1,-3)$ (iii) $(1,1)$, $(4,1)$, $(4,3)$, $(1,3)$ **14.** (b) (i) $(-2,1)$, $(-5,1)$, $(-4,3)$ (ii) $(-2,-1)$, $(-5,-1)$, $(-4,-3)$ (iii) $(0,1)$, $(3,1)$, $(2,3)$ **15.** (b) (i) $(-1,1)$, $(-3,1)$, $(-4,3)$, $(-2,3)$ (ii) $(-1,3)$, $(1,3)$, $(2,5)$, $(0,5)$ (iii) $(1,-1)$, $(3,-1)$, $(4,-3)$, $(2,-3)$ **16.** (b) (i) $(4,-1)$, $(6,0)$, $(8,-2)$ (ii) $(-2,3)$, $(-4,2)$, $(-6,4)$ (iii) $(-1,-2)$, $(0,-4)$, $(-2,-6)$ **17.** (i) $|QP| = 20$ (ii) $|PS| = 16$ (iii) $|MQ| = 15$ (iv) $|SQ| = 30$ **18.** (i) $x = 43$°, $y = 24$°   (ii) $x = 29$°, $y = 14$°   **19.** (i) $a = 3$, $b = 5$ (ii) $a = 10$°, $b = 100$°

Exercise 18.2

1. (i) $x = 7.5$ (ii) $x = 3$ **2.** (i) $x = 5$, $y = 6$ (ii) $x = 10$, $y = 20$ (iii) $x = 3$, $y = 13$ **3.** (i) $x = 7$ cm   (ii) $x = 10$ cm   **4.** (i) $\sqrt{7}$ cm (ii) $\sqrt{28}$ (or $2\sqrt{7}$) cm   (iii) $\sqrt{63}$ (or $3\sqrt{7}$) cm

Exercise 18.3

1. (i) $x = 2$ (ii) $x = 1\frac{1}{3}$ (iii) $x = 4.5$ (iv) $x = 7.7$ **2.** (i) $x = 2.4$ (ii) $x = 2.25$ (iii) $x = 1.2$ (iv) $x = 2.625$ **3.** (i) $|PS| = 18$ (ii) $|ST| = 4.5$ (iii) 4 : 1   **4.** (a) (i) 3 : 2   (ii) $|CE| = 10$ (b) No **5.** (i) $|DE| = 8.75$ (ii) $|FG| = 5$ **6.** (i) 5 : 2 (ii) 7 : 5   (iii) 2 : 7   **7.** (i) 3 : 4   (ii) 3 : 4   (iii) 4 : 7 **8.** Yes   **9.** No   **10.** (i) 441 m   (ii) 14 mins 42 secs

Exercise 18.4

1. (i) $x = 1.5$ (ii) $x = 4.8$ (iii) $x = 7.5$ (iv) $x = 22\frac{1}{3}$ **2.** (i) $x = 3.2$ (ii) $x = 12$ (iii) $x = 28$ (iv) $x = 28$ **3.** (i) $x = 8$, $y = 6$ (ii) $x = 19.2$, $y = 9.8$ (iii) $x = 1$, $y = 9$ (iv) $x = 10$, $y = 8$ **4.** (ii) $|PR| = 20$ (ii) $|RQ| = 16$ (iii) $|RS| = 8$ **5.** (i) $|EG| = 0.75$ (ii) $|GH| = 4.375$ **6.** (i) $|BC| = 8$ (ii) $|ED| = 2.4$ (iii) $|DC| = 3.2$ (iv) 25 : 4   **7.** (i) No   (ii) No   **8.** $y = 15.75$ **9.** 2.8 m   **10.** 7.224 m   **11.** $|PR| = 2.4$ m **12.** (ii) 653 cm   **13.** 6.38 m   **14.** $58\frac{1}{3}$ m **15.** (i) 19.7 m   (ii) 6,264 cm   **16.** (i) 3,742 m (ii) 7,937 m   **17.** (ii) 3.1 m   **18.** (i) A, E and C must be collinear; A, E and D must be collinear; [BE] must be parallel to [CD]   (ii) 36 m (iii) 50 m

Exercise 18.5

1. (i) $x = 5$ (ii) $x = 20$ (iii) $x = 6$ (iv) $x = 7$
(v) $x = 8$ (vi) $x = \sqrt{656}$ (vii) $x = 2\sqrt{119}$
(viii) $x = 4$ **2.** (i) $x = \sqrt{65}$, $y = 1$ (ii) $x = 4$,
$y = 7$ (iii) $x = 4$, $y = 7$ (iv) $x = \sqrt{5}$, $y = 3$
3. (i) $x = 15.6$ (ii) $x = 17.9$ (iii) $x = 6.93$
(iv) $x = 3.57$ (v) $x = 14.4$ (vi) $x = 2.83$
4. (i) No (ii) Yes (iii) No (iv) Yes **5.** (i) Yes
(ii) Yes (iii) No (iv) Yes **6.** (i) $|AB| = 50$
(ii) $|AB| = 130$ **7.** (i) $x = 11.09$ (ii) $x = 20$
(iii) $x = 5$ (iv) $x = 11.93$ **8.** (i) 158 cm
(ii) 39 cm **9.** (i) $p = 11$ **10.** 111.7 cm
11. 1,201 cm **12.** 5.2 cm **13.** (i) 3.6 m
(ii) 16.8 m (iii) 628 cm **14.** Radius: 60 mm;
Height: 120 mm; Slant height: 134 mm
15. 156 mm **16.** (i) 12.81 m (ii) 13.15 m
(iii) 9.43 m (iv) 9.90 m **17.** 33 cm
18. (i) 20 km (ii) 13 km (iii) 15 km
(iv) 20 km (v) 29 km

Exercise 18.6

1. (i) 40° (ii) 100° (iii) 90° (iv) 55° (v) 33°
(vi) 40° (vii) 50° (viii) 140° **2.** (i) $|\angle A| = 34°$,
$|\angle B| = 56°$ (ii) $|\angle A| = 220°$, $|\angle B| = 140°$
(iii) $|\angle A| = 144°$, $|\angle B| = 73°$ (iv) $|\angle A| = 129°$,
$|\angle B| = 258°$ (v) $|\angle A| = 76°$, $|\angle B| = 104°$
(vi) $|\angle A| = 48°$, $|\angle B| = 132°$ **3.** (i) $|\angle A| = 88°$,
$|\angle B| = 46°$ (ii) $|\angle A| = 50°$, $|\angle B| = 100°$
(iii) $|\angle A| = 70°$, $|\angle B| = 34°$ (iv) $|\angle A| = 64°$,
$|\angle B| = 58°$ (v) $|\angle A| = 46°$, $|\angle B| = 46°$
(vi) $|\angle A| = 30°$, $|\angle B| = 30°$ **4.** (i) $|\angle A| = 41°$,
$|\angle B| = 82°$ (ii) $|\angle A| = 50°$, $|\angle B| = 25°$
(iii) $|\angle A| = 59.5°$, $|\angle B| = 119°$, $|\angle C| = 59.5°$
(iv) $|\angle A| = 58°$, $|\angle B| = 116°$, $|\angle C| = 32°$
(v) $|\angle A| = 51°$, $|\angle B| = 102°$ **5.** (i) Yes (ii) No
(iii) No (iv) Yes **6.** (i) 38° (ii) 90° (iii) 71°
(iv) 52° **7.** (i) 118° (ii) 29.5° (iii) 29.5° (iv) 121°
8. (i) 116 (ii) 122° (iii) 61° (iv) 29°
9. Only a rectangle or a square can be
inscribed in a circle. **10.** 36° **11.** Possible
answers: Row 2, Seat 1; Row 2, Seat 7;
Row 5, Seat 5

Revision Exercises

1. (a) (i) $x = 50°$, $y = 30°$ (ii) $x = 50°$, $y = 70°$
(iii) $x = 40°$, $y = 25°$ (iv) $x = 18°$, $y = 85°$
(v) $x = 32.5°$, $y = 42.5°$ (b) 8 : 5

2. (a) (i) $x = 15°$, $y = 75°$ (ii) $x = 40°$, $y = 60°$
(iii) $x = 8°$, $y = 50°$ (iv) $x = 11°$, $y = 59°$
(b) (i) $a = 6$, $b = 8$ (ii) $a = 7.5$, $b = 5$
3. (a) (i) $x = 35°$, $y = 40°$ (ii) $x = 10°$, $y = 20°$
(iii) $x = 7.2°$, $y = 9°$ (b) (i) 8 units (ii) 3 units
(iii) No **4.** (a) (i) $|\angle A| = 80°$, $|\angle B| = 50°$,
$|\angle C| = 130°$ (ii) $|\angle A| = 42°$, $|\angle B| = 124°$,
$|\angle C| = 124°$ (iii) $|\angle A| = 105°$, $|\angle B| = 118°$,
$|\angle C| = 88°$ (iv) $|\angle A| = 40°$, $|\angle B| = 105°$,
$|\angle C| = 40°$ (v) $|\angle A| = 66°$, $|\angle B| = 48°$,
$|\angle C| = 90°$ (b) (iii) 1.5 (iv) 6 **5.** (a) (i) $x = 10.5$,
$y = 8$ (ii) $x = 5$, $y = 11$ (iii) $x = 21$, $y = 7$
(iv) $x = 13\frac{1}{3}$, $y = 10\frac{2}{3}$ (b) 3 m **6.** (a) (i) No
(ii) Yes (b) (i) Yes (ii) No (c) (i) Question 1
(ii) 34° **7.** (a) $|\angle A| = 21°$, $|\angle B| = 69°$
(ii) $|\angle A| = 98°$, $|\angle B| = 29°$ (iii) $|\angle A| = 35°$,
$|\angle B| = 75°$ (iv) $|\angle A| = 25.5°$, $|\angle B| = 30°$
(b) 4 m **8.** (a) (i) $x = 24$, $y = \sqrt{890}$ (ii) $x = \sqrt{40}$,
$y = \sqrt{19.75}$ (iii) $x = 4$, $y = \sqrt{89}$ (iv) $x = \sqrt{8}$,
$y = 4$ (b) 127 m **9.** (a) (i) No (ii) Opposite sides
of a paralleleogram must be equal in length but no
two strips are equal in length. (iii) She is correct.
(iv) 31.24 cm (b) (ii) 180 m **10.** (a) 14 cm
(b) (i) 101.6 cm (ii) Width: 89 cm; height: 50 cm
(iii) Area of 2nd TV screen (4 : 3) is 491 cm² larger
11. (b) A: central symmetry; B: axial symmetry;
C: translation; D: axial symmetry (c) $\alpha = 23.5°$,
$\beta = 83.5°$, $\gamma = 23.5°$ (d) (i) $|AB| = 5\sqrt{5}$
(ii) $x = 5$

Chapter 19

Exercise 19.1

3. Converse 2: False; Converse 3: False;
Converse 4: False **7.** (i) Yes (ii) Yes

Exercise 19.2

12. (ii) 30° **15.** (b) No

Exercise 19.3

10. (iii) 64 cm²

Exercise 19.4

11. (b) (iii) 2 : 1

Chapter 20

Exercise 20.1

1. (ii) $(-1,4)$ (iv) $2x - 3y + 2 = 0$ (v) $\left(0,\frac{2}{3}\right)$
(vi) $(-1,0)$ **2.** (ii) $(2,0)$ (iii) -1 (iv) $x + y - 6 = 0$
(vi) 16 units^2 **3.** (ii) $(4,1)$ (iv) $(0,2)$ **4.** (ii) $(1,5)$
(iv) $\left(-\frac{3}{2},0\right)$ **5.** (ii) $(2,6)$ **6.** (i) 10 units (ii) 1 km
(iii) 24 minutes **7.** (ii) $k = \frac{5}{3}$ (iii) Examples: $\left(\frac{2}{3},3\right)$,
$(2,-1)$, $(0,5)$ (iv) -3 **8.** (i) $y = 4x - 3$
(ii) $y = -3x + 5$ **9.** (i) $a = 4$, $b = -6$
10. (i) $x + 2y = 16$ (ii) $4x + y = 0$
(iv) $\left(\frac{6}{7},\frac{54}{7}\right)$ **11.** (a) $A(1,1)$, $B(11,1)$ (c) $(6,1)$
(e) (i) $|AD| = \sqrt{74}$; $|BD| = \sqrt{74}$ (f) ABD is
an isosceles triangle, as two sides are equal in
measure. (g) The triangles ACD and BCD are
congruent. **12.** (iv) Yes; opposite sides are equal
in length and the diagonals bisect each other.

Exercise 20.2

1.

Slope	Slope of parallel line	Slope of perpendicular line
$-\frac{1}{2}$	$-\frac{1}{2}$	2
$\frac{3}{4}$	$\frac{3}{4}$	$-\frac{4}{3}$
$-\frac{1}{3}$	$-\frac{1}{3}$	3
$-\frac{8}{11}$	$-\frac{8}{11}$	$\frac{11}{8}$
13	13	$-\frac{1}{13}$

2. $\frac{5}{4}$ **3.** $\frac{4}{3}$ **4.** $-\frac{1}{2}$ **5.** -4 **6.** $\frac{1}{3}$ **7.** (i) $m = -2$
(ii) $m = 3$ (iii) $m = 1$ (iv) $m = 1$ (v) $m = \frac{2}{3}$
(vi) $m = -\frac{4}{5}$ **8.** $3y = x + 18$ **9.** $x + 2y + 6 = 0$
10. $y = 2x + 2$ **11.** $x - 3y + 10 = 0$
12. $3x - 2y - 15 = 0$ **13.** (i) No (ii) No
(iii) No (iv) Yes (v) No (vi) Yes **14.** (i) $x = 1$
15. $5x - y - 23 = 0$ **16.** $2x + y + 6 = 0$
17. $7x - y + 10 = 0$ **18.** $x + y - 4 = 0$

Revision Exercises

1. (i) $\frac{6}{5}$ (ii) $\left(3\frac{1}{2},1\right)$ (iii) $\sqrt{61}$ (iv) $10x + 12y - 47 = 0$
(v) $(4.7,0)$, $\left(0,\frac{47}{12}\right)$ **2.** (i) $h = 1$; $k = 6$ (ii) $(3,4)$
3. (i) $(1,3)$ (ii) $\frac{1}{2}$ (iii) $2x + y - 5 = 0$
(iv) $(2,1)$ **4.** (i) $3x - 2y - 5 = 0$ (ii) $(-1,-4)$
5. (ii) $\sqrt{45}$ (iii) $\frac{3}{2}\sqrt{10}$ units^2 **6.** (i) $C(-5,0)$, $D(4,0)$
(ii) $E(0,3)$ (iv) 13.5 units^2 **7.** (i) $(0,-1)$

(ii) $y = x - 1$ **8.** (a) $l_1 = 11$; $l_2 = 8.5$
(b) Fuel consumption is lower at 60 km/h than
at 100 km/h. (c) It is €8.02 cheaper at 60 km/h.
9. (a) Line 4; slope $= 5$ (b) Lines 1 and 2 are
parallel; both have slope of 3 (d) Line 5
(e) Line 6 (f) $(3,-4)$ **10.** (a) $(1,4)$ (c) $(2,0)$
(d) $y = -2x + 4$ (e) -2 (f) $2x + y + 12 = 0$
(g) $1 : 1$ (h) Yes **11.** (i) $A(-3,0)$, $B(0,4)$
(iii) $3x + 4y - 16 = 0$ **12.** (i) $(2,4)$
(iii) $\sqrt{2}$ **13.** (i) $(2,6)$ (ii) $(8,0)$ (iii) $(0,5)$
(v) $\left(4,2\frac{1}{2}\right)$ (vi) $5x + 8y = 40$ **14.** p: slope is
positive; q: slope $= 0$; r: slope is undefined;
s: slope is negative; t: slope $= 0$ **15.** (i) $(2,-5)$
(ii) $-\frac{2}{3}$ (iii) $3x - 2y - 16 = 0$ (iv) $y = \frac{3}{2}x - 8$
(v) $(0,-8)$ **16.** (a) $y = 3x + 2$ (d) No
17. (i) $\frac{3}{4}$ (ii) $\sqrt{k^2 - 8k + 80}$ (iii) $k = 10$
(iv) 50 units^2 **18.** (i) 1 (iii) $x + y - 7 = 0$
(iv) $p = 2$ (v) 12 units^2 **19.** (a) 7.071 km
(b) 3 km (c) $3x - 4y + 31 = 0$
(d) $4x + 3y - 92 = 0$ (e) $(11,16)$ (f) 22 km
20. (a) $x - 2y - 4 = 0$ (b) $(0,-2)$ (c) $\frac{2}{3}$
21. Slope 2 $=$ line k; Slope $\frac{1}{8}$ $=$ line m;
Slope 0 $=$ line l; Slope $-\frac{1}{4}$ $=$ line j;
Slope -1 $=$ line n

Chapter 21

Exercise 21.1

1. (i) $x = 13$ (ii) $x = 37$ (iii) $x = 99$
(iv) $x = 9$ (v) $x = 60$ (vi) $x = 16$
2. (i) $x = 4.1$ (ii) $x = 14.7$ (iii) $x = 15.9$
(iv) $x = 5.9$ (v) 8.1 (vi) 6.6 **3.** (i) $56°$
(ii) $56°$ (iii) $30°$ (iv) $56°$ (v) $34°$ (vi) $71°$
4. $x = 4.0$, $y = 7.9$ **5.** (i) $y = 4$ (ii) $A = 18°$
6. $\frac{80\sqrt{3}}{9}$ cm **8.** 2,227 cm **9.** (i) $x \approx 26.42$ m
(ii) $y \approx 22$ m **10.** (i) No. For a given opposite
length, doubling the adjacent length does not halve
the angle – it halves the tangent of the angle.
(ii) 8.33 m **11.** (i) 41 m (ii) $52°$ **12.** (i) 4 m
(ii) 6.93 m **13.** (i) 34.08 m (ii) 3.4 m/s
14. (ii) $\sin A = \frac{4}{5}$; $\cos A = \frac{3}{5}$ **15.** (ii) $\sin A = \frac{3}{5}$;
$\cos A = \frac{4}{5}$ **16.** (i) $48°$ (ii) $7 - x$ metres
(iii) $h = x \tan 42°$; $h = (7 - x) \tan 48°$ (v) 348 cm
17. (i) $h = 10 \sin \theta$ (iv) $75\sqrt{3}$ cm^2
(v) $50 + 50\sqrt{2}$ cm^2 **18.** (i) SU is a tangent to the
circle and $[OU]$ is the corresponding radius;
a tangent and a corresponding radius make
a 90° angle with each other. (ii) $90° - \theta$

(iv) $|UC| = \sin\theta$ (v) $|OC| = \cos\theta$
(vi) $\sin^2\theta + \cos^2\theta = 1$ (vii) $|SU| = \dfrac{1}{\tan\theta}$

Exercise 21.2

1. (i) $2°\,30'$ (ii) $2°\,15'$ (iii) $2°\,45'$
(iv) $25°\,24'$ (v) $4°\,12'$ (vi) $15°\,30'$
(vii) $24°\,45'$ (viii) $36°\,15'$ (ix) $55°\,08'$
(x) $0°\,20'$ (xi) $0°\,45'$ (xii) $0°\,24'$
2. (i) $2.5°$ (ii) $10.67°$ (iii) $25.83°$
(iv) $70.37°$ (v) $11.6°$ (vi) $33.55°$
(vii) $42.17°$ (viii) $58.75°$ (ix) $56.5°$
(x) $82.2°$ **3.** (i) $6°\,45'$ (ii) $16°\,52'$
(iii) $68°\,10'$ (iv) $132°\,17'$ (v) $36°\,15'$
(vi) $6°\,38'$ (vii) $7°\,38'$ (viii) $13°\,40'$
(ix) $7°\,40'$ (x) $56°\,27'$ **4.** (i) $A = 45°\,16'$
(ii) $B = 59°\,12'$ (iii) $C = 165°\,5'$
(iv) $D = 74°\,40'$ **5.** (i) 15 km   (ii) $\approx$20 km
(iii) 66 km   **6.** (i) As $|\angle CBA| = 90°$, therefore α is
acute (only 180° in a triangle).   (ii) $\tan\alpha > 1$
if $45 < \alpha < 90°$ **7.** (i) $9'\,2''$
(ii) 2.445718857×10^9 metres   (iii) 8.15 seconds
(iv) 1.54×10^{10} metres   (v) 31,557,600 seconds
(vi) 488 m/s   **8.** (i) $29°\,43'\,26''$ (ii) $r + 90$ km
(iii) 6,336 km   (iv) 7,296 km   (v) 45,842 km
(vi) 1 hr 42 mins

Exercise 21.3

1. (i)

A	30°	45°	60°
$\sin A$	$\dfrac{1}{2}$	$\dfrac{1}{\sqrt{2}}$	$\dfrac{\sqrt{3}}{2}$
$\cos A$	$\dfrac{\sqrt{3}}{2}$	$\dfrac{1}{\sqrt{2}}$	$\dfrac{1}{2}$
$\tan A$	$\dfrac{1}{\sqrt{3}}$	1	$\sqrt{3}$

(ii) $x = 5$, $y = 5\sqrt{3}$, $z = \dfrac{10\sqrt{3}}{3}$ (iii) $x = 3\sqrt{3}$,
$y = 9$, $z = 9\sqrt{3}$ **2.** (i) 60°; Triangle CAB is
equilateral.   (ii) RHS   (iii) $\sqrt{3}$ (iv) $\dfrac{\sqrt{3}}{2}$
3. (i) $h = |DC|$ (ii) $\dfrac{1}{\sqrt{3}} = \dfrac{h}{4 + h}$
(iii) $h = 2(\sqrt{3} + 1)$ (metres)   **4.** $x = 2\sqrt{3}$, $y = 2$
5. (ii) x, x and $\sqrt{2}x$ (metres)   (iv) x, $8\sqrt{6} - x$,
$16\sqrt{6} - 2x$ (metres)   (v) -2 (vi) $x \approx 12.4$ m
(vii) 10.7 m   **6.** (i) Diagram 2   (ii) $4\sqrt{5}$ units
(iii) $\theta = 90° - \alpha$; $\beta = 90° - \alpha$ (iv) They both
contain a 90° angle and $\theta = \beta$ (vi) $8\sqrt{3}$
(vii) Yes   (viii) $[AB] = 8$ units; $[BC] = 10$ units
(ix) $[AD] = 2\sqrt{17}$ units, $[AE] = 4\sqrt{5}$ units,
$[AF] = 10$ units, $[AG] = 8\sqrt{2}$ units   **7.** 1
8. 4   **9.** $\dfrac{4}{3}$ **11.** (i) $4\sqrt{3}$ units   (ii) 8 units
(iii) 12 units   (iv) $48\sqrt{3}$ units^2

Revision Exercises

1. (i) 4.5   (ii) 3.0   (iii) 8.0   (iv) 3.6   (v) 10.0
(vi) 2.4   (vii) 4.2   (viii) 5   **2.** (i) 27°   (ii) 41°
(iii) 42°   (iv) 59°   (v) 37°   **3.** 26.4 units^2
4. (ii) 4.24 m   (iii) 3.16 m   (iv) 26.96 m
(v) €3,666.56   **5.** (i) 0.635   (ii) 42.34 m
(iii) 42.93 m   **6.** 60°   **7.** $54\sqrt{3}$ cm   **8.** 151.22 cm^2
9. $\sqrt{149}$ cm   **10.** (i) $h = x\tan 51°$; $h = (14.75 + x)$
$\tan 30°$ (iii) 12.95 m   (iv) 16 m   (v) 4 m
(vii) 16 m   **11.** (i) 56 m   (ii) 28°   **12.** (i) 18.93 m
(ii) 19.86 m   **13.** $\dfrac{1}{\sqrt{17}}$ **14.** 14 m   **15.** (i) 17°
(ii) 3 cm   (iii) 37 cm   (iv) 34 cm   **16.** (i) 60°
(ii) 2 m   (iii) 4.62 m   (iv) 2.31 m   **17.** (a) Incorrect
(b) Correct   (c) Incorrect   **18.** Suurhusen church
tower is more tilted.   **19.** (b) 125 m
20. (a) 109.2 cm   (b) (i) $h = \sqrt{3}.x$
(ii) $6\sqrt{3}$ m   **21.** (b) 1st estimate: 194.1750 m
(c) 2nd estimate: 194.0727 m; 3rd estimate:
194.1149 m   (d) 19,412 cm

Chapter 22

Exercise 22.1

3. (i) 7   (ii) $\dfrac{9}{4}$ (iii) -1 (iv) $x \geqslant 1$ **4.** (i) 8.1 m/s
(ii) $t = \dfrac{5}{3}$ seconds   (iii) 15 m/s   (iv) $t = 5$ seconds
5. (i) -6.25 (ii) $x = -1$ and -2 **7.** (iii) 9 m
(iv) 0.35 m or 5.6 m   **8.** (i) -3.25 (ii) $x = -1.6$ or
2.6   (iii) $-1.6 \leqslant x \leqslant 2.6$ (iv) -4.25
9. (ii) 5.01 m (iii) 51.25 m   (iv) 14.7 seconds
10. (i) -9.8 (ii) $x = 0.5$ or -6.5 (iii) $x = 0.74$ or
-6.74 (iv) $x = -7.1$ or 1.1   (v) -12
11. (ii) $t = 0.2$ or 4.1   (iii) $\max[h(t)] = 31.3$ m;
$\max[g(x)] = 20$ m   (iv) $h(t)$ ball: 2.5 seconds;
$g(t)$ ball: 5 seconds   (v) 4 seconds   **12.** (i) 5.75
(ii) $x = 0.7$ or 6.1   (iii) $x \leqslant 0.7$ or $x \geqslant 6.1$
(iv) $0.7 \leqslant x \leqslant 6.1$ **13.** (i) 5.75   (ii) $x = -3$
or 1   (iii) 6   (iv) $-3 \leqslant x \leqslant 1$ **14.** (i) $x = -2.6$
and 0.6   (ii) $x \leqslant -2.6$ or $x \geqslant 0.6$
15. (ii) At 2 seconds or 4 seconds   (iv) 0.2 seconds
after take-off   (v) 1.24 m above the ground
16. (ii) 500 units   (iii) €2,500   (iv) 400 units or
600 units   (v) It is more lucrative to produce
725 units.

Exercise 22.2

9. $a = 4$ **10.** $a = 2$ **11.** (i) $x < -2.1$ or $x > 0.6$
(ii) $-2.1 \leqslant x \leqslant 0.6$ **12.** (i) $-1.8 < x < 0$
(ii) $x \leqslant -1.8$ or $x \geqslant 0$ **13.** $x < -11.9$ or $x > -0.8$

14. $x \geqslant -0.2$ **15.** (i) 64   (iii) 16   (iv) 6 days
16. (iii) 5 days and 18 hours

Exercise 22.3

1. (i) $g(x)$: red graph   (ii) $h(x)$: blue graph
2. (i) $f(x)$: blue graph   (ii) $g(x)$: red graph
3. (i) $g(x)$: red graph   (ii) $f(x)$: blue graph
5. $f(x) = 3^{x-3}$ **6.** $g(x) = 3 + 2^{x+2}$

Revision Exercises

2. (i) $V = 5x$ (iii) $F = 45,000$
(v) $T = 45,000 + 5x$ (vii) $S(x) = 6x$

(ix) 45,000 units   **4.** (i) -4.75 (ii) $x = -1.2$ or 3.2
(iii) $-1 \leqslant x \leqslant 3$ (iv) -5 **6.** (ii) $g(x) = 2^{x-2}$
7. (iii) This is an exponential function.   (iv) Yes
8. (i) $f(x)$: black graph   (ii) $g(x)$: blue graph
9. $0 \leqslant x \leqslant 1$ **10.** $0.3 < x < 3$
11. (b) Ahmad should have drawn the line
$y = 2x + 7$, i.e. he subtracted 7 rather than adding
7.   (c) $y = 2x + 7$ **12.** (a) $x = -4$ and 2
(b) $k = -13$ (c) $k = 1$ (e) $k = -15$
13. (i) 17 hours   (ii) 14 hours   (iii) 13 hours
(iv) Yes   **14.** (a) $\frac{1}{2}x^2 + 3x$ (b) $x^2 + 6x - 7 = 0$
(d) $x = 1$ (e) Base = 3 cm; height = 3 cm
15. (b) Sarah   (c) $H = 4$ **16.** $(-2,-9)$